GREAT CARS
OF THE
20TH CENTURY

BY ARCH BROWN • RICHARD M. LANGWORTH
AND THE AUTO EDITORS OF CONSUMER GUIDE®

SMITHMARK

Louis Weber, C.E.O.
Publications International, Ltd.
7373 North Cicero Avenue
Lincolnwood, Illinois 60646

Permission is never granted for commercial purposes.

Printed and bound in Yugoslavia.

8 7 6 5 4 3 2 1

ISBN: 0-8317-3935-5

Library of Congress Catalog Card Number: 91-65673

This edition published by SMITHMARK Publishers Inc.,
112 Madison Avenue, New York, NY 10016
SMITHMARK books are available for bulk purchase for
sales promotion and premium use. For details write or
telephone the Manager of Special Sales, SMITHMARK
Publishers Inc., 112 Madison Avenue, New York, NY
10016, (212)532-660

The authors and editors invite your comments. Address
Great Cars of the 20th Century, c/o Publications
International, Limited, 7373 North Cicero Avenue,
Lincolnwood, IL, USA 60646.

Photography
The editors would like to thank the following people and organizations for supplying the photography that made this book possible. They are listed below, along with the page number(s) of their photos:

Reg Abbiss, Rolls-Royce Motor Cars Public Relations, USA: 20-21 **Les Bidrawn:** 68-69 **Scott Brandt:** 75, 142-143, 144, 145 **Henry Austin Clark:** 374-375, 376 **Chrysler-Plymouth Public Relations:** 394-395, 397 **Continental Motors** 388 **Jonathon Day, The National Motor Museum, Beaulieu, England:** 14-15, 22, 23, 28-29, 30, 31, 52-53, 54, 55, 100-101, 102, 174-175, 197, 246-247 **Mirco Decet:** 48, 49, 108, 109, 110, 116, 117, 129, 176, 177, 216-217, 218, 219, 220-221, 222, 248, 249, 274-275, 276, 277, 278-279, 280, 281, 282-283, 284, 285, 344-345, 346, 347, 356-357, 358, 359, 362, 363, 386-89, 404, 405 **Dodge Public Relations:** 396 **Elite Heritage Motors Corp., Elroy, Wisconsin:** 65, 66 **Maria Feifel, Mercedes-Benz Museum, Stuttgart:** 9, 63 **Steen Fleron:** 288 **Alex Gabbard:** 296-297, 298, 299, 300-301, 302, 303 **Thomas Glatch:** 126, 127, 200-201, 202, 203, 292-293, 324 **Eddie Goldberger:** 185 **David Gooley:** 154-155, 156, 307, 312-313 **Sam Griffith:** 62, 169, 184, 214, 228-229, 230, 231, 236-237, 238, 262-263, 268, 269, 294, 334, 335, 342, 343, 348-349, 350, 351, 366, 371, 384, 385, 388, 406, 407, 408, 409, 414-415, 416, 417 **Jerry Heasley:** 82, 83, 84, 85 **Fergus Hernandes:** 240 **Bud Juneau:** 40-41, 42, 43, 56-57, 58, 59, 112-113, 114, 132, 133, 141, 146-147, 148, 149, 178-179, 181, 224-225, 226, 227, 253, 258-259, 260, 270-271, 272, 273, 314, 360-361 **Milton Gene Kieft:** 64-65, 67, 70, 78-79, 80, 81, 96-97, 158-159, 160, 161, 194-195, 290, 304-305, 306, 370 **Steve Kimball:** 377 **Rick Lenz:** 99 **Dan Lyons:** 71, 136, 137, 232-233 **Vince Manocchi:** 74, 88, 89, 90-91, 94-95, 104-105, 106, 107, 122-123, 125, 130-131, 166-167, 180, 208-209, 210, 211, 245, 250-251, 252, 266-267, 326-327, 328, 329, 378-379, 380, 381, 382-383 **Mazda Information Bureau:** 410-411, 412 **Doug Mitchel:** 86, 87, 98, 121, 124, 138-139, 140, 150-151, 152, 153, 162-163, 164, 165, 166, 168,172, 173, 189, 190-191, 192, 193, 215, 239, 254-255, 256, 257, 261, 265, 289, 295, 308-309, 310, 311, 316-317, 318, 319, 336-337, 338 *Autocar & Motor* magazines: 402, 403 **Mike Mueller:** 32-33, 34, 35 **John Owens:** 354 **Klaus Parr, Porsche Archives, Stuttgart, Germany:** 204-205, 206, 207, 320-321, 325, 398-399, 400, 401 **Frank Peiler:** 416 **Maria N. Polleiner, Volkswagen United States, Inc.:** 198, 199 **Richard Spiegelman:** 254-255 **David Temple:** 134-135, 286-287, **Nicky Wright:** 10-11, 12, 13, 24-25, 26, 27, 36-37, 38, 39, 44-45, 46, 47, 50, 51, 60, 61, 72-73, 92, 93, 115, 121, 156, 157, 170-171, 182-183, 186, 187, 188, 196, 234, 235, 241, 242-243, 244, 322, 330-331, 332, 333, 352-353, 364-365, 367, 368-369, 372, 373 **Zoom Photographic:** 354, 355

Editorial
Packard Twelve article adapted from "The Mighty Twelve" by Maurice D. Hendry, *The Packard Cormorant*, 1978. **Lincoln K Series** article adapted from "Lincoln's Model K," by Ian Davidson (pen name for Maurice D. Hendry), *Car Classics*, June 1977.

Owners
Special thanks to the owners of the cars featured in this book for their enthusiastic cooperation. They are listed below along with the page number(s) on which their cars are shown:

Albie Albertshardt: 202, 203 **Auburn-Cord-Duesenberg Museum, Auburn, Indiana:** 118-119, 120 **Dale P. Aylward:** 150-151, 152, 153 **Ken Baker:** 334, 335 **Jack Bart:** 232-233 **Thomas W. Barrett III:** 60, 61, 115 **Paul Batista:** 250-251 **Fred Bausch:** 58 **Robert Beechy:** 370 **M.B. Belden, Lanton Classic Car Museum:** 78-79 **Raymond and Marilyn Benoy:** 254-255, 256 **John Bertolotti:** 40-41, 42, 43 **Blackhawk Auto Collection:** 112-113, 114 **Pete Bogard:** 262-263 **Joseph E. Bortz:** 124, 265 **Terry Buy:** 166 **J. Kim Callahan:** 286-287 **Robert Carlson:** 158-159, 160, 161 **Bejamin R. Caskey, Jr.:** 186, 187, 188 **J.F. Cassan:** 138-139 **Bernie Chase:** 382-383 **Henry Austin Clark:** 374-375, 376 **Collier Automotive Museum, Naples, Florida:** 32-33, 34, 35 **Rick Consiglio:** 371 **Ed Coughlin:** 336-337, 338 **Western Historical Reserve/Frederick C. Crawford Auto-Aviation Museum, Cleveland, Ohio:** 24-25, 26, 27, 36-37, 38, 39 **Duke Davenport:** 76 **Dells Auto Museum, Lake Mills, Wisconsin:** 292-293 **Michael Doyle:** 121 **Hugh Dixon:** 189 **Paul Eggerling:** 236-237 **Jerry Emery:** 132 **Bill and Jan Everitt:** 290 **Bev Ferreira:** 179-179 **John Finster:** 326-327, 328, 329 **Bob Gautschy:** 215 **Gary Gettlemen:** 224-225, 226, 227 **Richard Giacobett:** 342, 343 **Tom Griffith:** 314, 315 **Robert Halada:** 272, 273 **Torben Stiig Hansen:** 288 **Jack Harbaugh:** 86, 87 **William E. Harrah Foundation, National Automobile Museum, Reno, Nevada:** 10-11, 12, 13, 44-45, 46, 47, 50, 51, 103, 196 **Roger Hayes:** 253 **Barbara Hendrickson:** 324 **William S. Henry:** 194-195 **Bill Hentzen:** 156, 157 **David Hill:** 254-255 **Nancy and Philip Hoffman:** 132 **Harold Hofferber:** 130-131 **Owen Hoyt:** 56-57

Melvin Hull: 180 **Ken Hutchinson:** 169, 184 **Jerry Johnson:** 214 **Jonnie Keller:** 70 **Joe Kelly:** 316-317 **Knox Kershaw:** 80 **John J. and Minnie G. Keys:** 208-209, 210 **Steve Kimball:** 377 **Larry Klein:** 59 **Terry Knudsen:** 261 **Edward S. Kuziel:** 264 **Peter Lampert:** 99 **Ron Lipsey:** 134-135 **Bill and Pat Locke:** 308-309, 310, 311 **William Locke:** 354 **Dr. L. Philip Lufty:** 234 **Bud Manning:** 238 **Gerard & Lorraine May:** 71 **Raymond Maranges:** 355 **Ralph Marano:** 149 **Ed McCloughlin:** 366 **Ronald E. Miller:** 332, 333 **Tina Miller:** 330-331 **Tom Mittler:** 322 **Frank Monhart:** 294 **MotorTech, Inc., Barrington, Illinois:** 384, 385 **Dennis M. Murphy:** 172 **Gerald & Katherine Nell:** 126, 127 **Ken Nelson:** 348-349, 350 **Wayne Nelson:** 367 **Chuck Norris:** 350, 351 **Mike Nowicki:** 352-353 **Leo Oser:** 121 **Dan and Barb Pankratz:** 173 **Jack Passey, Jr.:** 88, 89 **David Patterson:** 82, 83, 84, 85 **Robert Peiler:** 257 **Rob Pelty:** 268, 269 **Robert Perez:** 270-271 **N. Gene Perkins:** 92 **Lloyd W. Pettigrew:** 252 **Edsel H. Pfabe:** 164, 165, 168 **Ron Pittman:** 239 **Richard V. Presson:** 228-229, 230, 231 **Hilary Raab, Jr.:** 364-365 **Dr. S. Radtke:** 354 **Terry Radey:** 64-65, 67 **Les Raye:** 304-304, 306 **Jim Regnier:** 372, 373 **Randall Renbarger:** 368-369 **Wayne Rife:** 241 **Carl M. Riggins:** 68-69 **Chuck Rizzo:** 200-201 **James L. Roman:** 258-259, 260 **Frederick J. Roth:** 211 **Otto T. Rosenbusch:** 242-243, 244 **R. Sauenschell:** 136, 137 **Ric and Miki Schug:** 360-361 **Bruce Sears:** 289 **Harold Sliger:** 93 **William Snyder:** 81 **Les Sterling:** 182-183 **Suburban Motors, Inc., Tucson, Arizona:** 185 **Eugene Tareshawty:** 148 **Mike Thraser:** 142-143, 144, 145 **Gene Troyer:** 133 **Jim Van Gordon:** 240 **Edward H. Wachs:** 62 **Charles and Charlotte Watson, Jr.:** 212-213 **Fred Weber:** 75 **R.S. Williams:** 274-275, 276, 277 **Sherman Williams:** 235 **Joe Witczak:** 318, 319 **Harry Wynn:** 141 **William Young:** 72-73 **P. Alvin Zamba:** 96-97

CONTENTS

INTRODUCTION...6

1901 MERCEDES 35 HP...8

1901-07 OLDSMOBILE CURVED-DASH...10

1902 PANHARD & LEVASSOR...14

1907 CADILLAC MODEL K...16

1907-26 ROLLS-ROYCE SILVER GHOST...20

1908-1927 FORD MODEL T...24

1908 LANCHESTER 20 HP...28

1911-1915 MERCER RACEABOUT, MODEL 35-R...32

1915 CADILLAC V-8, TYPE 51...36

1915-1922 STUTZ BEARCAT...40

1916-23 PACKARD TWIN SIX...44

1923-31 LANCIA LAMBDA...48

1924 CHRYSLER MODEL B-70...50

1926-32 BUGATTI TYPE 41 ROYALE...52

1927 LaSALLE...56

1927-32 MERCEDES S/SS/SSK/SSKL...60

1928-34 DUESENBERG J-SERIES...64

1928-31 FORD MODEL A...68

1930-40 CADILLAC SIXTEEN...72

1931-33 MARMON SIXTEEN...78

1932 FORD V-8...82

1932-39 LINCOLN K/KA/KB...86

1932-39 PACKARD TWELVE...90

1932-38 PIERCE ARROW TWELVE...96

1934-39 BUGATTI TYPE 57...100

1934-37 CHRYSLER AIRFLOW...104

1934-57 CITROËN "TRACTION AVANT"...108

1934-39 MERCEDES-BENZ 500K/540K...112

1935-39 ALFA ROMEO 8C 2900...116

1935-36 AUBURN SPEEDSTER 851/852 SUPERCHARGED...118

1936-37 CORD 810/812...122

1936-39 SS JAGUAR 100...126

1936-42 LINCOLN-ZEPHYR...130

1938-41 CADILLAC SIXTY SPECIAL...134

1940-41 LINCOLN CONTINENTAL...138

1940 OLDSMOBILE 90...142

1940-42 PACKARD-DARRIN...146

1940-45 WILLYS JEEP...150

1945-49 MG TC...154

1946-48 CHRYSLER TOWN AND COUNTRY...158

1947-52 CISITALIA 202 GRAN SPORT...162

1947-53 FERRARI 166/195/212...166

1948-54 JAGUAR XK-120...170

1948-71 MORRIS MINOR...174

1948 TUCKER "48"...178

1949 CADILLAC...182

1949 FORD...186

1949 OLDSMOBILE 88...190

1949-91 VOLKSWAGEN BEETLE...194

1950-55 NASH RAMBLER...200

1950-65 PORSCHE SERIES 356...204

1951-54 HUDSON HORNET...**208**

1951-55 KAISER...**212**

1952-55 BENTLEY R-TYPE CONTINENTAL...**216**

1953-67 AUSTIN-HEALEY 100/100 SIX/3000...**220**

1953 CADILLAC ELDORADO...**224**

1953-54 STUDEBAKER STARLIGHT/STARLINER...**228**

1954-63 MERCEDES-BENZ 300SL...**232**

1955-57 CHEVROLET...**236**

1955 CHRYSLER C-300...**242**

1955-75 CITROËN DS...**246**

1955-57 FORD THUNDERBIRD...**250**

1955-56 PACKARD CARIBBEAN...**254**

1956-59 BMW 507...**258**

1956-57 CHEVROLET CORVETTE...**262**

1956-57 CONTINENTAL...**266**

1957-58 CADILLAC ELDORADO BROUGHAM...**270**

1958-65 ASTON MARTIN DB4/DB5...**274**

1959-91 AUSTIN/MORRIS MINI...**278**

1959-62 LOTUS ELITE...**282**

1961-75 JAGUAR E-TYPE...**286**

1961-63 LINCOLN CONTINENTAL...**292**

1962-69 AC COBRA...**296**

1962-64 FERRARI 250 GTO...**300**

1963-65 BUICK RIVIERA...**304**

1963-67 CHEVROLET CORVETTE STING RAY...**308**

1963-64 STUDEBAKER AVANTI...**312**

1964-65 PONTIAC GTO...**316**

1964-91 PORSCHE 911-SERIES...**320**

1965-66 CHEVROLET CORVAIR CORSA...**326**

1965-66 FORD MUSTANG...**330**

1965-66 SHELBY GT-350...**336**

1966-74 FERRARI DINO 206/246...**340**

1966-71 JENSEN FF...**344**

1966-67 OLDSMOBILE TORONADO...**348**

1967-73 LAMBORGHINI MIURA...**352**

1967-77 NSU Ro80...**356**

1968-76 BMW 2002...**360**

1968-74 FERRARI 365 GTB/4 DAYTONA...**364**

1968-70 PLYMOUTH ROAD RUNNER...**368**

1970-73 DATSUN 240Z...**374**

1970-91 DeTOMASO PANTERA...**378**

1974-89 LAMBORGHINI COUNTACH...**382**

1975-91 FERRARI 308/328/348...**386**

1978-85 MAZDA RX-7...**390**

1984-91 CHRYSLER MINIVANS...**394**

1986-88 PORSCHE 959...**398**

1987-90 FERRARI F40...**402**

1990-91 CHEVROLET CORVETTE ZR-1...**406**

1990-91 MAZDA MX-5 MIATA...**410**

1991 HONDA/ACURA NS-X...**414**

INDEX...**418**

You might think *Great Cars of the 20th Century* a redundant term and thus a questionable book title. "Great cars of the Twentieth Century" as opposed to what? Great cars of the Eighteenth Century?

A moment's reflection, however, shows that the Automotive Age is unquestionably a phenomenon of the Twentieth Century, though the first automobiles in the now-accepted sense—that is, wheeled vehicles self-propelled by internal-combustion engines—are actually products of the Nineteenth Century. They

were, of course, tinkered up by the two Germans usually acknowledged as the automobile's "fathers," Gottlieb Daimler and Carl Benz, and it is because of their achievements that the world celebrated the centenary of the automobile in 1988.

Some would say the motorcar is closer to two centuries old, pointing to Frenchman Nicholas Cugnot's huge three-wheel steam-powered gun carriage of 1771 as an "automobile." But rather than debate technical definitions, let's just say that the work of Daimler and Benz was the culmination of at least 200 years of inventive searching toward the dream of mechanized alternatives to the horse and wagon. These scattered efforts, which can be traced all the way back to the Renaissance and Leonardo da Vinci, gained great impetus with the advent of practical steam power in mid-Eighteenth Century England. Among the most significant results of that development were the steam locomotives and river boats that carried settlers to the heart of the American interior, thus helping unite the new United States from sea to shining sea.

Yet the automobile as personal transportation would have remained a dream had not another German, Nicholas Gustav Otto, devised an engine both small enough and powerful enough for motorized vehicles to be sized for easy operation by one person. This, of course, was the four-stroke "Otto cycle" internal-combustion gasoline engine that became almost universal for automobiles and just as quickly consigned rival steam and electric power to the scrap heap of history.

Today, gathering social and environmental forces seem to threaten the same fate for Otto's surprisingly adaptable basic engine. But if nothing else—and getting

us back to book titles—*Great Cars of the 20th Century* suggests that there will be great cars in the *Twenty-First*, that the automobile itself will

survive despite a growing number of issues and problems that will surely change the kind of cars we're allowed to drive, if not the entire automotive landscape.

We're speaking here of air pollution, urban congestion, the continuing depletion of limited fossil fuels, the health hazards and financial perils of building and disposing of millions of automobiles each year, and similar problems. These, too, are products of the Automotive Age. Indeed, they testify to the worldwide pervasiveness the automobile has assumed during the Twentieth Century, to its enormous economic, social, and political importance in most developed nations. Surely Daimler and Benz would be be astonished, if not appalled, could they now see some of the consequences of what they wrought over 100 years ago: the choking, sooty pall that hangs over Mexico City and Los Angeles; the massive, daily traffic jams that afflict midtown Manhattan and downtown Tokyo; the heartbreaking environmental damage of oil spills from ocean-going tankers; the devastation of wars fought for control of fast-dwindling oil supplies; the personal economic hardship of fuel prices that now often fluctuate wildly and on mere whim; the struggle toward more ecologically "friendly" vehicles and manufacturing techniques that now occupies motor makers all over the globe.

Urgent and vexing though such problems are, they don't necessarily imply a grim future for personal motoring. Technology, especially the advent of reliable, sophisticated electronic systems, promises to keep all of us behind the wheel well past the millenium, though we may be there less often and we may not always steer. By the year 2000, new-age electric vehicles, piston engines redesigned for "clean" fuels like methanol and propane, and "smart cars" whizzing along computer-managed freeways at 80 mph will be facts of life—or at least very close to reality—in places like California. So, too, expanded and/or modernized light-rail and other mass-transit systems in most cities, perhaps mandatory car-pooling for those commuters not well served by mass transit and, inevitably, much higher prices for both cars and their fuels.

Of course, cars themselves will continue to become, dare we say, even more futuristic: sleeker and more complex, worthy of even the wildest "science fiction" prognostications. But it has always been thus. Indeed, the pace of the automobile's evolution over "only" 100 years has been nothing short of astounding. How Daimler and Benz would marvel at today's Mercedes 500SL and other descendants of their first fragile *motorwagens*. Equally certain is that the realities of our Twenty-First Century cars will be quite different from the fantasies, just as cars of the 1950s turned out to be nothing at all like the fanciful "Buck Rogers" visions paraded in the pulp press of the Thirties and Forties, though a few Detroit products certainly strained to imitate them.

Which in a roundabout way returns us to the subject of this book. Actually, there's little else you need know about *Great Cars of the 20th Century* except, perhaps, that the authors and editors have chosen 100 cars plus one to profile, one for each year of the century (though space limitations also dictated this number). The choices were both carefully considered and hotly debated, with special emphasis given to engineering innovation (as, for example, the first Chrysler), landmark styling (such as the Duesenberg J or the original Lincoln Continental), social and/or

commercial significance (hence the Ford Model T and VW Beetle), and simple all-around excellence (the "classic" mid-Fifties Chevrolets or Jaguar E-Type, to name two). We leave it to you to browse through the text and discover the precise reasons why each car here qualifies as a "great." And it should be mentioned that Classics and Milestones—with the capital letter as used in this book—are recognized by the Classic Car Club of America, which honors the "true" classics of 1925-48, and the Milestone Car Society, which caters to the finest of the postwar automobiles.

But as usual with books like this, it's important to sound the cautionary note that the selections here are *not* meant to be exhaustive, definitive, or entirely objective.

Any anthology always involves some limiting degree of personal judgment as to what's good or even "great," so you'll doubtless cheer some of our choices—and jeer others. That's fine. How dull this world would be if we all agreed on everything.

We've chosen to profile our historic hundred plus one with the simple, straightforward format that has proven so successful in two previous CONSUMER GUIDE® editions, *The Great Book of Sports Cars* and *Great American Cars of the 50s*. Each entry begins with a concise overview that not only presents key facts concerning the car's genesis, design, performance, and similar points, but that also attempts to place the car in a meaningful historical context. Following this is a short specifications table listing engine type, size, and output. Added to that are type of transmission, front/rear suspension and brakes; curb weight, top speed and 0-60 mph performance; and, finally, original production, usually broken down by model or calendar year. Data has been

painstakingly compiled using both original and modern reference works, plus the expert knowledge of the authors and editors.

The same expertise is reflected in the illustrations. Specially commissioned for this book from professional photographers, they depict carefully chosen specimens of the appropriate model or models, which in most all cases are restorations to perfect or near-perfect condition. Unlike some other books, this one supplements the expected exterior "glamour shots" with close-ups of important detail features such as interiors, engines, and so on.

And there you have it. We hope *Great Cars of the 20th Century* will spur you to delve further into those cars you may not be familiar with, and will broaden your appreciation of the entire sweep of automotive history. And a grand pageant it is. Happily, it seems destined to continue for a long, long time.

Arch Brown, Richard M. Langworth, and
The Auto Editors of Consumer Guide
June 1991

1901 MERCEDES 35 HP

Historians are not in agreement, but the bulk of opinion is that the products of Gottlieb Daimler and Karl Benz, working separately in Germany during 1886, were the first automobiles. Automotive history did not begin with Daimler and Benz, of course, because self-propelled vehicles had been known at least as far back as 1775. But until the mid-1880s all of them had been large, heavy, and inefficient, relying on steam power in one form or another. The technological breakthrough that allowed the "horseless carriage" to enter the modern age was the use of petroleum fuel in lightweight, high-revving engines—and this is exactly what Messrs. Benz and Daimler achieved— separately. Though they lived within 60 miles of each other, they were not acquainted, and the great company bearing both their names wasn't established until 1924. Gottlieb Daimler didn't even live to see the famous "Mercedes" name on one of his cars. He died in 1900, unhappily, protesting that he still had years of work to do.

The first "Mercedes," the great 35 HP of 1901, was conceived by Daimler's distributor in Nice, the formidable Emil Jellinek: Austria-Hungary's vice-consul in the city, a seller and sometime racer of Daimler machines, a scion of the Hapsburg establishment. Writer David Scott-Moncrieff described Jellinek as "a small, excitable man—in the matter of cars, like Toad of Toad Hall—whatever he had, he wanted something bigger and better." Jellinek especially wanted light cars, which was an uncommon idea in those days. He yearned for a "mechanical greyhound." Wilhelm Maybach and Daimler's talented son Paul set to work on a Daimler to meet his specifications. Jellinek encouraged them, promising to buy the first three dozen. He also selected the name Mercedes, after his 10-year-old daughter.

As often, things didn't quite go as planned. Daimler was able to complete only six cars by January 1901, and there was no time for a shakedown run before the Grand Prix of Pau in February, which was to be its racing debut. The race proved a fiasco. Both engine and gearbox were troublesome and the Mercedes retired after running only a few yards. But things were different at Nice, where the Mercedes of factory driver Wilhelm Werner dominated events. The 35-bhp Mercedes was fastest in both the sprints and hillclimbs, and also won the 393-km (244-mile) Nice-Aix-Senas-Nice road race that climaxed the proceedings.

Today, 35 horsepower from a six-liter engine in a car weighing 2,200 pounds seems very pedestrian, to put it mildly. But it was truly sensational by the standards of 1901. The four-cylinder engine, with its camshaft-operated intake valves, was quite advanced, and gave the car a higher power/weight ratio than most others of the time. Also, the Mercedes handled better than any other car yet seen. The secret was in its squat stance. The earlier Daimlers Jellinek had been racing were bulky,

Specifications	
Engine:	I-4 cast in pairs, T-head combustion chambers, 364.4 cid (5,973 cc), with cam-operated inlet valves, twin carburetors, Bosch low-tension magneto ignition, water-cooled, 35 bhp @ 1,000 rpm
Transmission:	4-speed, gate change
Frame:	Pressed channel-section side members
Brakes:	Internally expanding on the rear axle; hand brake on the gearbox countershaft
Drive:	Rear-wheel drive via sprockets and chains
Weight (lbs):	2,640
Top speed:	53.5 mph

over twice as heavy as the Mercedes, and relatively high on a short wheelbase. The resulting instability was thought to have caused the death of a driver in the La Turbie hillclimb of 1899. But the Mercedes was altogether lower and sleeker. Its hoodline was little higher than the tops of its front tires, the chassis side members rode at least six inches nearer to the ground, and its driver sat closer to the midpoint of a longer wheelbase and behind a considerably more raked steering column.

At one stroke with this car, automotive design made a complete break with the horseless carriage. By comparison with this Mercedes, contemporary Benz models seemed archaic. It is by no means exaggeration to say that the 35-bhp Mercedes was the key model in the evolution of the early automobile.

In general layout, the car faithfully followed the *Systeme Panhard*, except for its mechanically operated intake valves (most cars still relied on "automatic" induction). The T-head layout would look familiar to any lover of early American cars. So, too, would the cast iron block, with its cylinders cast in pairs, fixed to a light-alloy crankcase.

But several features made the Mercedes a true pacesetter. These included a pressed-steel chassis (at a time when many manufacturers were using wooden flitch-plate construction), a four-speed gearbox with gated linkage, pedal-actuated internally expanding drum brakes for the back axle, and a handbrake drum on the gearbox countershaft. While not revolutionary in layout, the transmission was already used by some other makers—and almost every make would adopt it in the next few years.

Immediately behind the transmission was the differential, from which two countershafts—actually driveshafts—ran to sprockets mounted outboard of the main frame members at either side. Final drive was by chain to the rear wheels, the wheel sprockets being mounted close to the drum brakes. On most cars that followed, the shift lever would also be outboard of the frame, but on the original racing Mercedes, with its skimpy two-seat body, the lever was pivoted at the base of the steering column.

The Mercedes-Benz archive describes this car as a 1902 Mercedes Simplex. Its T-head inline four was cast in pairs, and it developed 35 bhp from 364.4 cubic inches—quite impressive for its time. It was mated to a four-speed gearbox with gated linkage. A pressed-steel chassis was an advanced feature for the day.

With all this, no wonder the performance of the new car was so outstanding. So much so, in fact, that the secretary of the Automobile Club of France, Paul Meyan, was moved to say, "Nours sommes entres dans l'ere Mercedes"— "We have entered the Mercedes era."

The competition success at Nice and sales success that followed throughout the year proved to be a real watershed in the affairs of Daimler Motoren Gesellschaft. Many new Daimler models had been issued in the last years of the 19th century, but after 1901 there were no more. (Daimler Ltd. of Coventry, England, founded to build Daimlers under license, became independent after 1900.) From now on, the German company would produce the "Mercedes,"

which was adopted as its official name as soon as all legal formalities were ironed out. That name has graced most every Daimler and Daimler-Benz car ever since. The Daimler marque, therefore, passed from the scene in Germany just a year after its founder, though the name would survive proudly in the corporate title.

The story of Daimler in the next six years largely involved the big four-and six-cylinder cars that could be called the "Maybach generation." All were evolutions of the brilliant 1901 35 HP, and comprised both touring and competition types. Purists, incidentally, should note that while Jellinek's daughter always spelled her name with accents, they have never been used on the cars.

The unassuming Curved-Dash Oldsmobile is significant not only as the first best-selling American car of the 20th Century, but as a car that saved its maker. Had it not been as popular—or "rescued" from a disastrous fire—Oldsmobile might not have lasted past 1902. Just as important, the Curved-Dash was everything "horseless carriages" had to be to become a permanent part of this century's landscape: versatile, available, and most of all, reliable.

Its story begins with Ransom Eli Olds, born in 1864 in Geneva, Ohio. His father, Pliny Olds, repaired machinery, a trade "Ranny" began learning at an early age. By 1880, the family had settled in Lansing, Michigan, then a town of about 2,000, where papa Olds and his older boy Wallace set up shop as P.F. Olds & Son, "practical machinists" specializing in castings and steam engines. Ransom, meanwhile, attended high school and took an accounting course at a local business school, the latter enabling him to join the firm in 1883 as both machinist and bookkeeper. The business was incorporated in 1890, when Ransom bought out his brother's share. He became sole proprietor when their father retired four years later.

All the while, Ransom tinkered with horseless carriages, building a three-wheeled steamer by 1887, an even better four-wheeler in 1891, and another in '92. Yet that first car was enough to persuade Edward W. Sparrow and Samuel L. Smith, lumber and copper magnates, respectively, to give him $30,000 to start the Olds Gasoline Engine Works 1890. Despite its name, this firm made small steam engines, "gasoline" referring to the fuel that fired their boilers.

Still, Ransom recognized the internal-combustion gasoline engine as the most promising for motorcars, and in the summer of 1896 he built his first such automobile: a small machine with a five-horsepower water-cooled twin, chain drive, two-speed planetary transmission, and a top speed of 18 mph. Sparrow and Smith saw potential profit in this rig, and gave Ransom another $50,000 to set up the Olds Motor Vehicle Company that August. Ransom wanted "to build one carriage in as nearly a perfect manner as possible," but his workers managed four (some say five) within three months—then walked out. Sparrow soon followed, but Smith still believed, and in May 1899 put up $350,000 for yet another a new venture called Olds Motor Works, which absorbed the two previous companies. Because Smith and his sons Fred and Angus were Detroiters, Ransom became one, too, setting up a new plant—the first specifically erected for car production—on Jefferson Avenue near the Belle Isle bridge.

Over the next year, Olds Motor Works built some 11 cars, evident prototypes toward a two-cylinder seven-bhp "Oldsmobile" (a name registered in 1900) announced at $1250. But the new firm attracted little interest, and was soon looking terminal. Oddly, Ransom seemed

more interested in playing with electric cars (he built at least two around the turn of the century) and garnering more patents for various inventions like a crude self-starter, which would be perfected by Charles Kettering a few years after William C. Durant added Oldsmobile to his fledgling General Motors in 1908.

Destiny intervened in March 1901 when a fire ravaged the Olds factory. The losses, valued at a then-staggering $72,000, included all of Ransom's prototypes—save a "one-lung" single-seat runabout with a gracefully curved front, or "dashboard" in carriage parlance. A long-told story was that a worker risked life and limb to push this little car from a burning building, but subsequent research indicates the firm had already settled on this as its first product, and would have been able to build it from detailed drawings that survived the blaze.

Regardless, the Curved-Dash became the first production Oldsmobile, and was in production by late 1901—in Lansing. Though Olds Motor Works maintained a Detroit presence for a few more years, Ransom built a new factory near his hometown after the Lansing Chamber of Commerce simply gave the company the 52-acre site of the former state fairgrounds.

Appearance aside, the "Oldsmobile curved-dash runabout" was much like many other early century cars: simple and cart-like—truly a carriage without the horse. Its "drivetrain" followed that of Ransom's first gasoline car save for a single-cylinder engine, though still with side valves and water-cooling, and also placed beneath a two-passenger buggy seat. A horizontal radiator was mounted under the floorboard, where a foot lever was provided for controlling speed. The ignition system included dual batteries with a suggested life of 3-4 months. Supporting the body, with the then-customary wood-and-fabric construction, were 55-inch-wide tubular-steel axles mounted 60 inches apart and connected on each side by a long truss-shaped leaf spring that was flattened in the middle for attachment to a rectangular frame of channel-section steel. Steering was by tiller, the steering wheel being far from universal yet. Braking, or what passed for it, was by a foot pedal that caused a clutch band to grab a flange on the drive sprocket. There was also an emergency brake: a drum on the transmission jackshaft (between low and reverse) acting directly on the rear axle. Wheels were 28-inch-diameter wire- or wood-spoke units mounting three-inch-wide tires. With the four-gallon fuel and water reservoirs full, curb weight came to a feathery 700 pounds.

Easily repaired by most any blacksmith and able to withstand the rugged, rutted roads of contemporary rural America, the Curved-Dash found immediate acceptance at its $650 asking price—stiff, but not outrageous for the time. Only 386 were built in trouble-plagued 1901, but Olds turned out 2,500 in 1902, enough to claim the title as the best-selling car in the nation's infant auto industry. Olds repeated as number one in 1903 with higher sales of exactly 4,000. Useful accessories contributed to this success: a rear-facing "Dos-a-Dos" auxiliary seat ($25), folding top (with roll-up rear curtain) in either rubber ($25) or leather ($50), and a "storm apron," little more than a large, heavy blanket.

More significant to sales were the Oldsmobile's fine showings in the speed and durability trials so popular in the early years of "automobiling." In 1901, employee Roy Chapin— later of Hudson fame and one of several Olds people who would leave their marks at other companies—drove a Curved-Dash from Detroit to New York for the nation's second annual auto show as a publicity stunt. It took a week, but he made it, which in those days was all that mattered. The following year saw Oldsmobile taking victories in a Chicago endurance run, two five-mile contests in St. Louis, a Chicago Automobile Club meet, and first-in-class in a New York-Boston reliability trial. In 1903, a Curved-Dash made news by trekking from San Francisco to New York City in 60 days. Two years later, cars dubbed "Old Scout" and "Old Steady" were among the finishers in America's first transcontinental auto race, a 4,000-mile jaunt from Portland, Oregon, to New York.

Olds Motor Works naturally trumpeted such feats as proving its product's reliability, and the U.S. Post Office lent its endorsement by purchasing Oldsmobiles as the first mail "trucks." But the little car was also simply portrayed as a sensible substitute for skittish old Dobbin. "Nature made a mistake in giving the horse brains," said one ad. "Science did better and made the Oldsmobile mechanically perfect." Another ad touted the Curved-Dash as "the original and best [automobile]. Noiseless, odorless, speedy, sturdy, safe . . . flexible in gear, responds instantly to the will of the operator. Gets up and down stairs, and stops anywhere along the way."

The Curved-Dash also changed, if not very much, receiving a six-inch longer wheelbase and a bigger-bore seven-bhp engine for 1904, when it was redesignated Model 6-C (previously Model R). The price was still $650, but a pert $850 light-delivery "express" version arrived, and there was even a $450 "railway inspection" model with appropriate train-track wheels.

But bigger, more powerful cars were increasingly on the scene, and the Curved-Dash couldn't last forever. Ransom Olds disagreed, however, and departed the company in 1904, leaving money man Fred Smith to bring out the costlier, more elaborate Oldsmobiles he favored. These were just Curved-Dash variations at first, but two-cylinder cars bowed in 1906. By the time the last Curved-Dash was built, in 1907, Olds was offering four-cylinder cars and readying its first sixes.

Upshot Ransom ended up treading this same path when he moved—literally down the street—to start the Reo Motor Car Company in late 1905. Reo, a name obviously derived from Ransom's initials, was soon outselling Olds Motor Works, and would go on to become a major industry power, only to expire as an automaker in the Depression. Oldsmobile, meantime, fell from the number one sales spot after 1905—ironically, just as the ditty "In My Merry Oldsmobile" was becoming a hit—and has not reclaimed it since.

But the happy little Curved-Dash had saved Oldsmobile from an early grave while establishing a reputation that served the make well for years afterward. In fact, the Curved-Dash is still sometimes trotted out when the Oldsmobile Division of General Motors wants to remind people of its long history as an automotive pioneer. Any why not? Few makes can claim a more felicitous start.

Specifications	
Engine:	I-cylinder, side-valve, water-cooled **1901-03** 95.4 cid/1563 cc (4.50 x 6.00-in./127 x 152-mm bore by stroke), 4 bhp **1904-1907** 117.5 cid/1925 cc (5.00 x 6.00-in./127 x 152-mm bore x stroke), 7 bhp
Transmission:	2-speed, planetary
Suspension, front:	Beam axle connected by longitudinal leaf springs
Suspension, rear:	Beam axle connected by longitudinal leaf springs
Brakes:	Clutch band on main drive sprocket
Wheelbase (in.):	**1901-03** 60.0 **1904-07** 66.0
Weight (lbs):	approx. 700
Top speed (mph):	4,000
Production:	**1901** 386 **1902** 2,500 **1903** 4,000 **1904-07** unknown, but not significant after 1905; total vehicles were 5,508 in 1904, 6,500 in 1905 (all figures calendar year

Panhard was among the earliest automotive pioneers, and is credited with the *Systeme Panhard:* the front engine/rear drive format that would be all-but-universal for more than 50 years. Shown here is a 1902/03 model, along with some details of the "dash." Panhard adopted the steering wheel—as opposed to tiller steering—in 1898.

Many car enthusiasts know of the Panhard rod, the clever device that helps locate rear axles in the lateral plane. Few know about the company: Panhard & Levassor. It's understandable. Though the last Panhard wasn't built until 1967, the firm's glory days had passed a half-century before. Yet Panhard deserves to be appreciated for its historic contribution to automobile design, one made well before the 20th Century—this was the firm that pioneered "the horse before the cart," the front-engine/rear-drive format that would be all-but-universal for more than 50 years.

This *Systeme Panhard* was not conceived by René Panhard, but by fellow engineer Emile Levassor. Both had studied at the prestigious *Ecole Centrale des Arts et Manufacturers,* then met later in 1872 at *Perin et Pauwels,* a Parisian maker of woodworking machinery. When Perin died in 1886 they became sole owners of the renamed *Panhard et Levassor.* Both men knew about engines, but only Levassor was experienced in the budding business of designing and building them. And he had three important connections: the Otto and Langen Gas Engine Works of Deutz, Germany (Nickolaus Otto being the father of the four-stroke internal combustion engine), Gottlieb Daimler (who had worked at *Perin et Pauwels* around 1860), and friend Edouard Sarazin (Paris agent for the engines). Panhard & Levassor thus became a licensed producer of the Daimler-designed Deutz gas engine, which like other powerplants of its day was used mainly as a stationary source for running factory machines. P&L's contract ended when Deutz set up its own French factory, but Sarazin stayed in touch with Daimler even as the latter was setting up on his own in Canstatt. By 1887, the two were again seeking an engine builder for a new "high-speed" Daimler unit that could turn up to 750 rpm.

P&L might never have tried automaking had it not been for Sarazin's sudden death in late 1887—and for his wife, Louise. Sarazin had implored her to "continue to work with Daimler. No living person today has any idea of the possibilities of the Daimler patents." The widow Sarazin thus remained Daimler's Paris agent, struck up a friendship with Levassor, and married him in 1890 (giving him a financial interest in the Daimler engine).

At first, Levassor saw no future in making "auto-mobiles," as Daimler and Karl Benz were doing. Though one of the few who wasn't impressed by the Daimler "quadricycle"—a last-minute surprise at the 1889 Paris Exhibition—he *was* intrigued by its engine. And eventually, he concluded that P&L should make complete, specifically designed motor cars as well as engines.

Most early automobiles were cobbled together as motorized buggies, so engines were put in the only practical place: below or behind

wheel steering, pneumatic tires, and a new four-cylinder "Centaur" engine (1898); fin-tube radiators (1899). By 1903, Panhards boasted quadrant change for their four-speed transmissions, "automatic" intake valves, drip-feed lubrication, piano-type foot pedals, even electric ignition. This, plus continuing competition success and a "reputation for superb construction and unparalleled reliability...made the Panhard *the* car for the ultrarich," wrote Ralph Stein.

Nevertheless, Panhard soon turned out a bewildering variety of cars in all price ranges: three-, four-, and six-cylinder models ranging from 1.8 to no less than 11 liters in displacement and from eight to 50 horsepower. Further progress involved multi-plate clutches (1907), shaft drive and stamped-steel chassis (1908), monobloc engine (1909), and "gated" gearchange (1910). In 1912, Panhard introduced its first sleeve-valve engine—its mainstay for the next decade.

Panhard would occasionally capture the spotlight after World War I—as with that famous suspension rod in 1930—but was already on the wane. The firm came under Citroën's financial control in 1955, and both the name and the company vanished in 1967. But this long, sorry decline in no way diminishes the historic work of the forward-thinking Emile Levassor. On his death, a friend had described him as "very active, always working day and night; he dreamed only of carriages, alterations, improvements." That's a fine epitaph for anyone in the auto business, let alone one of its most visionary pioneers.

the operator's seat. Levassor did likewise. But dissatisfied with his rear-engine experiments, he hit upon a new formula by 1891: engine in front—Daimler's 1.2-liter, 3.5-bhp V-twin protected within a box—followed by a midships clutch and transmission.

Though it seems revolutionary now, Levassor's *systeme* was not viewed as such in the 1890s. As British writer Jonathan Wood observed some 90 years later in Britain's *Thoroughbred and Classic Sports Cars:* "There were no doubt many...who looked upon [Levassor's first car] as inferior to the rear-engine/belt-drive vehicles that far outnumbered it.... Engines at the time ran at a constant speed, and the Daimler power unit no doubt suffered from the vagaries of hot-tube ignition and poor carburetion. Thus, gear-changing [the only means for varying speed] involved much grinding of teeth both on the part of the machine and driver. [And] all the parts Levassor used were already in use on other vehicles...[but] the strength of *Systeme Panhard* [was] that it was capable of almost infinite development, whereas the rear-engine/belt

transmission soon represented an archaic backwater."

Panhards advanced rapidly: solid rubber tires in 1892 and, in 1895, enclosed gearboxes and a new Daimler-designed "Phenix" 2.4-liter, vertical-twin fed by a Maybach float-feed carburetor (instead of the old wick-type or "surface" carb). Yet engineering ever seemed to follow Levassor's two basic tenets: "Make it heavy and you'll make it strong," and "It's brutal, but it works."

Levassor entered his cars in the very earliest motor races. In 1894, his Panhard tied with a Peugeot as victor in the Paris-Rouen Trial. In 1895, he drove a Phenix-engine machine for some 53 hours all by himself to win the Paris-Bordeaux-Paris race, averaging 15 mph over 732 miles. In 1897, Levassor became the first casualty of motorsports when he died due to his fall in a Paris-Marseilles run the year before. René Panhard carried on, with Albert Krebs as new chief engineer, until his own death in 1908, when son Hippolyte Panhard became the firm's manager.

Technical progress continued apace: aluminum transmission cases (1897);

Specifications	
Engine:	**2-cylinder** sidevalve, inline, 104 cid/1.7 liters, approx. 7 bhp **4-cylinder** sidevalve, inline, 41 cid/673 cc (1.57 x 5.27-in./ 40 x 134-mm bore x stroke), approx. 15 bhp
Transmission:	3-speed sliding-gear
Suspension, front:	Solid axle on cantilevered elliptic leaf springs, friction dampers
Suspension, rear:	Solid axle on cantilevered elliptic leaf springs, friction dampers
Brakes:	Mechanical drum acting on rear wheels
Weight (lbs):	est. 2,000
Top speed (mph):	approx. 40 (4-cylinder)
Production:	NA, but likely no more than 250

1907 CADILLAC MODEL K

In the very early years of the automobile industry, Europeans accorded precious little respect to any of the various American marques. In no small measure, that attitude probably represented pure snobbery. But, of course, this country had yet to demonstrate that its products were the equal of Europe's best. All that changed during 1908—and the difference was due to two historic events.

The first of these was a race sponsored by the French newspaper *Le Matin*, in which six automobiles undertook a round-the-world trip from New York to Paris. In the dead of winter, often with no roads to follow, they were driven across the United States, after which they were shipped by steamer to Vladivostok, Russia. The cars then plodded on across Manchuria, and thence to Moscow, Berlin, and finally across Belgium and on into Paris.

Of the six cars entered in the contest, only four survived the journey across the North American continent. The original group consisted of three cars from France, one each from Italy and Germany, and one from the United States. And in the end the American car, a Thomas Flyer, was declared the winner. As auto historian John Bentley has written, that victory "set a new seal on the prestige of the infant American automobile industry. It proved that Americans could build a machine fully the equal of anything found in Europe."

In the meantime, over a two-week period commencing February 29, 1908, Cadillac scored an even more impressive triumph. Annually, starting in 1904, Britain's Sir Thomas Dewar had made a practice of awarding a trophy to the automaker deemed to have made the most significant advance in motor car manufacture over the preceding 12 months. The award, which took the form of an enormous silver cup, was considered to be the "Nobel Prize" of the automotive industry.

It happened that the first Cadillac to arrive in England had been imported by an aggressive young salesman named Frederick S. Bennett. And Bennett thought he knew how the Dewar Trophy might be captured, something no American car had managed to accomplish up to that time.

The secret lay in Cadillac's standardized parts. Parts interchangeability was literally unheard of in those days, either in England or on the Continent. For that matter, the concept had not yet been generally adopted in the United States, either. But Henry M. Leland, Cadillac's general manager, had been trained as a gunsmith during the Civil War and as a result of that experience he had developed very high standards of precision. Furthermore, he had learned how important it was to be able to substitute parts from one rifle in order to repair another. At Cadillac, he would apply the same principle to the manufacture of automobiles.

Cadillac's greatest contribution to the early motor car was parts interchangeability, masterminded by general manager Henry M. Leland. The cars seen here are a 1906 and 1907 Model K (*top right* and *center*), while the cutaway is of the 1905 Model E.

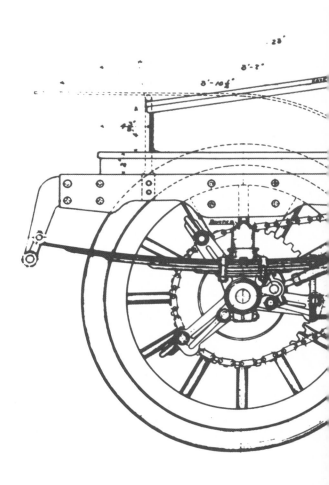

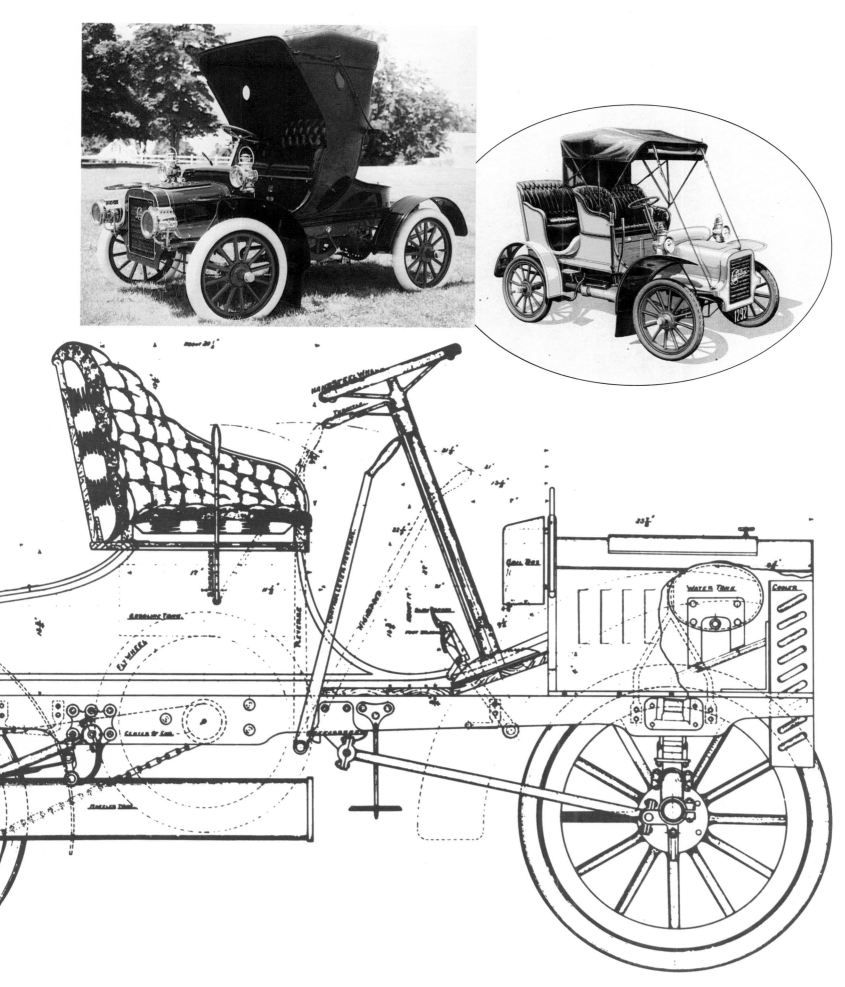

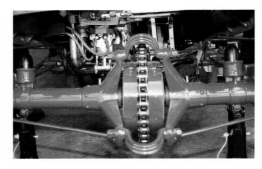

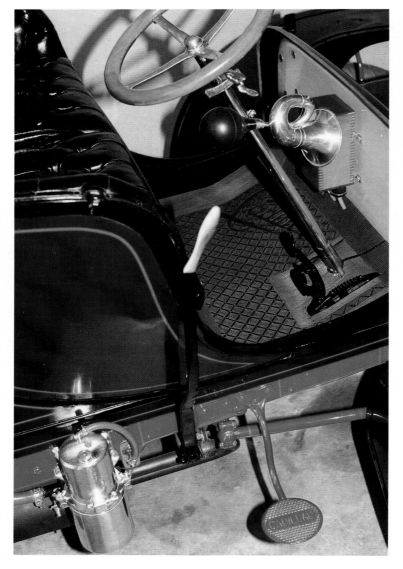

Some of the details of the 1906-07 Model K Cadillac included a one-cylinder water-cooled engine displacing 98.2 cubic inches. It had two main bearings and developed 10 horsepower. Other features included a two-speed planetary transmission and chain drive.

Commencing with the Model A, introduced at the New York Auto Show in January 1903, Cadillac had offered a variety of single-cylinder cars, all powered by the same Leland-built, 10-horsepower engine. Of square design, with both bore and stroke measuring five inches, the little one-lunger displaced 98.2 cubic inches. A two-speed planetary transmission was employed, and steering was by means of a wheel, rather than the then-commonplace tiller. Further, the car was sturdier and far more dependable than most of its contemporaries.

By 1905, Cadillac was building four distinct one-cylinder models in a total of seven configurations, and offering them at prices ranging from $750 to $950. Then, giving a glimpse of what the future would hold for the company, that year saw the production of 156 four-cylinder cars, along with nearly 4,000 of the single-cylinder jobs. Dubbed the Model D, this first Cadillac four-banger weighed nearly twice as much as the heaviest of the one-lungers, and it sold for $2,800—nearly four times the price of the one-cylinder runabout.

Bennett, thoroughly familiar with the product he was selling, knew that any part from a Cadillac could be installed, without hand-fitting of any kind, in another Cadillac of the same model. He was sure that the judges would find that concept impressive, and being something of a showman by nature he could see in this feature the possibility of an enormous publicity bonanza for Cadillac.

Bennett prevailed upon the highly skeptical officials of the prestigious Royal Automobile Club to oversee a test in which the interchangeability of Cadillac parts could be demonstrated. Three identical, single-cylinder Cadillac runabouts were selected from a shipment, recently arrived at a London dock. It

This photo of a 1907 Model K Cadillac—known for quality and dependability—clearly shows the flywheel (at mid-wheelbase). The Model K Victoria with top sold for $925.

might be noted that although this was 1908, the cars were actually late 1907 Model Ks. In any case, on Saturday, February 29, 1908, under RAC supervision, the cars were driven the 23 miles to the Brooklands race track. There, after 10 quick laps, they were locked up until the following Monday. At that point, again under the watchful eyes of the RAC's technical committee, the three Cadillacs were completely disassembled, down to the last bolt, nut, and screw. The committee then scrambled the parts, mixing them so completely that to identify any particular part with any one of the cars was out of the question. Finally, the parts were divided into three distinct piles. And then, in a further effort to make the demonstration convincing, 89 parts were set aside and replaced from dealer Bennett's over-the-counter stock. Included in this portion of the demonstration, according to Cadillac marque expert Maurice D. Hendry, were "such items as oil pump and transmission components, clutch bands and at least one piston, piston pin and rod."

And then the cars were reassembled. All three started and ran perfectly. Taken out onto the Brooklands track, they were driven flat-out for 500 miles, their average speed being a breakneck (for those days) 34 miles an hour over the duration of the run. Fuel mileage averaged 29.64 miles per gallon, a commendable figure considering that the cars had been driven at top speed. All three Cadillacs performed flawlessly for the duration of the run. The demonstration was enough to convince the Royal Automobile Club officials that Cadillac should be awarded the coveted Dewar trophy, the first time that honor had been bestowed upon an American company. It was a remarkable record, especially for an automobile selling for just $800!

Still, even this fine award wasn't enough for Frederick Bennett. Two of the cars that had participated in the contest were repainted and returned to stock, but the third Cadillac was locked away in the Royal Automobile Club garage immediately after the contest. The following June, that car was entered in an RAC-sponsored run, conducted in conjunction with the Scottish Automobile Club trial. "The route," according to Hendry, "led from London to Glasgow, then in the [Scottish Automobile Club] section for 772 miles on the Scottish Highland roads, back through the lake country, Welsh border district and Cotswolds to Brooklands, finishing with 200 miles at the [Brooklands]

motordrome. It included twenty-two miles of hill climbs and eleven timed hills, the total distance being 2,200 miles over a period of fifteen days."

Of course, there was a certain amount of risk in this undertaking, for should the Cadillac perform poorly—or fail to complete the test—the luster of the Dewar Award would have been severely tarnished. But there was no need to worry, for the little Cadillac completed the trial at the top of its class.

By the time this award was made, the one-cylinder Cadillac had entered its final year of production, having progressed through an alphabet of models: A, B, C, E, F, K, M, S, and T. From the day of its introduction in January 1903, the Cadillac had found immediate public acceptance, ranking that year as the third-best-selling automobile in America. By 1904, it had nudged Ford aside to take over second place, behind Oldsmobile, a position it retained for 1905. Between 1903 and 1908, Cadillac produced approximately 16,000 single-cylinder Cadillacs, several hundred of which still exist world-wide in the hands of enthusiastic collectors.

But of course, several years before it was awarded the Dewar Trophy, Cadillac had invaded the luxury market—again employing the principle of interchangeable parts. By 1908, the four-cylinder cars came in two sizes, with engines displacing 226.2 and 300.7 cubic inches, respectively. Prices ranged from $2,000 to $3,600, and although Cadillac still offered the one-cylinder cars on which its reputation had been built, they would be phased out by year's end.

Specifications[1]	
Engine:	1-cylinder horizontal, water cooled, 98.2 cid (5.00 x 5.00-in. bore x stroke), 2 main bearings, 10 bhp
Transmission:	2-speed planetary
Suspension:	Rigid axles, semi-elliptic springs
Brakes:	Mechanical, 2-wheel
Wheelbase (in.):	74.0
Overall length (in.):	110.0
Weight (lbs):	1,100
Tires:	30 x 3
Production:	1903 2,497 1904 2,457 1905 3,942 1906 3,559 1907 2,884 1908 2,377 (calendar year, all models, of which about 90 percent were one-cylinder models during the 1903-08 era)

[1]1907 Runabout

Charles Stewart Rolls (*top*) **and Frederick Henry Royce came from very different backgrounds. Yet, in 1904, they joined forces to build and sell motor cars. Two years later, the partnership produced the Silver Ghost.**

Henry Royce probably did not start out to create the "Best Car in the World" when he designed a new Six in the placid English summer of 1906. What he wanted was to replace his rough-running six-cylinder "Thirty" with something more reliable, something smoother and quieter. He succeeded so completely that the new car, introduced at the Olympia Motor Show and later named Silver Ghost, became the longest-running single model next to the Model T Ford (and, much later, the VW Beetle and the British Mini)—and certainly the most famous luxury car in history. The Silver Ghost remains to this day the most desirable model among antique (pre-1930) cars.

Rolls-Royce, founded in Manchester in 1904, was the amalgam of socialite entrepreneur Charles S. Rolls, who'd been selling Panhards and wanted something better, and the aforementioned Mr. Royce, whose previous experience had been with electric cranes. Early production involved a variety of cars in different sizes with two, three, four, and six cylinders, about as successful as bystanders expected from this unlikely duo. But those who thought the venture would fail did not reckon on Royce's acumen, nor his single-minded determination to build a better car than anybody else.

The Silver Ghost was renowned for its smooth, quiet running, achieved with a massive, seven-main-bearing crankshaft and stiff crankcase. Its cylinders were cast in two blocks of three, inclusive of heads, which eliminated head gaskets and the chances of their blowing. The specifications included full-pressure lubrication, an electrical system that really worked, and a precision carburetor made with the quality of a Swiss watch. Its reliability, at a time when "horseless carriages" were anything but reliable, was legendary. This was proven when a Silver Ghost emerged from a 15,000-mile trial in 1907, observed by the Royal Automobile Club, with highest marks. Four years later, on the London-Edinburgh-London run, a Ghost ran the entire distance in top gear with a fuel consumption of 24.32 miles per Imperial gallon (19 mpg U.S.), an astonishing performance for the time in such a heavy car.

Although the seven-liter side-valve engine's compression ratio was only 3.2:1, it developed 48 brake horsepower at 1,500 rpm, and would deliver 50-mph cruising speeds, which was more than an enthusiastic driver could do on almost any public road of the day. When a Ghost owner wanted to really let it out, he'd pay a visit to Brooklands, the huge banked oval in Surrey, built just after the first Ghosts. Brooklands' motto was "the right crowd and no crowding," which was certainly appropriate here: the Silver Ghost chassis alone cost £985, close to $5,000 at the time, five or 10 times what the average professional could expect to make in a year. Truly this was a car for the classes and not the masses.

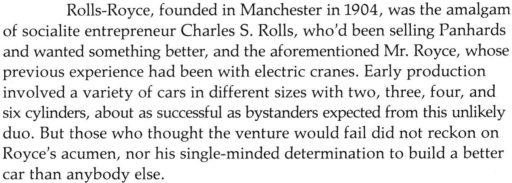

The Silver Ghost, which enjoyed a production run of two decades, was renowned for its smooth, quiet running. It was overbuilt, which is precisely why its reliability became legendary.

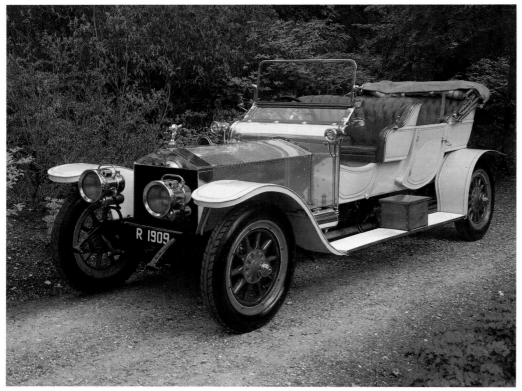

Because of the extraordinary quality built into the Rolls-Royce Silver Ghost, such as this 1909 model, prices were always extremely high, output low.

Henry Royce's success came at a key time, when the cash-poor company desperately needed a winner. So well received was it that the firm moved to more spacious quarters in Derby in 1908, simultaneously deciding to produce only this model—and so it did for the next 17 years.

The first mechanical change came in 1909, when an increase in stroke brought displacement to 7.4 liters and the original four-speed transmission was replaced by a three-speed unit. By 1911, when Rolls-Royce prepared a car for the London-Edinburgh run, compression was 3.5:1 and carburetion increases had brought horsepower to 58. The Ghost reverted to a four-speed transmission in 1913, when cantilever rear suspension was adopted. That was the year when Rolls-Royce was able to claim an honest 80 mph for the light, open-bodied Ghosts built for the Austrian Alpine Trials, where they finished ahead of all other rivals. Incidentally, the beautiful London-Edinburgh tourer survives, and recently changed hands at a Florida auction for $1,3000,000—a bargain compared to two other, less distinguished examples which sold for $2,005,000 and $2,600,000.

Limited production continued during the Great War, when many new and some old Ghosts were fitted with armored bodywork for running battles against the Turks in the Middle East, under such commanders as Allenby and Lawrence of Arabia. Others were used as staff cars and ambulances. Inflation saw the chassis price rise to £2,100 ($10,165) after the war, although this now included a chain-driven self-starter and four-wheel brakes with a servo assist. Brake horsepower of the 1919 and later models rose to 70.

In 1920, Rolls-Royce of America, Incorporated, was founded at Springfield, Massachusetts, in a plant purchased from the American Wire Wheel Company. The object was to build cars for the American market while avoiding high import tariffs, and the subsidiary enjoyed good success until the Depression closed it down in 1931. Silver Ghosts were built at Springfield beginning in 1921. Retaining their English right-hand drive, they offered the 7.4-liter engine rated at 80 bhp. In 1925, Springfield finally switched to left-hand drive, by which time the cars were developing 85 bhp at 2,300 rpm and could do 70-plus mph with the high-speed (3.25:1)

rear axle ratio. Two huge wheelbases, of 144 and 150½ inches, were available, and bodies were supplied by the cream of American coach builders, chiefly Brewster. Of the 2,944 Springfield Rolls-Royces built over 11 years, 1,703 were Silver Ghosts.

Paul Woudenberg, in his *Illustrated Rolls-Royce and Bentley Buyer's Guide* (1984), writes that the American Rolls had "no glaring weaknesses and, given regular maintenance and lubrication, has nearly unlimited life. The American Ghost has been given much attention in the *Flying Lady*, publication of the Rolls-Royce Owners Club, especially in the years after 1952, and owners will find back issues of this magazine (still available) a valuable guide in maintenance and troubleshooting." He adds that while the domestic version lacked the four-wheel brakes of the later British cars, it did feature valve covers, an important improvement over the exposed valves of the English models. The domestics can be recognized at a glance by their drum headlamps, tubular bumpers, and American componentry such as electrics, as well as left-hand drive after 1925. Finally, since Brewster built the vast majority of American bodies (and was itself bought by Rolls-Royce of America in 1923), the Springfield cars carry a far more uniform line of bodywork.

The Silver Ghost was superseded in Britain by the Phantom I in 1925, after a long and distinguished career. UK production since 1906 amounted to 6,173 chassis, making 7,876 altogether.

Specifications[1]	
Engine:	I-6, cast in 2 blocks, integral heads, side valves, 7,036 cc (4½ x 4½-in bore x stroke), 7 main bearings, dual ignition with magneto and trembler coil, 3.2:1 compression ratio, 48 bhp @ 1,500 rpm
Transmission:	4-speed, cone clutch multi-dry-plate clutch
Suspension, front:	Semi-elliptic leaf springs
Suspension, rear:	Semi-elliptic leaf springs with auxiliary transverse leaf spring
Brakes:	External contracting on the driveshaft
Wheelbase (in.):	135½ and 143½
Weight (lbs):	2,050-2,200 (chassis only)
Top speed (mph):	60
Production:	UK 6,173 US 1,703 (1907-26)

[1]1907

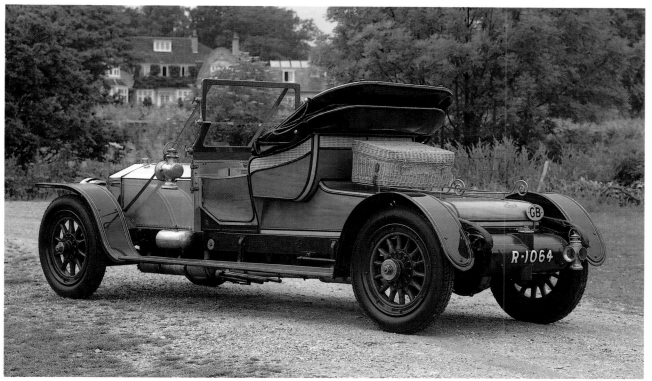

The very finest coach-builders in Europe and America provided bodywork for the Silver Ghost, this 1911 chauffeur-driven model (*above*) being a prime example. More sporting body styles included this replica of the 1911 40/50 HP "Balloon Car" (*left*).

It was on October 1, 1908, just about a month before William Howard Taft defeated William Jennings Bryan for the Presidency of the United States, that the Ford Motor Company unveiled the little machine that many historians think of as the most significant automobile of all time.

Henry Ford called it the Model T—hardly surprising since Henry had already run through the alphabet from A to S, though a lot of letters were skipped along the way. It was built only as a touring car at first, but within a few months a number of other body styles would be added to the line. Strictly a utilitarian vehicle, the Ford took no beauty prizes, and it won no speed contests. Still, its 22-horsepower, four-cylinder engine could propel the 1,200-pound car to a top speed of between 35 and 40 miles an hour, adequate for the mostly unpaved roads of the era. Cooling was by the primitive thermo-siphon method, lubrication via a splash system. The gas tank nestled beneath the front seat, its fuel being fed to the engine by the force of gravity. Meanwhile, the driver shifted the two-speed planetary transmission with foot pedals. The car didn't even have demountable rims at first, though in 1919 they became available for an extra $25.

Widely known as the "Tin Lizzie," the little Ford became the butt of a thousand jokes. But it was this machine, more than all the others combined, that was responsible for putting America—and ultimately the world—on wheels. On the strength of the Model T, Ford's yearly production would increase from 10,000 cars in 1908 to nearly two million 15 years later. As early as 1913, in fact, Ford was literally outproducing all the rest of the nation's automakers put together!

The formula for the Model T's success was a very basic one: It was simple, it was tough, and it was cheap (but not cheaply built). In some respects it was even ahead of its time. The engine, for example, was cast *en bloc* at a time when most manufacturers cast their cylinders singly or in pairs. Further, the cylinder head was removable, a daring innovation at the time. People, including many so-called experts, said it would leak, but it didn't. And Ford's metallurgy, under the direction of C. Harold Wills (who would later build the Wills Sainte Claire), was superior to that of most cars selling at many times the Model T's price. That figure, $825 at first, was steadily reduced as output increased, until by 1924 a brand new Ford runabout could be purchased for as little as $260!

By 1913, the year Ford production first topped the 200,000 mark, Henry had to abandon his original notion of using conveyor belts to bring component parts to the assembly point. Instead, he substituted a moving assembly line, operated at first by means of a windlass. By year's end he was able to assemble a complete car in 93 minutes, while most

Henry Ford built a fine car in the Model T, using only top-quality materials such as Vanadium steel. The 1909 Touring Car (*above*) listed at $850 and 7,728 were built. But the genius of Henry Ford—with help from others, to be sure—was the moving assembly line that allowed him to steadily reduce prices and thereby expand production so that the average man could afford a Ford. For example, by 1923 a five-seater Touring Car could be had for as little as $295, and over 900,000 were built.

The Model T used Henry Ford's beloved transverse leaf springs both front and rear. Tire sizes differed: 30 x 3-inches front, 30 x 3½-inches rear.

The Model T's two-speed planetary transmission was operated by foot pedals. The handbrake—such as it was—was located to the driver's left.

Relatively advanced when introduced, the Model T's L-head inline four was cast *en-bloc*. It developed 20/22 horsepower and 83 lbs/ft torque.

of his competitors still measured their production time in days.

It was in 1914 that Henry Ford is said to have issued his now-famous declaration that "the public can have any color it wants, so long as it's black!" There was a certain arrogance to the pronouncement, and indeed Ford could be an arrogant man. But in this instance the dictum made sense, for in those days the only available finish that would dry fast enough to keep up with the hectic pace of the Ford assembly line—now turning out more than 300,000 cars annually—was black Japan enamel.

In the early years one had to crank a Model T in order to get the engine started. And woe betide the driver who forgot to retard the spark before doing so—doctors had to set many a broken arm resulting from the Ford engine kicking back while being cranked. An electric starter was offered as optional equipment commencing in 1919, but it added $75—about 15 percent—to the price of the car. Many, possibly most, buyers elected to keep on cranking.

The technique of driving a Model T has almost become a lost art. Having cranked the engine into action, the driver had to advance the spark, then turn the ignition key from "battery" (used only for starting) to "magneto." At that point, he was ready to go.

The handbrake, located to the driver's left, was almost totally useless for stopping the car, nor would it hold the car very effectively if parked on a hill. Its real purpose was to disengage the gears, for once the brake was set the transmission was in neutral. Then as the driver released the hand brake, he opened the hand throttle a bit (there being no foot accelerator). At the same time, he depressed the left pedal, placing the car in low gear. Amid a shrill whining sound, the Ford got under way. Then at a speed of perhaps 10 miles per hour, the driver released that pedal so that the transmission would shift itself into high gear. In the hands of a novice, the shift often took place with a pronounced jerk, but with a bit of practice most operators learned how to accomplish it more smoothly.

Reversing the Model T required the coordination of both feet and the right

Early Model Ts came in red, gray, and green, with red being reserved mainly for the Touring Cars. It wasn't until 1914 that black became the one and only color. This 1909 Model T flaunts a generous amount of brass trim; later models wouldn't.

hand. The left foot depressed the "low" pedal halfway, thus releasing the transmission from high gear. The middle pedal (there were three) was then fully depressed, engaging the reverse gear. And of course the driver had to control the throttle with the right hand. Perhaps this helps explain why Henry Ford didn't bother to outfit the Model T with a foot accelerator, since a third foot would have been required in order to make use of it.

Then there was the service brake. Located in the transmission, it was operated by the pedal on the right. By modern standards it wasn't very effective, but truthfully it wasn't any worse than the conventional two-wheel binders used in those days by Chevrolet and other makes. There was just one problem—the brake band tended to wear out faster than the transmission's "low" or "reverse" bands. But that was solved if about every third time the driver slowed down he hit the reverse pedal, rather than the brake. No, this procedure wouldn't cause any damage, for the mechanism was tough enough to with-

stand a lot of punishment, and it helped assure that all three bands—low, reverse, and brake—wore out at about the same time.

Finally, we should mention the dashboard instrumentation. It consisted of an ammeter. Period. Of course, a speedometer was available to anyone willing to spend a few extra dollars. The fuel supply, meanwhile, was measured by dipping a stick, preferably a clean one, into the gas tank. And if the engine overheated, the driver was summarily notified by means of a geyser spouting out of the radiator. A gauge would have been superfluous! And since lubrication was by the splash system, an oil pressure gauge would likewise have been quite useless. As we've said, it's all very simple!

Henry Ford expected to continue producing the Model T indefinitely, making only minimal changes and improvements. But by 1924, the year the 10-millionth Model T was built, it had become apparent that a new car would have to be developed if Ford was to remain competitive. Ernest Kanzler, brother-in-law and confidant

to Edsel Ford, and himself a Ford vice-president, wrote a long letter to old Henry. In it he tactfully refrained from any criticism of the T, but he managed delicately to suggest that it was time for something new. Kanzler was exactly correct, of course, but that letter cost him his job.

Henry relented to the extent of introducing balloon tires as optional equipment in 1925. A few color choices were offered the following year, along with a larger brake band. There was even some nickel-plated trim on certain models.

But it was too little, and much too late. By the mid-Twenties, for an extra $150 the motorist could buy a Chevrolet instead. For that money, the Chevy came equipped with a three-speed sliding-gear transmission, and it was faster, quieter, more flexible, prettier, and a whole lot more comfortable than the Model T. And by that time it had come to be very nearly as tough.

Ford's market share had been falling for a number of years, and just as steadily as Ford sales were declining, those of Chevrolet were gaining. Chevrolet General Manager William S. "Big Bill" Knudsen, ironically a former Ford executive, had promised his troops in his Danish accent that Chevy would match Ford's production "vun for vun." It had become obvious, even to stubborn old Henry Ford, that Knudsen was about to make good on that pledge. So finally, on May 26, 1927, production of the Model T was ceased, as preparations were being made for the first really new Ford in nearly two decades: the Model A.

Specifications	
Engine:	L-head I-4, 176.7 cid (3¾ x 4-in. bore x stroke), 4.5:1 compression ratio, 20/22 bhp @ 1,600 rpm, 83 lbs/ft torque @ 900 rpm
Transmission:	2-speed, planetary, foot pedal controls, 24-26 disc clutch, torque tube drive
Suspension:	Rigid axles, transverse leaf springs
Brakes:	Contracting band in transmission, parking brake on rear wheels
Wheelbase (in.):	100.0
Overall length (in.):	134.5
Weight (lbs):	1,200 (touring car)
Top speed:	35-40 mph
Production:	15,007,033 between 1908 and 1927 (U.S. only)

The early century Lanchesters, seen here as a 1908 model, were not only innovative, they were also unconventional. Further, they were extremely well built and very expensive. The make was never very well known outside of its native England.

Lanchester has long since passed into the netherworld of half-forgotten automotive names. The company was little known outside its native Britain, and little appreciated even there by enthusiasts born after the Second Great War. Yet the unconventional brilliance of Frederick Lanchester resonates on after some 90 years in the disc brake and the counter-rotating engine "balance" shaft. The former, of course, has become nearly universal, and the latter has been embraced by no less than Germany's Porsche (albeit through a licensing arrangement with Mitsubishi of Japan).

Born in 1868, Fred Lanchester, unlike so many automotive pioneers, was something of a Renaissance man. Indeed, historian Ralph Stein described him as having a "da Vinci kind of mind... excited by many things. As early as the 1890s he had delved into the mysteries of heavier-than-air flight [and also] interested himself in optics and photography, music and poetry. [So] when he set his mind to designing a motorcar, he did it in his own unique way, owing nothing to what others had done before."

The result was not only the first all-British car, but one of the first designed *as* an automobile rather than being adapted from horse-drawn carriages. The production model did not appear until 1901, even though Lanchester had built a fully running and reliable prototype in 1894 (modified two years later). Why so long? As Stein records, "Lanchester was a perfectionist who [wouldn't] start building cars for sale until an entire system of production had been worked out. He was the first to insist on fully interchangeable parts, before Henry Leland of Cadillac, who is usually credited with this, and long before Henry Ford. To this end it was necessary to design and build specialized machine tools, go and no-go gauges, special jigs, and all the devices other manufacturers did not deem necessary until, years later, they turned to mass production."

Of course, *as* a perfectionist, Fred was less interested in building many cars right away as he was in building the one best car he could, and his fertile mind devised unusual but effective solutions to some of the major engineering problems of the day. For example, at a time when most every engine was a loud rattletrap threatening to shake everything apart, Lanchester's first engine, a horizontally opposed air-cooled twin, was inherently balanced and nearly vibration-free. This was accomplished by giving each cylinder its own flywheel and crankshaft assembly, mounted one above the other but turning in opposite directions, and by having three connecting rods per piston: two attached to each piston's own crank, the third to the opposite crank. The shafts were then geared together.

In addition, that first Lanchester engine employed a type of flywheel-magneto ignition that Henry Ford would more or less copy

Behind this badge (*right*) was a midships-mounted four-cylinder engine, which was rated at 30 horsepower and boasted overhead valves. It was capable of pushing the relatively large Lanchester to a top speed of some 50 mph, more than adequate for the roads of the 1908 era.

Although the Lanchester sported a generous sprinkling of brass trim, the laid-back, pushed-back radiator gave the car unusual proportions. In fact, early Lanchester design was totally original, and to many eyes not altogether aesthetically pleasing.

for his Model T of 1908. In addition Fred also designed a new type of igniter that fit like the breech block of a rifle, thus permitting instant changes without the danger of burning one's fingers. Equally unusual was the provision for adjusting spark externally with the engine running.

Lanchester's inventiveness didn't end with the engine. In contrast to then-prevalent two-speed sliding gear transmissions, he devised a three-speed planetary unit geared to the lower of the two crankshafts along with a cleverly combined clutch and brake. Instead of rudimentary chains, drive was by a sturdier and quieter worm gear. And the rear wheels turned on splined axle shafts with roller bearings—destined to be commonplace, but another of Fred's firsts. He even had to make his own bearings and machinery for cutting the splines. Springs, though conventional cantilevered elliptics, were unusually soft, with rates keyed to the rising and falling motion of a person walking. Also for comfort, seats were positioned so that passengers' eyes were level with those of passing pedestrians. Lanchester

felt this would make "automobiling" feel more natural as well as easing the driver's task of judging distances. Steering was by tiller, but Fred put his outboard, on the driver's right, rather than in the middle the car. He called it "side lever" steering because the driver operated it with his forearm, a design that also proved quite "natural."

Construction bordered on tank-like compared to contemporary cars. The original Lanchester chassis not only supported the body, but made up the lower 18 inches of it: a rigid girder-type structure of aluminum and steel members that forecast the fully unitized cars of some three decades later. Additional stiffness came from a steel plate beneath the midships engine and a full-width cylindrical gas tank that doubled as a transverse frame member. Partly embedded in that tank was a wick carburetor that Stein described as looking like "the business end of a floor mop...stuck vertically in a brass pail." Air was passed over combustible gases as they evaporated from the fuel through the wick for direct feed into the engine, thus avoiding any need for "cloggable piping."

Body construction was as unconventional as the chassis, comprising multiple panels that could be quickly removed without tools. What's more, they were designed like a Chinese puzzle so that each locked-in the one preceding it in a prescribed sequence that amounted to "no-fault" assembly.

Yet, there was still even more innovation. The transmission had a pre-select feature that predicted the much-later Wilson gearbox used on such cars as the American Cord 810 of the late Thirties. Stein recounted that "gear-shifting was easy" on the Lanchester, though controls were predictably unique: "On what Detroit would now call a 'console' stood two short levers on quadrants and a small pre-selector or 'gear change trigger.' Flicking these levers back and forth in various combinations changed pre-selected gears, and applied powerful brakes if either big lever was pulled all the way back. The system was quiet; there was nothing to do with your feet except to depress the accelerator or the bulb horn. Later, to satisfy fearful customers, Lanchester supplied optional foot brakes—discs, of all things! The first ever."

But whether because of high cost, relative complexity, or slow acceptance, most of these advanced ideas were soon washed away in the rising tide of conventionalism by the time of The Great War. It has been written that Fred Lanchester, like so many inventors, had a poor head for business. Perhaps he himself recognized this, for he didn't hesitate to resign as head of the Lanchester Engine Company when it found itself in severe financial trouble in 1904. Though Fred would continue as chief engineer, his younger brother George took charge of what was renamed the Lanchester Motor Company, and began pursuing profits by abandoning Fred's initial ideas one by one until only his basic transmission and worm-gear final drive remained.

A water-cooled twin had been offered in 1902, delivering 12 horsepower, two more than Fred's first air-cooled unit. In 1904, Lanchester added a 2.5-liter inline four-cylinder engine with overhead valves, pressure lubrication, and a rating of 20 taxable British horsepower.

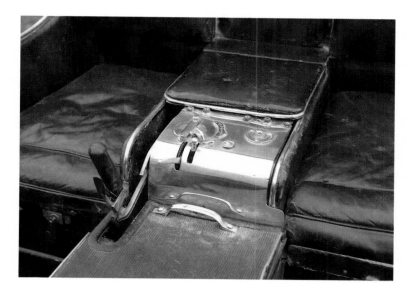

The Lanchester's transmission had a preselect feature. On what would today be called a console were mounted two short levers on quadrants and a small preselector "trigger." Once versed in the art, a driver could preselect the gears and operate the brakes via these controls.

The twins were gone by 1906, but a 28-bhp six was introduced that year. Wheel steering was offered beginning in 1907 (as an option); increasing vehicle weight then ended the "side lever steering" two years later. A new 38-bhp six arrived in 1911, followed a year later by a similarly uprated 25-bhp four-cylinder, by which time a single gearlever and three-pedal floor controls were in place. Midship engines persisted until 1914, when a new "Sporting Forty" debuted with a sidevalve six riding ahead of the passengers beneath a conventional "bonnet," Lanchester giving in to the by-then well-established *Systeme Panhard* at last.

Lanchester continued down the road of increasing orthodoxy in the Twenties, though its cars remained damn-the-cost products rivalled only by Rolls-Royce for craftsmanship and detail engineering, and built in similarly small numbers. By 1923, the large 6.2-liter "Forty" luxury tourer with overhead-cam inline six-cylinder power, introduced in 1919, had spawned a smaller, simpler companion, the 3.1-liter Twenty-One, which was replaced in 1926 by a bored-out 3.3-liter Twenty-Three. The Forty itself gave way in 1929 to the Thirty, powered by a 4.5-liter overhead-cam straight eight. But financial difficulties loomed again by 1931, and Lanchester was taken over by the BSA Group. As BSA owned Daimler, which was already catering to the "carriage trade" market, subsequent Lanchesters became smaller, much cheaper cars and, ultimately, little more than Daimlers with different badges

and less power. Lanchester managed to return in the postwar period, but would last only one decade, expiring in 1956. The last new production Lanchester was the Daimler-powered six-cylinder Dauphin, which saw minuscule production in 1953-54.

In its long, slow slide to obscurity, Lanchester mimicked the fate of Panhard and many other makes which became victims of forward-thinking that was simply too advanced to be commercially viable. It is a recurrent theme in automotive history, one with a lesson that many companies ignored to their ultimate peril: It literally doesn't pay to be too different. And more's the pity. Given today's enormous social and environmental challenges, the auto industry will need far less "group-think" and far more "Renaissance men" like Fred Lanchester if it is to have any hope of surviving long into the 21st Century. Fred would understand. Let's hope there's a new generation of automotive leaders willing and able to follow his example.

Specifications	
Engine:	Midships ohv I-4, 151.6 cid/2,485 cc (4.01 x 2.99-in./102 x 76-mm bore x stroke), 30 bhp (20 taxable)
Transmission:	3-speed planetary
Suspension, front:	Solid axle on cantilevered elliptic leaf springs, friction dampers
Suspension, rear:	Solid axle on cantilevered elliptic leaf springs, friction dampers
Brakes:	Single disc in unit with clutch
Wheelbase (in.):	113/125
Weight (lbs):	est. 2,500
Top speed:	approx. 50
Production:	NA, but likely no more than 500

Mention the name Mercer to almost any car buff and you'll get an instant response: "Raceabout." For of all the cars built by the Mercer Automobile Company during its 15-year (1910-25) lifespan, the sporty Raceabout was by all odds the most famous.

But not, perhaps surprisingly, the most numerous. Mercer was never a large-scale producer in any case, but the bulk of its output was comprised of more conventional body styles: roadsters, touring cars, sport phaetons, and sedans. There were even a few formal types, such as town cars and limousines, though coachwork of that sort must have seemed out of place on a chassis that was built primarily for speed, rather than comfort.

Mercer had its genesis in Trenton, Mercer County, New Jersey in 1909. Bankrolling the company was the Roebling family, builders of the Brooklyn Bridge, along with the Kusers, another very wealthy clan. It's not clear who designed the original Mercer automobiles, but in any case they appeared in 1910, powered by four-cylinder, L-head Beaver engines. Three body styles were offered: Toy Tonneau, Touring, and Speedster. Each was priced at $1,950, about 20 percent higher than the contemporary Cadillac Model 30. They were low-slung, fast, and rugged, as C.G. Roebling insisted they should be.

It was a respectable start, though hardly the stuff of which legends are made. But young Washington Roebling II, one of the financial "angels" of the operation, wanted something more. And at the same time, something less. That is, he wanted to build a very fast automobile, and if it happened to be short on creature comforts, so be it.

To design this new machine, Washington Roebling acquired the services of a talented engineer who's impressive name was Finley Robertson Porter. But Roebling himself played an important role in developing what was to become the original Mercer Raceabout. This is how automotive writer Ralph Stein describes its story:

"Much of the credit for the Raceabout's uniquely satisfying lines belongs to Washington A. Roebling II. . . . Young Washington . . . wanted the 35-R Mercer to be a low-slung machine. This insistence on lowness gave the car its own lovely shape and made every other bucket-seated, bolster-gas-tanked speedster look high and awkward. . . . The engine sat low between the tall wheels. This in turn raised the fender line in relation to the hood. Thus the rear line of the front fenders and the fronts of the rear fenders swept downwards at a sweetly shallow angle to the short, high running boards, which were far closer to the low chassis frame than on similar cars. The rake of the steering column, perforce, also had to be sharper in order to place the steering wheel comfortably in the driver's hands, since the low hood line allowed the cushions of the bucket seats to be set right on the floor without impairing visibility.

Though New Jersey-based Mercer was never a large-scale automaker, it achieved fame far beyond what that firm's modest size would have suggested. That was mainly because of the Raceabout, a low-slung, out-and-out speedster.

The result: perfection!"

Introduced late in 1910 as a 1911 model, the Raceabout was as light as it was low. A spartan machine, it had almost no body at all: just a pair of bucket seats, a 25-gallon fuel tank, and a five-gallon oil tank perched atop the frame. As Stein once observed, one didn't sit *in* the Raceabout; one sat *on* it.

Happily, the Raceabout *went* even better than it *looked*. It was powered by a 300-cubic-inch, T-head four-banger, with cylinders cast in pairs, after the common practice of the time. Officially rated at 34 horsepower, it was almost certainly good for more than 50—the figure 58 has been mentioned. A wet, multiple-disc clutch was used starting in 1914, replacing the original leather-faced cone type. And although a three-speed transmission was employed at first, by 1913 it was replaced by a four-speed gearbox, a welcome improvement.

In view of the almost total absence of a body, the Raceabout's $2,250 price was considered a stiff one. One could, if desired, have a similarly-powered four-passenger Toy Tonneau for another $500, but it is the Raceabout that has become almost legendary. And while these two high-speed models—Raceabout and Toy Tonneau—were finding

Befitting its dapper, driver-oriented attitude, the Raceabout was sparsely fitted, including even instrumentation, but a drum-type speedometer, odometer, and trip odometer were provided.

Part of the Raceabout spec included a Bosch dual coil ignition (*below*) with "Run" and "Start" positions.

Powering the 1912 Raceabout was an inline T-head four (*above*), which was cast in pairs. With a displacement of 300 cubic inches, it cranked out 58 horse-power, enough for a top speed of about 75 mph.

The 1912 Mercer Raceabout was still part of the brass-age era, which endears it to collectors. Note the dash, lights, and gas-filler caps. The seats were true buckets, the seating position quite low.

their place in the rapidly expanding automobile market, production of the more traditional Beaver-engined Mercers was continued for only one final season.

As Henry Ford had been quick to discover, the way to gain publicity for an automobile—almost *any* automobile—in those pioneer days was to take it to the racetrack. Washington Roebling understood the value of that sort of publicity, so during 1911 Mercer Raceabouts were entered in six major events, copping top honors in five of them—along with two seconds and one third place. Captain of the Mercer driving team was Ralph DePalma, one of the leading drivers of his generation. DePalma personally racked up eight new world's records during his time with Mercer.

The one contest in which the Raceabout failed to triumph, incidentally, was the very first "Indy 500," where Mercers placed 12th and 14th. But five out of six is a very creditable record for a brand new car. And in any case, in the grueling 500-mile contest at Indianapolis, just to finish *at all* was considered a major achievement.

By 1912 Mercers, thanks to their combination of speed and superior handling qualities, were winning races all over the country, securely establishing the make's reputation. But on April 15 of that year, tragedy struck: Washington Roebling II went down with the *Titanic* when it struck an iceberg off the coast of Newfoundland.

Mercers continued to race, and to win, following the death of Roebling, with Ralph DePalma still serving as the team's capable captain. But then in 1913, Finley Porter, evidently on the premise that two champions on the team were better than one, hired Barney Oldfield as a member of the Mercer team. DePalma, furious at what he considered to be a deliberate slight, quit in a huff and signed on with Mercedes, and it was in a Mercedes that he won the 1915 Indy 500.

DePalma's resignation was followed in 1914 by that of Finley Robertson Porter, who left in order to produce a car of his own. Named for Porter's initials, the F.R.P. was a big, expensive machine, powered by a 100-horsepower

A monocle windshield did little to protect the driver from the elements; goggles were highly recommended.

engine. Unhappily, it was not commercially viable, nor did its successor, the even costlier Porter, fare any better.

Meanwhile, with Mercer Raceabouts continuing to distinguish themselves on the nation's racetracks, a new chief engineer arrived at the Trenton factory. This was Brooklyn-born Eric Delling, who at a later time would produce a fine steam automobile under his own name. Delling took the company in a new direction, developing for 1915 a somewhat larger series of cars, powered by an L-head four-cylinder engine of his own design. The Raceabout was given a heavier, more conventional, and considerably more comfortable body, while the wheelbase was stretched from 108 to 115 inches.

The Delling Mercers were ahead of their time in a number of respects. Their 73-horsepower engine was fitted with a centrifugal water pump, instead of relying on the thermo-siphon system commonly used in those days. A drilled crankshaft facilitated full-pressure lubrication. Roller tappets were used, and both main and connecting rod bearings were of the insert type, bronze-backed and babbitt-lined. Pistons were made of aluminum. Also highly unusual was the latter-day Mercer's 1.8:1 stroke/

A Raceabout passed just about anything on the road in 1912. Mercer thus provided a foot-operated horn so that fast drivers could keep their hands on the steering wheel.

bore ratio. Connecting rods, we are told, measured 14 inches, center-to-center.

Other mechanical features of the Delling-designed Mercers included a dry multiple-disc clutch; four-speed gearbox; U.S.L. starting and electrical system, contained, remarkably enough, in the flywheel; service brake consisting of a huge drum on the driveshaft; and the industry's first hydraulic shock absorbers.

Delling left Mercer in 1916, although his steamer didn't appear until 1923. The Mercer automobiles were little changed for several years following his departure, however. By 1919, F. W. and C. G. Roebling had both followed Washington Roebling in death, and control of the company passed to a Wall Street syndicate. Joining with Simplex and Locomobile, it became a part of the short-lived Hare Motors, but two years later control was returned to a group of veteran Mercer staff members.

A Rochester-powered overhead-valve six appeared in 1923, a fine 84-horsepower car selling for as much as $5,000. But the Raceabout was gone. Production, which had never amounted to more than 500 cars a year, was halted in 1924. Re-started some months later, the factory stumbled on for a time, turning out no more than a handful of cars, doubtless assembled from stock on hand. And then, early in 1925, it was all over.

Specifications	
Engine:	T-head I-4, cast in pairs, 300 cid (4⅜ x 5-in. bore x stroke), 58 bhp
Transmission:	4-speed, selective
Suspension, front:	Rigid axle, semi-elliptic springs
Suspension, rear:	Rigid axle, semi-elliptic springs
Brakes:	Contracting; drum on driveshaft
Wheelbase (in.):	108.0
Weight (lbs):	2,850
Top speed (mph):	70-80
Production:	Less than 1,000 from 1911-15

By 1914, Cadillac's four-cylinder Model 30 had been in production for nearly five years, and the time had come for its replacement. Not that there was really anything wrong with the Model 30, for it was a very competent automobile. In fact, many years later when David Fergusson, long-time chief engineer for the Pierce-Arrow Motor Car Company, observed that "Cadillac for years had the reputation of producing the best medium-priced cars in the world," he was referring to the Model 30. One might question Fergusson's reference to the Cadillac as a "medium-priced" car, but in this world all things are relative—in 1914 a new Cadillac touring car could be purchased for just $1,975, while the least expensive Pierce-Arrow cost $4,300.

But despite its outstanding reputation for reliability and durability, the Model 30 had become seriously dated. The public had come to appreciate the smoothness of six-cylinder engines, and many—perhaps most—producers of cars in the Cadillac's price range had made the switch from fours to sixes. The competition was simply eating Cadillac alive. From 17,284 cars manufactured during 1913, the factory's output had plummeted the following year to just 7,818 units.

Fortunately, Cadillac's general manager, Henry M. Leland, had not been caught napping. For several years he'd been experimenting with various engine types, and as a result of his research he came to the conclusion that a V-8 would be preferable to a six. Presumably, the compact nature of the vee-type design appealed to him, for in some instances the long crankshaft that characterized the inline sixes had displayed an unfortunate tendency to whip at high rpm.

Admittedly, the V-8 was an unusual design in those days. Most people had never seen such an engine, but the type was not unheard of. More than a decade earlier, two French manufacturers had developed V-8's and used them to power racing machines, while in this country Howard Marmon had demonstrated an air-cooled V-8 as early as 1906. And then, in 1910, the respected French firm of DeDion had marketed a production V-8.

Charles Kettering, head of the Dayton Engineering Laboratories (DELCO) had purchased a DeDion V-8 for research purposes. With the help of his associate, Edward Deeds, Kettering disassembled the DeDion engine, examined it carefully, then put it back together and tested it extensively. Afterward, Kettering and Deeds built an experimental V-8 of their own design and submitted it to Henry Leland.

Leland immediately undertook to authorize the in-house development of a Cadillac V-8, using the Kettering-Deeds engine as its basis. To take charge of the project he hired D. McCall White, a Scottish-born engineer whose previous employers had included the prestigious firms of Daimler and Napier. There is some evidence that Cadillac's engineering

Cadillac sales had plummeted in 1914, and many would say this was because it had hung on to its Model 30 four-cylinder model for too long—after all, most other luxury makers were running with sixes. But Cadillac founder Henry M. Leyland decided to leapfrog his rivals with something even better: the Model 51 V-8.

Spartan instrument panels were the norm in 1915, and Cadillac's was no exception. The main instrument was a Warner drum-type speedometer with regular and trip odometers, but it was mounted out of the driver's line of vision at the center of the panel. The other gauges were to its left.

staff, a tight-knit group, took a dim view of having an outsider put in charge of so important a project, but obviously Henry Leland had his reasons.

First of all, the Cadillac people had had virtually no experience in building high-speed engines; in this respect, the better European firms were light years ahead of their American contemporaries. White was in a position to bring that expertise to Cadillac.

Then there was the matter of secrecy. Although he was very conservative by nature, Henry Leland was not without a sense of the dramatic, and he wanted to spring the new V-8 as a complete surprise. To keep the development of the new powerplant secret would have been quite impossible if the entire staff at the Cadillac factory had known what was going on.

So Leland housed the project in a small concrete block building, located a few miles out of Detroit in the community of Mt. Clemens, Michigan. The facility was out-of-bounds to all but a few carefully selected Cadillac employees, and those who were granted admittance were pledged to tell no one—even their wives—about the development of the new motor.

Introduced in September 1914 as a 1915 model, the new Cadillac V-8 was known as the Type 51. Nobody knows for sure how the model number was chosen, but it has been speculated that the digits may have represented a reversal of the year of introduction: 15. In any case, the car found instant popularity, with production reaching 13,002 units during its initial model year.

The engine was cast in two blocks of four cylinders each, located exactly opposite one another. Fork-and-blade connecting rods were fitted. The crankshaft was drilled, and full pressure lubrication was employed, while a single, centrally-located camshaft operated the valves. Water circulation was controlled by means of an impeller pump, with a thermostat located within each cylinder block.

Cadillac had advertised the old Model 30 at "40-50" horsepower, a respectable enough figure by 1914 standards. But the new 314.5-cubic-inch V-8 developed a rousing 70 horsepower, five more than even the Packard Model 38, a car costing nearly twice the price of the Type 51.

The clutch was of the multiple dry disc type, far superior to the leather-faced cone employed by the Model 30. A three-speed selective transmission was used, and the spiral bevel final drive utilized a ratio of 4.44:1. Steering was of the worm-and-sector type, and both internal and external brakes operated on drums fitted to the rear wheels.

The heart of the 1915 Cadillac was its new V-8, a 90-degree unit with a displacement of 314.5 cubic inches. It developed an impressive 70 bhp and 180 lbs/ft torque.

Cadillac didn't note on its hubcaps that its new "8" was actually a "V-8." That's likely because straight eights weren't on the market yet, so of course there was no reason to make a distinction.

Eight body types were offered, with the popular open styles selling for $1,975, exactly the same as the previous year's four-cylinder Model 30. Prices for the closed body styles ranged from $2,500 for the Landaulet Coupe to $3,600 for the prestigious Berline Limousine. In whatever guise, the Cadillac represented a phenomenal bargain, for the Type 51 proved to be a fine automobile, as durable as it was powerful.

Since the new engine was America's first mass-produced V-8, of course questions were raised about it. Cadillac countered with an advertisement that is still considered a classic. Appearing first in the January 2, 1915 issue of *The Saturday Evening Post*, the ad was titled "The Penalty of Leadership." It marked the beginning of a highly effective advertising campaign in which Cadillac, which already billed itself as "The Standard of the World," undertook to present its owners as a breed apart, people distinguished by their own superior taste.

In truth, however, the new engine wasn't completely above criticism. The problem had to do with the single-plane (180-degree) crankshaft. The Cadillac would cruise smoothly and remarkably quietly at speeds between 55 and 60 miles an hour. But between 40 and 50, a more appropriate speed range given the condition of the roads in those days, it exhibited the same secondary out-of-balance shaking force that characterized the four-cylinder engines of that time. Not until the coming of the 1924 models would Cadillac develop a solution to the problem in the form of an inherently balanced crankshaft.

In the meantime, however, the Cadillac V-8 gave an excellent account of itself despite the roughness, and in its second year on the market a 38.5-percent sales increase was recorded. For 1916, the Cadillac's already impressive power was increased by 10 percent. Meanwhile, prices on the popular open models went up as well, by $105, but the Cadillac was still one of the industry's best bargains.

By that time, of course, war was raging in Europe, and Cadillacs—in undetermined but apparently significant numbers—were ordered by the Cana-

The 1915 Cadillac V-8 found instant acceptance with luxury car buyers as output shot up from 7,818 units to 13,002. Riding a 125-inch wheelbase, the four-door touring model cost $1,975, compared to $3,750 for a Packard Six.

dian, British, and French governments for use as staff cars, ambulances, and the like. Then, in April 1917, the United States entered the conflict, and the Cadillac seven-passenger touring was adopted by both the U.S. Army and the Marine Corps as the standard officers' car. More than 2,000 of these sturdy automobiles were shipped overseas, along with a reported 300 Cadillac limousines, to be used by high ranking officers including General John J. Pershing, Commander of the American Expeditionary Force.

So well did these cars acquit themselves that some time later Colonel Edward J. Hall, co-designer of the Liberty aircraft engine, spoke of them as having given "better service than any other make of car in France." The colonel could not recall ever having seen a Cadillac "tied up for trouble of any kind," and in concluding his remarks he added, "One of the first things I did on my arrival home was to purchase one for my own use."

Cadillac, in those years, was not considered one of America's most prestigious automobiles. Historically, that honor had been more or less divided among the "Three Ps": Packard, Peerless,

and Pierce-Arrow. But after the conclusion of the Great War (as our grandparents called it), the gargantuan machines on which those companies had built their reputation fell rapidly out of favor. The electric starter, pioneered by Cadillac back in 1912, had come into general use, and women by the thousands had taken the wheel of the family car. They, and in time their husbands as well, turned increasingly to Cadillac as an automobile of impeccable quality in a manageable size.

Specifications[1]	
Engine:	90-degree V-8, cast in blocks of four, 314.5 cid ($3\frac{1}{8}$ x 5 $\frac{1}{8}$-in. bore x stroke), single plane crankshaft, 3 main bearings, 70 bhp @ 2,400 rpm, 180 lbs/ft torque @ 2,000 rpm
Transmission:	3-speed, selective, floor-mounted lever, 15-disc dry-plate clutch, shaft drive, 4.41 rear axle ratio
Suspension, front:	Rigid axle, semi-elliptic springs
Suspension, rear:	Rigid axle, platform springs, cross-spring
Brakes:	Mechanical, on rear wheels
Wheelbase (in.):	125.0 (special chassis, 145.0)
Tread, front and rear: (in.):	56.0
Weight (lbs):	4,000 (touring car)
Top speed (mph):	70 mph
Production:	20,404 (calendar year); 13,002 (model year)

[1]1915 Cadillac Type 51

Like the Mercer Raceabout, the Stutz Bearcat was a pure, early American sports car. The body was deliberately kept as light as possible so that performance would be maximized, as this 1918 model suggests. Note the step-over plate to the interior.

By the time Harry C. Stutz got around to the Bearcat, the car for which he is best remembered, he had been designing and building automobiles for at least six years. In 1906 he had been associated with American Motors of Indianapolis, where he designed a small but pricey 35-40 horsepower four-cylinder touring car. It was not, persistent legend and published reports to the contrary, the underslung model for which American would later become famous. Rather, Harry's chassis was entirely conventional. But it was a relatively fast automobile for its time.

Leaving American Motors in 1907, Stutz signed on as chief engineer of the Marion Motor Car Company, another Indianapolis firm, best known at the time as builder of the Marion Flyer, but remembered now primarily for its sporty 1913 Bobcat.

Then in 1910, with the backing of a financier named Campbell, Stutz organized the Stutz Auto Parts Company for the purpose of manufacturing a transaxle of Harry's own design. The business evidently prospered, but Harry Stutz wanted to build a car of his own—and he achieved that goal in 1911 with a racing machine, the very first Stutz car. Powered by a four-cylinder Wisconsin engine, driving through one of Harry's own transaxles, the racer bore no small resemblance to the later Bearcat.

Evidently Harry knew a thing or two about putting his name before the public, for he promptly announced that his car would go immediately, without trial runs or prior testing of any kind, to "the Brickyard," to take part in the first 500-mile race at the new Indianapolis Speedway. Presumably he knew his car couldn't win, since a number of its competitors boasted much bigger, more powerful engines than the Stutz's 389-cubic-inch T-head. But he had as his driver Gil Anderson, a big, rugged Swede who had competed successfully as a member of the Marion racing team. So Harry expected that his car would at least place within the first 10.

It didn't. Anderson came in just out of the money, in 11th place. Now when you think about it, that's not a bad record for a brand new, untried machine. Many a contestant failed to finish that grueling run at all. And the Stutz's time was creditable enough: 500 miles in 442 minutes, with, in Harry Stutz's words, "not a single mechanical adjustment." Flat tires didn't count, of course, and the Stutz had several of those, each one causing a delay while Anderson headed for the pits.

If Harry Stutz's spirits were dampened by his car's failure to win any money for its backers, that fact wasn't noticeable. He immediately billed his machine "The Car that Made Good in a Day." With the backing of Henry Campbell, his silent partner, he organized the Ideal Motor Car Company and commenced preparations for a series-built Stutz to be

The Bearcat's speedometer was in front of the driver, though mounted low. Even in 1918, Stutz favored right-hand drive.

offered to the general public.

The production Stutz, like the racing prototype, was powered by a Wisconsin engine that cranked out an advertised 50 horsepower. A powerplant of Harry's own design would have to wait. Five body styles were offered, including the Bearcat, a competitor to the highly regarded Mercer Raceabout. Like the latter, it was a bare-bones sporting vehicle consisting principally of frame, engine, steering wheel, bucket seats, and fuel tank. All of the earliest Stutzes shared a 120-inch wheelbase. Then in late 1912, a 60-horsepower, 468-cid six-cylinder series riding a 124-inch chassis was added to the line. This one, too, was available as a Bearcat.

In May 1913, Stutz Auto Parts and the Ideal Motor Car Company merged to form the Stutz Motor Car Company. Business was good, though its volume — like that of most higher-priced makes in those days — was modest. Between

mid-1911 and the close of 1913 some 2,000 cars were sold, yielding a profit of more than $400,000 — big money in those days before inflation and before the income tax!

The car was revised somewhat for 1914, with a brutal, leather-faced cone clutch replacing the earlier multiple-disc type in what appears, in retrospect, to have been a backward step. But on the other hand, electric starting and lighting were supplied as standard equipment that year. The Bearcat came in a choice of several vivid colors, an unusual practice for the time. Overall Stutz sales fell slightly, however, to 649, down from 759 the previous season.

There was a new, smaller Stutz for 1915, evidently intended for the motorist who couldn't afford a Bearcat. Known as the Model H.C.S. (for Harry's initials), it was a 23-horsepower roadster priced at $1,475. Production figures are not available, but the fact that the little

Stutz lasted only one season presumably tells us all we need to know about its salability. This car, by the way, is not to be confused with the H.C.S. automobile, an entirely separate marque, manufactured by Harry Stutz between 1920-25, after he left the Stutz Motor Car Company.

Harry Stutz entered three of his cars in the 1915 Indianapolis 500 race. As part of his strategy he made sure that the first two qualified at just under 97 miles an hour. Then the third car came along, qualifying for the pole position at 98.9 mph. Unfortunately, the lead Stutz broke a valve spring, so the first back-up car advanced to take the lead. But in the end, abnormal tire wear caused the two remaining cars to make repeated pit stops, which probably cost Stutz the race. Ralph DePalma, driving a Mercedes, took the checkered flag, while the two surviving Stutz racers placed second and third. At the close of the

1915 season Stutz retired from racing, perhaps because Harry's transaxle, though a strong unit and a great performer, abused the back tires unmercifully, forcing drivers to make overly frequent visits to the pits.

Sales, however, looked better than ever, with 1,079 Stutz cars finding buyers that year, followed by 1,535 sales during 1916 and 2,207 for 1917. The future looked promising.

To power his 1917 models, Harry Stutz at last trotted out an engine of his own design and manufacture. Featuring four valves per cylinder, similar to some of the better cars of the 1990s, it developed a whopping (for 1917) 80 horsepower. This revised T-head four would remain in production as late as 1924, replacing both the earlier four-banger and the six-cylinder line.

This new, four-cylinder Stutz borrowed the 130-inch chassis of the late, presumably unlamented Six. This represented a gain of 10 inches over the previous Four. Because the longer chassis was considered inappropriate for a car of sporting pretensions, the Bearcat alone continued to employ the 120-inch wheelbase.

But despite the good news on the sales front, trouble was brewing. Allen Ryan, described as "a young Wall Street sharpie," purchased control of the company. Speculation in Stutz Motor Car Company stock was rife, driving the price up, at one point, to over $700 a share. Harry Stutz sold out and moved to another part of town, where he commenced production of the H.C.S., a direct competitor for the original automobile that bore his name.

By 1921, a depression year, the Stutz Bearcat sold for $3,900, up from $2,300 in 1917. Or perhaps it would be more accurate to say that it hardly sold at all. The following season was no better, despite a $650 price cut. Ryan departed, becoming involved in the promotion of the Frontenac car, but his stock market manipulations soon caught up with him, and in a few short months he found himself broke.

For three years commencing in 1923, Stutz offered a line (eventually two lines) of six-cylinder cars designed by the firm's new chief engineer, Charles S. Crawford, formerly of the Cole Motor Company. Sales started off briskly, but soon tapered off sharply. The great overhead-camshaft

Vertical Eight followed in 1926. Sales that year spurted to more than 5,000 cars, but after that it was destined to be downhill all the way.

In the early 1930s Stutz marketed a model called the Super Bearcat, a bobtailed speedster powered by the 32-valve, 156-horsepower DV-32 straight-eight motor. It—along with the other DV-32s—was a superb automobile, but the grip of the Depression meant that it came too late to help Stutz. By 1934, production had skidded to just six cars, and the following year Stutz was bankrupt.

But Stutz left behind a legacy of great automobiles—notably the Bearcat.

Specifications[1]	
Engine:	T-head I-4, 360.8 cid (4⅜ x 6-in. bore x stroke), 16 valves, sohc, 80 bhp
Transmission:	3-speed transaxle; leather-faced cone clutch (multiple-disc prior to 1915)
Suspension, front and rear:	Rigid axles, semi-elliptic leaf springs
Brakes:	Internall expanding on rear wheels
Wheelbase (in.):	120.0
Top speed (mph):	85
Production:	NA, but probably about 1,000 from 1915-22

[1]1917 Bearcat

Stutz still ran with a four-cylinder engine in the 1918 Bearcat. It was a 360.8-cid T-head unit—but with four valves per cylinder, and it developed a whopping 80 horsepower. This was mated to a three-speed transaxle.

When Cadillac introduced its V-8 for 1915, Packard responded by one-upping Cadillac with its 1916 Twin Six. The 1920 Twin Six Limousine (*above*), a tall and very stately model indeed, rode a mammoth 136-inch wheelbase and cost a towering $7,900.

Packard built its early success as the standard American luxury car with the four-cylinder Thirty of 1907-12 and the mighty Six of 1912-15. But the model that really cemented Packard's reputation as a make of the highest rank was the Twin Six, which one-upped Cadillac's 1915 V-8 with four more cylinders and lasted with relatively few changes for eight years: a remarkably long run. In three series between 1916 and 1923, Packard built slightly more than 35,000 Twins, including numerous chassis for custom bodies. The Twin Six was the chief reason why, when the wealthy ordered a custom-bodied car, they tended to choose a Packard chassis.

Jesse Vincent, Packard's chief engineer, liked the 12-cylinder layout for three reasons: performance, smoothness, and silence. "A six-cylinder motor is theoretically in absolutely perfect balance," he wrote. "This is because the vibratory forces due to the rise and fall of one piston are neutralized by equal and opposite forces due to another. . . . Now it is only possible to cancel out forces in this way if they are tied together strongly." This meant a heavy crankcase and crankshaft and a rigid flywheel. But a Twelve or "Twin Six," Vincent continued, would provide the same rigidity and smoothness with less piston, crankcase, flywheel, and crankshaft weight—and provide more horsepower and torque, to boot. He preferred a V-12 to a V-8 because a V-8 would require a wider frame, larger turning radius, and more complicated steering gear.

The Twin Six engine duly embodied the above principles, with two banks of L-head cylinders set at a 60-degree angle (versus 90 degrees in Cadillac's V-8). This allowed accessories to be bolted just below the frame, where they were protected from road hazards, while keeping the valves accessible. Delivering 85 horsepower at 3,000 rpm, a bore and stroke at 3.00 x 5.00 inches resulted in a displacement of 424 cubic inches. Rockers were eliminated, with a separate cam for each valve, and all valves were located inboard of the cylinder blocks. A short, light crankshaft ran in three main bearings. Vincent proclaimed that torque was "50 percent better than it would have been with a V-8, and 100 percent better than the Packard Six. Six impulses per crankshaft revolution blend together so closely as to make it absolutely impossible to distinguish any pause between impulses, even at very low engine speeds. . . . The only thing I can liken it to is the action of steam."

Other Twin Six features were less radical, having been evolved on the previous 1912-15 Six, including many items we still find on cars today: ignition was supplied by a generator-charged storage battery; an ignition timer and distributor were fitted, with separate circuit breaker and distributor for each bank of six cylinders; the starter and lights were electric; the rear axle had spiral-bevel gears; cooling was by water pump; and the carburetor was located between the two banks of cylinders.

Twin Six headlights used fluted lenses. The bezels featured Packard's already famous "ox-yoke" design. The parking lights were located just below the headlights.

The 1920 Twin Six limo was a somber looking machine because it had no brass trim, and only a bit of shiny hardware. Intended as a chauffeur-driven conveyance for formal occasions, the driver's compartment was open and partitioned off from the rear. A tube was used to communicate between the two.

Bodies, on two different wheelbases, were up to date and offered in wide varieties, both closed and open. All Twins were expensive, but closed cars involved a lot more assembly work: while the touring, phaeton, and run-about listed at $2,750, the $3,700 coupe was the cheapest closed model and the Imperial Limousine cost nearly $5,000. Such figures represented small fortunes in 1916, yet to the Packard clientele they seemed amazing because they were hundreds less than the previous Six.

The introduction of the Twin Six on May 1, 1915 was the greatest single announcement in Packard's history to date. Testing one, *The Automobile* (a British motoring magazine) declared that it met Vincent's three design criteria: "No vibration was perceptible up to a road speed of well over 60 mph and the motor is hardly audible even at full revolutions . . . there is no sense of effort whatever in opening up from 3 mph in high gear . . . it was easy to accelerate from 3 mph to 30 mph in 12 seconds and on second speed in a much shorter time."

Demand for Twins was brisk and Packard's workforce increased 50 percent to nearly 11,000 in order to meet it. The factory on Detroit's Grand Boulevard underwent a $1.5 million expansion and now covered over 100 acres. In 1917, Frank Eastman, wry editor of the company's house organ, quipped: "We build a good car and charge a good price for it . . . ask the man who owes for one."

With 12 cylinders and a 3.00 x 5.00-inch bore x stroke, displacement of the L-head Twin Six came to 424.1 cid. In 1920, it was rated at 90 bhp at 2,600 rpm and was cast in two blocks of six cylinders each.

In July 1916, the 1917 model was announced (all previous models being 1916s). Designated the Second Series (2-25 for the short wheelbase car, 2-35 for the long), the Twin Six was little changed except in cooling: "In place of the water being expelled from the forward ends of the cylinder blocks, the gas intake manifold has been cored out to permit all water from the cylinder jackets to be circulated through it and thence to the radiator through a single tube." New also were detachable cylinder heads, "to insure a more perfect machining of the combustion chamber"; a faster running generator; a higher carburetor to keep it away from the manifolds; a low-current distributor; a lighter-pressure footbrake; and a redesigned gear shift with a ball end—another portent of the future. The Second Series looked lower, with its smaller wheels and deeper chassis.

Like its predecessor, the Second Series lasted a year. In the summer of 1917 Packard announced the 3-25 and 3-35 models, which would comprise the third and final series and cover six years, ushering in numerous body changes as the upright bodies of the Teens evolved to the sleeker, lower shapes of the Twenties.

This 1920 Twin Six sports a shiny Motometer cap atop the radiator.

Mechanical changes included a redesigned electrical system, improved heads for better breathing and cooling, and the "Fuelizer" intake manifold to help vaporize inlet gases with the help of its own spark plug. The ball-end gear lever was shifted to the center of the floor, where it would remain until the column shift in the late Thirties. The frame was

tapered slightly and the wheelbase increased; horsepower was now 90. Custom bodies began to appear for the first time: a coupelet, limousine, brougham, and landaulet by Derham; limousines by Caffrey and Judkins; a runabout and cabriolet by Fleetwood. From these the glittering array of custom-bodied Packards evolved during the later Twenties and Thirties.

Packard owners loved their Twin Sixes, sometimes to extremes. An oil-rich Osage Indian chief bought a custom-bodied 3-35, smashed it an hour after taking delivery, and telephoned the dealer for an immediate replacement. Czar Nicholas II of Russia owned a Twin Six with the front wheels replaced by skis for winter work. In 1921, Warren Harding used a Twin to become the first president to motor to his inauguration. In Japan, mechanics took the first car imported on a joy ride, ditched it in the moat of the Imperial Palace, and were fined for disturbing the royal goldfish—but the Emperor soon had one himself.

A lot of Twin Sixes are still around, because they were built to last. Many years later, an owner of a Twin Six he'd owned since new wrote the company: "It has twelve cylinders but I only need four. The rest of them came with the engine and I just let 'em run. The starter starts and the generator gens and the battery bats and the brakes brake and the seats seat and the top tops and the lights light. It will go from .001 mph to 75 on the same high gear. I love my old bus."

The '20 Twin Six limo carried a single spare tire upright at the rear; the vertical "tubes" seen at both the front and rear were vibration dampers.

Specifications[1]	
Engine:	L-head V-12, cast in 2 blocks, 424.1 cid (3.00 x 5.00-in. bore x stroke), solid valve lifters, 3 main bearings, 85 bhp @ 2,600 rpm
Transmission:	3-speed manual, selective sliding gear; multi-disc clutch
Suspension, front and rear:	Solid axle, longitudinal semi-elliptic leaf springs
Frame:	6-in.-deep channel section pressed steel
Brakes:	Mechanical, internal expanding, external contracting, rear wheels only, 262 sq. in. swept area
Wheelbase (in.):	125.0 & 135.0
Track (in.):	56.0
Weight (lbs):	3,910-4,715
Top speed:	70-75 mph
Production:	7,746 (model year)

[1]1916

47

Italian automaker Lancia is credited with introducing unit construction with its Lambda, here a 1924 model. The independent front suspension was a sliding pillar type.

The Lambda's bodyshell was made stronger by extending the sides upward, which meant that entry was gained only by stepping over high sills. The car itself was lower than just about any other, however.

N o one can look at the history of motoring without seeing the Lancia Lambda as a major technical milestone," wrote the late Michael Frostick. "Leaving aside its novel engine, its independent suspension, and a whole host of other minor innovations, its unique unitary construction, in which body and chassis were one, came a good ten years before Mr. Budd succeeded in selling his idea for a monocoque to Andre Citroën." The Lambda pioneered that method of car construction which today, 70 years later, is used by the majority of automobiles.

Exactly where Vincenzo Lancia, that brilliant pioneer, got the idea of a unit body-chassis is unknown. The only tale commonly repeated is that it glimmered aboard ship on the Atlantic, possibly from the way a ship's hull holds its structure together—which is probably about as true as the one about Isaac Newton and the apple. No matter, for the fact is that on the last day of 1918 Lancia filed for Italian patents on a car in which the body was "a self-supporting shell without a separate chassis," and had it in production four years later. If the Lambda represented a tremendous risk on the part of his company, it also emphasized Lancia's clean-slate approach to design.

One of his objectives was an extremely low center of gravity while retaining adequate ground clearance and suspension movement. Such a layout precluded the conventional separate chassis and body as known at the time. Lancia adopted a welded and riveted steel shell with a central open-bottom tunnel for the driveshaft and another tunnel at right angles to it for the rear axle, which simultaneously strengthened the overall shell. The tunnels in turn allowed for low-mounted seats, and footwells designed so that the seat cushions could rest even lower. The shell was made stronger by extending the sides upward—with the smallest possible doors—to form the body, while a removable hardtop provided weather protection and more rigidity. The independent front suspension was a sliding pillar system (still used by Morgan) with a transverse leaf spring; the engine a narrow, long-stroke V-4 of 2.1 liters developing 49 horsepower. The first Lambdas had three-speed gearboxes, but a four-speed was developed in 1925.

Displayed at the Paris Auto Salon in November 1922, the Lambda was instantly recognized as a new approach to cars. "Even those with no engineering interests had only to look at it to know that it was different," wrote Lancia historian Nigel Trow. "It was low and angular, with a quality of unity, of being 'all of a piece.' It looked deliberate, something that was designed from scratch by a team that knew exactly what was wanted. The car was a total departure from all previous practice."

Of course, not everything about the car was new, but certainly nobody else clapped so many innovations onto one model. The engine, for example, was unprecedented: a V-4 banked at a tiny 13-degree angle (later 14 degrees), with a flat cylinder-head face and combustion chambers in the block. Nobody had ever seen anything like it. The torpedo body, with pontoon or sweeping cycle fenders, looked more like a fanciful doodle than a production 1923 automobile. The brakes, to cite another attribute, operated on all four wheels. Designed by engineer Battista Falchetto, they were unorthodox in the extreme: conventional manufacture at that time tended to dictate rear brakes only. This was, incidentally, an example of Vincenzo Lancia's standards governing the car's development—he merely told his engineers that the brakes, whatever they were, must be capable of hauling the car down repeatedly from 100 kilometers per hour (62.5 mph). Falchetto suggested the use of front brakes by taking Lancia for a test drive in which the standard was met by a car fitted with front brakes *only*. Only later was it realized that front brakes do 80 percent of the work on any automobile.

The Lambda was faster over a twisty road than anything Lancia had hitherto produced, including the big Tri Kappa, an eight with twice the horsepower. It was soon being raced by privateers all over Europe. In 1924, the Lambdas of Riva and Gauderman finished 1-2 in the under 2,500-cc class in France's Routes Pavees race; another Lambda won the Indian Tourist Trophy at Simla in 1925; the Circuit of La Spezia in 1926; the Tunis-to-Tripoli race in 1927.

When Italy's famous open road race, the Mille Miglia, was instituted in 1927, a trio of Lancias took the first three places overall. The following year saw a Lambda entered by the factory, which prepared it merely by fine tuning a production model; it held second place most of the way and would have finished second to a more powerful supercharged Alfa Romeo had the engine not dropped a valve toward the finish. Gismondi, the Lambda driver, actually held the Alfa in average speed, thanks to Lancia's superior brakes, handling, long-range fuel tank, and modified fuel supply to prevent fuel starvation when ascending the mountains.

Over the production of 13,000 Lamb-

Lancia historian Nigel Trow wrote that the Lambda was "...low and angular, with a quality of unity, of being 'all of a piece.' It looked deliberate...."

das in nine series through 1931, the specification evolved gradually. Displacement was increased to 2.4 liters on the 1926 seventh series and to 2.6 liters on the 1928 eighth series. Also with the seventh series, Lancia parted with its revolutionary practice by offering the option of a separate chassis—a product of necessity and the pressure of custom coachbuilders.

The body makers had a complaint that would dog every unit-bodied car from the Lambda forward: the monocoque shell was very difficult to alter, and there was only so much the specialists could do with the factory bodies. (One of the loudest complaints came from Vincenzo Lancia's good friend, Battista Farina.) Also, some owners wanted to create more sporting bodywork for competition; this often took the form of shortening the wheelbase, which could not have been more disastrous. The alteration ruined the handling and seriously weakened the body.

So the Lambda had a problem. Simultaneous with its arrival had come a wave of prosperity in the mid- to late Twenties. There was a huge market for custom bodies, and this meant that a separate chassis option was crucial. "This is perhaps why enthusiasts lay so much

store by the seventh series Lambda," wrote Frostick, "since this was the last, and most highly developed version, of the original fascinating concept."

These later custom-bodied Lambdas led in time to the factory's own luxury model, the Dilambda, with a V-8 and separate chassis, independent front suspension, servo brakes, central chassis lubrication, and twin electric fuel pumps. Lancia built, 1700 Dilambdas; they in turn fostered other notable productions, including the prewar Astura and the postwar Flaminia.

Specifications	
Engine:	1923-25 13-degree ohc V-4, 2,120 cc/127 cid (75 x 120-mm bore x stroke), 49 bhp **1926-27** 14-degree, 2,370 cc/146 cid, 59 bhp **1928-31** 2,570 cc/156 cid, 69 bhp @ 3,500 rpm
Transmission:	1923-24 3-speed manual **1925-31** 4-speed manual
Construction:	Unit body
Suspension, front:	Sliding-pillar, transverse leaf spring
Suspension, rear:	Solid axle, parallel elliptical leaf spring
Brakes:	4-wheel mechanical, rear wheel handbrake
Wheelbase (in.):	122.0 (later 135.0)
Weight (lbs):	1,720
Top speed (mph):	72-78
Production:	12,530 or 12,999 (depending upon source)

The 1924 Chrysler's 211-cid inline six developed 68 horsepower at 3,000 rpm. It boasted a high 4.7:1 compression ratio (compared to Buick's 3.5:1).

Like many cars of its era, the '24 Chrysler placed the gauges in the center of the dash. The drum speedometer could easily be spun to show speeds of 70-75 miles per hour.

Specifications	
Engine:	6 cylinder, L-head, 211 cid (3 x 4¾-in. bore x stroke), 7 main bearings, solid valve lifters, 4.7:1 compression ratio, 68 bhp @ 3,000 rpm
Transmission:	3-speed selective, floor-mounted control
Suspension:	Rigid axles, longitudinal semi-elliptic springs
Brakes:	Lockheed 4-wheel external hydraulic
Wheelbase (in.):	112.75
Weight (lbs):	2,730 (touring car)
Top speed (mph):	70-75
Production:	Approx. 32,000 (calendar year)

He started out as a railroad man. And Walter P. Chrysler might have remained in that line of work had he not visited the 1908 Chicago Automobile Show.

On display there was a huge Locomobile touring car, finished in ivory white with red leather cushions. Chrysler was smitten on the spot. But the Locomobile was one of the most expensive automobiles on the market: $5,000, more than enough in those days to buy a comfortable four-bedroom home. And Walter, with a wife and two little girls to support, had $700 to his name. He was employed at the time as Superintendent of Motive Power for the Chicago Great Western Railroad, at a salary of $350 a month.

Nevertheless, to Chrysler it wasn't a question of whether, but rather of how, he was going to buy that car. In the end, he managed to persuade one of the railroad executives to co-sign his note, and the Locomobile was duly shipped to the Chrysler home in Oelwein, Iowa.

It should be noted that, so far as is known, Walter Chrysler had never driven an automobile. Presumably he didn't know how. One might expect, then, that his first order of business would have been to learn how to operate this big machine in which he had invested so much. But he didn't. Rather, he had the car delivered to the barn behind his house, and immediately set about disassembling it. For three long months he repeatedly took it apart and put it back together, studying every part of that Locomobile until he was sure he understood thoroughly how it worked. And then, at long last, with a cigar clenched between his teeth, he cranked up the car, drove it out of the barn, and took his family for their long-awaited first ride.

Three years later, Chrysler was drawing an annual salary of $8,000 as works manager for American Locomotive, and he had been promised a raise to $12,000—a king's ransom in those times. But when Charles W. Nash, president of Buick, offered him a job as Buick's works manager at half the salary he had been promised by his old employer, Chrysler took it. The lure of the automobile industry was irresistible.

By 1916, Walter Chrysler was president of Buick, at a salary of half a million dollars a year. Three years later he was appointed vice-president of General Motors, in charge of operations. But GM president "Billy" Durant was a mercurial character, quite impossible to work for, at least from Chrysler's point of view. He quit. Just 45 years old, he had plenty of money, and no plans. He told his wife he was going to retire, though it's doubtful that she believed him.

Walter's "retirement" was brief. In January 1920, at the behest of the bankers, he took over Willys-Overland, charged with straightening out that company's tangled affairs. His salary was a million dollars a year. Two years later, having set Willys-Overland on the road to recovery,

The 1924 Chrysler rode a 112¾-inch wheelbase, a bit on the short side for its price class. The five-passenger phaeton seen here listed at $1,395.

he accepted a similar assignment at Maxwell-Chalmers, taking his pay this time in stock options.

It happened that during his two years with Willys-Overland, Chrysler had become acquainted with a team of three young engineers: Fred Zeder, Owen Skelton, and Carl Breer. This group—Chrysler called them his "Three Musketeers"—had developed a car that ultimately became the basis for Billy Durant's new Flint automobile (that's a story in itself). But by the time Chrysler took the helm at Maxwell, the three men had established an independent consulting firm. Chrysler hired them at his own expense, charging them with the design of a new six-cylinder car to be built by Maxwell. Only this one wasn't to be a Maxwell. It would be a Chrysler!

The prototypes were ready by January 1924, just in time for the New York Automobile Show. But the new Chryslers were barred from being displayed there because they weren't yet in production. Learning that the Hotel Commodore would serve as headquarters for the show, Chrysler turned around and rented the Commodore's lobby, displaying his automobiles where nobody could possibly miss seeing them.

The new Chrysler, known as the Model B, was a sensation. Priced head-to-head with the Buick Six, it was more than 700 pounds lighter than its rival, and correspondingly more nimble. Its

engine boasted a 4.7:1 compression ratio, compared to the Buick's 3.5:1. Chrysler advertised that the new machine would accelerate from five to 25 miles an hour in seven seconds, which was considered phenomenal performance in 1924. It would do 70 to 75 miles-per-hour top speed, much faster than the Buick—and within five miles an hour of the new Packard straight eight, a car that cost more than twice as much as the Chrysler. Furthermore, the new Chrysler featured hydraulic brakes, giving it stopping power to match its speed.

Other innovations, most unheard-of in production automobiles at that time, included aluminum pistons, full-pressure lubrication, tubular front axle, air cleaner, oil filter with removable element, and Lovejoy hydraulic shock absorbers—all as standard equipment. The fully counterbalanced crankshaft was cradled in seven main bearings. Altogether, the new Chrysler stood out as a superb piece of engineering.

Compared to the competition, the Chrysler B-70, as it was called, was a relatively small car. The wheelbase was more than seven inches shorter than that of the Buick; overall, the Chrysler measured only 160 inches without bumpers, which was the way cars were delivered in those days. As a touring car, it weighed only 2,730 pounds, compared to the Buick's 3,455.

Worse, the Chrysler came to market at a time when competition was espe-

cially intense, forcing a number of veteran automakers—Revere, Stevens-Duryea, Winton, Premier, Dort, Dorris, and Columbia among them—to the wall. Skeptics said the new car would never sell. But it was peppy, capable of zipping from five to 50 miles an hour in just 13 seconds. It was maneuverable, handsome to look at, and a delight to drive. And of course, it was an instant success. The B-70 was so successful, in fact, that it remained in production until July 1925.

Nine body styles were offered, ranging from the popular five-passenger touring to a pretentious town car. There was even a sedan called the Crown Imperial, the first automobile ever to bear that famous title. All nine were fitted to the same 112.75-inch wheelbase and powered by the identical 68-horsepower, six-cylinder engine.

The new Chrysler was soon entered in competitive events, notably by the famed race driver, Ralph DePalma. Driving a stock B-70 touring car, on July 16, 1924, he climbed California's Mount Wilson in a record-breaking 25 minutes, 48 seconds, at times attaining a speed of 44 miles an hour in second gear. The contest involved a climb of 4,635 feet over a nine and a half mile course, with no fewer than 144 curves. Two months later, at Fresno, DePalma drove 1,000 miles in 1,007 minutes. Refueling stops excluded, his average speed was 68.3 miles per hour.

Meanwhile, the four-cylinder Maxwell had undergone a number of improvements. A three-bearing crankshaft was substituted for the earlier two-bearing job, which had an unfortunate tendency to whip at high rpm. Soon the car was being advertised as "The New Good Maxwell," which tells us all we need to know about the earlier models.

In June 1925, with Walter P. Chrysler firmly in control, the Maxwell Motor Company was reorganized as the Chrysler Corporation. By that time the Maxwell car was in its final season, though it would re-emerge in 1926 as the Chrysler 58. Eventually, the four-banger would metamorphose into a new marque, the Plymouth. But of course it was the B-70 on which the Chrysler reputation was built.

As the name implied, the Bugatti Royale was a "Car for Kings." Its mammoth 169-inch wheelbase and 6,000-7,000-pound curb weight also suggested that this car was something special. It's perhaps ironic then that no Royale was ever sold to royalty.

E ttore Bugatti died in 1947 after 66 years "full of frenzy and creation," to use journalist Ken Purdy's words. Thirty of those years he spent building some 7,800 cars—mostly lithe racers and sports-tourers unrivalled for handling, performance, and craftsmanship. How then could one explain his mammoth Type 41 Royale?

The answer lies in the man himself. All Bugattis mirrored their creator, but the Royale was perhaps the fullest reflection. Purdy described Ettore Bugatti as "an Italian who lived his life in France among Frenchmen, and was, they said, *un type*...a character...greatly gifted, proud, unswervingly independent, indifferent to any opinion but his own... aristocratic, impractical, profligate..." He was just as much the Michelangelo of motoring. Born the son and brother of artists, he believed "a technical creation cannot be perfect until it is perfect from an aesthetic point of view." How strong was that belief? Look no further than the simple visual elegance of most any Bugatti engine, or even front suspension.

But Ettore also possessed the great drive and native mechanical ability of a Henry Ford—and an equally monumental ego. The story is told of the Parisian Bugatti owner who, still dissatisfied with several details on his car after two visits to the dealer, went in again and met *Le Patron* himself. "You are the one who has brought his [car] back three times?" Bugatti asked. Thinking things would be put right at last, the customer said yes. "Do not," Bugatti huffed, "let it happen again."

By that time, as Purdy observed, Bugatti "had earned the right to be arrogant." He had, after all, built his first car from the ground up in 1898 at the age of only 17. A second car completed the following year won him a gold medal at a 1901 exhibition in his native Milan—and an engineering job with the French automaker De Dietrich. After brief stints at Mathis, Deutz in Germany, and Isotta-Fraschini, Bugatti decided to build his own cars based on a miniature chassis he'd constructed around 1908: a four-cylinder shaft-drive design evidently inspired by the contemporary Isotta *Coupe de Voiturettes*. With financial backing from a *Monsieur de Viscaya*, he set up in an old dye works near Molsheim, then in the Alsace-Lorraine region of France, later the Bas-Rhin district of Germany.

Like Enzo Ferrari in the late 1940s, Bugatti established his automaking credentials through racing. It started with the 1911 *Grand Prix du Mans*, where Ernest Friederich, Ettore's friend, associate, and mechanic, drove a tiny 1.4-liter Bugatti to second place behind a monstrous six-liter Fiat. "The disparity in size between the two cars made the victory most impressive," Purdy wrote. "Bugatti was famous from that day forward." After World War I, more impressive Bugattis turned in more impressive performances, including an outright Le Mans victory

Although the Type 41 Royale was an entirely different type of Bugatti than the successful racing cars usually associated with the name, the Royale did maintain the marque's tradition with its inverted horseshoe-shaped grille.

in 1920. In 1924-27, Bugattis racked up no fewer than 1,851 wins.

By that time, Molsheim had grown from 65 to over 1,000 employees—about a third of the town's population—who worked in greatly expanded physical facilities that Bugatti ruled like a kingly father—*Le Patron*. Besides a complex of one-story factory buildings (kept surgically clean at his insistence and fitted with identical door locks to which only he held the master key) there was a museum housing the sculpture of his brother Rembrandt, another for Ettore's carriage collection, a kennel, stables (horses were Bugatti's second love), vineyards, a family chateau, and an inn for favored clients, *L'Hostellerie du Pur Sang*: literally "hotel of the pure blood," as in thoroughbred horses—and motorcars. Each day, *Le Patron* toured his fiefdom by bicycle or electric car of his own design, dressed like some Hollywood mogul—and dispensing *nobless oblige* like a feudal lord.

A "Car for Kings" might be expected from so imperious an industrialist. One of the many stories woven into the fabric of the Bugatti legend concerns Ettore's dinner with a certain English gentlewoman who remarked (according to Purdy): "Everyone knows you build the greatest racing cars in the world, and the best sports cars. But for a town carriage of real elegance, one must go

to Rolls-Royce or Daimler, isn't that so?" Though the Type 41 allegedly sprang from this "challenge," correspondence indicates that Bugatti had been contemplating such a car since at least 1913. That it was delayed 13 years was due mainly to a lack of resources at the time, then the intervention of World War I, plus his desire that the "machinery" be "beyond any criticism."

The result was nearly beyond comprehension, so grand was its scale. The engine, for example, was a monobloc straight eight of by-then established Bugatti design, with a single overhead camshaft and three valves per cylinder (two intakes, one exhaust)—only it derived from Ettore's wartime Type 34 aero powerplant and was thus some five feet long and 770 pounds heavy. Pistons the size of coffee cans and a two-piece crankshaft, itself weighing 220 pounds, gave an astounding 12.8-liters displacement—and that was destroked from the planned 14.7-liter unit of the Royale prototype. Valve jobs meant removing crank, rods, and pistons, but Ettore didn't care. If you could afford a Bugatti, you could afford to hire out the dirty work.

The chassis was also typical Bugatti—and gigantic: a channeled pressed-steel affair varying in cross-section from one inch at the ends to 10 inches at the passenger compartment. Front suspen-

Given the Royale's size and weight, an elephant—particularly one rearing in defiance on its hind legs—was hardly out of place as the hood ornament of this grandest of all Bugattis.

The Royale's engine was as grand as the rest of the car: a monobloc 778.8-cid straight eight. It boasted an overhead cam, three valves per cylinder, and weighed 770 pounds.

Royale 41141 was bodied as a two-door coach by Kellner of Paris, and was the personal car of Bugatti's daughter. In 1950, American Briggs Cunningham bought it, and it was finally sold to a British collector for $9.8 million in 1987. As one might expect, Kellner did not skimp in fitting out the sumptuous interior.

sion was by semi-elliptic leaf springs poking through square holes in a hollow, tubular steel axle that provided "independence" by being in two pieces, joined in the middle, each free to move a little. At the rear were four upside-down quarter-elliptics, one pair ahead of the axle, the other behind, with trailing rods for added longitudinal location. The transmission, a three-speed "crashbox" in unit with the differential, took power from a combined flywheel/multiplate clutch mounted beneath the front seat to run in its own oil bath (actually a fine mist). And that power travelled a ways, for the wheelbase measured 169 inches—more than the overall length of today's Alfa Romeo Spider. Brakes were massive, beautifully cast 18-inch aluminum drums integral with 24 x 7-inch alloy wheels, each secured by 32 stud-bolts.

A car so exclusive that even brochures were deemed unnecessary, the Type 41 was sold only as a bare chassis at a price commensurate with its towering size and presence: $25,000, more than twice the cost of the best, fully bodied Rolls-Royce. Buyers, of course, were presumed financially able to furnish their own bodywork, which brought the final price to around $40,000—say around a half million dollars in today's money.

That implied a super-select clientele, but Ettore did the selecting, and you needed more than mere money to buy. Achievement and social standing counted greatly with him. It also helped to be royal, though even that didn't guarantee acceptance. King Zog of

Albania was refused a car because of table manners Le Patron judged as "beyond belief." The car was announced with word that Spain's King Alphonso XIII would be the first owner—hence La Royale, some say—but he was deposed before he could take delivery. Ironically, the "Car of Kings" was never sold to a monarch, reigning or otherwise.

The first production chassis wasn't delivered until some four years after announcement, by which time the Depression had forced cutting the planned 25 units to only six, including the prototype chassis. The latter, Number 41100, began with modified touring bodywork from a contemporary Packard Eight, then went through three more bodies (including a lovely prize-winning Weymann coach) before Ettore wrecked it. Fully repaired, it was given an elegant town car style penned by Ettore's talented eldest son Jean. This Coupe Napolean survives today at France's Musee Nationale de l'Automobile, the former Schlumpf brothers collection in Mulhouse.

The five production Royales also survive, and have equally involved histories. Number 41111 was built as a beautiful Jean Bugatti roadster, then received Coupe de Ville bodywork by Henri Binder of Paris, retained to this day. Royale 41121 resides at the Henry Ford Museum with its original two-seat cabriolet coachwork by Ludwig Weinberger of Munich. Number 41131 has also had but one body: a six-window "D-back" limousine type with sporty sidemount spares by Park Ward of London; it, too, now lives at the French

museum. Royale 41141, bodied as a two-door coach by Kellner of Paris, remained in Molsheim for years after Le Patron's death as the personal car of his daughter L'Ebe; it was purchased in 1950 by American Briggs Cunningham, and remained in his collection until 1987, when it sold at auction to an unnamed British collector for $9.8 million. That was the highest price ever paid for a car at the time, eclipsing the previous record set by . . . another Royale. This was 41150, the odd Berline de Voyage "cabriolet-limousine" once part of the Harrah Collection (along with 41111), acquired in late 1986 for $8.1 million by American pizza baron Tom Monaghan.

The few who've actually experienced a Royale report it surprisingly easy to drive. Of course, those heroic proportions make for cautious maneuvering like that required in a semi-trailer truck, but the steering is pleasantly manageable, performance adequate, ride firmly sporting, and handling of such a high order that the beast actually seems to shrink around you after awhile.

But the Royale was less a car for driving than for arriving: one to be seen in, one to make you the envy of all whom you'd deign to survey—the ultimate automotive statement. Then again, what else from Ettore Bugatti, a man whose life, as Ken Purdy wrote, was "full of such gestures. Indeed, his whole life was a gesture. A sweeping, magnificent gesture."

Specifications	
Engine:	sohc I-8 **prototype** 898.6 cid/ 14,726 cc (4.92 x 5.91-in./125 x 150-mm bore x stroke), output NA; **"production"** 778.8 cid/12,763 cc (4.92 x 5.11-in./125 x 130-mm), 200 bhp @ 1,700-2,000 rpm
Transmission:	3-speed manual in unit with final drive
Suspension, front:	Tubular axle on semi-elliptic leaf springs, friction/hydraulic dampers
Suspension, rear:	Solid axle on dual inverted quarter-elliptic leaf springs, dual radius rods, friction/hydraulic dampers
Brakes:	Cable-operated front/rear drums (integral with wheels)
Weight (lbs):	6,000-7,000, depending on body
Top speed (mph):	100
0-60 mpg (sec):	est. 18.0
Production:	6, including prototype

The LaSalle deserves its place in automotive history because it was the first production car worldwide to have been consciously "styled." The convertible coupe body style, another LaSalle first (with seven other automakers!), sold for $2,635.

For years, Cadillac had been America's best-selling luxury car. But by the mid 1920's Packard began playing catch-up, and by 1925—largely on the strength of its price-leading six-cylinder line—Packard was commencing to eat Cadillac alive.

It happened that in May of that year, Lawrence P. "Larry" Fisher—third of the seven brothers of Fisher Body fame—was appointed Cadillac's general manager. And Fisher, determined that under his leadership Cadillac would again be number one, found several major tasks awaiting him.

For one thing, the Cadillac's styling was stodgy. In fact, it always had been. Henry Martyn Leland, the division's first general manager, had known nothing about the subject and cared even less. His concerns were for precision workmanship and unimpeachable quality. Cadillac's reputation was built on these qualities, and it was a heritage that Larry Fisher was careful to preserve. But as far as looks were concerned, the Cadillac was tall, square, old-fashioned, and ungainly—which, of course, didn't suit Larry Fisher at all.

And that was only for openers. An even more serious problem had to do with the competition. In September 1920, Packard had augmented its huge Twin Six series with a smaller, lighter car known as the Single Six. Intended for the owner-driver rather than for chauffeur use, it offered traditional Packard quality in a more manageable package, and it quickly developed a loyal following, especially among women drivers. It was comparatively costly at first, but by April 1922 prices had been reduced to the point that this new Packard could be purchased for as little as $2,485. Cadillac prices, meanwhile, *began* at $3,100.

By 1925, prices of both cars had risen a little, but the spread between the cost of a Packard Six and that of the Cadillac remained the same: $2,585 versus $3,185, a $600 difference—which is to say that for the price of the Cadillac, the buyer could have both a Packard and a Chevrolet, with $75 left over. Or, to put the matter another way, the Cadillac sedan cost just over twice as much as a Buick Master Six in the same body style. For the upwardly mobile Buick owner, that was simply too great a jump. Thus, as customers circumstances improved, some of them left the General Motors "family" and defected to Packard.

The solution was obvious to both Larry Fisher and General Motors President Alfred P. Sloan, Jr.: GM would have to develop an automobile to fill that gap. Of necessity, the newcomer would have to be a high-quality car, more prestigious than the Buick, but its price would have to be pegged considerably under Cadillac's cheapest offerings.

Since the new car was intended to compete against the Packard Six, logic dictated that of GM's five automaking divisions, Cadillac should be the one to produce it. Thus, since it was to be a "companion" car to the Cadillac, it was logical that Cadillac's usual engineering practices should be followed in its construction—including the landmark L-head V-8 that Cadillac had pioneered back in 1915.

This association also suggested that the name of the new car should in some way reflect its relationship to Cadillac. And since the senior car had taken its title from Antoine de la Mothe Cadillac, the 17th century French explorer who founded the city of Detroit, it seemed appropriate that the new car should honor another French pioneer: René Robert Cavalier de la Salle, who in 1682 had claimed Louisiana for King Louis XIV.

A new engine was designed for the LaSalle. It was a handsome powerplant, characterized by ribbed cylinder heads. Company flacks claimed that the ribs were "for improved cooling," but the fact of the matter is that they were for looks—they had absolutely nothing to do with dissipating heat.

In those days the Cadillac V-8 engine was comprised of two cylinder banks, separate castings set at a 90-degree angle from one another. Fork-and-blade connecting rods were employed so that the two banks could be located directly opposite each other. However, the fork-and-blade layout was an expensive way to go, so in an effort to control costs Cadillac engineers sought a more economical design. In the end, the right

cylinder bank of the LaSalle engine was located an inch and three-eighths forward of the left, permitting the rods to be fitted side-by-side on the crankpins. Happily, the new design, in addition to being more economical to build, proved to be superior in every way to the original.

With development of the new engine under way, Larry Fisher turned his attention to the field he knew best—styling. On a visit to the West Coast he had visited a custom body shop operated by Don Lee, Cadillac's California distributor. There, he had become acquainted with 31-year-old Harley J. Earl, the firm's body designer. Earl had turned out a number of stunning custom designs, many of them specifically for the Cadillac chassis. Equally impressive were some of his new techniques, such as the use of modeling clay to develop the various forms he was seeking to create.

Larry Fisher invited Harley Earl to come to Detroit on a consultant basis, in order to design the new LaSalle. Supposedly this was to be a short-term assignment, but Earl stayed on at GM until his retirement in 1958. Not only was the LaSalle the first production car worldwide to have been designed by a stylist, but it marked the beginning of General Motors' Art and Colour Section, the industry's first full-scale styling department—headed, of course, by Harley Earl.

Earl made no bones about the source of his inspiration in creating the design of the LaSalle. In his view, the most beautiful automobile in the world at the time was the Hispano-Suiza. Thus, the new GM marque emerged with a tall, narrow radiator; sweeping clamshell fenders; plus unusual, and thoroughly pleasing, two-tone effects—all clearly reflecting the Hisso's influence.

Nor was performance neglected. The LaSalle engine, officially rated at 75 horsepower, probably developed more; it was easily capable of propelling the car to 70 miles per hour. And even more, at least in roadster form, particularly when tall gearing was employed. At the GM proving grounds a LaSalle roadster, fitted with high-compression cylinder heads and a special camshaft, averaged 95.3 mph over a 951.8-mile run—which said something for the car's durability as well as its speed.

Five body styles were offered initially, all by Fisher. They rode a 125-inch wheelbase, seven inches shorter than that of the 1927 Cadillac. Model for model, the LaSalle was about 180 pounds lighter than the Caddy, and correspondingly more nimble. Six additional Fisher bodies joined the roster at mid-year, three on the original 125-inch wheel span, and three on a longer 134-inch chassis. In addition, four semi-custom models, featuring coachwork by Fleetwood, were introduced on the shorter

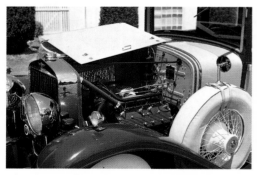

The '27 LaSalle was powered by a 90-degree L-head V-8. With 303 cubic inches, it cranked out 75 horsepower. The standard compression ratio was 4.8:1; a 5.3:1 ratio was optional.

Above is an example of the 1929 LaSalle 328, which had a 328-cubic-inch V-8 that was good for 86 brake horsepower at 3,000 rpm. The four-door sedan, one of 22,961 LaSalles built that year, sold for $2,595 and weighed 4,490 pounds.

All 1930 LaSalles rode a 134-inch wheelbase, including the $2,590 convertible coupe. The engine was bored ¹⁄₁₆ inch to 340 cid (same as the Series 341-B Cadillac) and 90 bhp.

chassis. The Fleetwood jobs were very costly, ranging in price from $4,275 to $4,700, compared to a range of $2,495 to $2,975 for the short-chassis Fisher-bodied cars. Yet, interestingly enough, Harley Earl's Fisher-bodied cars were far better looking.

It should perhaps be noted that although the LaSalle sold for several hundred dollars less than the Cadillac, it was still considered an expensive automobile at a time when a new Chevrolet roadster sold for $525, and a perfectly respectable Buick Standard Six sedan could be had for $1,295.

When the 1928 models went on display, the LaSalle's influence on Cadillac was readily apparent. Styling of the senior car this year was the work of Harley Earl, and the result was extremely attractive. And under the Cadillac's hood was a 341-cubic-inch version of the engine introduced by LaSalle the year before. As for the LaSalle, it was little changed, although several additional models were offered on the 134-inch chassis.

In succeeding years, the original LaSalle concept of incorporating Cadillac quality in a smaller, more maneuverable package became lost. By 1929, only three Fisher and two Fleetwood models remained on the 125-inch wheelbase, while a total of 14 were available on the longer chassis. And by 1930 the entire line had the longer wheelbase.

Not surprisingly, the LaSalle fell upon very difficult times during the Depression, with production falling to as low as 3,290 units for the 1932 model year. A smaller, much less expensive model, borrowing most of its components from the Oldsmobile Division, brought better sales during 1934-36, but the LaSalle didn't hit its stride again until 1937, when a new V-8 led to sales of 32,005 units—LaSalle's all-time high.

By that time, however, there was a smaller Cadillac, the Series Sixty, priced as low as $1,445. At this time, the LaSalle was still an extremely attractive automobile and an excellent value for the money, and it boasted a loyal following. But it made no sense for Cadillac to offer two

automobiles that essentially competed with each other. Thus, at the end of the 1940 model run, the curtain came down and the LaSalle was no more.

Ironically, back in 1687 René Robert Cavalier de la Salle was killed by his own men. During the summer of 1940 the same thing happened to the automobile that bore his name.

Specifications	
Engine:	90-degree L-head V-8, 303 cid (3⅛ x 4¹⁵⁄₁₆-in. bore x stroke), 4.8:1 compresssion ratio (5.3:1 opt.), mechanical valve lifters, 3 main bearings, 75 bhp
Transmission:	3-speed selective, floor-mounted lever, 11-disc clutch, torque tube drive
Suspension, front and rear:	Rigid axles (rear ¾ floating), longitudinal semi-elliptic springs
Brakes:	4-wheel internal mechanical, 14-in. drums
Wheelbase (in.):	125.0 (most models); 134.0 (Imperial)
Overall length (in.):	185.0 (short wheelbase)
Weight (lbs):	3,755-5,100 (depending on body style)
Top speed (mph):	70 +
Production:	12,000 (model year); 16,850 (calendar year)

The great supercharged Mercedes Sports of 1927-32 were among the fastest cars, and some of the most beautiful, ever to put rubber to road. Ever. They were triumphant on road and track, magnificent to look upon, and faster than any contemporary automobile that might qualify even part-time as a street sports car. Yet the young Ferdinand Porsche, only 48 when he became technical manager of Daimler-Benz, had arrived to engineer them almost by accident, succeeding Paul Daimler, son of the firm's co-namesake. Yet all the work was not done by Porsche. Hans Nibel—who replaced Porsche and had been a D-B employee since 1904—also deserves credit for the series.

Daimler had won acclaim for his 1908 Grand Prix Mercedes racer and 1914 4.5 liter, but his greatest accomplishment was the supercharged Mercedes engine. His first blown unit was a Daimler aircraft engine, built from 1915-18, with a Roots-type blower driven by a gear on the flywheel. Its technology led to the first supercharged auto engine in 1919, which three years later had evolved into a production four-cylinder unit of 2.6 liters, the 10/40/65 (10 taxable bhp, 40 bhp unblown, 65 bhp blown). Similar was the 28/95 supercharged six with 120 bhp, never installed in a production model, but important in helping Mercedes return to international racing at the 1921 *Targa Florio*. Subsequent racers were unsuccessful, however, and Daimler resigned at the end of 1922. Porsche was then charged with developing the masterful supercharged engines Daimler left behind into race winners and extremely capable street sports cars.

Fast touring cars had always been Mercedes' stock in trade, but after the last 28/95s were built in 1924 the lineup had lacked a worthy replacement. Porsche's first steps were to shorten the chassis of the Model 24/100/140 (a 6.3-liter monster weighing 3,400 pounds) and to boost

The Mercedes-Benz SSK, basically a lighter model S (by 66 pounds), went into production in late 1927. It remained available through 1931.

its underwhelming performance. The result was the Model K (for *kurz* or "short"), introduced in 1926 as a Mercedes (not a Mercedes-Benz), weighing only 3,153 pounds. Its two spark plugs per cylinder (one fired by coil and breaker ignition, the other by magneto) and a 5.0:1 compression ratio gave 110 bhp without a blower or 160 bhp with blower engaged: officially 24/110/160. The gearbox was unaltered, but final drive ratios were lowered numerically to reduce engine revs in relation to road speed, which was a little over 90 mph. The K was an admirable touring car, but being tall and ungainly, it was certainly no sports car.

Its successor was.

Directly derived from the K, the 1927 model S (Sport) had impressively low construction and looked as fast as it was. The engine was bored to 6.8 liters; the Roots blower was gear-driven and set to run at three times crankshaft speed. This boosted maximum power to 180 supercharged and made the SK a genuine 100-mph car. It also

The exhaust pipes exiting from the hood suggested power. And indeed, the 1928 Mercedes-Benz SSK was endowed with a seven-liter (431.4-cid) inline six. It boasted a single overhead cam, dual carburetors, and a Roots-type super-charger with a 10-psi boost. All of this was good for 225 horse-power at 3,200 rpm. Top speed came in at about 120 miles per hour—amazing for 1928.

featured a new four-speed gearbox with very low numeric ratios (2.76:1 standard, 2.5:1 and 3.08:1 optional), and its light roadster body gave it a curb weight of only 2,867 pounds.

The racing impact of the S was tremendous. During its career it racked up 53 racing victories and 17 speed records, including a German national mark for passenger cars of 110.3 mph. It was expensive, of course, and thus uncommon: most estimates put the total at 149, all built in 1927-28.

At the end of 1928, Porsche left Daimler-Benz for Steyr in Vienna, and in 1930 he set up his own engineering firm in Zuffenhausen, where he became involved in the Volkswagen project. Meanwhile, he was replaced at Daimler-Benz by his former assistant, Hans Nibel,

another brilliant technician. Nibel's credits included the great 200-bhp "Blitzen Benz" speed record car of 1910 and a host of fine touring cars in the early Twenties.

Porsche was still at the helm when an even more formidable sporting Mercedes went into production in late 1928: the SS (Super Sport), basically a lighter S (by about 66 pounds) with a more powerful, seven-liter engine. Its blower, providing eight psi boost, was shared with the S, but compression was raised and valves and ports were larger. Maximum supercharged horsepower now rose to 200, top speed to 115 mph, and 0-60 took less than 15 seconds. Such numbers seemed like fiction in the world of 1928, but they were valid enough.

The SS remained in production up to 1933, but very few were constructed after the end of 1929. Total production is estimated at only 109 cars. Next step was the yet-hairier SSK, a short-wheelbase derivative of the SS built alongside it in 1928. As with the 1926 Model K, the letter denoted *kurz* (short). Its chassis was lighter still at 2,680 pounds. In addition a bigger blower delivering 10 psi boost, gave the SSK engine more power. With the supercharger engaged

The "K" in SSK stood for *kurz*—short. This meant that the SSK rode a shorter wheelbase than the 136-inch SS, and it was lighter, too—just 2,680 pounds. The SSK enjoyed a brilliant competition career, but the total number produced is estimated at only 31.

it put out 225 bhp at 3,200 rpm, good for a sizzling 120-mph top speed under test conditions with perfectly tuned factory examples.

The SSK enjoyed a brilliant competition career. Caracciola scored its first victory at the Gabelbach hillclimb in 1928, then repeated Model S wins at Frieburg and Semmering. In 1930 he won the Irish Grand Prix in an SSK against a host of open-wheel racing cars.

On track or road the SSK was truly a supercar. Britain's *The Motor* published a test in June 1931 and said the results (0-90 in 45 seconds, top speed 103.2) fell short of expectations. Considering the state of the art in the early '30s, the editors must have expected a great deal, for such performance was then unequalled by any other car in the world. The number of SSKs built is estimated at 31, all from 1928 to 1931.

Near the end of the run in 1931, a lightweight SSK made its appearance, not as a production item but as a special, reserved for the factory racing team. Only six of these cars, known as the SSKL, were built. The "L" stood for *leight* or "light," because the frame and many other components were drilled to remove excess metal. Chassis weight accordingly went down to about 2,640 pounds. At the same time, horsepower went up—way up.

The major modification was adoption of an "elephant" compressor delivering 12-psi boost, but the SSKL also had a lighter crankshaft and flywheel, special valves, high-lift camshaft, and high-compression pistons. The factory recommended using a fifty/fifty mixture of gasoline and benzol to avoid local overheating in the cylinder head. Maximum output was 300 horsepower at 3,300 rpm. A special streamlined single-seater was built on the SSKL chassis in 1931 for Manfred von Brauchitsch to drive at Avus. It was the fastest car present, completing the race at an average speed of 121.6 mph. Its top speed was not far short of 150.

One measure of the SSKL's performance was provided in 1960 by *Road & Track* magazine. Geared with a 2.76:1 rear axle, the test car's top speed was 120 mph. Out of deference to its age, acceleration was calculated on the basis of power/weight ratio: 9.5 seconds for 0-60 mph, 41 seconds from 0-100. That was quite a performance for a 30-year-old veteran—and there wasn't a car of its era that could have touched it.

Specifications[1]	
Engine:	ohv I-6, 431.4 cid/7,069 cc (3.94 x 5.9-in/100 x 150-mm bore x stroke), sohc, 2 updraft 1-bbl M-B carburetors, 140 bhp @ 3,000 rpm; with Roots-type supercharger (8-psi boost): 200 bhp @ 3,000 rpm
Transmission:	Non-synchro 4-speed manual; multi-dry-plate clutch
Chassis:	Pressed-steel frame, channel-section side members, pressed or tubular cross members
Suspension, front and rear:	Forged solid front axle, half-elliptic leaf springs front and rear, torque-tube rear axle, lever or friction shock absorbers
Brakes:	Shaft-and-rod operated 4-wheel drum (vacuum assist opt.)
Tires:	6.50 x 20
Wheelbase (in.):	136
Overall length (in.):	185
Track, front and rear (in.):	58
Weight (lbs):	approx. 2,800
0-60 mph (sec):	14-15
Top speed (mph):	115
Production:	est. 109 SS; approx. 300 total S/SS/SSK/SSKL

[1]1928 27/140/200 SS

The Mercedes-Benz SSK was endowed with 175 horsepower, and if that wasn't enough, it trotted out 225 eager ponies "mit Kompressor"—amazing for its era.

With a supercharger, the 1927 M-B Sportwagen S boasted 180 horses. Even without one, it still cranked out 120 bhp.

The '31 M-B "Sportwagen Mannheim" hummed along with a more humble 75 horsepower, which was respectable for its time.

At the opening of the New York Salon, on December 1, 1928, one car stood out above all the others that were on display. It was the new Duesenberg. In fact, it was Duesenberg J-101, the very first of the J-Series cars and the only example that had been completed at that point. And what a gorgeous machine to behold! Finished in silver and black, it was a dual-cowl phaeton, bearing coachwork by LeBaron. The price wasn't specified, except to say that the bare chassis sold for $8,500. Figure at least $2,500 for a coachbuilt body and a buyer would have been looking at a price tag equivalent to 22 Model A Fords.

Left to his own devices, Fred Duesenberg would never have produced anything so pretentious. But financial problems had overtaken the Duesenberg Motor Company of Indianapolis, and control of the firm had been acquired in 1926 by Errett Lobban Cord, president of the Auburn Automobile Company. Cord wisely left Fred Duesenberg and his brother, August, in charge—but he made it clear that he wanted the Duesenbergs to develop the "World's Greatest Motor Car."

Fred Duesenberg had been building automobiles of his own design as early as 1906, though in those days the name of his backer, Edward R. Mason, appeared on the radiator badge. He had gone on to build marine engines, and marvelously successful racing machines powered by a four-cylinder "walking beam" engine of his own design. Then, during World War I, Duesenberg turned to the production of aircraft engines and powerplants for artillery tractor units.

And finally, in 1921, the first Duesenberg passenger car appeared, the Model A. A highly advanced machine, it was powered by America's first series-produced straight eight, a 259.6-cubic-inch job featuring an overhead camshaft and rated at 88 horsepower. This at a time when Cadillac advertised its fine V-8 at 60 bhp. Speeds as high as 85 miles an hour were possible for anyone foolhardy enough to drive at such a pace on the comparatively primitive roads of the day. And to assure the driver that the Duesenberg would stop as well as it would go, four-wheel hydraulic brakes were fitted—another industry "first."

But at $6,500, that original Duesenberg was an expensive automobile, more than twice as costly as a Cadillac. Demand was never high, and by 1926 production was down to one or two cars a week. It was at that point that E.L. Cord entered the picture, and work commenced on the development of the mighty Model J.

The J was an enormous automobile. Two wheelbase lengths were offered: 142.5 and 153.5 inches. And the cars were heavy— the lightest of them, the open styles on the shorter wheelbase, weighed close to 5,500 pounds. But under the hood was a fabulous 419.7-cubic-inch, dual-overhead-camshaft straight eight. Fitted with four valves per cylinder, it produced a mind-boggling 265 horsepower and 374 pounds/feet torque.

The Duesenberg Model J stood out above all other cars when it was introduced at the New York Salon on December 1, 1928. One of the earlier cars off the line was a convertible coupe bodied by Murphy.

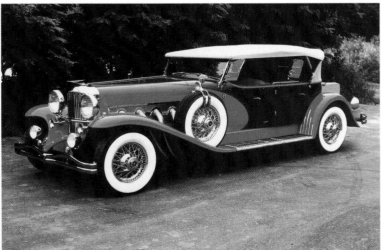

In the Eighties, Elite Heritage Motors Corporation, of Elroy, Wisconsin, built a Model J replica (actually the SJ—supercharged) called the Duesenberg II Royalton.

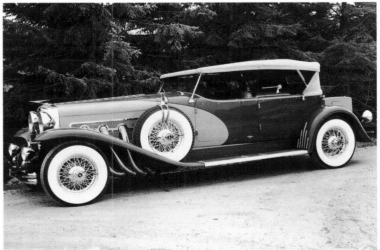

As can be seen by comparing the Model J and the Duesenberg II, Elite Heritage Motors took pains to be sure that the Royalton was a faithful reproduction of the original.

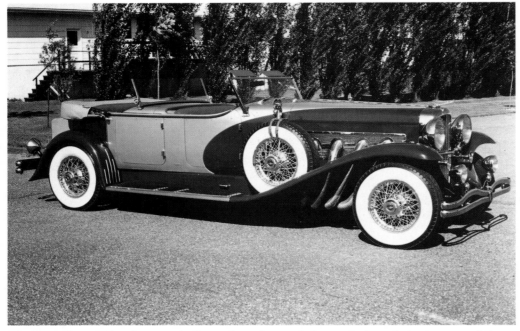

The Duesenberg II Royalton was built as a long, low, and elegant dual-cowl phaeton, one of the body styles most desired by modern-day collectors.

By comparison, America's second most powerful production car in 1929 was the Pierce-Arrow, rated at 125 bhp. Duesenberg advertised that "with a standard touring body and with top and windshield up and fenders on, this car has attained 116 m.p.h., while a maximum speed of 89 m.p.h. has been reached in second gear."

The big engine, designed by Fred Duesenberg and manufactured by Lycoming (a Cord-owned company), was as smooth as it was powerful. The drop-forged crankshaft, cradled in five oversized main bearings, was made of double-heat-treated chrome nickel steel. It was counterweighted, and statically and dynamically balanced. And then, just to be doubly cautious, there was a vibration damper consisting of two cartridges, each containing 16 ounces of mercury. Any vibrations that might be set up in the shaft were damped out almost instantly by the movement of the mercury in the cartridges.

Nobody talked about gas mileage. Those who had to ask obviously couldn't afford a Duesenberg anyway. Fuel was fed to the big 1½-inch Schebler carburetor by no fewer than four fuel pumps, one of them mechanical, the others electric. Full pressure lubrication was accomplished by means of a gear-driven oil pump with a capacity of 22 gallons per minute. Meanwhile, an eight-gallon cooling system made sure there were no problems with overheating.

A hypoid axle, highly unusual in those days, helped make possible the new Duesenberg's low profile. Ross cam-and-lever steering was used, and under-girding the chassis was a frame stout enough to support a freight car. As for the brakes, they were probably the best in the industry—hydraulics, of course, with huge 15 x 3-inch drums. Shortly after introduction time an adjustable vacuum booster, controlled from the dash, was supplied, making it possible for the driver to match the big Duesenberg's braking action to the conditions of the moment—anywhere from gentle, for icy pavement, to very abrupt.

Bodies were supplied by some of the nation's leading coachbuilders: Murphy, Holbrook, Derham, LeBaron, Willoughby, and Weymann, to name but a few. Then as the Duesenberg's fame spread, coachwork came from overseas. Fernandez et Darrin, Franay, Gurney Nutting, Saoutchik, and other top-ranking firms were represented.

And then there were the LaGrande bodies, most of them phaetons and all of them gorgeous. The late Gordon Buehrig, Duesenberg's chief stylist from 1929 to 1933, explained: "The LaGrande Phaeton was a product of the Depression, and it exemplifies the struggle [Duesenberg vice-president] Harold Ames made to keep the Duesenberg company in business.

"The Union City Body Company of Union City, Indiana, who built the body shells for the LaGrande phaeton, was not a prestige carriage builder. They had built some bodies for Auburn, but they also built seats for movie theatres and other non-automotive products. However, they could build bodies and they had a low wage scale. Ames was able to buy phaeton bodies from them for less than he could from LeBaron or Derham.

"At the Duesenberg factory we had good trimmers and painters, equal in fact to those in the prestige custom shops. Thus, the LaGrande bodies were purchased 'in the white,' then decked, trimmed and painted at Duesenberg. This arrangement had the extra advantage of keeping our own craftsmen busy....

"LaGrande, incidentally, was a name coined by Harold Ames to be a prestige body nameplate because Union City... was not a recognized carriage builder. The LaGrande name was also used later for all bodies received at the factory 'in the white,' which included unfinished bodies from Weymann, Walker, Brunn and others. While a LaGrande body plate was struck, it was not normally used, and these vehicles were usually delivered with no body plate affixed, as they were referred to as Duesenberg's own coachbuilder. They are credited with producing twenty-one bodies, of which nineteen were LaGrande phaetons."

In fact, the LaGrande phaeton was basically Gordon Buehrig's adaptation of the LeBaron design that had appeared on Duesenberg J-101, though Buehrig incorporated some of the features of the later Derham Tourster, a body he had personally designed. The LaGrande version was suitable for use on either the 142.5- or 153.5-inch chassis, though most of them appeared on the shorter wheelbase.

By 1931, with the nation locked in the grip of the worst Depression in history, the market for automobiles of the Duesenberg's calibre—and price—had just about dried up. Even those few people who could still afford such an automobile were, more often than not, reluctant to flaunt their prosperity in the face of such widespread poverty. Still, there was a small but loyal clientele, many of whose members came from the celebrity world. Over the years Gary Cooper owned two of them. So did Mae "Come Up and See Me Sometime" West, while chewing gum magnate Philip Wrigley owned five! Harlem evangelist Father Divine had a huge Duesenberg "Throne Car," built on a special wheelbase of 178 inches. Cardinal Mundelein, who must somehow have overlooked his vow of poverty, owned a Duesenberg. So did Howard Hughes, New York Mayor Jimmy Walker, playboy Tommy Manville, pharmaceutical magnate Eli Lilly, publisher William Randolph Hearst, and Hearst's great-and-good-friend Marion Davies.

Duesenberg's response to its shrinking market was twofold. First, the price of the chassis was raised from $8,500 to $9,500, presumably on the premise that the extra $1,000 wouldn't mean a great deal to anyone who could afford such an expensive piece of equipage in the first place. And second, a supercharged version was under development.

Introduced in May 1932, the supercharged SJ series developed a neck-snapping 320 horsepower. Priced at $11,750 in bare chassis form, it was fitted with flashy, chrome-plated external exhaust pipes (which were soon adopted by owners of non-blown Duesys, of course). The factory claimed that an SJ phaeton with the top down would do 104 miles an hour in second gear, 129 in top.

Tragically, however, just a month after the SJ's debut, Fred Duesenberg died of pneumonia, resulting from injuries sustained in an automobile accident in which he was driving an SJ. His brother, Augie, took over Fred's duties as chief engineer. Soon afterward, Gordon Buehrig left to join Harley Earl's staff at General Motors, though he would return later to design the fabulous Auburn speedster of 1935-36 and the Series 810/812 Cords of 1936-37.

But by that time E.L. Cord's automotive empire was crumbling. Auburn packed it in following the 1936 season, and a year later both Cord and Duesenberg were gone. Well, almost gone—between 1938 and 1940 one final Duesenberg was assembled from leftover parts.

A number of years ago, the late Ken Purdy wrote: "The fact that a whole new generation still recognizes his cars as 'the finest thing on four wheels' would please [Fred Duesenberg], which is perhaps the best monument that he could have."

Specifications[1]	
Engine:	dohc, 32-valve I-8, 419.7 cid/6.9 liters (3¾ x 4¾-in./95 x 121-mm bore x stroke), 5.25:1 compression ratio; 5 main bearings, 4 fuel pumps (3 electric, 1 mechanical), full pressure lubrication; Schebler carburetor, 265 bhp @ 4,250 rpm
Transmission:	3-speed selective, floor-mounted lever
Suspension:	Rigid axles, semi-elliptic springs, Watson stabilators (front), Delco Lovejoy shock absorbers (rear)
Brakes:	4-wheel hydraulic drum type (vacuum assisted beginning 1930)
Wheelbase (in.):	142.5
Shippingweight(lbs):	5,460
0-100 mph (sec):	21
Top speed (mph):	116 (89 in second gear)
Production:	approx. 480 (J, SJ, SSJ, and JN combined)

[1]1929 model, J-101

An elegant hood ornament helped set the tone for the fabulous Model J.

The Model J dash was complete, including even an altimeter gauge.

The Duesenberg Model J was powered by a 419.7-cid straight eight that featured dual overhead cams, four valves per cylinder, four fuel pumps—and a mighty 265 horsepower at 4,250 rpm.

This '35 Duesenberg Speedster-Roadster was bodied by the British firm J. Gurney Nutting & Company and delivered to the Maharajah Holkar of Indore, India.

1928 FORD MODEL A

The Model A's instrument panel was basic, and it was placed in the center of the dashboard. The speedometer was a revolving drum, and both an odometer and a trip odometer were provided, as was an amp gauge.

The 1928 Ford Model A roadster sold for $480. For that the buyer even got a rumble seat, not to mention an all-new Ford that served as the replacement for the venerable Model T. With twice as much power as the T, the Model A could do an honest 65 mph—and some owners claimed 70.

The suspense had been building for months, ever since the announcement was made that after more than 19 years Ford would at long last introduce a brand new car. And when the Model A finally made its debut, on December 2, 1927, its introduction literally created more excitement than any similar event in the history of the automobile. It was estimated that in the United States alone, 10 million people flocked to Ford showrooms to inspect the new car, and in some instances police were called upon in order to control the crowds.

The Model A's coming was even celebrated in a popular song:

Lay off people, lay off folks,
None of your sarcastic jokes,
HENRY'S MADE A LADY OUT OF LIZZIE!

No more bruises, no more aches,
Now she's got four-wheel brakes,
HENRY'S MADE A LADY OUT OF LIZZIE!

Talk of this and talk of that,
Boys you must take off your hat,
HENRY'S MADE A LADY OUT OF LIZZIE!

Has she plenty, has she much?
Got the tin you love to touch,
HENRY'S MADE A LADY OUT OF LIZZIE!

She's like all the other vamps,
Pretty shape and lovely lamps,
HENRY'S MADE A LADY OUT OF LIZZIE!

Since she's taken on some weight,
Honest, folks, she's looking great,
HENRY'S MADE A LADY OUT OF LIZZIE!

. . . and so on, for something like 18 verses!

For the new Ford really *was* new. Announcing its arrival in a $2 million advertising blitz, Henry Ford noted that "conditions in this country have so greatly changed in the last few years that further refinement in motor car construction is desirable. So . . . we have built a new and different Ford to meet new and different conditions.

"We believe the new Ford car . . . is as great an improvement in motor car building as the Model T Ford was in 1908 . . . ."

And indeed it was. The Model A's wheelbase was longer by three and a half inches, and the new car outweighed the old one by more than 350 pounds. The new engine, a 200.5-cubic-inch four, developed 40 horsepower, up from 20/22 in the Model T. A centrifugal water pump replaced the Model T's antiquated thermo-siphon cooling

Inside, the Model A roadster featured a bench seat, floor-mounted shift lever and hand brake, and a spartan dashboard. The choke knob was awkwardly placed to the right.

The Model A's 200.5-cid four developed 40 horsepower at 2,200 rpm and 128 lbs/ft torque at a lazy 1,000 rpm. Other details: a two-venturi carb and a 4.22:1 compression ratio.

system, and the T's primitive ignition system yielded to a high tension battery-and-distributor arrangement. The pedal-operated, two-speed planetary transmission of the earlier car was replaced by a conventional clutch and three-speed selective gearbox, both scaled-down counterparts of the Lincoln units. Four-wheel brakes took the place of the single brake band acting on the Model T's transmission.

Speed was increased, too, from a top of 35 or 40 mph in the Model T to about 60-65 in the Model A—some claimed up to 70 mph, but that was optimistic. Acceleration was outstanding: 5-25 miles an hour in just eight and a half seconds. Most six- and eight-cylinder cars couldn't match that in 1928. There was even a dashboard fuel gauge, a laminated safety glass windshield, automatic windshield wiper, Houdaille hydraulic shock absorbers all around, a dome light in the rear compartment of the closed cars, a speedometer, and a rear view mirror—all standard equipment. Ford even included front and rear bumpers in the purchase price.

As well, the new cars were handsome. Henry Ford admittedly knew nothing

The 1929 Model A Leatherback Sedan sported a leather-like sun visor, and as with other Model As, the windshield could be opened. Note the gas cap.

and cared even less about styling, but by the late Twenties he had belatedly come to realize that automobiles were sold as much on good looks as on good engineering. On the other hand, his son Edsel, a patron of the arts, was genuinely talented in that area. And so the attractive appearance of the Model A Fords, which bore no slight resemblance to the then-current Model L Lincolns, was a monument to Edsel's good taste. Even the senior Ford, who was never one to scatter compliments about indiscriminately, was moved to comment, "We've got a good man in my son. He knows style—how a car

ought to look . . . ."

Eight body styles were offered at first, or nine if the taxicab is included. Each was available in a range of four attractive colors in addition to the traditional black—an unusual feature at a time when the color choice in a low-priced car was often dictated by the body style. Upholstery, in the closed models, was of attractive hairline-stripe cloth. Prices began at $460 for the standard phaeton and ranged as high as $585 for the Fordor sedan. In between, there were two roadsters, three coupes, and—at $550—a Tudor sedan, by far the most popular of the lot. True, these figures were higher than those of the 1927 Model T, but the difference, in the case of the popular Tudor, came to only $55. Perhaps even more to the point, Ford's prices were still well below those of Chevrolet.

The early Model As, oddly enough, served as status symbols for their owners. In very short supply, they were eagerly sought after, even by those who could afford much more expensive automobiles. And fortunate were those who were able to acquire an early example. One of the first of the smartly styled sport coupes, for example, was

A Model A could look quite elegant with a fancy hood ornament—this one being functional as well—and a stone guard over the radiator. On the $625 Leatherback Sedan, the fabric covered both top and the rear panel.

The 1930 Model A five-window coupe cost $495 in standard guise, but a DeLuxe coupe—with its cowl-mounted parking lights—listed at $545. A two-passenger model, it weighed 2,265 pounds; 29,777 copies of this model found customers.

purchased by screen star Douglas Fairbanks for his wife, Mary Pickford. Other notables among the owners of this new Ford included New York Governor Franklin D. Roosevelt, inventor Thomas Edison (who received his as a gift from his friend, Henry Ford), homespun philosopher Will Rogers, and such screen luminaries as Dolores Del Rio, Joan Crawford, Wallace Beery, Lon Chaney, and Lillian Gish.

Of course, there were the inevitable glitches in the early production cars. The multiple-disc clutch that had performed so well in the Lincoln proved to be less suitable to the Ford. It was replaced before the end of the year by the single-plate type. The original starter, a Ford design, displayed a nasty habit of chewing up the teeth on the flywheel gear. It was soon superceded by a more satisfactory Bendix unit. Even the brakes had to be modified in order to meet the standards of the District of Columbia and the Commonwealth of Pennsylvania.

By 1929, there were no fewer than 18 Ford body styles, not including the taxi. Among the most interesting were the convertible cabriolet, which sold

for $670 including the rumble seat; a hardwood-bodied station wagon; and an open-front Town Car, built for those who wanted to combine manageable size with the snob appeal of an open chauffeur's compartment. That one sold for $1,400—more than twice as much as the convertible, Ford's second most costly car.

Reconversion of the Ford factories for production of the Model A had slowed production sharply during 1928, so for the second year in a row Chevrolet ranked first in sales. Ford regained the lead in 1929, however, claiming 33.75 percent of the market on a calendar year output of 1,507,132 cars—half a million more than Chevrolet. Of course, that number was still a bit shy of the Model T's 1923-25 figures. But Ford sales momentum was building, and prospects looked very good indeed—that is, until the Wall Street crash that October.

Changes for 1929 had been minimal, especially in terms of styling. But for 1930 the Model A's good looks became even better. The radiator was taller, suggesting the appearance of the handsome new LaSalle. Brightwork was done

in stainless steel rather than nickel plate. Wheels were reduced in size from 21 to 19 inches, lowering the Ford's profile significantly. And at mid-year a couple of new body styles debuted. A smart four-passenger Victoria featured a slanting windshield, while the new two-door deluxe phaeton would ultimately become a special favorite with collectors.

Alas, the Depression was taking its toll. Ford's production, though still comfortably ahead of Chevrolet's, was down by about 350,000 cars, a drop of more than 23 percent. And there was worse news yet to come.

Styling was little changed for 1931, though the Town Sedans and the convertible cabriolet were given slanted windshields like the Victoria. Further, a particularly smart new body style, A-400, bowed as a convertible two-door sedan. To the modern collector, it is the most valued and sought-after of all Model As.

It was during 1931 that the six-cylinder Chevy, first introduced in 1929, really came into its own. Advertising "A six at the price of a four," it outsold the Model A by more than 85,000 cars that season, in spite of a well-earned reputation for snapping axles. Chevrolet had at last established its sales supremacy, to be edged out by Ford only once more during the prewar era.

But if Ford was more or less marking time publicly during 1931, big things were going on behind the scenes. This would become apparent in 1932, when Henry Ford stunned the world with the first V-8 in the low-price field.

Specifications[1]	
Engine:	I-4 L-head, 200.5 cid (3⅞ x 4¼-in. bore x stroke), 4.22:1 compression ratio, 3 main bearings, Zenith or Holley double-venturi carburetor, 40 bhp @ 2,200 rpm, 128 lbs/ft torque @ 1,000 rpm
Transmission:	3-speed selective, floor-mounted control
Suspension:	Solid axles, transverse leaf springs
Brakes:	4-wheel internal mechanical
Wheelbase (in.):	103.5
Tread, front and rear (in.):	56
Weight (lbs):	2,050-2,495
Tires:	4.50 x 21
Top speed (mph):	60-65
Production:	1928 633,594 1929 1,507,132 1930 1,155,162 1931 541,615 (all numbers calendar year)

[1]1928 Model A

When 37-year-old Lawrence P. "Larry" Fisher was appointed general manager of the Cadillac Motor Car Company in 1925, he came with the determination that under his leadership Cadillac would replace Packard as America's premier motorcar.

To achieve that goal, Fisher knew that he would have to expand his line at both ends. On the one hand he needed a more moderately priced luxury car, to compete with the Packard Single Six. And at the other end of the scale he needed an automobile that would be unrivaled in power, smoothness, and luxury, without consideration for price—a car whose mystique would presumably lend an extra measure of prestige to the firm's lesser models.

The latter, it was determined, would take the form of a 16-cylinder car, with development getting under way early in 1926. Heading the "multi-cylinder" project was Owen Nacker, an experienced engine designer who had previously worked with both Alanson Brush and Howard Marmon. His selection proved to be an inspired choice.

Work commenced under carefully guarded secrecy. A 12-cylinder engine was being developed simultaneously, and Fisher used that one as a decoy. Word of the Twelve's development was deliberately leaked. Then security was tightened to a degree unprecedented in the industry, and Nacker was instructed to get cracking on the V-16. Drawings, specifications, and even supplies were labeled "Truck" or "Coach." And as far as Cadillac's suppliers and most of its employees knew, that's what the project was all about.

Then on December 10, 1929, Larry Fisher wrote a letter to his dealers telling them that a fabulous new 16-cylinder Cadillac was about to receive its first public showing. It was suggested that the dealers might wish to share this knowledge with prospective customers. Evidently this announcement had been planned to come some weeks earlier, but the Wall Street debacle that October created so much anxiety that the introduction was delayed. A modest recovery was experienced in November, optimism returned—for a time—and plans for the big event went forward. The debut finally took place the following January fourth at the New York Automobile Show, where a gorgeous Imperial Landau Sedan was displayed.

It was a fabulous machine, the likes of which the industry had never seen. Essentially, the engine was comprised of two eight-cylinder inline blocks positioned at a narrow 45-degree angle to one another and mounted on a common crankcase. Each bank was perfectly balanced and could be run independently of the other. Smoothness of operation was enhanced by the use of a fully counterweighted crankshaft. Unlike the eight-cylinder Cadillacs, which retained the firm's traditional L-head configuration, the V-16 used overhead valves, equipping them with

Cadillac stunned the world when it announced its new V-16 engine on December 10, 1929. It was a bold move and a grand car, but it arrived at just about the same time as the Great Depression. One of the most desirable models was the cabriolet coupe, which rode a massive 148-inch wheelbase.

73

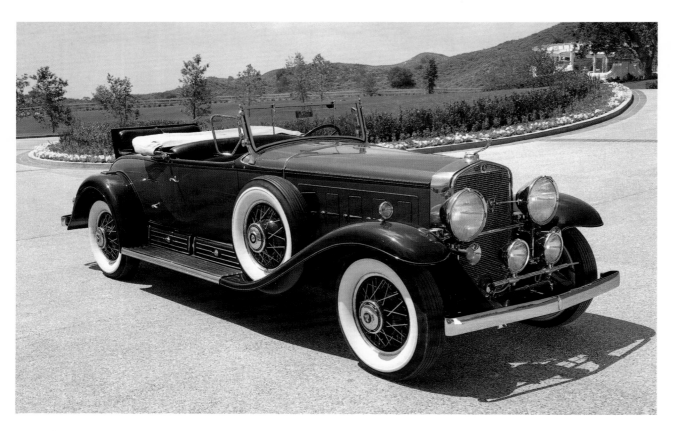

Probably the raciest-looking of the series 452 V-16 Cadillacs of 1930-31 was the two/four passenger roadster. It retailed for $5,310—enough to buy a nice house at the time—and weighed 5,350 pounds. With its windshield folded down, it provided a thrilling ride for young blades.

Golfers appreciated the special provision made to accommodate golf bags, probably almost as much as they liked the smooth, turbine-like power of the V-16. With a 45-degree angle between the banks of cylinders, it displaced 452.8 cubic inches and cranked out 165 horsepower.

hydraulic valve-lash adjusters which offered nearly silent valve train operation.

With the bore and stroke measuring three by four inches, the new engine displaced 452.8 cubic inches. Horsepower was advertised, no doubt conservatively, at 165 (though at least one early advertisement claimed "175-185" bhp). Torque was listed at 320 pounds/feet. The single camshaft was located in the crankcase, and twin vacuum tanks and updraft carburetors fed the two cylinder banks separately.

The V-16, in addition to its virtues of smoothness and power, was one of the most dramatic-looking engines ever produced. As Walter McCall has observed, "It was the first automobile engine anywhere to bear the mark of a stylist. The new V-16 was a truly beautiful creation of bright chrome, polished aluminum, porcelain and gleaming black enamel. There wasn't a trace of unsightly wiring or hoses; everything was tidily out of sight or under appropriately detailed covers."

It was a huge automobile, mounted on a 148-inch wheelbase and stretching 216 inches from bumper-to-bumper. It weighed, depending on body style, anywhere from 4,625 pounds (for the roadster) to as much as three tons. To

The badge proudly touted the V-16 and the fact that it was made by the "Cadillac Motor Car Co." Alas, the Depression put a severe damper on sales, but even so 3,251 were built for the 1930-31 model years.

take account of differences in weight, and with an eye perhaps to the different sorts of terrain on which the cars might be driven, a choice of final drive ratios was provided. Standard issue was 4.39:1, with 4.75:1, 4.07:1 or 3.47:1 optional at no additional cost, the last being intended, solely for the roadsters.

Styling was outstanding. Fisher Body, since 1929 a wholly owned subsidiary of General Motors, had purchased Fleetwood, a highly respected Pennsylvania coachbuilding firm, in 1926. And with Fleetwood's help, Larry Fisher undertook what has been called the "most expansive and varied catalogue custom body program of all time." No less than 54 distinct body styles were offered! The most glamorous of these were the 11 "Madam X" models, which took their mysterious-sounding name from a popular play of the day. These high-styled cars featured slender pillars and roofs, sharply raked and visored windshields, and belt moldings said to have been inspired by Hibbard and Darrin of Paris.

The level of quality represented by the Cadillac V-16 did not, of course, come cheap. Prices for "catalogued customs" in 1930 Series 452 and the nearly identical 1931 Series 452-A started at $5,325 for the roadster, and ran all the way to $9,700 for the Transformable Town Brougham, described as "probably the most ostentatious production Cadillac ever built." To put these figures into

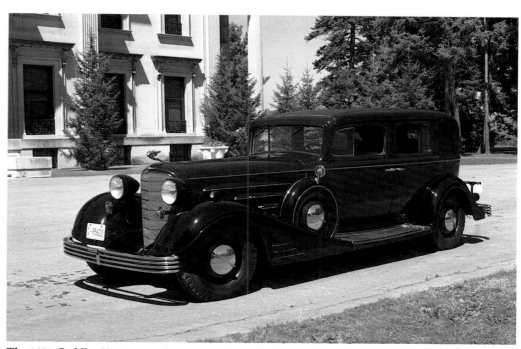

The 1933 Cadillac V-16 sported more aerodynamic styling: skirted fenders, horizontal hood louvers, and "speed lines" on the front fenders. Cadillac said it would build only 400 V-16s for '33, but in fact only 126 were sold.

context, bear in mind that in 1930 a new Oldsmobile sedan cost only $995, and the most expensive Buick limousine sold for $2,070.

The initial reception was enthusiastic, with 3,251 (some sources say 3,250) Sixteens sold in the 1930-31 model years, 2,887 of them during 1930. At least one of these cars was purchased by the United States government for use by the White House. George Tolan, a White House chauffeur for some 30 years, recalled a trip to the Presidential retreat

at Camp Rapidan, in Virginia. President Hoover, himself an engineer, was riding in a limousine of another make, but when he saw the remarkable way in which the Cadillac V-16 tackled the hills, he commandeered it for his own use. (In those days of innocence, of course, armor plate and bullet-proof glass for presidential limousines was unheard of.) So greatly did the President admire that car that when he left office, in 1933, he arranged to buy it from the government.

The only phaetons offered on the Cadillac V-16 chassis for 1932 were built by Fisher. Priced at $4,695 and weighing a road-hugging 5,400 pounds, reportedly only six were built. The one seen here is a dual-cowl model. Note the vertical hood "doors," which would be dropped after 1932.

For 1937, the Cadillac Series 90 V-16 received fresh, new styling. Highlights included squared-off fenders and an eggcrate grille, the latter a styling device still seen on current models. The lineup comprised a dozen models, among them a $7,250 Town Sedan, of which only three were built.

The instrument panel of the '37 V-16 was dominated by a large speedometer that read up to 110 mph and an equally large clock.

In 1938, Cadillac introduced an all-new V-16, a flathead engine displacing 431 cubic inches, 21 less than the old unit. Even so, it churned out 185 horsepower, just as before. Styling changes were minor for 1939, and only 18 convertible sedans, priced at $6,000, were built that year.

The deepening Depression prompted Cadillac to offer a smaller, Fisher-bodied V-16 for 1932. Although it sold for as little as $4,495, it apparently had little effect on sales. Only 364 V-16's had been sold during 1931, and for 1932 the total dropped to 296, with even worse results yet to come. Hard times, combined with competition from the excellent V-12 that Cadillac had introduced for the 1931 model year, had simply devastated the market for the 16-cylinder models.

For 1934, the standard wheelbase was stretched to 154 inches, and weight was increased by nearly 350 pounds. In order to maintain the V-16's customary level of performance, the compression ratio was increased to 6.0:1, raising the advertised horsepower to 185. In 1933, Cadillac had optimistically announced a policy of restricting production of the V-16 to 400 cars annually, but total output that year came to only 125 units, and in 1934 that figure plummeted to a miserable 56.

The succeeding years were even worse. Output sank to just 50 cars for 1935, and despite improvements that included a seamless steel "turret" top in 1936 and hydraulic brakes for 1937, the totals for those two seasons amounted to just 52 and 49 units, respectively.

The wonder is that Cadillac didn't pack it in, right then and there, as far as the multi-cylinder program was concerned. Many people expected that the division would. Instead, for 1938 GM's finest unveiled a brand new V-16, redesigned in every respect. Half a ton lighter and almost a foot and a half shorter than the 1937 version, it was powered by a new 135-degree L-head engine. Intended as a replacement for both the V-16 and V-12 of prior years, it was priced $2,400 lower than the previous Sixteen.

The new engine, which had fewer than half as many parts as its predecessor, was far more economical to build than the overhead-valve V-16 had been. In addition, it gave the stylists the lower profile they had been wanting, and it made possible the use of twin downdraft carburetors. Displacement was a little smaller at 431 cubic inches, but horse-

power remained at 185. And if it lacked something of the classic appearance of the earlier models—both externally and in the engine compartment—at least the new Sixteen was somewhat more economical to operate.

From the start, the Cadillac V-16 had been a favorite with the Hollywood crowd. A 1933 convertible phaeton, built for Al Jolson, is displayed now at the Harrah Foundation's National Automobile Museum in Reno, Nevada. Robert Montgomery had a '33 convertible victoria, while Marlene Dietrich owned a '35 town car. Among the owners of the "second generation" V-16's were Gary Cooper, Eddie Cantor, and W.C. Fields (who had two of them, one with a built-in bar!). Al Capone owned a 1940 formal sedan, and even the Vatican owned a 1938 town car.

There is little doubt that Cadillac lost money on every V-16 it built. But over its 11-year production span the 16-cylinder car accomplished its major objective, for by the time the last of these great cars left the assembly line, it was Cadillac—not Packard—that was recognized as America's top-ranking luxury car.

The '39 V-16 convertible sedan was a trunkback model sporting taillights that were partially integrated into the fenders, a trend that would continue in the future. The dashboard featured a woody look, with a large chrome speaker grille in the center. Instruments ran one alongside the other in a horizontal strip.

Specifications[1]	
Engine:	45-degree ohv V-16; 452.8 cid (3.0 x 4.0-in. bore x stroke); 5.35:1 compression ratio (later 5.11:1, 4.98:1 opt.); hydraulic valve lifters; twin coils, distributors, and updraft carburetors; 165 bhp @ 3,400 rpm; 320 lbs/ft torque
Transmission:	3-speed selective, synchronized 2nd and 3rd gears
Suspension:	Rigid axles, semi-elliptic springs, Lovejoy double-acting shock absorbers
Brakes:	4-wheel mechanical, 16.5-in. drums, vacuum-assisted
Wheelbase (in.):	148
Weight (lbs):	5,325 to 6,020, depending on body style
Top speed (mph):	84 to 100, depending on gear ratio and weight
Acceleration (sec):	5-25 mph: 7.88; 10-60 mph: 21.1 (7-pass. sedan with standard 4.39:1 rear axle)
Production:	1930 2,887 1931 364

[1]1930-31 Sixteen

F or years the 16-cylinder automobile has been identified in the public's collective mind exclusively with Cadillac. But there was another fine Sixteen back in the early Thirties: the Marmon. It was an exciting car, and in a number of respects it was superior to the Cadillac. That fact was duly recognized at the 1932 New York Automobile Show when the Society of Automotive Engineers declared the Marmon Sixteen engine to be "the year's most noteworthy automotive accomplishment," an honor that Cadillac has yet to receive.

Marmon had been building automobiles ever since 1902, when Howard Marmon, the company's vice-president of engineering, constructed an air-cooled V-2 for his own use. The second Marmon, built the following year, ran with a V-4. Half a dozen of these cars were built and sold that season, mostly to friends of Howard Marmon and his older brother, Walter. Production rose to 25 cars in 1905, and a one-off V-6 was also built that year. By 1906, Marmon had come up with a big 65-horsepower, air-cooled V-8. It was a pioneering effort, produced nearly nine years before the first Cadillac V-8, but it failed to get beyond the prototype stage.

In 1909, a pair of conventional water-cooled, T-head, four-cylinder Marmons made their debut. One of these, the Model 32—a very advanced car for its time—would remain in production as the company's mainstay as late as 1914. In all of these early cars, Howard Marmon insisted upon two characteristics: light alloy construction and perfect lubrication. While virtually all of Marmon's competitors clung to the old dipper-and-splash method, the Model 32 featured a gear-driven oil pump with pressure delivery to all bearings.

A major boost to the Marmon reputation for performance came with the introduction, in December 1915, of the Model 34. This car was powered by a highly advanced overhead-valve six. Displacing 339.7 cubic inches, it developed 74 horsepower. Block and crankcase were an integral aluminum casting, something virtually unheard of at that time. Pistons, intake manifold, pushrods, even the water pump were made of aluminum alloy. Iron was used only for the head and cylinder liners.

Nor was the use of aluminum confined to the engine. The transmission case and differential housing, plus the body, hood, and even the fenders were made of lightweight aluminum alloys. As a result, the Model 34 weighed in some 700 pounds lighter than the contemporary Cadillac, giving it a substantial performance edge. It was also the more expensive of the two. In 1916, for example, the Model 34 Marmon touring car sold for $2,900, while a Cadillac in the same body style could be purchased for $2,080.

Cadillac beat Marmon by about a year with a V-16, and by the time Marmon got its V-16 on the market, the Depression was full-blown. Even so, that didn't stop Marmon from touting its Sixteen as "the world's most advanced motor car."

The Marmon Sixteen rode a 145-inch wheelbase, three inches shorter than Cadillac's. And due to extensive use of aluminum, the Marmon weighed about 500 pounds less. The Victoria Club Coupe (*opposite*) listed at $5,270.

Competitors predicted problems would arise with Marmon's aluminum engine block, for aluminum was known in those days as "the trouble metal." Unfortunately, they were correct, so for 1920 an iron engine was used, cast in two blocks of three cylinders each. But Howard Marmon retained his faith in the lighter metal, and kept working on ways to make its use more practical. Eventually his efforts would bear fruit, but that success would not come for another decade.

The automobile operation was really a sideline at Marmon in those days. The company's principal source of revenue came from the manufacture of milling machinery, a field in which Marmon was probably the leader. And a good thing, too, for the cars were not selling well. In 1924, the automobile business was spun off and a new management team, headed by George M. Williams, was called in. Williams, with an eye to the volume market, hired Delmar G. "Barney" Roos, formerly chief engineer at Pierce-Arrow, to design a medium-priced straight eight. Howard Marmon, who took a dim view of any product that fell short of his own meticulous standards, withdrew at that point from active participation in the firm.

Which is not to say that the Little Marmon, as the new model was called, was a bad car. It was probably at least as good as competing machines in its under-$2,000 price field. But it clearly

The Marmon Sixteen sported free-standing taillights, and this '32 Convertible Sedan is fitted with an add-on exterior trunk.

was not comparable to Marmons of yore—nor to the current Model 74, successor to the Model 34.

Meanwhile, Howard Marmon was by no means idle. Working in his own laboratory, he devoted much of his energy to the fulfillment of a long-held dream: the development of what would eventually be billed as "The World's Most Advanced Motor Car," the Marmon Sixteen.

Observe, by the bye, that Howard Marmon never referred to his car as the "V-16" the way Cadillac did. It was simply the Marmon Sixteen. Still, in

concept the Marmon and Cadillac engines had much in common. Both were comprised of two straight-eights fitted to a single crankcase. In both cases the cylinder blocks were located at an angle of 45 degrees to one another, which in a 16-cylinder engine guaranteed an even firing order. Both employed full-pressure lubrication, overhead valves, dual exhausts, and six-volt electrics.

But there were major differences as well. While the Cadillac used cast iron exclusively, the Marmon engine featured aluminum alloys throughout, including the cylinder blocks, resulting in a considerable savings in weight. To allay any anxiety on the part of the public, Marmon advertisements proclaimed, "Case-hardened, file-hard steel cylinders are used"—meaning, of course, the cylinder liners. Howard Marmon's long years of research had paid off: the new engine could claim all the advantages of aluminum construction with none of the penalties experienced with the early Model 34.

And there were other distinctions. The Marmon, for instance, used rubber engine mountings. Its cylinder blocks and crankcase were a single casting, while Cadillac cast the three pieces separately. Comprised of an alloy of aluminum and copper, the material used by Marmon was developed by a Pennsylvania foundry. And in lieu of offset engine blocks, which made possible Cadillac's use of side-by-side connecting rods, Marmon used the more costly fork-and-blade arrangement.

Like the Cadillac, the Marmon engine was based on a four-inch stroke. But the Marmon's 3⅛-inch bore was an eighth of an inch greater than that of the Cad, resulting in a slight advantage in displacement: 490.8 versus 452.8 cubic inches. The Marmon's compression ratio—highest in the industry at that time—was 6.00:1, compared to the Cadillac's 5.50:1, and its duplex downdraft carburetor was more efficient than its rival's dual updrafts. Taken together, these factors gave the Marmon a 35-horsepower advantage: 200, compared to 165 for Cadillac.

And what a performer the Marmon Sixteen was. Its power-to-weight ratio was the greatest of any automobile on

The Convertible Sedan is probably the most-prized Marmon Sixteen model. In 1932, it set a Depression-weary buyer back $5,950. Marmon's V-16 was made of aluminum alloy and advanced for its day, developing an even 200 horsepower.

The Marmon Sixteen's interiors were as elegant as one would expect. Only the finest materials were used, as on this elegant 1933 five-passenger sedan.

Marmon prices were lowered for 1933 as the four-door sedan went from $5,700 to $4,975, but in the end it didn't matter as Marmon was on the ropes and there would be no 1934 models. In total, only about 390 Sixteens were produced.

the American road, save only the Duesenberg. Torque, though never advertised, has been reliably estimated at between 380 and 400 pounds/feet, providing the Sixteen with phenomenal hill-climbing ability. A San Francisco newspaper reporter declared, "We've never driven a luxury automobile that can climb hills like a Marmon 16!"

Top speed was in excess of 100 miles per hour. In fact, upon taking delivery of a new Marmon Sixteen, the buyer received a certificate indicating that his car's chassis, fitted with a test body that simulated the weight of a fully equipped car, had been driven 210 miles at the Indianapolis Speedway, the last 10 miles being run at "Wide open throttle at not less than 105 miles an hour." A further requirement of the test run was that the driver must have downshifted from high to second at 80 mph without gear clash.

A 5,100-pound, 100-plus-mph automobile obviously needed superior brakes, and Howard Marmon was not one to overlook anything so important. He used the mechanical, duo-servo type, vacuum-assisted and self-energizing. Sixteen-inch drums were used, and at 353¾ square inches, the lining area was nearly 64 percent greater than that of the Cadillac V-16.

To style his magnificent new luxury-liner, Marmon called upon Walter Dorwin Teague, a New York-based industrial designer. It was a puzzling choice, for Teague had had no previous experience in automobile styling, nor was he particularly interested in automobiles. In fact, at that time he didn't even know how to drive. Chances are he was hired because he was a close

personal friend of the Marmon brothers, and no doubt he agreed to do the job on the cheap, for by that time the company was in desperate financial condition.

In any case, the actual design was evidently the work of Teague's son, Walter Dorwin, Jr., 18 years old at that time and a freshman at the Massachusetts Institute of Technology. Young Teague borrowed ideas from both Ray Dietrich and Frank Hershey, the latter an employee of the Walter M. Murphy Company in those days. His design, somewhat controversial at the time, appears now to be clean, sleek, and more modern-looking than most luxury cars of the early Thirties.

But of course the timing of the Marmon Sixteen's introduction could hardly have been worse. First, although a prototype was displayed at the New York Salon in December 1930, actual production didn't get under way until April 16, 1931. By that time the Cadillac V-16 had been on the market for more than 15 months, which took the edge off the excitement of the Sixteen's debut. And then there was the condition of the nation's economy, by then approaching its nadir.

In the circumstances, it can hardly come as a surprise that production of this great automobile was severely

limited. Although eight LeBaron body styles were catalogued, according to the best available estimates only 390 Marmon Sixteens were built: 223 in 1931, 111 in 1932, and 56 in 1933. Marmon had contacted a number of custom coachbuilders in the hope that some of them might use the big Marmon's chassis, but apparently only three custom jobs were ever produced: two phaetons by Waterhouse and one, a victoria, designed by Count Alexis de Sakhnoffsky and built by the Hayes Body Company.

By May 1, 1933, the company was in receivership and the great Marmon Sixteen was history.

Specifications	
Engine:	45-degree V-16, ohv, aluminum alloy block, 490.8 cid (3.125 x 4.00-in. bore x stroke), 200 bhp @ 3,400 rpm, 380-400 lbs/ft torque (est.)
Transmission:	3-speed selective, synchronized on 2nd & 3rd
Suspension:	Rigid axles, semi-elliptic springs, 2-way hydraulic shock absorbers
Brakes:	Duo-Servo with vacuum booster, 16-in. drums, 353.75 sq. in. effective area
Wheelbase (in.):	145
Tires:	7.00 x 18
Weight (lbs):	5,090-5,480, depending on body style
Top speed (mph):	105
Acceleration 5-60 mph (sec):	20
Production:	est. 390 total

When rumors concerning a forthcoming Ford V-8 were permitted to leak out of Dearborn in the fall of 1931, the public's reaction for the most part was one of incredulity. A low-priced V-8? Nobody had ever heard of such a thing—and nobody thought it could be done.

But this time, for once, the rumors were true. In fact, development of the V-8 engine had commenced more than two years earlier. The work took place under a cloud of secrecy at the Edison Institute, secluded behind the walls of Ford's Greenfield Village. Carl Schultz and Ray Laird, two of Ford's most gifted engineers, participated in the project from the start, having been charged with laying out a small V-8 that might be suitable for mass production. They were joined during the summer of 1930 by another engineer, a bright young man named Emil Zoerlein, whose particular task was to design an ignition system for the new engine. And, of course, Henry Ford himself kept his hand in the game, every step of the way. Equipment was amazingly primitive, given the resources at the Ford Motor Company's command, for Henry Ford firmly believed in challenging his engineers with nearly impossible tasks.

Always a man of contradictions, Henry Ford on the one hand had stubbornly clung to his Model T long after it had become hopelessly outmoded; on the other hand, in the mid-Twenties he had instructed some of the members of his engineering staff to work up plans for an X-8 engine. A radical design, the X-8 had two pairs of cylinders facing up and two pairs facing down, after the manner of two V-4's joined at the bottom by a common crankshaft.

Henry Ford was responsible for three great cars: the Model T, the Model A, and the V-8. Not only did the '32 Ford boast the world's first low-priced V-8, but son Edsel saw to it that it received new, and very attractive, styling. The optional quail hood ornament added a touch of class and is very much prized by collectors.

The proposal proved to be totally impractical for a number of reasons: the lower spark plugs tended to become fouled, the block was excessively heavy, and production costs would have been impossibly high. So Ford eventually turned to the V-8 as an alternative.

Logic might have suggested that Ford should follow Chevrolet's lead and develop a six of its own. But Henry Ford's experience with the 1905-08 Model K, his only six-cylinder car, had left him with a deep-seated prejudice against that engine type. That was because the Model K, a big car with a 405-cid engine and a lofty $2,500 price tag, had been a rolling disaster all the way.

So it was to be a V-8. But still, even when word got out about the new engine, it was impossible to determine exactly what the old man had in mind. Hardly anyone in those days, apart from Henry Ford himself, really believed that it was possible to build such a powerplant at a competitive price. Thus, the question: Was the V-8 to be a companion car to the Model A, or *what*? Surely the old man didn't expect to be able to offer an eight-cylinder car at the price of a four.

Henry Ford's nifty V-8 cranked out 65 horsepower and 130 lbs/ft torque in 1932. It featured a cheap-to-produce one-piece block. The engine-turned instrument panel was more elegant than that of the Model A. A manual choke and throttle were standard.

The highly respected journal, *Automotive Industries*, speculated that the V-8 would most likely be an intermediate-sized car riding a wheelbase of 117 inches, more than a foot longer than the Model A. Which, of course, further suggested that it could be expected sell in a higher price range.

Speculation was rife. But Henry, as usual, wasn't talking.

Henry Ford's prejudice aside, there was a certain logic to the idea of going to a V-8 rather than a six, since Ford's Lincoln Division had been building V-8 engines for more than a decade. But in a low-priced car? Impossible! For according to the conventional wisdom of the day, the V-type engine was extremely expensive to build. Standard practice at Lincoln—and at Cadillac, for that matter—called for the two cylinder blocks to be separately cast, then meticulously machined, bench-assembled, and bolted to the crankcase. A lot of precision work was involved, but of course Cadillacs and Lincolns cost many times the price of a Ford.

Still—despite the cost considerations— Henry Ford was determined to have his V-8, and he remained sanguine regarding the cost factor. In any event,

something drastic had to be done, for the six-cylinder Chevrolet was already eating Ford alive on the sales charts. The Model A had been sensationally popular when first introduced, but the public was becoming enchanted by the smoothness of Chevrolet's six-cylinder engine, and the Model A's four suffered by comparison. The trend was ominous: In 1930 Ford had held a comfortable 77-percent sales lead over Chevrolet, but that advantage had suddenly disappeared during 1931. By year's end, Chevy would rank as America's most popular automobile.

The first big problem confronting Ford and his team of engineers was how to design a V-8 block that could be cast in one piece, for only thus could costs be contained. General Motors' Oldsmobile and Oakland/Pontiac Divisions had introduced monobloc V-8's during 1929 and 1930, respectively, but neither had been particularly successful—and in any case these cars cost from two to three times as much as a Ford.

At first even Edsel Ford, nominally president of the company, and production chief Charles Sorensen had been denied access to the V-8 project. But early in the summer of 1931 they were let in on the secret, along with Lawrence Sheldrick, head of Ford's engineering department. Sorensen's participation was especially critical, particularly with respect to the development of the one-piece engine block, for such was his expertise in that field that he would become widely known as "Cast Iron Charlie."

Henry Ford still produced a four-cylinder car in 1932 (upped to 50 horsepower), but the V-8 models strutted their own special hubcaps.

The '32 Ford V-8 convertible coupe came with a rumble seat included in the $610 base price. It weighed a modest 2,390 pounds, only 20 more than the four-cylinder Model B.

The pace had been leisurely enough at first because Henry Ford was toying with a number of ideas. But as the 1931 sales figures began to come in, the development of the V-8—known as the Model 18—took on a new urgency, with the staff working long hours and Henry Ford himself devoting virtually full time to the project.

The result, as every aficionado knows, was a remarkable little engine. Displacing 221 cubic inches, it was officially rated at 65 horsepower. That figure was evidently conservative, however, for the car proved to be very fast, a favorite with bank robbers and law enforcement officials alike.

Among the firm's customers, as Henry Ford well knew, there still were diehard devotees of the four-cylinder engine. Accordingly, while the V-8 engine was under development, work was under way on an improved version of the Model A's familiar four-banger. Dubbed the Model B, the new four was given, among other things, a stronger crankshaft, a higher compression ratio, and an improved lubrication system. Horsepower was thereby increased by 25 percent, from 40 to 50.

Even apart from the two new engines, the '32 Fords received a number of significant improvements. Rubber engine mounts were employed for the first time to cut down on vibration. The wheelbase was stretched from 103.5 to 106 inches, and the spring base (the distance between the transverse-mounted springs) was lengthened, leading to a lowering of the car's profile and a smoother ride. A heavier frame was employed, the fuel tank was relocated from the cowl to the rear of the car, and the brakes were enlarged. Further, a new transmission boasted synchronized second and third gears, and the steering ratio was increased. And so it went.

Edsel Ford and Joe Galamb, who had been responsible for styling the Model A, took on the same task for the new car, with the help of body builders Murray, Budd, and especially Briggs, Ford's principal body supplier. Once again, the car resembled a scaled-down Lincoln in appearance, except that the grille—said to have been styled by Briggs and originally intended for Plymouth— was unique to the Ford. Offerings

Running boards were still standard fare in 1932, but they were more smoothly integrated than on the Model A.

comprised 16 standard and DeLuxe types, each with a choice of four- or eight-cylinder power.

The revised four-cylinder car was ready by late 1931, but the V-8 wasn't. Since the two new models were essentially identical except for their engines, early introduction of the Model B would have diluted the impact of the V-8, so Henry Ford wisely chose to wait. Dealers, meanwhile, had to scrape by on a dwindling supply of 1931 Model A's.

The pace of preparations must have been feverish, but finally—on March 10, 1932—production got under way on the Model 18, to be followed shortly by the Model B. The public's reception was enthusiastic. When the V-8 first went on display, on March 31, nearly six million people visited Ford showrooms for a first-hand look. But availability was extremely limited at first; not until early May was Ford able to supply even one car to each of its dealers. And in any case, in those severely depressed times, only a fortunate few had money enough to buy a new car.

Unfortunately, the haste with which the V-8 engine was rushed to completion exacted a toll in several ways. Casting problems were so severe that for a time half the blocks ended up as scrap. Pinholes developed, even in some of the engines that had passed the initial

inspection. The early units burned oil— as much as a quart every 50 miles. And the twin problems of overheating and vapor lock soon asserted themselves.

Excessive engine temperatures, which would plague the flathead V-8 throughout its long lifetime, resulted from Ford's practice of routing the exhaust ports right through the engine block to a pair of outboard-mounted exhaust manifolds. This was a clever arrangement, but one that tended to generate a great deal of internal heat. Even an 84-percent increase in the capacity of the cooling system failed to solve the problem entirely. As to vapor lock, that too resulted from a design flaw because the fuel pump was mounted at the rear of the vee, where it was the recipient of much of the heat generated by Ford's unique manifolding arrangement.

Then there were the rumors, the most widespread of which was also the most peculiar. It was said that because the pistons lay more or less on their sides, wear on the cylinder walls would be both excessive and uneven. Remarkable, isn't it, that no such charge had been made regarding the Lincoln or the Cadillac.

But most of the problems of the L-head Ford V-8 were eventually solved, and the same basic engine remained in production through the 1953 model year (1954 in Canada), a remarkable record of longevity. And of course the 1932 Ford V-8—the fabled "Deuce"— remains a collector's favorite worldwide.

Specifications	
Engine:	90-degree L-head V-8, 221 cid (3 1/16 x 3 3/4-in bore x stroke), 5.5:1 compression ratio, 3 main bearings, mechanical valve lifters, 1-bbl downdraft carburetor, 65 bhp @ 3,400 rpm, 130 lbs/ft torque @ 1,250 rpm
Transmission:	3-speed selective, synchronized on 2nd & 3rd, floor shift, single dry-plate clutch
Chassis:	Pressed-steel frame, channel-section side members, pressed or tubular cross members
Suspension:	Rigid axles, transverse leaf springs
Brakes:	4-wheel internal mechanical
Wheelbase (in.):	106.0
Overall length (in.):	165.5
Tread, front/rear (in.):	55.2/56.7
Tires:	5.25 x 18
Weight (lbs):	2,203-2,568, depending on body style
Production:	193,891 V-8s plus 89,036 4-cylinder cars (model year)

I f it hadn't been for the patronage of Edsel Ford, the great Model K Lincolns of the 1930s would surely never have been produced. The irony, of course, is that the greatest Lincolns—and the other Classics as well—were produced in the worst of times. The period from 1929 to 1934, generally held to have delivered the most purely beautiful automobiles of all time, was an era of unprecedented economic catastrophe and a Depression whose depths have not, thankfully, been approached since. An example of such ironies was the K-Series Lincolns, the most luxurious ever to bear the name: fabulous V-8s and V-12s that set new standards of performance, refinement, and accoutrement—yet found few buyers in threadbare times.

By the early Thirties that wonderful Classic era was rapidly fading. Mass production methods had made it possible to build excellent machines at relatively reasonable cost—and even to supply them with a remarkably high grade of trim. No longer was it necessary to lay out at least three times the price of a Buick in order to purchase a really high-grade car. Nor was it possible any longer for the automaker to ignore the cost factor and remain in business—that is, unless the firm was blessed with a financial angel.

In the case of the Lincoln, it was Edsel Ford who made it all happen. Evidently, Edsel had persuaded his father, Henry Ford, to purchase the Lincoln Motor Company in 1922 after its founders, Henry and Wilfred Leland, ran into financial difficulties in the 1920-21 recession. Thereafter, Lincoln was always Edsel's special pride, for he had a keen appreciation of the fine engineering that went into its design and the superb crafts-manship that characterized its construction.

Unlike Henry Leland, Edsel Ford also had a keen eye for styling. Soon after he took charge, Lincoln began offering "catalogued custom" designs by Brunn, Fleetwood, and Judkins. Bodies were supplied in lots of 10, 25, or more, resulting in greatly reduced costs compared to the traditional one-off custom jobs.

In 1925, Lincoln opened a body plant of its own, this to keep up with rapidly increasing demand. And seeking a more modern image, Edsel Ford lured Ray Dietrich away from LeBaron, in New York City, and set him up in Detroit as Dietrich, Inc. Regarded by this time as a fashion leader in the industry, Lincoln offered a wider selection of semi-custom bodies than any of its competitors, including the designs by Dietrich, as well as Holbrook, Willoughby, Locke, and LeBaron. Production that year reached 8,451 cars.

Sales began to slip a little in 1927. Even the introduction of an enlarged 384.8-cid V-8 for the 1928 models failed to stop the slide. Clearly, it was time to replace the Model L with something entirely different.

Among Classic cars, the dual-cowl phaeton body style is highly coveted. It can be seen why here, because even in a chauffeur-driven car the Lord and his Lady had the luxury of adjusting the dual-cowl apparatus to let in the amount of fresh air they desired.

Although the Model L had been a fine car, the 1931-40 K-Series cars represented Lincoln's finest hour. In 1931, only a 120-bhp V-8 was offered, but Ks would be powered by V-12s for the rest of the decade. Only 77 dual-cowl phaetons were built for 1931.

By 1939, styling of the big Lincoln K had evolved into a more aerodynamic shape than in the early '30s. The convertible sedan, bodied by LeBaron, sold for $5,828, or $6,028 if one added the partition window. This model rode the longer 145-inch wheelbase. LeBaron turned out only nine of these magnificent cars.

Thus was born a brand new Lincoln, the Model K, which wasintroduced in January 1931. Its V-8 engine was still built to Henry Leland's original design, even to the costly fork-and-blade connecting rods that Cadillac had abandoned in 1928. But horsepower was raised from 90 to 120, thanks to a higher compression ratio, dual downdraft carburetion with mechanical pump feed, and a redesigned intake manifold. Other mechanical innovations included a new double-plate clutch, synchromesh transmission with free-wheeling, Houdaille double-acting shock absorbers all around and worm-and-roller steering replacing the worm-and-sector type.

But from a sales standpoint, probably the most important feature of this new Lincoln was its fresh new styling. Standard wheelbase was stretched from 136 to 145 inches, overall height reduced, and the stance widened, giving the car a sleek—and more imposing—appearance. A handsome new grille adorned the front end, complemented by more sweeping fender lines. Meanwhile, bowl-shaped headlamps added to the bolder look, and the dual trumpet horns offered the driver a choice of "town" or "country" settings.

Fourteen "factory custom" styles were offered, in addition to nine standard bodies. Prices ranged from $4,400 to $7,400, a substantial premium over the price tag of a Cadillac. In fact, the Model K Lincoln V-8 actually cost several hundred dollars more than Cadillac's new V-12!

Sales increased by about 10 percent for 1931, despite the tightening grip of the Depression, but the figure of 3,540 cars produced for the model year was less than half the number recorded just five years earlier. There is little doubt that the Lincoln operation was losing money, but Ford's bookkeeping methods were so inadequate in those days that no firm figures have ever been calculated.

For the first time in its history, Lincoln presented two distinct car lines for 1932. The Model KB, which some authorities consider the greatest of all classic Lincolns, retained the 145-inch chassis of the 1931 car, but was powered by a brand new engine: a 447.9-cubic-inch V-12. A 65-degree unit, this huge powerplant weighed 1,070 pounds and was rated at 150 horsepower. Features included a seven-main-bearing forged steel

crankshaft fitted with a torsional vibration damper, plus Lincoln's traditional fork-and-blade connecting rods. Remarkably enough, prices for the Model KB were slightly lower than those of 1931's eight-cylinder Series K.

Very few cars could still be ordered with side-mounted spare tires in 1939, but the Lincoln K was one of them.

But it was the other series, the Model KA, that helped make the Lincoln more competitive. There were no "factory custom" bodies for these cars, and they rode a shorter 136-inch chassis—and they cost about $1,400 less, model-for-model, than the big KB. This is not to say that the KA was inexpensive, for it cost at least $300 more than the Cadillac V-8.

Another new "twelve" replaced the V-8 engine in the 1933 version of the KA. This was the first Lincoln engine to use offset engine blocks, permitting the connecting rods to be placed side-by-side on the crankshaft journals. Wilfred Leland is said to have been scornful of this departure from his father's fork-and-blade design, but this was a much more modern engine than that of the KB. The number of main bearings was reduced from seven to four, in the interest of reduced length. Insert bearings were fitted, a pioneering effort on Lincoln's part, and aluminum pistons were utilized.

A new mesh grille, more slanted than before, helped to give the 1933 Lincolns a more rakish appearance, and many models featured the skirted fenders then coming into vogue. And despite the addition of four cylinders in the KA models, prices were unchanged. But by this time the Depression was taking a serious toll on all luxury makers; in Lincoln's case, production of the KA models dropped 44 percent from 1932's already depressed figures, while the big KB took a 65-percent tumble.

With output reaching just 2,007 cars for the 1933 model year, clearly some consolidation of models was in order. So for 1934 both the KA and KB models shared just one engine. This was a bored version of the KA unit, displacing 414 cubic inches and rated at 150 horsepower. It was generally regarded as smoother, faster, and more economical than the larger KB engine—and it was also less expensive to produce. Styling changed little, though prices were shuffled a bit: somewhat higher for the KA, slightly lower for the KB. Production for the year climbed by about 46 percent.

By 1935, Lincoln was concentrating exclusively on the upper end of the market. The KA and KB nomenclature

Lincoln dressed up the dashboard of the K with four horizontal chrome strips. Note the floor shift.

was abandoned; thenceforth, though Lincoln continued to offer two wheelbase lengths, all cars would be designated simply Model K. And the least expensive car in the line cost about $1,000 more than the comparable 1934 unit. All models were completely and very attractively restyled, from a handsome new grille and bullet headlamps up front to a sloping rear. In addition, the bodies were moved forward on the chassis, providing a more comfortable ride for rear-seat passengers.

A number of custom coachbuilders had fallen by the wayside by this time, victims of the Depression. Lincoln nonetheless hung on as the last major sponsor of custom body designs. Still, at least 12 "Factory Custom" styles remained available on the Lincoln chassis, sporting designs by Brunn, Judkins, LeBaron, and Willoughby.

Changes were minor for 1936 (aside from the introduction of the medium-priced Lincoln-Zephyr, of course). The windshield was more sharply raked, pontoon fenders were adopted, and pressed steel wheels replaced the earlier wires. Mechanical changes, meanwhile, were limited to the deletion of free wheeling and an increase in the steering ratio.

The classic Lincoln's last major restyling took place in 1937. Bulky and

impressive in appearance, it has been labeled "bulbous" by some critics. Four standard body styles and 17 Factory Customs were offered, but fewer than a thousand of these fine cars found buyers. Hydraulic valve lifters were fitted, but otherwise there were no major mechanical changes. Horsepower was still advertised at 150, though thanks to a revised camshaft the 1937 engine was faster than its predecessors.

Production of the nearly identical 1938 Lincolns fell once again, and 1939 proved to be even worse. And then . . . . Let Lincoln expert Paul Woudenberg provide the epitaph: "Production of the mighty Model K Lincoln had dribbled to a close in 1939, the few chassis left over being presented as 1940 models with black Lincoln medallions, a fitting funereal color to commemorate what many believe to be the finest-quality car produced in America in the Thirties."

But even in its waning days, the Model K Lincoln was paid the ultimate compliment in 1939 when a special 160-inch-wheelbase unit was delivered to the White House. Called the "Sunshine Special," and intended for parades and other official functions, it was used by Presidents Roosevelt and Truman. Boasting armor-plated doors, bullet-proof glass, siren, and flashing lights, as well as handgrips for bodyguards, this historic Lincoln lives on in retirement at the Henry Ford Museum in Dearborn, Michigan.

Specifications[1]	
Engine:	67-degree L-head V-12, 414 cid (3⅛ x 4½-in. bore x stroke), 6.38:1 compression ratio, 4 main bearings, hydraulic valve lifters, 2-bbl downdraft carburetor, 150 bhp @ 3,800 rpm
Transmission:	3-speed selective, floor-mounted lever, double dry disc clutch
Suspension, front:	Rigid axle, 42 x 2¼-in. semi-elliptic springs
Suspension, rear:	Rigid axle, 62 x 2½-in. semi-elliptic springs
Shock absorbers:	Houdaille double-acting
Brakes:	Front/rear mechanical drum type
Wheelbase (in.):	136 or 145, depending on body style
Tread, front/rear (in.):	60
Weight (lbs):	5,172-5,801, depending on body style
Tires:	7.50 x 17
Top speed (mph):	95+
0-60 mpg (sec):	est. 20
Production:	977

[1]1937 Model K

Packard called its first V-12, built from 1916-23, the Twin Six. The new V-12 was also called the Twin Six in 1932, but after that it was known as the Twelve.

ackard's Twelve exactly coincided with Lincoln's Twelve and competed directly with it. It also faced competition from Cadillac's Twelves and Sixteens, the Marmon Sixteen, and other multi-cylinder Classics. All of them were virtual prisoners of their time, conceived in the Roaring Twenties but born in the Terrible Thirties, and soon cast aside. Destiny did not favor them, yet they were among the greatest cars of all time.

Developed by a crack team at Packard, the Twelve had not begun as a clean-slate proposal. Indeed, it didn't even originate at Packard, but on the outside. It had been part of a package including another radical concept: front-wheel drive.

Packard began experimenting with fwd when racers like Tommy Milton were singing its praises, driving Ruxtons and Cord L-29s at prodigious speeds at Indianapolis. Tommy Milton's friend Cornelius Van Ranst, principal designer of the L-29, was looking for more work along the same lines, and Milton introduced him to Packard chief engineer Jesse Vincent. Van Ranst set to work, but the Depression, development delays, and Cadillac's one-two announcement of a V-16 and V-12, forced the company's hand. President Alvan Macauley decreed that front drive be dropped, but the V-12 continued. It was duly introduced for 1932, carrying an honored name brought back out of Packard history: Twin Six.

The Twelve ran with four main bearings and the foundry work must have been advanced, for its cylinder blocks and crankcase were cast integrally. Among contemporary multi-cylinder engines, only the Marmon V-16 could claim similar distinction. Advanced also were its dual downdraft carburetion and manifolding. The 67-degree V-angle was a departure from the old 60-degree Twin Six, but in line with modern thinking. Displacing 445 cubic inches and boasting 160 horsepower, it produced a level of performance very similar to the Lincoln KB.

The 1933 or "Tenth Series" Packard had a massive new X-frame and 17-inch wheels. After seven hours of engine testing, each car received a 250-mile test run at the Packard Proving Grounds. There were few changes in design, though one magnificently styled and appointed custom, the Dietrich-bodied "Car of the Dome," thrilled visitors at the Chicago World's Fair. The Twin Six name was dropped this year, as dealers worried that it was anachronistic; and through the final models in 1939, it would remain simply the Packard Twelve.

Packard didn't plan to build many Twelves, which was just as well, given the economic conditions. Still, the firm managed 549 Ninth Series cars and 520 Tenth Series, which was reasonably consistent. In 1934, business picked up a little, so 960 Twelves were produced, but after 1934 Packard no longer catalogued its traditional wide range of custom body styles. Instead, it relied mainly on slightly modified

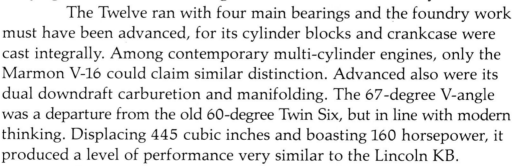

The 1934 Packard was an Eleventh Series model. The magnificent Twelve, with prices starting at $3,820 and soaring beyond $7,700, found only 960 buyers willing to indulge themselves in those tough economic times. Seen here is the sporty dual-cowl phaeton.

The hardware for the '34 Twelve dual-cowl phaeton included adjustable side windows to maximize comfort.

The Twelve's dashboard featured woodwork, plus an instrument panel with a large speedometer and clock.

Packard's V-12 was a 445.5-cubic-inch L-head unit running through four main bearings. Output was 160 bhp in 1934.

The '34 Packard Twelve Convertible Victoria listed at $4,590. It weighed 5,440 pounds and rode a 142-inch wheelbase. Its mascot was the cormorant ($20 extra), and was seen on Packards for many years.

The hood louvers aided engine cooling, but were stylish as well. Design changes for '34 included front fenders that curved down closer to the bumper.

versions of its regular line. This—plus increasing emphasis on the One Twenty (introduced in 1935)—rendered the Twelve rather peripheral as a product, though it still remained Packard's flagship.

In 1935, the engine was stroked to 473 cubic inches, giving 175 bhp at 3,200 rpm. Dual rows of narrow streamlined hood ventilators, a raked radiator, extended fenders forming a transverse front apron, bullet headlights, and more streamlining characterized the styling. Exactly 721 Twelfth Series (1935) cars were built. Packard was superstitious, so the Thirteenth Series was skipped and the '36s were called the Fourteenth Series. Changes on these were minimal, and 682 were built for the model year.

By contrast, the 1937 Fifteenth Series was a completely redesigned car with independent front suspension. Packard's Safe-T-Flex design, the system was adapted from the smaller Packards introduced in 1935, and gave a splendid ride, making it possible in 1937 to delete the bumper balance weights. Hydraulic

brakes were adopted, though the Bijur lubrication system was abandoned, and—as was the industry trend—steel disc wheels replaced wires.

Safe-T-Flex was a modified version of the Short/Long Arm type introduced in 1934 by Cadillac. While it never gained the worldwide acceptance of the Cadillac system, several British makes (Bentley, Daimler, Lanchester, Rover, and Rolls-Royce) paid Packard the compliment of adopting a version of Safe-T-Flex, that of the postwar Rolls-Royce and Bentley being virtually a direct copy.

The Twelve's best year was 1937: no fewer than 1,300 were built. Two reasons for this success were the improved ride thanks to Safe-T-Flex and the three-model lineup (1506, 1507, 1508), which replaced the previous two-model lineup (1407, 1408), giving buyers a wider choice. The addition was a 132-inch-wheelbase sedan priced at $3,940, hundreds of dollars less than the previous low price. In particular, the Rollston Body Company was very busy working for Packard during 1937, and other custom firms still providing Packard bodies were Brunn, LeBaron, Dietrich, and Kellner. In addition, the Darrin body made its first appearance on Packards this year.

The Sixteenth Series (or 1938 model, introduced in September 1937), featured a few styling changes, but basic bodies were identical to the previous run. There was a new vee windshield, an attractive new instrument panel, and new body hardware. External hardware was stainless steel. New front fenders and a redesigned grille and hood were featured. Twelves were now identifiable by the new arrangement of three adjustable louvers along each side of the engine compartment. Also the radiator filler now hid under the hood. The 144-inch wheelbase was dropped—and each surviving wheelbase reduced by five inches. Weight distribution and geometry changes resulted in excellent handling and maneuverability. Coupled with the already superb ride, the 1938 Twelve's handling and general attributes made it truly grand in every sense of the word.

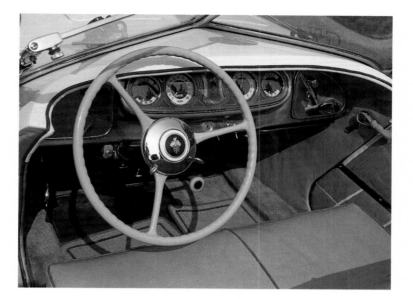

This Fernandez & Darrin '36 Packard was constructed in the summer of 1935 from a 1929 Auburn 120 Speedster body mated to a 135-inch-wheelbase Packard chassis. The body had to be widened at the cowl to fit the frame, and the grille had to be narrowed to accommodate the cowl. The Packard front fenders were narrowed, made more pointed, and given special trim at the ends as there were no running boards.

This 1936 Packard Twelve Gentlemen's Tailback Speedster was custom-bodied by Fernandez & Darrin of Paris. Though the car's heritage was in doubt for years, Dutch Darrin after checking the facts was happy to authenticate the car as "one of my creations."

93

A total of 566 cars were built for 1938, spread over two wheelbases: 134 inches (1607) and 138 inches (1608).

The last Twelves of 1939 were almost identical with the '38s, the only changes being an optional column gearshift, a pushbutton radio, and minor styling and interior alterations. For its final year, the Twelve was offered in 10 different body styles, all built to individual order only, total production being 446.

The final Packard Twelve was built on August 8, 1939, just three weeks before the outbreak of World War II. In many ways, it was probably the right time to go, for cars like it were by then passé, undeniably inappropriate for the impending era of rationed gas and tighten-your-belt war effort. But the Twelve will ever rank among the greats: it would do close to 90 mph and 0-60 in 20 seconds—remarkable for its bulk—in utter silence. It responded, especially after 1937, to a light touch with precision and efficiency. Its generous doors clicked shut like a bank vault. Its interiors, as journalist Griff Borgeson wrote, were "tiny palaces." The passing of the Twelve marked the close of an era of American motoring grandeur, the like of which has never been known before or since.

Specifications[1]	
Engine:	67-degree V-12, L-head, 473 cid ($3^7/16$ x $4^1/4$-in. bore x stroke), 6.0:1 compression ratio (6.4:1 and 7.0:1 opt.), 4 main bearings, mechanical valve lifters, dual downdraft Stromberg carburetion, 175 bhp @ 3,200 rpm (180 bhp opt.)
Transmission:	3-speed, synchromesh on 2nd & 3rd, floor-mounted lever, single plate vacuum-assist clutch
Suspension, front:	Safe-T-Flex independent, coil springs
Suspension, rear:	Solid axle, leaf springs
Brakes:	4-wheel hydraulic
Wheelbase (in.):	132, 139, or 144
Weight (lbs):	5,255-5,790
Tires:	8.25 x 16
Top speed:	95 +
Production:	1,300

[1]1937

Packard debuted its Fifteenth Series models in September 1936 for the '37 model year. At the top of the lineup was the 1507 series Twelve with a 139-inch wheelbase and 175-bhp V-12. This special Convertible Victoria was custom-bodied by Dietrich.

N ot infrequently, hard times bring out the best in us—in corporations as well as in individuals. Consider the case of the Pierce-Arrow Motor Car Company.

In the years leading up to World War I, and for a time thereafter, the Pierce-Arrow was one of America's leading luxury motor cars. More than a few authorities considered it, in fact, to be the best of the lot. Engine displacements, at one time, were as great as 825 cubic inches, and prices for the big Model 66 ranged as high as $8,000, more than twice the cost of corresponding Cadillacs.

But Pierce fell behind the times during the 1920s. While Cadillac was making strides with its fine V-8, and others, notably Packard, set new sales records with powerful straight eights, Pierce-Arrow clung stubbornly to its fine—but outmoded—T-head six-cylinder powerplant. A more reasonably priced six, the Series 80, was introduced in 1924, but Pierce's production methods were so leisurely (and yes, painstaking) that it cost at least $300 more than the corresponding Packard Six.

It wasn't until the 1929 models appeared that Pierce-Arrow caught up with the times. Offered that year were two lines of smartly styled straight eights, more powerful than any contemporary American automobile, save only the Duesenberg. And with prices beginning at $2,775, the new model was actually less expensive than its smaller, six-cylinder predecessor.

That year, the company's Buffalo, New York factory was literally unable to keep up with demand. Even after the stock market crash that October, demand remained comparatively strong, enabling Pierce-Arrow to post a 1930 profit of $1.3 million. But then came the inevitable—sales dropped off sharply, and red ink was seen once more in the company's ledgers. By 1932, production was down to fewer than 2,700 cars, about a third of the 1929 figure, and losses totalled $3 million, a staggering sum for so small a company.

This was all, of course, during the very pit of the Great Depression, hardly the most propitious time for any company to introduce a new, more powerful, more expensive model. But that's what happened in November 1931: Pierce-Arrow announced that two new lines of 12-cylinder cars would soon be put into production, alongside the existing straight eights.

In reality, competitive conditions required that Pierce take such a step. Cadillac had announced its spectacular V-16 two years earlier, and followed it after some months with a fine V-12. Packard was in the process of reviving the Twin Six, Lincoln would have a Twelve of its own for 1932, and of course Marmon was building its superb Sixteen. The new Pierce-Arrow Twelve would be the equal of any of them.

One of the more memorable things about Pierce-Arrow—aside from its famed "bug-eye" headlights that were partially integrated into the fenders—was its archer mascot.

Pierce-Arrow was in trouble in 1933, but that didn't stop the firm from producing the magnificent Model 1247 convertible sedan. Riding a 147-inch wheelbase, it set the buyer back $5,700 ($6,100 with partition window). Only 143 Model 1247s of all body styles were produced in 1933.

One could argue that the Pierce-Arrow had one of the most beautiful dashboards of its era (*far left*), what with all the wood, the gauges nicely integrated in their own panel, and just the right touch of bright trim. This car still has its original "Made for Pierce" key.

Like the other Classics, the '33 Pierce-Arrow convertible sedan was heavy: about 5,500 pounds. But it had a 462-cid V-12 generating 175 horses to pull it along.

Classic-era cars were noted for their fine detailing, as on the pin-striping seen here. The '33 hubcap for the Model 1247 read simply "Pierce 12."

For 1933, Pierce bored out its V-12 from 429 to 462 cid. An 80-degree unit, it utilized seven main bearings and dual downdraft carburetors.

As noted, there were two series of Pierce Twelves. That is to say, there were two 12-cylinder engines. The first of these displaced 398 cubic inches and was rated at 140 horsepower; the second, bored to 429 cubes, developed 150 bhp. Three distinct wheelbase lengths were used, with the 137- and 142-inch chassis employing the smaller engine, while the 147-inch cars received the 150-horsepower version. The 125-bhp straight eights, meanwhile, could be mated with the two shorter chassis.

The two cylinder banks of the V-12 engines were set at an unusual angle of 80 degrees to one another. The compression ratio of 5.1:1 was considerably lower than that of the Packard engine, and the twin Stromberg E-2, 1¼-inch carburetors were fed by a camshaft pump. In all of the 1932 Pierce-Arrows, the previous four-speed transmission was replaced by a three-speed unit, which was fitted with a free-wheeling unit.

Performance of the 398-cubic-inch V-12 proved to be disappointing, for it offered little discernable advantage over the 366-cid eight—though it added $800 to the price tag. For 1933, that engine was dropped, so the smaller Twelves used the 429-cubic-inch block, now raised to 160 horsepower. The increase came compliments of a larger intake manifold, a new dual downdraft carburetor, and a compression ratio raised

to 5.5:1. For the larger cars, Pierce increased the bore, raising the displacement to 462 cubic inches and the output to an impressive 175 horsepower. By now, any of the 12-cylinder Pierce-Arrows was capable of cruising for extended periods at speeds as high as 80 miles an hour.

A major development for 1933 was the introduction of self-adjusting hydraulic tappets, an industry "first" developed by Pierce-Arrow engineer Carl Voorhies. Other new features included Stewart-Warner power brakes, a Stromberg automatic choke, and tinted glass. The Startix automatic starter was carried over from the previous year.

Meanwhile, out on Utah's Bonneville Salt Flats, over a two year period commencing in September 1932, modified Pierce-Arrow Twelves driven by Ab Jenkins had been racking up a number of new records for both speed and endurance.

The really big news for 1933, however, was the Silver Arrow. Phil Wright, formerly of the Murphy coachbuilding firm and by then a freelance stylist, had prepared a proposal for a streamlined luxury sedan. He presented his sketches along with a clay model to Pierce-Arrow vice-president Roy Faulkner, who took the matter up with Studebaker management. It was agreed that five of the cars would be built on the 139-inch chassis of the Model 1236 seven-passenger sedan and powered by the 175-bhp engine of the larger Model 1247.

By the time the decision was made to build the Silver Arrows, only three months remained before the New York Auto Show, posing an almost impossible deadline. Because more adequate facilities were available at South Bend, it was decided that the five cars would be built at the Studebaker plant, though the work was done by a hand-picked crew of Pierce-Arrow craftsmen. The first car was completed on schedule, with the others following by mid-February. Only the five hand-built cars were ever produced.

The Silver Arrow was, as Pierce authority Bernard J. Weis has commented, "a far cry from the stately and staid vehicles for which Pierce-Arrow had previously been noted. The traditional fender headlamps, of stock Multibeam design, were retained but were mounted high in flush-sided front fenders which flowed past the doors and swept downward to an almost-pointed tail. Mounted in the front fender on each side, but concealed by a hinged panel, was a spare tire. The panel latch was released by pulling a handle located inside the car...."

By anyone's standards, the Silver Arrow was a sensational automobile. Its price was likewise sensational: $10,000, more than three times the tab for the sedan on which it was based. Or, to put the matter in a different perspective, that figure would have covered the cost of 20 Ford V-8 Tudor sedans.

Since mid-1928, the venerable Pierce-Arrow Motor Car Company had been owned by the Studebaker Corporation. The combination had appeared, initially, to be of enormous benefit to both organizations, providing the combined companies with coverage of the entire automobile market except for the lowest-priced field. But Studebaker's aggressive president, Albert Russel Erskine, over-extended his organization's resources by paying huge dividends out of capital reserves during the Depression, while simultaneously attempting to acquire control of White Motors. As a result,

A 1936 Model 1602 Club Berline shows off its "quad" headlights. The outside units were more smoothly integrated into the fenders than previously.

Studebaker lapsed into receivership in 1933, and shortly thereafter Albert Erskine shot himself to death. The future of Pierce-Arrow, as well as that of Studebaker, hung in the balance.

In August of that year a group of Buffalo businessmen purchased Pierce-Arrow from Studebaker's receivers. The price was one million dollars. The new owners calculated that with a bit of belt-tightening they could make the company profitable on an annual production level of as few as 3,000 cars. A degree of optimism returned to Buffalo.

Sadly, however, that goal of 3,000

cars a year was never reached. Only 2,152 Pierce-Arrows were built during 1933, and after that it was downhill all the way. The cars were restyled for 1934, the line including a fastback model bearing the Silver Arrow name—but unfortunately not its panache. Production, including all models, totaled just 1,740 cars, dropping to 875 the following year.

There was one final effort. For 1936 the company produced what Bernie Weis has called "the finest Pierce-Arrow ever built." Styling, after the fashion of the times, was more streamlined than before. The box girder frame, reinforced by a massive X-member, was stout enough to support a railroad car. The V-12 engine, thanks to a higher 6.4:1 compression ratio, produced 185 horsepower. A Borg-Warner overdrive was fitted to the transmission, permitting speeds as high as 90 miles an hour without strain. From 40 miles per hour, the brakes—the largest of any car on the market—would stop the three-ton Pierce within 68 feet and 2.3 seconds.

But it was all to no avail. Sales that year came to just 787 units. No significant change was made for 1937, as sales continued to slip, this time to 167 cars. And of the nearly identical 1938 models, evidently only 17 were built before the factory was forced to close its doors. The company ceased to function in March 1938, and another great name in automotive lore became history. But at least it had produced great cars, right up to the very end.

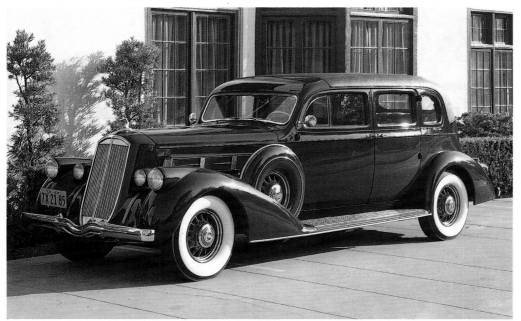

Pierce-Arrow produced only a handful of 1938 models, its last cars. Most sources peg actual production at less than 40 units. Seen here is the Model 1803 limo.

Specifications	
Engine:	80-degree V-12; L-head; 5.1:1-6.4:1 compression ratio; twin Stromberg carbs at first, dual downdraft with automatic choke beginning 1933 **1932** 398 cid, 140 bhp; 429 cid, 150 bhp **1933** 429 cid, 160 bhp **1933-35** 462 cid, 175 bhp **1936-38** 462 cid, 185 bhp
Transmission:	3-speed manual, initially with free wheeling; overdrive 1936-38
Suspension:	Rigid axles, semi-elliptic springs
Brakes:	Internal mechanical, power-assisted beginning 1933
Wheelbase (in.):	136, 137, 139, 142, 144, 147, depending upon model
Weight (lbs):	4,650-6,000
Top speed (mph):	90 +
Production:	**1932** 2,692 **1933** 2,152 **1934** 1,740 **1935** 875 **1936** 787 **1937** 167 **1938** 17 (includes 8- and 12-cylinder cars)

The Type 57 was not only Bugatti's last production car but, in the view of many, it was the best. It was certainly the fastest, and among the most sweepingly lovely, eloquent testimony to the talent of Jean Bugatti, *Le Patron* Ettore's eldest son. Just as important, the 57 was the most civilized and practical Bugatti—the smoothest, the quietest, and the most reliable. Jean had worked hard to make it so, realizing that Bugattis had to be more like Bentleys, Mercedes, Delahayes, and Delages to compete in a late-Thirties market that had scant room for barely tamed race cars or extravagant fantasies like the huge Royale.

Nevertheless, the 57 was no less a *pur sang* Bugatti. Its bloodline flowed directly from the giant-killing Type 51 and mid-Twenties Type 35 racers back to the very first Bugattis of 1909-10. As ever on a Molsheim car, front suspension comprised a tubular-steel axle with semi-elliptic leaf springs pegged through square holes (the machining process for which was never revealed). At the rear were Ettore's time-honored inverted quarter-elliptics. Brakes remained large-diameter cable-operated drums with chain tensioners.

For all this familiarity, the Type 57 marked several departures from Bugatti custom. The engine, still with *Le Patron's* usual monobloc construction, was essentially a reworked version of the twincam 3.3-liter from the 1930 Type 49 sports-tourer. The reworking involved the cylinder head, where valves— still four per cylinder—no longer sat vertically in a line but inclined at 90 degrees to cluster around a more central spark plug location, thus giving higher specific output. Valve operation was through articulated rocker arms; cams were driven by helical gears at the rear of the crank.

Equally significant, the gearbox was again behind the engine instead of in a rear transaxle, and a single-plate clutch replaced the usual twin-plate unit. The gearbox itself was a non-synchronized four-speed with dog clutches engaging all forward ratios save first. The rear axle, still on Bugatti's usual torque tube, was beefier than on the previous roadgoing T55, essentially that of 1930's 5.3-liter Type 46 "baby Royale."

Noting the advent of independent front suspension at Auto Union, Mercedes, *et al*, Jean Bugatti devised a simpler setup for the T57 with twin transverse leaf springs. Even hidebound Henry Ford would have approved, but not Ettore Bugatti, who cared only that an idea worked, not that it was "modern." When Jean drove one of two prototypes to the Swiss Grand Prix at Berne in 1934, his father heard about its "radical" front suspension and ordered it scrapped for a proper "Bugatti" axle. As it turned out, the 57 didn't even have the usual two-piece semi-articulated axle at first, just a simple welded-up beam.

Ettore had been a reluctant convert to supercharging, having given in—with spectacular results—on the 130-horsepower straight-eight

With a long 138-inch wheelbase and 5.3-liter straight eight, the Bugatti Type 46—the "baby Royale"—preceded the Type 57.

Type 35C racing engine of 1926. The 57 would also get a blower, though not right away.

Meantime, *Bugatti et Fils* were content to present the new sports-tourer with their widest ever choice of bodies, some striking, all attractive. The tamer offerings comprised notchback Ventoux coupes with "two-light" and "four-light" window treatment; four-door "Galibier"

sedan; and the "Stelvio," a blind-quarter convertible cabriolet. More rakish by far was the two-seat Atalante coupe and Jean Bugatti's masterful Atlantic (a.k.a. *Atlantique*), available as a convertible built by the Gangloff works and as a super-streamlined fastback. The last was notable for body panels hammered out of ultra-light "electron" magnesium alloy, necessitating boldly exposed rivets along the body and fender centerlines (welding would have melted the metal). Equally unusual were doors cut high into the roof (foreshadowing the American Tucker by some 14 years), a prominent ridged "spine" running back from the windshield divider bar (previewing the Corvette Sting Ray some 30 years distant), and belt/windowlines shaped to match fender curvature.

There was even something intriguing about the sober Galibier, least initially: no B-posts (or external rear door handles), which with center-opening doors provided an unobstructed entrance to front and back seat. This wasn't exactly a new idea, Chrysler having shown a similar experimental DeSoto in 1933, a year before the 57 appeared. Still, there must have been reservations about structural strength at both companies, for the DeSoto never reached production (the Airflow was at hand anyway) and

the pillarless Galibier gave way within a year to a conventional fastback design where all four doors were hinged on evidently stout B-posts. But this second sedan was quite handsome: close-coupled and Bentley-like; even its lefthand sidemount spare looked right. Like all 57s, it wore Bugatti's famous horseshoe radiator, albeit with new thermostatically controlled shutters and a conventional core instead of the traditional honeycomb.

There's been much haziness about Bugatti power ratings over the years, but most sources suggest initial Type 57 horsepower at no more than 140 and probably more like 130-135. It was adequate in any case. A reporter for England's *Motor Sport* reported 95 mph all-out with closed bodywork and 39 seconds for the standing kilometer—and that was riding with team driver René Dreyfus, with Jean Bugatti at the helm. "All this," he said, "was carried out with hardly a murmur from the engine . . . . The exhaust note is subdued and even when all out there is nothing more than a slight rumble." This, of course, was in relation to previous "Bugs," as the 57 was still no threat to Cadillac.

Motor Sport's man also praised low-speed flexibility, the "smooth pick-up," and—this being a Bugatti—handling,

The Bugatti Type 57 was introduced at the Paris Auto Show in 1933, but deliveries to customers didn't begin until 1934. Various body styles were offered, but enthusiasts liked the Type 57S, seen here as a 1936 model. Its straight-eight engine boasted dual overhead cams and four valves per cylinder.

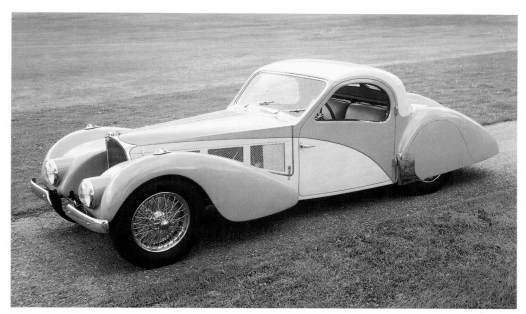

Among the body styles placed on the Type 57 chassis was this striking two-seater coupe, a '37 model. Note the set back radiator and thrust-forward headlights.

of course. With Dreyfus driving he went "down a minor road at 75, slowed to 60 . . . and took a 60-degree bend without any reduction in speed. The car neither rolled, slid or gave any indication that the maneuver was at all unusual. . . . Without doubt, this latest product from the Molsheim factory is '*une voiture de pur-sang*,' and no one can deny the benefits of racing when they experience the high performance and ease of handling which are directly derived from high-speed international competition." In short, racing had again improved the Molsheim breed.

Bugatti improved the 57 starting in late 1936 with "Series 2" models boasting rubber engine mounts, a heavier frame with extra cross-bracing, and a revised instrument panel with more instruments. Arriving alongside it was the 57C *avec compresseur*, the belated supercharged version with the same changes plus a modified exhaust manifold to accommodate a Roots-type blower run off the cam drive. Maximum power was in the vicinity of 160, top speed up by some 10 mph.

There was also a new 57S, a "Sport" —or perhaps "short," as wheelbase was trimmed from the standard 130 inches to 117.3, and ride height was markedly lowered by routing the rear axle *through* the frame. The straight eight here was unsupercharged, but higher compression (8.5:1) plus revised cam and spark timing

combined for some 170 bhp, good for a top end of at least 110 mph. The split front axle was revived for the S, and increased engine torque prompted the addition of trailing front radius rods as well as the return of a twin-plate clutch.

A supercharged Sport seemed inevitable, and it debuted in mid-1937 as the 57SC. Packing some 200 bhp, it could sail to 120-plus mph, *very* impressive for the day. Like the S, it bore a lowered, slightly vee'd horseshoe grille—and, of course, that ground-hugging stance.

Alas, the S and SC were cancelled at the end of 1938. The likely reason, according to H.G. Conway in *Bugatti: Les Pur-Sang des Automobiles*, was low sales and high manufacturing costs. Then too, the long-wheelbase *Normale* and C were selling well. In fact, the 57 would prove one of Bugatti's higher-volume series with some 685 produced, including an estimated 40 S-models.

As the S/SC bid adieu, other 57s were treated to two major updates: modern Bugatti-Lockheed hydraulic brakes with twin master cylinders, and telescopic Alliquant shock absorbers to replace the costly and complicated De Ram friction/hydraulic units of yore. Though production may have continued into 1940, the 57 and all other Bugatti enterprises were soon halted by advancing Nazi forces. Just as tragic, the firm lost one of its leading lights in August 1939, when Jean Bugatti was killed

swerving his prototype 57G "tank racer" to avoid hitting a cyclist on a public road.

Jean's death and the crushing work of rebuilding the company postwar were ultimately too much for *Le Patron*, who died in August 1947. Under son Roland and his two sisters, the firm slowly returned to normal operations, mainly the manufacture of tools, appliances, and similar necessities, many the inventions of papa Ettore (who amassed over 1,000 patents in his 66 years).

Finally, in 1951, Molsheim announced its return to automaking with the Type 101, essentially a modernized 57 with new slab-sided bodywork by Gangloff. There were grand plans for a coupe, cabriolet, and even a sedan, but financial difficulties proved insuperable, and no more than six were built. Bugatti also managed a few postwar racers, including the midships T251 *monoposto* for the mid-Fifties Grand Prix formula.

The late 1980s brought word of a new Bugatti company formed in Italy to build a midships exotic with V-12 power and a six-figure price. We've yet to see it at this writing, but it will need be quite spectacular to be worthy of the hallowed Bugatti name. Even then, it can never erase memories of the Type 57 and Ettore's other cars. Immortals all, they remain unique in the annals of Twentieth Century motoring.

Specifications	
Engine:	I-8 sohc, 198.7 cid/3,257 cc (2.83 x 3.93-in./72 x 100-mm bore x stroke); **57** (1934-39): 130-135 bhp @ 5,000 rpm **57C** (supercharged, 1936-39): 160 bhp @ 5,000 rpm **57S** (1936-38): 170 bhp @ 5,500 rpm **57SC** (supercharged, 1937-38):, 200 bhp @ 5,500 rpm; all figures approximate
Transmission:	4-speed manual (integral with rear axle)
Suspension, front:	Tubular axle on semi-elliptic leaf springs, hydraulic shock absorbers
Suspension, rear:	Solid axle on inverted quarter-elliptic leaf springs, hydraulic shock absorbers
Brakes:	Front/rear drums
Wheelbase (in.):	117.3 (S/SC), 130.0 ("Normale"/C)
Weight (lbs):	2,700-3,000
Top speed (mph):	95-110 +
Production:	685 (incl. est. 40 S-models); some sources list 670 total, others 750-800

103

I t has been called "the most influential car of the 1930s." And no doubt it was—but in its own time the Airflow very nearly spelled disaster for Chrysler.

It was Carl Breer, one of the "Three Musketeers" of Walter P. Chrysler's great engineering triumvirate, who supplied the inspiration for the project. According to company legend, one day Breer was watching what he took to be a flock of geese in flight. But as they approached he came to realize that what he was seeing wasn't geese; he was observing a squadron of military aircraft on maneuvers.

It was one of those illuminating moments. If the airplane, or for that matter the bird, was shaped in such a way as to minimize wind resistance, could not the same principle be applied, Breer wondered, to ground transportation: to trains, to trucks, to passenger cars? Especially to passenger cars, for by that time (late 1927) some of the better automobiles were capable of speeds as high as 80 or even 90 miles per hour. Breer was just beginning to recognize the handicap posed by wind resistance.

With Walter Chrysler's blessing, work got under way on the development of a streamlined automobile. A wind tunnel was constructed at Dayton, Ohio, and there Breer and his cohorts, Fred Zeder and Owen Skelton, undertook their research under a cloak of secrecy. By the end of 1932, a prototype was on the road. Dubbed the "Trifon Special" in honor of an engineering laboratory employee, it was a semi-fastback four-door sedan. Carl Breer had originally proposed seating for three in front, two in the rear, but that idea was quickly shot down by the marketing people.

However, many of Breer's other proposals *were* incorporated into the Trifon Special. For instance, passengers were moved forward 20 inches from their traditional position. This had the effect, first, of reversing the previous weight distribution of approximately 45-percent front, 55-percent rear. Second—and even more importantly—this positioning cradled all the passengers within the axles, largely eliminating the bouncing sensation that had typically been experienced by rear-seat occupants. And finally, it made possible the use of roomy, 50-inch-wide seats.

Taken for a demonstration ride in the prototype car, Walter P. was impressed by its comfort and performance. Oliver Clark took over the role of chief stylist, in charge of the streamliner's exterior design, and by the time the curtain was raised on the auto shows in January 1934, the Airflow was ready.

The original idea had been that the Airflow would be introduced only as a DeSoto. But as the car began to take shape, Walter Chrysler became increasingly enthusiastic about it. "I sincerely believe," he said,

The '36 Airflow C10 was powered by Chrysler's largest engine, a 323.5-cubic-inch straight eight. Like all Chrysler engines, it was an L-head, and with a bore and stroke of 3.25 x 4.88 inches, it developed 130 horsepower.

Chrysler's middle Airflow offering for '36 was the Imperial C10. This four-door retailed at $1,475 that year and saw 4,259 copies produced. This was a big car riding a 128-inch wheelbase and weighing in at a hefty 4,175 pounds.

The Airflow incorporated many forward-looking engineering features, but the styling—especially up front—was of the love-it or hate-it variety; not enough people loved it.

The Airflow was a relatively expensive car, so it's hardly surprising that it left the factory well dressed. One nice touch was the "wings" decorating the rear fender skirts.

The Series C1 was the least costly of the '35 Airflows. Of the three models offered, all priced at $1,245, the four-door sedan accounted for over 90 percent of sales. In fact, the two-door six-passenger coupe seen here (there was also a two-passenger business coupe) found only 307 buyers.

"it will bring about a whole new trend in personal transportation." Of course, he wanted an Airflow with *his* name on it! The introduction of this revolutionary new automobile would be, he believed, an appropriate way to celebrate the upcoming 10th Anniversary of the founding of the Chrysler Corporation.

In the end there were four Chrysler Airflows, each with its own wheelbase, and all with straight-eight powerplants. In addition, DeSoto fielded a six-cylinder Airflow. The Chrysler Division's two six-cylinder lines retained their conventional styling, but DeSoto placed all its bets on the success of the Airflow—with dismal results, as we shall soon see.

The Airflow's structure, appropriately enough, was designed by Dr. Alexander Klemin, chief of the Guggenheim Foundation for Aeronautics. Bodies, as author George Dammann has noted, "were constructed around a cage-like steel girder network, to which the body panels were welded." This was not, strictly speaking, "unit" construction; that would have to wait until the introduction of the 1941 Nash 600. Nor did it result in reduced weight, for the Airflows were heavier by several hundred pounds than their conventionally styled 1933 counterparts. The structure was, however, a tightly integrated body-and-frame design in which the welded body contributed substantially to chassis rigidity. Chrysler was at pains to point out just how stout the Airflow really was. In one demonstration, an Airflow sedan was sent over a 110-foot cliff. Falling end over end over the face of the cliff, it landed on its wheels at the bottom—whereupon it was driven away under its own power.

Performance was another selling point. Out on Utah's Bonneville Salt Flats a Series CV coupe ran the flying mile at 95.7 miles per hour, averaged just over 90 mph over 500 miles, and did 84.43 mph for 24 hours—ample testimony to the car's durability, as well as its performance.

Initially, the Airflow received an enthusiastic reception. It was the sensation of the auto shows, where visitors are said to have placed orders in record numbers. The press, however, gave the new car mixed reviews. Dr. Klemin pronounced it "Splendid"—but then, he was hardly an unbiased source. Carolyn Edmundson, fashion artist of *Harper's Bazaar*, found the Airflow "breathlessly different-looking," which may or may not have been a compliment, depending upon how one looked at it. Britain's *The Autocar* gave it muted praise: "The more one sees of [them] the more they are apt to grow on one." And on this side of the Atlantic, *MoToR* suggested, "Look at the Airflows for two or three days and suddenly they will look right and conventional cars will look strange."

Unfortunately for Chrysler, the public's initial enthusiasm for the Airflow was short-lived. Increasingly, prospective buyers looked, then turned away without giving this radical new

The Series C1 Airflow four-door sedan (*opposite*) was selected by 4,617 buyers in 1935. It rode a 123-inch wheelbase and came with Chrysler's least powerful version of the 323.5-cid straight eight: 115 bhp. An optional high-compression head boosted output to 120 bhp.

The Airflow was one of the first cars to completely integrate its headlights into the fenders rather than having them free-standing as was the industry norm. Note the Art Deco styling.

While the Airflow sedans sported an externally mounted spare tire, the coupes were among the first cars with a completely integrated trunk. That being said, there really wasn't room enough for anything but the spare tire.

car a fair trial. Chrysler loyalists purchased the company's conventionally styled six-cylinder cars; others turned to Oldsmobile, which scored an impressive 128-percent sales gain during 1934. In 1933, 45 percent of all new Chryslers had been straight eights, but with the coming of the Airflow that figure dropped to 31 percent. Meanwhile, DeSoto—with no conventional cars to offer—was hurting badly. While most of the industry enjoyed a partial recovery that year from the effects of the Depression, DeSoto sales were off by nearly 39 percent.

The best seller among the Airflow Chryslers was the price-leading Series CU, which rode a 123-inch wheelbase and was powered by a 298.7-cubic-inch, 122-horsepower straight eight. At $1,345, it was priced midway between the "50" and "60" series Buicks. The CU came in four body styles: four-door sedan (by far the most popular), Town Sedan (with blind quarter panels), Brougham (two-door sedan), and coupe. The last, easily the best-looking of the lot, was a true fastback, with the spare tire enclosed within the trunk; on the other body styles the spare was mounted externally.

The three larger Airflow series all bore the Imperial name. Wheelbases measured 128, 137.5, and 146.5 inches, respectively, for the Imperial Series CV and the Custom Imperial CX and CW. The first two used a 323.5-cid, 130-horsepower engine, while the CW, the

largest car Chrysler had ever built, employed a 384.8-cubic-inch straight eight rated at 150 bhp. Imperial prices started at $1,625 and ranged all the way to $5,145 for the Series CW limousines—the latter a figure $350 higher than a Cadillac V-12 in the same body style.

Once the initial enthusiasm had died down—and that didn't take very long—it quickly became apparent that Airflow sales would not come up to expectations. Design consultant Norman Bel Geddes was called in to "fix" the styling. He endowed the 1935 models with a new hood, which extended forward to a vee-shaped grille. Decorative hood louvers were added, the bumpers were redesigned, and the Brougham—which had not been at all well received—was dropped from the line.

All of which didn't help very much. Chrysler Airflow production, which had totalled 10,839 for 1934, fell to 7,751 in 1935. Fortunately for its dealers, Chrysler rushed two new conventionally styled cars to market for 1935. Known as the Airstream Six and Eight, these were particularly attractive cars, helping pace the division to a 35 percent sales increase for the year.

The Airflow received another facelift for 1936, this time featuring a prominent diecast grille. A humpback trunk was added to the sedan's rear, allowing the spare tire to be tucked inside. The Town Sedan followed the Brougham into oblivion as Airflow sales continued to

fall, this time to 6,275 units. Again it was the Airstreams that kept the corporation and its dealers alive. Overall, Chrysler production rose that year by nearly 43 percent.

Only one Airflow series was offered for 1937, the ill-fated streamliner's final year of production. Though it actually represented a continuation of the 1934-36 Imperials, it was known simply as the Chrysler Airflow (the company had other plans for the prestigious Imperial title). Sedan and coupe styles were offered, both priced at $1,610, a $135 increase over the previous year. Alas, sales continued their downward trend, totalling just 4,600 for the season.

Or rather, 4,603. The big Custom Imperial CW still had its cadre of loyalists. Three more of these enormous cars were run up on special order during the Airflow's farewell season, one of them for Major Edward Bowes, host of radio's popular *Amateur Hour* show.

And then it was all over. Walter Chrysler, by then in his final illness, must have wondered what went wrong. Richard M. Langworth and Jan Norbye, in their *Complete History of Chrysler 1924-1985*, offer this explanation: "The normally canny Walter Chrysler approved this advanced concept without much apparent regard for whether the public would accept it. And that would prove to be Chrysler's—both the man's and the company's—first serious mistake."

Specifications[1]	
Engine:	L-head I-8, solid valve lifters, 1-bbl carburetor (CW, 2-bbl) **CU** 299 cid (3¼x 4½-in bore x stroke), 6.5:1 compression ratio, 122 bhp @ 3,400 rpm **CV & CX** 323.5 cid (3¼ x 4⅞-in.), 6.5:1 c.r., 130 bhp @ 3,400 rpm **CW** 384.8 cid (3½ x 5-in.), 6.5:1 c.r., 150 bhp @ 3,200 rpm
Transmission:	3-speed selective, floor shift (CW, 4-speed; overdrive optional on other series after March 1934)
Suspension:	Rigid axles, semi-elliptic leaf springs
Brakes:	Lockheed hydraulic drum type (CW vacuum assisted)
Wheelbase (in.):	CU 122.8 CV 128 CX 137.5 CW 146
Weight (lbs):	3,716-5,935
Tires:	7.50 x 16 (CW, 7.50 x 17)
Top speed (mph):	95 + (Series CV)
Production:	1934 CU 8,389 CV 2,277 CX 106 CW 67 1935 7,751 (all series) 1936 6,275 1937 4,603

[1]1934 Airflow

Y ou've seen it in dozens of movies: ever-present in scenes depicting the mid-Thirties to the late Fifties. It's the Citroën *Traction Avant*, as much a universal symbol of its native land as champagne, *gendarmes*, and the Eiffel Tower. And why not? It lasted 23 years, and was at least that far advanced on its 1934 unveiling. True, unitized construction was its only genuine "first" among volume production models. But combining that with front-wheel drive, overhead-valve power, and torsion-bar suspension in a single car—let alone an affordable one—was nothing short of revolutionary when most everything else had orthodox rear drive, side-valve engines, and separate cart-spring chassis.

Then again, this daring automobile only mirrored André Citroën, whose talent for making profits was exceeded only by a fondness for taking risks. Though not an engineer, Citroën had studied at the Ecole Polytechnic, France's premier technical school, then served as chief engineer for the Mors car company before starting a gear-making business in 1913 that soon made him very rich—and worsened his unfortunate addiction to gambling. The double-chevron emblem still seen on Citroën cars symbolizes the gears built by André's factories on Paris's *Quai de Javel*.

The *Traction Avant* looked decidedly out of the Thirties from the rear because of its externally mounted spare. Note, however, the decklid.

More improtantly, Citroën was also fond of America, especially Henry Ford and his mass-production techniques, and became acquainted with both in several Stateside visits. He put his new technical know-how to good use—and to increasing his personal fortune—by boosting French munitions output during The Great War. He then applied it to his first automobile, the 1919 Type A: a small, simple 1.3-liter four-cylinder job that carried with it definite Ford Model T influence. It sold well, and within two years *Societe Automobiles André Citroën* was building 10,000 cars annually at no fewer than six Paris plants.

In 1922 came the even smaller 856-cc 5CV that vaulted Citroën to the top ranks of French automakers. Opel in Germany, it might be noted, thought enough of it to build a near-duplicate, the whimsically named *Laubfrosch*—"tree frog"—which proved just as popular. By 1929, Citroën was number three in France, behind Peugeot and Renault, and building 100,000 vehicles a year, mostly 1.5-liter four-cylinder sedans, but also a 2.4-liter Six. The early Thirties brought new four-cylinder models that added "floating power" engine mounts, licensed from Chrysler Corporation, to such now-established Citroën features as synchromesh transmission, four-wheel servo brakes, and all-steel bodies built on the principles of American Edward Budd.

It was Budd who encouraged Citroën to take his biggest gamble, what André called his "future miracle—a car of entirely fresh conception." He would do what American automakers had only talked about: weld body and chassis together to create a car of extraordinary strength without

Although the *Traction Avant* looked much like other cars of its era because of its separate fenders and free-standing headlights, unit construction and front-wheel drive allowed it to take a much lower stance than most of its contemporaries.

The speedometer housing on the Citroën's instrument panel also made room for little gauges in the corners and a tiny clock in the center. The steering wheel lacked any trim whatever, but the center of the dash sported a bit of shiny trim.

extraordinary weight. What's more, he would pick up where the American Cord L-29 had just left off by giving it front-wheel drive—but with a fully *automatic* transmission. Just as incredible, the impatient Citroën set what seemed an impossible deadline for the finished product: just 18 months. It was all eerily similar to the hurried work then under-way toward Chrysler's Airflow—and fraught with the same enormous perils. As British journalist Peter Robinson observed in 1989: "[Coming from] Citroën, its reputation established on...robust, simple cars that sold cheaply, the sheer arrogance of this radical car was breathtaking in its boldness."

Fortunately for Citroën, the team he'd assembled was well up to their daunting task. Engine designer Maurice Sainturat drew a new, moderately undersquare four with pushrod-operated overhead valves and removable wet cylinder liners. Maurice Julien penned a suspension featuring full frontal independence via double wishbones and longitudinal torsion bars (used under Porsche patent), plus odd, star-shaped friction dampers; out back, a simple beam axle rode transverse torsion bars, with location by parallel arms and angled trailing rods. Putting it all together was chief engineer André Lefebvre, who'd already

worked on a front-drive car with aviation pioneer Gabriel Voisin. Here, his drivetrain followed L-29 practice in slinging the transmission ahead of the differential and engine. Power was taken back over the differential by shaft to the gearbox, then forward by bevel pinion to the final drive. Halfshaft joints, initially a sticking point, ended up as twin Hardy Spicer units that functioned like costlier constant-velocity joints, but whose necessarily limited operating angle made for an unduly wide turning circle (some 43 feet). Steering was by an overly complex worm-and-nut mechanism, brakes by all-wheel drums.

Lefebvre supervised Raoul Clinet in engineering the unitized steel structure, which was tooled in America by Budd. Early *Tractions* had traditional fabric roof inserts, but solid canopies were substituted almost immediately. Later came still another predictive feature: a sliding metal sunroof.

Styling was entrusted to an artist, Flaminio Bertoni, who actually worked in a prototypical Parisian garret—provided by Citroën. Front drive permitted a rakishly low stance of just under 60 inches, some 18 inches below the contemporary norm, and Bertoni emphasized it by omitting running boards. Wheels which were pushed out to the car's extreme corners made for excep-

tional interior space, plus a smooth ride and, with fairly broad track dimensions, terrific stability. Overall, the *Traction* looked like a '34 Ford sedan chopped and channeled hot rod-style; the derivative 2+2 coupe and convertible were even snazzier.

André's beloved automatic transmission quickly proved impossible, which was just as well. The design, by Seneaud de Levaud, was too involved for quality volume assembly and good on-road reliability. As well it promised snail-like performance with the 1.3-liter 32-horsepower engine. The *Traction* thus bowed in March 1934 with a conventional three-speed manual gearbox that Lefebvre designed literally overnight on his kitchen table, owing to lack of time. To save money, he salvaged the automatic's aluminum case, though it dictated an awkward shift pattern. Forecasting a Chrysler feature 21 years distant, the gearlever poked out from the dashboard instead up from the floor.

For all its relatively untried features, the *Traction* was surprisingly trouble-free. An exception was its six-volt electrical system, which could strand one with a dead battery at inopportune times, hence the provision for old-fashioned handcrank starting.

In a day when L-head engines were the norm, Citroën saw to it that his four-cylinder engines had overhead valves.

Citroën modestly announced the *Traction Avant* as being two years ahead of its time, but in fact the engineering was so superior that the model remained in production until 1957. Over its lifetime both fours and sixes were offered.

Weak performance was the main deficit, however, which explains why Citroën quickly supplemented the initial "A-series" 7CV *Traction* (CV referring to taxable French horsepower) with bored-out 1.5-liter 7B models in June 1934. Alas, these had only three more horses, so both engines were stroked late in the year, resulting in 1.6- and 1.9-liter units of 36 and 46 bhp for the new 7C and 7S. At the Paris Salon that November, Citroën showed a 22CV with a 100-bhp 3.8-liter V-8, essentially two 1.9s bolted together. Like the automatic, though, this was precluded by tooling costs that had long spiraled out of sight, leaving André Citroën $190,000 in debt—a good deal of money in those days.

And sadly, it was that debt on top of his continued gambling losses that forced the sale of SA Citroën to its chief creditor, the Michelin tire interests, in early 1935. In July that year, André Citroën died, a broken man, his fortune squandered. Some say he died of a broken heart, believing he had failed to deliver his "future miracle," that he had gambled once too often.

How ironic, then, that the *Traction* went on to be his most successful creation

of all. Assured of further improvements by Michelin's money and faith, the lineup was expanded beginning in November '34. Joining the 7C was the 11, a renamed 7S available as a four-place *legere* ("light") on the original 114.5-inch wheelbase, a five/six-seat *normale* on a 121.5-inch chassis, and a seven/nine-passenger *familiale* with a 129-inch span and a liftup rear-end panel—one of the first hatchbacks. The last was also sold in *commerciale* form with removable seats. A five-seat, five-window *coupe de ville* was announced at the same time, but would see only very limited production.

The next major changes came in 1937, when steering was switched to rack-and-pinion and the friction front dampers were replaced by hydraulic units (thus matching rear shocks). The following year brought a new six-cylinder 15CV on the middle wheelbase, offering 77 bhp from a 2.7-liter engine that amounted to a 1.9 with two cylinders tacked on. Twin downdraft carbs replaced single instruments on 1939 engines. Then came World War II, halting further progress for some six years.

But the *Traction* was far from out-

moded, and returned postwar with few changes save cancellation of the 7CV and—shades of Henry Ford—color choices, all cars being painted black. By 1953, louvers had replaced the original hood-side flaps, dashboards had been restyled, heaters standardized, and the familiar "flat-back" styling bulged into "trunkbacks" for additional luggage space. Beginning in 1954, the 15CV/Six gained a radical new self-leveling oleo-pneumatic suspension system as a trial run for the replacement DS19, unveiled the following year. Even so, the *Traction* wasn't fully supplanted by the futuristic DS until July 1957, when assemblies stopped at over three-quarters of a million units, including prewar British-built models and some 50,000 Sixes (the final 3,000 or so of which had the oil/air suspension).

Citroën modestly announced the *Traction Avant* as being two years ahead of its time. "In truth," as Robinson records, "it wasn't until well after World War II that any rival attempted to match [its] technical specification. . . . From that day on, the cars of the double-chevron would always be regarded as *avant garde*, even bizarre. . . . André Citroën would have approved. By then we knew that if the gambler had lost, the world had certainly won."

Specifications	
Engine:	I-4, ohv, except I-6 15 CV **1934 7A:** 79.5 cid/1,302 cc (2.83 x 3.15 in./72 x 80-mm bore x stroke), 32 bhp **1934 7B** 93.3 cid/1,529 cc (3.07 x 3.15-in./78 x 80 mm), 35 bhp **1934-41 7C:** 99.3 cid/1628 cc (2.83 x 3.94-in./72 x 100-mm), 36 bhp **1934-57 7S** and **11CV** 116.6 cid/1,911 cc (3.07 x 3.94-in./78 x 100-mm), 46/56 bhp **15CV Six** 175 cid/2,867 cc (3.07 x 3.94-in./78 x 100-mm), 77 bhp
Transmission:	3-speed manual in front transaxle
Suspension, front:	Independent, upper and lower wishbones, longitudinal torsion bars, tube shocks (friction 1934-37)
Suspension, rear:	Beam axle on transverse torsion bars, twin parallel arms, angled links, tube shocks
Brakes:	Front/rear drums
Wheelbase (in.):	114.5 (7CV, 11 *legere*), 121.5 (15, 11 *normale*), 129.0 11 *familiale/commerciale*
Weight (lbs):	2,650-2,950
Top speed (mph):	61-84
0-60 mph (sec):	21-29
Production:	4-cylinder 708,339 6-cylinder 50,518

They've been called great—also magnificent, imposing, stupendous, noble, arrogant, thrilling, and—inevitably—unique. Yet, as one writer observed, "no single word can adequately define" the late-Thirties Mercedes-Benz 500K and 540K. How true. Daimler-Benz has never been given to halfway measures, and this sports-touring series, coming at the close of motoring's "Golden Age," was the culmination of everything the company had learned since Gottlieb Daimler and Karl Benz had built the world's first true automobiles a half-century before. Inspiring to behold and experience, Mercedes' last big sporting cars of the prewar period remain, as Britain's *The Autocar* said at the time, "master car[s] for the very few"—towering machines from an era of giants.

The 500K and 540K were spiritually descended from the awe-inspiring, supercharged six-cylinder S, SS, SSK, and SSKL of the late Twenties. In engineering terms, however, they built on the 380 model introduced at the 1933 Berlin Auto Show, which was itself a modernized replacement for the earlier (and rather boring) Nurburg as the junior eight-cylinder Mercedes. History records the 380 as the first series-production car with independent front suspension by means of coil springs and transverse wishbones or "A-arms." One of the most acceptable and durable designs, it remains in use nearly 60 years later. But it was only one of two contributions by Hans Nibel, who had replaced the redoubtable Ferdinand Porsche as Mercedes chief engineer in 1929. The other was a new-design 3.8-liter inline eight with pushrod-operated overhead valves, similar to that of the big contemporary 770 *Grosser*, save a block cast in one piece instead of two.

Like the S-models, the 380 employed a supercharger—*kompressor* to the Germans—driven from the front of the crankshaft by a multi-plate clutch that engaged when the accelerator was floored. A Roots-type unit of the sort then used by a good many others, the blower literally boosted horsepower from a nominal 90 to 120. But that wasn't enough for good performance, because the 380 was Teutonically and crushingly heavy. The chassis alone, a beefy box-section edifice with near-straight siderails and a Porsche-designed swing-axle rear suspension, weighed a ton and a half; with bodywork—typically a factory-built cabriolet, though coupe and sedan styles were also available—it flattened the scales at well over 5,000 pounds.

More displacement was the obvious answer, which explains why the 500K bowed in 1934, again at Berlin, to replace the 380 (after just 134 were built, none designated as *mit kompressor*, incidentally). There were still three factory body types available: a quite sober-looking Cabriolet, a very rakish new Sports Roadster, and a fastback coupe labelled *Autobahn Kurier*. The engine became less a "stroker" as the bore was widened by 6 mm, swelling capacity to a full 5.0 liters.

The large and imposing Mercedes-Benz 500K was built from 1934-36 and only 354 were produced. Seen here is a 1936 model.

The 1936 Mercedes-Benz 500K roadster rode a 129.5-inch wheelbase and weighed 5,000 pounds. It came equipped with a supercharged five-liter straight eight.

Horsepower rose commensurately—by 10 without the blower and by no less than 40 with it engaged—so performance was much improved. *The Autocar* reported 0-60 mph in 16.5 seconds and a top speed of about 100 mph, which was not only impressive for a 2.5-ton car but among the best showings of any mid-Thirties car.

Typical of Mercedes, the 500K gearbox was rather over-engineered: a non-synchronized three-speed with dogclutch engagement of second and third gears (helical-cut, like first), supplemented by a "Maybach system" fourth-speed overdrive via a set of straight-cut gears that didn't mesh until their rotational speeds matched, thus obviating the need for declutching. The overdrive usefully lowered effective final gearing from 4.88:1 to 3.03:1, thus allowing surprisingly quiet and restful medium-speed cruising *sans* blower to be combined with that phenomenal full-bore acceleration.

Flooring the throttle to kick in the supercharger made a 500K "another machine altogether," as *The Autocar* put it. "...An almost demoniacal howl comes in.... The rev counter and speedometer needles leap round their dials. There is perhaps no other car noise in the world so distinctive as that produced by the Mercedes supercharger...." Let up on the gas and "a multi-

disc brake [has] precisely the opposite effect to that when engaging the blower, stopping the supercharger drive and rotors instantly."

Despite its heft, the 500K was not clumsy. To the contrary, it handled "magnificently" in *The Autocar's* opinion. "Its very weight gives it a solidity that helps toward safe road holding, and the independent suspension...does not permit any disturbing degree of roll or side sway.... [S]afe limits are not easily discovered...." The steering, though tiresome around town, had "a wonderfully firm 'feel' [that makes] for absolute accuracy when travelling very fast." Only "oversensitive" brakes spoiled an otherwise matchless motoring experience, much of it due to what *The Autocar* termed "the sheer insolence of [the 500K's] great power."

The sports-touring Mercedes became even more insolent when the 540K appeared in 1936 as a companion to the 500. A half-point gain in compression to 6.0:1, plus increased bore and stroke (by 2 and 3 mm, respectively) turned the straight eight into a 5.4-liter beast with 115/180 bhp (still breathing through a single two-barrel Solex carburetor). To be sure all that power reached the ground without starting the back-end to dancing, the 540 chassis was given four horizontally situated coil springs as torque "compensators,"

one pair behind the differential, the other ahead of it—the same idea as "traction bars" of a later age, but more elegant.

At the same time, factory body styles expanded to include no fewer than three Cabriolets (A, B, and C, all five-seaters but differing in body lines and spare-tire placements), five-seat Open Tourer and two-door sedan, and a three-place Convertible Coupe (supplied with both folding soft top and a lift-off steel accessory roof) in addition to the Sports Roadster. Of course, this was still an ultra-premium conveyance—at $12,000-$14,000, the German equivalent of America's mighty Duesenberg J and about twice as expensive as a contemporary Packard Twelve or Cadillac V-16. Predictably, then, a few 500/540 chassis were treated to custom bodies—anything their wealthy buyers wanted—which brought the typical delivered price up to a cool 20 grand. The best known of these specials—certainly the most desired today—are the rumble-seat roadsters crafted by Berlin builder Erdmann & Rossi, with their mile-long hoods, jaunty tails, delicately scalloped doors, and swooping French-curve front fenders.

Road & Track editor Ron Wakefield got the chance to drive just such a car in 1973. After getting over some understandable nervousness at piloting the near-priceless machine in the madding urban crowd, he found the steering unduly heavy ("though at road speed it's thoroughly manageable"), the brakes even more so. The ride, he noted, "which must have been good by contemporary standards, is both too hard and too soft by today's—somewhat floaty on gentle undulations but cracking harsh on sharp bumps." The steering wheel was close, and there was little legroom.

But oh, the driving. Though not a quiet car, Wakefield reported the 540 was "easy to get underway. There's plenty of torque, and 1st gear is a 'grandma' speed.... [O]ne must make shifts slowly and deliberately. Aside from the graunching, though, the big floor lever is easy to handle and the clutch is smooth enough that clean shifting comes quickly. You're soon into 3rd, but it's not a road gear; the engine sounds quite busy yet. Time for 4th...."

The blower enters the picture when you've pushed the gas pedal an extra three inches or so past wide-open throttle, and there's enough extra pressure required . . . that you really have to want to do it—because your foot is actually doing the physical work of engaging the multi-plate steel clutch that drives it. That done, up comes the blower speed and now there's a strong whine from the unit, proportional to engine speed. . . . In addition, two extra carburetor jets are brought in (there are five sets of jets altogether in this pressurized carburetor!) and the fuel tank gets some of the blower pressure. I kept my foot in it. . . . The surge of extra power from the blower isn't startling, but you won't miss it either. It must have been great to let the 540K have its head on an *autobahn* in the 1930s."

Wakefield wasn't able to run "his" 540 like that, but a 1937 test by Britain's *The Motor* showed 0-60 mph in 15.5 seconds and a top end near 115 mph, both sensational for the day. Yet, as Don Vorderman observed after a similar 1970 drive for *Automobile Quarterly*, the 500K and 540K "were not meant to be high-performance cars. Their best feature was a sense of style, even flamboyance—both curiously un-German characteristics—that set them apart from anything else on the road in the Thirties. . . . My most memorable impression. . . aside from its glorious looks, was one of enormous strength and rigidity—two qualities, by the way, that you can also find in any modern Mercedes. Some people, it seems, still do build them the way they used to."

Alas, Daimler-Benz built too few of these supercharged *Uberwagens:* just 354 of the 500s and 406 of the 540s through 1939, when a madman named Adolf Hitler put an end to them—and many other things. Still, as author Richard M. Langworth said in CONSUMER GUIDE's® *Mercedes-Benz: The First Hundred Years:* "Those who never knew them should be glad there are still a few around to admire, a few that occasionally bellow their own kind of Wagnerian song through the rotors of wide-open superchargers." Like many pictures, that song is worth a thousand words, "adequate" or otherwise.

For the 540K, seen here as a '39 model, the 5,020-cc straight eight was enlarged to 5,401 cc (329 cid). With the supercharger it developed 180 horsepower, enough for a top speed of about 115 mph. What the 500K/540K were noted for, however, was their style.

The external exhaust pipes and fender-mounted spare tires added to the flashy good looks of the 540K. Only 406 were built from 1936-39.

Specifications	
Engine:	I-8 ohv, supercharged **500K** 306 cid/5,020 cc (3.39 x 4.25-in./86 x 108-mm bore x stroke), 100/160 bhp @ 3,400 rpm(with/without supercharger) **540K** 329 cid/ 5,401 cc (3.46 x 4.25-in./88 x 108-mm), 115/180 bhp @ 3,300 rpm (with/without supercharger)
Transmission:	4-speed overdrive manual; 5-speed overdrive manual optional 1939 540K)
Suspension, front:	Independent, upper and lower A-arms, coil springs, lever shocks
Suspension, rear:	Independent, swing axles, trailing arms, dual coil springs, lever shocks; on 540K, double compensating springs fore and aft of differential
Brakes:	Front/rear drums
Wheelbase (in.):	129.5
Weight (lbs):	5,000-5,500
Top speed (mph):	**500K** 101 **540K** 105
0-60 mph (sec):	**500K** 16.5 **540K** 15.5.-16.4
Production:	**500K** 354 (1934-36) **540K** 406 (1936-39)

enry Ford used to say that every time an Alfa Romeo passed he would tip his hat. The record suggests that he said it before Alfa produced the 8C 2900, but it is hard to think of anything more appropriate for hat-tipping. In this book of great cars, it is difficult to name one that is more desirable.

Built in the exasperating quantity of only 43, the 8C 2900 is quite simply one of the four or five ultimate road cars. It was the fastest prewar sports car. It maintained a superlative racing record. Each example was devastatingly beautiful, aggressive, and competent beyond adjectives. And, it carried with it a subtle mystique surrounding its history. Sports car expert Don Vorderman wrote, "to drive it is to experience the vintage car developed to its highest form." Warren Fitzgerald called it "a car to quicken the pulse." It was a masterpiece.

Its engine, like those of all Alfas from 1931 until World War II, was the ultimate variant of Vittorio Jano's brilliant design that won 110 firsts in every form of competition (and more seconds and thirds than are possible to list) from hillclimbs to Grands Prix, Le Mans, and the *Mille Miglia*. The 2.9-liter version was in fact conceived to maintain Alfa's dominance of the *Mille Miglia*, which had obligingly changed its rules to allow any car with fenders, electrics, and two or more seats to compete. Anything could be entered up to and including thinly disguised Grand Prix cars. Such a 2.9 Alfa won the famous Italian road race in 1935, driven by Carlo Pintacuda for Enzo Ferrari's Scuderia.

The 2.9 was also necessary to maintain Alfa's strength in sports car racing, which by the mid-30s was hotly contested. Yet the 29001, as the first version was called, was a genuine sports car, suitable for use on the road as well as the track by a very limited number of very wealthy owners: it cost nearly $14,000 at the time, equivalent only to the most esoteric cars on the market today.

As you consider the 2900A's characteristics, bear in mind that we are talking about a car produced in 1935-36. Its chassis, with independent front suspension via trailing links and coil springs and independent rear suspension via swing axles, transverse leaf, and transaxle, was derived from the 8C 1935 Alfa Grand Prix car. Its engine was a straight eight with twin overhead cams and twin superchargers, one serving each group of four cylinders. It developed 220 brake horsepower at 5,300 rpm—a figure that can only astonish in a period when 50 horsepower was considered powerful. Since it weighed only 1,870 pounds, its performance was everything one would expect: 125 mph flat out, rocketing to three-figure speeds as fast as its driver could shift, and making in the process some of the most glorious noises in all motordom.

Most 2900s used open bodies by Carrozzeria Touring of Milano, with its patented "superleggera" construction method. A few others were

This view of the engine vents and louvers only hints at what might lie under the hood of the Alfa Romeo 8C 2900—the fastest prewar sports car.

The 8C 2900's straight eight boasted 2,095 cc, dual overhead cams, and twin superchargers. Despite low 5.75:1 compression, 180 horses were on tap.

The Alfa 8C 2900 was fast enough to win many races, such as the *Mille Miglia*. It was also designed with something of an aerodynamic look about it, and it possessed an all-independent suspension. It's a pity that only 43 were built.

built by Farina, and Ramsiers of Switzerland made at least one. Better than half of the run survives, and most of these have been located.

The 2900 was built to race—and race it did, entering the Tenth *Mille Miglia* for Scuderia Ferrari in April 1936: three 2900s with cycle fenders and big, oval grille openings with little racing windscreens and single spare tires. They finished 1-2-3. They also scored 1-2 at the Brazilian Grand Prix, and won the 24 Hours of Spa, Belgium. The 1937 *Mille Miglia* was again dominated by the 2.9.

The following year Alfa announced an "improved version," the 8C 2900B, which seems to have been much the same car, with certain modifications to the engine for a rating of 180 bhp at 5,200 rpm. Four spiders with Touring bodywork were prepared for the formidable factory team, still under Enzo Ferrari's management: Clemente Biondetti, Emilio Villoresi, Nino Farina, and Carlo Pintacuda. (Pintacuda's car, brilliantly restored, is now in the Brooks Stevens Collection in Wisconsin.)

Biondetti's car had a Tipo 308 Grand Prix engine with even greater horsepower, but any one of the four could win: the *"Mille"* almost had to be won by an Italian, familiar with the roads, and Pintacuda had already won it twice, in 1935 and '37. It was a classic contest, the signal event for the 8C 2900.

The *Mille Miglia*, usually spanning 1,000 miles from Brescia south to Rome and back to Brescia again, was the greatest open road race in history. It spanned the period 1927 to 1957, interrupted by war and, on occasion, public outrage. This very event in 1938, for example, was marred when a Lancia Aprilia spun loose in the middle of Bologna, killing 10 people including seven children as it careened into the crowd. The 1939 *"Mille"* was canceled as a result. It is a shame that such a classic race was never accompanied by adequate safety measures, but with such a long route on entirely public roads it was nearly impossible to ensure the safety of every spectator.

Typically, the slower cars were flagged off in the dark hours of the morning, while the Alfas left with the Maseratis and Mercedes as dawn was breaking. Pintacuda departed two minutes before Biondetti. Their Alfas were hitting 140 mph on the straightaways, but Pintacuda, the experienced twice-champion, had a superior knowledge of the route and was soon dominating the race. At Bologna, halfway to Rome on the outward run, he had averaged 112 mph—faster than he'd ever run before. Through the passes of the mountains he extended his lead; down along the flat west coast toward Rome he averaged over 130 mph in one section. There was a saying, though, or a superstition: "Who leads at Rome will not lead at the finish." It was true this time.

At Terni, not far out of Rome on the northward leg, the brakes locked. While Pintacuda's mechanic feverishly labored to free them, Biondetti flashed by into the lead. Pintacuda lost a desperate 14 minutes—to win he would have to finish at least two minutes ahead, since Biondetti had left two minutes after he did.

The two Alfas roared toward Bologna, where they briefly crossed the southward track and then streaked northeast toward Venice before doubling back toward Verona and Brescia. Pintacuda was eight minutes behind. "Rounding the corner" at Treviso north of Venice, he was three minutes behind. Screaming toward Brescia and the finish they were virtually side by side. But there just wasn't enough time and Biondetti won it in the GP-engined 2900. This is not to discredit him in the least: he had run it in less than 12 hours, the fastest time on record, at a record 83.9 miles per hour, the first average speed over 80. It was one of the classic encounters between these superb cars—the greatest roadgoing Alfa Romeos.

Specifications	
Engine:	I-8 dohc, 2,095 cc (68 x 100-mm bore x stroke), 5.75:1 compression ratio, dry sump lubrication, twin superchargers, 180 bhp @ 5,200 rpm 8C 2900 A: 220 bhp @ 5,300
Transmission:	4-speed, multi-plate clutch
Suspension, front:	Independent, with coils and trailing links
Suspension, rear:	Independent, with swing axles, transverse leaf
Wheelbase (in.):	110/122
Weight (lbs):	approx. 2,500 (1,870 in racing form)
Top speed (mph):	125
Production:	43 (all models)

117

T he automotive supercharger originated in America (on the Chadwick in 1907), yet was uncommon on American cars as late as 1930. When it was used, however, the transformation tended to be profound—sometimes astonishing. A blower made the hitherto workaday Grahams capable of 112 mph in 1935, for example—a speed which journalist Ken Purdy observed was beyond the capability of most drivers. Blowers, of course, did wonderful things for the Duesenberg and Cord, which would have been impressive enough without them. And they certainly did a lot for Auburn. The unbelievable fact was that Auburn's alleged price for an 851 speedster, with its magnificent boattail bodywork and supercharged straight eights, was only $2,245. (As a matter of fact, one might be right not to believe it—about which more in due course.)

Auburn was founded in 1900 and, though never a high volume manufacturer, was well run and usually showed a profit. It produced nothing memorable, however, until 1924, when it joined Errett Lobban Cord's burgeoning empire with Cord, Duesenberg, and the Lycoming Engine Company. Lycoming-engined Auburns were sprightly performers and Auburn's styling was attractive to boot. In 1931, with the Depression two years old, Auburn built more cars than DeSoto, or Packard and Cadillac combined, and stood an unaccustomed 13th in production. Auburn was still in the black while most independents were losing money heavily. This was, however, its high water mark.

An expensive retooling program for the 1934 models didn't pay off in sales, and the board of directors appointed Duesenberg president Harold T. Ames as executive vice-president. Ames immediately asked Duesenberg chief designer Gordon Buehrig to create a facelift that would salvage Auburn's fortunes in 1935. A supercharger, Ames said, would be one inexpensive way to boost performance quickly. Could Buehrig first create a "special" or show car that would get people into the showrooms? Yes, he could.

Auburn had built a V-12 Speedster in 1933, and about 100 unused bodies were available. Buehrig mounted one on a chassis designed by August Duesenberg, its supercharged engine sporting chrome external exhaust pipes. The body was extremely narrow, so Buehrig had to design a new hood and radiator shell, which were grafted onto the 1933 body at the scuttle. He also shaped the lovely pontoon fenders, which were banged out over hardwood forms and individually finished at considerable expense—this was one of the reasons why Auburn never made money on the Speedster. Another was the fact that the body comprised no fewer than 22 individual sections, which had to be hand formed, filed, fitted, filled, and sanded.

There was very little money available, Buehrig recalled, so he

Auburn eight- and 12-cylinder cars have long been recognized as true Classics, and the most desired of the lot has long been the 1935-36 Speedster (here a '35). Designed by the late Gordon Buehrig, the appeal of the Speedster has withstood the test of time.

Other cars in the late Twenties and early Thirties received "boattail" bodies, but none were nearly as rakish as the Auburn Speedster. Unfortunately for collectors, only an estimated 500 were ever built.

The Speedster's cabin was a bit tight, but the dash featured sporty engine-turned trim panels. Aided by a supercharger, the 280-cid straight eight developed a healthy 150 horsepower, and sent its exhaust through pipes that exited via the side of the hood.

had to skip any ideas for elaborate trim. He did manage to slice the Auburn "flying lady" hood ornament down the middle, however, so that it could be applied to each side of the car just behind the doors: the only trim unique to the Speedster. He recalled that he would have liked to fit the Speedster with a beautiful engine-turned metal dashboard and plethora of instruments, as on his famous Cord 810 of 1936—but there wasn't anything to pay for it.

The Speedster was more than a pretty face. To prove it, veteran racer Ab Jenkins took one on test to the salt flats at Bonneville, Utah, where he scored 104.17 mph for the flying mile and covered 500 miles at a 103-mph average. Jenkins and test driver Wade Morton ostensibly tested each car as it was built, for each carried a plaque attesting that it had been driven at a certain speed—always just over 100 mph. But Buehrig told this writer that he had seen workmen tacking the plates on dashboards before the bodies had even been mounted on the chassis. It doesn't matter: the Speedster was a genuine 100-mph automobile, allegedly available for a paltry $2245.

We'd better get that price business out of the way. Many writers have marveled over the bargain it represented, and wondered why Auburn didn't sell 10,000 copies. The reason is that few if any could be bought at anywhere near $2,245. *Road & Track* found the records of a Speedster sold in Hartford, Connecticut, for $3,745, tax and freight

included—which was considerably more, especially in 1935 when a Ford V-8 cost $500.

When the Speedster first appeared, people loved it. Ames thus decided to make it a production model rather than a limited-production show car, and began producing copies 25 at a time. When people found that it took closer to $4,000 than $2,000 to own one, however, their enthusiasm tailed off. In all, about 500 were built, as the 1935 Model 851 or the 1936 Model 852.

If it disappointed Ames in terms of sales, the Speedster did serve to build showroom traffic as he'd originally hoped. Most of the time, Auburn buyers left as owners of an Auburn Six, which started around $800 and rarely cost more than $1,000. This was a good looking, well built, middling priced car that represented fine value for money. In fact, sales for 1935 rose 20 percent compared to the dismal results of 1934, so it would be fair to say that the Speedster helped Auburn—though only briefly. Perhaps it helped it too much, since it brought E.L. Cord back.

Cord had left active management of his empire in 1934 when he packed his family and moved to England, allegedly because of kidnapping threats against his children. When business picked up, he was quick to rethink his position. In 1936, he returned to the helm, a prodigal anything but welcome back home in Indiana. The Internal Revenue Service was investigating his finances, the Secu-

rities and Exchange Commission his stock dealings. By mid-1937, he had sold out to Wall Street financiers backing a new management team led by L.B. Manning, who had run his companies during his absence.

Manning took one month to assess the situation, and then announced that Auburn—along with Cord and Duesenberg—would build cars no longer. Thus, Auburn's last year turned out to be 1936, during which only 4,300 cars were built between January and October.

Remarkably, Speedsters today are still the bargains, relatively speaking, that they claimed to be back in 1935-36. Compared to other rakish bodies of the Classic era, they are positive bargains, especially since the collapse of the collector car bull market in 1989-90. Maybe that's the justice they deserve.

Specifications	
Engine:	L-head I-8, 279.9 cid (3.06 x 4.75-in. bore x stroke), Schwitzer-Cummins supercharger, 150 bhp @ 4,000 rpm
Transmission:	3-speed, floor-mounted shift lever
Suspension:	Rigid axles, longitudinal semi-elliptic leaf springs, dual ratio rear axle
Brakes:	4-wheel hydraulic, 194 sq in.
Wheelbase (in.):	127
Weight (lbs):	3,706
Tires:	6.50 x 16
Top speed (mph):	100 +
Production:	approx. 500

In 1936, the 852 Series lineup comprised 24 models. Though all shared a 127-inch wheelbase, prices ranged from $995 to $2,245 for the Speedster. Seen here is the Supercharged Eight Dual Ratio phaeton sedan, which sold for $1,725.

The '36 Auburn 852 series were the Eight, Custom Eight Dual Ratio, Salon Eight Dual Ratio, and the Supercharged Eight Dual Ratio. Among the last was a very nice two/four-passenger cabriolet, for which Auburn dealers asked $1,675.

The late Gordon Buehrig designed the stunning 1935 Auburn Speedster, and he also penned the immortal Cord 810/812.

Having pulled the veteran Auburn Automobile Company back from the brink of disaster, Errett Lobban Cord undertook during the late Twenties to develop and market a car bearing his own name.

Not yet out of his twenties when he became Auburn's general manager, and only 32 years of age when he was appointed president of the company, Cord had managed in a few short years to give the Auburn a dashing, youthful image. His cars were among the style leaders of their day, and they were among the first in the medium-price range to feature straight-eight power. To match their speed, Cord had even provided them with hydraulic brakes—something most of his competitors wouldn't introduce for another decade.

So, of course, when Cord decided to field an automobile bearing his own name, it was to be expected that it would be both different and daring. Which indeed it was. It came to market in August 1929 as America's first series-produced front-wheel-drive car. Styled by Al Leamy, it stood only 61 inches high, at least nine inches lower than any of its major competitors. Its smart vee-shaped radiator would inspire a host of imitators, notably the Chryslers of 1931-33. And the long, sweeping front fenders established a new trend in automotive design. In short, the L-29, as that first-generation Cord was called, was one of the most beautiful automobiles ever to put rubber to the road. It was not, however, a commercial success. In some respects it wasn't an engineering triumph, either, but that's another matter. Suffice it that early in 1932, after about 5,000 of these beauties had been produced, the Cord L-29 was taken out of production.

E.L. Cord's enthusiasm for front-wheel drive was undimmed, however, and he certainly never lost sight of his goal of producing an automobile carrying his own name. So in 1936 there came another front-wheel-drive car, the Cord 810. And if the L-29 had been a beauty, the 810—designed by the late Gordon Buehrig, formerly chief stylist at Duesenberg—was a styling tour-de-force.

As a matter of fact, however, when work had begun on this car back in 1933, it was intended to be neither a Cord nor a front-wheel-drive machine. It was to have been a "baby Duesenberg," a thoroughly conventional car based on Auburn straight-eight components, intended to bring the Duesenberg's prestige to a broader market.

By February 1934, a prototype had been completed. Then there followed a brief hiatus during which time Buehrig was called upon to redesign the 1935 Auburn, an assignment which included styling the stunning Series 851 speedster. When Gordon Buehrig returned to the Duesenberg project several weeks later, he was told that all previous bets were off: This car was to be a front-wheel-drive job. And it was to be a Cord, not a Duesenberg.

In drumming up prospects for the 1936 Cord 810, an ad was placed in the November 1, 1931 issue of *Forbes* magazine (*top*) proclaiming that the new car would be at both the New York and Los Angeles auto shows that week. In another promotional piece it was noted that the 810 had "Quality in every detail."

123

By December 1934, the design of the new Cord was essentially complete. Buehrig, pleased with the result, got married and departed on his honeymoon. But the Auburn Automobile Company, and indeed all of E.L. Cord's industrial empire, was skirting the edge of bankruptcy by that time. Upon his return, Buehrig learned that the Cord project had been scrubbed for lack of financing.

Six months later, Buehrig was hastily summoned to a meeting of the Cord Corporation board of directors. There he learned that the manufacture and sale of steel kitchen cabinets, most of them going to Montgomery Ward, had replenished the corporate coffers to some extent, and the front-drive Cord project was being revived.

So much for the good news. The bad news was that the cars were to be displayed at the New York Auto Show on November 2, 1935. That left less than four months in which to build and test a prototype, tool up, and get the cars into production. It was literally an impossible task. Under the rules of the Automobile Manufacturers Association, no automobile could be exhibited at shows under their jurisdiction unless a minimum of 100 cars had already been produced. Since time didn't permit tooling up for normal production, this

Although the 1937 Cord 812 looked like the '36 810, supercharging became available for '37, boosting the horsepower of the Lycoming V-8 from 115 to 170. And of course, the exterior exhaust pipes added a bit of dash.

meant that the 100 cars had to be built by hand, a hideously expensive procedure.

Somehow, the deadline was met. But the display cars wouldn't run, for they had no transmissions. These were four-speed gearboxes of a brand new design, and there simply hadn't been time enough to get them on-line.

If the first 100 cars had been laboriously—and expensively—hand-built, numerous economies were effected with the production units. In order to save

tooling costs, the left front and right rear doors used the same stampings. The same applied to the right front and left rear. When brakes failed due to heat trapped behind the wheel discs, George Ritts, head of Cord's experimental garage, simply punched a dozen holes around the perimeter, thus solving the problem while creating an attractive styling highlight. Interior hardware, gauges, and steering wheels all were adapted from obsolete stock, obtained on the cheap from various suppliers. Even with those constraints, Buehrig managed to give the new Cord a svelte, expensive look.

Body and frame construction was rather like that of the Camaro, 30 years later. That is, the engine (as well as, in this case, all driving components) was carried on a forward sub-frame, while the body itself was of single-unit, all-steel construction. Three basic styles were offered: a four-door sedan known in standard form as the Westchester and in deluxe guise as the Beverly; a four-passenger convertible called the Phaeton; and a two-passenger ragtop popularly, though unofficially, called the Sportsman.

Powering the Cord 810 was a brand new V-8 from Lycoming, another part of E.L. Cord's empire. An L-head of comparatively modern design, it featured a stroke/bore ratio of just 1.07:1. Displacement was 288.6 cubic inches, a

In designing the Cord 810/812, the instrument panel was not overlooked. Gauges and controls were placed against a purposeful-looking engine-turned metal panel with everything arranged symmetrically—perhaps too symmetrically.

The '37 Supercharged 812 Westchester sedan makes clear the enduring appeal of Gordon Buehrig's basic design. Few closed cars have stood the test of time so well. This model, riding a 125-inch wheelbase, sold for $2,860 when new.

trifle larger than the Packard One Twenty's straight eight; horsepower was advertised at 125. The power-to-weight ratio was closely comparable to that of the junior Packard.

The trickiest problem in engineering the new Cord was the question of how to control the transmission. With the gearbox placed ahead of the engine, shifting gears mechanically would have required a very complex arrangement of rods and levers, so in the end Cord adopted the new Bendix electro-vacuum system. A fingertip control was mounted under the steering wheel, and gears could be pre-selected at any point, with the shift taking place when the clutch was depressed. In proper working order, the remote-control shift was very effective and a joy to use. But if something were go wrong with its enormously complex mechanism, the driver was left stranded by the roadside, quite helpless.

But, of course, the Cord's major selling point was neither its engine nor its transmission. It wasn't even the car's unusual construction. It was the Cord's remarkable good looks. Buehrig had devised a wraparound "coffin-nose" grille, the likes of which Detroit had never seen before. Running boards were hidden out of sight, as were the door hinges; headlamps, concealed in the

fenders, were raised by means of small cranks, one at each end of the handsome, engine-turned dashboard. Standing several inches lower than the competition, the total effect of the Cord was smooth and sleek.

At its introduction, the new Cord—designated Model 810—was the runaway hit of the show. Delighted Cord salesmen busied themselves taking orders. But getting the cars into production proved to be another matter. Weeks went by, and still the cars weren't ready. To keep customers interested, Cord ordered 1/32-scale models and supplied them to anyone who had put down a deposit on the new car. But as the delay continued, not a few customers defected to other makes—perhaps especially the handsome new Cadillac Series Sixty, which undercut the Cord's price by $300.

Production finally got underway on February 15, 1936. Inevitably, "teething" problems began to appear: engines overheated, transmissions jumped out of gear, the constant-velocity U-joints were noisy. All of these maladies were amenable to solution, but the defects in the early production units did terrible things to the Cord's reputation.

Basically, however, the Cord was a good automobile. Had it been spon-

sored by a stronger company, and had there been more time for development and testing, the story might have had a happier ending. But by 1937, Cord was in deep trouble. A new Auburn was announced that season, but never produced; Duesenberg production had sputtered to a halt. Thus, E.L. Cord's hopes were pinned entirely on his namesake car, now designated the Series 812 and available with an optional supercharger, which raised the V-8's horsepower to 170. Also available were Custom Beverly and Berline four-door sedans on a stretched 132-inch wheelbase.

But the odds against the Cord's success were simply overwhelming. Production ground to a halt early in August 1937—and it was all over. Fewer than 3,000 of the 810/812 cars had been produced.

Gordon Buehrig believed to the end of his life that had it not been for the six months of inactivity during which development of the second-generation Cord was halted, regular production cars could have been ready for delivery at show time. There would have been ample opportunity to correct any mechanical deficiencies, and even the very first cars would have been good ones. "It is very probable," Buehrig declared, "the whole venture would have been a complete and lasting success."

Buehrig just may have been right!

Specifications	
Engine:	Lycoming 90-degree V-8, L-head, 288.6 cid (3½ x 3¾-in. bore x stroke), 6.5:1 compression ratio, Stromberg dual downdraft carburetor, 125 bhp @ 3,500 rpm. Supercharged (1937 only): 170 bhp @ 4,000 rpm
Transmission:	4-speed selective, synchromesh on top three gears; Bendix "Electric Hand" electro-vacuum remote control; 10-inch semi-automatic dry=plate clutch
Chassis:	Pressed-steel frame, channel-section side members, pressed or tubular cross members
Suspension, front:	Independent, transverse leaf spring
Suspension, rear:	Tubular axle, semi-elliptic springs
Brakes:	Front/rear drums
Wheelbase (in.):	125; Custom: 132
Overall length (in.):	195.5; Custom: 202.5
Overall height (in.):	58.0-60.0
Weight (lbs):	3,715-4,170
Top speed (mph):	92.8; Supercharged: 98.9
0-60 mph (sec):	20.1; Supercharged: 13.2
Production:	Under 3,000 total

Today's Jaguar XJ-S is descended from the SS Jaguar 100, the best of William Lyons' prewar sports cars, which set his traditions of "grace, space, pace"—and value for money. The "SS" stems from Lyons' original Swallow Sidecar Company, Limited, which originally built motorcycle sidecars, then bodies on other peoples' chassis, then cars in its own right which were later called Jaguars. The designation "SS-100" usually applied to this car is incorrect: all 100s were SS Jaguars, but not all SS Jaguars were 100s. (After World War II, of course, the "SS" initials were abandoned and the cars were simply called Jaguars.)

To properly trace the model hierarchy, it's necessary to go back to 1932 and the SS-1, Lyons' first car. Originally offered as a closed coupe with 2.1- and 2.6-liter sidevalve engines, the SS-1 rode an under-slung chassis supplied by the Standard Motor Company. Bodies were built to Lyons' design, early models having cycle front fenders and later ones the "clamshell" style. All had long, elegant hoods and beautifully curved fenderlines, apparently at the insistence of Lyons himself, who had a fine eye for design. A touring convertible appeared in 1933, followed by a sedan in 1934-35. The undistinguished chassis featured beam axles at each end and cable-operated mechanical brakes.

The SS-1 looked good, but could barely get out of its own way, puffing hard at around 80 mph, even with the larger engine. Its first competition appearance, at the 1933 Alpine Trials, was a fiasco in which the entire team retired. But Lyons came back the following year and took a third in class, which was sufficient consolation. He also hired Bill Heynes away from Humber to be his chief engineer. Their object was to build something that would win a European rally outright. Their answer was the SS Jaguar 90, the 100's direct forebear.

Introduced in early 1935, the 90 used the largest available engine of 2.7 liters and the smallest available chassis with a 104-inch wheelbase. It was pretty, but still not quick enough, and it failed even to finish in its debut at the 1935 RAC Rally. Only 21 were built before Jaguar revised the spec again, introducing the SS Jaguar 100 in the autumn of 1935.

The 100 set the tone for future Jaguars by bringing together the brilliant triumvirate of Lyons, Heynes, and cylinder-head wizard Harry Weslake, who would later conspire to create the stupendous XK engine of 1948. For the 100, they designed a smooth-running, seven-main-bearing 2.5-liter engine with overhead valves and twin SU carburetors. Lyons had wanted to get 90 bhp out of it; with Weslake's head and overhead valves he got 102. This was the first of the Jaguar engines, used through 1948. Though by no means as singular as the XK's six, it exemplified the high standards of power, smoothness, and efficiency that would mark all Jaguar engines in the future.

The '37 SS Jaguar 100 had a 2.5-liter inline six with overhead valves, seven main bearings, and twin SU carbs. Designed by Jaguar, it was smooth running and developed 102 horsepower. This gave the 100 a top speed of just about 100 mph. That was pretty much academic, in any case, because the 100's styling stopped people in their tracks, for it did indeed look fast just standing still.

For 1938, the SS Jaguar 100 was treated to an all-new 3.5-liter six that offered better cooling and breathing and larger valves—and 125 horsepower. This was exactly the tonic the 100 needed for it would now easily cross 100 mph and sail along to 110. Further, a 0-60-mph dash now took in the area of 10-12 seconds.

over 110 and gave 0-60 times in the realm of 10-12 seconds. For this quantum leap forward in performance, SS Cars demanded the premium of £50 ($250) over the cost of the 2.5-liter model. At $2,165, the 3.5-liter 100 was just as remarkable a buy for the money as the E-Type was at $5,500 a generation later.

While Lyons was perfecting the SS Jaguar 100, Britain's Prime Minister Chamberlain was meeting Hitler at Munich, so there wasn't much time left for rallying. While peace lasted, the 100 did very well. The 2.5s won the 1937 RAC Rally to Hastings outright and finished 1-2-4-5, handily winning the manufacturer's prize; they also won the Welsh Rally and its manufacturer's prize that year. Similar events fell to 3.5s 12 months later. In 1939, Jack Harrop, one of the top factory drivers, achieved 10th place in the punishing Monte Carlo Rally and five other SS cars finished. In the RAC Rally that year, 100s took four out of the first seven positions, and a 3.5 dominated Shelsley Walsh again, beating every unsupercharged car that showed up.

The 100 had minor influence on future Jaguar styling as well as engineering: in 1938, at the Earls Court Auto Show in London, SS Cars displayed a new coupe version with a smooth, louverless hood and large, pontoon fenders. Aside from the long bonnet, it bore little resemblance to the SS Jaguar 100, but the coupe body resembled that of the XK120! The latter was then still 10 years into the future, but it showed the way William Lyons was thinking. There's one thing you can't take away from the old boy: consistency.

The 100's chassis was conventional enough, a rigid X-member frame with rod-actuated Girling mechanical brakes and center-lock wire wheels. The suspension was likewise: semi-elliptic leaf springs front and rear. A four-speed gearbox was mounted behind the engine. Stock 100s typically failed to do an honest 100 mph, though one test car just made it in 1938. Still, 98 mph was plenty quick in those days, particularly when combined with a 0-60 time of as low as 12 seconds. There certainly wasn't much to touch a 100 in England.

Mechanical details aside, the 100's body stopped people in their tracks. Its voluptuous curves, huge Lucas P-100 headlamps with stoneshields, long louvered hood, and honeycomb radiator made it look fast just standing still. The leather bucket seats and array of black-on-white instruments spread across the gullwing dash beckoned one behind the classic, close-to-your-chest steering

wheel. The first cars were offered in maroon, cream, dark blue, black, gray, and two shades of green—lighter colors worked best. Remarkably, all this sold for only £395, about $2,000 at the time—Jaguar was establishing its tradition of value for money.

There's no substitute for cubic inches, of course, and the 2.5 was hardly on the market when Lyons was seeking more power. This was duly introduced on the 1938 models: a 3.5-liter engine developing 125 bhp at 4,250 rpm. The same engine in a prototype had made the best time for an unsupercharged car at the famed Shelsley Walsh hillclimb the previous autumn. A clean-slate design rather than an enlarged 2.5, it offered better cooling and breathing, and larger valves. Bolted to it was a new transmission, designed to handle the added power. The 3.5 was offered on all SS cars including saloons in 1938; on the 100 roadster it put the top speed

Specifications[1]	
Engine:	I-6, ohv, 3,485 cc (82 x 110-mm bore x stroke), 7.2:1 compression ratio, twin SU carburetors, 125 bhp @ 4,250 rpm
Transmission:	4-speed, manual
Suspension:	Solid axles, semi-elliptic springs
Brakes:	4-wheel Girling drums
Wheelbase (in.):	104
Track, front and rear (in.):	63
Tires:	5.25 x 18
0-60 mph (sec):	10.4 (The Autocar, September 1938)
Top speed (mph):	110
Production:	309

[1]1938 3.5-liter

Enthusiasts remember the 1936-39 SS Jaguar 100s best, but the firm also produced other models—and often in larger volume— such as four-door sedans and this attractive '38 1.5-liter convertible.

By 1932, Charles Sorensen, Henry Ford's production chief, was openly advocating the termination of the Lincoln Motor Company. A money-maker during the prosperous Twenties, the division had become a fiscal liability as the grip of the Great Depression tightened.

That prospect was a matter of major concern to Edsel Ford, for he took special pride in the high style and superb quality that Lincoln represented—and besides, this was the one area in which his father had given him a considerable degree of autonomy. Obviously, if disaster were to be averted a less expensive Lincoln would have to be developed.

By that time, it was common knowledge in the industry that both Cadillac and Packard were planning "companion" cars to sell in the medium-price range. Cadillac's entry, a LaSalle straight eight based largely on Oldsmobile components (as opposed to the greater use of more expensive Cadillac components earlier), would be ready in 1934. And Packard, having hired some first-rate talent away from General Motors, would enter the mass production field for 1935. Clearly, it was time for Lincoln to follow suit.

In the meantime, the Briggs Manufacturing Company, builders of bodies for both Ford and Chrysler, had become concerned about the declining volume of their Ford Motor Company account. And so when Briggs recruited the talented John Tjaarda from General Motors, the firm did so in the hope of developing a highly advanced design that might be sold to Edsel Ford as a smaller, lower-priced Lincoln. Tjaarda, Dutch-born and British-trained, had cherished for some years the hope of building his "ideal" car. It would be aerodynamic in shape, with body and frame constructed as a single unit. He hoped to place the engine at the rear, and four-wheel independent suspension figured in his thinking as well.

The whole thing came together when Edsel Ford expressed an interest in Tjaarda's sketches. The green light was given for the construction of three prototypes. One of these, powered by a rear-mounted Ford V-8 engine, was displayed at Chicago's Century of Progress Exposition in 1934, where it received generally favorable reviews. The one reservation expressed by the public had to do with that unfamiliar rear engine, and the stubby, sloping front end.

This prototype streamliner, by the way, could be said to have resembled a scaled-up Volkswagen "bug," a car whose introduction was still three years away. The resemblance may not have been entirely coincidental, for although VW designer Dr. Ferdinand Porsche didn't visit the United States until 1936, Tjaarda's rear-engined car created such a sensation when it was displayed in Chicago that it received worldwide publicity.

The streamlined Lincoln-Zephyr debuted for the '36 model year. Its styling was far more successful than the Chrysler Airflow.

Even before the prototype was put on display, Edsel Ford had secured his father's permission to proceed with the development of a small Lincoln, based on Tjaarda's concepts. There were strings attached, of course; given old Henry's temperament it could hardly have been otherwise. The new car, the elder Ford insisted, would have to follow established Ford Motor Company engineering practices, which included mechanical brakes, rigid axles, and the archaic transverse suspension. Further, it would stick with the conventional forward-mounted engine.

The restrictions posed no particular problems from a design standpoint. Ford stylist E.T. "Bob" Gregorie provided ample space for the engine by grafting a vee-shaped prow onto Tjaarda's streamlined body, and the effect was strikingly attractive.

From an engineering standpoint, the Lincoln-Zephyr was far more Ford than Lincoln. But in keeping with Lincoln practice at that time, it received a 12-cylinder engine—a 75-degree L-head job—in lieu of the V-8 that Tjaarda had originally envisioned. Although Lincoln engineers were responsible for its design, old Henry Leland, Lincoln's founder, would never have recognized the Zephyr engine because it was derived from the Ford V-8, not from any Lincoln powerplant. In fact, its stroke was identical to that of the Ford, and many parts interchanged between the new V-12

The 1941 Lincoln-Zephyr was priced from $1,478 to $1,858. Model year production came to 20,094 units.

and its V-8 parent. A monobloc casting displacing 267.3 cubic inches, it was rated at 110 horsepower at 3,900 rpm.

The Zephyr engine is looked upon today as something less than an engineering masterpiece, primarily because inadequate crankcase ventilation gave it a tendency to accumulate oil sludge, particularly in stop-and-go driving. But it proved to be an extremely smooth engine, happiest at high rpm, and if properly treated it was capable of providing excellent service—and of delivering remarkably good gas mileage as well, particularly in combination with

the optional Columbia two-speed rear axle.

Of the three "companion" cars of 1936—LaSalle, Packard One Twenty, and Lincoln-Zephyr—the Zephyr was the lightest. The Packard outweighed it by about 100 pounds, the LaSalle by double that figure. Although the Zephyr boasted four more cylinders than either of its competitors, the Packard held the edge in both piston displacement and horsepower. Perhaps even more importantly, the One Twenty enjoyed a distinct price advantage as well. At $1,115 for the popular four-door Touring Sedan, it was $205 cheaper than its newest competitor, a difference of more than 18 percent. Not surprisingly, then, the small Packard outsold Lincoln's junior edition by something like two and a half to one during the 1936 season.

Nevertheless, the Lincoln-Zephyr must be counted as a distinct commercial success. Nearly 15,000 units were turned out in the first year of production, placing it comfortably ahead of the well-established LaSalle.

The Zephyr was a success in a number of other respects, as well. For example, its top speed came in at just over 90 miles per hour, accommodations were roomy and comfortable, and the ride was amazingly smooth considering the car's comparatively primitive suspension. And in terms of styling, the Lincoln-Zephyr represented the first really successful streamliner to be offered by an American manufacturer. Its proportions were right, its lines and curves graceful—and the public loved it.

Twin horizontal grilles and a new front section marked the '38 Lincoln-Zephyr. The '39 got vertical grille bars. That year the convertible coupe sold for $1,747; only 640 were built.

For 1937, the Lincoln-Zephyr lineup was expanded with the addition of a Town Sedan and a three-window coupe. The latter cost $1,165 and 5,199 were sold.

Two additional body styles were offered for the Zephyr's second year of production. Bowing was a handsome coupe and a Town Limousine. Intended to be chauffeur-driven, the latter came with a divider window. Styling changes for 1937 were minimal, consisting chiefly of new bumpers and five sets of double bright bars placed in the grille at evenly spaced intervals. The pace of production picked up, however, with 29,997 cars turned out for the model year. As time would tell, that figure would prove to be the Lincoln-Zephyr's high-water mark.

A new front section, with twin horizontal grilles, characterized the 1938 Zephyr. That made for a very effective facelift, better looking than the original in the eyes of most observers. Two- and four-door convertibles joined the line that year, and the two-door sedan was given a new title: Coupe-Sedan.

Mechanical modifications that year included a hypoid rear axle and hydraulic valve lifters, both welcome improvements. Unfortunately, the economy fell into a steep recession during 1938, so Zephyr production dropped to 19,111 units. But even at that level, the "baby Lincoln" suffered less than many of its competitors.

Sales picked up slightly for 1939, with the model year total coming to 20,905 units. A more modest facelift was undertaken this time, with the twin grilles featuring vertical—rather than

horizontal—bars, a minor but attractive change. The lower body panels now enclosed the running boards, and a new custom interior option was offered at about $150 additional. The big news, however, had to do with the brakes—Henry Ford had at last relented, and an excellent set of hydraulics was fitted.

The first major restyling for the Lincoln-Zephyr came in 1940, and it was a beautiful job. Notably, glass area was increased by 22 percent, seats were wider, and the trunk was expanded by about 30 percent. The Zephyr looked more massive than before, although its weight was actually reduced slightly. This basic styling, subject to periodic updating, would serve Lincoln until the introduction of the 1949 models.

The Coupe-Sedan and Convertible Sedan were dropped from the roster for 1940, but a handsome Club Coupe was added. The gearshift lever was moved to the steering column, while the engine was bored to 292 cubic inches, boosting the horsepower to 120 at 3,500 rpm.

Only minor changes attended the 1941 models. Nonetheless, longer and wider springs provided improved ride quality, a wider rear tread promoted greater stability on the road, and for the first time Borg-Warner's excellent overdrive joined the options list. The Town Limousine, always a slow seller, was deleted from the line at the same time the Club Coupe was gaining in popularity. Over-

all, however, model year sales fell slightly from the 1940 figure, probably because of competition from the new Cadillac Series Sixty-One.

A major facelift was undertaken for 1942, featuring a horizontal-bar grille that some critics have described as "too busy." The public reacted favorably, however, and sales were strong until the assembly lines were shut down by early February due to the conversion to military production.

Two mechanical disasters occurred that year, however. The first was an extremely complex semi-automatic transmission known as Liquimatic. It proved so unsatisfactory that virtually every unit was recalled and replaced—at no cost to the owners—by the stick-and-overdrive combination. The other problem area had to do with the engine. The '42 Zephyr was at least 250 pounds heavier than the 1941 edition, so in order to maintain the car's performance the engine was bored again, this time yielding 305 cubic inches and 130 horsepower. Unfortunately, there wasn't enough meat in the engine block to deal with the larger bores, and serious problems resulted. Early in 1946, Lincoln would revert to the 292-cid engine.

When production resumed following the war, the Lincoln-Zephyr returned essentially unchanged—except in name. Henceforth, it would carry the proud name of Lincoln.

Specifications	
Engine:	75-degree monobloc V-12, L-head, 2-bbl downdraft carburetor **1936-39** 267.3 cid (2.75 x 3.75-in. bore by stroke), 6.7:1 compression ratio, 110 bhp @ 3,900 rpm **1940-41** 292.0 cid(3.88 x 3.75-in.), 7.2:1 c.r., 120 bhp @ 3,500 rpm **1942** 305.0 cid (2.93 x 3.75-in.), 7.0:1 c.r., 130 bhp @ 4,000 rpm
Transmission:	3-speed selective; optional: Columbia 2-speed axle, Borg-Warner overdrive (1941-42), Liquimatic semi-automatic (1942); single dry plate centrifugal clutch
Suspension:	Rigid axles, semi-elliptic transverse springs
Brakes:	**1936-38** 4-wheel mechanical **1939-42** 4-wheel hydraulic
Wheelbase (in.):	**1936-37** 122 **1938-42** 125
Weight (lbs):	3,289-4,130
Top speed (mph):	90 +
0-60 mpg (sec):	16
Production:	**1936** 14,994 **1937** 29,997 **1938** 19,111 **1939** 20,905 **1940** 21,536 **1941** 20,094 **1942** 6,118

It was December 1935 when 23-year-old Bill Mitchell arrived in Detroit—a far more important event than most people could have known at the time. By the following year he would be appointed chief stylist at Cadillac, and eventually he would replace the legendary Harley Earl as chief of design for General Motors.

Most of Cadillac's 1938 styling was pretty well locked up by the time Mitchell arrived, but he saw an opening for a brand new series. What he had in mind was an upscale, high-fashion version of Cadillac's newly introduced price leader, the Series Sixty. It would be far more daring—and less traditional—than any previous Cadillac. And it was with Harley Earl's full blessings that Mitchell set about to bring his concept to reality.

Not surprisingly, the new car's mechanical components were identical to those of the Series Sixty, though its double-drop frame was lower and more rigid than that of the less expensive series. A more elaborate grade of trim was used throughout, and hardwood was employed for main sills and seat frames, which of course added to both weight and cost. Still, given the quality this new model represented, it was a bargain at just $2,090.

The '40 Cadillac Sixty Special flaunted the usual Cadillac crest, but in this case it was surrounded by a "V" emblem. Cadillac was advertising itself in those days as "The Standard of the World."

Powering this beauty was the monobloc V-8 that Cadillac had first introduced for 1936. With a displacement of 346 cubic inches, it developed 135 horsepower at 3,400 rpm. Basically, this was the engine that would see later service in the military tanks that were deployed all over the world during World War II.

Since the new car was based on the Series Sixty, it was known as the Sixty Special. And as it began to take shape, there were those who felt some trepidation. Don Ahrens, head of Cadillac sales at the time, later recalled his own misgivings: "I do not need to remind automobile men," he had said, "that the Cadillac market is ultra-conservative. The bulk of our business is conducted with sound and substantial families. How would this revolutionary car affect our position in the industry? Was it too startling for our price class? Was it too rakish for our reputation?"

Indeed, this new car *was* rakish and revolutionary, especially by traditional Cadillac standards. For example, running boards were eliminated, a daring move that enabled Mitchell to widen the body to the full tread of the wheels. Thus, more spacious accommodations were provided. By means of the new, double-drop frame, overall height was reduced by three inches compared to the Series Sixty.

Pontoon fenders, doubtless inspired by those of the 1934-36 LaSalle, gave the car a massive appearance and added to the illusion of length. All four doors were hinged at the front, a practice that would be widely copied in the years ahead. The low beltline, tall windows,

Cadillac held the price of the Series Sixty Special four-door sedan steady at $2,090 for 1940. Of the 4,597 Sixty Specials built that year, 4,472 were the four-door sedan, 110 the division sedan, and only 15 were Town Cars.

Befitting its $346 premium over the Series Sixty-Two sedan, the Sixty Special featured a fancier interior.

Not too many automakers still offered side-mounted spare tires in 1940, but Cadillac did with the Sixty Special.

The '41 Cadillac Sixty Special sported new front-end styling. Its eggcrate grille is still a Caddy trademark.

and slim pillars provided a startlingly different visual effect, one that would later come to be associated with "hardtop" styling—though in this instance a slim center pillar was retained.

Brightwork was sparingly applied, in sharp contrast to the then-customary practice of laying on as much chrome as possible. An extended deck, one of the first for a production automobile, transformed the trunk from a clumsy

A novel feature of the '41 Cadillac Sixty Special was that the gas cap was hidden under the taillight on the driver's side of the car.

afterthought to an attractive styling feature. And, by 1941, to the confusion of many a filling-station attendant, the gas filler was hidden under the left taillight.

Radical though it may have been, the Sixty Special was tastefully done and strikingly handsome. And in the years ahead it would be widely imitated — probably more so than any Cadillac before or since. The copywriters had a field day. "There has never been a car like the Cadillac Sixty Special," they enthused. "A car with such definite modernity of line, yet so obviously right in taste . . . a precedent-breaking car prophetic of motor cars not yet on other drawing boards, yet a car wholly devoid of freakish trappings."

Still, for all the high-flying hyperbole there was genuine cause for concern. The reason was that the Sixty Special sold at a premium of nearly 25 percent over the price of its mechanical twin, the Series Sixty, and 1938—the year of its introduction—saw the coming of a severe economic recession. Furthermore, the new model's appeal would presumably be restricted by the fact that it was offered in just one body style, a four-door, four-light sedan. There would be

no coupe, no convertible—not even a two-door sedan.

The powers that be needn't have worried, however, because the public loved the Sixty Special. Loved it so much, in fact, that it outsold the less expensive Series Sixty sedan by a margin of nearly three to one.

With the coming of the 1939 model year, two variants were offered in addition to the original model. The first of these featured a sunroof; the other was a formal Imperial, complete with divider window. Styling was little changed for the most part; after all, it would have been less than prudent to mess around with a winner. Nonetheless, a new prow-shaped grille was featured, and the headlamps were repositioned, higher and closer to the radiator. And once again, the Sixty Special was Cadillac's best selling model.

Two additional variations were built that year, exclusively for the use of company executives. First was a smart, one-off coupe that General Motors President William S. Knudsen drove for a number of years. In addition, four convertible sedans were run off. One of these went to Knudsen, the others to Harley Earl, GM Chairman Alfred Sloan, and Research Director Charles Kettering. The bodies were built by Fleetwood, rather than Fisher, starting in 1940. But output of the Sixty Special was eclipsed that year by the total sales of the new Series Sixty-Two. This was another Bill Mitchell design, clearly inspired by the Sixty Special and utilizing the new, bustle-backed General Motors C-body. Offering more than a touch of the Sixty Special's styling for $345 less—a savings of 20 percent—it naturally cut into the sales of the more expensive car, replacing it as the division's best-selling series.

Then there was another new Sixty Special variant for 1940. Or rather, two of them. Both were open-front town cars, one with a leather back, the other done in metal. In contrast to the standard sedans, whose base price held steady at $2,090 (unchanged from 1938), these two sold for $3,820 and $3,465, respectively. Think of it this way: For the price of the leather-backed Town Car, a buyer could have opted instead for

Legroom in the rear seat of the '41 Sixty Special was generous, to say the least. The C-pillars were rather thick, which gave back-seat passengers extra privacy. Note the three-piece rear window.

need to change. No car from any American manufacturer, with the exception of the Lincoln Continental, presented such a striking appearance.

There was big news under the hood, however, as well as in the Sixty Special's styling. Thanks chiefly to an increase in the compression ratio, horsepower was raised from 135 to 150. And for an extra $125, the buyer could opt for Hydra-Matic drive, the first fully automatic transmission to be installed in a luxury car.

Inevitably, the price was increased by a hundred dollars for 1941. America wasn't yet officially at war, but most of the rest of the world was, and inflationary pressures were already mounting. The Town Cars were dropped that year. Only six of the leather-back jobs and nine metal-back examples had been sold during the 1940 model year, so they could hardly have been a paying proposition. And Cadillac was too busy at that point to be bothered with small numbers. The LaSalle had been deleted from the line following the 1940 model run, and for 1941 its place was taken by a new, fastback Series Sixty-One. In response, Cadillac's overall model year sales were nearly double the combined 1940 total of Cadillac and LaSalle.

A brand new Sixty Special bowed for 1942, but it was a very different breed. Though beautifully finished inside and out, it was simply a stretched, upscale version of the Series Sixty-Two sedan. It wasn't unattractive—but neither was it the stuff of which legends are made.

Even on a prestige make like the '41 Cadillac, a heater was an option: $59.50-$65.00, depending on model. The controls were very easy to understand and use.

two Cadillacs: a Sixty Special sedan and a Series Sixty-Two coupe. And he'd have had $45 left over. But then, the owner would have to forego the status that presumably was conferred upon him by the practice of leaving the chauffeur out in the weather.

During an interview some years ago with this writer, Bill Mitchell declared in reference to the 1941 model: "That was the first Cadillac to really have its own image!" Its wide, massive grille was conceived by Art Ross, a member of Bill Mitchell's styling staff. Extending into the fenders on either side, it made a powerful statement, and it too would be a major influence on other marques in the years to come.

Rear fender skirts were standard issue. The pontoon fenders extended onto the front doors, but aside from the grille and fenders the styling remained basically unchanged for 1941. Nor did it

The instrument panel of the '41 Sixty Special was symmetrical, with a large speedometer on the left and an equally large clock on the right. The radio and speaker were in the center.

Specifications	
Engine:	90-degree monobloc V-8, L-head, 346 cid (3½ x 4½-in. bore x stroke), 6.25:1 compression ratio, 3 main bearings, hydraulic valve lifters, 135 bhp @ 3,400 rpm (1941: 7.25:1 compression ratio, 150 bhp @ 3,400 rpm)
Transmission:	3-speed selective, column-mounted
Suspension, front:	Independent coil springs
Suspension, rear:	Rigid axle, semi-elliptic springs
Brakes:	4-wheel hydraulic, 12-in. drums
Wheelbase (in.):	127.0
Overall length (in.):	207.63
Weight (lbs):	4,170 (1938) to 4,365 (1940 Town Car)
Tires:	7.00 x 16
Top speed (mph):	est. 90-95
Production:	1938 3,703 1939 5,506 1940 4,600 1941 4,100

Architect Frank Lloyd Wright, who knew as much as anyone about good design, called it "the most beautiful car of all time." It ranked among the top 10 in *Time* magazine's list of the 100 best designed commercial products. And in 1951, more than 11 years after its introduction, the Lincoln Continental of 1940-41 was one of eight automobiles recognized by the Museum of Modern Art "for their excellence as works of art." *No* other automobile has ever been granted such widespread recognition.

It's not that the Lincoln Continental was by anybody's definition a masterpiece of engineering. Its chassis was that of the medium-priced Lincoln-Zephyr, and its 12-cylinder engine was basically a Ford V-8 plus four. Developed hastily, the V-12 had its share of shortcomings. As Lincoln expert Paul Woudenberg has noted, "The oiling system was never [its] strong point." Owners' complaints ranged from overheating to vapor lock to excessive oil consumption. Crankcase ventilation was inadequate and there was a tendency for the engine to build up sludge, especially in stop-and-go driving.

Yet in fairness it must be noted that the Zephyr-cum-Continental V-12 was one of the smoothest engines on the market—and if treated properly it was capable of giving satisfactory service. It was also, claims of the competition to the contrary, remarkably economical of fuel.

The Continental's suspension was by means of rigid axles and transverse leaf springs, simply a refined version of the type used for the Model T Ford. Brakes were skimpy, their 168 square inches of lining area being only four percent greater than that of the Ford, though the Continental was the heavier of the two cars by more than 900 pounds.

For that matter, although the various derivatives of the Zephyr— including the Continental—were the only 12-cylinder cars on the American market after 1939, they weren't particularly powerful, either. Displacement was 292 cubic inches and the horsepower rating came in at 120, compared to 356 cubes and 160 horsepower for the Packard One Sixty straight eight—though the Continental cabriolet cost $1,065 more than the Packard ragtop.

So it was styling that made the Lincoln Continental memorable. And the inspiration for the design came from none other than Edsel Ford. Edsel and his wife, Eleanor, had been traveling on the Continent during the summer of 1938. Returning to Dearborn, Edsel asked stylist E. T. "Bob" Gregorie to design a one-off convertible for his own use— and to have it ready in time for his Florida vacation, scheduled for the following March—an absurdly short time frame. It wasn't the first time Edsel had asked to have a special car prepared; after all, he was president of the company—even if his father, the irascible Henry, still held the reins of power.

Many people consider the 1940-41 Lincoln Continental to be one of the most beautiful cars of all time. Designed for—and under the direction of—Edsel Ford, it was basically a heavily reworked Lincoln-Zephyr, but with its own roofline on the coupe, and unique rear-end styling as well. An exterior-mounted spare was a noteworthy feature.

Much hand work went into building the '41 Lincoln Continental, which is why the cabriolet listed at $2,778, compared to $1,801 for a Zephyr ragtop. Surprisingly, it weighed only 20 pounds more than the Zephyr.

Edsel Ford wanted a "continental" look for his specially built Zephyr, so designer E.T. "Bob" Gregorie gave it an exterior-mounted spare tire. The V-12 that powered it was basically a Ford V-8 with four extra cylinders. It developed 120 horsepower at 3,500 rpm and was one of the smoothest engines on the market.

The elder Ford was consistently critical of his son, permitting him little authority while relying on him to attend to administrative detail. The one area where he appears to have recognized Edsel's talents was that of styling. Industrial designer Walter Dorwin Teague recalled in later years: "Here his unique ability was in his father's eyes both mysterious and highly respected, not to be interfered with."

Which was as it should have been. For Edsel Ford, though he lacked any formal art training—his father would never permit any such nonsense!—was a lifelong patron of the arts and a man of impeccable taste. And he had a genuine talent when it came to automotive styling. It was Edsel who had been primarily responsible for the good looks of the Model A Ford. It was he who saw to it that the Lincolns of the 1930s were among the handsomest automobiles of the Classic era. And it was Edsel who set the parameters for the Lincoln Continental, specifying among other things that the spare tire was to be left exposed "in the continental manner."

Taking the 1938-39 Lincoln-Zephyr as his base, Gregorie went to work. He sectioned the body at the belt line, lowering it by three inches. The passenger compartment was shifted rear-

As one might expect, the Continental featured a deluxe interior with gold trim. Entry was via a pushbutton. The convertible weighed in at 3,860 pounds, 30 less than the coupe.

The Lincoln Continental boasted a prow-shaped front end, fender skirts, and badging mounted just ahead of the doors. For 1941, just 400 convertibles and 850 coupes were produced. In 1940 the numbers were 350 ragtops and 54 coupes.

ward, and seven inches were added to the length of the hood. A squared-off, top-loading trunk brought up the rear, creating the long hood, short-deck effect that was employed so effectively a generation later when the first Mustang appeared.

Thus was conceived the Lincoln-Zephyr Continental, as it was called initially. It was completed ahead of schedule and delivered to its delighted owner in February 1939. Now it certainly wasn't Edsel Ford's intent to create a stir—that was simply not his style. But word of this stunning new automobile spread rapidly, especially among the Fords' circle of friends, and before long a number of people expressed an interest in owning a car like Edsel's. A second prototype was built, and by April 1939 the decision had been made to produce the Continental on a limited basis for the 1940 model year.

The first production cabriolet rolled off the assembly line in September 1939—based, this time, on the Zephyr's new, 1940 bodyshell. There was a formal introduction at the Ford Rotunda at Dearborn on October 2, 1939, followed by presentations two weeks later at the New York and Los Angeles auto shows.

The price—$2,840 at introduction time—was steep, yet because of the hand work involved in building the Continental, there is no possible way the

company could have made money on it. Rather, this car was intended as a image-builder. Production of the classic K-Series Lincolns had ceased by that time, and Lincoln needed a prestige line to augment the medium-priced Zephyr. At first, only the cabriolet was offered, but in May 1940 a coupe joined the line. This was a genuine "hardtop" in the sense that it was derived from the cabriolet body, though it did have B-pillars. If anything, it was even better looking than the original.

Production really *was* limited. Only 350 cabriolets and 54 coupes were built during the 1940 model year. For 1941, styling was little changed, but the word "Zephyr" was dropped from the Continental's title. The numbers grew that year, too, and the ratio between cabriolets and coupes was reversed. Output came to 400 cabriolets and 850 coupes.

A heavily facelifted Lincoln Continental was introduced for 1942. Seven inches longer and 170 pounds heavier than its predecessor, it featured a grille that critics have described as "busy." Yet it was popular with the public, and it sold rather well until the conversion to war production brought the assembly lines to a halt.

Early in January 1942, the V-12 engine was bored "to within an inch of its life," in author Tom Bonsall's phrase, yielding 305 cubic inches displacement.

Horsepower was thus raised to 130, but there were not only far too many casting failures but owners would eventually discover that it was virtually impossible to bore the block. Early in 1946, the factory reverted to the 1941 dimensions, raising the compression ratio and adjusting the gear ratios in order to maintain a reasonable level of performance.

Apart from a massive diecast grille, there was little change in the 1946-48 Lincoln Continentals. Production continued, still on a limited basis, until March 1948, when the line shut down as preparations got under way for production of the true "postwar" models—none of which could even come close to matching the beauty of the original Lincoln Continental.

Specifications[1]	
Engine:	75-degree V-12, L-head, 292 cid (2⅞ x 3¾-in. bore x stroke), 7.2:1 compression ratio, 4 main bearings, hydraulic valve lifters, Holley downdraft 2-bbl carburetor, 120 bhp @ 3,500 rpm, 220 lbs/ft torque @ 2,000 rpm
Transmission:	3-speed selective, column-mounted lever; Columbia 2-speed axle or Borg-Warner overdrive optional
Suspension:	Rigid axles, transverse semi-elliptic springs
Brakes:	4-wheel hydraulic, drum type
Wheelbase (in.):	125
Overall length (in.):	209.8
Tread, front/rear (in.):	55.5/60.75
Weight (lbs):	3,860 (cabriolet), 3,890 (coupe)
Tires:	7.00 x 16
Top speed (mph):	90
0-60 mph (sec):	16
Production:	1940 350 cabriolets, 54 coupes 1941 400 cabriolets, 850 coupes

[1]1941 model

F or years, Oldsmobile had the dubious distinction of being the "also ran" of the General Motors family. Take 1926, for instance: Buick built 266,753 cars that year, making it the industry's third-best seller, while Olds production came to only 57,862 units—hardly more than a fifth of Buick's total. Even the Oakland Division outproduced Oldsmobile that season by two and a half to one, though it did so largely on the strength of upstart Pontiac.

One has to wonder why Oldsmobile wasn't more successful during those years. The product was a good one, and more often than not Oldsmobile's styling was far more attractive than Buick's. In 1929, for example, while Buick was struggling with the infamous "Pregnant Six," Oldsmobile offered a line of cars that was as sleek and smooth as anything on the market. Furthermore, the Olds could boast of a better power-to-weight ratio than the Buick—and best of all, it enjoyed a $345 price advantage. Buick sales were off sharply off that year, but even so, the total was nearly double the figure at Oldsmobile.

The 1940 Oldsmobile featured pleasantly rounded styling, but the big news was the availability of a fully automatic transmission: Hydra-Matic. It dispensed with the clutch pedal and had four forward speeds. Further, it was priced the first year at only $57.

With the coming of the Depression, Buick fell upon hard times, and the intra-corporate rivalry was intensified. By 1934, Oldsmobile—offering both six- and eight-cylinder models—had actually overtaken Buick in the sales race, only to lose its lead once again three years later.

Historically, Olds had been positioned a notch below Buick and somewhat above Pontiac on General Motors' carefully constructed price ladder. But by the mid-Thirties, the price distinctions had begun to blur. The 1934 introduction of its Series 40 "Special" took Buick into a new, lower-price range, where it actually undercut by $70 the price of the eight-cylinder Olds. And then, to further confuse the issue, Olds offered a smaller model for 1939, the Series 60, priced almost head-to-head with the least expensive Pontiac.

Meanwhile, Olds had been in the forefront of an important engineering advance. Starting in 1937, the division had offered—as a $90 option in its eight-cylinder L-37 line—the "safety automatic" transmission. This was actually a semi-automatic device, retaining the traditional clutch pedal and requiring, in the company's coy words, "a certain amount of manipulation of the gear selector." Oddly enough, this new transmission was built not by Olds, but by the Buick Division, which made it available on its own cars only in 1938, confining it even then to the Special series. Oldsmobile, on the other hand, offered the semi-automatic through 1939, extending its availability to the six-cylinder lines after 1937.

But, of course, the Automatic Safety Transmission was only a first step. Prominent on the options list when the 1940 Oldsmobiles went on display was Hydra-Matic: a four-speed, fully automatic planetary gearbox. "No gears to shift . . . No clutch to press," touted the ads.

Available in any Oldsmobile, it was so reasonably priced at $57 that it is understood to have been subsidized. Oldsmobile's use of a 3.63:1 final drive ratio, in lieu of the 4.30:1 cogs employed in combination with the standard gearbox, helped Hydra-Matic-equipped Oldsmobiles achieve remarkably good fuel mileage. Despite some misgivings on the public's part—the result of the mechanism's admitted complexity—the new automatic was highly popular from the start.

Development of the Hydra-Matic was clearly a team effort, at Oldsmobile and throughout General Motors. The groundwork was laid by Earl W. Thompson, who had started work on the project at the Cadillac Division back in 1934. Supposedly a secret operation at that time, it was billed as the "Military Transmission Project." But although Hydra-Matic did eventually give excellent service in GM-built World War II tanks, the original intent was to make it available for passenger car use by any GM division that wanted it.

As the project progressed, Oldsmobile general manager Charles McCuen, formerly the division's chief engineer, took an intense personal interest in it, but it was Harold Metzel, Oldsmobile's transmission engineer, who led the final development effort. It was also Metzel who, in 1939, sent a fleet of 5,000 Hydra-Matic-equipped Oldsmobiles around the country for evaluation.

With the introduction of the 1940 models, for the first time since 1923 Oldsmobiles came in distinct sizes, using three different bodyshells. The price-leading Series 60 shared with Chevrolet the Fisher A-body. Powered by a 230-cid, 95-horsepower L-head "six," it was relatively light (as little as 2,950 pounds), giving it an excellent power-to-weight ratio. At prices ranging from $807 for the business coupe to $1,042 for the station wagon (a new model for Olds with a hardwood body by Hercules), it was priced less than $100 dollars above the Chevrolet Special Deluxe—an easy step for the upwardly mobile motorist.

Next came the Series 70, sharing the B-body of Buick's Special and Century models. Heavier by about 170 pounds than the Series 60, and four inches longer

The '40 Olds could boast about a fairly roomy trunk, and it was nicely lined, but the spare tire hampered loading and unloading. A Custom Cruiser 90 club coupe was priced at $1,069 and some 10,243 were built for the model run.

As the top-of-the-line series, the Custom Cruiser 90 featured high-quality, long-wearing upholstery. A standard radio listed at $45.00, but the deluxe model sold for $56.60. A 30-hour clock cost just $5.50.

in wheelbase, it shared the engine of the smaller car and cost $64 more. An outstanding value at $963 for the four-door sedan (which is to say, $33 less than the cheapest Buick), it proved to be Oldsmobile's best-seller for the second year in a row.

The flagship of the 1940 Oldsmobile lineup was a newcomer, the Series 90 Custom Cruiser. A hundred and sixty pounds heavier and 11 inches longer overall than the Series 70, the biggest Oldsmobile was powered by a 110-horsepower, 257.1-cubic-inch L-head straight eight. Incidentally, Olds had offered inline eights since 1932, but this particular powerplant—larger of bore and shorter of stroke than the original—dated only from 1937. Examination of its specifications suggests that it must have been derived from Ben Anibal's excellent Pontiac straight eight. It would remain in production through 1948.

The Custom Cruiser was truly a luxury automobile, employing—like the Buick Super and Roadmaster, Cadillac, LaSalle, and, in an interesting switch, the new Pontiac Torpedo Eight—the sleek, roomy, and very modern-appearing Fisher C-body. Extra wide, extra deep lounge seats were padded with foam rubber and beautifully upholstered in mauve-tone broadcloth. Exterior two-tone colors were especially effective when used with the Series 90 coupes and sedans.

Four body styles were offered in the Custom Cruiser line, at prices ranging from $1,069 to $1,570. By far the most popular of the four was the sedan, but Olds also offered a club coupe, convertible coupe, and a stunning convertible phaeton. The last was extremely rare, even in its own time: only 50 examples were built during the 1940 model run.

The big Olds and its counterpart from the Buick Division, the Super series, make an interesting comparison:

	Olds 90	Buick Super
Price (sedan)	$1,131	$1,109
Wheelbase (in.)	124.0	121.0
Overall length (in.)	210.75	208.0
Weight, sedan (lbs)	3,555	3,790
Engine	Straight 8	Straight 8
Valve configuration	L-head	OHV
Displacement (cid)	257.1	248.0
Horsepower/rpm	110/3,600	107/3,400
Torque (lbs/ft)/rpm	200/2,000	203/2,000
Compression ratio	6.2:1	6.1:1
Carburetor	1-in. Stromberg	1¼-in Carter
Braking area (sq in.)	170.5	158.7
Horsepower per cid	.428	.431
Weight per horsepower	32.3	35.4
Production, this series	43,658	128,736
Production, all models	192,692	238,404

Note that although the Olds was longer than the Buick, it was the lighter of the two cars by 235 pounds, giving it a slight edge in its power-to-weight ratio. Observe also that despite its extra weight, the Buick had much less braking area than the Olds. Yet in terms of sales, it was no contest. Buick had long since recovered from its slump of a few years earlier, and was firmly in fourth place, just behind the "Big Three" of the low-priced field and comfortably ahead of Oldsmobile.

Olds would continue with the same three lines for 1941, this time offering the Custom Cruiser with six- as well as eight-cylinder power—though the Series 96, as it was called, found few buyers and would be dropped at year's end. The Hydra-Matic transmission was increasingly popular, however, especially among buyers of the eight-cylinder cars, which helped Olds overtake Dodge to become the industry's number six nameplate.

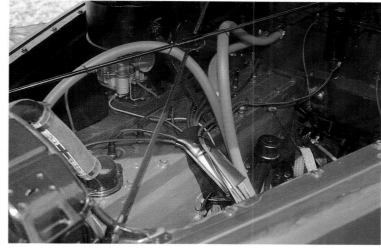

Some might have thought the grille on the '40 Olds a bit busy, but the overall effect was pleasing enough. For 1940, the headlights were more closely integrated into the fenders, and for 1941 they would be completely integrated.

Specifications	
Engine:	I-8, L-head, 257.1 cid (3¼ x 3⅞-in. bore x stroke), 6.2:1 compression ratio, 5 main bearings, dual downdraft carburetor with automatic choke, 110 bhp @ 3,600 rpm
Transmission:	Hydra-Matic 4-speed automatic planetary (opt)
Suspension, front:	Independent, coil springs, hydraulic shocks
Suspension, rear:	Rigid axle, coil springs, hydraulic shocks
Brakes:	Hydraulic, front/rear drums
Wheelbase (in.):	124
Overall length (in.):	210.75
Tread, front/rear (in.):	58.0/59.0
Tires:	7.00 x 15
Top speed (mph):	est. 90
Production:	43,658 (Series 90 only)

The '40 Olds Custom Cruiser 90 ran with a straight eight: 257.1 cubic inches and 110 horsepower. Of course it required regular maintenance.

The late prewar collaboration between Packard and designer/ coachbuilder Howard A. "Dutch" Darrin was a proverbial match made in heaven. If it was a long time coming, it was only because neither had any real need for the other until diminishing sales opened Packard's eyes to the importance of styling—the kind of pleasing, contemporary design that had long been Dutch's calling card. Unfortunately, Darrin's involvement with Packard was too brief, but it has left us a great legacy in a handful of exquisitely beautiful customs, plus one landmark production car.

In the public mind, Packard in 1940 was still very much the aristocratic purveyor of quality automobiles it had been since the turn of the century: "the supreme combination of all that is fine in motorcars." But Packard had lately remade itself into a rather different company, the Depression having forced a change in focus from custom and semi-custom luxury to a reliance on medium-priced cars. The same sort with which rivals Cadillac and Lincoln also survived "hard times"—and without which Stutz, Marmon, Peerless, and Pierce-Arrow did not. Beginning with the eight-cylinder One Twenty, then augmented by the even cheaper One Ten/Six, Packard made a historic transformation from the slow, old-fashioned builder of "motorcars" into an efficient high-volume producer, vaulting from fewer than 6,300 units in calendar 1934 to over 52,000 in '35, then to nearly 81,000 and onto what would prove an all-time record: 110,000 in 1937.

But this evident success exacted a heavy price: the blurring of Packard's strictly patrician image, the very thing that would lead to the make's demise some 20 years later. Indeed, trouble was apparent as early as 1938, when sales in that recession year plunged 50 percent and the previous year's $3 million profit turned into a $1.5 million loss.

Yet Packard had not squandered its good name. Yes, years of stuffy styling were beginning to hamper sales, but not a golden reputation for engineering excellence, painstaking craftsmanship, and an enlightened approach to customers and employees alike. What's more, as *Automobile Quarterly* observed, the firm still "did not have to look for talent, the talent came to Packard."

Enter Dutch Darrin. Dutch began his career as an electrical engineer with Westinghouse and Willys in the Teens and then got into auto design when he chanced to meet Tom Hibbard. The latter joined with Ray Dietrich to found the famed LeBaron coachworks in 1921. A commission for several custom bodies on the Belgian Minerva chassis encouraged them to form Hibbard & Darrin in Dutch's beloved Paris the following year. To Dutch's great surprise, they sold quite a few similar specials, and by the late Twenties their custom bodywork was in great demand for all manner of European and American chassis—including

The 1940-41 Darrin, here a '40 Custom Super Convertible Sedan, filled the glamour gap left by the demise of the Packard Twelve.

The '40 Packard Darrin Sport Sedan was "built for those who look to Packard to . . .create the newest, the finest, the most luxurious in motor car transportation."

The trunk rack at the rear of the '40 Packard Darrin Sport Sedan was probably there more for looks than for function. Note the free-standing taillights.

the occasional Packard.

Things went well until 1931, when Hibbard joined Harley Earl's new "Art & Colour" design studio at General Motors in Detroit, leaving Dutch to soldier on in Paris with backing from a Mr. Fernandez. Darrin continued to be dogged by botched deals and misunderstandings with auto moguls like Edsel Ford and Errett Lobban Cord—hence his nickname: He always seemed to be in "dutch." But he kept rubbing elbows with the rich, famous, and influential— and more superb creations established him as a designer *par excellence* in his own right by 1937. That's when another lucky break, an introduction to film producer Darryl Zanuck, prompted a move to California.

Setting up as "Darrin of Paris" on Hollywood's Sunset Strip, Dutch turned out custom-bodied cars that became the favorites of filmdom's elite. Among these was a raffish two-seat sport convertible on the One Twenty chassis for actor/crooner Dick Powell. A great advertisement for Dutch's talents, it led to several similar efforts in 1938-39, and response there encouraged Darrin to interest Packard itself in cataloging his wares on a special-order basis. In the summer of 1939, he managed to get the Powell car parked at the Packard Proving Grounds, where it was roundly cheered by dealers attending their annual

sales meeting. Here, it seemed, was just the thing to fill the glamour gap being left by the demise of the mighty Twelve (after '39), and to bring buyers into Packard showrooms as never before.

The result was a quartet of low, long-hooded, virtually handbuilt Packards by Darrin. Most glamorous by far was the two-door Convertible Victoria. An evolution of the Powell design on Packard's mid-range, 127-inch wheelbase, it was available in $3,800 One Twenty form or as a $4,953 offering in the Custom Super 8 One Eighty series, the 1940 replacement for the flagship Twelve as Packard's coachbuilt line in the grand tradition. A 138-inch-wheelbase Custom Super Convertible Sedan was also listed, at $6,332, and a companion closed

Sport Sedan was announced as "virtually a request car—built for those who look to Packard to . . .create the newest, the finest, the most luxurious in motorcar transportation." Heady stuff, but apropos considering that $5,000 still bought a very nice house in those days.

Save sectioned radiators and hoods, the Darrins wore unique body panels and lacked running boards, a fixture Dutch detested, though they were literally fast-fading anyway. The Sport Sedan was a handsome "gentleman's" car with a semblance of Bill Mitchell's 1938 Cadillac Sixty Special in its curved blind-quarter roof, chrome-edged windows, and sharp beltline. But the real eye-catcher was the sleek Victoria, with cut-down windshield and an abrupt kickup into the rear flanks from a gradually sloped doorline—the famous "Darrin dip." Alas, Dutch's insistence on style prompted substitution of the radiator-support member with a thin strap that made for marked body wobble and rather dodgy handling.

With that, plus Packard's highest 1940 prices and the deliberately limited pro-

Plastic was considered a miracle material in 1940, and it was beginning to find its way into the interiors of cars, as on this '40 Darrin Sport Sedan. Note the large "banjo" steering wheel.

duction (at the old Auburn plant in Connersville, Indiana), sales were minuscule. Only 50 Victorias were built and a mere 12 Convertible Sedans (of which nine survive today). The Sport Sedan never got going, dropped after only two were completed at Dutch's shop. Packard built two "Darrinized" sedans with stock 1940 front ends, but they weren't nearly as pretty, and also led nowhere.

With a singular exception, 1941 was another year of mostly detail engineering and cosmetic refinements at Packard. The Darrins shared in these, but there was only one Darrin now, as the Convertible Sedan and One Twenty Victoria failed to return. The Custom Super Victoria retained its general lines save minor trim, a slightly different "notch" treatment, and what for Packard was a big styling innovation: headlamps set firmly within the fenders (shared with other '41s). Also new were lowered floors, suitably revised suspension, larger motor mounts, steel-backed conrod bearings, and an oil-bath air cleaner. Power, as before, came from Packard's ultra-smooth, ultra-strong 356-cubic-inch straight eight, again delivering 160 horsepower.

Overdrive was still optionally available throughout the Packard line, but it could also be teamed for 1941 with an "Electromatic" clutch that disengaged by manifold vacuum on releasing the accelerator to permit "clutchless" driving in second gear, which covered most day-to-day use; the pedal could still be floored to select first. As *AQ* described it, "depressing the accelerator would move the car forward, and at speed [its] momentary release would bring the overdrive into operation which, in connection with second, would approximate high gear. At the next stoplight, the foot would naturally be removed from the accelerator to operate the brake, automatically cancelling out the overdrive and making ready for the sequence to be repeated."

But Packard saved its biggest news of 1941 for mid-season, at which point it unveiled the Clipper. A single four-door sedan sharing the 127-inch wheelbase and 282-cid straight eight of the "junior senior" One Sixty series, it looked

Probably the sportiest of the Darrin Packards was the Convertible Victoria, here a '41, which listed at $4,595 in the Custom Super 8 One Eighty series.

like no Packard before—a bold and unexpected bid for industry design leadership. Smooth and utterly modern, the Clipper bore the unmistakable Darrin touch, though it was actually a joint project, with contributions from Packard's own stylists plus several other stellar outside consultants. It was mostly Darrin, though, as seen in its descending beltline, tapered tail, and long prow-front with Packard's trademark "ox-yoke" radiator (albeit slimmer than ever). Predicting postwar styling at Packard and elsewhere was a nearly flush-sided "envelope" body with front fenderlines "swept-through" into the doors—and width that exceeded height.

Amazingly, Dutch dashed off the Clipper in just 10 days to meet Packard's deadline, but he never got a promised $10,000 fee. As he later revealed, "Packard's purchasing agent . . . said to me, 'Now, Dutch, you know the real money is in your custom Packards. So let's just up your order for them by a substantial amount.' This they did, and then later quietly canceled it."

Which was poor form, because despite its late debut the Clipper alone garnered 22 percent of Packard's '41 sales, encouraging the firm to proceed as planned with making its Darrin styling virtually linewide for 1942. As for the Darrin Victoria, its production was transferred from California to Cincinnati, where ambulance/hearse builder Sayers and Scoville crafted 35 as 1941 models and

another 15 to little-changed 1942 specifications. Then it was gone, a victim of Packard's turn to war production and the now scant demand for custom-bodied cars after the long Depression.

Dutch would move on to other projects (including some more of his "disasters"), and Packard would offer a few coachbuilt postwar models, though nothing so grand as these Darrins—certainly not grand enough to prevent its demise in 1958. Today, the Packard-Darrins are *bona fide* Classics all, and every bit the dream machines they were in 1940-42: rare and expensive rolling artwork that many appreciate—but few can own.

Specifications	
Engine:	L-head I-8; **120 Victoria:** 282 cid/4,621 cc (3.25 x 4.25-in./82.6 x 108-mm bore x stroke), 120 bhp @ 3,600 rpm, 225 lbs/ft torque @ 1,700 rpm **Custom Super 8 One Eighty** 356 cid/5,834 cc (3.50 x 4.63 in./89 x 118 mm), 160 bhp @ 3,500 rpm, 292 lbs/ft torque @ 1,800 rpm
Transmission:	3-speed manual, overdrive optional
Suspension, front:	Upper and lower wishbones, coil springs, lever shocks
Suspension, rear:	Live axle on semi-elliptic leaf springs
Brakes:	Front/rear drums
Wheelbase (in.):	127 (Victoria), 138 (sedans)
Weight (lbs):	3,920-4,200
Top speed (mph):	est. 85
0-60 mpg (sec):	est. 18.0
Production:	1940 Victoria 50 Convertible Sedan 12 Sport Sedan 2 prototype Sport Sedan 2 1941 Victoria 35 prototype Sport Sedan 1 1942 Victoria 15

The World War II Jeep was one of the most versatile vehicles ever built. A total of 644,287 were built by Ford and Willys.

It was Ernie Pyle, easily the most beloved of American war correspondents, who described it as "the greatest discovery of World War II," adding, "I don't see how we could continue this war without the jeep!"

Pyle was not alone in this appraisal. General George C. Marshall, Chief of Staff of the United States Army, called the Jeep "America's greatest contribution to modern warfare."

Lyman M. Nash, writing in *The American Legion Magazine*, explained why: "The jeep laid smoke screens and furnished hot water for shaving. It served as mobile command post, front line ambulance, field telephone station, fire engine and snow plow. It delivered fresh socks and C-rations, towed artillery and airplanes, and its broad, flat hood was used as a map table, dining table, and an altar for religious services. The jeep also revolutionized land warfare, permitting troops to reach the front without being overburdened by supplies and ammunition." Or, one is tempted to add, oats for the horses.

The Jeep became as familiar to the rich and famous as it was to the ordinary GI. Madame Chaing Kai-Shek toured Cairo in a Jeep, with General Claire Chennault as her chauffeur. Queen Elizabeth, now the Queen Mother, used a Jeep in her wartime visit to Northern Ireland. President Franklin D. Roosevelt rode in a Jeep as he reviewed the troops in Morocco. Prime Minister Winston Churchill sat in a Jeep as he watched the historic landings at Normandy. General George S. Patton chose a Jeep in preference to a staff car for his trip to Fedala, Morocco, when he accepted the surrender of the French resident general there.

Of course, Hollywood got into the act, and so did Tin Pan Alley. Songs, all of them eminently forgettable, unfortunately, included such gems as "A Jerk in a Jeep" and "I'll be Jeeping Back to You." Meanwhile, on the silver screen the world was treated to *Four Jills in a Jeep*, a piece of fluff starring Kay Francis, Martha Raye, Carole Landis, and Mitzi Mayfair. The plot, such as it was, was loosely based upon a 1943 USO tour undertaken by the same four ladies.

It all added up to unprecedented recognition for an inanimate object, one that has been described by Lyman Nash as "short, squat and ugly as sin . . . an inelegant, incredible and virtually indestructible little vehicle, not much bigger than a fair-sized doghouse." But somehow this remarkable machine "bounced its way into GI hearts back in 1941 to kindle the hottest romance since Antony and Cleopatra pitched woo by the Nile. From buck private to star-glazed officer it was a case of love at first sight."

The Jeep is associated in the public's collective mind with Willys-Overland, and so it should be for reasons that we'll come to presently. But the little quarter-tonner was actually based on a design

Given their role in life, Jeeps were basically quite spartan. They could be equipped in various ways, but this one carries a rear-mounted spare tire and spare gas can. It's also equipped with a blackout headlamp.

This wartime Jeep came with a shovel and axe mounted on the side of the body. At 2,337 pounds, the Jeep was relatively light, a plus for maneuverability on tough terrain.

The bodywork on a Jeep looked almost crude, and every piece was meant to be functional. This is a 1945 model, so it's likely that it saw little, or perhaps no action on the war front.

developed over a three-day period in July 1940 by an engineer named Karl Probst, then employed in a consultant capacity by the American Bantam Car Company of Butler, Pennsylvania.

Representatives from both Willys-Overland and Ford were given the opportunity of inspecting Karl Probst's American Bantam prototype before submitting proposals of their own. Thus it's hardly surprising that when orders for 1,500 vehicles apiece were placed with the three firms—Bantam, Ford, and Willys—all three makes looked very much alike.

In the end, a slightly modified version of the Willys design was chosen for standardization, the selection being based primarily upon the outstanding performance of the Willys engine—an interesting development, in the light of the checkered history of that particular powerplant.

Originally developed for the 1927 Overland Whippet, the 134.2-cid flat-head was rated in those days at just 30 horsepower. By 1933, as fitted to the Willys "77," it developed 48 horses. But it had also developed a dismal reputation, one that may not have been entirely deserved. Both the Whippet and the little Willys were very light cars, each weighing about 2,000 pounds. So in combination with a numerically high axle ratio, the little four-banger

supplied plenty of pep. In the hands of lead-footed drivers the cars were beaten unmercifully, with the result that they became known for excessive oil consumption, fried bearings, water pump failures, and leaking cylinder heads.

By the mid-Thirties, financier Ward M. Canaday had become chairman, as well as principal stockholder of Willys-Overland. And Canaday, seeking to improve the image of his product, hired Delmar G. "Barney" Roos as executive vice-president and chief engineer. Roos, who had held similar posts with Pierce-Arrow, Locomobile, and Studebaker, was one of the finest engineers in the industry. Had he signed on with a stronger company, no doubt he would have preferred to design a new engine from scratch. But Willys had recently gone through bankruptcy and cash was in short supply, so Barney undertook to beef up the existing engine.

The Jeep's engine was called the "Go-Devil." It was an inline four that developed 60 horsepower at 4,000 rpm and 105 lbs/ft torque at 2,000 rpm. The engine had a good reputation for durability.

Roos wrought a low-cost miracle with the aging Willys engine. He tunneled out the intake ports and increased the diameter of the intake manifold. A Carter 1¼-inch plain tube downdraft carburetor was fitted. The compression ratio was boosted from 5.70:1 to 6.48:1. Aluminum pistons replaced the old cast iron jugs. Cleveland graphite micro precision bearings and manganese valve springs were fitted. The crankshaft was strengthened and counterweighted. A quieter air cleaner and fan were devised. Taken together, these modifications resulted in much greater durability, as well as a 25-percent increase in horsepower.

Roos called his revised engine the "Go-Devil." And just to be sure that he had it right, Barney directed his staff to run test engines wide open (4,400 rpm) continuously for 100 hours. That kind of abuse would have destroyed the original engine in short order. In fact, a test in which one of the older jobs was run for 22 minutes at 3,400 rpm had resulted in scored cylinders and burned-out bearings. But the Roos-designed version held up admirably and came back for more.

The selection of the Willys design was not a matter of great moment to the Ford Motor Company. Truthfully, Ford wasn't terribly interested in the project, having been awarded a number of other military contracts. But by October 1941 it was apparent that the Jeep's versatility and usefulness would far exceed the Army's original expectations. A second source was sought, partly in order to increase the supply, but apparently in large measure as insurance against the possibility of sabotage at the Willys plant.

Bypassing Bantam, Quartermaster General E. B. Gregory sought out Edsel Ford with the unprecedented request that his company manufacture Jeeps according to the Willys design—including Barney Roos' "Go-Devil" engine. All parts, Edsel was told, were to be interchangeable between the Willys vehicles and their Ford-built clones.

Edsel Ford agreed without hesitation, and early in January 1942 the contract was signed and Willys turned over to Ford its patents, specifications, and drawings. It was an almost unparalleled

The seats in the World War II Jeep were hardly luxurious, and the cushions were flat, so they didn't exactly cradle the driver in place.

example of wartime cooperation between two competing firms. The agreement may even, in fact, have been illegal—but it was considered vital to the war effort.

By war's end, Willys-Overland had built 362,841 Jeeps, while Ford had turned out 281,446. And Bantam, the company that had started it all, had been eliminated from the project after having built 2,643 units. Bantam president Frank Fenn had lodged a protest, pointing out—correctly—that his company had literally subsidized the Jeep's development. To be left out of the production schedule was highly unfair, he said. Which of course it was, but given the shaky financial condition of the Bantam organization, not to mention the limited capacity of its factory, the decision to go with Willys and Ford—however harsh it might have seemed—was probably a wise one.

In its August 1943 issue, *Popular Science* magazine offered cash prizes for the best ideas on "Peacetime Jobs for Jeeps." The money involved was almost ludicrous, even judged by the modest standards of the time, but nearly 1,200 entries were received. Based on these replies, the editors concluded that "the jeep's reward for its part in winning the war is likely to be, for the most

The steering wheel shows just how spartan the Jeep really was; the dash had only the basic instruments.

part, a lifetime of work down on the farm."

And so it was, to a considerable extent, although the civilian Jeep proved to be even more versatile than anyone could have anticipated. In July 1945, with military production still under way, Willys announced its first peacetime Jeep, the CJ-2A. Two weeks later, the government contract with Ford ended, and the Jeep reverted exclusively to Willys-Overland.

Since that time, many revisions have been made to the Jeep. Meanwhile, the company's ownership has passed from Willys to Kaiser to American Motors and now to Chrysler Corporation. It is an unprecedented sequence of events, for while three great companies have disappeared from the scene, their product—the Jeep—soldiers on.

Which, when you think of it, is just what you might expect from the indestructible Jeep.

Specifications	
Engine:	I-4, L-head, 134.2 cid (3⅛ x 4⅜-in. bore x stroke), 6.48:1 compression ratio, 60 bhp @ 4,000 rpm, 105 lbs/ft torque @ 2,000 rpm
Transmission:	3-speed, selective, floor-mounted lever; 2-speed transfer case; 4-wheel drive
Suspension:	Rigid axles, semi-elliptic springs
Brakes:	Hydraulic drum type, 9-in. drums
Wheelbase (in.):	80.0
Overall length (in.):	132.5
Width (in.):	62.5
Tread, front/rear (in.):	49.0/49.0
Weight (lbs):	2,337
Ground clearance (in.):	8.8
Tires:	6.00 x 16
Top speed (mph):	65
Production:	644,287 during World War II (Willys and Ford)

153

The MG TC was "the sports car America loved first," and it rewarded many Americans with the sheer joy of driving.

In 1964, the author heard a summary that perfectly captures the essence of the MG TC, in an argument between two officers at the Coast Guard base in Yorktown, Virginia: "I can do 120 mph in my '55 Eldorado," one said—"he gets his TC up to 60 mph on the Colonial Parkway and thinks he's in heaven."

That was it, you know—that was what separated the TC person from the rank-and-file, bigger-is-better, V-8 nut in Sixties America. And, indeed, Fifties and Forties America. It wasn't speed that mattered to the TC person—nor, contrary to detractors, was it the semblance of speed. It was the sheer, unadulterated beauty of the machine—the way of its going. It was the way the rain beaded on the hood, if you were foolish enough to be caught in the wet ("weather protection," as MG called it, was rudimentary at best). It was the stance of the TC: those big, 19-inch wire wheels, the inevitable right-hand drive, the foursquare radiator grille, with a cap you really did unscrew to add water. With that and 60 mph, you were "motoring."

Aesthetically, the TC was the best MG of the postwar years. Even the elegant MGB couldn't beat its perfection of line—and for many it was the very definition of the term, "sports car." Together with the Jaguar XK-120, the TC started the sports car boom in America after World War II. Yet it was not an "import" in the sense we know it today—a foreign car carefully designed to appeal to Americans, brought in and sold by a well-organized dealer network. The first TCs arrived almost by happenstance, in the possesion of GIs returning from their stations in England, where they had been wooed and won by the spindly, underpowered, noisy, haphazardly assembled—yet unique and beautiful—products of the Morris Garages of Abingdon-on-Thames, Oxfordshire. There wasn't a serious sales organization in America until almost the end of the TC's production run.

Neither was the TC the first of a type, having evolved from a line of MG Midgets that had begun 15 years earlier. Cecil Kimber, founder of MG, conceived of an affordable sports car built using off-the-shelf parts from a mass production small car, the Morris Minor. The TC's forebear was Kimber's M-type, the first of which was built in March 1929. Its most direct progenitor was the Type J2 of 1933, by which time MG had adopted the unique double-hump cowl, cutaway doors, slab-mounted fuel tank, rear-mounted spare tire—and those delicate, elegantly swept, clamshell fenders.

The TC was directly preceded by the TA and TB of the later 1930s, but fewer than 400 TBs had been built before World War II shut down production. After the war, Kimber was gone, and new managing director H.A. Ryder had never made an automobile. Cecil Cousins, an early MG employee who rose to works manager, recalled asking Ryder,

"What will we make?" Ryder replied, "We'd better make the TB again." Then, Cousins added, "somebody wisely said we'd better find out what's wrong with it.

"So they went through the records to determine the largest number of service complaints," Cousins continued. "The only two things that anybody could point to were that it wasn't wide enough and the sliding shackles were the biggest service item. So they made the body four inches wider across the cockpit and replaced the sliding trunions with rubber shackles to get over the other problem. And that was how the TC came to be. We announced it in October of 1945 and had built 81 by the end of the year."

In a day when little traffic wiggled along what Chesterton called the "drunkard's roads" of Britain, the TC seemed a quantum leap into the automotive future. *The Autocar's* famous road tester, Montague Tombs, said it had "a dashing sort of performance, smartness off the mark and quick acceleration...the little car is rock steady and stable, and handles with a satisfying accuracy. It is quite charming to drive the car fast." (Tombs hadn't even tried it on the Colonial Parkway!)

The MG TC wasn't very powerful—its little 1,250-cc four-banger cranked out only 54.4 horsepower. Thus, the 0-60-mph romp took over 20 seconds and top speed was only around 75 mph.

The TC's 1,250-cc four was a piddling engine by world standards even then, developing 54.4 horsepower. But it was a torquey little job and dead reliable, capable of cruising at about 70 mph, which was pretty close to its maximum speed. Coupled to it was a beautifully balanced gearbox with four well-spaced ratios and a decent synchromesh in the top three gears; a 5.13:1 rear axle ratio perfectly matched its quick-off-the-line character.

The first official MG importers in America were the Collier brothers, Sam and Miles, via their Motor Sport, Inc. of New York City. J.S. Inskip took over from Motor Sport in 1948, at which time the TC began to be seen in serious numbers. We are speaking relatively: officially, only 2,001 of the 10,002 TCs

The styling of the MG TC was already dated in the late Forties, but sports car fans loved it for its honest, purposeful look. The spare tire was hung out at the rear, but that's a plus in the eyes of modern day collectors.

The influence of the MG TC on Americans was far out of proportion to its production, which was only 10,002 units.

built were exported to the United States. But an unknown number of the British (3,408) and world (4,591) market production got in the back door, as returning personal property. The great Tom McCahill, father of the modern road test through his articles in *Mechanix Illustrated*, first tried one in January 1949, and pronounced it good. Racing a TC in his '49 Mercury, McCahill said he could beat the TC on the straightaway or up hills, but the rest of the time it "made me feel like an idiot." Cecil Cousins likewise compared the TC to bigger cars as a knife to an axe: "If you want to cut something you can take an ax and if you hit the thing enough you'll wear through. With a good knife, you want to hone it until it's at the point where it will do exactly what you want of it. That's the way it is with an MG."

The Collier brothers' big interest was road racing. They were prominent in the Automobile Racing Club of America, the prewar forebear of the Sports Car

Club of America, and they competed in TCs from the first SCCA race meeting, at Watkins Glen on October 2, 1948. Here, despite an unlimited field comprised of much more powerful iron like Alfa Romeos, six TCs finished in the top 10, Haig Ksayian averaging 59 mph in his supercharged TC, with Sam and Miles close behind in similar models.

That was the beginning. TCs were prominent finishers at the early Bridgehampton, Long Island road races, the Sebring Twelve Hours endurance race in Florida, Elkhart Lake in Wisconsin, and at events on the West Coast, where one early driver was Phil Hill, later America's first world champion driver. Other future greats who ran their first races in TCs included Carroll Shelby, Ken Miles, John Fitch, and Richie Ginther. As late as 1955, a TC actually won the SCCA Class G-Production national championship—six years after the last one had left the factory.

In retrospect, one can apply without

hesitation an old cliché to the MG TC—it was not so much a car as a way of life. What it spawned—the realization that brute force isn't everything, that finesse and balance and purity of line also count—are values that are with us yet.

Specifications	
Engine:	I-4, ohv, 1,250 cc (66.5 x 90-mm bore x stroke), 7.25:1 compression ratio, twin SU carburetors, 54.4 bhp @ 5,200 rpm, 64 lbs/ft torque @ 2,600 rpm
Transmission:	4-speed, synchronized on top 3 gears
Suspension:	Rigid axles, half-elliptic leaf springs, Luvax hydraulic lever-arm shock absorbers
Brakes:	4-wheel hydraulic drums
Wheelbase (in.):	94
Overall length (in.):	139.5
Tread, front/rear (in.):	45.0/45.0
Weight (lbs):	1,735
Tires:	4.50 x 19
0-60 mph (sec):	22.7[1]
Top speed:	75[1]
Production:	10,002

[1]As tested by *The Autocar*

You will often hear the term "Land Yacht" used to destcribe American cars, but it probably fits the Chrysler Town and Country better than any other model. Chrysler itself was first to make the comparison, in a 1946 brochure: the Town and Country, it said, "has the grace and elegance of a yacht. In fact, the wood paneling is quite similar to the planking of a ship both in construction and treatment . . . . Just as any yacht is refinished every season, so should the beauty and luster of the wood body be maintained by periodic varnishing."

Today the Town and Country is one of the most coveted American cars of the Forties, probably the single most valuable domestic convertible built in that decade, desired by at least 10 times the number of people who actually own one. In its day, it was the darling of Hollywood—but only in its day, for it was dropped by Chrysler after 1950, except as a nameplate for a series of station wagons. Also, the 1949-50 models were really postscripts: the best Town and Country Chryslers were built for only three years after World War II.

The origins of the name most likely lie in a proposal by the Boyertown (Pennsylvania) Body Works to Chrysler, in the mid to late Thirties, for a line of wood-bodied station wagons Boyertown wished to build under contract. Paul Hafer, later president of the firm, recalled sketching many of the designs, and actually using the name on one of them, though he does not claim with certainty to have been the first: "The steel front end looked 'town' and the wood portion looked 'country,' so I thought it natural to use that title." It fitted the role handsomely— and was the only one of Hafer's titles Chrysler picked up. (The other two were the somewhat less alluring "Country Club Sport" and "Country Gentleman.")

Chrysler Division first offered a Town and Country in 1941, advising prospects how the "utility of the Station Wagon was blended with the beauty of custom body creations to produce . . . a car that was at once a sensation." These car-like T&C estate cars of 1941-42, with their clamshell rear doors and smooth, steel rooflines, were startling contrasts to the boxy wagons of their day, but built in limited quantity. Numbers aside, they proved excellent "traffic builders" in Chrysler-Plymouth dealerships, where the public would come to admire a Town and Country and leave clutching an order slip for a Royal or a Windsor— or even, if necessary, a Plymouth.

During the car-less years of World War II, when manufacturers laden with defense work merely doodled ideas for postwar auto production, Chrysler toyed with the idea of a complete line of Town and Countrys as soon as the war was over. Stylist Buzz Grisinger recalled that the eventual program was "a hurry-up thing. . . . There weren't any clay models or production prototypes; we just designed up a series of

Like all 1946-48 Chryslers, the '47 Town and Country convertible featured a shiny "harmonica" grille. It rode on the New Yorker's 127.5-inch wheelbase and was powered by an L-head straight eight that cranked out 135 horsepower.

The Chrysler Town and Country convertible required a lot of maintenance to keep the wood looking beautiful, and it was also an expensive car to build. That's why one cost $2,998 in 1947, compared to $2,447 for a New Yorker soft top.

Chrysler didn't have an automatic transmission in 1947 like Cadillac did, but it did have a four-speed semi-automatic that it called Fluid Drive. It came standard on the Town and Country.

were, however, the Town and Countrys Chrysler did build: the six-cylinder four-door sedan and the eight-cylinder, longer-wheelbase (127.5 inches) convertible coupe.

The ragtop, which lasted with only detail changes through 1948, was manifestly beautiful. Somehow, the T&C treatment overrode the mundane looks of the standard body, and the woodwork was what did it. Maybe it was a little hokey, with whizzy rearview mirrors, heavy daubs of chrome, and that huge "harmonica" grille common to all Chryslers. But it didn't matter—the result was a delight. You drove your T&C convertible top down, soaking up the sun, or relaxing before the twin-blower heating system with its jumbo air scoops on the quarter panels.

That was living—if you could afford it. At $3,395 in its 1948 permutation, the T&C ragtop commanded the price of a Cadillac, and a year's salary for a lot of people. Nevertheless, the T&C convertible was by far the more popular of the two production models, production amounting to 8,380 units over the three-year period.

Sharing a somewhat smaller sector of the spotlight was the Town and Country sedan, complete with chrome or wood roof rack surrounding wood rub rails, and the same white ash framing around mahogany inserts on doors and trunk lid. While convertibles featured interiors of full leather, leather and bedford cloth, or a variety of one-off custom upholstery styles, the more workaday sedan used full leather, or vinyl and Saran plastic or cloth. In place of the convertible's matching leather/fabric side panels, the sedan went all the way with wood, which was seen on door panels as well as on the headliner support bows.

Chrysler seemed blithely unconcerned that these termite traps might create maintenance problems, and went so far as to say that the white ash framing, actually one of the strongest and most durable of woods, would hold up as well as steel—"if properly cared for." Service publications reminded dealers that care was complicated: a T&C "should be thought of in terms of boating rather than motoring. . . . Of the two,

different styles and brushed on white ash and mahogany trim where we thought it looked best aesthetically. Sales took it from there." Indeed, Sales did.

A June 1946 brochure announced no fewer than five Town and Country models, three of which never appeared: a three-passenger roadster and two-door Brougham on the Windsor (six-cylinder) chassis, and a hardtop "Custom Coupe" on the straight-eight New Yorker. Of these, only one experimental Brougham and seven hardtops were built, although at least one of the hardtops has survived. There was also one experimental short-wheelbase T&C convertible, built on a Windsor chassis, whereabouts unknown.

What rocked the showrooms and the country in the early postwar years the requirements imposed on the protective finish of the Town and Country car are the more severe considering weather extremes, flying gravel, mud splashing, dust and grit, road salt, tar, and the many other conditions of ordinary driving."

Treat your T&C like the land yacht it was and you'd have no trouble: Chrysler recommended varnishing every six months, "with special attention paid to all joints, which at all times must be kept thoroughly sealed against moisture." These urgent precautions suggest how much work is involved in a T&C restoration today—how much effort the owners of perfect examples have expended to get them or keep them the way you see them here. But it's a labor of love.

The halcyon late Forties were good years for Chrysler. About 6,000 Town and Countrys were sold in 1946, and again in 1947, and then only 4,500 for 1948—not significant in terms of a division selling over 100,000 cars a year, but enough to bring the prospects into the showrooms. And that, of course, was the whole idea.

In 1949, Chrysler reduced the T&C line to a single convertible model, though a hardtop was proposed and actually went into production—in place of the convertible—for 1950. This was the last use of the name except on station wagons for many years. In 1966, Chrysler offered a decal wood appliqué for non-wagon models which reinvoked the image, but not the genuine wood, of the original Town and Country. It served mainly to remind us of what we had lost.

Not only did Chrysler announce Fluid Drive on its center-mounted rear brake light, but it was also noted on the steering wheel. The center of the dashboard was heavily chromed.

Specifications	
Engine:	**Sedan** L-head I-6, 250.6 cid (3.44 x 4.50-in. bore x stroke), 6.6:1 compression ratio, 114 bhp @ 3,600 rpm **Convertible** L-head I-8, 323.5 cid (3.25 x 4.875-in.), 6.7:1 compression ratio, 135 bhp @ 3,400 rpm
Transmission:	4-speed Fluid Drive semi-automatic
Suspension, front:	Independent, with coil springs
Suspension, rear:	Solid axle, semi-elliptic leaf springs
Brakes:	4-wheel hydraulic drums
Wheelbase (in.):	**Sedan** 121.5 **Convertible** 127.5
Weight (lbs):	**Sedan** 3,917 **Convertible** 4,332
Tires:	**Sedan** 6.50 x 15 **Convertible** 7.10 x 15
Production:	**Sedan** 7,950 **Convertible** 8,380 (1946-48)

With a sunny day and a '47 Chrysler Town and Country convertible, how could one go wrong? The woodwork on the T&C was very labor intensive, as can be seen by the detail work around the doors.

The Cisitalia was a style leader, as recognized by New York's Museum of Modern Art, where one is on permanent display.

Without too much exaggeration, Italian automobile designers can claim a direct descent from the artistic traditions of Michelangelo and Leonardo da Vinci. Their automobiles—the best of them—are poetry in motion, clean and classically uncluttered. Each car bears the unmistakable stamp of its designer, a mark that connotes a subtle mixture of craftsmanship, intelligence, and appreciation of and sensitivity to the beauty of form. Each car shows the care of hand and mind at work, not the impersonal rendering of a machine. If indeed it has been rightly said that Italian cars are not always reliable, with unreliable electrical systems and infamous susceptibility to rust as part of the package—an added mystique that makes their designs all the more desirable.

The best known Italian auto designer has long been Pinin Farina. The son of a coachbuilder, he was 12 years old when he began working for his brother, and prospered moderately as the "horseless carriage" became popular. With the advent of the airplane, Farina glimpsed new vistas of automobile design, but it wasn't until 1937 that his studies of aerodynamic theory led him to build what could be called the prototype of the streamlined models his firm produces today.

Pininfarina (the trade name contraction came later) designed racing cars that broke record after record. Typical in the early Sixties was the Fiat-Abarth SYD, which set 16 world's records, an Abarth 500 with 23 new records, and a Fiat-Abarth 1000 which broke another record on the Monza track in October 1960.

But whether on the race track or highway, a Pininfarina-designed automobile is easily recognized by its simplicity of line and minimum of chrome and lustrous finish. Well aware of mechanical limitations, but not oppressed by them, Pinin Farina the artist brought elegance, comfort, and safety to the automobiles which carried his insignia, as do modern products of the firm which continues to bear his name.

Pinin Farina never actually built an automobile; he was a designer of bodies, not motors. This is not to say that he was indifferent to the physical specifications of motors or the size of a given chassis. "In order to understand Farina," a friend once said of the founder, "you must think of him as an artist in the same way that a painter is. A painter, in committing his art to a mural, fills up a certain portion of space with design. Farina does the same thing. He fills up a space given him by a chassis builder with certain bits of steel, wood, chromium and paint. The result is a picture."

Pinin Farina, then, was an artist. What, by contrast, can we say of Piero Dusio, founder of Cisitalia, its name an acronym for *Consorzio Industriale Sportivo Italia*, the maker of tennis rackets, bicycles, swimsuits, and uniforms for Mussolini's army? Well, that he was both smart and rich—qualities that are not always complementary. And that

A dash-mounted rear view mirror was one of the Cisitalia's interior features, as was in this case a painted maroon dashboard with yellow knobs. Note the banjo steering wheel and the long, narrow door handle.

Buick adopted "portholes" in 1949, but the Cisitalia had them, too. Buick used three or four, the Italian two.

The Cisitalia's engine came from Fiat, a 1,089-cc inline four with dual downdraft Weber carbs and 70 bhp.

and barely missed winning outright against powerful Alfa competition, while Piero Taruffi won the Italian championship in a Cisitalia roadster.

Curiously, the famous 202 coupe evolved almost by accident, after Dusio sent a chassis to the young, small firm of Pinin Farina—not with particularly great expectations. To his delight, the finished car won the grand prize at the *Coppa d'Oro* show at Lake Como in September 1947. From there, the 202 became the star of the show at the Paris salon, where its name was already well established from racing. And, in due course, Arthur Drexler of New York's Museum of Modern Art selected Cisitalia as one of eight cars in his design excellence exhibit in 1951. Today, the Cisitalia is the only car still on permanent display.

It is worth quoting from Drexler's original catalogue: "The Cisitalia's body is slipped over its chassis like a dust jacket over a book...the openings Farina cuts into the jacket provide some of the most skillfully contrived details of automobile design...to maintain the sculptural unity of the entire shape, its surfaces are never joined with sharp edges, but are instead wrapped around and blunted. The door is minimized. The back of the car, particularly the fender, is lifted at an angle rising from the strict horizontal base line which gives stability to the design. Thus both ends of the car gain an extraordinary tension, as though its metal skin did not quite fit over the framework and had to be stretched into place. This accounts, in part, for that quality of animation which makes the Cisitalia seem larger than it is." In the longevity of its display, the Museum obviously holds this car the most important single piece of design work in the history of the automobile.

Like many great names, the Cisitalia's story does not end sweetly. In 1947, with abundant demand for 202 coupes (at $6,800 retail in New York City) plus racing cars and car accessories, Piero Dusio ransomed Ferdinand Porsche from the French government, which was holding him on trumped-up charges of Nazi war crimes. Now this would have been well and good had Dusio sent Porsche back to his Gmünd, Austria

he kept his war profits intact long enough to offer to Il Maestro, Pininfarina, the alluring chassis of the Cisitalia 202, from which "Pinin" crafted the most celebrated automotive shape of the postwar era.

Cisitalia automobiles began when Dusio hired a moonlighting Fiat engineer named Dante Giacosa to design a monoposto racing car he hoped would become a one-design racing class—the first of its kind, a Formula Vee of the Forties. Applying the age-old formula of off-the-shelf borrowing, Giacosa mated Fiat 1,100-cc components to his own tubular chassis (the chrome-moly tubes came from a pile of stock Cisitalia had left from its prewar bicycles). Although Cisitalia single-seaters never established their own class, they raced well. Dusio soon built a two-seater out of Giacosa's tube frame and coaxed 70 bhp from the 1,100 engine which, in this light application, would do 110 mph. That was something! In 1947, for example, Tazio Nuvolari averaged nearly 100 mph for the 90 minutes of the *Mille Miglia*,

The Cisitalia has long been a recognized Milestone car by the Milestone Car Society. Unlike so many cars of the late Forties, the Cisitalia has aged well. The design work was done by none other than Pinin Farina.

factory with instructions to build the VW-based sports car Porsche dreamed about. But what Dusio wanted him for was a world-conquering Cisitalia Grand Prix car.

That project died aborning. Porsche spent five times the budget Dusio gave him to produce but one totally uncompetitive Formula car. Dusio hocked his business to support the vain project, and by 1949 Cisitalia was bankrupt. Ferdinand Porsche and son Ferry then left for Gmünd, fame, and fortune. Dusio sold the remains of his company to an Argentine firm, which used it to make diesel trucks. He went to Argentina with it, almost as if he wished personally to witness the crash of his empire.

Still, as writer Rich Taylor put it, you have to look at the bright side: Dusio "built works of art for museums of the world—when Nuvolari was his driver, Taruffi his race chief, Porsche his engineer and Pininfarina his stylist. It's not every Italian playboy who gets to lord it over four legends all at once, and finance the creation of a fifth."

Specifications	
Engine:	Fiat I-4, ohv, 66.4 cid/1,089 cc, 2 downdraft Weber carburetors, 70 bhp @ 5,500 rpm
Transmission:	4-speed manual
Suspension, front:	Lower A-arms, transverse leaf spring
Suspension, rear:	Live axle, semi-elliptic leaf springs
Brakes:	4-wheel hydraulic drum
Wheelbase (in.):	NA
Weight (lbs):	1,960
Top speed (mph):	approx. 100
Production:	Coupe 153 Cabriolet 17

Although the Cisitalia could claim only a modest 70 horsepower, the car was light enough (1,960 pounds) and sleek enough that it could do about 110 miles per hour at the top end.

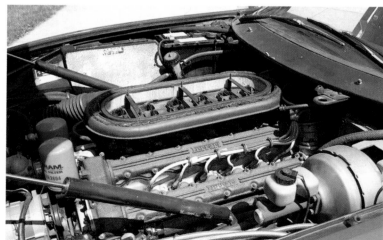

The 1950-53 Ferrari 212s were powered by a single-overhead-cam V-12 of 2,562 cubic centimeters. Horsepower of the Export model came in between 150-170 at 6,500 rpm.

As would befit a racing-inspired car, the Ferrari 212 Export placed its large, round tachometer closest to the driver. The speedometer was actually nearer the passenger.

The venerable Ferrari 212 Export was competition oriented and ran on a wheelbase of 88 inches. It could be ordered with a trio of 32 DCF Weber carburetors. This car was bodied by Touring.

Enzo Ferrari has been rightly termed "The Caesar of Speed." Still, it is faintly remarkable that his very first cars rank among the greatest of motoring's first century. Seldom have automobiles been so "right" from the start.

Ferrari had made his mark in the Twenties as a team driver, then team manager, for Alfa Romeo, before becoming the driving force behind the independent Scuderia Ferrari team that built and raced modified Alfas in the Thirties. After World War II, with the patronage of Enrico Nardi, he moved swiftly toward dual-purpose sports-racing cars of his own design.

Enzo set up shop in his hometown of Modena, in the Po River valley of northern Italy. Despite Nardi's backing, his facilities were quite small, so the earliest Ferraris were virtually handcrafted customs. Just three were built in all of 1947, followed by nine in '48, and 30 in '49. All were powered by the now-classic, long-revered small-displacement V-12 designed by Gioacchino Colombo in 1946.

The three 1947 cars were initially 1,500-cc road racers labeled *Tipo* (Type) 125. Two of these later received bored-out 1,902-cc engines and the Type 159 designation. Those engines were enlarged again in 1948, to 1,995 cc, to create the Type 166, the first of the true road-going Ferrari sports cars.

By the early Fifties, Enzo Ferrari had settled on Vignale and Pinin Farina as his primary body suppliers, but Carrozzeria Touring also bodied some of the 166/195/212 models.

Until recently, Ferrari model numbers always reflected the rounded-off cubic-centimeter displacement of each cylinder (Type 166s had precisely 166.25 cc). Designations also included letters, which could mean different things at different times. For example, the first cars carried the suffix "C," for *Corsa* ("race"), and were indeed designed more for track than road. Later, Ferrari used "C" (*Competizione*) on single-seat racers and substituted "I," for "Inter," on sports-racing models. Just to confuse things, there was also an early 166 Sport (no more than two built, both compact notchback coupes) and the lovely Spyder Corsa, a cycle-fender two-seat open racer.

Serial numbers initially had three digits (later four), with odd numbers reserved for "street" machines and even ones for competition types. However, the dual-purpose nature of early Ferraris quickly rendered this distinction academic.

The 166 made an auspicious competition debut in April 1948, when an open-body Sport driven by Clemente Biondetti won Sicily's gruelling *Targa Florio* road race. Biondetti won the *Mille Miglia* a month later with the same car (albeit rebodied as a coupe by Allemano). It was the first of what would be eight outright Ferrari wins in the demanding *Mille Miglia*, and Enzo commemorated it by using the "MM" designation on subsequent examples of this chassis.

Ferarri capitalized on the versatility of the 166 MM (*Mille Miglia*) chassis by using it as a foundation for numerous cars, here a dual-windshield roadster.

Now widely termed the "Colombo engine," the 166 V-12 would, with further development, be a Ferrari mainstay until well into the Sixties. A 60-degree design, it employed a single chain-driven overhead camshaft on each cylinder bank to operate two inclined valves per cylinder via rocker arms and finger followers. Each valve was closed by two hairpin-type springs. Carburetion was by a single twin-choke Weber instrument on Inters and Sports, triple twin-choke Webers on MMs. Both fed through siamesed intake ports. Block, heads, and sump were cast of aluminum alloy, but there were separate cast-iron cylinder liners. The six-throw crankshaft ran in seven plain bearings, as did the conrods (although one car, the 1949 Le Mans-winning 166 MM, had needle bearings in the rod big-ends). The rods were split at 40 degrees to the centerline, which permitted removing both rod and piston through the cylinders.

Horsepower of the 166 engine has been variously quoted as between 110 and 150 bhp at 7,500 rpm. This is explained not only by the two carburetion setups employed, but different compression ratios, some high enough to permit running on alcohol fuel. Regardless, a single dry-plate clutch and five-speed non-synchromesh transmission (later 166 MMs had synchronized third and fourth gears) carried power to a live rear axle.

The 166 also set the pattern for roadgoing Ferrari chassis that would persist for many years. Though wheelbase varied with model, all 166s employed a tubular-steel ladder-type frame with oval-section main tubes and round-section cross-tubes. Front suspension was independent via unequal-length A-arms and a transverse leaf spring, while the rear axle was located on each side by a semi-elliptic leaf spring and a pair of parallel trailing arms. Houdaille vane-type lever-action hydraulic shock absorbers were standardized after the first few cars had been built. Brakes were large-diameter aluminum drums with cast-iron liners and hydraulic actuation. Steering was of the worm-and-peg type. Reflecting Enzo's racing orientation, all 166s had right-hand drive.

Though the 166 Sport was Enzo's first attempt at a road car, the Inter was the first Ferrari to see serious production—if you call 37 units "serious." Carrozzeria Touring seems to have supplied most 166 bodies, but virtually every Italian coachbuilder of the day contributed a few: Allemano, Bertone, Ghia, Ghia-Aigle (a Swiss firm), Pinin Farina, Stabilmenti Farina (founded by Pinin's brother), and Alfredo Vignale.

Of all 166 styles, the most famous and popular is Touring's "Barchetta" roadster. The nickname (which did not appear in Ferrari literature) means "little

boat," and was prompted perhaps by the full-length bodyside crease suggesting a "waterline." Tojeiro of Britain would later emulate it for the AC Ace and its later Shelby Cobra evolutions. (The Barchetta would also be stretched for use on Ferrari's later 212 Export and 340 America chassis.)

In 1950, continuing competition both on and off the track prompted Ferrari to bore out the Colombo V-12 twice more: first from 60 to 65 mm for 2,341 cc, then to 68 mm for 2,562 cc (stroke remained 58.8 mm). The results were two new *Tipos*, the 195 and 212, respectively. Again there were sporty road-going Inter versions, plus 195 Sport and 212 Export editions aimed solely at competition. Frame, suspension, steering, and brakes were as for the 166, but tracks were widened on both series (to 49.8 inches front, 49.2 rear). Wheelbases also followed the 166 series. The shortest 86.6-inch span was reserved for the 195 Sport, while the 166 MM's 88.6-inch measure was used for the 212 Export, and a still-longer 98.5-inch dimension was specified for all Inters.

Except for their increased bores, the 195 and 212 engines were almost identical with the 166 V-12. Inters had the single twin-choke Weber, Sport and Export the triple twin-choke arrangement (reportedly adopted for 1953 212 Inters as well). Drivelines were also carried over unchanged. In fact, the

In 1950, Ferrari introduced a 2.3-liter (2,341-cc) engine with about 170 horsepower for a car he called the 195 S. Note the prancing horse emblem.

195/212 differed so little from the 166 mechanically that most chassis and engine components were apparently interchangeable.

None of this is really surprising. In its early years Ferrari was a small concern whose primary business was competition, so "production" cars were largely a sideline, built to special order for a discerning, monied clientele. Enzo actually disliked having to bother with road cars, but they did bring in the extra money he sometimes needed to support his racing activities.

Though Ferrari continued offering a wide variety of custom coachwork on the 195/212 chassis, he had settled on Vignale and Pinin Farina as his primary body suppliers by the early Fifties. Unlike the 166, there was an attempt at "standardizing" 195/212 production around just two body styles: a coupe, a.k.a. *berlinetta* ("little sedan"), and a convertible coupe, usually referred to as a "spyder." Even so, there were again many variations in both detail appearance and overall shape. Right-hand steering persisted until 1952, when a left-hand-drive Ghia coupe and Pinin Farina convertible were previewed at the Paris Salon. At the same time, both Vignale and Farina bodies adopted one-piece curved windshields. Touring's bodies retained two-piece vee'd windshields, though a curved screen appeared on one of its last berlinettas, whose styling was otherwise dated.

Good though it was, the 195 was always overshadowed by the bigger-engined 212—and the even more potent

The Ferrari 212 Export ran with a triple-carb V-12. This car was raced in the United States in the late '50s.

340 America, which arrived in 1951. Of course, there was a reason for this as they all cost about the same, around $9,500. Enzo soon realized he had one too many entries for such a limited market, so the 195 was dropped after just one year and no more than 25 units. A few race wins might have prevented its early demise, but it had to run in the same grouping as the 212 and was thus handily outclassed.

No such problem for the 212, which enjoyed almost immediate competition success. In Europe alone, Pagnibon and Barraquet drove to victory in the inaugural *Tour de France* (the car was later sold to American world driving champ Phil Hill), Vittorio Marzotto and Piero Taruffi ran 1-2 in the Tour of Sicily, Luigi Villoresi won the *Coppa Inter-Europa*, and Piero Scotti came home third in the *Mille Miglia*—all in 1951. That same year, Taruffi paired with

Luigi Chinetti and Villoresi with Alberto Ascari to place first and second in the fabled *Carrera Panamericana* Mexican Road Race.

There's little point in detailed comparisons among the 166, 195, and 212 because they're all so similar aside from bodywork (and, as noted, with similarities there, too). Moreover, Enzo wanted to "win the race" outright, which is why everyone—racers and buyers alike—opted for his biggest and fastest models. In the end, even the 212 (built through 1953 alongside the 166 MM) was outshone by the 340.

Interestingly, most 166, 195, and 212 production seemed to find its way to the United States, where privateers could usually count on winning their class and, quite often, overall victory. Subsequent Ferraris would improve on their formula, but would not fundamentally depart from it for more than a decade. So as the progenitors of the great touring and sports-racing thoroughbreds that conquered one and all both on and off the track, the 166, 195, and 212 deserve their honored place in the pantheon of automotive immortals—timeless chariots befitting a "Caesar of Speed."

This 1952 Ferrari 212 Export *berlinetta* has a one-off body by Vignale/Michelotti. Vignale went on to use this design—including the two-tone paint scheme—for the Cunningham C-3, a grand touring car conceived by American Briggs Cunningham.

Specifications	
Engine:	V-12, sohc **166** (1947-53): 122 cid/1,995 cc (2.36 x 2.31-in./60 x 58-mm bore x stroke), 110-150 bhp @ 7,500 rpm (variable with compression and carburetion) **195** (1950-51): 142.8 cid/2,341 cc (2.56 x 2.31-in./65 x 58-mm), 130 bhp @ 6,000 rpm (Inter), 160-180 bhp @ 6,000 rpm (Sport) **212** (1950-53): 156.3 cid/2,562 cc (2.67 x 2.31-in./68 x 58-mm), 130 bhp @ 6,000 rpm (Inter), 150-170 bhp @ 6,500 rpm (Export)
Transmission:	5-speed non-synchromesh manual
Suspension, front:	Unequal-length A-arms, transverse leaf spring
Suspension, rear:	Live axle, parallel trailing arms, parallel semi-elliptic leaf springs
Brakes:	Hydraulic, front/rear drums
Wheelbase (in.):	**166 MM** Barchetta, **195** Sport 86.6 **166 MM** berlinetta, **212** Export 88.6 **166** Sport 95.3 Inter 98.5-103.1
Weight (lbs):	**166** approx. 2,000 **212** approx. 2,100
Top speed (mph):	**166** 99-140 **195** 110 **212** 120
Production:	**166** Inter (1948-53) 37 (some sources list 38) **166 MM** (1949-53) approx. 32, incl. 12 closed models **166** Sport (1947-48) 2 **195** (1950-51) 25 (some sources list 24) **212** Export (1950-53) 24-26 **212** Inter (1950-53) approx. 80

When it was introduced at Earls Court in October 1948, the Jaguar XK-120 stirred people's souls with its sleek styling.

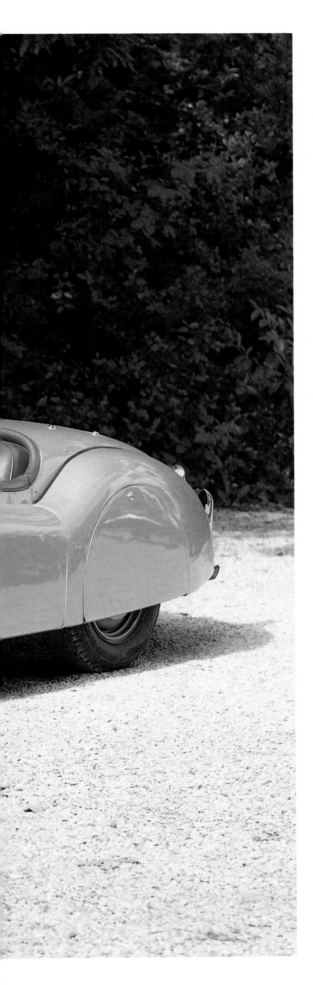

Some few miles from Kenilworth, amidst the rolling Warwickshire countryside, lies Wappenbury Hall, a baronial estate commanding 500 acres of lush farmland. When this writer visited there in the hot summer of 1976, a 90-degree heat wave, almost unknown in England, was at its peak. The grounds were parched, the aphids swarming, and the Lord of the Manor concerned. "We're spraying the fields with an airplane this morning," he said. "If that doesn't work we'll have to plow everything under."

It was hard to believe that this vigorous, white-haired gentleman farmer had ever spent time beyond his rural acreage. There was youth in his step and sparkle in his eyes that belied years of struggle in less hopeful times, now only a memory. Yet this was no farmer at all, not at least in the terms which define a life's work. He was a retiree from 50 years in the car business, 50 of the most exciting years, from 1922 to 1972. For Sir William Lyons of Jaguar made a mark in that industry akin to Schweitzer's in medicine, and Bach's in music.

It was easy to imagine Sir William still running things at Browns Lane, Coventry, because he was as up-to-date on matters Jaguar as any practicing executive. At that particular moment, the Japanese had raised their stiff emissions standards, and Jaguar was the only British car still able to meet them. Sir William knew all about it, right down to the hydrocarbon levels. Somehow, one expected him to know.

As quickly as civilities permitted, the subject was changed from new cars to old: to the early years when young Bill Lyons ran a fledgling business devoted to motorcycle sidecars and special bodies for other people's chassis. There's a long, long road awinding from the Swallow Sidecar and Coachbuilding Company to the XK-120, though the story is pretty well known. Lyons founded the firm in 1922, built custom bodies starting in 1927, and eventually introduced the SS make in 1931, the forebear to Jaguar.

Cycle-fendered and close coupled, SS cars had a rakish look but were uninspired performers. To juice them up, Lyons had help from two brilliant engineers: Harry Weslake, followed by Bill Heynes, who would be instrumental in the XK sports car project. Sir William said, "I made a deal that Harry would get so much [pay bonus] per horsepower—however much he could wring out of the 2.5-liter engine—so I was on a reasonably safe wicket! He produced a very good engine indeed, developing as I remember around 35-bhp per liter." This was the SS Jaguar 90, with 90 bhp and 90 mph. Then Bill Heynes stroked the Standard Six to 3,485 cc and created the SS Jaguar 100, the first Lyons car capable of 100 mph. Few of his cars have failed to achieve that mark since.

171

The XK-120 made Jaguar's reputation in the United Sates. Here was a car that could do 120 mph right off the showroom floor, and it sold for less than $4,000! Everybody who was anybody owned one.

The great XK engine of 1948 was conceived during the Blitz, as Lyons and Heynes watched the *Luftwaffe* flatten Coventry from the roof of their factory. If they survived this war, Heynes said, they must build a clean-slate engine based on all their experience—strictly their own design. After the war, Lyons bought an engine plant from Standard, acquiring the tooling and personnel. The result—and this is on the late Sir William's personal authority—was his own all-time favorite Jaguar, the XK-120.

Think back on all the tales that you remember of the Jaguar XK-120. It debuted at Earls Court in October 1948, the ultimate, perfect sports car. It was

While Jaguar was pushing its traditional-looking Mark V sedan as "The finest car of its class in the world," it was the sleek XK-120 roadster that everyone wanted. Eventually a coupe and a convertible would join the lineup.

staggeringly beautiful. It was powered by a gem of an engine, the 3.4-liter XK six, with twin carbs, double overhead cams, and 160 horsepower. It was guaranteed to do 120 mph off the showroom floor. It sold in the USA for less than $4,000 and it literally made the sports car's reputation. Everybody who was anybody from Clark Gable to Dave Garroway drove one.

There was no gainsaying this car's abilities. Six months after introduction, test driver Ron Sutton recorded 132.596 mph at the Jabbeke Road in Belgium, a celebrated speed-test highway. From there the XK went on to sweep production racing victories through 1952. Even

after it was out of production it was running and winning on road courses throughout the world.

One of those who recalls the XK-120 is Stirling Moss, who buried all challengers in the 1950 Tourist Trophy, the 120's first important long-distance victory. "I remember this race terribly well because it was really raining like hell," Moss said, "and because the Jaguar was to me fairly difficult to drive; it was a very fast and large car. I think it was the big turning point in my career because I went from driving professionally...to heading up what was then the world's leading sports car racing team." Moss, incidentally, averaged 77.6 mph on the tortuous course in near-hurricane conditions: a typically impressive performance.

The heart of every great sports car is its engine, and here Heynes, Weslake, and Wally Hassan came brilliantly together. Heynes insisted on overhead cams, Weslake on hemispherical-head combustion chambers and cross-flow design, Hassan on inclined valves and duplex chain-drive camshafts. Its 83 x 100-mm bore and stroke made the engine relatively square among British powerplants. The crank was massive, made of 65-ton steel, and ran in seven main bearings. The block was a light casting of cylinders and crankcase, webbed for strength in all the right places. The induction system, with its twin SU carburetors, was designed by Weslake "to achieve maximum filling of the cylinders throughout the wide range of engine speed. [Thus] it is possible to obtain high power output without a very high compression ratio." The XK's ratio was a mere 7.0:1, so it could almost run on kerosene. It produced 195 lbs/ft torque at 2,500 rpm. Withal, it was delightful to the eye, with polished aluminum cam covers, enameled exhaust manifolds, superb surface finish. During the XK-120's tenure, Jaguar also offered a "Special Equipment" 180-bhp engine, a 210-bhp alternative called C-Type (after Jaguar's contemporary sports-racer), as well as a variety of other competition-inspired performance options.

Relative to the engine, the XK-120 chassis was unsophisticated, but immensely strong. It was made of box section steel, had wishbone and torsion-bar independent front suspension (Heynes' work, Citroën-inspired), and a carefully placed live axle with semi-elliptic springs at the rear. Steering was by recirculating ball, and brakes were 12-inch drums. The four-speed Moss

gearbox, derived from military vehicles, was an abomination, with dreadfully slow synchromesh. The only reason for it was that no other box in Britain was able to cope with 160/180 bhp.

Originally, Jaguar Cars Limited ("SS" was dropped for obvious reasons, after World War II) had also intended to build a two-liter four called the XK-100, but demand for the XK-120 outstripped all resources. The idea had been to build about 200 roadsters, using easy-to-work aluminum bodies over ash frames, as a trial balloon—and steel bodies only if they sold. But public acceptance rolled like a tidal wave. By the end of 1950, Lyons had moved to larger quarters at Browns Lane, Allesley, Coventry— Jaguar's present home. By then serious production had started, with nearly 90 percent of output going overseas. Two additional models eventually joined the roadster: a beautiful fixed-head coupe in 1951 and a drophead cabriolet with roll-up windows and better weather protection in 1953. Also in 1953 was recorded the fastest speed ever by an XK-120: 172.412 mph at Jabbeke, by Norman Dewis in a modified, stream-lined roadster.

At the end of that day in Warwick-shire, we asked Sir William about Jaguar's future. "They'll probably carry on for a bit," he winked—already knowing what was in store. Carry on they have... but the carryings on of their predecessors weren't half bad, either.

The chassis of the XK-120 wasn't terribly sophisticated, but it was strong. The car weighed about 3,000 pounds, so it could accelerate from 0-60 mph in just 10 seconds, quite outstanding for the late Forties. Some 7,631 roadsters were built altogether.

The XK-120's engine was a dual-overhead-camshaft inline six that produced 160 horse-power at 2,500 rpm, or 180 in Special Equipment tune.

Specifications	
Engine:	I-6, dohc, 210 cid/3,442 cc (83 x 100-mm bore x stroke), 7.0:1 compression ratio, 7 main bearings, 2 SU carburetors, 160 bhp (SAE) @ 5,000 rpm, 195 lbs/ft torque @ 2,500 rpm (180 bhp and 203 lbs/ft with optional Special Equipment engine)
Transmission:	4-speed, synchromesh on top 3 gears
Suspension, front:	Independent, with double wishbones, torsion bars, anti-roll bar
Suspension, rear:	Live axle on semi-elliptic leaf springs
Brakes:	4-wheel hydraulic, 12-in. drums
Wheelbase (in.):	102.0
Weight (lbs):	2,855-3,080
0-60 mpg (sec):	10.0
Top speed (mph):	120 +
Production:	Roadster 7,631 Coupe 2,678 Convertible 1,769

The Morris Minor was one of those cars whose total was more than the sum of its parts. It survived for two dozen years.

William Morris, who—like many other British entrepreneurs— entered the car business from the cycle business, saw the need for affordable private transportation only a few years after his American counterpart, Henry Ford. Built it. And sold it as the "Oxford." Morris' first car was powered by a small one-liter four. Consistency was a Morris characteristic: the Minor 1000, the last genuine Morris product, also displaced about one liter, albeit with rather more horsepower.

Morris remained an independent purveyor of popular-priced cars through 1951, when it merged with Austin—largely at the behest of the British government—to form British Motor Corporation (BMC). Unfortunately, there was no neat meshing of resources, and for years later duplicate departments remained, fiddling around and quarreling. With the firm also remained parallel lines of competing Austin and Morris cars. Here was the future undoing of what later became British Leyland, and with it the British car industry as a whole.

Immediately after the merger, BMC management scrapped the entire Morris engine development program in favor of Austin engines. Yet post-merger Morrises retained their SU carburetors and electric fuel pumps, whereas Austins stayed with Zeniths and mechanical pumps. These are examples of exactly the wrong kind of rationalization: BMC would have been better off standardizing supplier-built components while retaining individual engines.

The Morris Minor, which had been in production for five years before the BMC merger, was less affected by corporate changes than most other models in the line because it was so distinctive—right from the start. Through 1948, Morris had produced two models, both of them holdover prewar designs, so the Minor was not only new when it appeared at Earls Court that year, but a breath of fresh air. Dubbed the Series MM, it was Morris' first genuine postwar product. It combined an American-style envelope body with state-of-the-art engineering by Alec Issigonis and Jack Daniels: unit body/chassis, torsion-bar independent front suspension, hypoid rear axle, and rack-and-pinion steering.

The MM Minor rode a wheelbase of only 86 inches, eight inches shorter than the prewar-based Morris Eight (and the Volkswagen Beetle). Yet the MM was four inches longer, and equally spacious on the inside. It was greeted with high acclaim; Britain's *The Motor* magazine, for example, affirmed with characteristic phlegm that it was "a very good 8-hp car indeed."

That "8-hp" referred to the old Royal Auto Club (RAC) rating for taxable horsepower (dropped in 1949), and also to the only part of the car that wasn't new. The Minor's sidevalve engine (918.6 cc), taken directly from the predecessor Morris Eight, produced 27.5 net bhp at 4,400 rpm. This was not a lot: 0-50 mph took no less than 24 seconds

Compare this 1953 Morris Minor with the 1949 model on the preceding page. The headlights were moved from the grille to the upper part of the front fenders because they had been mounted too low to satisfy the law in some export markets.

After 1959 the Morris Minor was the only "true" Morris left, the others by this time being badge-engineered Austin products. The last Minor left the factory in October 1970. It had been the first British to sell more than a million copies.

of hard shifting/flogging. Still, the Minor returned 40 miles to the Imperial gallon (30 mpg U.S.)—and in petrol-short postwar Britain this was a welcome compromise between economy and performance.

Unfortunately, Issigonis and Daniels had been forced by budget constraints to abandon a new flat-four engine they had hoped to provide for the car. Had the money been granted them, the Minor would have been unbeatable. As the late Michael Sedgwick wrote, "the aged 8-hp unit looked out of place in these sophisticated surroundings. Even a good Fiat Topolino could beat a Minor to 30 mph. Handling, however, set new standards, and the tuners were soon at work on the Minor. Modifications ranged from special cylinder heads to heart transplants, among these latter the Austin A40 and overhead-camshaft Coventry-Climax units. The Minor could take it."

The new body, far more streamlined than its predecessors, allowed higher gearing: 4.55:1—high where Morrises were concerned. Finally, post-merger in 1952, a more appropriate engine

arrived in the form of an overhead-valve 803-cc four, part of the Austin rationalization policy, on what Morris called its Series II. This was in fact the engine of the Austin A30. While it was not the distinctive engine that could—and should—have been applied in the first place, it was a modern step in the

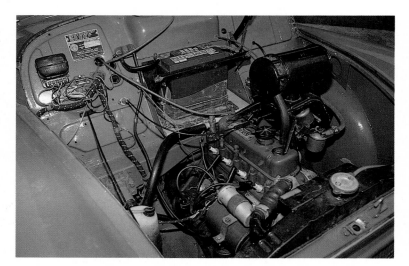

Various engines powered the Morris Minor over its long lifetime, but in 1953 it was an overhead-valve inline four of 803 cubic centimeters. It developed a modest 28 horsepower. Later editions would have up to 48-bhp.

right direction. It lasted through 1956, by which time BMC had fielded a new Minor 1000 with the now-familiar 949-cc, 37-bhp powerplant. This finally gave it a genuine 70-mph capability for the first time. Bored and stroked to 1.1 liters in 1963, this engine lasted through the final Minors.

The initial MM Minor was offered as a two-door sedan or drophead tourer only. A four-door sedan was added in 1951, a station wagon called Traveller in 1954. The handsome wood-trimmed wagons, along with the convertibles, long ago became "cult" cars in Britain, and are popular in the United States as well. In both countries, unconscionable sums are spent on their restoration, and the best of those set very high standards indeed.

After the Pinin Farina-designed Oxfords brought massive body sharing to Morris in 1959, the Minor was the only distinctive Morris product left in the line. From 1960 on, there was a Morris-badged counterpart to numerous Austins, including the Mini and Mini-Cooper, 1100/1300, 1800, 2200, and Marina. The Minor outlived all but the last two of these pretenders.

The 250,000th Minor was delivered in the spring of 1954, the 500,000th in June 1957, the millionth in January 1961. A special run of distinctive lavender cars, badged "Minor 1,000,000" were built to celebrate the latter occasion. Like the VW Beetle and Citroën 2CV, Minors of the late Sixties had become nostalgia pieces and buyers simply kept demanding them. The last one left the factory in October 1970, car number 1,582,302.

In 1990, a retiring Jaguar executive whose career had been spent in U.S. export sales of most BMC and British-Leyland makes opined that the Morris Minor could have licked Volkswagen in the United States "if only we had kept the price down." One wonders how far down he thinks it ought to have been kept. In 1962, which was the last year Minors were imported, the two-door sedan listed for $1,295, against $1,595 for the two-door VW Beetle. Meanwhile, the neat little Minor Estate wagon cost only $1,669, against $2,275 for the much larger VW Kombi.

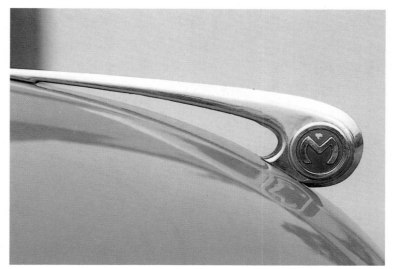

Considering that the Morris Minor rode a short 86-inch wheelbase, it was quite roomy inside. The dashboard, as on so many economy cars, was quite spartan. A stylized "M" was engraved into the sides of the hood ornament.

The Minor failed in the United States not because of its price, but because of the same afflictions that were so common to so many other British cars: poor liaison between importer and factory; second-rate dealerships, which were not required to stock adequate parts or properly train mechanics; and certain qualities of the cars themselves, such as unreliable electrics. More telling, one could run a Beetle on American highways at 70 mph for months at a time because its design enabled its cruising speed and top speed to be the same. Minors couldn't take a 70-mph pounding for such a long duration; they came from a land where the first modern superhighway was only opened in 1959.

Nevertheless, the Morris Minor was a car of great character and distinction, and it will be remembered.

Specifications	
Engine:	1948-52 I-4, sidevalve, 918.6 cc, 27.5 bhp @ 4,400 rpm 1952-56 I-4, ohv, 803 cc, 28 bhp 1956-62 I-4, ohv, 949 cc, 37 bhp @ 4,800 rpm 1962-71 I-4, ohv, 1,098-cc, 48 bhp
Transmission:	4-speed manual, synchromesh in top 3 gears
Suspension, front:	Independent, with torsion bars; rack-and-pinion steering
Suspension, rear:	Solid axle, semi-elliptic leaf springs
Wheelbase (in.):	86.0
Tires:	5.00 x 14
0-50 mph (sec):	24 (918.6-cc engine)
Top speed (mph):	70 + (949-cc engine)
Production:	1,582,302

Anybody who combines the skills of a top-drawer film producer with blind enthusiasm tends to be a loose cannon on the quarterdeck of history. Francis Ford Coppola owns two Tuckers, and after a decade of planning he produced a film about his favorite car, a film which received laudatory reviews in the old car press a couple of years ago. It was certainly entertaining. It was also lousy history.

The film's theme was that Preston Tucker, ingenious inventor of a revolutionary car, was walloped by the faceless moguls of Detroit, who knew that if the Tucker succeeded they'd have to spend millions to redesign their own products. It incidentally vests Mr. Tucker with extraordinary prescience. At one point he says that if America doesn't wise up, the Germans and Japanese will one day be building our toasters, radios, and automobiles. Had he really had such clairvoyance, Tucker would have raised billions, instead of the $12 million he drummed up with his misleading claims and empty promises.

There's no doubt that oddballs fascinate, and the Tucker "48" was both odd and intriguing. Styled by Alex Tremulis, the sleek fastback four-door sedan boasted an unusual 335-cid aluminum alloy flat-six engine mounted ahead of the rear wheels; four-wheel independent suspension; aircraft-like doors cut into the roof; a central headlight that pivoted in the direction of the front wheels; a padded safety dash surmounting a carpeted "storm cellar"—or "Safety Chamber"—where Tucker said the occupants could shelter in the event of a crash. Fuel injection, automatic transmission, unprecedented power, 150-mph speeds, seat belts, and disc brakes were all promised. None showed up. Yet all but two of the 51 Tuckers built have survived, and are regularly heralded as the cars Detroit should have built to save itself from the erstwhile foreign devils. We interrupt this program with some facts. . . .

The first Tucker engine, designed by chief engineer Ben Parsons, was a huge 589-cid unit, installed only in the prototype, which was dubbed the "Tin Goose." That was enough. An ordinary electrical system couldn't turn it over—starting it required 30 to 60 volts of external power. (This episode the film got right; occasionally its producers stumbled over the truth, but then they picked themselves up and hurried on as if nothing had happened.) The 589 also lacked, according to Tucker historian Richard E. Jones, a satisfactory hydraulic valve mechanism and fuel injection—curious, since Parsons ran the Fuelcharger Corporation, which was supposed to be providing Tucker's promised injection system.

When the 589 engine became a cropper, Tucker contracted with the Jacobs Aircraft Company to furnish 25 light, horizontally opposed 361-cid sixes. Jacobs' engines were to have cost $1,500 each, which is another curiosity, since Tucker had promised a retail base price of $2,450 for the whole car. Then in February 1948, Tucker told Jacobs to stop

The Tucker "48" ran with a rear-mounted engine, so a rear fender vent was fitted to cool the helicopter-based flat six provided by Aircooled Motors.

Innovation was the name of the game with Tucker, although certain features (such as disc brakes) never did make "production." In all, only 51 cars were built, including the prototype.

The Tucker's "trunk" wasn't terribly accessible because of the very high lift-over height. Note the spare tire.

Taillights for the Tucker were mounted atop the virtually flat rear fenders, and were visible from the sides.

As can be told by the door handles, the rear doors opened "suicide" style—they were hinged at the rear.

The Tucker's dashboard featured a large speedometer that also housed the gauges. Note the aircraft-style controls mounted at the far left.

A stylish touch was that the rear bumper had three scallops on each side to accommodate the exhaust pipes. The C-pillars (below) were extremely wide.

The Tucker was a large car mounted on a 128-inch wheelbase (a half inch longer than a Chrysler New Yorker), and it weighed about 4,200 pounds (200 more than that same New Yorker). This car rides on the more modern narrow-band whitewall tires.

development because the 361 didn't fit the Tucker engine compartment—yet another curiosity for a company developing a revolutionary, world-beating new car.

Finally, Tucker opted for the 335-cid six built by Aircooled Motors, which Preston said would have 275 horsepower and deliver speeds up to 150 mph. Neither the claims nor the price proved viable: Jones determined that the average cost of the 91 engines delivered through the end of August 1948 was $1,418 each. Subtracting that from $2,450 leaves $1,032 for the rest of the car—retail. Out of which Tucker promised to wring features like the swivel third headlamp, disc brakes, seatbelts, independent rear suspension, not to mention body, chassis, and upholstery.

Tucker realized the impractical cost levels of the 335 engine in August 1948, so he assigned engineer David Doman to create a cheaper alternative, the "335U." The dreamlike quality of the Tucker episode is nowhere better illustrated than by Doman's brief: provide the same horsepower and displacement as the original, but do it for one-third the cost.

Doman tried, using a two-piece crank and cylinder block and two heads covering three cylinders each, but there was never any sign that the 335U could meet Tucker's requirements. So Tucker reverted to the original 335, ordering another 125 units at $1,500 each. Richard Jones correctly summarizes what turned out to be the only engine ever fitted to

Tucker cars: ". . . one of the most impressive automobile engines of that day or this [whose] quality and aircraft standards precluded mass production."

Similar questions arose over the rest of the drivetrain. Former GM engineer and president Ed Cole, interviewed in 1973, mentioned Tucker's first configuration of "driving the rear wheels with a pair of converters and transmitting axle torque through a converter," a system Tucker had to abandon. John R. Bond, late publisher of *Road & Track*, said, "You had all that weight out back and a pretty long wheelbase . . . the handling was catastrophic." Most of those who have driven one agree that a Tucker is perfectly safe—provided you are prepared to cope with drastic oversteer.

Writer Tom Murray has observed that "Tucker feature-packed his car because he had no former production model to worry about, but I think many [features] would have contributed to much user dissatisfaction if produced." The famous swiveling center headlamp would have been banned as a hazard to navigation, frying the eyeballs of oncoming drivers at the apex of every curve. Several states had already banned it while Tucker was promoting it—the company issued metal shields to cover it up. The cut-in doors looked exotic, but would have soaked passengers in a downpour since there were no rain gutters. The Safety Chamber compartment, however impractical, was a fallback safety angle after his sales people convinced Preston that seatbelts would

imply to the public at that time an unsafe car. (In fact that's what happened when Nash tried to offer them in 1950.) But, like the disc brakes he also vainly promised, seatbelts seemed to have been forgotten by the time Tucker framed his promotion.

The Tucker venture concluded with a Securities and Exchange Commission investigation and a trial which correctly acquitted Tucker and several colleagues of willful fraud—they were guilty only of an excess of enthusiasm—while ending any hope of production. The most accurate summation of the Tucker episode remains that of writer Michael Lamm in 1973: "Preston Tucker was a small-time promoter who'd gone big-time. He was out of his pond. He remained a stranger and perhaps even a threat to the SEC, and he didn't know anyone in government. He was careless in some of his pencilwork, perhaps in a bit of his talk, too, and when the SEC jumped on him about irregularities, those irregularities did exist."

Having done justice to history, it remains to be said that the Tucker, conceptually, was a marvelous car, bristling with ideas. Tucker's concepts of minimal wind drag, elegant lowness, lightweight alloy engine, and safety features—however undeveloped—were all worthy of study. He simply lacked the business acumen to find enough time and money to develop them properly.

One could perhaps guess that the Tucker had a rear-mounted engine because of the grille above the back bumper. For a car as modern as the Tucker, it's surprising that the rear window was so small. The center headlight was intended to swivel in tune with the steering wheel, but some state laws would have nixed that feature.

Specifications

Engine:	H-6 (horizontally opposed), ohv, 335 cid (4.50 x 3.50-in. bore x stroke), 7.0:1 compression ratio, 166 bhp, 372 lbs/ft torque
Transmission:	4-speed transaxle
Suspension, front:	Independent, with unequal-length A-arms, tubular shock absorbers
Suspension, rear:	Independent, with trailing links, tubular shock absorbers
Brakes:	4-wheel hydraulic, 11-in. drums
Wheelbase (in.):	128.0
Overall length (in.):	219.0
Height (in.):	60.0
Width (in.):	79.0
Tread, front/rear (in.):	64.0/65.0
Weight (lbs):	approx. 4,200
0-60 mpg (sec):	est. 10
Top speed (mph):	est. 120
Production:	51, including the prototype

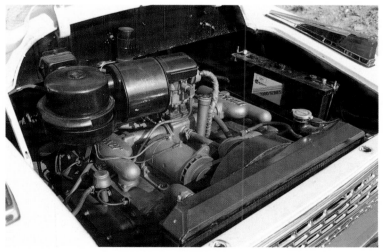

The Tucker's engine was a horizontally opposed unit that boasted 335 cid, just slightly larger than Chrysler's straight eight. On 7.0:1 compression, it developed 166 horsepower (135 for the Chrysler) and 372 lbs/ft torque.

There were only two viable candidates as *Motor Trend* prepared to announce its first "Car of the Year" award in 1949. The reason was that only Cadillac and Oldsmobile, at the time, could boast of newly engineered, state-of-the-art powerplants. While the competition carried over old prewar designs, both of these GM divisions had introduced, just that season, highly efficient short-stroke, overhead-valve V-8s, setting off what would become a trend for the entire industry. By the mid-Fifties, it would be a stampede, so influential were the new high-efficiency engines.

In many ways, the results of Cadillac's and Oldsmobile's research and development efforts bore a close resemblance to each another, though *MT*'s John Bond was quick to note that "the engines are not by any means the same. The Cadillac, with 10 percent more piston displacement, develops 18.5 percent more b.h.p. and weighs a few pounds less."

The two V-8s had, in fact, been more or less parallel developments, although Cadillac—whose research had commenced during the late 1930s—was first to undertake the project. Not unexpectedly, the work at Oldsmobile appears to have been influenced by what was going on at its sister division. Harry Barr, who was Cadillac's engine engineer during the time the new V-8 was under development, and would eventually become GM's engineering vice-president, later recalled that at the time Olds was getting under way with the development of its engine, Tony Waters, Barr's counterpart at the Oldsmobile Division, was shown the entire Cadillac design. It would be highly unrealistic to suppose that he hadn't been influenced by what he saw.

In any case, the award went to Cadillac—and deservedly so!

There were those who wondered, at the time, why Cadillac had gone to the enormous trouble and expense of developing a brand new engine. The division's monobloc L-head V-8, first introduced in 1936, was still at the height of its success. Smooth, sturdy, and powerful, it had given an excellent account of itself in military applications as well as in civilian passenger-car use.

But the truth is, the old flathead had reached the limit of its potential. To increase the compression ratio beyond 1948's 7.25:1 would have invited rough idling and detonation problems, characteristics that luxury car buyers have never accepted kindly. Years of research had clearly demonstrated that the overhead-valve configuration was the way to go.

Overhead valves were nothing new to Cadillac, by the bye. The great 12- and 16-cylinder engines of 1930-37 had used that setup. But in a sharp departure from the usual practice at Cadillac (and throughout the industry, for that matter), the new V-8 was of over-square design, having a stroke/bore ratio of 0.955:1.

The Cadillac was completely restyled for 1948. For 1949, it received a mild facelift, but the "Standard of the World" still had something up its sleeve. Two things, actually: a modern high-compression overhead-valve V-8 and a brand-new hardtop called the Coupe de Ville.

The '49 Cadillac featured a bolder-looking grille, but was otherwise little changed externally. As in the past, the gas cap was hidden underneath the left taillight. The Series Sixty-Two convertible listed at $3,497, and 8,000 were built.

In no small measure, the key to the new engine's success lay in its use of "slipper" pistons, designed by piston specialist Byron Ellis. With a half-moon section cut from either side of the lower skirt, the piston could neatly drop between the crankshaft counterweights. This made possible the use of very short, and correspondingly light, connecting rods, which in turn led to a 30-pound reduction in the weight of the crankshaft. The block, heads, and crankcase were also lighter than those used in the L-head engine, and the required cooling capacity was substantially less. Altogether, the new engine was reduced five inches in length and four inches in height. The latter would become significant as overall height was reduced during the Fifties. Further, the "wet" weight of the engine and radiator, taken together, was reduced by a full 220 pounds.

Piston travel, thanks to the short-stroke design, was cut by 20 percent. This resulted in reduced friction, which contributed to longer engine life as well as to greater fuel economy. At least 15 percent was added to Cadillac's gas mileage.

Naturally, the improved breathing resulting from the use of overhead valves led to increased power, although the engine's displacement was reduced from 346 to 331 cubic inches for 1949. The compression ratio was set at 7.50:1, an appropriate figure considering the fuels available at the time. This hardly began to tap the engine's potential, however, for Cadillac engineers boasted that with no major modifications to the engine the ratio could have been set as high as 12.0:1.

Horsepower was increased from 150 in 1948 to 160 in the 1949 engine. Top speed of the new Cadillac was about 100 miles an hour, and it could accelerate from 0-60 miles per hour in just 12 seconds, three seconds faster than the earlier model. This was phenomenal performance for a luxury car in 1949. Passing times were similarly impressive; the Cadillac would accelerate from 45 to 75 mph in only four seconds. And at the same time, the Caddy's already smooth performance was made even silkier, thanks to the use of a five-main-bearing crankshaft.

Meanwhile, Packard soldiered on, as it would until 1955, with its time-proven L-head straight eights: a 327-cid, 145-bhp job for the Super Eight; a 356-cubic-inch, 160-horsepower version for the Custom Eight. These were excellent engines, and the nine-bearing power-plant of the Custom models was especially smooth, but both it and the 145-bhp unit were becoming hopelessly dated and—like the L-head Cadillac V-8—about at the limit of their potential.

Like Cadillac, Lincoln could lay claim to a new V-8 for 1949, and it was a welcome improvement over the somewhat anemic V-12 whose place it took. But it was an old-fashioned, long-stroke flathead, developed originally as a truck engine and destined to be phased out after only three seasons.

No doubt about it—as far as engines were concerned, Cadillac was ahead of the competition by a country mile!

There was another engineering feature that was extremely popular with the public. This was the Hydra-Matic transmission, a well-proven unit first offered by Cadillac in its 1941 models. Technically a $174 option—it didn't become standard equipment on the popular Series Sixty-Two until 1950—it was fitted to something like 98 percent of all 1949 Cadillacs. At the start of the model year, Cadillac was still the only luxury car to offer a fully automatic transmission, which must have been a major plus for the sales personnel. Lincoln would follow suit at mid-season, however, having contracted with

General Motors for the purchase of Hydra-Matics, and late in the year Packard would introduce its own automatic, a torque-converter unit called Ultramatic.

And then there was the matter of styling. Cadillac's was carried over with only a new grille and a few minor trim changes to distinguish it from the 1948 model. Still, it was the freshest and best-looking design of any luxury automobile. Packard's styling, also carried over from 1948, was an adaptation of the prewar Clipper, modified with flared sides and a low, squat grille that retained the familiar Packard "ox-yoke," yet somehow lacked the elan of the earlier version. Packard had received rave reviews from some quarters, initially, for this rendering, but it is best remembered today as the "bathtub" or, even worse, the "Pregnant Elephant"—which isn't much of a compliment.

Lincolns came in two sizes for 1949, both completely new designs. The smaller of the two was barely distinguishable from the Mercury, whose bodyshell it shared. And though impressive in appearance, the larger Cosmopolitan—priced just a little higher than the Cadillac Sixty-Two—somehow lacked the grace of later Lincolns. Or of the earlier ones, for that matter. Another design from the "bathtub" school of design, it dated quickly.

Caddy's new V-8 displaced 331 cid and developed 160 horsepower at 3,800 rpm.

There were four Cadillac series, which used three distinct chassis lengths. Serving once again as the division's price leader was the Series Sixty-One, available as either a sedan or a fastback coupe. Next up was the Series Sixty-Two, essentially a dressed-up version of the Sixty-One.

In addition to the sedan and coupe styles, the Sixty-Two—by far the most popular Cadillac series—came in convertible form, and during the late spring of 1949 the Coupe de Ville, Cadillac's first "hardtop," was introduced as a member of this series. Both the ragtop and the two-door hardtop were equipped with hydraulically powered windows and seats as standard. Called by writer Walter McCall "one of the most beautiful production Cadillacs ever built," the Coupe de Ville was the first series-produced hardtop in the luxury field

(although it should be noted that the senior Buicks and Oldsmobiles got hardtops at the same time). Although production was limited by its late introduction, Cadillac's hardtop would quickly prove to be extremely popular.

The Fleetwood Sixty Special was, as it had been since 1942, a stretched, upmarket version of the Series Sixty-Two. All of these—the Sixty-One, Sixty-Two, and Fleetwood Sixty Special—carried over the styling theme that had first been introduced in 1948, including the tailfins that were said to have been inspired by the World War II P-38 fighter aircraft. The big Fleetwood Seventy-Five cars retained their basic prewar styling for this one additional year.

Cadillac was already on a roll. But with the help of the new V-8, sales far exceeded all previous records. The 1949 model year total came to 92,554 cars, up from 52,706 for 1948 and an all-time record for the division up to that time. Or to put the matter another way, Cadillac production for 1949 was more than half again as great as the combined total of the senior Lincolns and Packards.

It happened that the very last 1949 Cadillac to come down the production line—a Coupe de Ville—marked an important milestone: the one-millionth car to be built by the division. It had taken 47 years for Cadillac to reach that point; only nine years would be required for the second million to be produced. Cadillac's dominance of the luxury field was clearly established.

It was Cadillac that started the tailfin era with these modest units of 1948-49. The Sixty-Two sedan sold for $3,050.

Specifications	
Engines:	V-8, ohv, 331 cid (3.80 x 3.63-in. bore x stroke), 7.5:1 compression ratio, 5 main bearings, hydraulic valve lifters, Carter 2-bbl carburetor, 160 bhp @ 3,800 rpm
Transmission:	Hydra-Matic 4-speed automatic planetary (optional)
Suspension, front:	Independent, coil springs, tube shocks
Suspension, rear:	Live axle, leaf springs, tube shocks
Brakes:	4-wheel hydraulic drums
Wheelbase (in.):	Sixty-One, Sixty-Two 126 Sixty Special 133 Seventy-Five 136.25
Overall length (in.):	Sixty-One, Sixty-Two 214 Sixty Special, Seventy-Five 226
Tread, front/rear (in.):	59.0/63.0
Weight (lbs):	3,880-4,720, depending on series and body style
Top speed (mph):	100 (lighter models)
0-60 mph (sec):	12.0
Production:	92,554

I t was make-it-or-break-it time for Ford Motor Company when the 1949 models were introduced on June 18, 1948. The company had been creaking along losing money for years, as much as $10 million a month at one point. Henry Ford II had brought in a new management team headed by Ernest R. Breech, formerly of General Motors' Bendix Division, to straighten out the administrative tangle left by his grandfather. But he needed saleable new products—and quickly—if the company bearing his name was to survive.

A crash program was thus undertaken, with the result that the new Ford was developed in less than two years. It was a remarkable achievement, for at the outset Ford maintained virtually no engineering staff, and testing facilities were totally inadequate. By the time the task was completed, $72 million and 10 million man hours had been consumed in getting the '49 Ford into production.

There was no lack of public interest in the goings-on at Ford, so perhaps it wasn't too surprising that more than 28 million people visited Ford showrooms during the first three days following the 1949 model's debut. More than 100,000 orders were placed during the first day of the showing. Not since the Model A replaced the Model T, back in December 1927, had any new Ford created such a stir.

What the public saw represented a radical departure from all previous Fords, even though the wheelbase remained at 114 inches and the buyer could still choose between a 226-cid, 95-horsepower six-cylinder engine or the 100-bhp, 239-cubic-inch V-8. But in virtually every other respect the new Ford really *was* new.

In fact, even the hoary flathead V-8 had been substantially revamped by an engineering crew headed by vice-president Harold Youngren, a recent recruit from Oldsmobile, where he had been chief engineer for 15 years. Improvements included more effective cooling, reduced oil consumption, better breathing, and stronger bearings.

Coil springs and wishbone-type independent suspension were employed up front, with longitudinal semi-elliptics at the rear—a radical departure from the rigid front axle and archaic transverse springs that Ford had used front and rear ever since the days of the Model T. Airplane-type tubular shocks contributed to stability. Meanwhile, the old torque tube was superceded by Hotchkiss drive, a hypoid axle helped reduce overall height, and for the first time Borg-Warner's excellent overdrive became an available (and popular) option.

Other improvements included a lightweight ladder frame in lieu of the earlier X-type, which helped account for a 230-pound reduction in the new Ford's weight. Smaller-diameter brake drums helped facilitate ventilation, while braking area was increased by nearly nine percent. The engine, moved forward five inches, placed the rear seat passengers

Rumor has it that Pontiac had planned a "spinner" grille similar to the one on the '49 Ford, but since the Ford came out first, Pontiac was forced to change its design at the last moment.

The '49 Ford was a crucial car to Ford because the company had been losing money, and the new Ford would make or break it.

The '49 Ford station wagon was still a woody. Like other '49 Fords, it rode a wheelbase of 114 inches, but it cost $233 more than even the Custom ragtop: $2,119. New features included an independent front coil suspension and longitudinal leaf springs in back.

Caleal, who had previously been a member of the Raymond Loewy styling team at Studebaker, recruited two of his former associates, Robert Bourke and Holden "Bob" Koto to assist in the project. Working on their own time, reportedly in Caleal's kitchen, they developed a quarter-scale clay model that came very close to the final proposal. George Walker added a final touch, replacing Caleal's vertical taillamps with a pair of horizontal pods. And of course the "spinner" theme of the '49 Ford grille was echoed a year later—in more extreme form—in Bourke's design of the 1950 Studebaker.

The clay mock-up was completed shortly before the elder Henry Ford's death in 1947, and it is said that both old Henry and his wife, Clara, were pleased with the result. Clara, in fact, found the model so realistic that she grabbed a door handle and inadvertently broke it off!

Space utilization represented a considerable improvement over earlier Ford models. Overall height was cut by nearly three and a half inches. Width and length were both reduced slightly, yet the car appeared longer than before. Headroom remained about the same, while legroom was increased. More significantly, seats measured six inches wider than before, and luggage space was nearly doubled.

The styling can best be described as "slab-sided." The proportions were good,

ahead of the axle for a more comfortable ride. "Super balloon" tires on 15-inch wheels were supplied with the Custom models, further contributing to a smooth ride.

Preliminary plans had called for two sizes of Ford cars for the postwar market, but in the end it was feared that the larger proposal was too big and would cost too much to produce. That car became the 1949 Mercury. The smaller model, using a compact 97-inch wheelbase, was eventually assigned to Ford of France, where it became the popular Vedette (later the Simca).

New design proposals were solicited, both within and without the company, and it was independent stylist George Walker who brought in the winning proposal. On the strength of it, Walker was ultimately appointed Ford's styling director, but in point of fact it was mainly his associate, Dick Caleal, who was responsible for the design that was so enthusiastically received by Ford executives.

Ford's V-8 received some engineering improvements for 1949, but it was still rated at 100 horsepower. That was enough to give the '49 a top speed of over 90 and a 0-60-mph time of about 14 seconds, though *Popular Science* did it in 12.3.

There were only nine models in the '49 Ford lineup, four standards and five Customs. The Custom convertible was the sportiest of the lot, retailing for $1,886. Buyers snapped up 51,133 ragtops that year.

and the net effect was so attractive that the car won the Fashion Academy Award; some years later the '49 Ford was selected for *Motor Trend*'s Hall of Fame.

Prices came in about $200 higher than the corresponding 1948 models, a difference of nearly 14 percent. But the same was true of the newly restyled Chevrolets and Plymouths, so Ford remained quite competitive. The top-line Custom four-door sedan, for instance, cost $1,638 with the V-8, or $1,559 with the six-cylinder engine. By way of comparison, the Chevrolet Styleline and Fleetline DeLuxe sedans sold for $1,539, while the Plymouth Special Deluxe listed at $1,629.

Nine models were offered in two trim levels, standard and Custom. The former series, upholstered in very plain fabrics and characterized by a minimum of brightwork, came in four body styles: two- and four-door sedans, and club and business coupes.

The upscale Custom series, which cost an extra $92 model for model, were far more attractively trimmed both inside and out. Not surprisingly, they outsold the plain-Jane cars by a margin of better than four-to-one. In fact, the Custom two-door sedan outsold any two other Ford models put together! In addition to the two- and four-door sedans and the club coupe, the Custom line included a convertible and a wood-trimmed two-door station wagon. The business coupe, however, was exclusive to the standard series. Most '49 Fords were fitted with the popular V-8 engine, although the flathead six was available at a savings of $79.

Ever since the introduction of the company's first V-8, back in 1932, high performance had been a Ford characteristic. The '49 model carried on that tradition. It's believed that at 100 horsepower the newly revised V-8 was underrated, for the car would easily exceed 90 miles an hour. And when fitted with the optional overdrive it would cruise comfortably, hour after hour, at 75 mph. According to *Popular Science* magazine, 0-60 took about 12.3 seconds, a phenomenal—and probably somewhat optimistic—figure for 1949.

But for any company, success or failure is found on the bottom line, and that is where any lingering doubts about the future of the Ford Motor Company were laid to rest. Output for the calendar year came to 841,170 cars, an increase of 53 percent over 1948. The extended model year, thanks to the early introduction date, allowed for the production of 1,118,762 cars. But best of all, after many years of hemorrhaging red ink, Ford Motor Company was making money once again. Profits for the year totalled $177 million—with even better times yet to come.

Specifications	
Engine:	V-8 L-head, 239 cid (3.19 x 3.75-in. bore x stroke), 6.8:1 compression ratio, 3 main bearings, Holley 2-bbl carburetor, 100 bhp @ 3,600 rpm **Six** L-head, 226 cid (3.30 x 4.40-in.), 6.8:1 c.r., 4 main bearings, Holley 1-bbl carburetor, 95 bhp @ 3,300 rpm
Transmission:	3-speed selective, column-mounted lever; overdrive optional; semi-centrifugal clutch
Suspension, front:	Independent, coil springs, tubular shocks
Suspension, rear:	Rigid axle, semi-elliptic springs, tube shocks
Brakes:	4-wheel hydraulic drums
Wheelbase (in.):	114.0
Overall length (in.):	196.8 (208.0 wagon)
Overall width (in.):	72.8
Weight (lbs):	2,871-3,563, depending on body style, engine
Top speed (mph):	90 + (V-8)
0-60 mph (sec):	12.3
Production:	841,170 (calendar year); 1,118,762 (model year)

For a number of years, Oldsmobile had been recognized as the pioneer among the five General Motors automaking divisions. Some even called it the corporation's "experimental" branch. For example, in 1937 Olds had offered, as an $80 option on its eight-cylinder models, the Safety Automatic Transmission—so called because it enabled the driver to keep his hands on the wheel instead of having to shift gears. This somewhat cumbersome unit could best be described as a semi-automatic—rather than a fully automatic—gearbox. No matter, it was a major step toward "shiftless" driving, and although it was built by the Buick Division, Oldsmobile was responsible for its development. By 1938, advanced in price to $100, the Automatic Safety transmission's availability was expanded to the division's six-cylinder cars.

Then Hydra-Matic was introduced, the first fully automatic transmission to be offered by an American automaker, and certainly one of the most important innovations ever to come along. Jointly developed by the Olds and GM engineering staffs, it was first offered on the 1940 Oldsmobiles. Not for a full year would it be available in any other make, at which point it was adopted by Cadillac. Hydra-Matic was a sturdy, efficient unit whose design provided the basis for the automatic transmissions in popular use today. And remarkably, although it was more complex than the Automatic Safety transmission, it was priced at just $57 at introduction time.

By the end of World War II, it was apparent that the time had come for a new engine. Cadillac had been working on a modern V-8 since 1936, and under the leadership of engineer Gilbert Burrell, Oldsmobile undertook in 1946 to play catch-up. It was quickly determined that Oldsmobile's new engine must be of oversquare design because the large bore permitted the use of larger valves, with the added benefit that the short stroke helped to reduce friction. This led to the conclusion that to continue with the eight-in-line configuration that Olds had used since 1932 would be out of the question; the engine block of a big-bore straight eight would be unacceptably heavy as well as excessively long.

So it was to be a V-8. In recent times, Oldsmobiles had been powered exclusively by inline L-head sixes and eights. But Olds was no stranger to the V-type layout, having built L-head V-8's from 1916-23. Then in 1929-30 there had been the Viking, a short-lived companion car designed and built by Oldsmobile and powered by a horizontal-valve V-8. However, in both of these instances the numbers were limited, and the experience was of little value in the development of a modern powerplant.

Burrell and his staff knew from experimental work conducted at Cadillac that, in terms of compression ratio, the practical limit of the L-head engine was about 8.0:1. Based on research conducted by

Oldsmobile's '49 lineup of 88s comprised 10 models, among them the $2,559 convertible coupe. A total of 5,434 were built for the model year.

Styling of the '49 small Oldsmobiles was all-new, although the grille carried over the theme of the 1946-48 models, but with only half the number of grille bars. Scoops beneath the headlights were a new styling theme.

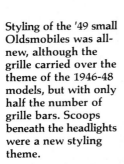

The 88's dash featured a fan-type speedometer and a high-mounted clock in the center. Both the 88 and 98 series came with Hydra-Matic standard.

Oldsmobile's new overhead-valve V-8 developed 135 horses, but since the 98 outweighed the 88 by about 350 pounds, the 88 was the faster of the two.

Charles F. Kettering, GM's legendary "Boss Ket," it was anticipated that within a few years very high octane fuels would become readily available, so that ratios as high as 12.5:1 would be feasible. Accordingly, it was determined that an overhead-valve layout would be required.

Like the new Cadillac engine, Oldsmobile's "Rocket" V-8 featured a rigid crankshaft cradled in five main bearings. The compression ratio was a comparatively modest 7.25:1. Eventually that figure would go as high as 10.25:1, as high as available fuels would permit; the hoped-for goal of 12.5:1 was never achieved.

"Slipper" pistons nestled neatly between the crankshaft throws, and hydraulic valve lifters were employed. Displacement was 303.7 cubic inches, while the stroke/bore ratio was .917:1. In addition, a new side-draft carburetor was designed to minimize vapor lock. Horsepower was rated at 135, and the engine developed 263 pounds/feet torque. By way of comparison, the

stroke/bore ratio of the old flathead eight had been 1.19:1. It displaced 257.1 cubic inches, from which it developed 110 bhp and 210 lbs/ft torque.

For nearly a decade, Oldsmobile had marketed three series of cars using three different body shells. The Series 60 shared the GM A-body with Chevrolet, while the B-body was employed for the Series 70 as well as—among others—the Buick Special. Either series was available with a choice of six- or eight-cylinder power. The Series 90, meanwhile, used GM's C-body, basically the same unit assigned to the Buick Super and Roadmaster and the Series Sixty-Two Cadillac. With the exception of the 1941 model year, when a six-cylinder version was offered (but found few takers), this senior Oldsmobile was powered exclusively by the straight-eight engine.

Changes were in the wind as 1949 approached, however. The original intent was that only two basic series would be built. The Series 70, to be offered in a choice of notchback or fastback body styles, would use the old flathead six. Called the "Big Six," it was to be bored and stroked to 257.1 cubic inches— almost exactly the displacement of the former straight eight. The V-8 engine was to be exclusive to the biggest Oldsmobile, the luxurious Series 98.

But then Sherrod E. Skinner, Oldsmobile's shrewd general manager, came up with the idea of mating the new V-8 to the smaller A-body series, resulting in a weight savings of some 350 pounds. Reportedly, there was some resistance on the part of GM's high command, but in the end, Skinner's proposal was accepted. Thus in February 1949—a couple of months following the introduction of the 76 and 98 models—the sensational Olds "Rocket 88" appeared. It shared the 119.5-inch wheelbase of the six-cylinder car, but model-for-model it was about 275 pounds heavier. It was also $395 more costly, but the price included the newly revised "Whirlaway" Hydra-Matic transmission, a $185 option on the Series 76. Despite its late introduction, the Rocket 88 proved to be Oldsmobile's most popular series during the 1949 model year—and that was only the beginning, for during 1950 nearly 65 percent of all new Oldsmobiles were Rocket 88's.

This hot little number had a power-to-weight ratio that was almost without parallel in those times: as little as 26.3 pounds per horsepower, compared, for instance, to a minimum of 29.1 for the Ford V-8. Whether or not it had been Sherrod Skinner's deliberate intent to create a new stock car champion may be open to question because Olds took no part—at least officially—in the racing game. Perhaps the men at Lansing preferred to let the car's performance speak for itself. But it wasn't long before the high-stepping Rocket 88s, under private sponsorship, were turning up in contests all over the country.

In those days, "stock car" racing meant exactly that because the cars one saw on the tracks were virtually identical to those on the dealer's showroom floor. And as Beverly Rae Kimes and Dick Langworth have noted in their excellent Oldsmobile history, "more than one driver merely removed his road wheels and license plates and stuck a bit of

The '49 Olds 88 shared its bodyshell with Chevy and Pontiac, but it rode a 119.5-inch wheelbase (115 for Chevy) and boasted unique Olds styling touches.

tape over the headlamps before taking to the track to keep his date with his Rocket Eight."

The box score for 1949 was that out of nine NASCAR (National Association for Stock Car Automobile Racing) races entered, the Olds 88 won six. There were even more wins to follow during the 1950 and '51 NASCAR seasons. And in the 1950 *Carrera Panamericana*— the 2,178-mile road race running the length of Mexico over all sorts of roads— an Oldsmobile took top honors out of a field of 132 cars, which included such estimable marques as Lincoln, Cadillac, Delahaye, and Alfa Romeo.

Six basic body styles were offered, four of them available in either standard or DeLuxe trim. These were the fastback four-door Town Sedan and two-door Club Sedan, and the bustleback four-door sedan and club coupe. The convertible was offered only in DeLuxe form, while the station wagon was a standard model, available at first with either an all-steel or partial wooden body.

Prices, ranging from $2,025 to $3,120, were roughly parallel to those of the Chrysler Royal. DeLuxe models, priced $125 higher than the standard cars, were embellished with such refinements as two-tone upholstery, foam rubber seat cushions, deluxe floor mats front and rear, deluxe instrument cluster, clock, glove box light, special external mold-

ings, deluxe steering wheel, wheel trim rings, and turn signals.

In later years, the Olds 88 moved away from its original concept as a relatively light, high-performance machine. By 1957, it would be six inches longer and more than 500 pounds heavier than the 1949 edition, and its engine—bored and stroked to 371 cubic inches—would be more than twice as powerful as the original. Yet it is that first Rocket 88 that ranks as one of the most significant automobiles of the postwar era.

Specifications	
Engine:	V-8, ohv, 303.7 cid (3.75 x 3.4375-in. bore x stroke), 7.25:1 compression ratio, 5 main bearings, Rochester GM dual downdraft carburetor, 135 bhp @ 3,600 rpm, 263 lbs/ft torque @ 1,800 rpm
Transmission:	Hydra-Matic 4-speed automatic planetary
Suspension, front:	Unequal A-arms, coil springs, anti-roll bar, double-acting lever shocks
Suspension, rear:	Rigid axle, coil springs, control arms, anti-roll bar, lever shocks
Brakes:	4-wheel hydraulic drums
Wheelbase (in.):	119.5
Overall length (in.):	202.0
Tread, front/rear (in.):	57.0/59.0
Weight (lbs):	3,550-3,945, depending on body style
Top speed (mph):	92
0-60 mph (sec):	12.2
Production:	88 99,276 total Oldsmobile 287,710

Ferdinand Porsche's most important invention, the VW Beetle has racked up a number of impressive accomplishments: the longest-running and best selling single model in the history of the automobile (about 21 million through 1990); a transformation in the automotive tastes of an entire nation; a reincarnation for a shattered German car industry; a revolution in business methods among American car dealers; and car advertising that used honest photographs rather than exaggerated drawings. We haven't by any means exhausted the VW's credits, but these will do for a start.

An irony of history is that Volkswagen is one of two things—the *autobahn* is the other—for which Germans can thank Adolf Hitler. The dictator who plunged Germany into the greatest catastrophe of its history happened to be a car nut. He attended most all the Berlin motor shows, where he proclaimed that every German needed a car. And shortly after he had come to power, Hitler selected Ferdinand Porsche to design it: a people's car, a Volkswagen. Porsche got the nod by the process of elimination, according to auto historian Erik Eckermann: When Hitler's minions asked a Berlin engineering meeting to cite three persons who could develop a *volkswagen*, somebody named Joseph Ganz, Edmund Rumpler, and Porsche: "There followed an icy silence, because Ganz was a Jew, and so was Rumpler. That left Porsche."

Himself totally apolitical, Porsche simply wanted to design automobiles. He had been in business, heading his own engineering firm, for three years when Hitler called him to Berlin in late 1933. The brief was simple: a small car that would deliver good fuel economy yet hold a family of four or five, capable of cruising at 100 kph (62.5 mph), air-cooled because of the lack of service facilities in Germany, and priced below 1,000 *reichsmarks*, or $250 at the current exchange. (At the same meeting Hitler gave Porsche another assignment: to develop a winning Grand Prix car. The result was the great rear-engined Auto Unions which vied with Mercedes for GP championships in the later Thirties.)

Porsche had already been working on a similar theme with NSU, the German motorcycle firm, and had evolved a prototype called Type 32, with a rear-mounted air-cooled flat four, an alloy-cased transaxle, fully independent torsion-bar suspension, and a body not now unfamiliar. The Hitler commission spurred this process, and by 1934 several running prototypes had been developed. Then NSU dropped out of the picture after it agreed to manufacture cars under license from Fiat—and Porsche was further demoralized when Hitler rejected his plans because his projected price was 50 percent too high. Eventually, the Volkswagen project was assigned to the RdA (Society of German Automakers), but Porsche was retained as chief engineer.

Somehow, Volkswagen arose from the rubble of World War II. The heart of this "people's car" was its understressed, air-cooled, 1.1-liter flat-four. Made of alloy, it was extremely light, and the amazing thing about the 25-bhp VW was that its cruising speed—about 65 mph—was also its top speed.

The shape of the VW Beetle is familiar, but this 1946 model has two Euro-spec features rarely seen in the U.S.: pop-up turn signals and a speedometer calibrated in kilometers per hour. VW didn't begin importing Beetles to the U.S. until 1949.

Compared to the '46 Beetle seen on the preceding page, this '47 model sports chrome bumpers and hubcaps. It has the split rear window—much prized by collectors—which would persist for a few more years. The rear-mounted engine got a new choke valve with a swing handle, while the "trunk" continued to house the spare tire and gas tank.

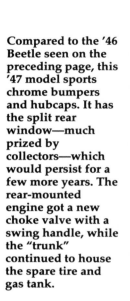

By 1935, Hitler was spouting enthusiastic promises that a car of the people would soon be available, much to the ire of the RdA and Porsche, who thought it would take years to produce anything at all. Many prototypes were indeed alive by late 1936, mainly because Porsche and his staff just kept plugging on. Porsche was convinced he could do anything, including designing a car that would sell for $250.

A year later, Hitler concluded that producing the VW would require a state-run, independent company—for which he handily confiscated some appropriate property with good transportation access in southern Saxony. Thus was founded the factory at Wolfsburg, a planned community of 150,000, the kernel from which a mighty Volkswagen would grow after the war.

Porsche's design was locked up in 1938 and a small number of hand-built cars were built, mostly for Nazi VIPs. A barrage of propaganda promised all Germans a copy of the new car, labeled "KdF" for *Kraft durch Freude* (Strength Through Joy)—the slogan of the *Deutsche Arbeitsfront*, or Nazi labor organization. This nameplate never took hold, however, and the KdF continued to be referred to by all and sundry as the

Over the next five years, the outlook changed dramatically. So did the car. Though it didn't look much different from Porsche's prototypes, the Volkswagen received endless improvements. Among the more important were hydraulic brakes (1950), synchromesh on upper gears (1952), one-piece rear window (1953), key-starting (1954), directional lights instead of semaphores (1955), bumper guards and twin tail pipes (1956), tubeless tires (1957), steering damper and contoured seatbacks (1960), full synchromesh (1961), gas gauge instead of reserve fuel tap (1962), cranked steel sunroof instead of fabric (1964), 1,300-cc 50-bhp engine (1966), 1,500-cc 53-bhp engine and back-up lights (1967), external gas filler and automatic stick shift (1968), true independent suspension instead of swing axles (1969), VW Diagnosis service program (1970), Super Beetle with coil spring front suspension and a 1,600-cc 60-bhp engine (1971), and inertia-reel seatbelts (1972).

In 1972, the Beetle broke the Model T Ford's record as the highest-production single model in history, but its days were numbered, or so it seemed, at least. VW was now preparing more modern formulas involving front-wheel drive and water-cooled engines. By 1975, the Rabbit and Scirocco had arrived, and by 1977 the convertible (specially built since 1953 by Karmann of Osnabruck) was the only Beetle still sold in the United States. Coupes continued in production in such places as Nigeria, Brazil, and Peru into the late 1980s. And the Beetle is still being produced in Mexico, where amazingly it was that country's most popular car in 1990 with nearly 85,000 units sold—and also Mexico's least expensive car at just over $5,000.

Why was such an ancient formula, dating back to 1933, so successful for so long? VWs were great fun to drive, beautifully built, incredibly economical by American standards, and backed by the most formidable sales and service organization established up to that time by any import. They also had the cachet of an inverse status symbol—and a unique character which will continue to render them popular nostalgia pieces.

Specifications[1]	
Engine:	Rear-mounted 4-cylinder, horizontally opposed, ohv, air-cooled, 91.1 cid/1,500 cc (3.27 x 2.72-in bore x stroke), 7.5:1 compression ratio, 53 bhp @ 4,200 rpm, 78 lbs/ft torque @ 2,600 rpm
Transmission:	5-speed synchromesh
Suspension:	Torsion bars, fully independent
Brakes:	4-wheel hydraulic
Wheelbase (in.):	94.5
Overall length (in.):	158.6
Weight (lbs):	1,808
0-60 mph (sec):	23.0
Top speed (mph):	78
Production:	approx. 21 million worldwide through 1990

[1]1969 model, U.S. spec

A feature of the Super Beetle was air vents behind the rear side windows. The '74 Super Beetle (*above*) carried a 12-month/20,000-mile warranty, while the "VW Owner's Security Blanket with Computer Analysis" plan included 24-month/24,000-mile coverage on internal engine and transmission parts, "Our Fault" transportation, a "rent-A-Bug" plan, and quick, while-you-wait service for small jobs.

The dashboard of the '51 Nash Rambler was relatively plain, but there was just enough chrome trim to avoid a cheap, stripped-down look.

Though George Mason had gone back to the early part of the century in naming the new Rambler, the cars overall design bore a distinct Nash look.

One could argue whether the Rambler Custom Landau Convertible was a "true" ragtop because of the "Bridge-beam" siderails above the doors.

Introduced on April 14, 1950, the pert little Nash Rambler rode a compact 100-inch wheelbase. It was priced at $1,808, but the virtually identical 1951 model seen here listed at $1,993. Weight came in at 2,430 pounds, 950 pounds less than the '51 Chevy convertible.

On the face of it, one might have thought there wasn't a cloud on the horizon for Nash-Kelvinator back in 1949. The company's appliance business was booming, and Nash automobiles—characterized by the new, designed-in-a-wind tunnel "Airflyte" styling—were selling in greater numbers than ever before. Production for the year would come to 142,592 units, topping Nash's previous all-time record, which had been set way back in 1928.

But George Mason, Nash's far-sighted president, understood all too well that there were difficult times ahead for the nation's independent automakers. Three years earlier he had attempted to persuade Hudson, Packard, and Studebaker that the time had come for the four leading independents to join forces to form a GM-style combine—and do it without waiting for trouble to descend upon them. In combination, the four companies held nearly 18 percent of the market at that time. All four were solvent, and although Hudson and Studebaker were somewhat shaky, both Packard and Nash boasted excellent cash positions. To fail to take prompt action, Mason feared, would ultimately mean being pushed to the wall by the superior resources of the "Big Three": General Motors, Ford, and Chrysler.

The taillights on the Rambler were similar in shape to those on the big Nash Statesman and Ambassador, which helped to maintain a "family" identity. The gas filler cap didn't have to be removed very often because the Rambler got up to 30 miles per gallon.

Alas, Mason's proposal fell on deaf ears. After nearly four years in which no new automobiles had been manufactured, demand was at a record high. Every automobile manufacturer could sell as many cars as it could build, and executives of the other independent companies were smugly confident that their firms would continue to prosper. George Mason, however, saw a different scenario. He sensed the futility of a small company trying to compete head-on with the giants of the industry, once competition was fully restored. But his was the proverbial voice crying in the wilderness.

If Nash had to go it alone, Mason concluded, the best bet was for his company to appeal to a specialized market, one that was essentially being ignored by the competition. So George Mason began to think small. Now a small automobile really made a lot of sense in the light of current driving conditions, for studies had demonstrated that the typical American driver traveled mostly within a radius of 50 miles from home. And a big road locomotive just wasn't suitable for that kind of duty.

But there was a problem. What the public *needed* wasn't necessarily what it *wanted*. Several attempts had been made, over the years, to interest American motorists in small cars. But in the American lexicography, *small* was equated, more often than not, with *cheap*. And nobody wanted the neighbors to think he was driving a small car because he couldn't afford a big one.

George Mason's solution to this marketing dilemma was a brilliant one. His new small car would be marketed, at least at first, in

Two-toning was the industry rage in 1955, so in mid-year the Rambler got some fancy two-toning of its own. The Custom Cross Country wagon sported a unique roofline; it was priced at $2,098. Note that this Rambler wears a Hudson badge in the center of the grille.

Powering the '55 Rambler was an inline L-head six. Displacing just 195.6 cid, it developed 90 bhp, enough to give the Rambler lively performance.

Pinin Farina had been involved with the design of the big 1952 Nash; since the '55 Rambler was styled along similar lines, it got Farina badging.

the most prestigious body styles, and it would come with deluxe equipment throughout—in other words, all "dressed up." It would not be intended for the penny-pinching economy buyer. Rather, its appeal would be to people who could afford whatever sort of motor car they might choose. It would be driven by professional people, by executives, and their wives. It would be seen at country clubs; it would share garage space with the Lincolns and the Cadillacs of Beverly Hills and Grosse Pointe.

The result of this strategy was America's first really successful compact car, the Nash Rambler. The name recalled the company's pioneer days, for in the early years of the century the Thomas B. Jeffery Company, predecessor to Nash Motors, had built one of the most popular cars in the country, an automobile known as the Rambler.

Mason produced this second-generation Rambler on a wheelbase of just 100 inches (compared to Chevy's 115 inches), and borrowed the 82-horsepower, 176.2-cubic-inch flathead six that had powered the Nash 600 of 1941-49.

And when the Nash Rambler was first introduced, officially on April 14, 1950, it bowed as a smart little Custom Landau Convertible. Dressed to the teeth, it came complete with a radio, heater, clock, directional signals, white-sidewall tires, chrome wheel covers, and even a power top, all as standard equipment. There was absolutely nothing austere about it. Nor was it particularly cheap—plenty of full-sized cars could be bought for less money.

The Rambler ragtop's price, in fact, came in at $1,808, just $10 less than that of the 1951 Chevrolet convertible. Which may not sound like much of a bargain, unless one takes into account all the goodies—nearly $300 worth—that came standard with the Rambler, but cost extra on the Chevy.

Two months after the convertible's debut the Rambler line was expanded to include an all-steel two-door station wagon. Also priced at $1,808, it proved so popular that by 1951 more than one-fifth of all new U.S.-built station wagons wore Rambler nameplates.

The third body style, a smartly styled

hardtop coupe called—appropriately—the Custom Country Club, debuted in June 1951. Befitting its name, it was a deluxe car all the way, and at $1,968 it cost $54 more than the Chevy Bel Air.

Not until 1953, by which time the Rambler had firmly established itself as an automobile that almost anyone would be happy to own, did Mason allow the Rambler to be "undressed" with an inexpensive, bare-bones two-door sedan. Mason's hunch proved correct, for when Kaiser brought out the compact Henry J in 1951 (also on a 100-inch wheelbase), it was undressed. Offered only as a two-door coupe, base models didn't even have a trunk or glovebox lid—not even sun visors. It died in early 1954.

Like the senior Nashes, the Ramblers featured all-steel unitized construction. This posed a challenge when it came to designing the convertible, but Nash's solution was a clever one. "Bridge-beam" siderails were retained above the doors, thus lending structural rigidity while at the same time simplifying the operation of the top. The latter's mechanism was both simple and effective, raising and lowering the canvas by means of cables, driven by an electrically-powered windlass. And best of all, the unit was virtually rattle-free.

The proposal to build a small car got a poor reception from most of the members of George Mason's staff. Sales of the big Nash Ambassador and Statesman models were continuing at a brisk pace during 1950, and to some the Rambler appeared to be a high-risk venture. George Romney—then special assistant to George Mason and later president of Nash's successor company, American Motors—tells of being approached by one company official who pleaded, "Can't you get Mason to kill this car? It'll ruin us!"

But of course it didn't. Instead, it literally saved the company. By 1951, the little car was accounting for more than 35 percent of Nash's total volume, and its popularity was continuing to grow. In addition to its attractive appearance and convenient size, the Rambler quickly became noted for its economy of operation. With the optional overdrive engaged, 30 miles to the gallon

Rambler four-door models, including the Cross Country wagon, rode a longer 108-inch wheelbase. The roof rack was standard equipment on this model.

was not at all uncommon. A major advantage here, in addition to its fuel-stingy engine, was the Rambler's weight-saving "unitized" construction.

Furthermore, the little car was surprisingly comfortable because the suspension was soft without being mushy. Further, available space was utilized to maximum advantage. Twenty-two inches shorter over-all than the Chevrolet, the Rambler lacked only half an inch of the Chevy's width, and its front legroom was only a quarter of an inch shorter.

And while the Rambler was never intended as a high-performance car, its acceleration was pleasantly brisk. Its power-to-weight ratio, in fact, was more than a match for the competition. Comparing the 1950 Rambler Convertible Landau with the other low-priced ragtops, here's how it stacked up:

	bhp	weight	lbs/bhp
Nash Rambler	82	2,430	29.63
Chevrolet	90	3,380	37.56
Ford V-8	100	3,263	32.63
Plymouth	97	3,295	33.97
Stude. Champion	85	2,900	34.12

In 1954, Nash-Kelvinator merged with the Hudson Motor Car Company to form American Motors Corporation. Then in the spring of 1957, the aging full-sized Nashes and Hudsons were

The door windows of the '55 Rambler were neatly framed. Unlike the big Nashes, the Rambler didn't adopt a wraparound windshield for 1955.

dropped from the lineup, so the AMC compact no longer used the Nash (or Hudson) name—it became simply Rambler. And by 1960—standing alone now, but offered on three distinct wheelbases—the Rambler had become America's third most popular car, exceeded in the sales race only by Chevrolet and Ford.

For more than 30 years now, we have seen a proliferation of small American cars. But it was the 1950 Nash Rambler that pointed the way, opening up a market that many so-called experts believed didn't exist.

Specifications[1]	
Engine:	I-6, L-head, 172.6 cid (3⅛ x 3¼-in bore x stroke), 7.25:1 compression ratio, 4 main bearings, solid valve lifters, Carter 1-bbl carburetor, 82 bhp @ 3,800 rpm
Transmission:	3-speed selective, column shift; overdrive optional
Suspension, front:	Independent, coil springs above upper A-arms
Suspension, rear:	Rigid axle, semi-elliptic springs
Brakes:	4-wheel hydraulic, 8-in. drums
Wheelbase (in.):	100.0
Overall length (in.):	176.0
Tread front/rear (in.):	53.25/53.0
Weight (lbs):	2,430-2,515, depending on body style
Tires:	5.90 x 15
Top speed (mph):	80.0
0-60 mph (sec):	21.0
Production:	1950 11,428 1951 70,003 1952 53,000 1953 30,260 1954 36,231 1955 56,023 (model year)

[1]1950 model

The 1950 Porsche 356 boasted unit construction, with the floorpan welded to a boxed, pressed-steel chassis. Also featured was an all-independent suspension and, for 1950, hydraulic brakes.

G reatness often has humble beginnings, and so it was with the Porsche 356. At first little more than a sporting version of the unassuming (if technically advanced) Volkswagen, it was slowly, patiently, and expertly evolved into a sports car of great ability that still engenders respect—and fond memories—nearly 40 years after the last one was built.

Its father was Dr. Ferdinand Porsche, who like Henry Ford was present at the automobile's birth and dreamed of cars for the common man. As an engineer for Austro-Daimler, Daimler-Benz, NSU, and Auto Union in the Twenties and Thirties, Porsche won fame for inventiveness—and all-conquering competition cars. But designing Adolfh Hitler's inexpensive "people's car" only won him an unwarranted two-year imprisonment in France, after which he returned to Gmünd in his native Austria. There, with son Ferry, he created the first Porsche.

This project, number 356 for Porsche's design company, harked back to his prewar Type 114 "F-Wagen," itself conceived as a sporting evolution of *Der Fuhrer*'s bug-shaped *volkswagen*. The prototype, a spartan mid-engine roadster, was built in 1947, then reconfigured as a cabriolet with an air-cooled engine placed behind the rear wheels, VW-style; a beetle-backed companion coupe was also developed. Production was underway by 1948, when *Porsche Konstruktionen GmbH* completed just four of these "356/2" cars, followed by 25 in '49 and 18 in 1950, all hand-built.

In 1949 the firm started moving operations to Zuffenhausen, a suburb of Stuttgart in the new war-created nation of West Germany, and began serious production. By April 1950, when the first German-built cars were delivered, the company had changed its name to *Dr. -Ing. h.c. F. Porsche KG* (KG denoting a limited partnership). It was the start of a modern dynasty the great Ferdinand barely lived to see, for he died in January 1951 after suffering a stroke the previous November, just two months into his 76th year.

The 356 followed VW practice in many ways. For example, it utilized the same type of unit construction, with the floorpan welded to a boxed, pressed-steel chassis, and similar all-independent suspension with transverse torsion bars, twin parallel front trailing arms, and flexible, single rear arms (for longitudinal location). Gmünd cars had cable-operated mechanical brakes, but VW's new 1950 hydraulic brakes were adopted for Stuttgart production. Power was initially supplied by the VW's 1,131-cc flat-four, albeit with Porsche-modified heads. Drive was via a single dry-plate clutch to VW's non-synchronized four-speed transaxle.

With the move to Stuttgart, the 356/2 became just 356 and received cleaner styling: a larger two-piece windshield with slightly curved

By 1956, the Porsche 356 had evolved into the 356A. Production set a record that calendar year as 4,201 cars were produced. Porsches now rode on 15-inch wheels.

outboard ends, a higher beltline, no wing vents, plus a reworked dash with an oil temperature gauge and relocated clock. There was still no gas gauge, Porsche relying on VW's reserve-tank arrangement and a wooden measuring stick.

Further improvements began coming thick and fast. By 1951, brakes had changed to twin-leading-shoe drums, tube shocks had replaced lever-action at the rear (matching the front), and a bored-out 1,286-cc engine option was available, with aluminum cylinder liners (replacing cast iron) and a rousing four extra horsepower. October brought a 1,488-cc alternative with roller-bearing rod journals, along with bigger brakes, full Porsche-patent split-ring synchro-mesh, and a slightly vee'd one-piece windshield.

The following year, some 20 "America" roadsters, lightweight 1.5-liter specials intended mainly for racing, were built at the behest of U.S. import-car baron Max Hoffman, who sold most of them. Engines expanded to six in 1954: 1100, 1300, 1300S (Super), 1300A, 1500, and 1500S; only the last two went to the States. September saw introduction of another Hoffman idea: the sporty, loveable Speedster, a detrimmed cabriolet with cut-down windshield priced at $2,995 (1500) or $3,495 (1500S). Sales were initially restricted to the U.S. Like most early 356s, it carried Reutter bodywork, though Heuer built some cabriolets and Glaser the 1952 Americas.

Production was up to 12 cars a day by 1955, when U.S. models were badged Continental—but that year only because Lincoln, which "owned" the name, objected. Few Porsche components interchanged with Beetle parts anymore, the 356 having moved rapidly away from its proletarian parent in this respect.

The 356A, introduced in late 1955 as a '56 model, moved even further. Rocker rubrails appeared on coupes and cabrios, and all models received one-piece curved windshields and inch-smaller 15-inch wheels. Inside, the original center-bulge metal dash was discarded for a flat-face panel with padded top and a large tachometer between speedometer and a combined fuel level/oil-temperature gauge. A floor lowered 1.5 inches provided more leg-room and easier entry/exit, and sound insulation was added in strategic places. The suspension was softened a bit, too, but worked with the smaller wheels and tires to actually improve roadholding.

Initial 356A engines comprised 1300N (Normal) and Super for Europe, plus a new 1600N and S—bigger-bore versions of the previous 1500. All retained overhead valves actuated by pushrods. Topping the chart was the potent 1500GS, a detuned version of Porsche's twincam 550 Spyder sports/racing engine from 1954—and dubbed "Carrera" in honor of its competitive prowess in the famed Mexican Road Race (*Carrera Panamericana*). Features included a Hirth

built-up crankshaft with one-piece conrods, roller bearings for both mains and rods, and dry-sump lubrication. Output was an impressive 100 DIN horsepower (115 SAE gross).

Several detail revisions appeared in the spring of 1957, including exchanged speedo/combination gauge positions, teardrop taillights (replacing four little round ones) and a license plate/backup lamp bar moved from above to below the plate. The next year, ventwings materialized in cabrio doors, coupes sprouted windwings, exhaust tips were poked through the vertical bumper guards, a double-bow front-bumper overrider replaced the former single-bow item, soft tops received larger windows, and a lift-off fiberglass roof was made a factory option for the Speedster.

There was predictably more engine upgrading in '58. The 1300s vanished, the 1600s reverted to plain bearings, and cast-iron liners returned on the 1600N to reduce both cost and noise. The Carrera unit grew to 1,588 cc and also got plain bearings—though 1.5s were still built, some with plain bearings, some with rollers. Elsewhere, carburetors switched from Solex to Zenith, a diaphragm clutch replaced the former coil-spring unit, and the old worm-and-peg VW steering finally gave way to a Ross-type ZF mechanism.

Alas, August 1958 saw the end of the much-loved Speedster. In its place was a pudgier Speedster D bearing a taller, chrome-framed windshield and a top somewhere between the original low, simple design and the cabrio's deluxe padded affair. Bodies were built by Drauz, hence the "D." The name was changed to Convertible D before sales commenced.

The next major step was the 356B for 1960, easily spotted by higher bumpers with large vertical guards that better protected the relatively delicate body. Some say they improved looks, too, but not everyone agreed. Brake-cooling ducts were cut in below the front bumper, and headlights were raised so that fenderlines ran almost straight back. The Convertible D was again renamed, becoming the Roadster. Inside, a lowered rear seat increased headroom slightly, and its folding backrest was newly split. All models gained door vent windows, and defroster vents were added below the backlight.

Underneath, the familiar drum brakes with circumferential fins were replaced by cast-aluminum units with radial fins and cast-iron liners held in by the Alfin process. Engines were almost unchanged save for a new 1600 Super 90 (named for its rated DIN horsepower), though it was delayed until March 1960.

For 1961, Koni shock absorbers were specified for 1600S and Super 90 models, and rear roll stiffness was reduced via slimmer torsion bars. A transverse leaf spring, or "camber compensator," became standard on S90s, optional elsewhere, this to tame the lift-throttle oversteer typical of tail-heavy cars. D'Ieteren Freres joined Drauz in supplying bodies for the Roadster (which would be axed during model-year '62), and Karmann in Osnabrück began turning out a fixed-roof notchback coupe looking much like the cabriolet with its optional lift-off top in place. Reutter, meantime, built lightweight GT coupes with Carrera-tune engines for 1960-61 (the first Porsches with 12-volt electrics).

Subtle appearance updates marked the '62s: flatter front "trunklid," a second engine-lid grille, external fuel filler (beneath a flap in the right front fender), and enlarged back windows on coupes.

Spring brought the last and fastest of the 356 Carreras: the 2.0-liter Carrera 2. The hottest roadgoing Porsche yet, it had all-disc brakes of the same Porsche design used on the firm's single-seat Formula 1 racers.

Few additional changes were made through July 1963, when the replacement 356C appeared, a visual twin to the B save flat-face hubcaps covering standard all-disc Dunlop brakes supplied by Ate. Porsche had experimented with these as well as its own discs since 1958, but chose the Dunlop system for volume models because of its lower cost. Engines were trimmed to three: Carrera 2, 1600C, and 1600SC, the last two respectively derived from the 1600S and Super 90 and equipped with positive crankcase ventilation for U.S. sale. All engines were available in both coupe and cabriolet models.

After more than 15 years and 76,303 units, the 356 was honorably retired in September 1965. Porsche had come a long way with this basic design since its struggling days in Gmünd, achieving international fame as a builder of fast, durable, superbly engineered performance machines at home on road and track alike. But even greater renown, prosperity, and corporate growth lay ahead. With the new six-cylinder 911, Porsche would succeed in ways its founder could scarcely have imagined.

The 356B debuted in 1960, although the car seen here is a '63 356B 1600. That year was a memorable one for Porsche because output exceeded 10,000 for the first time.

Specifications	
Engine:	All ohv flat-four except Carrera (dohc) **1100** (1950-54): 66.3 cid/1,086 cc (2.89 x 2.52-in./73.5 x 64-mm bore x stroke), 40 bhp (DIN) @ 4,200 rpm (46 SAE), 50 lbs/ft torque @ 2,800 rpm **1300** (1951-57): 78.7 cid/1,286 cc (3.14 x 2.52-in./80 x 64-mm), 44 bhp (DIN) @ 4,200 rpm (50 SAE), 58 lbs/ft @ 2,500 rpm **1300 Super** (1953-59): 78.7 cid/1,286 cc, 60 bhp (DIN) @ 5,500 rpm (70 SAE), 63 lbs/ft @ 3,600 rpm **1500** (1951-52): 90.6 cid/1,488 cc (3.14 x 2.91-in./80 x 74-mm), 60 bhp (DIN) @ 5,000 rpm (70 SAE), 73 lbs/ft @ 2,800 rpm **1500/1500 Super** (1952-55): 55/70 bhp (DIN) @ 4,400 rpm (64/82 SAE), 76/77 lbs/ft @ 2,800/3,600 rpm **1500GS/GS GT Carrera** (1955-57): 90.6 cid/1,498 cc (3.35 x 2.60-in./85 x 66-mm), 100/110 bhp (DIN) @ 6,200 rpm, 85/88 lbs/ft @ 5,000 rpm **1600** (1955-63): 96.5 cid/1,582 cc (3.24 x 2.91-in./82.5 x 74-mm), 60 bhp (DIN) @ 4,500 rpm (70 SAE), 78 lbs/ft @ 2,800 rpm **1600** (1963-65): 75 bhp (DIN) @ 5,200 rpm (88 SAE), 88 lbs/ft @ 3,600 rpm **1600 Super/1600C** (1955-63): 75 bhp (DIN) @ 5,000 rpm (88 SAE), 83 lbs/ft @ 3,700 rpm **1600 Super 90** (1960-63): 90 bhp (DIN) @ 5,500 rpm (102 SAE), 86 lbs/ft @ 4,300 rpm **1600 SC** (1963-65): 95 bhp (DIN) @ 5,800 rpm (105 SAE), 88 lbs/ft @ 4,200 rpm **1600 Carrera/Carrera GT** (1958-65): 96.9 cid/1,588 cc (3.45 x 2.60-in./87.5 x 66-mm), 105/115 bhp (DIN) @ 6,500 rpm (121/132 SAE), 86 lbs/ft @ 5,000 rpm **1600 Carrera** (1963-65): 96.5 cid/1,582 cc (3.24 x 2.91-in./82.5 x 74-mm), 90 bhp @ 5,500 rpm, torque NA **Carrera 2** (1961-64): 120 cid/1,966 cc (3.62 x 2.91-in./92 x 74-mm), 130 bhp (DIN) @ 6,200 rpm (150 SAE), 116 lbs/ft @ 4,600 rpm
Transmission:	4-speed manual in rear transaxle (non-synchromesh 1950-52)
Suspension, front:	Independent, twin parallel trailing arms, laminated transverse torsion bars, tube shocks, anti-roll bar
Suspension, rear:	Independent, swing axles, transverse torsion bars, tube shocks (lever shocks 1950-51), anti-roll bar
Brakes:	Hydraulic, front/rear drums; 4-wheel disks on Carrera 2 and 356C
Wheelbase (in.):	82.7
Weight (lbs):	1,675-2,250
Top speed (mph):	95-130
0-60 mph (sec):	9.2-15.4
Production:	1950 410 1951 1,169 1952 1,297 1953 1,941 1954 1,891 1955 3,970 1956 4,201 1957 5,241 1958 5,994 1959 6,980 1960 7,559 1961 7,996 1962 7,930 1963 10,032 1964 9,772 1965 1,688 (calendar year; figures include Carrera models)

The hot Hornet, new Hollywood hardtops in each series, and Hydra-Matic were the big news for the outwardly little changed 1951 Step-down Hudsons. The Hornet emblem rode on the front fenders and decklid.

One night at the Hudson Motor Car Company, PR man Frank Hedge was working late. A guard came into his office and announced a visitor named Marshall Teague: "He's been trying all day to get into Engineering. He's waited and waited and he has to see somebody." Hedge offered to see what he could do.

"I took Marsh and a friend of his to dinner," Hedge recalled. "The next day I phoned Engineering and got him some manifolds. Hudson's advertising director, Bob Roberts, was scratching around for some excuse for publicity, and this appealed to him. Suddenly Advertising was really interested, and I was traveling around the country to these races. And then we started winning. . . ."

That was the start of what has come to be revered as the "Fabulous Hudson Hornet." A more roadable American car may never have been built in the Fifties.

For four years in a row, the Hornet was a force *majeure* in American stock car racing: 11 national wins in 1951, second to Oldsmobile because of a late start; 27 wins in 1952-53, a record virtually unbeatable; eight more outright wins in 1954, retaining the championship with its H-145 six-cylinder L-head engine still vanquishing the more modern rival overhead V-8s. If such an engine bespoke a certain conservatism on Hudson's part, it nevertheless flew in the face of convention and all probability by truly trimming such V-8 rivals as the Olds 88 and Chrysler Saratoga on the NASCAR or AAA ovals—and on America's highways.

It seems improbable that Hudson would simply bore and stroke its big six in 1951, when others were thinking about "clean slate" V-8s. Chief engineer Stuart Baits explained: "Hudson had six-cylinder manufac-turing equipment, the V-8 was not yet so dominant and cost was certainly a factor." The Hornet six was evolutionary—a displacement increase on the understressed, easy-revving, tremendously durable Super Six. The big change was torque: 30 percent more than in the Super Six, and 18 percent more horsepower, now 145. This compared favorably with 135 bhp for Oldsmobile's Rocket 88 (in a 100-pound lighter car), but paled a bit beside the brand-new 180-bhp Chrysler Hemi V-8 (in a 350-pound heavier body). Still, Hudson could claim—and did—that it built "The most powerful six-cylinder automobile engine in production." This resulted in a pounds-per-horsepower ratio of only 24.8:1 for the two-door Hornet, astonishing in a big American car—no matter how many cylinders.

Since 1948, Hudson had touted its immensely strong "Monobilt" unit body/chassis and "Step-down" design. The latter utilized a recessed floorpan nestled between the frame's siderails, which allowed the height

Although Hudson offered two-door sedans, hardtops, and convertibles, the four-door sedan, here a '52 Hornet, was easily the best seller year after year.

of the car to be lowered to 60⅜ inches, giving Hudson the lowest center of gravity in the industry. This allowed Hudson to offer handling with greatly reduced body roll, along with big-six performance that was hard to match—a winning combination. Likely, there was no better balanced American car offered to the public in the early Fifties.

The 1951 Hornet effectively replaced the old Super Eight, leaving the Commodore with Hudson's only eight-cylinder engine—but it was far more lively than the Commodore. Style for style, the Hornet exactly matched the Commodore's price: $2,543 base for the coupe up to $3,099 for the convertible. A new body style was the Hollywood hardtop; with "Hudson-Aire styling" it was the first of this type for the venerable Detroit automaker.

Motor Trend's Walt Woron said the Hornet "hums, buzzes, zooms and [does] practically everything else any self-respecting hornet would do except fly [but] the top speed isn't far from take-off speeds. It's powerful, fast in the getaway, is easy to handle and gives a comfortable ride." Woron ran 0-60 in 14 seconds and approached 100 mph in his Hydra-Matic-equipped Hornet sedan. He praised the inherent safety of its unit-construction, all-welded body/frame: "If you've ever seen one after an accident, you've seen the greatest advantage."

As good as it was, the Hornet didn't sell particularly well, garnering about a third of Hudson's sales in a poor year. In 1951, Hudson recorded its first loss since 1939. Production was hampered by a shortage of steel owing to U.S. involvement in the Korean conflict, and there was confusion about government-mandated price ceilings, and more than a few strikes. The company consoled itself by its track performance, thanks largely to the aforementioned Marshall Teague.

Teague ran a Daytona garage where he tuned engines and followed neigh-

boring NASCAR racing. His relationship with Hudson established, he convinced North Carolina truck farmer Herb Thomas to switch to Hornets from the Olds 88s he'd been driving. Gregarious and unassuming, the two worked closely with Hudson engineers. Without any cheating, Marsh could get 108-112 mph from a certifiably stock Hornet—and this was 1951, before the announcement of "severe-usage components" or Twin-H-Power manifolding, which would make the Hornet even more formidable. He did it through hairline timing and precise clearances, taking everything apart: engine, transmission, differential, wheels, steering.

Teague's final preparations were crude by today's standards, though effective enough then. He removed the rear seat, taped the headlights, tied down the hood with cord, and strapped the doors shut. On the dashboard, chalk lines were marked to represent race laps; as Teague finished a lap he would rub out a line with his finger. Finally, after the hubcaps and muffler were removed, the "Teague-mobile" was track-ready.

The Hudson Hornet was also pretty fair at long-distance, over-the-road enduros. In November 1951, Marshall Teague finished a respectable sixth in the car-breaking 2,000-plus-mile *Carrera Panamericana*, contested over the worst imaginable Mexican roads from the Guatemala border to Texas. Though

The triangle was a Hudson symbol, seen here in stylized form as the '52 hood ornament. The '52 Hornet sedan listed at $2,769, $206 more than a Buick Super sedan. In that price range, one expected relatively lavish interiors, and the Hudson Hornet didn't disappoint.

overwhelmed by Ferraris on the straights, Teague actually held them on the corners, to the *"Carambas!"* of spectators and the amazement of the Italians.

Before the 1952 season was half over, the Hornet had become the dominant racing stock car—yet the "Teague-mobiles" were almost innocently "prodified." The best known "severe usage" item was Twin H-Power, introduced on April 1, 1952, though on Hudson shelves since 1944. It consisted of a dual manifold and dual carburetors, providing a very even measure of fuel-air mixture to the cylinders, which in a standard induction arrangement is not ideally suited to six-cylinder configurations. Hudson claimed that Twin H-Power "accurately measures the gasoline and evenly distributes it to each cylinder, and thoroughly vaporizes the fuel with air, providing what the engineers call far better 'breathing' and better combustion than has heretofore been obtainable on regular grade gasoline."

The highest development of Hudson racing was the 1953-54 "7-X," a dealer-installed engine option. Highlights included a minimum overbore of .020 inches, a special hand-reworked head with higher than standard compression, a studded block to hold it on, Twin H-Power, and a split dual-exhaust manifold and header pipe. One member of

The '54 Hornet dashboard sported plenty of chrome trim; the speedometer read up to 120 miles per hour. A ragtop listed at $3,288 that year.

the Hudson-Essex-Terraplane Club rates these engines at 210 horses. This was certainly the highest state of tune for an L-head six in automotive history—and a credit to Hudson.

Hardly any changes were made to the 1952 Hornets: the hood ornament moved forward, rub rails extended and

swept downward following the bodyside sculpturing, taillights were lowered and wrapped around, and the rear window was enlarged. Sales were off—production limits set by the government that year hurt the entire industry—and weren't much better in 1953, when output limits were lifted and Hudson offered only another extremely mild facelift. Strut bars were eliminated from the grille, a dummy airscoop appeared on the hood, and new upholstery fabrics were fitted. A more extensive facelift occurred for 1954—the most serious seen on the 1948-54 Step-downs—resulting in "Flight-Line" styling: a bold, simple horizontal-bar grille; crisper hood and deck lines; squared-off rear fenders; and large triangular taillights. Hudson advertised that the Hornet was "... more powerful than ever for '54. With its Instant Action Engine (featuring Super Induction) the Hudson Hornet rules the road!" A hotter camshaft and higher 7.5:1 compression gave the stock Hornet 160 bhp, 170 with Twin H-Power.

As good as it was, though, the Hornet couldn't ward off the competitive pressure of V-8s and more the easily restyled separate body/frame construction of its Big Three rivals. On May 1, Hudson merged with Nash to form American Motors, and the Step-down Hornet was dropped—replaced by a Nash-based design for 1955.

The '54 Hornet/Hornet Special rode a 124-inch wheelbase. Just 24,833 Hornets were produced that year, and they would be the last of the Detroit-built Hudsons.

Specifications	
Engine:	I-6, L-head, chrome-alloy block **1951-53** 308.2 cid (3.81 x 4.50-in. bore x stroke), compression ratio 7.2:1 (6.7:1 opt.), 4 main bearings, solid valve lifters, Carter 2-bbl carburetor, 145 bhp @ 3,800 rpm **1952 ½-53** 160 bhp with Twin H-Power **1953-54** dealer-installed 7-X option: 341.0 cid (4.01 x 4.50-in.), est. 200-220 bhp
Transmission:	3-speed manual, column shift; overdrive ($100) and 4-speed Hydra-Matic ($158) optional
Suspension, front:	Independent, coil, springs, tube shocks
Suspension, rear:	Live axle, semi-elliptic leaf springs, tube shocks
Brakes:	Hydraulic, front/rear drums
Wheelbase (in.):	124.0
Overall length (in.):	208.5
Tread, front/rear (in.):	58.5/55.5
Weight (lbs):	3,505-3,800
Tires:	7.10 x 15 or 7.60 x 15
0-60 mph (sec):	12.0-14.0; 11.0-12.0 (modified)
Production:	1951 43,666 1952 35,921 1953 27,208 1954 24,833

A new Kaiser bowed for 1947, and it would use that basic bodyshell through 1950. Styling was all-new for 1951 as seen here.

When car collectors saw the 1991 Chevrolet Caprice, their reaction was instantaneous: "The Kaiser's back!" Actually, the new Caprice is a quirky blend of Kaiser and Nash—if you shrouded its front wheels, it would look more like a Nash than a Kaiser. The curious thing is that the Kaiser was a truly beautiful car—while few people are raving about the new Caprice.

There is no doubt that the 1951-55 Kaiser represented one of the great styling landmarks in the industry. Even today, 30 years since its introduction, it is still clean and rakish from every angle. Its problem was its association with a whole funky order: Henry J. Kaiser and his Sunshine Boys from California, who came east to Willow Run, Michigan to build automobiles—but hardly knew a steering wheel from a life preserver. The topsy-turvy decade of Kaiser-Frazer was filled with some of the most bizarre contraptions ever to spring from the hand of man: a forklift engine made into an automobile powerplant, a four-door convertible that didn't quite convert, a "hardtop" that was really a sedan, a compact car designed by a car seat manufacturer. Nevertheless, the heft of opinion among those who ought to know is that the 1951-55 Kaiser was a styling tour de force.

In fact, it ought to have been. Styling was Kaiser-Frazer's strongest suit. Its own design department was built on an heroic scale, including some of the best people in the business. There were separate studios for Kaiser, Frazer, and Advanced Design, headed respectively by Buzz Grisinger, Bob Robillard, and Herb Weissinger—each a brilliant tactician. The team included Alex Tremulis of Briggs, Ford, and Tucker fame. K-F also had consultant contracts with both Dutch Darrin and Brooks Stevens. Its Styling Department had a healthy budget, courtesy of general-manager-then-president Edgar Kaiser, for whom design was a kind of outlet, a relaxation. All of this came together on the 1951 Kaiser.

The car itself was the product of a design competition between the in-house team, consultant Darrin (assisted by Duncan McRae), and consultant Stevens. Darrin's prototype was chosen, then honed to perfection by Darrin himself, McRae, and the K-F designers, though its lines remained little changed throughout the process. Its advanced features included a tipsy windshield slant of 52 degrees (45 degrees was the average for the day), a glass area of 3,541 square inches (the Buick Special had 2,858), a beautiful padded dash with safety-recessed instruments, and a windshield designed to pop out in a crash, rather than crack your skull.

The glass area and narrow "A" pillars combined with a daringly low beltline to provide a crow's nest feel to the occupants. Indeed, the Kaiser beltline remained lowest in the industry until Chrysler's "Forward Look" designs of 1957. Incredible for the period, K-F didn't muck the

213

The 1953 Kaiser Golden Dragon seen here was the show car at that year's Chicago Auto Show. Dragons featured plush interiors, a vinyl top, and a lot of gold trim. Kaiser referred to it as a "hardtop," but of course it wasn't. A '53 Dragon cost $3,924.

car up with chrome. The only bright metal of significance was a stainless steel molding along the bottom of the body, which both Darrin and Stevens had conceived of, to protect and decorate the sides of deluxe models. The clean lines were announced by a grille which wasn't a grille at all, but a functional air scoop set out by horizontal bars.

Defying the contemporary fad of annual styling changes, successive models evolved almost scientifically. The major 1952 change was to the taillights, crafted by Darrin: neat teardrops that followed and extended the fenderline. Aside from a "sabre jet" hood ornament and small chrome rear fins, the '53 was little altered. For 1954, Herb Weissinger and Buzz Grisinger applied a handsome front end using a concave vertical-bar grille and large oval big headlamp/ parking lamp housings (a design similar to the Buick XP-300 show car) and an extraordinary "Safety-Glo" taillamp ensemble: huge teardrops with extended lenses running along the tops of the rear fenders, visible from the sides, the rear, and above. The '54 also featured an aircraft-inspired dashboard, crash panels for rear as well as front passengers, and a wrap-around backlight giving the car nearly 4,000 square inches of

glass area. Aside from a slightly modified hood ornament, the '55 was identical.

The most luxurious Kaiser was the Dragon, a special trim option in '51 and a separate series in 1953, conceived by K-F's brilliant fabric-color specialist, Carleton Spencer. Before publication of the history of Kaiser-Frazer in 1975, Spencer was virtually unknown; today, anyone interested in automotive design is aware of his contributions: beautiful embossed "bambu" vinyls for Dragon interiors and padded tops, imaginative interior fabrics, color combinations

All Kaisers from 1947-55 ran with a 226.2-cubic-inch inline six. It was initially rated at 100/112 horsepower, but it was up to 118 in 1953. A supercharger upped that to 140 in 1954-55.

which were always tasteful, and usually elegant.

Lest we leave the impression that styling was all that Kaiser had going for it, we should note its engineering sophistication. This was not in the engine department: the 226.2-cubic-inch L-head six, derived from industrial applications, was uninspired and archaic, even after a McCulloch supercharger wrung 140 horsepower out of it in 1954-55. But engineers like Ralph Isbrandt and John Widman combined to produce unusual body and chassis features which put Kaiser handling in a class by itself.

Widman rejected unit construction as expensive and heavy-handed, but came close to its rigidity by using far more body mounts than other cars. The frame was light but strong; on it, Isbrandt located the engine, oil pan, and steering, using the frame for protection. The wheel rate was 112 pounds rear and 100 pounds front, different from the norm, and even impressed engineering-conscious Chrysler. A visiting Chrysler engineer drove an early '51 and told Isbrandt that "It rides like one of our 4,500 pound cars." The Kaiser weighed in as low as 3,100 pounds.

Isbrandt also adopted extra long rear springs to enhance steering control. He recalls that the cars could be thrown into a skid at 60 mph by a 180-degree twist of the wheel, only to correct themselves and straighten out instantly.

Had Henry Kaiser only spent the money for a V-8 engine (one was worked on, but never made producton), the 1951-55 Kaiser would have been a one-car revolution. Even so, he sold 170,000 copies during the first two years of production, and for a time dealers couldn't get enough of them. Of course, mistakes were made. Too many 1951s had piled up by the '52 model year, and some of these were rebadged as 1952 "Kaiser Virginians" before the true '52s arrived. The same thing happened with the '53s, which were sold as 1954 "Kaiser Specials" in advance of the true '54 Specials (only the latter, and the '54 Manhattan, had wrap-around rear windows). In 1951 there were too many models: club coupes that sold poorly; two- and four-door Travelers with opening rear hatches and folding rear

seats, a nice idea but not worth the money it took to build. By 1954, Kaiser was down to just two- and four-door sedans—but imagine what a convertible would have looked like on this body! (Actually, a prototype ragtop was built, but Kaiser lacked the money to put it into production.)

After 1955, the Kaiser dies were sent to Argentina, where the four-door sedan was produced through 1962 as the Carabela. Even then, it still looked up to date. Not many Detroit designs lasted 11 years, and in such longevity lies the greatest tribute to Kaiser's design excellence.

Specifications	
Engine:	I-6, L-head, 226.2 cid (3.31 x 4.38-in. bore x stroke), 4 main bearings, solid valve lifters, Carter 2-bbl carburetor **1951-52** 115 bhp @ 3,650 rpm **1953-54** 118 bhp @ 3,650 rpm **1954-55** supercharged, 140 bhp @ 3,900 rpm
Transmission:	3-speed manual, column shift; overdrive and 4-speed Hydra-Matic optional
Suspension, front:	Independent, coil springs, tube shocks
Suspension, rear:	Solid axle, semi-elliptic leaf springs, tube shocks
Brakes:	4-wheel hydraulic drums
Wheelbase (in.):	118.5
Overall length (in.):	210.4-213.8
Weight (lbs):	3,061-3,375
Tires:	6.70 x 15
0-60 mph (sec):	approx. 15.0-16.0, 13.0-14.0 (supercharged)
Top speed (mph):	90-98
Production:	1951 139,452 1952 32,131 1953 27,652 1954 8,539 1955 1,291

The 1951-55 Kaisers have long been noted for their outstanding styling. The '53 Manhattan four-door sedan listed at $2,650, compared to $2,696 for a Buick Super with a 164/170 horsepower straight-eight engine. The back seat was nicely trimmed and roomy.

There's an old wive's tale abroad in the land, among many with which we are amused and benighted, that they never built a "real" Bentley after Rolls-Royce took over in the early Thirties. As near as can be ascertained, the theory is that W.O. Bentley, that legendary genius, took the greatness of the marque with him when he left. Bentley without W.O. (and without the great supercharged 4.5-liter cars) was akin to Mount Vernon without George Washington. That there were better cars than the Blower Bentley, and even better Bentleys, is conveniently ignored. We order up another Pimms No. 1 and drink to the demise of old excellence. . . .

Though the Blower 4.5 was one helluva car, Bentleys in its image have continued to emerge from Rolls-Royce-controlled Bentley Motors. The Mulsanne Turbo is a recent example. Equally qualified are the Bentley Continentals.

The first postwar Bentley was the 1946-51 Mark VI, a car that typified all the fastidiousness and craftsmanship for which Rolls-Royce has always been known. It of course added impetus to the wive's tale: the Mark VI was not a Bentley, really, but a rebadged Rolls-Royce standard steel saloon—a quiet, dignified motorcar to be sure, but not the Bentley of old. Yet the Bentley Continental grew out of the Mark VI and its successor, the R-type saloon—so in this relatively mundane sedan was the seed of one of the finest Bentleys ever produced.

In 1950, word came down from the Rolls-Royce factory at Crewe, Cheshire, to chief stylist J.P. Blatchley and chief project engineer H.I.F. Evernden, to design a companion to the Mark VI, "not only to look beautiful, but possess a high maximum speed coupled with a correspondingly high rate of acceleration, together with excellent handling qualities and roadability." The result, as we now know, was what the home office first called the "Corniche II," a striking car bearing registration number OLG490, for which it was nicknamed "Olga." This historic car has long been owned by the Bentley Drivers Club honorary president Stanley Sedgwick. It is historic because it was the prototype of the Continental series.

Although the R-type Continental (the Mark VI had been re-designated by the time it appeared in 1953) was designed to be a sporting automobile, it had to retain all the extraordinary refinement and dignity of what Rolls-Royce called "The Silent Sports Car." While Evernden was allowed to increase the power of the 4½-liter six, therefore, he could not make it a fire breather, or do anything to interfere with its notable smoothness. Aside from raising its compression, it is obscure exactly what he did do to increase performance—but improve it he did.

From the design standpoint, Olga's advantages were only too obvious: a wind tunnel-tested fastback shape; a wind-splitting, traditional

The fastback Bentley R-Type Continental, which was built from 1952-55, proudly carried a traditional bluff Bentley grille, but was otherwise quite aerodynamic for its time.

A long hood and low-set headlights combined to give the R-Type a much fleeter look than that of the Bentley sedans. The auxiliary lights added a sporty touch. A 63-inch overall height also aided the Continental's good looks.

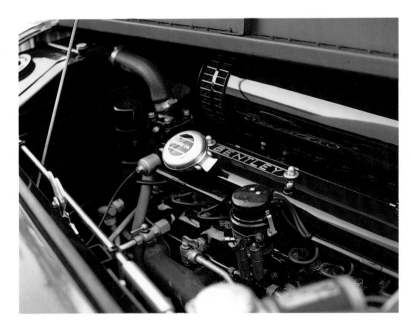

An inline six provided motivation for the R-Type Continental. Initially it had 278.6 cubic inches and approximately 150 horsepower. In mid-1954 the engine was enlarged to 298 cid, and the horsepower moved up to an estimated 170. A tool kit was a nice touch.

Bentley front end; a body only 63 inches high, built of aluminum alloy; a car that weighed only 3,640 pounds at the curb, against 4,100 for the standard Mark VI saloon.

Olga was delivered to the Montlhery, France race track for evaluation in September 1951, where the talent of Evernden and Blatchley—and Mulliner, who built its body—was underlined. The car delivered close to 120 mph lap after lap. Later, *The Autocar* found that a Continental would deliver 0-60 sprints in 13 seconds, 0-100 in 36. Since the hemi-head Chrysler Saratoga ran out of steam at a little over 100 mph at that time, the Continental R-type was undoubtedly the fastest full-size sedan in the world. Even the Jaguar XK-120 was only marginally quicker. True to character, Rolls-Royce did not publicize such a claim, preferring to recommend people who inquired to the results of press tests.

Some detractors say that the R-type Continental was really copied from the designs of General Motors, specifically GM's A-body fastbacks of the late Forties and early Fifties. A Bentley copied from a Chevrolet! In fact, the resemblance is coincidental, but it is certainly no disgrace. Those GM cars had one of the most successfully contrived shapes, from the point of view of streamlining; that Bentley came up with a similar solution is only indicative of the consistency of its value.

Of 208 R-type Continentals built, 193 had the fastback Mulliner body. The rest were treated to the work of individual coachbuilders including Franay, Graber, Park Ward, and even Pinin Farina. Interiors were invariably finished in Connolly leather; burled walnut dashboards contained full instrumentation, including a tachometer.

Continentals were broken down into arbitrary sub-series A through E, each standing for minor modifications made during the production run. The most noteworthy was a new, bored-out engine displacing 4,887 cc, starting with the "D" model in May 1954. Performance was somewhat improved, although it was hardly necessary. In power as in looks, the Continentals were stunning.

"The discerning instinctively felt that this car was the first offspring that the marriage between the two finest names in British motoring had labored twenty years to produce," wrote Richard Busenkell—"the tremendous Bentley performance combined with Rolls-Royce craftsmanship, elegance and silence. By comparison, every preceding Bentley had been merely a sporting Rolls, including the first Continental, a lightweight, high-performance version of the Phantom II.

"The cost of the Continental was very steep—£4,890 in England, before the exorbitant sales tax, or about $17,000 delivered and taxed in the United States—but there was simply nothing like it available anywhere. Nor had there ever been."

Incidentals: 43 R-type Continentals were equipped with GM's Hydra-Matic transmission, which says something about the latter—but only 28 of these were sold in the United States. The first bumpers were aluminum, about which the late Dennis May commented: "It's doubtful whether there are still many R's in circulation with the original aluminum bumpers fitted. They were as light as loofahs and just about as much use in a shunt."

The original R-type Continental concluded in 1955, after 2,320 R-type Bentleys had been produced in all—so fewer than 10 R-types in 100 were Continentals. At that point, the company introduced the new S-type, along with the parallel Rolls-Royce Silver Cloud. This represented a major—though evolutionary—change in specification, a longer wheelbase, softer suspension, and new body; also, Hydra-Matic (R-R-built) was now standard. The R-type Continental's successor was therefore a break with the sporting temperament of the original: a lovely car in its own right, but not the same.

From the rear and rear three-quarter view, the R-Type looks a lot like the GM fastbacks of 1949. But with only 208 built from 1952-55, it was far rarer than the GM models.

Specifications	
Engine:	I-6, ohv 278.6 cid/4,566 cc (3.625 x 4.5-in./92.1 x 114.3-mm bore x stroke), 7.27:1 compression ratio, twin SU carburetors, approx. 150 bhp @ 4,000 rpm. From mid-1954: 4,887 cc/298 cid, 7.25:1 c.r., est. 170 bhp (horsepower figures never officially announced)
Transmission:	4-speed manual; GM 4-speed Hydra-Matic optional beginning in 1953; 11-in. single dry-plate clutch
Suspension, front:	Independent, coil springs, hydraulic lever-type shock absorbers
Suspension, rear:	Solid axle, half-elliptic springs, lever-type shocks
Brakes:	4-wheel hydraulic, with mechanical servo assist
Wheelbase (in.):	120.0
Overall length (in.):	206.5 (for U.S. export cars)
Curb weight (lbs):	3,640-3,800
Tires:	6.50 x 16
0-60 mph (sec):	13.0
Top speed (mph):	approx. 120
Production:	208 (1952-55)

The Austin-Healey 100/4 went into production in the spring of 1953, which ended up forcing back the introduction of what would become the MGA. Like a proper sports car, it featured a large tach and speedometer. They were calibrated to 6,000 rpm and 120 mph, respectively.

Sporting British roadsters have captivated the world for most of motoring's first century, none more than the postwar Austin-Healey 100s and 3000s. Like many "great cars," they're unmistakably individual—tangible expressions of their creator's soul. All the more remarkable, then, that they were built not in tiny numbers by some small "cottage" specialist, but in the tens of thousands by one of Britain's biggest companies.

The "Healey," of course, refers to Donald Healey, the ace 1920s rally driver who became technical chief at Triumph, then helped Invicta and Riley win the famed Monte Carlo Rally and other competitions in the Thirties. In 1946, he decided to pursue a long-held dream of building his own cars, and set up shop near Coventry, then the heart of Britain's motor industry. A lack of capital precluded tooling his own drivetrains and bodies, so the former were purchased—mostly from Riley and Alvis— the latter farmed out to Elliot, Duncan, Tickford, Abbott, and Westland. Donald did, however, manage his own chassis: a sturdy, box-section design with an odd trailing-arm front suspension inspired by those of prewar Auto-Union and ERA single-seat racers.

Early Healeys were frumpy four-seat coupes, fixedhead and drophead. The singular exception was the Riley-powered 2.5-liter Silverstone, a racy cycle-fendered roadster in the time-honored dual-purpose tradition. Simplicity, lightness, and functionality were its hallmarks—as were a jolting ride and a decided lack of amenities. But the Silverstone could see 100 mph, quite credible for the late Forties, and did well in motorsports. Alas, it did little for Donald, who ended up building just 781 cars (including 105 Silverstones) over eight years, a reflection of limited resources and slow, handbuilt assembly methods.

That promised to change when Healey chanced to meet Nash-Kelvinator president George Mason aboard the *Queen Elizabeth* in late 1949. Mason wanted a sports car, and he knew about Healey. Together they hatched a slab-sided open two-seater powered by Nash's big Ambassador overhead-valve six that Donald would assemble in England for George to sell Stateside. But this Nash-Healey was expensive and proved tough to sell, garnering only 506 orders from 1951 through '54. As Healey had greatly expanded his facilities for much higher volume, this failure left him wondering what to do with them.

One answer seemed to be a new car using more proprietary components so it could sell at a lower price and, therefore, in greater numbers. Thinking Austin's largish A90 sedan chassis a suitable starting point, he shortened it for a sleek, envelope-bodied prototype roadster. Leonard Lord, head of Austin's parent, the recently formed British Motor Corporation, saw this "Healey 100" at the 1952 London Motor Show, liked the idea (doubtless because A90s weren't selling well), and decided

Author Richard Newton has called the Austin-Healey 100S "the King of the Healey Hill.... The S was for Sebring, and that was meant to play to the American market." Only 55 of these BN1 racing models were built.

to take it under BMC's wing. Which is how it came to be an Austin-Healey, built at Austin's big plant near Birmingham. Well, most of it. Though the body was ostensibly separate from the box-rail chassis, they were actually welded together, a job ultimately contracted to brothers Dick and Alan Jensen in nearby West Bromwich.

Aside from its handsome looks—Donald's own work, refined by Tickford—the 100 was orthodox, if appealingly sturdy and simple. Its driveline consisted of the A90's 2.7-liter all-iron four mated to a four-speed gearbox with first blanked off (ample torque made the ultra-low "tractor" cog superfluous), though standard Laycock de Normanville electric overdrive on second and third gears effectively gave five forward ratios. Suspension comprised coil-sprung double wishbones fore and a live axle on semi-elliptic leaf springs aft, with a Panhard rod for lateral location. Mounting the axle above the chassis siderails limited vertical movement—to the detriment of ride; antiquated all-around lever shocks didn't help. Center-lock wire wheels were standard, as was a three-position windshield that could be folded down flat or tilted back from vertical to a rakish angle.

Production commenced in spring 1953 (with some aluminum body panels at first, gradually changed to steel). U.S. exports quickly followed, and assemblies were soon 100 units a week. A good

thing, that, as demand was strong everywhere, thanks to looks, performance, and handling matched by few other cars at the price. Indeed, the A-H was dynamically closer to Jaguar's sexy, upmarket XK120 than Triumph's small and cheap TR2—easily able to reach the magic "ton" (hence "100"). There were just two problems, both noted right away: excess engine heat inside, and scant ground clearance due to a low-hanging exhaust system. Neither would be fully solved over this basic design's 15-year life span.

Though built for only 3½ years, the four-cylinder A-H saw four distinct variations. The original BN1 model ran through late 1955. Then came the BN2, the same car with first gear restored. Meantime, the Healey works, not BMC, devised a racing BN1, the 100S (Sebring), with stripped all-aluminum bodywork

sans bumpers, plus a much-modified 132-bhp engine. Only 55 were built, all in 1954-55. Most went racing, as intended, and usually fared well. There were also 1,159 examples of a 100M, a BN2 with 110 bhp, duo-tone paint, and assorted body and chassis modifications.

The 100 quickly established a fine reputation, especially in the U.S., where it greatly appealed for having everything contemporary that MGs didn't. In fact, America bought most of the 14,000 four-cylinder cars ultimately built, thus making the Austin-Healey a permanent part of the sports-car scene.

BMC managers had been quick to embrace it as a permanent part of their line; to them, building 100 such cars a week was quite something. But the American market was demanding more cockpit room, and the Austin four was woefully obsolete. Accordingly, Healey

The 100S was built of aluminum bodywork to keep the weight down, and it didn't come with side windows or a top. It was one of the first cars to use four-wheel disc brakes, however, and a 140-mph speedometer was provided because the engine was tweaked to 132 bhp at 4,700 rpm.

was asked to modify the car for six-cylinder power and freshen it.

The result bowed in 1956 as the 100 Six (earlier A-Hs were then retrospectively called "100/4"). Stretching the wheelbase two inches (to 92) and repositioning some components allowed squeezing in a pair of "+2" rear seats as a nod to the U.S., though they couldn't carry anything much larger than parcels. Appearance was mercifully little changed, but the delicate shell-shaped grille was replaced by a shiny oval affair, the hood acquired a central bulge with a small frontal air intake, steel-disc wheels became an alternative to wires, and the windshield, sadly, was fixed. Finally, overdrive was now an extra-cost option.

Supplying power was BMC's corporate C-series six, which shared some design points—but few components—with the B-series four of the new 1955 MGA sports car. Like the old A90 engine, it was a heavy, cast-iron job, but not that much larger or more potent, giving just 12 more horsepower. And as curb weight ballooned by nearly 300 pounds, the new BN4 was decidedly less lively than the BN2. It didn't handle quite as well, either.

Help arrived in late 1957 with a revised cylinder head and more efficient manifolding that not only booted horsepower to 117, but provided a more sporting torque spread. The real-world differences were more marked than the paper ones suggested, for road tests reported an eight-mph gain in top speed and acceleration restored to near BN2 levels.

Meantime, BMC had decided to build all its sports cars at MG's quaint Abingdon works, so A-H assembly moved 50 miles south. Soon afterwards, the two-place Healey was revived (by simply omitting the back seats) as the BN6, the kind of "second thoughts" backpedaling that would increasingly characterize BMC marketing. But enthusiasts didn't mind, and not even the advent of a cheap A-H in 1958, the winsome little "frog-eye" Sprite, could dilute the "big" Healey's appeal.

On the contrary, that appeal was only enhanced by the 1959 announcement of the "3000," named for its larger

The Austin-Healey 100 Six debuted in 1956 boasting an overhead-valve six that developed 102 bhp. Riding a 92-inch wheelbase, it carried a pair of small "+2" seats and sported a revised grille and a bulged hood.

six with seven more horsepower, though displacement was actually closer to 2,900 cc. Front-disc brakes were adopted for both the two-seater (BN7) and 2+2 (BT7), along with a return to vertical grille bars. "Mark II" versions arrived in 1961 with a new gearbox case and improved linkage, plus an extra carburetor that swelled horsepower to 132. But performance was little affected, and the triple-carb setup was tricky to tune, so BMC reverted to twin pots for the replacement Mark II Convertible, announced in summer 1962. Offered only as a 2+2, it sported ventpanes, roll-up door glass, and an integral fold-down top—"modern" touches that purists judged sacrilegious. Spring 1964 brought the tuned Mark III with 148 horses and sub-10-second 0-60-mph performance, though it tilted even more toward touring with a center console and restyled wood-paneled dash. Arriving later that year was a "Phase II" version with trailing-arm rear axle and increased suspension travel.

Sales remained strong, but the big Healey was quite dated by then—too dated to meet pending U.S. safety and smog rules without costly changes that BMC just couldn't justify. Thus, after total production of nearly 72,000 units, this winning sports car was quietly consigned to history at the end of 1967.

Surprisingly—but happily—it was reborn in 1989 under the auspices of a new, independent Healey Motor Company. Offered in convertible "Mark IV" and side-curtained "Silverstone" models (the latter with 100 Six-type grille), it retains classic Healey styling but packs Rover's 3.5-liter V-8 and five-speed

gearbox, a new tubular "backbone" chassis with independent rear suspension (by wishbones and trailing arms), rear disc brakes, a modern climate system, and more generous equipment. And with 190 bhp, it's the fastest Big Healey ever, with a claimed six seconds 0-60 time and 140 mph all-out.

How fitting that this memorable British roadster should live again to captivate the world.

Specifications	
Engine:	100/4 I-4, ohv, 162.3 cid/2,660 cc (3.44 x 4.38-in./87.3 x 111.1-mm bore and stroke), 90 bhp @ 4,000 rpm, 144 lbs/ft torque @ 4,000 rpm **100M** as for 100/4 except 110 bhp @ 4,500 rpm, torque NA **100S** as for 100/4 except 132 bhp @ 4,700 rpm, torque NA **100 Six** ohv I-6, 161 cid/2,639 cc (3.13 x 3.50-in./79.4 x 88.9-mm), 102/117 bhp @ 4,600/4,750 rpm ("early"/"late"), 142/144 lbs/ft @ 2,400-3,000 rpm **3000** ohv I-6, 177.7 cid/2,912 cc (3.28 x 3.50-in./83.4 x 88.9-mm), 124/132/148 bhp @ 4,600/4,750/5,250 rpm, 162/167/165 lbs/ft @ 2,700/3,000/3,500 rpm
Transmissions:	3-speed (1953-55 only) or 4-speed manual with Laycock de Normanville electric overdrive on top two gears
Suspension, front:	Independent double wishbones, coil springs, lever shocks, anti-roll bar
Suspension, rear:	Live axle on semi-elliptic leaf springs, Panhard rod (trailing arms from 1964), lever shocks
Brakes:	Hydraulic, front/rear drums
Wheelbase (in.):	**100/4** 90.0 **Six, 3000** 92.0
Weight (lbs):	2,015-2,550
Top speed (mph):	103-121 (100S: 126)
0-60 mph (sec):	9.8-12.0 (100S: 7.8)
Production:	**BN1** 10,668 (incl. 55 100S) **BN2** 3,924 (incl. 1,159 100M) **100 Six BN4** 10,289 **BN6** 4,150 **3000 "Mk I"** 13,650 **Mk II** 5,450 **Mk II Convertible** 6,113 **Mk III** 17,704

Cadillac was a slow starter as a collector car, decades ago during the early Classic car movement, as well as in more recent times during the "special interest" boom. The true Classics, as defined by the Classic Car Club of America, were mostly spoken for ages ago, and there aren't that many Cadillacs from the antique period around either. So the interest today is heavily concentrated on "special interest" Cadillacs, specifically postwar models through about 1970, among which the 1953 Eldorado ranks supreme, or nearly supreme—on par with the 1957 Eldorado Brougham as a technological masterpiece, with the 1949 V-8 as a mechanical triumph.

It's impossible to underrate the importance of the tailfinned Cadillacs, which began in 1948 with the first complete restyle since before World War II. They ushered in not only a styling fad but a new tradition of Cadillac design, which would persist until modern times—distinctive rear contours plus an unmistakable front end, with a grille, usually of the eggcrate pattern, that was higher in the middle than at the sides. Actually this grille shape originated in the Thirties, but the '48 was the first Cadillac to translate the idea into modern form.

By now nearly everyone knows that Cadillac tailfins were inspired before America entered the war, when GM styling chief Harley Earl took his designers to see the then-still-secret Lockheed P-38 fighter aircraft. Originally, Cadillac design models imitated the whole plane, with fanciful cribs from pointed noses to pontoon fenders. Conservatives prevailed and knocked out the more radical ideas, but the tailfin—after some upper management indecision—lasted. Once introduced, it took the public by storm, and it wasn't long before accessory houses were offering "Cad Fins" to bolt onto the rear ends of Chevys and Pontiacs. The idea was successful, Harley Earl said, "because ultimately Cadillac owners realized that it gave them an extra receipt for their money in the form of a visible prestige marking for an expensive car." It was both unfunctional and essential—like Mercedes' three-pointed star. This was important: After the war, Packard searched for a long time in vain for a similar hallmark, and by the time it found one—the famous "cathedral taillight"— it was too late. On the other hand, it took more than tailfins to make a Cadillac.

Beginning in 1950, the finned Cads started to get heavier and shinier, and by 1953 they were sprouting what the British disdainfully called the "dollar grin." Never mind the Brits' hypocrisy: the Rolls-Royce grille actually carried more square inches of bright metal. But 1953 did see a very special Cadillac in the Eldorado, purposely limited to only 500 copies, and priced at a stalwart $7,750—equivalent to at least $50,000 in today's money.

Under the hood was the most powerful V-8 Cadillac had yet developed: 210 horsepower with 8.25:1 compression. Its advanced

The '53 Cadillac Eldorado was both expensive and exclusive: $7,750 and just 532 built. While it featured the basic styling of the other '53 Caddys, it got a "Panoramic" windshield and wire wheels as two exclusives.

styling, shared with the Buick Skylark and Olds Fiesta, was—and is—its most important contribution. Highlights included a leather-cowled instrument panel, Cadillac's first wrap-around windshield, wire wheels, a lowered beltline, and a fully disappearing top that dropped into a well behind the rear seat. It was then covered by a metal boot, giving the deck an ultra-clean appearance. The convertible top came in black or white Orlon, the body in Aztec Red, Azure Blue, Alpine White, or Artisan Ochre. Interiors were color-keyed in full leather. Chrome wire wheels and frameless windwings were standard, exclusive to the model. Eldos were instantly recognizable via their cut-down doors, metal boot covers, gold "V" with Cadillac crest on hood and deck, and full leather upholstery.

It is of passing interest to note that the Eldorado was not broken out as a separate Cadillac model. Technically, it was part of the Sixty-Two Series, although it cost about double the price of a conventional Sixty-Two ragtop. This situation continued until 1959; since then, Eldorados have all been distinctive models within the Cadillac line.

A swank and daring car with a host of new ideas, the Eldo cost an up-and-coming film star or oil mogul a cool piece of change, and at that price only a few were sold. But it had everything

to excite the buyer of those days, and it retains tremendous appeal among collectors today. From the collector standpoint it is the most important Cadillac built during the period between the first overhead valve V-8s in 1949 to the Eldorado Brougham of 1957. It is also the most expensive postwar collector Cadillac you can buy at least through the '58.

Some 300 pounds heavier than the stock convertible, the Eldorado was the slug of the 1953 Cadillac line in performance, but this was merely relative: with 210 brake horsepower there was more than enough power for jack-rabbit starts and smooth cruising at any speed you cared to travel, provided it was in a relatively straight line. Roadholding, which was so good on the 1949 Cadil-

One nice feature about the '53 Eldorado was that it had a fully disappearing top that dropped into a well behind the rear seat. It was then covered by a metal boot, giving the deck an ultra-clean appearance. "Dagmar" bumper guards were in evidence.

lacs, had deteriorated as the cars added length, width, and weight in the early 1950s. It was no better or worse on the Eldorado than on any of the other '53 models, which means it was pretty awful. The Eldo was thirsty too, returning about 12 miles to the gallon, as might be expected of any 4,800-pound V-8-powered car. But when premium gas cost 20 cents a gallon, this hardly seemed extravagant, and nothing could beat it for sunny-day cruising.

Collectors have several caveats about buying and owning 1953 Eldorados, some of which are exclusive to this vintage. If you can afford one, you're probably braced for the expense of maintenance, but you'll find replacement parts exclusive to the Eldo (like doors, for instance) to be non-existent: anything that gets damaged has to be rebuilt or recreated. Low production volume resulted in few spare body parts even being made by the factory, and the special trim that went into the Eldorado simply doesn't exist. However, there's hardly anything that can't be made, given resourcefulness and bucks, so this problem is relative. As to longevity, the Eldorado is as good as its more standard Cadillac counterparts, and not especially prone to rust.

Like all limited-production exotics, the 1953 Cadillac Eldorado will continue to appreciate in direct proportion to its rarity and the steady, high demand. The money one spends on it today is probably as well spent as it would be if you bought a certificate of deposit. Of course, you can't drive a CD, let alone put the top down.

The '53 Eldo was 300 pounds heavier than the stock convertible, but with 210 horsepower that didn't matter too much. Styling touches included a sleek hood ornament, the traditional Cadillac crest and "V" up front, and a snazzy padded dashboard. Power windows were standard, of course, and the rear seat allowed plenty of room.

Specifications	
Engine:	V-8, ohv, 331 cid (3.81 x 3.63-in. bore x stroke), 8.25:1 compression ratio, 5 main bearings, hydraulic valve lifters, 4-bbl carburetor, 210 bhp @ 4,150 rpm
Transmission:	4-speed Hydra-Matic
Suspension, front:	Independent, coil springs and tubular shock absorbers
Suspension, rear:	Solid axle, semi-elliptic leaf springs
Brakes:	4-wheel hydraulic
Wheelbase (in.):	126.0
Overall length (in.):	215.8
Curb weight (lbs):	4,799
0-60 mph (sec):	approx. 13.0-14.0
Top speed (mph):	approx. 110
Production:	532

People speak of them as the "Loewy" coupes. Which makes a certain amount of sense, since Raymond Loewy was Studebaker's design consultant back in the early 1950s when these gorgeous automobiles were developed.

Loewy, of course, was a world-famed industrial designer, so it was naturally in Studebaker's interest to have his name attached to this radical new car. But it was actually Bob Bourke, Studebaker's chief designer in those days, who was mainly responsible for styling the low-slung and strikingly beautiful 1953 Starliner hardtop and its pillared companion, the Starlight coupe. At the same time, Raymond Loewy clearly deserves recognition, for without his enthusiastic support Bourke's graceful designs would never have gotten off the drawing board.

In the project's early stages, during the spring of 1951, it was generally understood that Bourke was developing a "show" car, a one-off intended for display purposes only, not for series production.

But Bob Bourke had other plans. Or at least he had ambitious hopes. As the clay model developed, he later confessed that "In the back of my mind. . . was the thought that if the result was practical enough, and well designed, it might have some production potential." Others, notably Studebaker President Harold Vance, were dubious at first, but Raymond Loewy endorsed the idea wholeheartedly.

Studebaker's traditional mainstays were two- and four-door sedans. For the first time since 1947, they were to be completely restyled for 1953, under the direction of Bob Bourke and Holden "Bob" Koto, the man who had been largely responsible for the design of the 1949 Ford. Following the practice first established by Studebaker in 1951, the six-cylinder Champion and the Commander V-8 shared the same wheelbase—116.5 inches, in this instance. The sole exception to this was the Commander Land Cruiser, an upscale sedan built on a stretched 120.5-inch chassis. And of course the sedans were the primary concern of Studebaker's conservative management. Not until preparations for their production were well under way did Harold Vance finally give the green light to the idea of building Bob Bourke's highly advanced coupes. That delay, unfortunately, would prove to be a costly one.

Good design, as the late Gordon Buehrig used to say, is largely a matter of proportion. And so in designing his handsome coupes, Bourke made use of the longer Land Cruiser chassis. Overall length measured 201 15/16 inches, more than four inches longer than the then-current Ford. Then by using a "cowbelly" frame, whose siderails flared out behind the cowl, he was able to lower the car's profile so that its overall height was only 57¾ inches, compared to 61⅝ and 64⅞ inches for the new Studebaker sedans and the 1953 Chevrolet, respectively. The result was a low, slinky, ultra-modern look that appears remarkably contemporary

Studebaker was known mainly for sedans, so the European-influenced '53 Commander Starlight hardtop came as a surprise.

even today.

Recognized early on as a certified Milestone Car, the Starliner hardtop has been described by auto journalist Michael Lamm as "the most beautiful car ever mass-produced in America." It was available in either the Champion or Commander series. Meanwhile, its lower-priced pillared companion, the Starlight coupe, was likewise available in both series, and unlike the Starliner it could be had in a choice of DeLuxe or Regal trim.

For Studebaker's board of directors to have authorized the production of the two coupes represented a high-stakes gamble because it required that the factory tool up for two distinct types of automobile. So distinct that virtually no body panels interchanged between the coupes and the more sedate sedans. The investment was therefore a huge one, particularly in relation to Studebaker's perilously slim resources.

But perhaps President Harold Vance and the rest of the company's management could foresee the accolades that Bob Bourke's neo-classic design would receive. Certainly they must have realized that he had produced a masterpiece. But just as surely nobody in the organization—including Bourke himself—

The '53 Starlight featured gauges mounted low on the instrument panel. Bucket seats might have been more comfortable than the bench provided.

could have foreseen its longevity. With periodic modifications that transformed it first into the 1956 Studebaker Hawk and then into Brooks Stevens' remarkable 1962-64 Gran Turismo Hawk, the coupe was destined to remain a part of the Studebaker lineup for 12 seasons!

Unfortunately, the 11th-hour decision to produce the coupes meant that when the first 1953 Studebakers started coming down the assembly line, three days before Christmas in 1952, they were all sedans. The disappointed dealers had expected the Starliners and Starlights to be their showroom "draw," so South

Bend was under tremendous pressure to bring the coupes on line as soon as possible. Vance announced that they would be ready in March, a month ahead of his original schedule.

The result, inevitably, was a rash of problems, having to do chiefly with poor fit and generally shoddy quality control in the earliest units. This was quite out of keeping with Studebaker tradition, and it did the company's reputation no good. And in any case, by the time the coupes arrived in showrooms around the country, some of Studebaker's prospective customers, impatient with the delay, had gone shopping elsewhere.

Which, of course, was most unfortunate. That's because not only did the Starliner and Starlight coupes exhibit highly advanced and extremely attractive styling, they were also very competent automobiles. This was especially true of the Commander. While the lower-priced Champion retained the aging and underpowered L-head "six," which dated back 14 years to the original 1939 Studebaker Champion, the Commander offered one of the most advanced V-8 engines then on the market.

First introduced for 1951, the Studebaker V-8 was a short-stroke, overhead-valve design. Remarkably similar to the new Cadillac engine, it was of course much smaller, and it lacked the Caddy's "slipper" pistons and hydraulic valve lifters. Displacement was 232.6 cubic inches (almost the same as the Ford V-8), from which it derived 120 horsepower. Some camshaft problems emerged with the earliest units, but these were quickly corrected and the V-8 proved to be a sturdy powerplant, lively and very economical.

Had things gone according to plan, the future should have brought greater power to both the Commander and the Champion. A smaller V-8, never produced, had been planned for the latter, and it was understood that 120 horsepower represented only a fraction of the Commander V-8's potential. According to author Mike Lamm, in anticipation of the "super fuels" that most engineers believed to be forthcoming, the new V-8 was built to handle compression ratios as high as 14.0:1, a modification

Studebaker introduced an automatic gearbox in 1950, and a new overhead-valve V-8 for '52. It ran with 120 horses.

The extremely low hood and the narrow grille openings contributed to the European look of the Starlight. Provision for allowing enough air into the engine compartment was via an opening under the bumper. Studebaker built 20,858 Commander Starlights for '53.

that could have been accomplished simply by shaving the block decks.

But those super fuels never materialized, and unfortunately Studebaker hadn't provided for very much enlargement potential of its new V-8. Periodic increases in the stroke would bring its displacement to 289 cubic inches by 1956, but at that point the block had about reached its limit (it ultimately went to 304.5 cid in 1964). Studebaker would fall seriously behind the competition in the cubic-inch derby as the Fifties progressed.

It's not as though Studebaker's engineers had been idle at the beginning of the decade, however. For instance, the veteran South Bend firm was the second of the independent automakers to offer an automatic transmission mostly of its own (Packard had brought out Ultramatic in 1949). Optional at an extra $231, it had been jointly developed by Studebaker and Borg-Warner and was first introduced in 1950. An excellent

unit, it incorporated a unique anti-creep device that locked the transmission when the car was at idle. It was good enough, in fact, that Ford tried to purchase the rights to this transmission, but Studebaker—evidently in the hope of reaping some publicity value from it—declined. One suspects that Studebaker officials later came to bitterly regret that decision, for Ford promptly developed an automatic of its own—also in collaboration with Borg-Warner—and Studebaker lost out on the royalty money that would have been extremely helpful in the lean times that lay ahead.

It is not our purpose here to recount the sad story of Studebaker's decline and eventual fall, but over the years this pioneer company had scored its share of triumphs in both styling and engineering. And surely the introduction of Bob Bourke's Starliner hardtop and Starlight coupe ranked as one of the high points in the firm's long and distinguished history.

Specifications	
Engine:	Commander V-8, ohv, 232.6 cid (3.38 x 3.25-in. bore x stroke), 7.0:1 compression ratio, 5 main bearings, solid valve lifters, Stromberg 2-bbl carburetor, 120 bhp @ 4,000 rpm **Champion** I-6, L-head, 169.6 cid (3.00 x 4.00-in.), 7.0:1 c.r., 4 main bearings, solid valve lifters, Carter 1-bbl carburetor, 85 bhp @ 4,000 rpm
Transmission:	3-speed manual, column shift lever; overdrive or Studebaker Automatic Drive optional
Suspension, front:	Independent, coil springs
Suspension, rear:	Rigid axle, semi-elliptic springs
Brakes:	4-wheel hydraulic drums
Wheelbase (in.):	120.5
Overall length (in.):	201.9
Tread, front/rear (in.):	56.5/55.5
Tires:	**Champion** 6.40 x 15 **Commander** 7.10 x 15
0-60 mph (sec):	16.9 (V-8, automatic transmission)
Top speed (mph):	95.6 (V-8, per *Motor Trend*)
Production:	1953 Champion Starlight 25,488 Starliner 13,058 **Commander** Starlight 20,858 Starliner 19,236 1954 Champion Starlight 12,167 Starliner 4,302 **Commander** Starlight 6,019 Starliner 5,040

The Mercedes-Benz 300SL is appreciated for its fine, aggressive styling. Too bad it's so rare a car that few will ever enjoy one.

You can't touch a Mercedes-Benz 300SL Gullwing now for much under half a million dollars, and for good reason. Not only was it always a very limited-production car, it was a truly historic one—"the 1954 equivalent of a Porsche 959 and Porsche 962 rolled into one," as *Car and Driver*'s Csaba Csere wrote 35 years later.

Like the Jaguar E-Type of 1961, the 300SL was conceived as a sports/racer, not a road car. As well, both were startlingly advanced for their respective days. Unlike the British car, the German one proved its competition mettle well before the production model appeared. In subsequent years, 300SLs would even notch an impressive number of rally wins.

It began with 10 racing SL prototypes built in 1952 under the beaming gaze of board chairman Vilhelm Haspel, his signal to the world that Mercedes was not only back in business after the agony of war, but ready to reclaim its former competition eminence. There was no money for a new purpose-designed engine, so chief engineer Fritz Nallinger, assisted by legendary team manager Alfred Neubauer and test engineer Rudolph Uhlenhaut, appropriated the basic drivetrain from the big new 300-series passenger models of 1951 and wrapped it in a complex, multi-tube space-frame chassis overlaid with special coupe and spider bodies. Because full-height side-opening doors would have compromised rigidity in this high-sided structure, half-doors—hinged at the roof center to lift upward—were developed for the coupes, necessitating the now-famous "Gullwing" design.

Though costly, the new chassis was deemed necessary to minimize weight as a means to victory for Stuttgart's first postwar racers, hence their revival of the famed SL ("Sports Light") designation. Competitive considerations also prompted Uhlenhaut to modify the basic 3.0-liter 300-series single-overhead-cam inline six. Top-end power and high-speed aerodynamics were paramount, which implied the lowest possible hoodline, so he first canted the engine 45 degrees to port, then a highly unorthodox measure. This dictated a new sump, which was duly fabricated along with new tuned manifolds, special competition camshaft, and larger valves and ports. With triple Solex carburetors, the result was 165 horsepower, versus 115 for the production unit. Subsequent adoption of dry-sump lubrication and Bosch direct mechanical fuel injection, the latter a world first, boosted output to around 175 bhp in racing trim. The later production SL was more potent still, arriving with an advertised 215 DIN/240 SAE bhp. Suspension, final drive, and a four-speed fully synchronized gearbox were lifted more or less intact from the 300-series.

Among the most potent racing cars of their time, the SL prototypes could easily top 130 mph. As planned, they did their job with

Compared to the '55 300 SL Gullwing on the preceding pages, the '56 was little changed. Designed as a sports/racer, it was built with an eye to keeping the weight low. It was also very costly—$6,800 at first.

crushing Germanic efficiency, placing second and fourth in the '52 *Mille Miglia* and winning that year's Le Mans 24 Hours outright, as well the marathon *Carrera Panamericana* in Mexico.

The SL story might have ended there had it not been for American import-car impresario Max Hoffman. Ever quick to spot a "good thing," Hoffman pleaded with Daimler-Benz to offer a production Gullwing, and put his money where his mouth was by ordering 1,000 of them. That was enough for D-B, and Wilfert and Uhlenhaut set about modifying the racing coupe for road use. The fruit of their labor proved an absolute sensation when unveiled at the New York Auto Show in February 1954.

It cost a bunch—initially $6,800, as much as a Cadillac limousine—but was worth every penny. Solid and handsome, it laid fair claim to being the world's fastest series-built road car. This was despite an interim weight increase caused by switching bodywork from light-alloy to more practical steel, save for hood, doors, and trunklid, which remained aluminum. It might be noted, however, that all-aluminum competition bodies were available to special order. Nothing could outpace a Gullwing except the occasional Ferrari, which was hardly a "production" car then. Aside from the fuel injection and a new cylinder head, changes from prototype form were quite modest: mainly requisite road equipment (bumpers, proper lighting, etc.) and a fully trimmed, but still very race-car-like, interior.

As most enthusiasts know, the Gullwing was replaced at mid-1957 by a 300SL Roadster with a space-frame redesigned for conventional doors. Respective total production came to

just 1,400 and 1,858 units. The peak year was 1955, with 867 Gullwings; annual volume after 1958 was only 200-250, reflecting high price as much as the car's low-volume, highly specialized nature.

But it's that very nature that enables the Gullwing especially to do what we expect of "great cars"—stand the test of time. *CD*'s Csere proved as much in a 1989 retrospective test of a restored '57 coupe. Though the cockpit was too narrow by modern standards, noise levels unacceptably high (there wasn't much sound insulation), and steering effort in hard corners sufficient to tax Arnold Schwarzenegger, he judged the Gullwing "surprisingly refined" overall: "The shifter arcs through its longish travel with little pressure and precisely telegraphs the engagement of the gears to your hand. The clutch takeup is smooth and even. The ride is astonishingly plush. The SL glides over minor road imperfections but remains well-damped over bumps. And the steering is accurate and light at moderate pace."

Interestingly, Csere put the lie to what was long perceived as the Gullwing's one major dynamic problem: "snap" oversteer caused by sudden, wide camber changes in hard cornering by the relatively simple "high-pivot" swing-axle rear suspension then favored by Mercedes. This proved "not nearly as diabolical as we expected," Csere reported. "The SL's tail did ooze out at the limit, but could be easily controlled with mild oppposite lock. The mythical sudden and uncontrollable oversteer never showed up." Mythical or not, the tendency was deemed serious enough in the Fifties for D-B to give the Roadster the new "low-pivot" arrangement designed for its W196 Grand Prix car, with a transverse compensating spring that increased roll stiffness to keep the rear wheels from hopping around *in extremis*.

Two undeniable Gullwing drawbacks related to its doors: poor water-sealing and awkward entry/exit. The latter stemmed partly from the high, wide sills and partly from the huge arc the doors had to scribe, which meant they couldn't be opened fully if you were parked close to, say, a wall. All these

Entry/exit were for the nimble due to the high, wide sill. Removing the luggage from inside was a chore, but the trunk was filled by the spare tire.

The 300SL roadster came on stream for 1957, although the sample pictured here is a '58 model. The 2,996-cid inline six churned out 240 horsepower and 210 lbs/ft torque that year. The roadster weighed about 3,000 pounds, 250 more than the coupe, and because the doors were lower, entry/exit was easier.

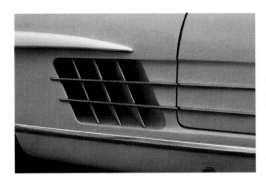

factors prompted development of the Roadster, which came with a folding, lined soft top and could be ordered with a lift-off steel top.

At least the Gullwing's doors moved easily enough, thanks to dual assist springs, and though the cockpit was cozy, editor Csere judged legroom plentiful and the driving position good. One interesting feature was a steering wheel hinged at the base of its hub to tilt almost upside down—doubtless to ease entry/exit for more amply proportioned folk like Herr Neubauer. Both coupe and convertible were strictly two-seaters, of course, with ample stowage space behind and typical Mercedes dashboards dominated by a high-set speedometer and tachometer and plenty of chrome.

Styling hardly needs comment, except to note that it was far lower and sleeker than that of concurrent Mercedes sedans, especially the baroque 300-series. Distinguishing features such as the big tristar grille emblem, wheelarch "eyebrows," and eggcrate front-fender louvers are well-known, and the gullwing doors would be imitated by all sorts of later cars without a tenth of the SL's class—notably the ugly mid-Seventies Bricklin and the disastrous early Eighties DeLorean.

Performance deserves fuller comment. Csere's retrospective test listed Gullwing curb weight at near 2,900 pounds and SAE *net* horsepower of around 170. Though the latter was somewhat below the original claim, he noted that mid-Fifties power ratings were often inflated

for advertising purposes, and that "the official power curve for the 300SL was run on an engine with a high-performance camshaft, which was fitted to only 29 of the 1,400 Gullwings produced." Still, his 8.6-second 0-60-mph time and standing quarter-mile of 16.5 seconds at 86 mph were hardly shabby considering he had "less off-the-line traction than a modern suspension and tires would provide." Indeed, braking was the only real disappointment—a lengthy 319 feet from 70 mph—though the big multi-shoe drums of his restored '57 were "somewhat out of adjustment."

In retrospect, the 300SLs were a mixed blessing for Mercedes. On the one hand, they were tremendous symbols of D-B's engineering prowess and terrific image-leaders for the rest of its passenger-car line. On the other hand, they were hardly profitable, and there was the memory of Pierre Levegh's racing 300SLR flying into the grandstand at Le Mans '55, which hastened D-B's retirement from motorsports.

But none of this dims the luster of the 300SLs, long since enshrined in the automotive hall of fame for their performance, heritage, and sheer presence. They will always be counted among the very greatest of cars.

Specifications	
Engine:	I-6, sohc, 183 cid/2,996 cc (3.35 x 3.46-in./85 x 88-mm bore x stroke), Bosch mechanical fuel injection **1954-57**: 8.55:1 compression ratio, 240 bhp (SAE gross) @ 6,100 rpm, 210 lbs/ft torque @ 5,000 rpm **1957-63**:9.5:1 c.r., 250 bhp (SAE gross) @ 6,200 rpm, 228 lbs/ft @ 5,000 rpm
Transmission:	4-speed manual, fully synchronized; single dry-plate clutch
Suspension, front:	Upper and lower A-arms, coil springs, tube shocks, anti-roll bar
Suspension, rear:	**Coupe:** High-pivot swing axles on radius arms, coil springs, tube shocks **Roadster:** Low-pivot swing axles
Brakes:	Hydraulic, front/rear drums
Wheelbase (in.):	94.5
Tread, front/rear (in.):	**Coupe** 54.5/56.5 **Roadster** 55.0/57.0
Weight (lbs):	**Coupe** 2,750 **Roadster** 3,000
Tires:	**Coupe** 6.50 x 15 **Roadster** 6.70 x 15 (both super sport)
Top speed (mph):	130-150+
0-60 mph (sec):	7.6-8.8
Production:	**Coupe** 1,400 (1954-57) **Roadster** 1,858 (1957-63)

Chevy ads in 1955 proclaimed "New Look! New Life! New Everything!" And indeed, Chevy had cast off its old, staid "Stovebolt" image.

The overwhelming popularity of the 1955-57 Chevy can be either logical or inexplicable, depending on how one looks at it. Logically, any car that could sell nearly five million copies in three years ought to be popular with latterday collectors. As Pat Chappell put it in her history of the breed, "almost everybody had one once." Furthermore, as Chevys go these were particularly good cars, bristling with innovation and the most exciting since the war—maybe the most exciting to date. For example, they had sprightly new styling, vivid two-tone color combinations, the first successful Chevy V-8 (which eventually offered one genuine horsepower for each cubic inch of displacement), good quality of construction, and some interesting new models ranging from the four-door hardtop to the Nomad wagon.

On the other hand, more levelheaded students of history are forced to admit that they were no better generally than the concurrent Fords and Plymouths, definitely inferior to their sister GM makes (because Chevy occupied the lowest rung on the ladder), and not particularly timeless as designs. Still, nothing says "Fifties" so well as a charcoal and coral Bel Air. And that car is 10 or 20 or 30 times as popular with collectors as the timeless Continental Mark II or the stunning 1953 Studebaker Starliner.

The fact of the matter is that a lot of people did "have one once," or their parents did, and a lot of people in the collector avocation are predisposed to like Chevys. Give them a singular and exciting period—1955-57 was both of those things—and they'll love it. Well over 30,000 people today collect 1955-57 Chevys, and the best of these cars command prices that exceed those of almost every other American mass-production car of their era.

The package which so electrified people in their day and ours involved two-pronged innovation: all-new styling and mostly new engineering. To the snazzy, Ferrari-like grille, hooded headlamps, acres of glass, and dipped beltline of Clare MacKichan and the Chevy styling studio was added the brilliant 265 small-block V-8 conjured up by Ed Cole and Chevy Engineering. These were the blockbuster ingredients—but many little niceties iced the cake. Engineering also provided the slick Powerglide automatic, Power-Pack V-8s with dual exhausts and later multi-carbs, and the option of fuel injection by 1957. Styling chipped in with the distinctive and glamorous Nomad hardtop-like station wagon and one of the best looking four-door hardtops produced in the Fifties, the 1956-57 Bel Air Sport Sedan.

In all three years, Chevrolet followed a three-series hierarchy, much as did its rivals—the time of "limited editions" like the first Impalas or special power/trim options like the Super Sports was still in the future. The top-of-the-line series was the Bel Air, the ultimate "classic Chevy,"

237

Flashiest of the '55 Chevys was the $2,206 Bel Air ragtop. Note the hooded headlights, sleek hood ornament, and "twin-cove" dash. The hot new V-8, extra chrome trim, and continental tire cost extra.

today the most desirable standard Chevrolet model on the collector car market. Fine styling, high performance, and good build quality created a huge collector following for the Bel Air, which was the only series in which the convertible and the Nomad were offered.

Style-wise, the '55 Bel Air was the purest and the most timeless, but its Ferrari grille was not particularly well liked at the time, and the '56 with its more glitzy and conventional front end was quickly substituted. Today's collectors tend to favor neither of these compared to the '57, which in its time was looked upon only as a facelift to keep sales moving until the all-new '58s were ready. But the '57 had more aggressive, extroverted styling, with sporty tailfins and an aggressive combination bumper-grille—these are very popular now.

The mid-range series was the Two-Ten, with less deluxe trim than the Bel Air, but more sparkle than the baseline One-Fifty. The advantage of the Two-Ten today is that it's far more affordable than comparable Bel Airs—and there are two- and four-door hardtops to choose from, if not Nomads and convertibles. Fewer were sold than Bel Airs, and proportionally fewer are around. Though the full range of engines up to '57's 283 with 283 bhp was available, Two-Tens were basically workaday Chevys and usually came with sixes or the base V-8.

However, bottom of the line doesn't mean undesirable when it comes to these cars. Excellent styling and V-8s up to the 283 by 1957 make plain-Jane One-Fiftys definite collector's items. But one has to be choosey when picking one, which means looking for a hairy engine and a stick shift. Curiously, there are more big-engined One-Fiftys around than Two-Tens, perhaps because a lot of people liked the idea of an unassuming (and slightly lighter) car that could blow the wheels off fancier rigs. Most such sleepers carried the multi-carb 270-bhp set-ups in 1957, as very few standard-size Chevy passenger cars were equipped with fuel injection. There are, in fact, more fuelie Chevys on the market now than Chevrolet built new—*caveat emptor.*

"Loves to go . . . and looks it!" boasted Chevy in '56. And if ever there was a wagon with that sort of spirit, it was the '56 Nomad. Its hardtop-style design, deluxe interior, and sporty exterior set it totally apart from normal workaday wagons.

"Sweet, Smooth, and Sassy!" That was the '57 Chevy with its more powerful 283-cid V-8, velvety Turboglide automatic, and styling more akin to a Cadillac than ever before. The Bel Air Sport Coupe started at just $2,299, and 166,426 were produced.

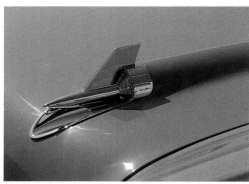

Although factory-sponsored racing was brought to a halt in early 1957 when the auto manufacturers agreed to downplay racing in a misguided attempt to appease the safety lobby, Chevys did very well while it lasted. In the new Short Track Division of the National Association for Stock Car Auto Racing (NASCAR), the '55 Chevy held more winning points than any car in its price class. In American Automobile Association (AAA) racing, Marshall Teague, having departed from Hudson, was leading the league with a Chevrolet. At NASCAR's Darlington 500 in September 1955, Herb Thomas and Jim Reed romped home at 90-mph averages, well ahead of the vaunted Chrysler 300s, and Chevys occupied six places among the top 10 finishers.

Fuel injection, which didn't arrive until a few months before the Automobile Manufacturers Association anti-racing decision, never really had its bugs worked out, and "fuelie" cars suffered from many breakdowns. Still, in February 1957, the SEDCO stable of Chevys under Vince Piggins and Dick Rathmann ran away with the first three places in their class (213-259 cubic inches; these were special debored 265s) at the Daytona Speed Weeks flying mile, seven seconds ahead of the nearest Ford. The same day in Class 5 (259-305 cid) Chevrolet captured the first 33 out of 37 places, with Paul Goldsmith averaging over 131 mph. In the same class for measured-mile standing-start acceleration runs, 1957 Chevys took the first 18 places. Even Chevy sixes did well at Daytona, taking six of the first seven positions in Class 4 acceleration tests. "The Hot One," as Chevy called it, was truly hot—and it remains so in the affections of a great many Americans to this very day.

Although collectors seek out the '57 Chevy Bel Air hardtops and convertibles, the Bel Air four-door sedan was far more popular when new. Listing at $2,290, some 254,331 were built for the model run. The interior featured a new dashboard, while the 283 V-8 came in ratings from 185-283 horsepower. Twin "windsplits" on the hood were a neat styling touch.

Specifications

Engine:	1955 I-6, ohv, 235 cid (3.56 x 3.94-in bore x stroke), 7.5:1 compression ratio, 1-bbl carburetor, 123 bhp @ 3,800 rpm (136 bhp with Powerglide); V-8, ohv, 265 cid (3.75 x 3.00-in), 8.0:1 c.r., 162-bhp @ 4,400 rpm (2-bbl), 180 bhp @ 4,600 rpm (4-bbl, dual exhausts) 1956 I-6, 235 cid, 140 bhp @ 4,200 rpm; V-8, 265 cid, 8.00:1 c.r.: 162 bhp @ 4,200 rpm (2-bbl), 170 bhp @ 4,400 rpm (2-bbl), 205 bhp @ 4,600 rpm (4-bbl), 225 bhp @ 5,200 rpm (9.25:1 c.r., 2 4-bbl carbs) 1957 I-6, as in 1956; V-8, 265 cid, 162 bhp @ 4,400 rpm (2-bbl); 283 cid (3.88 x 3.00-in): 185 bhp @ 4,600 rpm (8.5:1 c.r., 2-bbl), 220 bhp @ 4,800 rpm (9.5:1 c.r., 4-bbl), 245 bhp @ 5,000 (9.5:1 c.r., 2 4-bbl), 270 bhp @ 6,000 (9.5:1 c.r., 2 4-bbl), 250 bhp @ 5,000 (9.5:1 c.r., FI), 283 bhp (10.5:1 c.r., FI)
Transmission:	3-speed manual; overdrive and 2-speed Powerglide opt.; 2-speed Turboglide opt. 1957 only; 3-speed close-ratio manual on selected high-performance engines
Suspension, front:	Upper and lower A-arms, coil springs
Suspension, rear:	Live axle, longitudinal semi-elliptic leaf springs
Brakes:	Hydraulic, front/rear drums
Wheelbase (in.):	115.0
Overall length (in.):	196.5-200.8
Weight (lbs):	3,070-3,561
0-60 mph (sec):	8.0-15.0
Top speed (mph):	85-120
Production:	1955 1,704,667 1956 1,567,117 1957 1,505,910

I t could be said with some justice that it was the new overhead-valve V-8s from Cadillac and Oldsmobile that started the "horsepower race" back in 1949, though the pre-war Buick Centurys had been pretty rapid machines in their own right. But it wasn't until Chrysler got into the act with the fabulous FirePower engine in 1951 that the game really began to get serious.

The FirePower was Chrysler's first V-8, a heavy, enormously complicated piece of machinery, featuring not only overhead valves, but more efficient hemispherical combustion chambers and double rocker-arm shafts. Horsepower was rated at 180, a mind-boggling figure in those days, representing a full 20-bhp advantage over Cadillac's V-8.

Walter P. Chrysler, had he still been on the scene, would have been delighted. That's because advanced engineering was at the top of his agenda, and in no small measure the reputation of the original Chrysler automobile had been built on its performance. Introduced in 1924, that car had been priced nose-to-nose with the Buick Six. But the Chrysler was the lighter and nimbler of the two. Its power-to-weight ratio was 23 percent better than that of its rival from Flint, which gives a pretty good indication of its speed and agility.

There came a time after the founder was gone, however, when performance seemed to become a secondary consideration at Chrysler. In 1941, for instance, the year after Walter P.'s death, the Chrysler New Yorker carried 14 percent more weight in relation to its horsepower than the comparably priced Buick Century. Then—to make matters worse—Chrysler suffered because of the sluggish performance of its Fluid Drive semi-automatic transmission, a unit noted not only for slippage, but also for the interminable time it took to shift into fourth gear.

Then there was the matter of styling. The classic Custom Imperials of the early Thirties had been absolutely stunning automobiles, among the handsomest on the road. They were followed by the aero-dynamic—but commercially unsuccessful—1934-37 Airflows, which were in turn followed by several generations of ultra-conservative and uninspired boxy designs. K.T. Keller, Walter Chrysler's successor as president of the corporation, understood nothing whatsoever about styling, which was bad enough. What was worse was that he took an intense personal interest in the subject. So Chrysler's position relative to the competition had gradually become seriously eroded. Clearly, Chrysler had some catching up to do, in more ways than one.

As matters developed, the 1951 introduction of the FirePower engine was just for openers. Stylist Virgil Exner was finally let out of his cage. On the Chrysler payroll since 1949 as head of Advanced Styling, he had designed some gorgeous "show" cars, as well as several

The "300" badges front and rear on a '55 Chrysler meant that this was a very special car. First off, it was a limited-production model. Second, its front-end styling set it apart from other Chryslers. And third, this car had a 300-bhp Hemi V-8 under the hood.

From the rear, the C-300 sported "Twin Tower" taillights like other '55 Chryslers. Under the hood, however, was that 300-bhp Hemi V-8, the most powerful production auto engine in the world. Even the hubcaps wore 300 badges.

magnificent "Parade Phaetons," but he had been effectively walled off from participation in the design of production vehicles. Belatedly appointed during 1953 as Director of Styling for the corporation, he had barely 18 months in which to replace his predecessor's unimaginative work with handsome new designs that would become known as "The Forward Look."

By 1955, Chrysler styling was equal to—or better than—the best the competition had to offer. And for the Windsor DeLuxe, Chrysler's high-volume line, a new "poly-head" V-8 appeared to replace the now-obsolete flathead six. Horsepower, rated at 188, represented an impressive 58-percent increase over the 119 of the 1954 model. In addition, the recently introduced—and fully automatic—PowerFlite transmission came as a welcome improvement over the tough, but clumsy and inefficient, "M-6" semi-automatic unit.

What was needed now was a car that would, in some dramatic way, call attention to Chrysler's sparkling new image—one that would build showroom traffic, so that potential buyers might see for themselves the full line of high-styled, fast-moving new cars that the division had to offer.

It happened that Bob Rodger, chief engineer at the Chrysler Division, had been thinking along the lines of just

such a car, one whose performance would clearly outshine the competition. Using the New Yorker St. Regis hardtop coupe as his base, Rodger made a number of highly effective modifications. For starters, increased spring rates and other chassis modifications gave this car superior handling qualities. The ride was firm—some might have even called it harsh—but Rodgers' car steered with precision and cornered with aplomb.

The Chrysler "Hemi," still retaining its original 331.1-cubic-inch displacement, featured a special full-race camshaft and solid lifters, not to mention dual four-barrel carburetors. Output, which at 250 horsepower in the New Yorker and Imperial models was already second only to the Packard Caribbean's 275 and the Cadillac Eldorado's 270, was raised to an even 300 at 5,200 rpm. The idle was a little lumpy, but not intolerably so, and the performance

trade-off made it worthwhile. After all, the new model was the most powerful full-sized car built anywhere in the world at that time. It was also the first American production automobile to reach the magic figure of 300 horsepower. Hence its name: Chrysler C-300.

The PowerFlite transmission was supplied as standard equipment; no manual gearbox was available for the C-300 (though one was offered in the '56 300-B). Final drive gearing of 3.36:1 was normally used, but for those with special needs four optional ratios were available: 3.54, 3.73, 3.91, and 4.10. "Safe Guard Hydraulic" power brakes were also standard issue.

As might be expected, special styling touches were provided for this high-performance Chrysler. The bold, chrome-plated grille of the Imperial substituted for the more modest front end of the New Yorker, while the Windsor's less

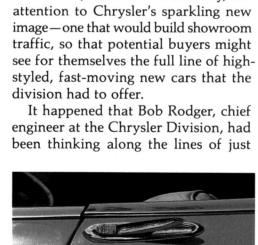

With 1,725 sales to its credit, the '55 C-300 was continued for 1956 as the 300-B. The B sprouted fins at the rear, and the 331.1-cid Hemi was bored to 354 cid and 340/355 thundering horses.

elaborate side trim gave the C-300 a neatly tailored appearance.

The interior was lavish, featuring "Natural Cowhide" leather upholstery and a handsome dash panel, identical to that of the Imperial except that its speedometer was calibrated all the way to 150 miles per hour—an optimistic figure, even for this very fast automobile.

Exterior color options were limited to Platinum, Tango Red, or Black, and there were no two-tones. Exner reportedly didn't like them, and provided them only reluctantly for the rest of the Chrysler line. Chrome wire wheels, surplus stock from the slow-selling 1954 Imperials, were an attractive option. Other available equipment included Chrysler's "Full-Time" power steering, four-way power seat adjustment, power windows, Solex glass, radio, heater, and clock. *Not* on the available list were backup lights and an outside rear-view mirror, evidently because a mirror would have increased wind resistance. Nor was air-conditioning offered, reportedly because there wasn't room under the hood for the compressor—though at least one car is known to have left the factory with refrigeration installed. Cool air officially joined the options list when the modestly facelifted 300-B was introduced.

Immediately upon its introduction

the Chrysler C-300 commenced tearing up the nation's race tracks. Before long it was being advertised as "The Car that Swept Daytona," and by season's end it had taken 37 first-place awards in NASCAR and AAA-sponsored events of 100 miles or more.

The automotive press was duly impressed. "Uncle" Tom McCahill, writing in *Mechanix Illustrated*, called it "a hard-boiled, magnificent piece of semi-competition transportation, built for the connoisseur," adding that it was "as solid as Grant's Tomb and 130 times as fast!" (How's that again? A hundred and thirty times as fast as Grant's tomb?) In any case, at Daytona the C-300 covered the flying mile at a little better than 127 mph, which spelled *speed* in any language in 1955.

Not surprisingly, this brawny new Chrysler drew plenty of attention from the public, though it was obviously aimed at a very limited market. It sold, after all, for $4,110, 11 percent more than the St. Regis hardtop, and its rock-solid suspension wasn't to everyone's taste. For that matter, the C-300 couldn't have been intended as a money-maker for its manufacturer, either. Rather, it was an image-builder—and an effective one! Even so, 1,692 of these great road machines found domestic buyers, in addition to 32 cars and one bare chassis built for export. Meanwhile, the public obviously paid close attention to the entire Chrysler line, for the division scored a near-record production increase of 73 percent during 1955.

With the introduction of the 1956 Chrysler 300-B, the high-performance Chryslers became known as the "Letter Series," and for several years they continued their winning ways on the NASCAR circuit and in other competitive events. Production was continued through 1965's Series 300-L, though beginning with the '62 300-H the cars lost some of their performance edge— and some of their distinctive appointments as well.

But by the mid-Sixties it was the intermediate-sized cars that were the hot ticket, both in racing and in sales. The Chrysler Letter Series had served its purpose, and it was time for something different.

Specifications	
Engine:	V-8, ohv, hemispherical combustion chambers, 331.1 cid (3.81 x 3.63-in. bore x stroke), 8.5:1 compression ratio, full-race camshaft, solid valve lifters, 2 4-bbl carburetors, 300 bhp @ 5,200 rpm
Transmission:	PowerFlite 2-speed automatic planetary with torque converter
Suspension, front:	Independent, lateral control coil springs, heavy duty shock absorbers
Suspension, rear:	Solid axle, parallel longitudinal semi-elliptic leaf springs, straddle-mounted heavy duty shock absorbers
Brakes:	Hydraulic, front/rear drums, power-assisted
Wheelbase (in.):	126.0
Overall length (in.):	218.8
Curb weight (lbs):	4,005
0-60 mph (sec):	9.8
Top speed (mph):	127
Production:	1,725

Specialist Henri Chapron debuted a sleek Citroën DS convertible in 1960. Built in limited numbers, the one shown here is a 1966 model.

Breathes there a man with a soul so dead, who never before to himself has said, what in the world is that weird looking car? No one has ever failed to react strongly to the Citroën DS— *Desirée Spéciale*—sedans, wagons, and convertibles. To some it really is a "Special Desire." Others hate it like poison. "The simplest way to characterize the DS," said *Motor Trend* years ago, "is to say that it is the first technological, as opposed to mechanistic, car ever to go into production."

Time has marched on and a lot of the car's once-singular characteristics are now widespread, but in its day it was unique. Consider Citroën's one-spoke steering column (the spoke was an extension of the column, bent away from the driver), its lateral bracing (like GM adopted with much ballyhoo 20 years later), its remotely located fuel tank (now required by law), its eye-level turn indicators (now often seen), its disc front brakes (the first in mass production, mounted inboard to reduce unsprung weight). Those brakes could panic-stop all day long with only the time required to accelerate back up to 60 mph for cooling down.

The DS body shape had the lowest drag coefficient among production four-door sedans 20 years after its introduction. It was capable of delivering one mile per hour for every horsepower: routine enough for 70-mph econoboxes, but not so common among cars with 115 or 125 DIN horsepower—which the DS offered from its four-cylinder, two-plus-liter engines after 1968.

It was introduced at the Paris Auto Show in October 1955 as "Tomorrow's Car Today." The fact that tomorrow's car came from Citroën was, however, taken for granted because Citroën was never a tradition-bound company. From its 1913 origins, when André Citroën founded the Citroën Gear Company to produce double helical tooth gears of particular smoothness, through the *Traction Avant* front-wheel-drive model of 1934, the ubiquitous 2CV of 1948, the more recent SM and CX, innovation has always been part of the Citroën character.

The DS benefited from previous technology in three areas. Front-wheel drive, of course, had been a Citroën feature for 20 years. A second carryover was a centrifugal clutch, first used on the 1954 2CV, the first French car mass produced with a semi-automatic transmission. Finally, there was the hydropneumatic suspension, which had been introduced on the 1953 *Traction Avant*: a unique system combining the action of a gas and a liquid for a perfect combination of smooth ride and tenacious handling. Constantly adjusting itself with almost human moans and sighs, the suspension had side benefits: with an override switch one could raise it to its maximum, 11 inches above the ground, insert a jack, and lower it again to change a wheel (held, by the way, on a spline with a single lug nut). When parking, the car could be left in the "high" setting

Citroën's station wagon variant of the DS-19 bowed in 1957, two years after the sedan's debut. Like other DS models, it had front-wheel drive and Citroën's unique hydropneumatic suspension, but at 198 inches overall the wagon was 7.5 inches longer than the sedan.

to protect against bumper-bashers. If left to itself, it sighed softly and settled like a relaxed cat, ending just 3.5 inches above ground level.

The designation DS-19 signified the 1,911-cc overhead valve "stroker" four with 75 bhp (60 DIN), inherited from the *Traction Avant*, which was retained until 1966. Chrysler engineers would have recognized its hemispherical-head combustion chambers. The 1.9 never gave lightning acceleration, taking about 18 seconds to amble up to 60 mph, but it would cruise at high speeds all day. When a new 2.1-liter, oversquare engine option arrived, the resulting DS-21 became the only car capable of 118 mph on a mere 119 horsepower.

Citroën wasted no time in proving the car's mettle. Six months after announcement, a DS taken at random from the first 500 off the assembly line came in first in class in the punishing Monte Carlo Rally. From then on, the DS was a serious force in European rallying. In 1961, the team of Bianchi and Harris in a DS-19 won the Liége-Sofia-Liége *Marathon de la Route*, a rugged 3,400-mile loop including 90 hours of uninterrupted flat-out driving.

Of 85 cars entered, it was one of only eight that survived: three were Citroëns. By the mid-Sixties, Citroëns were winning numerous rallies outright. Finland's Pauli Toivonen was proclaimed the 1962 Scandinavian rally champion because of his numerous victories with a DS-19. The following year, the DS was the outright winner in Finland's Snow Rally, the *Routes du Nord*, Lyon, and Norway again. By then Citroën held the Manufacturers Cup in the Monte Carlo and Liége-Sofia-Liége.

Road tests reported qualities which made the DS a winner on the street as well as in competition. *The Autocar* said it "could be hurtled round corners, braked violently, accelerated violently, with nothing untoward." But it was styling, not performance or competition, that most intrigued enthusiasts of the *Desirée Spéciale*. It was not so much a statement of style as of honest, uncompromising function.

The designers, Bertone of Turin, Italy, produced a shape unlike anything else

Some detractors thought the Citroën DS weird looking; others criticized it for being underpowered. At first, a 1.9-liter four delivered 75 bhp, good for 0-60 mph in about 18 seconds. Later, a 2.1-liter four developing 119-bhp pushed the DS to a top speed of nearly 120 mph.

The Citroën DS Estate was both roomy and practical. Note the single-spoke steering wheel and the unusual two-piece tailgate assembly.

on the road. To begin with, there was "half-door construction"—the door structure ended at the beltline and the windows were free-standing. In 1955, this was a new concept (shared only with VW's Karmann Ghia), and almost impossible to do well. The problem was that side windows without frames tended to flex, though Citroën's didn't. Combined with high, curving glass and a tall windshield, the DS had exceptional visibility. Another unique aspect was the minimal overhang. Despite a long 123-inch wheelbase—the same as a '55 Lincoln—the car was only 189 inches long, a couple of feet less than the typical 123-inch-wheelbase car of its time (26.6 inches shorter than that same Lincoln).

The sloping, grille-less nose, streamlined front fenders, and sloping deck were designed with aerodynamics as the paramount consideration. It was a stable form, almost unaffected by cross

winds, offering amazing cruising speeds and high mileage. Driven at a steady 40 mph the DS could deliver 35 miles per gallon; at 60 it gave 27. Citroën said that 2-3 mpg and about six mph were owed to the plastic coated canvas air passage, which ducted air to the radiator, eliminating the usual underhood air friction.

After the initial DS sedan, Citroën added the detrimmed ID series in 1956. A station wagon called the Safari (with family, ambulance, and commercial fittings) and a deluxe Prestige DS-19 sedan arrived in 1957, and a sleek convertible by Henri Chapron in 1960. Chapron also produced a Majesty razor-edged DS in 1964, special versions of which were built for French President de Gaulle. The most luxurious DS-21 was the Pallas, with interior trim remindful of a Parisian drawing room, though Chapron continued to produce even

more opulent one-offs on the 2.1- and 2.3-liter chassis.

D-series Citroëns were quickly recognized by the art community. In 1958, the Illinois Institute of Technology asked 100 leading architects, designers, and instructors to choose the 100 best mass-produced designs of modern times. Only 14 cars were named, but Citroën was one of them—along with the Cisitalia GS, first-generation Ford Thunderbird, VW Karmann-Ghia, Porsche 356, and the 1947 and '53 Studebaker coupes. That's pretty good company.

Specifications[1]	
Engine:	I-4, ohv, 2,175 cc/132.7 cid (90 x 86-mm bore x stroke) 8.75:1 compression ratio, 109 bhp @ 5,500 rpm, 128 lbs/ft torque @ 3,000 rpm
Transmission:	4-speed manual, front-wheel-drive transaxle
Suspension, front:	Independent, parallel semi-leading arms, hydropneumatic struts with height control, anti-roll bar
Suspension, rear:	Independent, single trailing arms, hydropneumatic struts with height control, anti-roll bar
Brakes:	4-wheel hydraulic, inboard-mounted front discs, outboard-mounted rear drums
Wheelbase (in.):	123.0
Overall length (in.):	190.5 (wagon 198.0)
Tread, front/rear (in.):	59.0/51.0
Weight (lbs):	2,855
Top speed (mph):	118.0
0-60 mph (sec):	est. 14.0
Production:	1,456,115 (all types, 1955-75)

[1]1968 DS 21, U.S. spec.

The always provocative Tom McCahill, writing in *Mechanix Illustrated*, called it "the finest production American sports car ever built, bar none." But of course the two-passenger Thunderbird of 1955-57 wasn't really a sports car at all. Ford described it, much more accurately (most of the time), as a "personal" car, one in which "even routine driving becomes thrilling entertainment."

Which isn't to say that the "Little Bird" didn't have some of the attributes expected of a sports car. For one thing, it was fast. Its 292-cubic-inch V-8 was borrowed from the Mercury, though the T-Bird was lighter than the Merc by at least 500 pounds. Horsepower was posted at a generous 193 or, in combination with the Ford-0-Matic transmission and a slightly higher compression ratio, 198 bhp. Top speed approached 120 miles an hour, and cars equipped with the stick shift would go from rest to 60 mph in less than 10 seconds.

Further, the new Thunderbird handled well. Balance was a good deal better than the average car—in McCahill's words, it cornered "as flat as a pool table." McCahill, in fact, was so impressed that he bought a T-Bird for himself, the very car that Ford confirmed to be the first T-Bird the factory equipped with the overdrive transmission.

It's quite true, of course, that the late 1953 introduction of Chevrolet's Corvette had a lot to do with inspiring Ford Motor Company to come up with a sporty car of its own. Nowhere has the art of industrial espionage become more highly refined than in the automobile business, so when Chevrolet commenced work on the development of its fiberglass-bodied two-seater, that fact didn't remain a secret for very long. Naturally, among the first to get wind of the Corvette project was Franklin Quick Hershey, Ford's talented styling director. Inspired by the idea, he and a young associate named Bill Boyer began, without fanfare of any kind, to develop some renderings.

That was in 1951. That fall Lewis Crusoe, general manager of the Ford Division, was traveling in France. During October, he and George Walker, head of the freelance styling team credited with the design of the 1949 Ford, attended the Paris Salon. There Crusoe became fascinated by some of the two-passenger sports cars being displayed by various European manufacturers. Walker told him—diplomatically but not altogether truthfully—that his staff was already at work on just such an automobile.

A series of trans-Atlantic telephone calls followed, so the story goes, with instructions that both Hershey's and Walker's staffs get cracking. The result was the '55 Ford Thunderbird, and to this day there are conflicting claims as to who masterminded its design. Some credit Bob Maguire, head of the Ford passenger car studio. Others point to a Ford stylist named Damon Wood. But in retrospect it seems certain that

Although the '55 Thunderbird was to be a Corvette fighter, Ford called it a "personal" car and gave it a host of luxury features.

it was Hershey and Boyer who were chiefly responsible for the end product.

The Little Thunderbird was not really expected to be a money maker for Ford. Rather, its mission was that of an image builder. And just to make sure the public got the point, the sporty car echoed the styling theme of the full-sized '55 Fords. Actually, the ads put it the other way around, trying to impart some of the T-Bird's glamorous sporty image to the regular workaday Fords. In any case, annual sales of 10,000 were projected— a ridiculously small figure by Ford standards. But the T-Bird did far better than that, as first-season output totaled 16,155 cars.

This little jewel didn't come cheap. The base price at first was $2,695, $391 more than the full-sized Fairlane convertible. Further, most buyers appear to have loaded the Thunderbird with options. Included among the popular extras were Ford-O-Matic; power steering, brakes, windows, and seat; white sidewall tires; and of course radio and heater. All of which ran the price up pretty rapidly. With a full load of accessories, the price crept very close to four grand. And by 1957 the options list had grown to include, among other goodies, automatic windshield washers,

a Dial-O-Matic power seat with a seven-position fore-and-aft and five position up-and-down memory, a radio whose volume automatically advanced as engine speed increased—even an Auto-home electric shaver.

The horsepower race was going full bore during the mid-Fifties, so it was more or less obligatory that the Thunderbird receive even more "Trigger-Torque 'Go'" for 1956. Thus, the standard

compression ratio was raised from 8.1:1 to 8.4:1, boosting the base engine's output to 202 bhp. And a larger 312-cid V-8, also borrowed from Mercury, was fitted to T-Birds equipped with either overdrive or Ford-O-Matic. Horsepower in this instance was rated at 215 with overdrive, 225 with the self-shifter. Or, for the all-out performance buff, a rarely installed 260-horsepower, four-barrel edition of the 312 was available at extra cost late in the year.

Other mechanical modifications included a slightly slower steering ratio and a somewhat softer ride, the latter resulting from the use of four- rather than five-leaf rear springs.

That first Thunderbird had been criticized for its minuscule luggage compartment, so for 1956 the spare tire was mounted on the outside, "continental" fashion. Not only did this provide a rather substantial boost in cargo capacity, but by shifting the weight slightly to the rear it tended to improve further the car's already superior balance.

A second criticism had to do with the "blind" spot created by the bolt-on hardtop. That fiberglass top was standard issue, by the way—it was the convertible canvas top that cost extra ($290

The '56 Thunderbird sported a standard continental spare tire, plus front fender ventilation flaps. Portholes for the hardtop were also new. For 1957, the T-Bird got a handsome new dashboard (above), and the 312-cid V-8 could be supercharged for 300 bhp or ordered with twin four-barrel carbs (as shown) for 270 or 285 horses.

Many two-seat T-Bird fans consider the '57 model to be the best looking of the lot. It was also the most popular, with 21,380 built. The base price for 1957 was $3,408.

in 1955). Bill Boyer solved that one with "portholes," a popular no-cost option which also added a neat styling touch. And flip-open cowl vents on the front fenders were added, helping to counteract the engine heat that tended to gather in the engine compartment and find its way into the cabin.

After record sales in 1955, the '56 model year was a downer for the automotive industry. Still, the Thunderbird fared better than most, though it in fact suffered a modest 3.2-percent drop in production to 15,631 units.

Meanwhile, a much more extensive restyling was under way for 1957. After the fashion of the time, fins were added—modest, canted appendages in this instance, beginning at the door handles and extending to the rear fender tips. The effect was surprisingly good. A combination front bumper and grille, proposed earlier by Bill Boyer but considered too radical at that time, was substituted for the original, Vignale-inspired grille. Further, the rear deck was extended five inches and the spare tire moved back into the trunk, all of which did good things for the car's proportions.

Other changes included larger, more competent brakes. And following an industry-wide trend, 14-inch wheels replaced the previous 15-inchers, thus slightly lowering the T-Bird's profile. In an about-face, five-leaf rear springs replaced the four-leaf units.

Power was increased again for 1957. The 292-cid V-8 was rated this time at 212 horsepower, thanks to an increase in the compression ratio from 8.4:1 to 9.1:1. The 312's output, meanwhile, was raised to 245 bhp with 9.7:1 compression and a four-barrel carb. Options included a pair of dual four-barrel carb editions, rated at 270 and 285 horsepower, the latter with the aid of a "Racing Kit."

And then there was one more Thunderbird: the supercharged, limited-production "F" series. Modified with reinforced cylinder heads, special combustion chambers with lowered compression ratio, dual-point distributor, a hotter camshaft, and a special fuel pump, these little hotshots were officially rated at 300 horses. However, as expert Ken Gross has noted, with a little fine tuning they were actually good for somewhere between 325 and 340.

Needless to say, the supercharged "F" series Thunderbird was expensive. With a normal complement of accessories, the tab exceeded $5,000, which was just about enough in 1957 to cover the price of a new Cadillac convertible. Ergo, it was the rarest '57 T-Bird of all. There is

some disagreement as to exactly how many of the blown T-Birds were built, but the figure wasn't much above 200.

The 1957 Little Birds proved to be the most numerous of all. Almost since the fall 1954 introduction of the original Thunderbird, plans had been underway for a four-place successor that became the '58 "Squarebird," much to the dismay of purists. But the larger T-Bird wasn't ready until February 1958, which gave the '57 edition an extended model year. Production of the final version of the two-passenger job totaled 21,380 units.

And then the two-seater Bird was gone. The corporate bean-counters were right, of course: the larger four-seater was more popular and certainly far more profitable for the company. But when it comes to charm you can't beat the Little Bird. It was, as Ford correctly advertised in 1955, "Seventh heaven on wheels."

Specifications	
Engine:	V-8, ohv, 312.1 cid (3.80 x 3.44-in. bore x stroke), 9.0:1 compression ratio, 5 main bearings, Holley 4-bbl carburetor, 225 bhp @ 4,600 rpm, 324 lbs/ft torque @ 2,600 rpm[1]
Transmission:	3-speed manual; overdrive and 3-speed Ford-O-Matic automatic planetary with torque converter optional
Suspension, front:	Independent, A-arms, coil springs, ball joints, link stabilizer bar, tubular shock absorbers
Suspension, rear:	Rigid axle, longitudinal leaf springs, tubular shock absorbers
Brakes:	Hydraulic, front/rear drums
Wheelbase (in.):	102.0
Overall length (in):	185.0 (incl. Continental kit)
Tread, front/rear (in.):	58.0/56.0
Curb weight (lbs):	3,570
Tires:	6.70 x 15 tubeless
Top speed (mph):	113.9 (Road & Track)[1]
0-60 mph (sec):	9.3[1]
Production:	1955 16,155 1956 15,631 1957 21,380

[1]1956 model with Ford-O-Matic

In the Fifties, every manufacturer tried to produce a "flagship" or limited-edition model to bring people into the showrooms, where it was hoped they would be inspired to purchase one of the run-of-the-mill models. Of course, most companies were happy to sell a flagship to those who had the money, and a lot of Packard customers did. The problem with Packard's *grand luxe* supercar was that *Packard* didn't have the money—not enough of it, anyway. The company tooled to build only 500 Caribbeans in 1955 and 539 in 1956, though the evidence was great that it could have sold many more. By comparison, Cadillac showed more entrepreneurship by down-pricing the Eldorado from its 1953 heights, thus selling an increasing number of Eldos: 3,950 in 1955 and 6,050 in 1956.

The first Caribbean arrived in 1953 (as did the first Eldorado), styled by young Dick Teague along the lines of the Pan American show cars, which had been designed and built for Packard by the Henney Company. The '53 and its successors were handsome enough, but the Caribbean really flowered in 1955, when Packard produced a number of engineering innovations to go with it: adjustable torsion-bar suspension for a "Torsion-Level" ride, the most powerful V-8 in the industry except for the Chrysler Hemi, and an extensive facelift that injected new excitement into the hitherto fairly staid Packard bodies. Caribbeans were offered only as convertibles in 1955, but about half of the '56s were hardtops.

Unlike earlier Caribbeans, the '55 rode Packard's senior 127-inch wheelbase, up from 122. Cash-short since the early Fifties, the company had been unable to tool a long-wheelbase convertible. However, it finally managed in 1955 thanks to plastic tooling, a new process which took a lot of time and about 60 percent of the cost out of the tooling process. Plastic tooling also allowed for the production of the Four Hundred, Packard's first 127-inch-wheelbase hardtop, on which the Caribbean hardtop was based.

Along with Teague's line-wide eggcrate grille and "cathedral taillights," the Caribbean featured a unique hood with twin dummy scoops and (in most cases) a three-tone paint job—very upmarket in 1955. To this Packard threw in as standard every option except wire wheels ($325), tinted or shaded glass, and air conditioning. Thrown in for good measure were leather upholstered, specially contoured seats; twin radio antennas; and gold anodized nameplates. Then again, Packard was charging $5,932 base for the car, and people who spent that kind of money wanted to be noticed. Most of them, anyway—one who didn't was Howard Hughes, who presented a white-pink-black Caribbean to his future wife, actress Jean Peters. That car has survived in pristine condition.

As in 1953-54, the Caribbean served as Packard's flagship in '55. The styling was all-new (though the bodyshell under it wasn't), with hooded headlights, massive "cathedral" taillights, an eggcrate grille, and bright new colors.

254

This Caribbean was probably a late '55 because it has the '56's straked hood scoops. The padded dash sported a full-width gold-tone textured applique, set off by a deluxe, two-tone steering wheel. Leather covered the seats and twin antennas graced the rear fenders.

The '55 also featured a highly tuned version of the new 352-cubic-inch V-8 developing 275 horsepower, more than every other 1955 car except the limited production Chrysler 300, and just enough more (five bhp) than Cadillac to one-up Packard's long-time rival. This was achieved by bolting on two Rochester four-barrel carburetors, which drank 20-cents-a-gallon premium gas to the tune of about 10 mpg.

All of the styling and engineering changes resulted in a '55 Caribbean "as smart and exhilarating as the island domain for which it was named. A car designed for thrills, excitement and pure pleasure." Not surprisingly, dealers were crying for more Caribbeans when the meager '55 supply ran out—so much so that Packard coaxed some agencies to specially trim Four Hundreds, a few of which have emerged over the years as ersatz '55 Caribbean hardtops.

For 1956, Packard decided to offer a genuine Caribbean hardtop (Cadillac also added an Eldo hardtop that year), but made the indefensible decision again to produce only about 500 units, including convertibles, the exact breakdown being 276 ragtops and 263 hardtops. From a financial standpoint, the firm need not have bothered, for it lost money on every one. From a collector standpoint it's great that they built at least those few: the 1956 Caribbean is today one of the most desirable postwar cars.

To the established three-tone paint job and special styling features the new Caribbean added the '56 facelift features: more deeply hooded front fenders, wider bumper guards, a new "V and Circle" hood and deck ornament, and a minor trim shuffle. A practical new feature was reversible seat cushions: seats and seatbacks upholstered in leather on one side and fabric on the other, instantly changeable and unique, as far as we know, to this model alone. Packard also added a gold anodized fine-mesh grille background to the Caribbeans and other '56 Packards early in production, when the '56 Cadillac appeared with similar gold accents.

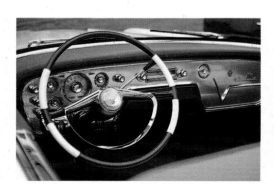

Engineering also featured in the 1956 Caribbean package. New were power door locks, pushbutton Twin Ultramatic transmission, Twin-Traction limited-slip differential, negative instead of positive ground and, once again, a highly tuned engine built specially for the Caribbean. All 1956 Packards went to a 374-cubic-inch V-8 in 1956, but whereas Patricians and Four Hundreds made do with 275 bhp, the dual four-barrel Caribbean gave 310 horses and 405 lbs/ft torque—both figures were just high enough to eclipse the new 365-cid Cadillac.

Packard had a lot of service troubles in 1955—torsion-level motors that didn't work, bad differentials, troublesome Twin Ultramatic transmissions—and a few more in 1956, like electric woes with the new pushbutton transmission selectors. A problem unique to the Caribbean involved the reversible seats, which seemed like a good idea at the time but were really more trouble than they were worth. To make up for the rigidity lost by the lack of integral cushions, interior designers produced a very heavy seat frame, which tended to flop forward under even light braking, crushing anything on the front seat, like butter or eggs. Packard then devised

As in 1955, the Caribbean was treated to colorful leather upholstery in 1956, but this time with unique reversible seat cushions with fabric on the flip side.

a knob to restrain the seatback, which had to be pulled to fold it forward—a crude version of the mandatory seatback locks on modern cars. This worked, but once wear set in the seatbacks began flopping down again. "The cushion covers had zippers, so theoretically one

could remove the covers and have them dry-cleaned (forget it)," Packard authority George Hamlin has noted. "The seats ended up costing Packard a lot of money. Not only were they produced in limited quantity and subject to the restraint problem, but some early purchasers complained that the cushions were too hard. . . . Take a snappy left turn in a Caribbean with the leather side up, and you risked being slammed against the right door, from which position it can be difficult to control the car. To fix that complaint, Packard released kits to make the seat cushions softer. The cost of this project is impossible to calculate . . . ."

It's curious how companies knee deep in trouble spend money on inconsequentia, but there it is. Studebaker-Packard Corporation was fast running out of money in 1956, and by August of that year all potential sources had dried up. S-P signed a management contract with the Curtiss-Wright Aircraft Corporation, which mainly mismanaged the firm over the next two years, when pseudo-Packards were built using Studebaker bodies. The Packard name was retired after 1958, the Caribbean name after 1956. At least the Caribbean left on a high note.

At $5,995, the facelifted '56 Caribbean ragtop featured more deeply hooded headlights, wider-spaced bumper guards, and a fine gold mesh behind the eggcrate grille.

Specifications	
Engine:	V-8, ohv, 5 main bearings, hydraulic valve lifters, 2 4-bbl Rochester carburetors **1955** 352 cid (4.00 x 3.50-in. bore x stroke), 8.5:1 compression ratio, 275 bhp @ 4,800 rpm **1956** 374 cid (4.125 x 3.50-in.), 10.0:1 c.r., 310 bhp @ 4,600 rpm, 405 lbs/ft torque
Transmission:	2-speed Twin Ultramatic with gear-start and lock-up torque converter **1955** column-mounted shift lever **1956** column-mounted electric pushbutton control
Suspension, front:	Independent, longitudinal torsion bars
Suspension, rear:	Live axle, longitudinal torsion bars, interconnected with the front; electric self-leveling
Brakes:	Hydraulic, front/rear 11-12-in. drums
Wheelbase (in.):	127.0
Overall length (in.):	218.5
Tread, front/rear (in.):	60.0/61.0
Weight (lbs):	4,590-4,960
Tires:	8.00 x 15 tubeless
Top speed (mph):	120
0-60 mph (sec):	11.0-12.0
Production:	**1955** cvt 500 **1956** cvt 276 htp cpe 263

The BMW 507, designed by Count Albrecht Goertz, is best remembered for its styling: "beautiful and timeless," said one journalist.

Today, the Bavarian Motor Works in Munich builds Mercedes-Benz rivals, but BMW has had a topsy-turvy history, embracing everything from motorcycles to egg-shaped bubble cars. Before the Hitler war the only BMW automobiles of significance were the powerful six-cylinder 327 and 328 sports cars, whose engines later powered Bristols, along with Arnolts, ACs, and Frazer-Nashes. After 1945, the firm kept itself busy building the basic-transportation BMW-Isetta 300 and 600 bubbles, plus a handful of big cars, the 501 and 502.

By 1956, the company was showing a new sporting coupe and cabriolet based on the 2.6-liter 502 and called, logically, the 503. Powered by an enlarged V-8 of 3.2 liters, the 503 had been shaped by Count Albrecht Goertz—an important designer who came to the BMW project fresh from a stint at Raymond Loewy Associates. The 503, an expensive indulgence to get BMW back into sporting, or semi-sporting, machinery, had been first shown in prototype form in 1954. But it didn't appeal to the U.S. importer, Max Hoffman—canny New York City retailer of BMWs, among numerous other high-pedigree European makes.

Before the war, Max Hoffman had been an Austrian Rolls-Royce/Bentley dealer and an amateur racer, especially of motorcycles. When the hostilities started he moved to America, where he founded a plastics factory and developed a metalized plastic that corralled a lucrative business with the War Department. After the war, he used his wealth to reestablish his car business, choosing the best location he could conceive of in the sure knowledge that the market for expensive European luxury cars was wide open. Hoffman was the first importer and/or the conceiver of such memorable cars as the Mercedes-Benz SLs, the Facel Vegas, and the Porsche Speedster. In 1954, he helped shape the most important BMW of the early postwar years: the 507. It is not inaccurate to say there would never have been one without him.

According to Eric Dahlquist, writing in *Collectible Automobile*, every 507 development story connects Hoffman with designer Albrecht Goertz: Hoffman "saw some sketches of a new sports car BMW was working on, though it's unclear whether this was the forthcoming 503 or something completely different. What is clear is that Hoffman didn't like it. He also felt strongly that the kind of dour, traditionally Teutonic styling embodied in the 'Baroque Angel' wouldn't even get a second glance on Park Avenue or Sunset Boulevard, which is where it counted in this league. So, according to the designer, Hoffman urged Goertz to submit ideas for a two-seater. He did, the powers in Munich were intrigued, and Goertz had the assignment by November 1954."

The 507's aluminum V-8 has been denounced by one writer as "totally conventional," and if this means a simple design that got the job done, it will have to plead guilty. Standard tune offered 150 DIN

horsepower (10 more than the 503), with 160 bhp optional. That was pretty good for just 193 cubic inches in 1956. A Detroit company would have rated it at close to one bhp per cubic inch, box office news when Chevrolet announced it in 1957. Though the 507 wasn't light, it was geared for *autobahn* work with a 3.7:1 standard axle ratio that would deliver 128 mph. Those who spent all their time on *autobahnen* could specify a 3.42:1 ratio and 10 more DIN horsepower, good for 138 mph. Stirred by a smooth four-speed transmission and held down by large, capable drum brakes, the standard axle yielded 0-60-mph sprints in seven seconds, and a reported 24 miles per gallon at cruising speeds. Not bad for a conventional engine.

The 507 also handled well, thanks to a torsion bar independent front suspension and a well-located live rear axle with transverse Panhard rod. Its sophisticated tubular chassis gave it great rigidity compared to most open roadsters of the day. Its rack and pinion steering was crisp and precise. Mechanically, it was exactly what BMW needed at the time: capable and uncomplicated.

So far, what we have here is an interesting, well-built, competent—but overpriced—car which cost more new than a Mercedes-Benz 300SL Gullwing. So why are original 507s today priced in the stratosphere, when one can be found one at all? Styling is the first reason. It is also the second and the third reasons.

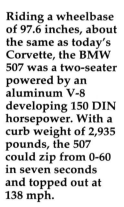

Riding a wheelbase of 97.6 inches, about the same as today's Corvette, the BMW 507 was a two-seater powered by an aluminum V-8 developing 150 DIN horsepower. With a curb weight of 2,935 pounds, the 507 could zip from 0-60 in seven seconds and topped out at 138 mph.

Like any proper German sports car, the 507 roadster came equipped with bucket seats and placed a large speedometer and tachometer directly in front of the driver.

The 507, auto journalist Rich Taylor wrote, "is easily the most beautiful and timeless German car since the Sturm und Drang Porsche-designed SSKs. There is nothing in particular to rave about: Goertz's car simply looks right. It is thin in section, yet not at all dachshundlike. It's long and low, but unsquashed. The [optional] lightweight, lift-off roof is perfectly shaped and proportioned, yet it dominates nothing. The pointed nose with twin nostrils echoes the classic twin grilles of early BMWs, yet it is perfectly right and totally integrated into one of the smoothest, classiest bodies ever. It could be powered by twisted rubber bands and no one would care a whit." It could also be built today and not give away much, design-wise.

If it was so good, why didn't it sell? Hoffman figured that at $5,000 the 507 would sell at least 5,000 units a year, which would be more than adequate for a handsome profit. Alas, by the time he got 507s to sell, the price had risen to $9,000, nearly the cost of two Cadillacs at the time. Hoffman had a hard time getting rid of them even in his exalted location. Production over the course of a four-year model run amounted to only 254 chassis, all but

three fitted with the production body. The other three were the Goertz prototype, the "Loraymo" special built by Raymond Loewy and used as a bench mark for the Studebaker Avanti, and a Vignale body built by Scaglietti.

During the collector car boom years of 1988-89, 507s came up surprisingly often at auction, setting record after record for high bids, and a fair proportion sold. The prices have since leveled off, for the time being at least, but they're still good investments because they are so scarce that demand is always bound to be strong. Longtime collector Gilbert Steward says every one is worth restoring, no matter what its condition: "Restoration won't be easy, of course, because every 507 is, in a sense, a 'custom' job because of hand labor variations from one to the next and because mechanical components were changed on an as-needed basis." And this is hardly the sort of car you run across every day.

Estimates vary widely on the number of survivors. In 1975, a longtime 507 owner, John Kessler of Richmond, Virginia, compiled a register listing 180 examples, but the German BMW Vintage Club has more recently accounted for about 200.

Specifications	
Engine:	Aluminum V-8, ohv, 193.3 cid/3,168 cc (82 x 75-mm bore x stroke), 7.8:1 compression ratio, 2 Zenith carburetors, 150 bhp @ 5,000 rpm, 173 lbs/ft torque @ 2,000 rpm; 160 bhp opt.
Transmission:	4-speed manual
Suspension, front:	Independent, with wishbones, torsion bars, anti-roll bar
Suspension, rear:	Live axle, radius rods, A-bracket, torsion bars
Brakes:	Hydraulic, front/rear drums (front discs 1958-59)
Wheelbase (in.):	97.6
Tread, front/rear (in.):	56.9/56.1
Weight (lbs):	2,935
Tires:	6.00H x 16
0-60 mph (sec):	7.0-8.8, depending upon gearing
Top speed (mph):	128-138
Production:	254, incl. the prototype

The "greatness" of the 1956-57 Corvette, here a '57, was that it proved to the world that Chevy was truly serious about "America's" sports car.

ike Hollywood movies, American cars may not always be the best in the world, but the world always seems to love them. That's particularly true of America's sports car, the Chevrolet Corvette. For almost 40 years, it has been changing and improving—sometimes dramatically—yet has never lacked the ability to stir souls and fire imaginations.

Popularity alone doesn't make any car "great," of course, never mind securing it a place in the pantheon of motoring's first century, so one must be selective even among Corvettes. Viewed dispassionately, the second-generation 1956-57 models were the first that honestly deserved to be called "greats." Not coincidentally, they were also the first Corvettes the world could take seriously.

As most everyone knows, the Corvette came about because General Motors design chief Harley Earl liked sports cars, knew Chevrolet needed something flashy to reverse its solid-citizen image, and had the clout to make it happen. The original 1953 model was a curious blend of old and new. Styling was straight from GM's futuristic Motorama shows—which, in fact, is where it was first seen: clean, but oh-so-trendy, with its wrapped windshield, jet-pod taillamps, toothy grille, and Euro-style mesh headlamp guards. On the other hand, old-fashioned side curtains substituted for proper roll-down windows, and though a convenient hard cover hid the soft top, door handles were conspicuously absent. The open two-seater body was made of fiberglass, the new postwar "wonder" material that promised to revolutionize consumer goods from fountain pens to travel trailers, but the essential underpinnings were mundane passenger Chevrolet: an orthodox inline six that had been around since the Depression, a decidedly unsporting two-speed automatic transmission, and the usual kind of GM frame. Granted, the engine was tuned to a fare-thee-well and the chassis ended up virtually all-new, but as a technical package the Corvette was far removed from the likes of Jaguar's sophisticated XK120.

Worse, for Chevrolet at least, this dream-car-come-true quickly turned into something of a nightmare. Assembly line problems with the complex body (no fewer than 46 separate pieces) and lack of plant capacity held 1953 production to just 315 cars. Yet, the person on the street couldn't really buy one because they were earmarked for VIPs and dealer promotion. The '54 edition changed little, but was more readily available because Chevy had transferred production from its Flint, Michigan plant to larger facilities in St. Louis. But though output increased 10-fold for 1954, it came to less than a third of projections. More troublesome was that some 1,500 Corvettes remained unsold at year's end.

Happily, 1955 brought the brilliant new overhead-valve V-8 that would prove to be the Corvette's salvation. Developed for

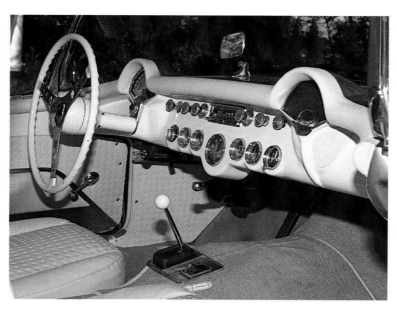

One feature of the '56 Corvette often criticized was the dashboard—gauges were scattered across its width and the tach was too low and at the center of the dash.

that year's all-new passenger Chevys by Harry Barr and division chief engineer Edward N. Cole, this efficient, high-revving 265-cubic-inch unit weighed 30 pounds less than the old six, but packed 30 percent more horsepower for the 'Vette—195 bhp versus 150. Performance was utterly transformed, and even the purists suddenly took notice. They were also pleased to note the new three-speed manual transmission option announced late in the model run, plus some adroit chassis tuning by recently hired Belgian-born engineer Zora Arkus-Duntov. Yet for all that, plus a major price cut from $3,523 to $2,799, only 674 of the '55s were built.

Profit-minded GM bigwigs were ready to kill the Corvette right there, but Earl and Cole pleaded for a stay of execution. Ford, meanwhile, helped their case by releasing its posh new "personal" car, the 1955 Thunderbird—a competitive challenge GM couldn't ignore. The Corvette was duly granted a reprieve.

Earl, Cole, and Duntov were prepared, for the all-new car they brought forth for 1956 marked a Corvette renaissance that continues to this day. With it, Chevrolet could rightfully proclaim itself as builder of "America's only true sports car," as indeed it did. Ironically, the decision to make the Corvette a genuine high-performance sports car came just as Ford was taking off in another direction, making the Thunderbird a lush, four-seat showboat.

Compared to the slab-sided first generation Corvette, the '56 was stun-

ning. Earl fashioned fresh new styling with show car-inspired elements like elliptical bodyside indentations, eventually called "coves" by 'Vette folk. The overall result was tasteful for that age of garishness—yet sexy, low-slung, distinctly American, and still recognizably Corvette. The only questionable elements were phony air scoops atop the front fenders, dummy knock-off hubs on the wheel covers (retained from 1953-55), and a dash that remained more flash than function.

While the '56 looked decidedly more like a serious sports car, it was also more civilized. Featured were comfier seats covered in a new "waffle-weave" vinyl (also found on door panels), roll-up windows (electrically operated at extra cost), exterior door handles, and an optional lift-off hardtop (previewed on a 1954 Motorama Corvette) for sedan-like weather protection. Even the convertible top was better: tighter, more integrated, rounded at the rear to echo the new French-curve rear fenders, and now blessed with power operation.

Beneath this finery was a chassis heavily reworked by engineering wizard Duntov. Without upsetting the near-equal front/rear weight distribution of the previous models (52/48 percent), he tightened up both steering response and handling. Though understeer was still a tad excessive and the cast-iron all-drum brakes "faded into oblivion" in hard stops, as one magazine stated, the 'Vette was now as quick through turns as it was on the straights.

And quick it was. The superb small-block V-8 had been an option fitted to all but six '55 Corvettes. Now it was standard—and up to 210 horsepower in normal tune or 225 bhp with a "Power

The '56 'Vette received more conventionally mounted headlights and bodyside "coves," which were usually two-toned. Wind-up windows were a welcome feature.

At the rear, the 1956-57 Corvette (here a '57) gave up the "jet pod" taillights with the mini fins for a neater, more rounded look. The optional hardtop is much coveted nowadays.

Pak" comprising a high-lift cam, twin four-barrel carbs, and dual exhausts. Better yet, an optional over-the-counter "Duntov cam" upped output to 240. The old six? Gone for good, and *Motor Life* expressed the sentiments of many by asking, "Who cares?" Also standard now was the close-ratio manual three-speed (still with non-synchronized first), the Powerglide automatic having been shunted to the options sheet at $189. Further enhancing performance were an improved differential and a larger, stronger coil-spring clutch replacing a diaphragm-spring type.

With all this, the most potent '56 could hit 60 mph from rest in a swift 7.5 seconds and approach 120 mph. *Sports Car Illustrated*'s Karl Ludvigsen was enthusiastically impressed, proclaiming the new Corvette "fully as much a dual-purpose machine as the stock Jaguar, Triumph or Austin-Healey. Without qualification, General Motors is now building a sports car."

There was no need to change the handsome styling for 1957, but Chevy upped performance by boring the V-8 from 3.75 to 3.875 inches while retaining the 3.00-inch stroke. The result was 283 cid in five engines offering from 220 bhp to an amazing 283 bhp, the latter courtesy of new "Ramjet" fuel injection. A new four-speed Borg-Warner manual arrived in May as a $188 extra,

and when combined with axle ratios as short as 4.11:1 the "fuelie" '57s were thunderingly fast. Road tests showed 0-60 mph in 5.7 seconds, 0-100 in 16.8 seconds, the standing quarter-mile in 14.3 seconds at 96 mph, and a maximum of 132 mph plus. Alas, mechanical bugs and a $500 price tag limited Ramjet installations to only 240 Corvettes, one of the reasons they're now among the most prized cars of the Fifties.

Chevy also whipped up a $725 "heavy-duty racing suspension" package for '57, comprising high-rate springs and shocks, front anti-roll bar, quick steering, and ceramic-metallic brake linings with finned ventilated drums. With this and one of the high-power engines, a Corvette was virtually ready to race right off the showroom floor.

All '57 Corvettes ran with a V-8 bored to 283 cid. Fuel injection was now available, but most 'Vettes were ordered with a four-barrel carb, 220-bhp setup.

And indeed, these were the years when the Corvette began to make its mark in international competition. Dr. Richard Thompson won the Sports Car Club of America C-Production national championship in 1956, then took the '57 crown in B-Production, where the 'Vette qualified that year by dint of its larger engine. John Fitch's '56 was the fastest modified car at that year's Daytona Speed Weeks, a Corvette finished ninth in the gruelling 12 Hours of Sebring in '56, and another came home second (behind a Mercedes 300SL) at Pebble Beach that same year. Chevy's 1957 Sebring assault saw production Corvettes finish 1-2 in the GT class and 12th and 15th overall.

It was all symbolic of a dramatic metamorphosis. Said one European writer: "Before Sebring...the Corvette was regarded as a plastic toy. After Sebring, even the most biased were forced to admit that [it was one] of the world's finest sports cars...."

That included buyers, who happily snapped up 3,467 of the '56s and 6,339 of the '57s, a far cry from the dismal figures of 1955. It had taken some time, but the Corvette was no longer trying to imitate anything from Europe. And from here on, it would never again be confused with anything else on the road.

Specifications	
Engines:	V-8, ohv **1956** 265 cid/4,343 cc (3.75 x 3.00-in./95.2 x 76.2-mm bore x stroke), 210/225 bhp @ 5,200 rpm, 270 lbs/ft torque @ 3600 rpm; 240 bhp with opt. Duntov cam **1957** 283 cid/4,638 cc (3.875 x 3.00-in./98.4 x 76.2-mm), 220 bhp @ 4,800rpm, 300 lbs/ft @ 3,000 rpm; 245 bhp @ 5,000 rpm, 300 lbs/ft @ 3,800 rpm; 250 bhp @ 5,000 rpm, 305 lbs/ft @ 3,800 rpm; 270 bhp @ 6,000 rpm, 285 lbs/ft @ 4,200 rpm; 283 bhp @ 6,200 rpm, 290 lbs/ft @ 4,400 rpm (FI)
Transmission:	Close-ratio 3-speed manual; 2-speed Powerglide automatic opt., 4-speed manual opt. beginning May 1957
Suspension, front:	Unequal-length A-arms, coil springs, tube shocks, anti-roll bar
Suspension, rear:	Live axle on semi-elliptic leaf springs, tube shocks
Brakes:	Hydraulic, front/rear drums
Wheelbase (in.):	102.0
Weight (lbs):	2,730-2,764
Top speed (mph):	**1956** 121-129 **1957** 115-130
0-60 mph (sec):	**1956** 7.3-8.9 **1957** 5.7-8.0
Production:	**1956:** 3,467 **1957:** 6,339

The Continental Mark II was the product of the Continental Division of Ford Motor Company. Its styling was elegant and understated.

By the time the opening guns of World War II were heard, a fabulous era in the automobile business was, to all intents and purposes, over. Gone was the magnificent custom coachwork from firms such as Judkins, Locke, Dietrich, Murphy, and others. Gone, too, was the meticulous craftsmanship, the painstaking hand work, the precision of fit and finish that had been the special province for the privileged few—those who could afford the very best. Gone were the distinctive lines that set apart the cars that we now know as the "Classics."

By the time the war was over and the production of automobiles commenced once again, Cadillac and the senior Packards were hardly more than shadows of what they once had been. Lincoln was little more than a 12-cylinder Mercury, and one had to look twice to distinguish an Imperial from a Dodge. The great names lived on, but the Classic car was dead.

Except in a limited sense, for there was an exception in those immediate postwar years. That's because early in 1946 Ford resumed production—in modest numbers—of Edsel Ford's fabled Lincoln Continental. Mechanically it was anachronistic, and certainly its body was not built to true coachwork standards, but such was the beauty of the Continental that nobody seriously disputed its designation as a *bona fide* Classic.

But then, in the spring of 1948, production of the Lincoln Continental was discontinued, having just barely outlasted the 1946-47 Packard Custom Super Clipper, which later became about the only other postwar car recognized as a Classic. Now, with the demise of the Continental, the Classic era was truly over.

By the early Fifties, however, Lincoln was preparing to mount a serious challenge to Cadillac's ever-growing domination of the luxury-car market. Lincolns had established an enviable performance image by dominating the famed *Carrera Panamericana* Mexican Road Race, but performance doesn't necessarily sell high-priced automobiles. Prestige does, and in that respect the Lincoln was simply no match for Cadillac.

The obvious solution was to introduce a new Continental, so in July 1952 a small group of engineers and stylists was assembled under the leadership of 26-year-old William Clay Ford, youngest of Edsel Ford's three sons. Known as the Special Projects Operation, this organization was formed for the express purpose of developing just such a car. Its intent, as *Motor Life* magazine noted, was to carry on the original Continental's reputation for excellence of design, but to add to it unsurpassed quality of engineering and construction.

It should be noted that the car this group developed was never referred to as a *Lincoln Continental* by Ford Motor Company, nor should it have been by anyone else—though that happened all too often.

The Mark II came only as a hardtop coupe, and listed at $9,645. A fake "continental" spare tire-look was seen up back, mimicking the 1940-48 Mark I. Interiors featured Bridge of Wier leather. Note the gas cap hidden behind the taillight.

Properly, it was (and remains) simply the Continental Mark II. By the time it was first introduced to the public at the Paris Auto Show on October 6, 1955 (October 21 in Dearborn for the U.S.), Continental was a separate division of Ford Motor Company. It boasted its own officers and staff, housed in sumptuous new quarters, and had its own manufacturing facility designed with quality, rather than volume, in mind.

The general characteristics of the original Lincoln Continental's styling were retained in the new car: long hood, short deck, and a very low center of gravity. An overall height of just 56 inches was achieved with no sacrifice in headroom by means of a three-joint driveline and a double-ladder "cowbelly" frame, which permitted recessing the floor panels between the frame rails. Ground clearance was maintained by routing the muffler inlet pipes around the outside of the frame.

The most distinguishing feature of the original Lincoln Continental had been its outboard-mounted "continental" spare tire. There had been a host of imitators from various manufacturers, some as factory equipment, others as after-market accessories—but none had come close to the smart design of Edsel Ford's original.

To have followed the same practice with the Mark II would have been to imitate the imitators, and this Bill Ford and his design group wisely refused to do. Instead, the decklid was formed so as to "suggest" the continental tire, while the actual spare was mounted inside the trunk, utilizing—at the expense of accessibility—the space provided by the humped deck.

Once the design had been determined, the Special Projects group turned its attention to the mechanical components from which the car was to be assembled, and to techniques of construction and finish appropriate to an automobile that was expected to become a modern American classic.

The engine selected was basically the 285-horsepower, 368-cubic-inch V-8 of the 1956 Lincoln, but for this application special pains were taken. Following the usual dynamometer tests to which all Lincoln engines were subjected, those units destined for the Continental were partially disassembled, minutely inspected, and then carefully reassembled. Automatic transmissions, also stock Lincoln Turbo-Drive units, were road tested in a vehicle before being shipped to the Continental assembly plant, there to be mated to the engine and tested twice more: first on a dynamometer, then on the road in the completed car.

Meanwhile, other components were selected with equal care. Sheetmetal was inspected at supplier plants by Continental quality control engineers. Matched hides for the luxurious leather interiors were imported from Bridge of Weir, a section of Scotland where the cattle were reputed to be of especially gentle disposition—the point being that there would be no imperfections in the leather as the result of the poking of bovine horns. Nor would there be any scars from barbed wire, which wasn't used there. Carpeting, identical in the passenger compartment and the trunk, was 1.5-inch deep-pile rayon (blended with 10 percent nylon), the kind that invites a barefoot romp.

Then came the final fit and finish. All body panels and sheet metal were assembled and fitted, then removed for simultaneous painting, thus assuring accurate color matching. Several primer coats were applied, followed by a double surfacing coat and two separate double coats of hand-rubbed lacquer. Buyers could choose from 14 solid colors and five two-tone combinations. Chrome plating was applied over successive layers of copper and nickel—three times as durable as SAE standards required. Nuts and bolts were hand-torqued to aircraft standards. And finally, each Continental Mark II was shipped in its own fleece-lined cover.

Thus, the Continental Mark II was intended to represent a return to the standards of quality that had character-

The 285-bhp, 368-cid Lincoln V-8s used in the Mark II were tested extensively before installation.

ized the "factory customs" of the Thirties. The company boasted that more time was spent in metal-finishing and painting each car than was normally required for the complete assembly of other high-quality automobiles.

And the Continental was loaded. Standard equipment included automatic transmission, power steering, power brakes, power windows, four-way power front seats, radio, dual heaters, engine compartment lamp, slatted wheel covers with individually-fitted vanes, white sidewall tires, full instrumentation including tachometer, map lights, fuel warning light, undercoating, and polished aluminum rocker-arm covers. The only available extra, and seemingly the only possible addition to such a fully-equipped car, was air conditioning, with the ducting built into the headliner.

Of course, the Continental Mark II didn't come cheap. The price was $9,645, or $10,430 with air conditioning, figures close to double the price of a Lincoln Premier.

Given its ponderous weight—nearly two and a half tons—and its relatively tall (3.07:1) gearing, the Mark II was never intended to be a "banker's hot rod." Zero-to-sixty took a full 14 seconds. But Floyd Clymer, road-testing a Continental for *Popular Mechanics*, reported a top speed of 118 miles per hour. Even today a 35-year-old Mark II will cruise effortlessly and silently, all day long, at speeds far in excess of the legal limit.

Sales during the first weeks after introduction must have brought joy to the heart of young Bill Ford. The break-even point had been calculated at about 1,600 units annually, and the initial output was proceeding at more than

twice that rate. Even so, a long waiting list was reported in some parts of the country. In a few instances dealers demanded, and got, a $1,000 premium over the list price.

But then the bubble burst. Compared to the first optimistic weeks, the pace of sales was about one-third slower during the first quarter of 1956, and from that point on it was downhill all the way. By the first quarter of 1957, demand had dried up to such an extent that only 200 Mark IIs were built, and by the time production ceased, on May 8 of that year, only 3,000 Continental Mark IIs had been built. It is estimated that the company lost $1,000 on each one produced.

But then, the Mark II hadn't been intended as a money maker. It was intended to be America's number one prestige car, the assumption being that some of its glamour would rub off on the handsome new Lincoln Premier. And perhaps in that sense it did succeed, for during 1956 Lincoln celebrated an 85-percent increase in output.

There's an interesting postscript to the Mark II story. When the Special Projects operation was terminated, its imposing executive offices were taken over by another new division of the Ford Motor Company, one that seemed sure to be a winner. They called it the Edsel.

Specifications	
Engine:	1956 V-8, ohv, 368 cid (4.00 x 3.66-in bore x stroke), 9.5:1 compression ratio, Carter 4-bbl carburetor, 285 bhp @ 4,800 rpm, 401 lbs/ft torque @ 2,800 rpm 1957 10.0:1 c.r., 300 bhp
Transmission:	3-speed Turbo-Drive automatic with torque converter
Suspension, front:	Independent, unequal A-arms, coil springs, ball joints, link stabilizer bar, tubular hydraulic shocks
Suspension, rear:	Rigid axle, longitudinal semi-elliptic springs, tubular hydraulic shocks
Brakes:	Hydraulic, front/rear drums, power-assisted
Wheelbase (in.):	126.0
Overall length (in.):	218.5
Overall width (in.):	77.5
Shipping weight (lbs):	4,797
Tires:	8.00 x 15 (8.20 x 15 with air)
0-60 mph (sec):	14.0
Top speed (mph):	118 (per Floyd Clymer)
Production:	1955 1,231 1956 1,325 1957 444 (calendar year)

For years, Cadillac had dominated the luxury car field. But not since the demise of the great V-16, back in 1940, had the division built what might be termed a "Super Car." Chances are it wouldn't have built one in 1957, either, but for the recent introduction of the Continental Mark II. For a sort of low-profile game of one-upmanship was going on in those days between the two giants of the American automobile industry, General Motors and Ford—and GM wasn't about to be upstaged!

For several years, General Motors had been sponsoring elaborate "Motoramas," traveling road shows in which certain of the corporation's production automobiles were displayed alongside some exotic "concept" cars. In 1954, for example, there were three of these futuristic machines, a coupe known as the El Camino, a roadster named La Espada, and a four-door luxury sedan called the Park Avenue. And although the coupe and the roadster— both built on a shortened, 115-inch wheelbase—were flashy, it was the more sedate Park Avenue that drew the most attention.

The same thing had happened a year earlier, when the Orleans, a pillarless four-door hardtop, had upstaged—at least as far as the moneyed crowd was concerned—a slinky prototype convertible called the LeMans.

By the time the 1954 Motorama was staged, Ford's plan to introduce a new Continental was no longer a secret. The general parameters of the Mark II had been established, and estimates of its very high price were being rumored. For competitive reasons, a response from General Motors was almost mandatory. So, with a shove from chief stylist Harley Earl, the Park Avenue became the basis for Cadillac's new Super Car, the Eldorado Brougham. Introduced in December 1956 as the flagship of the 1957 Cadillac line, the Eldorado Brougham followed, in general, the Park Avenue's styling theme. But a number of changes were made. For example, the display car's aluminum roof was replaced by brushed stainless steel, and massive stainless steel skirts covered the lower rear fenders. The side pillars were eliminated, transforming the sedan into a four-door hardtop.

Air intakes were built into the tops of the front fenders, and "quad" headlamps—still illegal in some states—were fitted. There were slim, understated chrome moldings sweeping back from the tips of the front fenders to louvered vertical moldings located midway in the rear doors. Three "seashell" horns were backed up by a large trumpet. All four sounded simultaneously, creating a sound that was every bit as impressive as the Brougham's appearance.

Like the Series Sixty-Two and de Ville Cadillacs, the Eldorado Brougham used a tubular X-type frame. More rigid than the previous type, it had the further advantage of permitting the car's overall height to be lowered by about three inches. Unfortunately, however, little

Though based on the 1954 Cadillac Park Avenue show car, the 1957-58 Eldorado Brougham (here a '58) was a four-door hardtop sporting a stainless steel roof. It was the first production car to feature air suspension.

Underneath the front-hinged hood of the Eldorado Brougham resided a 325/335 bhp V-8 (1957/58). Inside, a glovebox vanity featured magnetized tumblers, cigarette case, tissue dispenser, lipstick, cologne, and more, while the six-way power seat boasted a "favorite position" memory. The battery was housed in the trunk.

protection was offered the passengers in the event of a side-impact collision.

The engine was that of Cadillac's other Eldorado models: the Seville hardtop, and the Biarritz convertible. Fitted with two four-barrel carburetors (in place of the single four-throat used by the other Cadillacs), it developed 325 horsepower, 40 more than the Continental Mark II and 25 more than the less exotic Cadillacs.

But the most unusual—and controversial—of the Brougham's mechanical features had nothing to do with its engine or driveline. For this was the first production automobile, world-wide, to feature air suspension. (And no, we haven't forgotten the Citroën—the French car's system was actually hydropneumatic.)

Air suspension had been used by General Motors' bus division since 1952, so the company was not without experience in that area. The bus system proved to be inappropriate for passenger car use, however, so a new mechanism was developed in-house by Cadillac engineers. The editors of *Motor Life* magazine explained how it worked: "The air suspension system features air spring units at each wheel. Air is supplied to the spring units thru leveling valves so the car remains level with varying loads and road conditions. This contributes to easy handling and exceptionally smooth riding qualities." Cadillac's suspension system was modified so as to accept either coils or air springs, and anti-dive characteristics were built into the ball-joint front end in order to keep the car from nosing down during hard stops.

But *Motor Life* to the contrary, on smooth pavement the air suspension appears to have done little for the Cadillac's already excellent ride, and its effect on cornering ability was, if anything, somewhat negative. The air springs were at their best on very bumpy roads, where a lift valve actuated by the driver could fully pressurize the suspension, thus increasing road clearance. But of course that's the sort of terrain on which pickups are seen much more frequently than Cadillacs. Truthfully, the air suspension's major advantage had to do with its self-leveling capability.

As a safety feature, the center-opening doors of the Cadillac Eldorado Brougham locked automatically when the car was put into gear. Only 704 cars were built in two years.

Manager James M. Roche called it "the finest car possible," and priced it accordingly: $13,074, nearly three times the cost of a Series Sixty-Two coupe and $3,000 more than the Continental.

Sales of the Eldorado Brougham were disappointing as just 400 were produced for the 1957 model year. The 1958 model was little changed except that a slightly higher compression ratio and triple two-barrel carbs increased the horsepower from 325 to 335. Output fared even worse as sales dropped to 304 units. Thus, Cadillac marketed a different version of the Brougham for 1959 and '60. This one was hand-built in Italy, a handsome automobile but far less distinctive than the original. Production suffered accordingly as only 200 examples were built during its two-year life span.

From a strictly business perspective, the Eldorado Brougham of 1957-58 would have to be counted a failure—Cadillac is estimated to have lost $10,000 on every one they built. And in a final touch of irony, the Continental Mark II, against which it was pitted, was withdrawn from production just a few months after the Brougham's introduction. But the Eldorado Brougham was the first postwar Cadillac to be awarded Milestone Car status, so perhaps it paid its way, after all, in prestige value.

Unfortunately, there was also a major disadvantage. With the passage of time, one of two things inevitably happened to the air springs: either they blew out, causing the car to fall suddenly on its axles, or—more frequently—they developed leaks. Usually the leaks were slow, at least at first, so the compressor could manage to keep the car on an even keel. But as auto writer Mike Lamm has noted, "It's awkward to hop into a car whose body is resting on the street and sit there until it resurrects itself."

It's fortunate that Cadillac had made the air springs interchangeable with steel coils, for within a relatively short time most owners of the Eldorado Broughams had found it prudent to convert their cars to conventional springs.

The Eldorado Brougham's list of standard equipment was impressive, if not excessive. Included were obvious features such as air conditioning; Hydra-Matic transmission; and power steering, brakes, and windows. But some of the other items were highly unusual, and in some instances several years ahead of their time. For example, individual front and rear heating systems were employed, along with under-seat blowers. The six-way power front seat was equipped with a "favorite position" memory, and it moved automatically in order to facilitate entry and exit. Automatic power door locks were used, and a dashboard control raised and

lowered the trunk lid electrically. There was an automatic headlight dimmer, and polarized sun visors that became darker when tilted. As Walter McCall has commented, "The Eldorado Brougham bordered on technological overkill!"

And there was more. Forged aluminum-center wheels were fitted with premium wide-oval tires, an industry "first." With the ignition on and the transmission lever in Park or Neutral, the engine started automatically. And the center-opening doors locked automatically when the car was put into gear.

Passenger comfort was catered to in every possible way. Four cigarette lighters were provided, two in front, two in the rear compartment. Front and rear radio speakers were supplied, an unusual feature in 1957, and an automatic disappearing antenna was installed. The glovebox vanity was furnished with six magnetized tumblers, a fold-out shelf with mirror, cigarette case, tissue dispenser, lipstick, and stick cologne. There were center armrests front and rear, the latter including a storage bin with note pad, pencil, mirror, and a perfume atomizer stocked with Arpege, Extrait de Lanvin.

Buyers could choose among 15 special exterior colors and 45 standard and two special-order trim and color choices. Carpeting was of genuine mouton or high-pile Karakul. Cadillac General

Specifications	
Engine:	1957 V-8, ohv, 364.4 cid (4.00 x 3.63-in. bore x stroke), 10.0:1 compression ratio, 5 main bearings, hydraulic valve lifters, 2 Carter 4-bbl carburetors, 325 bhp @ 4,800 rpm **1958** 3 Rochester 2-bbl carburetors, 335 bhp @ 4,800 rpm
Transmission:	Hydra-Matic 4-speed automatic planetary
Suspension, front:	Unequal A-arms, self-leveling airbags, tubular hydraulic shock absorbers
Suspension, rear:	Lower trailing control links, upper single control yoke, self-leveling air bags, tubular hydraulic shock absorbers
Brakes:	Hydraulic, front/rear drums, power-assisted
Wheelbase (in.):	126.0
Overall length (in.):	216.3
Curb weight (lbs):	5,420
Tires:	8.40 x 15 high-speed
0-60 mph (sec):	12.9
Top speed (mph):	110-115
Production:	**1957** 400 **1958** 304

With only 1,110 Aston Martin DB4s ever produced, it was always rare; with just 95 DB4 GTs built, it was rarer still. The GT rode a shorter 93-inch wheelbase.

A mong numerous baths taken by unwary investors when the great collector car bull market of the late '80s turned to bust, Aston Martin may have scrubbed them more than most. Cars that had sold for a couple hundred thousand a year or so before were down by 50 percent or more by 1990, and at this writing they're barely holding their own. At the muddy Hershey swap meet in September of that year, a pristine navy blue DB6 with the desirable ZF five-speed gearbox was being offered at $65,000—a bargain even in that depressed market.

Astons have always been dicey investments. As one European dealer remarked, in the Sixties you paid the same $10,000 for a new Aston Martin as you did a Ferrari, but today that Ferrari is worth three or four times as much as the Aston. Still, Aston Martin has never built a dull automobile, and the DB4 and DB5 series represent two of that firm's finest efforts.

"DB" stands for David Brown, the millionaire tractor builder who rescued the established—but not prosperous—Aston Martin company after World War II. The marque name came from founder Lionel Martin and the Aston Clinton hillclimb, a bash known mainly in England, but respected as a challenger and sometime-wrecker of motor cars. When Brown bought the company in 1947, Aston had been bankrupt at least twice. By the time he sold the firm in 1976, it was nearing bankruptcy again, and has since been bailed out twice again—in business, Aston Martin is like a mini-Chrysler Corporation.

Brown's first postwar car, the DB1, was scraped together using a leftover prewar chassis and an uninspired two-liter engine, and he didn't build more than a score. What Brown had in mind was something considerably more impressive. He had also bought Lagonda Cars Limited, which provided a powerful 2.6-liter, dual-overhead-cam six. This Brown inserted in the Aston chassis, clothed it in an aluminum coupe body by J.J. Mulliner, and dubbed it the DB2.

The DB2 set the Aston Martin standards that are still with us. It was big, fast, and handled beautifully, giving the performance, say, of a contemporary Ferrari. Further, it was trimmed out like a Rolls-Royce, with Connolly leather and West of England cloth and thick-pile woolen carpeting. More than 400 were built, all by hand, banged out in aluminum over steel forms and trimmed by Tickfords in Newport Pagnell, Buckinghamshire, where Brown later moved his main operations. The DB2/4 2+2 hatchback, which succeeded the DB2 in 1953, evolved through Mark II and Mark III models, ending in 1959 with a 195-bhp three-liter engine and disc brakes. All these evolutions retained the original, aging DB2-style body. In 1955, Aston Martin began planning its replacement, which was introduced in 1958 as the DB4.

Aston Martin's DB4 was introduced in 1958; the DB4 GT followed in 1959. The latter was a two-seat fastback coupe for the truly serious enthusiast. The instrument panel placed the speedometer and tach high and directly in front of the driver, with the other gauges nearby. The front-end design couldn't be mistaken for anything but an Aston.

Though the DB4 emerged from an alleged clean slate, it was evolutionary, not revolutionary. The engine, designed by Tom Marek, was again a dohc six, heavy and expensive to build, rated at 240 bhp, or 266 bhp in Vantage form—which figures, competent sources say, were exaggerated for advertising purposes. To a straightforward platform frame and steel-tube cage, Carrozzeria Touring in Italy applied a body that was not exotic, but smooth and purposeful looking. Aston's hammer bangers built the chassis and bodies and Tickford again trimmed them to a high standard. The DB4 was no styling *tour de force* like the Cisitalia or the Pinin Farina Ferraris, but it looked miles better than the contemporary Jaguars and Corvettes, and it literally went like hell. Aston Martin claimed with honesty that it would do 0-100 *to* zero in 27 seconds flat—right off the showroom floor. And until the big-block Corvettes and Cobras came along, there wasn't anything to match it. Top speed was 140 with conventional gearing, 0-60 came up in seven or eight seconds, and the bill for a new one came to $10,000, thank-you-very-much-for-not-buying-a-Ferrari.

Between 1958 and 1963 the company built 1,110 regular DB4s including the Vantage, which combined a streamlined

"FT" nose with the regular DB4, built from 1962 onward and offered for $11,200 by importer J.S. Inskip in New York.

The DB4 GT which followed in 1959 was a two-seater with a claimed 302 bhp and a verifiable 150-mph top speed. A year later 25 short-wheelbase GYT chassis were turned over to Zagato in Italy, which produced an aluminum coupe of exceptional lightness--only 2,000 pounds—and a smooth, aerodynamic shape. With 314 bhp via triple Weber carbs, Aston Martin could now rejigger its acceleration-deceleration claim: the Zagato did 0-100-0 in a mere 20 seconds. It looked like the ideal car for long distance endurance racing, but experience showed that its mechanicals weren't up to that kind of punishment. Zagatos remained high-speed 160-mph grand tourers of exceptional merit, limited availability, and greatly desired by collectors of the marque.

Of the 95 DB4 GTs built, 75 were straight Newport Pagnell models and the rest Zagatos. Together, they represent the most sought-after Aston Martins in history, commanding in the range of $800,000 for the straight GT and up to $2 million for the Zagato—even in the current depressed market. They represent the high point in street machinery for the company, which in later years moved steadily away from performance and more toward high-speed executive transport.

The DB4 series was replaced in late 1963 by the DB5, produced for two years with a total of 1,021 standard models, including 123 Volante convertibles. Nobody was looking for a radical change with this one: the chassis, basic running gear, and bodyshell (with a minor styling update) was identical to the DB4. A bore increase brought displacement on Aston's twincam six to nearly four liters. As with the last DB4s, a choice of engine tune was available, either 282 or 314 bhp, depending on how much the customer thought he or she could handle. Four transmission choices were offered, including a five-speed ZF manual and Borg-Warner automatic. A much-modified DB5 put this model on the map in the United States and elsewhere when it was used as James Bond's spy car in the movie *Goldfinger*.

Curiously, DB5s do not tend to be priced as high as DB4s, although they are virtually the same cars. Though the aforementioned Hershey example was amazingly cheap, a mid-1990 review by a respected investment newsletter pegged a top-condition DB5 at $100,000-150,000, $25,000 less than the comparable range for the DB4. These prices, for coupes, had dropped considerably six months later. Volante convertibles are about evenly priced in both models.

What price guides don't tell you, of course, is that Aston Martins are devilishly difficult and expensive to maintain and to keep running in top form, as they always have been. Nevertheless, a strong body of enthusiasts and good club support makes them attractive to many collectors. Bought right, the DB4 and DB5 in particular are rated as excellent investments for the 1990s.

Specifications[1]	
Engine:	Aluminum I-6, dohc **DB4** 3,670 cc, 8.25:1 compression ratio, 2 SU carburetors, 240 bhp @ 5,500 rpm; Vantage: 9.0:1 c.r., 3 SU carbs, 266 bhp @ 5,750 rpm; GT: 9.0:1 c.r., 3 Weber carbs, 310 bhp @ 6,000 rpm; GT Zagato: 314 bhp **DB5** 3,995 cc, 8.9:1 c.r., 3 SU carbs, 282 bhp @ 5,500 rpm; Vantage: 3 Weber carbs, 314 bhp @ 5,750 rpm
Transmission:	DB4 4-speed manual; overdrive opt.; 3 automatics reportedly installed DB5 4-speed manual, overdrive, 5-speed ZF manual, Borg-Warner automatic
Suspension, front:	Independent, coil springs, unequal wishbones
Suspension, rear:	Rigid axle, coil springs, parallel trailing links, Watts linkage
Brakes:	4-wheel hydraulic, Dunlop discs all-around (later Girling)
Wheelbase (in.):	98.0 (DB4 GT and Zagato: 93.0)
0-60 mph (sec):	DB4 7.0-8.0; Zagato: 6.0 DB5 8.0
Top speed (mph):	DB4 140; GT: 150; Zagato: 160 DB5 145
Production:	DB4 1,110 (incl. 70 cvt, 95 GT) DB5 1,021 (incl. 123 cvt, 12 estate wagons)

[1]Please note that there are many variations within these models

The DB4 GT interior featured fine leather, of course, but the heart of the matter was Aston's aluminum dual-overhead-cam six. In GT form it developed just over 300 bhp, good for a 150-mph top speed.

277

Every five years on another anniversary of the Mini, salubrious tributes attest to its longevity as the inevitable product of genius—Alex Issigonis' elegant solution to transporting four adults in a spacious compartment within the smallest possible exterior dimensions. Without taking anything from the Mini's influential concepts—transverse engine, wheels at the extreme corners, integral engine-cum-gearbox, subframe support structure—the reason it's lasted so long is its sheer practicality.

Anyone who has driven extensively in Britain lately knows how heavy the traffic is and how inadequate the roads are. It is said that if all the cars in Britain came out on the road at the same time, there wouldn't be any space to move on public pavement from Land's End to John O'Groats. A 10-foot-long car on 10- or 12-inch wheels that will stop on a dime, corner as if on rails, and deliver decent performance with high fuel economy is the only sensible solution for dealing with that kind of traffic on a regular basis. Its engineering made the Mini practical; its endearing shape made it a cult car (even in Japan!).

Issigonis, who already had the postwar Morris Minor to his credit, was given a difficult brief by the British Motor Corporation in 1957: design the smallest possible car capable of carrying four people, new from the ground up, don't cost us more than 10 million pounds to set up the factory to build it. Ultimately, the budget decided much of the specification. For instance, a radical two-cylinder air-cooled engine was seriously considered, but would have probably cost half the budget alone just to develop properly. So Issigonis, thinking he could change engines later, chose an off-the-shelf unit: the ancient, water-cooled Austin A-series engine designed by William Appleby, which had started life at 25 bhp in 1952—but had potential. Issigonis never got an all-new engine, but 30 years later in the MG Metro Turbo, derivatives of Appleby's design were producing 93 bhp.

And the engine was the only "old" thing about it. Issigonis conceived of a wholly radical, never-before-done combination of transverse-mounted engine with a gearbox, using the same lubrication oil. This, along with front-wheel drive, gave him the most compact drivetrain possible, plus excellent traction and road holding. A component manufacturer, Hardy Spicer, supplied a constant-velocity joint borrowed from submarine design, which transmitted drivetrain power-steering wheel jerk or "snatch" common to some similar front-drive small cars at that time.

The Mini's roller skate wheels were dictated by the incredible smallness of the body, which with larger wheels would have produced unacceptable wheel arch intrusion into the passenger compartment. As it was, the front wheel arches were considerable and the pedals con-

Over its three-plus decades, the Mini hasn't changed much in looks. The mid-life 1976 model seen here wears just a "Mini" nameplate, though earlier models came under the marque names of Austin and Morris, while upmarket versions strutted Riley and Wolseley badges.

The performance Mini was the Mini Cooper, seen here as a '65 (*right*), '68 (*below*), and '69 (*center right*). It used a tuned one-liter four, while the Cooper S—the '65 and '69 pictured—ran with a 1,275-cc engine boasting 75 bhp. This '76 Mini (*bottom*) was powered by the 850-cc four.

siderably offset toward the center to compensate. Nobody in the industry had 10-inch tires, but Dunlop agreed to develop them. Ten-inchers were used on every Mini until the 1974 1275 GT went to 12-inchers, which were finally standardized on all Minis in 1984—they only just fit. In the beginning, Issigonis argued properly that a more conventional tire would have looked ridiculous on a car as small as the Mini anyway.

A lot of things had to be miniaturized on this car for the same reasons as the tires and wheels: the size of the thing demanded it. Brakes, for instance: seven-inch drums at first, and they did the job. But in 1961, when the hot Mini-Cooper was released, Lockheed conjured up seven-inch front discs, which were unprecedented. As Mark Steward wrote in his history of the Mini, "Lockheed were more than happy to help [development engineer] John Cooper as he convinced them that if the system could

The 1991 Mayfair is the current upmarket Mini. It is identified outside by its wheel trim and signature under the rear side windows, and inside by its higher-level trim.

work on the Mini using tiny seven-inch discs it would be a great advertisement for them." Later, in 1963, the discs grew to 7.5 inches for the Mini-Cooper S and to 8.4 inches for models with 12-inch wheels.

Limning the makes, models, and variations of the Mini over its 30-plus years of production requires a lot of space, but it is important to mention the highlights. The original Minis, and most of those built until the Seventies, carried Austin or Morris badges; after that they acquired the marque name "Mini." The Riley Elf and Wolseley Hornet, introduced in 1961 and produced through 1969, were badge-engineered luxury Minis with traditional upright radiator grilles, extended trunks, and posh interiors including polished woodwork. Significantly, they introduced the roll-up windows adopted by all Minis in 1964, and the one-liter engine used with such effectiveness by the Mini-Cooper.

Conceived by a World Champion race car manufacturer, the Mini-Cooper carried a tuned one-liter engine with 55 net horsepower and handling modifications. It was fast, stuck to the road like glue, and stopped and steered with precision. Before long, the Cooper was dominating its class in sedan racing and making a serious impact on the European rally circuit. A further development was the 1963 Mini-Cooper

S, with a 1,275-cc engine and 75 bhp, a truly impressive performance car built and raced with great success through 1969.

Another unique Mini was the Moke, first built in 1964 with the military in mind: a light transporter with minimal body and weather protection. Mokes appealed more to the surfer set than the army. After BMC was merged into British Leyland the Moke was dropped from the home market, but factories in Australia and, later, Portugal kept it alive until the 1980s. Mokes are still common transport in many warm climes and often enjoyed by visitors to the Caribbean islands, where they are ideal for the climate, terrain, and high-priced gas.

The first attempt to seriously restyle and upgrade the Mini was the Clubman, arriving in 1969 with a four-inch-longer nose and all-around upmarket trim. The Clubman body provided the 1970 replacement for the Mini Cooper S, the 1275 GT, but by that time British Leyland was in charge and management had stopped thinking in terms of performance Minis. After the demise of Leyland, the Mini business went to Austin-Rover, rump remnant of the mass-volume manufacturer. The latest Mini craze in Britain has been for "limited editions" like the recent "Park Lane" with special trim, paint, and identification.

Exactly how long the present line of economical "City" and upmarket "Mayfair" Minis will continue to run is anybody's guess. The Mini has racked up five million sales since 1959, which puts it in company like the VW Beetle and the Model T Ford. Along the way, a cult of addicts has grown up to customize and hot-rod thousands of Minis, and to support a massive aftermarket providing everything from badge bars to turbochargers. It's a car with great character, and it will probably be around a good many years to come.

Specifications[1]	
Engine:	I-4, ohv, transverse mounted, 60.9 cid/998 cc (2.54 x 3.00-in/ 64.6 x 76.2-mm bore x stroke), 8.3:1 compression ratio, SU carburetor, 38 bhp @ 5,200 rpm, 51 lbs/ft torque @ 2,000 rpm
Transmission:	4-speed manual transaxle
Suspension, front:	Independent, wishbones, Hydrolastic rubber cone springs, telescopic shock absorbers
Suspension, rear:	Swinging longitudinal trailing arms, Hydrolastic rubber cone springs, telescopic shock absorbers
Brakes:	4-wheel hydraulic drums
Wheelbase (in.):	80.25
Overall length (in.):	120.0
Overall width (in.):	55.5
Tread (in.):	47.25
Weight (lbs):	1,318
Tires:	5.20 x 10
0-50 mph (sec):	17.2
Top speed (mph):	75
Production:	5,000,000 +

[1]1967

281

Volkswagen of America was noted for whimsical advertising in the Fifties, but Lotus of America arguably did them one better by depicting an Elite at an altar, being married to its new owner. That was the way owners felt about their Elites, and today they're just as enthusiastic.

They deserve to be. The Elite was unarguably one of the industry's great shapes. Though modern classics like the Cisitalia, Studebaker Starliner, BMW 507, Mark II Continental, and Karmann Ghia still look good today, they are all obviously products of their time. The Elite *still* looks like it was built yesterday. Many automotive writers who have thought about it, including this one, think it is the single most perfect shape among all postwar automobiles.

Type 14 in the Lotus project evolution, the Elite was the firm's first serious road car—everything before it, including the grasshopper-like Seven, was built specifically for the track. An exercise in clean slate thinking, it was designed by Lotus founder and visionary Colin Chapman, aided by John Frayling and Peter Kirwan-Taylor. Its object was to explore the possibility of fiberglass as a structural as well as body-shaping material. Production models of course had sub-frames and some reinforcement around the A-pillars, but the rest was held together entirely by fiberglass. The body actually varied from wafer-thinness to three-fourths of an inch, according to the load-bearing needs in different areas. Allowing fiberglass to do the work of steel gave the Elite incredible lightness: from 1,300 to 1,500 pounds, almost unbelievable for a grand touring coupe even of its modest proportions.

Chapman's smooth, natural styling was marked by a low-set oval air intake, sloping hood, fixed plexiglass door windows, and a neat, cut-off (but not squared-off) tail. The permanent windows were an anomaly dictated, as on many Lotuses, by Chapman's uncompromising demand for aerodynamics. "Windows that don't roll down can't affect airflow," he said. He did compromise to the extent of allowing the windows to be removable; special bags were provided to house them behind the seats.

The chassis featured fully independent suspension, four-wheel disc brakes, and a British BMC four-speed transmission as used on the MGA (Series I models, through July 1960) or a German ZF unit (a major improvement, on Series II models). Suspension on the Series I was taken directly from the preceding project, the Lotus Twelve *monoposto* racing car with its so-called "soft rider" suspension: independent front suspension with steep-angle coil springs encasing tubular shocks and tube steel double-wishbones. The rear suspension was a MacPherson-type called "Chapman strut" by Lotus, which ex-Lotusman Graham Arnold describes as "high-mounted at the top pick-up point and traditional long stroke through

Many automotive writers contend that the 1959-62 Lotus Elite is the single most perfect shape among all postwar automobiles.

The Elite's four-cylinder powerplant began life as a fire pump engine. Spartan described the snug interior of the Elite, but its racing heritage saw to it that the gauges were well placed.

the combined spring and shock absorber. The independently sprung, universally jointed drive shafts formed an integral part of the rear triangulation, needing only a kinked trailing arm to complete the system. As on the front, 9½-inch discs handled the rear braking, and rubber bushes were used to absorb some of the harsher vibrations and road noises. Second series models adopted a revised rear-suspension locating system, with the kinked trailing arm replaced by a simple wishbone system joined to the body/chassis by a fragile, rubber-insulated ball-and-socket joint." This was evidently a cost-cutting measure, as was a detail of the later disc brake design: iron instead of aluminum caliper housings. Wheels were 15-inch Dunlop wires mounted with Firestone P100, Michelin X, or Pirelli Cinturato tires.

Power was supplied by an aluminum overhead cam four supplied by Coventry Climax and offered in various states of tune from 71 to 105 bhp. This famous unit is one of the industry's milestone engines. "Its reported origin as a unit

Designed by Lotus founder and visionary Colin Chapman, the Elite's smooth, natural styling was marked by a low-set oval air intake and sloping hood. Fixed plexiglass door windows were the result of Chapman's uncompromising demand for aerodynamics.

for a fire pump, like so many of those anecdotal stories, contains a grain of truth," says Arnold. "Those involved in its production knew full well that their engine had amazing potential for cars and even boats. However, the only crock of gold to plunder was in a defense contract for a fire pump engine." When the Climax did get into cars it provided astonishing power for its piddling 74 cubic inches. In the Elite, it delivered from .96 to 1.4 horsepower per cubic inch!

These specifications ought to suggest how astonishing the Elite was in the world of 1957. Until such materials as Kevlar and carbon fiber appeared in the 1970s, it was in Arnold's words, "as near to a pure fiberglass monocoque as could be achieved. . . . The car's good looks attract attention but the handling and fine balance is something to savor. An Elite feels more 'up on its toes' than later sporting Lotus cars because of its 15-inch wheels and rather high stance. However, there is no body roll at all— not even in the fastest turns. Brake pressure is heavy by today's standards due to the absence of a servo but there is more than enough stopping power available. It certainly gets no aerodynamic braking effect from the body design. The car can be run up to 100 mph on a flat road, then with the engine off it will maintain that speed for quite a while and only gradually slow down."

The Coventry-Climax four displaced only 74 cubic inches (1,216 cc), but in various states of tune it developed from 71 to 105 bhp. In the ultra-light Elite that meant 0-60 in 6.6 seconds and a top speed of 130 mph in racing form.

Elites built purposely for racing carried flush-fitting windshield glass, light unstressed door and body panels. However, a "street" Elite could race competitively merely with the addition of an oil cooler, competition tires, and racing disc pads. The best-known racers were named for their British number plates: Les Leston's "DAD10" and Graham Warner's LOV1, which fought many a road race on English circuits in the late Fifties and Sixties. "LOV1," which was fitted with a stump-pulling 4.90:1 rear axle ratio for Brands Hatch, still delivered 130 mph, and its acceleration was phenomenal: 0-60 in 6.6 seconds, 0-100 in 17, the standing quarter-mile in 15.1—all on 74 cubic inches. That

must be the best performance for so few cubes on record in a street automobile.

On the street, frankly, the Elite was not so much fun. The interior was spartan, furnished with cheap materials, very snug and—because of Chapman's fetish for lightness—almost completely uninsulated. Fiberglass' natural property of noise transmission makes riding in an Elite like traveling under a galvanized trash can powered by a mixmaster. That's the car's big disadvantage, and it has been enough to keep many collectors out of an Elite. A shame, because they're missing a lot.

Officially, Lotus built 986 Elites in six years of production, but a least 50 more were built with stock bodyshells fitted with Ford or Lotus engines, and others from parts. It's a pity there weren't more.

Allowing fiberglass to do the work of steel gave the Elite incredible lightness: from 1,300 to 1,500 pounds, amazing even for a modestly sized grand touring coupe.

Specifications	
Engine:	Coventry-Climax aluminum I-4, ohc, 74.2 cid/1,216 cc (3.0 x 2.63-in./76.2 x 66.6-mm bore x stroke), 1 or 2 SU or 2 Weber carburetors, 71-105 bhp
Transmission:	MG 4-speed or ZF 4-speed manual
Suspension, front:	Independent, wishbone, coil springs, tubular shocks, anti-sway bar
Suspension, rear:	Independent, Chapman struts, trailing arm
Brakes:	Hydraulic, 4-wheel discs
Wheelbase (in.):	88.0
Overall length(in.):	148.0
Curb weight (lbs):	1,450
Wheels:	15-in. wires, knock-off hubs
0-60 mph (sec):	6.6 (racing model)
Top speed (mph):	118 (83 bhp)
Production:	986

1961-75 JAGUAR E-TYPE

There was no doubt which automobile was Car of the Year in 1961. With its long-awaited E-Type ("XKE" in the United States), Jaguar reached its peak of perfection in roadgoing sports cars. Never before, and certainly not since, has such perfection of design and engineering been reached, though as time went on the shape evolved downward as government regulations tore into its aesthetic and design excellence.

It had been a long time coming. By the time the E-Type was formally introduced to the British press in March 1961, people had been wearing a path of letters to the company's door asking for something like it, fed up with the aging, overweight XK150S that Jaguar was flogging by the late Fifties. They wanted something along the lines of the XK-SS, the "street version" of the D-Type built in limited quantities and abruptly abandoned. Of course they wanted more luggage capacity and creature comforts, the flexibility for city and country driving, and the bargain price for which all Jaguars were known. By all accounts they got it. Said *Road & Track:* "The car comes up to, and exceeds, all of our great expectations."

At about $5,600 the E-Type was a bargain. There wasn't anything remotely near its price that would go 150 mph, and a Ferrari, which would, cost double the money. The contemporary Corvette looked like a kiddie car by comparison, and though a though a well-tuned fuelie 'Vette could shave an E's acceleration times, it couldn't outrun one, nor return 20 miles to the gallon driven more moderately.

The sleek design underlined its ancestry, the racing D-Type and the XK-SS, yet comprised in whole the most pleasing shape to emerge from Coventry since the XK120 in 1948. Sir William Lyons had his usual control over the design, but the E-Type was strongly influenced by Malcolm Sayer, an aero engineer from Bristol Aeroplane, who developed the car's shape using the Farnborough wind tunnel. Yet the E didn't look a compromise in favor of aerodynamics—like, say, the Citroën DS-19. It was slippery, all right, but it was also elegant. Even those pieces it needed to qualify for the street—lights, bumpers, and the like—were blended carefully into the pattern. They of course failed to meet the demands of the subsequent safety lobby, and were duly replaced in time by hulking five-mph bumpers, uncovered sealed beam headlamps, and outsized tail and parking lights.

Inside, the E was a feast to the eye, with a traditional large rev counter and speedometer mounted behind a wood-rimmed adjustable wheel. A central panel housed all the secondary instruments above a row of toggle switches, while grabby leather bucket seats beckoned both driver and passenger. Complementing the roadster was a beautiful coupe, with a hinged backlight and a large carpeted area aft of the seats for

The '61 Jaguar E-Type—XKE in the U.S.—created quite a stir when first introduced. It had style, power, and even creature comforts. The '63 model seen here had changed little because there was little reason to tamper with a winner.

The purity of line of the early E-Types was eroded under the burden of U.S. regulations. The '68 model, for example, wore side marker lights, upright exposed headlights, and clumsier bumpers—and it took a larger 4.2-liter engine to develop the same 265 bhp.

luggage. Many thought the coupe was more elegant than the roadster; some say it is the most notable single product of Sixties automotive design.

In construction the E benefited from competition experience, its new independent suspension based on an experimental prototype raced by Briggs Cunningham in the 1960 Le Mans 24 Hours. Both coupe and convertible used a stressed-skin monocoque body from the firewall back—a hull so stiff that no sub-floor reinforcement was required on the open model. "Main load carrying members are the rigid and massive scuttle structure," wrote *The Autocar*, "and, just forward of the rear wheels, a deep box section assembly; bracing these points is a deep boxed sill at each side. Midway along the sills is another top-hat section cross member, and there are two additional longitudinal floor members running from the bulkhead to the rear cross member structure."

If the monocoque body and full-independent suspension were new, there was nothing unfamiliar about the E-Type's powerplant: the respected 3.8-liter six kept from the XK150S, with its 70-degree inclined angle, hemispherical combustion chambers, and 9.0:1 compression ratio. Induction was via three SU carbs with manual choke, feeding into straight ports in the aluminum head. The engine was exceptionally smooth throughout its working range and unusually quiet. Acceleration was everything the road testers expected: 0-60 took about seven seconds, 0-120 just 26 seconds; second gear took the car to 78 mph, third to 116 mph. With the standard 3.31:1 rear axle ratio the E-type would do almost exactly 150 mph, although ratios of 2.94 and 3.07 permitted higher top speeds and 3.54 better acceleration. With the 2.94:1 ratio this was a genuine 180-mph car—the fastest cars they'd ever tested according to the editors of *The Motor*. It still ranks near the top by today's supercar standards.

Perhaps *The Motor*'s comparisons with ordinary cars best illustrates the nature of the E-Type: "A good medium-powered family saloon will accelerate from 10-30 mph in top gear in about 10-11 seconds. The E-Type will do 110-130 mph in this time and, despite

Like the '68 E-Type, the '69 roadster sported larger parking and taillights, and headrests were now part of the package, too. But even though burdened with the myriad changes forced on it, the E-Type still looked sexy. Note the SU triple carbs that fed Jag's dohc six.

The 2+2 coupe rode a 104.7-inch wheelbase, nearly nine inches longer than the original E-Type. This 1970 model shows the Coventry cat on the front bumper and steering wheel hub, the uncovered headlights, the safety-inspired rocker switches on the dash, and the hatchback-like access to the cargo hold. The 2+2 may not have been as sleek as the early E-Types, but it still cut a mean figure.

its very high top gear, 10-30 mph in half the time; on one occasion it climbed a 1-in-6 hill in top, travelling quite slowly and using only part throttle. This initial rate of acceleration, about 4 mph every second, is maintained in one steady effortless sweep all the way up to 100 mph, but for real exhilaration when emerging from a 30 mph speed limit, second gear will spin the speedometer needle round to the mid-seventies in about 7 sec. to the accompaniment of a very subdued but delightfully hard exhaust hum and considerable strain on the neck muscles, whilst another 6 sec. in third brings up the hundred mark.

"The sheer elegance of line which Jaguar seems able to produce by total disregard for fashion trends is allied to a combination of performance, handling and refinement that has never been equalled at the price and, we would think, very seldom surpassed at any price." Of course certain compromises had to be made to allow that price, and many were made at the cost of quality and reliability, "I'd rather be driving my Jaguar," read a famous bumper sticker, "but it's in the shop."

The first revisions were good ones: a larger 4.2-liter engine and all-synchro-

mesh transmission in 1965. Then in 1966 came a stretched wheelbase coupe with 2+2 seating and less lithe appearance. Starting in 1968, U.S. models gradually added side marker lights, clumsier bumpers, and upright exposed headlights. The six-cylinder E-Type continued through 1971, when it was replaced by the new, powerful but thirsty V-12 designed by Jaguar's Harry Mundy: 5.3 liters, 325 horsepower (gross). To accommodate this powerplant Jaguar adopted the longer wheelbase of the 2+2 coupe and the weight went up to more than 3,200 pounds. Twelves were recognizable with their larger hood bulge, wider tires mounted on slotted wheels with hub caps, a cross-hatch grille insert, and more ungainly bumpers. Offered only as a 2+2 convertible and roadster, it was quite fast for the Seventies, delivering performance approximately equal to the original 3.8 despite massive emission controls. In 1976, doomed by the design compromises inflicted by regulation and the energy shortages of the mid-Seventies, it was replaced by the XJS four-seat coupe, which is still in production, also as a convertible. But it's the slinky E-Type that most everyone loves best.

What is referred to as the Series III XKE boasted a 314-bhp V-12, larger hood bulge, eggcrate grille insert, and bigger bumpers that would get even bigger before the mid-Seventies demise of the beloved E-Type.

Specifications

Engine:	Series I I-6, dohc, 230.6 cid (3.43 x 4.17-in. bore x stroke) 3 1-bbl SU carburetors, 265 bhp @ 5,500 rpm, 260 lbs/ft torque @ 4,000 rpm Series II 258 cid (3.63 x 4.17-in.), 265 bhp @ 5,400 rpm, 283 lbs/ft @ 4,000 Series III V-12, sohc, 326.0 cid (3.54 x 2.76-in) 4 2-bbl Zenith carbs, 314 bhp @ 6,200 rpm, 349 lbs/ft @ 3,800 rpm
Transmission:	4-speed manual; Borg-Warner automatic opt. beginning in 1966
Suspension, front:	Independent, with torsion bars, wishbones, anti-roll bar
Suspension, rear:	Independent, double spring/shock units, transverse lower links, longitudinal radius arms, anti-roll bar
Brakes:	4-wheel disc, rears inboard mounted
Wheelbase (in.):	96.0/104.7
Overall length (in.):	175.3/184.4
Curb weight (lbs):	2,720-3,220
0-60 mph (sec):	7.0 (1961)
Top speed (mph):	150 (1961)
Production:	72,507 (all models)

Many collectors consider the 1961 Lincoln Continental a modern-day classic. So even did Lincoln in its 1961 advertising, which promoted the car's "pure elegance," boasting that it was "a classic automobile of enduring value." The convertible's top mechanism borrowed technology from the '57 Ford retractable and the '58 Thunderbird.

Committees really can design a horse that doesn't look like a camel, they just have to have the freedom to. The 1961 Lincoln Continental proves it.

Every year members of the Industrial Designers Institute meet to present their annual awards in recognition of "noteworthy and fresh approaches to design and function." Though cars are not common award winners, a prominent exception was the 1961 Lincoln Continental, which received one of the IDI gongs that year. Seven Ford designers collected it: Eugene Bordinat, Don DeLaRossa, Elwood Engel, Gayle Halderman, John Najjar, Bob Thomas, and George Walker. They all had something to do with it. Here was one committee design that not only worked, but was outstanding.

The basic parameter in the '61 Lincoln program was the sharing of front structure through the cowl (housing the electrical system, air conditioning and many other components) with the 1961 Ford Thunderbird. This purposeful economic decision allowed two relatively low-production automobiles to share an expensive component, freeing up more funds for other areas. Both cars were brand new for 1961, so a great deal of money had to be spent on each.

Component sharing was not new even then, but this program was unique because the Continental and Thunderbird were significantly different in size, style, and body type. The T-Bird was a two-door hardtop and convertible; Continental wanted a four-door sedan—and the first four-door convertible since the Frazer Manhattan back in 1949-51.

The concept of a clean, smooth, full-length body was explained in retrospect by Bob Thomas: "We wanted the car to be a statement of elegant simplicity. There was a discussion at the time that the car should be like an elegant lady in a simple black dress, with her jewelry nothing more than an uncomplicated diamond necklace." The task was to make a heavy, stable car appear so, while making it smaller than its predecessor in actual size. This required close attention to every detail.

"Since the more stable a car looks, the more comfortable it will be to drive, we wanted to fill out the usable area," John Najjar said. "Most cars before this time had their maximum width halfway down the side and sloped inward at the top of the body. By creating the top edge of the body side and defining it as we did with thick chrome trim, the appearance of stability and width was achieved. An additional benefit of this clearly defined longitudinal edge appeared from the driver's seat. The fenderline was visible from front to back, so you knew where the edge of your car was at all times."

The wide-shouldered width of the top edge had another benefit. It helped give the greenhouse a "nestled" appearance, adding to the impression of stability. The nestled look was achieved by maximizing

For reasons of structural integrity, the Lincoln had "suicide" rear doors that opened outward from the front. The vent in the center of the dash had to be opened manually when the air conditioner was used. The '61 Continental was "alone, among all American fine cars . . . now warranted for two full years or 24,000 miles."

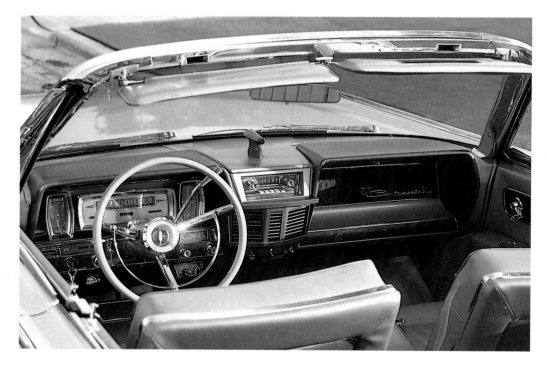

the angle of "tumblehome." Looking at a cross-section, take a point at the bottom of a side window: if the glass is absolutely vertical up to the roof, the tumblehome angle is zero. Now hear John Najjar: "The window glass on all cars slopes inward toward the top, and the greater the angle of the slope, the more nestled and stable the greenhouse area appears to be. By introducing curved side glass, we were able to achieve what was probably the greatest angle of tumblehome yet on a car of this type."

To better achieve the appearance of width and stability, the designers decided to make the new Lincoln's roof and rear deck surfaces as flat as possible. A conflict has always existed between designers and production engineers over the degree of crown (curve) required on a piece of sheetmetal in order for it to hold its shape. If a roof panel could be rounded, like the top of a '49 Mercury for example, it would hold its shape beautifully and be easy to produce, but would not be consistent with the rectilinear design of the '61 Lincolns. The roof panels were thus made as flat as possible while retaining sufficient crown to hold their shape.

The four-door convertible created challenges of its own. Lincoln resorted ultimately to 11 electric relays working with mechanical and hydraulic linkage to open the rear deck, unlatch the convertible top, and lower it in such a way that it would fold into the trunk. "This gave us an opportunity to bring the rear deck styling into the passenger compartment," said Najjar. "With the top down the area blends in perfectly and looks like the car never had a top, nor was intended to have one." The ingenious top design owed much to the 1957 Ford Skyliner retractable, whose hardware had already been successfully applied to the 1958 Ford Thunderbird convertible.

An aspect unique to these Continentals, not seen for quite a few years until they arrived, was the center-opening doors. Some people thought they had been inspired by the dual-cowl phaetons of Lincoln's classic era. Perhaps—but the designers really had no choice. The lack of a "B" pillar made it necessary to hinge the rear doors at the rear on the

A 1963 Lincoln Continental ad boasted that "It is unquestionably the finest car in the world. Its classic look scarcely changes from year to year." Indeed, the Continental didn't change much in the Sixties. It was "Timeless in styling ... exciting to drive ... more lasting in value."

convertible, and it made no sense to alter this for the sedan.

Many other engineering aspects of these Lincolns are worthy of note. The 1961 Continental employed the most rigid unit frame and body ever produced to that time, the most thorough sound insulation and shock-damping ever applied to a production automobile, extremely precise fits and tolerances in all sheetmetal and mechanical components, the most thorough product testing yet applied, minimum service intervals, completely sealed electrical components, and new precautions to prevent rust and corrosion. Most impressive of these features was the insulation and shock damping, which was the class of the industry. The idea was to use every known means of eliminating road shock and noise transmission, and then to spare no expense to insulate or isolate whatever got through. Rubber was used liberally throughout the suspension, and the variety of sound deadeners and insulation material would take pages to describe. Even the tires were specially engineered to reduce noise transmission.

Power for Continentals came from the established Lincoln 430 V-8, but

the testing each engine now received bore no relationship to pre-1961 practice—and is probably why so many Contis survive in fine original condition. Each engine, as it came off the line, was test run for three hours on a dynamometer, the latter part at 3,500 rpm (equivalent to 98 mph); then the engine was torn down, inspected, and reassembled. The automatic transmission received similar treatment. Each car off the line got a 12-mile road test, during which the driver checked off some 189 separate items. Finally, the car was run over a pit where black light was used to detect oil leaks, reflecting a fluorescent dye mixed in the lubricants. All of this attention to detail helped Lincoln win *Car Life* magazine's 1961 Engineering Excellence Award and gave Ford the confidence to offer a 24-month/24,000 mile warranty, this in the days when the average was 90 days or 3,000 miles.

Continentals were marvelous cars that saw modestly increased sales in a down market, though Lincoln's sparser dealer force and the lack of more body styles prevented it from rivaling Cadillac sales. About 90,000 were built during the first generation (1961-63) run, 10 percent

being convertibles. They were replaced by a longer-wheelbase but very similar line in 1964, which ran with little alteration to 1969. It is the Lincolns of the early Sixties that will be remembered not only for their timeless styling and impeccable quality, but also as the cars that began a renaissance that ultimately led to Lincoln's being able to challenge Cadillac's once dominant position in the luxury-car field.

Specifications[1]	
Engine:	V-8, ohv, 430 cid (4.29 x 3.70-in. bore x stroke), 10.0:1 compression ratio, Carter 2-bbl carburetor, 300 bhp @ 4,100 rpm
Transmission:	3-speed Turbo-O-Drive automatic
Suspension, front:	Independent, ball joints, upper and lower struts, coil springs, tubular shock absorbers
Suspension, rear:	Live axle, longitudinal leaf springs, tubular shock absorbers
Brakes:	Hydraulic, 11 x 3-in. front/rear drums
Wheelbase (in.):	123.0
Overall length(in.):	212.4
Weight (lbs):	sdn 4,927 cvt 5,215
Tires:	sdn 9.00 x 14 cvt 9.50 x 14
0-60 mph (sec):	approx. 12.0
Top speed (mph):	approx. 115
Production:	1961 sdn 22,307 cvt 2,857 1962 sdn 27,849 cvt 3,212 1963 sdn 28,095 cvt 3,138

[1]1961 model

The AC Cobra was masterminded by ex-racer Carroll Shelby, who mated the British AC Ace roadster with Ford's then new small-block 260 V-8. Needless to say, the Cobra soon went racing.

Carroll Shelby is a hero now, but in 1961 when he rang up Dave Evans at the Ford Motor Company and conned him out of a pair of thinwall small-block Fairlane V-8s he was only an East Texas ex-dump truck operator and chicken farmer who liked cars and drove them fast. After a bright racing career which included winning Le Mans in 1959, Shelby developed heart trouble and had to give up active racing for passive—as passive as he'd let it get, which wasn't much.

By 1961, Shelby was running a racing driver school, flogging Goodyear tires to the West Coast competition crowd, and playing with mechanical ideas at Dean Moon's Speed Shop in Los Angeles. The Fairlane V-8 intrigued him. It also made him famous.

The AC Ace roadster, though still the handlingest sports car made in Britain, was on its last legs by then, still winning races but not selling in even enough quantity to maintain its village blacksmith operation in tiny Thames Ditton, Surrey. It looked terrific, though—always did—and Shelby knew that it didn't lack anything that good old American cubic inches couldn't cure. He'd no sooner evaluated the new Fairlane engines than he was off to England to sell Derek Hurlock, head of the old family firm of Autocarriers, Limited, an AC-saving combination: Hurlock's car, Ford's engines, and Shelby's brains. The result was the AC Cobra, first with the 260-cube V-8, then the 289, finally the hells-bells 427. It's a cliché to say this, but they proved legends in their own time.

The real stroke of fortune was Ford's acquiescence in all this. Once Lee Iacocca had taken over Ford Division from Bob McNamara, after lackluster years when Ford cars bore every impress of McNamara except his steel-rimmed glasses, Ford went racing in a big way—every kind of event from rallying to Le Mans, Indianapolis to NASCAR. Ford backed Shelby to the hilt, covering the overhead, providing test facilities, loaning engineers like Danny Jones, who refined and made the AC Cobra buildable. Before 1962 was out, the Cobra was in production, homologated as a GT car, and actually selling—in small quantities—for about the price of an E-Type Jaguar. It cost more than a Corvette, but it also buried the Corvette in every form of competition—which suited Ford to a tee, of course. You think they were in this for fun?

Shelby built Cobras in the old Venice, California "factory" that had once turned out Scarabs for Lance Reventlow. They weren't sophisticated, with spartan interiors, minimal weather protection nobody ever put up anyway, spindly nerf bumpers that wouldn't ward off a well placed kick, and that delicate AC body. But the cars did have flow-through ventilation: the air flowed in and the air flowed out. But they looked fantastic—the AC roadster always did—and they simply went like hell.

The 289, which ultimately developed 306 bhp, gave 0-60 times in the five-second range with the right axle—one road test actually claimed 4.8 seconds, while the AC's sturdy tubular chassis and all-independent transverse leaf suspension produced hard but controllable and predictable handling.

Shelby hired Ken Miles, the brilliant English racing car developer, and Pete Brock, who had helped design the Corvette Sting Ray, to evolve competition Cobras. Early attempts at Daytona and Sebring were unsuccessful, but by 1964 Cobras were dominating Class A-production in Sports Car Club of America events, winning the manufacturers and drivers championships in the U.S. Road Race of Champions, even finishing seventh overall at Le Mans—a marvelous performance in a field dominated by purpose-built sports racers.

All out racing Cobras had 370 bhp, Borg-Warner T-10 four-speed gearboxes, and a menu of final drive ratios from 2.72:1 (180 mph) to 4.56 (for drag racing and 0-100 in 13 seconds). Except for the Corvette Grand Sport, temporarily fielded by a dubious GM which was still officially *not* backing competition, Cobras simply ran right past Corvettes every time they met on the street or track.

Problem: the Cobras didn't sell well! The Ford dealers who *did* offer them mainly didn't understand them. Buyers with six grand to spend wanted performance, all right, but they also wanted roll-up windows, tops that worked, comfortable interiors—air conditioning, even. The production total for the 1962-65 small-block Cobra came to only 654, including 75 with the 260, 39 competition roadsters, and six competition coupes. So much for the small-block.

The 1965-68 427 Cobra was another animal entirely. People who drove the thing came away spellbound. Here was a car no bigger than a Ford Pinto, weight not much over a ton, packed with a mighty engine developing at least one bhp per cubic inch. Remember when the Jaguar XK120 advertised 0-100 in 25 seconds? When Aston Martin made everybody sit up by announcing 0-100-0 in 27? When the fuel-injected Corvette cut 0-100 down to 14? All of these in their day were *very* impressive accomplishments—still are.

Well, the 427 Cobra would go from 0-100 *to* zero in 14 seconds flat. It would do 160 mph almost before you could think about it. But wait. Although the ultimate Cobra was always known as the 427, it seems that some of them

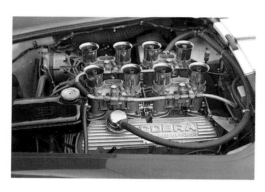

The Cobra, which Carroll Shelby built in his Venice, California "factory," was homologated for racing as a GT car. It sold in small numbers for about the price of an E-Type Jaguar, and thus cost more than a 'Vette, which it buried in every type of competition.

Purposeful road-and-track car that the Cobra was, it was also a good looker. Both bumper and weather protection were minimal.

were actually built with the low-stress low-output 428 engine, which had completely different cylinder dimensions and cylinder head castings. The 427 was a racing engine, while the 428 was designed for the big Galaxie and Thunderbird passenger cars—considerably heavier than the 427 and by no means as "tuneable."

The 427 Cobra would also—despite what everybody says—handle extremely well, as long as you knew what you were doing. The body resembled the Cobra 289, indeed the same old recognizable shape as the original 1954 AC Ace, except for the extra hood scoop and extractor vents and outside pipes and bulging wheel wells. Underneath, there was a beefed-up frame to handle the V-8's unprecedented torque, coil springs in place of the old transverse leafs, and fatter tires to lay as much rubber as possible to the road. It would handle, all right. As long as you knew what you were doing. Otherwise you might find yourself trying to steer a Cobra while watching the rear end come around and pass up the front.

A very good driver once pointed out that a 427 Cobra was not only faster in a straight line than every other street car and most competition cars, it was also faster over *any* kind of a road you cared to choose. And just when you thought you'd found its limit, it simply dug in and kept going faster. But it was a wild beast that sensed the nature of the nut holding its wheel. Everything— steering, braking, cornering, and above all accelerating—happened so all-fired fast that it took only a moment's lapse to lose it completely. One percentage point over your capability and you'd be nose to tail or upside down—in a car the size of a Pinto.

A specialist in hyperbole once compared driving this beast to "riding bareback aboard a thundering V-8 engine carrying somewhere over 500 bhp." Well...officially, the 427 had 425 bhp, but there's evidence to suggest that figure was purposely low, to reassure the insurance companies. They didn't reassure. The rate of insurance levied on Cobra 427s helped sink them as civilian automobiles, not that they had

much more appeal to the general public than the 289s. Government emissions and safety regulations did the rest. By December 1968 they were gone.

Specifications	
Engine:	All Ford U.S. ohv V-8s **260** cid/4,261 cc (3.80 x 2.87-in. bore x stroke), 260 bhp @ 5,800 rpm, 269 lbs/ft torque @ 4,800 rpm **289** cid/4,727 cc (4.00 x 2.87-in.), 271 bhp @ 6,000, 314 lbs/ft @ 3,400 rpm **427** cid/6,997 cc (4.24 x 3.78-in.), 390 bhp @ 5,200 rpm, 475 lbs/ft @ 3,700 rpm **428** cid/7,014 cc (4.14 x 3.98-in.), 355 bhp @ 5,400 rpm, 420 lbs/ft @ 3,200 rpm (all bhp SAE gross)
Transmission:	4-speed manual
Suspension, front:	**260/289** Independent, double wishbones, transverse leaf spring **427/428** coil springs
Suspension, rear:	**260/289** Independent, double wishbones, transverse leaf spring **427/428** coil springs
Brakes:	Hydraulic, front/rear discs
Wheelbase (in.):	90.0
Weight (lbs):	2,100-2,530
Top speed (mph):	138-165
0-60 mph (sec):	4.2-5.5
Production:	260 V-8 75 289 V-8 51 "Mk II" 528 "Mk III" AC 289 27 427/428 348 (numbered chassis)

The prancing horse has been the Ferrari symbol for many years now. Probably no car ever wore it more proudly than the 1962-64 250 GTO, a model built for the track, but able to live on the street.

The 250 GTO served as Ferrari's *gran turismo* of the early Sixties, and it was the ultimate evolution of the "small V-12" series begun in 1954. The 2,953-cc engine developed about 300 horsepower and was mated to a five-speed manual gearbox.

Built for the track but able to live on the street. A legend in its own time, a near-priceless treasure in ours. A handsome brute, but not brutish to drive. A classic example of form following function and racing improving the breed. That's the greatness of the Ferrari 250 GTO. More than just the ultimate evolution of the "small V-12" series begun in 1954, it was Ferrari's ultimate *gran turismo* of the early Sixties. But though formidable in competition, it was doomed to be cut down in its prime. Born in the dawn of the mid-engine age, the GTO would not only be the last race-and-ride "production" Ferrari but Maranello's last purpose-designed, front-engined factory racer.

Its genesis was the two-seat 250 berlinetta that dominated mid-Fifties GT competition and was nicknamed "Tour de France" (TDF) after winning that grinding, high-speed rally three years straight (1956-58). Seeking greater success with a lighter, more agile car, Enzo Ferrari trimmed length between wheel centers some seven inches to create a Short-Wheelbase Berlinetta, long since known as the 250 SWB. Introduced in 1959, it retained the TDF's sturdy multi-tube chassis as well as its 3.0-liter version of the reliable "small-block" 60-degree V-12 (a Ferrari staple since Gioacchino Colombo had designed it back in 1946, a year before Automobili Ferrari was established). Taut, closely coupled Pinin Farina styling completed a beautiful—and beautifully balanced—package offered as both a steel-bodied road car (dubbed *Lusso*, "luxury") and a semi-stripped, aluminum-paneled competition special weighing about 100 pounds less.

Of course, both versions went racing in the grand "dual-purpose" tradition, and the factory took its share of the numerous victories with 22 supertuned "SEFAC" models. But the SWB was the end of an era. As author Pete Lyons observed in CONSUMER GUIDE®'s *Ferrari: The Man and His Machines*, "From this point on, the company's products [would become] ever more specialized, designed for road *or* track, but not both."

The GTO began this changing of the Maranello guard. Its impetus was a decree by the FIA—*Federation Internationale de l'Automobile*, the world motorsports governing body—that the 1962 Manufacturer's Championship would be fought with series-built grand touring cars. That spelled trouble for Ferrari because, fast though it was, the SWB just wasn't slick enough to achieve the higher top speeds this change implied. But the ever-wily Enzo was quick to spot a loophole allowing "evolutionary variations in body style" to be homologated—that is, accepted as "production." Though Enzo had no intention of building the required 100 copies, he got the FIA to let him run SWBs with the new, more aerodynamic bodywork he was planning, arguing that he'd already built more than 100 of the regular models.

Ferrari created a few four-liter GTOs to race in the prototype class in 1962. The cars are identified by a prominent hood bulge.

In 1960 he'd built a pair of streamlined SWB experimentals, one of which was race-tested at Le Mans the following year. After some additional fine tuning of this fastback shape—created not by PF but by Ferrari's own engineers under Giotto Bizzarrini (who had access to a wind tunnel at the University of Pisa) —Enzo introduced his homologated GT in February 1962. Its soon-to-be-famous initials allegedly stemmed from a factory paper referring to a "GT-O," indicating the car was officially *omologato*. However the name started, it stuck.

Like the vision of the car itself. Though blessed with long-hood/short-deck berlinetta proportions, the GTO was strikingly unique: purposeful but pretty— uncommonly so for a competition machine. From low, rounded nose to high, clipped "Kamm" tail (then coming into favor because it diminished air turbulence off a relatively short car), the GTO looked ready to run. And its distinct wedge profile forecast the shape of racing cars to come.

Weight-saving was evident throughout: aluminum body panels, no bumpers or sound insulation, plastic rear window and sliding door "glass," a trunk barely

big enough to enclose a spare tire. The cockpit was fairly well trimmed—for a racer—but any copilot had to share space with a bulky battery, an intrusive frame brace, and an oil tank (usually quite warm).

Save altered body mounts, plus lighter tubing in places and a switch from antiquated lever shocks to modern tubular hydraulics, the GTO chassis was much like the SWB's, right down to wheelbase. However, more tubes were used to form an even stiffer structure that was close to a pure space-frame. Though Bizzarrini had wanted independent rear suspension, he settled for the SWB's live axle (all the better to qualify as "production") but supplemented its existing quartet of trailing arms with a Watt linkage for more secure lateral location.

Equally new was a five-speed gearbox with full Porsche synchronizers to replace the SWB's four-speed unit. Even better, it bolted to the full-house dry-sump racing engine from the mighty 250 Testa Rossa, complete with aluminum-alloy block, magnesium cam covers, and no fewer than six twin-choke Weber carburetors—a barrel for each

cylinder. By spring 1962, Ferrari had built a pair of 4.0-liter GTOs to contest the Prototype class. Except for a dry-sump rendition of the contemporary 400 Superamerica engine beneath a prominent hood bulge, they looked much like the 3.0-liter cars.

Interestingly, chassis had the odd serial numbers traditionally reserved for road-going Ferraris, not the even numbers applied to competition models. Nevertheless, the GTO was clearly a racer, and it immediately lived up to its winning looks in spectacular fashion. Debut 1962 saw GTOs run fourth overall in the *Targa Florio*, 1-2 at Silverstone, second in the Nurburgring 1000 Kilometers (a 4.0), 1-2-3 in the British Tourist Trophy, and 1-5 in the 1000 Kilometers of Paris. In the ultimate test, the Le Mans 24 Hours, GTOs acquitted themselves admirably, finishing second overall (behind a 4.0 Ferrari spyder) as well as third, sixth, and ninth. The 1963 season brought more of the same: first overall in the three-hour Daytona Continental, 4-5 in the Sebring 12 Hours, fourth in the *Targa* (also sixth, eighth, and 13th), runner-up at the 'Ring (also 6-7), 1-2 in the TT (as well as fifth and eighth), second at Nassau, and second and fourth overall at Le Mans. The GTO also gave Ferrari its eighth consecutive *Tour de France* by coming home first in the '63 contest.

But competitors were looming. Joining Jaguar's lightweight E-Types as a 1964 threat were the new ultra-light Ford-powered AC Cobras of former Ferrari pilot Carroll Shelby. To maintain an edge, Maranello devised a "Series II" GTO. Also known as "GTO 64," this crowned the existing chassis with a new Scaligetti-built body featuring a lower nose, reshaped tail, shallower and wider windshield, and a shorter, more set-back cab with "flying buttress" sail panels and inset back window (a roofline destined to be duplicated for the 1968 Corvette). The result was slightly better air penetration and a bit less weight, as the "64" was 4.3 inches shorter, 2.3 inches wider, and 2.1 inches lower than the "Series I."

To the delight of *Ferraristi*, GTOs again checked the opposition during 1964. Notchbacks won the Daytona 2000 Kilometers, came seventh overall at Sebring, and finished fifth in the *Targa*, second at the 'Ring, second at

Paris, and fifth overall at Le Mans. The fastbacks continued doing well too, with high placings in all these events and outright victory in the *Tour de France*—Ferrari's ninth consecutive.

Yet the GTO's day had already passed. Ford's GT40 was at hand, destined for greatness. And Maranello itself was about to join the midships revolution in international endurance racing with the 250 LM, which looked like nothing so much as a reconfigured GTO 64.

But Enzo had left us pearls of great price in the masterful GTOs, if precious few of them. Marque expert Dean Batchelor lists total production as 25 Series Is (including two 4.0-liters) and 10 Series IIs (including one 4.0)—just 35 in all. There were also three so-called "pseudo" GTOs cobbled up on modified SWB chassis by Piero Drogo's Modena Sports Cars, with technical help from *Ingegnere Bizzarrini*. The most famous of these was the striking "breadvan," with its straight-through horizontal roof. It survives today, as do the other two—all "uglier and less successful than the [factory GTOs] they were hoping to beat," in Batchelor's view.

Great rarity, plus a great racing record,

explains why GTOs have become all-but-untouchable today. From about $20,000 new, prices went as low as $6,000-$7,000 in the Seventies, only to skyrocket when U.S. Customs seized one particular GTO in a 1988 drug action and auctioned it off for $1.6 million. That same car later changed hands for a reported $2.1 million, and the new owner was said to have refused a subsequent bid of $4.1 million. As we said, pearls of *great* price.

And thus hardly for everyone, though always a thrilling experience. *Car and Driver*, testing a Series II 20 years later, clocked 0-60 mph at 5.8 seconds, 0-100 in just 12.7, and the standing quarter-mile in 14.4 seconds at 108 mph. "An honest and forthright piece of machinery," the magazine aptly termed it, with "light, direct" steering, heavy but "effective" brakes, handling still surprisingly modern, responses "telegraphed from the chassis...with an accuracy that Western Union couldn't match," and a cockpit at once quirky and taxing. But its sounds were "mechanical music. Whining gears, whirring chains, and crackling exhaust tips beg for more throttle. Twelve unfiltered carburetor throats roar for air at 4,000 rpm; by 6,000, the 'ripping canvas' shriek from the exhaust drowns out every other sound in the world."

This, too, is the greatness of the 250 GTO. For one brief shining moment it dominated the sports-car landscape with towering authority. Some say it always will.

The engine for the four-liter GTOs was a 3,967-cc V-12 from the 400 Super America that had been brought up to Testa Rossa sports-racer standards. Horsepower was estimated at 375-400.

Specifications	
Engine:	V-12, dohc, 180.0 cid/2,953 cc (2.88 x 2.31-in./73 x 58.8-mm bore x stroke), 295/300 bhp @ 7,400 rpm, 250 lbs/ft torque @ 5,500
Transmission:	5-speed manual
Suspension, front:	Independent, unequal-length A-arms, coil springs, tube shocks, anti-roll bar
Suspension, rear:	Live axle on semi-elliptic leaf springs, parallel trailing arms, Watt link, tube shocks
Brakes:	Hydraulic, front/rear drums
Wheelbase (in.):	94.5
Weight (lbs):	approx. 2,500
Top speed (mph):	165-170 +
0-60 mph (sec):	5.8
Production:	"Series I" 25 (1962-63, incl. 4.0-liter prototypes) "Series II" 10 (1964) "Psuedo" 3

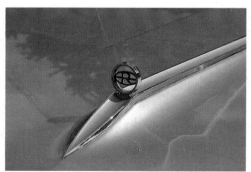

You could think of it as "The Buick that Started Out to Be a Cadillac." Because according to William L. "Bill" Mitchell, General Motors' styling chief and the man who designed the 1963 Riviera, the original intent had been for it to represent a revival of the LaSalle—and it was to have been built by the Cadillac Division.

According to Mitchell's account, GM stylists built several prototype "show" cars—four- and five-passenger coupes—for display at the Motoramas, General Motors' traveling road shows. Harley Earl, Bill Mitchell's predecessor and mentor, had wanted to demonstrate to corporate officials that the public was ready to accept something new and different. "He'd show a special car," Mitchell explained, "and people would say, 'Why don't you build it?' That's how the Corvette was born.

"We didn't bother much about it," Mitchell recalled, "but we did know that Ford came in and measured these cars at night. And the next thing we knew, the [four-passenger] Thunderbird was born! And the dealers started to raise hell about that, saying 'We need an answer!' And that's how come we did the Riviera.

"Now when we did the Riviera we did it for Cadillac," Mitchell continued, "and I called it the LaSalle. That's why the two grilles are on the ends of the fenders—to look like the LaSalle. But Cadillac didn't want it, didn't need it. They could sell everything they made. But in the B-O-P lines, Chevrolet was knocking the hell out of Buick, Olds, and Pontiac with their Impala. So Buick, Olds, and Pontiac bid for [the Riviera.]

"DeLorean was at Pontiac then. He wanted to screw it up. And Olds wanted to put something on it, and I fought it! I had it all done, designed. And the only one who ever saw it was [General Motors President John F.] "Jack" Gordon. And no way would I let 'em change it! Ed Rollert was head of Buick then, and he said, 'I'll take it the way it is!' So that's how Buick got it."

Buick needed it. Needed something, anyway, for between 1955 and '59 the division's production had plummeted by just over 70 percent, dropping its standing in the industry from third to seventh place. And so the car that started out to be the "LaSalle II" became the Buick Riviera instead, introduced in October 1962 as a 1963 model.

The distinctive, razor-edge roofline had been suggested by a Rolls-Royce that Bill Mitchell had seen at the Claridge, in London, dimly outlined in the fog. Working with stylist Ned Nickles, Mitchell developed a low-silhouette design featuring a long hood and short deck. Lines were smooth, and brightwork was sparingly applied. Door glass was frameless, an innovation in 1963, and bucket seats for four were supplied.

Mechanical components, including the engine, were borrowed from the big Buick Electra 225. Standard displacement was 401.2 cubic

The 1963 Buick Riviera, which was brought out to do battle with Ford's incredibly successful four-seater Thunderbird, was recognized immediately as a styling *tour de force*. The little changed '64 model seen here shows off its distinctive, razor-edge roofline, long-hood/short deck proportions, and impeccable detailing.

For 1964, Buick's 425.5-cid, 340-bhp V-8 became standard, with 360 horses optional. Passengers were coddled in a truly luxurious bucket-seat interior.

inches, from which the engine produced 325 horsepower, the same output as the contemporary Cadillac. For an extra $50, the buyer could specify a bored, 425.5-cid version, rated at 340 horses. The standard transmission was Buick's smooth-as-silk Dual-Path Turbine Drive—which John Bond, writing in *Car Life*, described as "the best automatic made." *Motor Trend*'s Jim Wright was equally enthusiastic, describing the unit as "hard to beat, either in smoothness or performance." No manual gearbox was offered at first, though by 1964 a four-speed unit would become available. Standard final drive gearing was 3.23:1, with ratios of 2.78, 3.36, 3.58, 3.91, or 4.45 on the options list.

Also supplied as standard issue were power steering, power brakes, and heater. Optional equipment included air conditioning, tinted glass, power windows, power seats, remote trunk release, adjustable steering wheel, cornering lights, radio, deluxe wheel covers, and white sidewall tires. Base price was a remarkably reasonable $4,333, fully $112 lower than Ford's Thunderbird.

Suspension, in the Buick tradition, was comparatively soft, with coil springs at all four corners. Yet so well balanced was this car that Tom McCahill, writing in *Mechanix Illustrated*, was able to report that "This Buick Riviera will corner with any car made today, which means it's not only more roadable than most other cars but a helluva lot safer when a driver goofs and finds himself going into a turn or switchback at a much faster clip than he realized. This is truly a fine handling car, as good as any made in this country today. . . . The Buick Riviera has true top roadability, a statement I never thought I'd be writing about this particular brand of car." Still, heavy-duty springs and shock absorbers were available for those who wanted them.

Finned, 12-inch aluminum front brake drums with cast-iron liners combined with cast iron rear drums to give the Riviera superior stopping power. John Bond described the binders as "just about the best in the business." *Motor Trend* recorded a stopping distance of 151 feet from 60 miles an hour—nine feet shorter than the contemporary Thunderbird, as tested by the same magazine.

The Riviera's frame was a cruciform (X-type) unit, adapted from that of the Buick Electra. Wheelbase measured 117 inches, nine inches shorter than that of the Electra 225, and overall length was the shorter of the two cars by 13.7 inches. At 53.2 inches, the "Riv" stood 3.8 inches lower than the Electra, and it weighed a couple of hundred pounds less. And at the insistence of engineer Phil Bowser, special tires were developed, designed for higher cornering speeds and higher lateral forces. All of which contributed to the superior handling about which McCahill, among others, wrote so enthusiastically.

Performance was remarkably brisk for what was, after all, a big, heavy automobile. Road testing a car powered by the base 401.2-cid engine, *Motor Trend* covered the standing quarter-mile in 16.01 seconds, ending the run at 85.71 miles an hour. Top speed for that car was 115.5 miles an hour, while the 340 horsepower job tested by *Car Life* topped out at 123 mph. And thanks to the combination of a relatively short wheelbase and a quick steering ratio with just 3.5 turns lock-to-lock, the

Riviera was really quite nimble.

Taken all-in-all, the Riviera was a superb automobile. Even *Ward's Automotive Yearbook*, a publication not given to hyperbole, was moved to call it "a marvelously balanced prestige car."

Few visible changes were made for 1964—one almost has to be a Buick aficionado to tell the '63 and '64 models apart. But under the hood the 425.5-cid, 340-horsepower engine became the standard powerplant, with a twin four-barrel, 360-horsepower version optional. There was a new automatic transmission, the Super Turbine, which was said to be even better than the earlier unit. Power seats were available, and a new Electro-Cruise Speed Control System became a $57 option.

Bill Mitchell's original intent had been to stack the Riviera's headlamps vertically and hide them behind the LaSalle-like grilles in the leading edge of the front fenders. That idea had been shot down by top management, initially, as too expensive, but it was finally adopted when the 1965 model appeared. That year, the Riv reverted to the 401.2-cid engine as its standard powerplant, though the 425 was available at extra cost. A clever way to hide a price increase, perhaps?

In 1965, Buick offered something special for performance buffs: the Riviera Gran Sport. Standard equipment on this model, in addition to its dressed-up interior decor, was the 360-horsepower engine, a transmission specially calibrated for higher shift points, a 3.42:1 positive-traction axle, stiffer springs and shocks, a heavier front roll bar, and faster steering. "They've kept the excellent ride and luxurious comfort," observed Bob McVay, Assistant Technical Editor of *Motor Trend*, "but vastly improved performance and handling."

Which, given the reputation of the original Riviera, was quite a recommendation.

Specifications[1]	
Engine:	V-8, ohv, 401.2 cid (4.188 x 3.641-in. bore x stroke), 10.25:1 compression ratio, 4-bbl carburetor, 325 bhp @ 4,400 rpm. Opt.: 425.5 cid (4.312 x 3.641-in.), 340 bhp
Transmission:	Dual-Path Turbine Drive, console-mounted lever
Suspension, front:	Coil springs with upper and lower control arms, anti-roll bar, direct-acting tubular shocks
Suspension, rear:	Rigid axle, coil springs, leading control arms, track bar, direct-acting tubular shocks
Brakes:	Hydraulic, front finned 12-in. aluminum drums/rear 12-in. cast iron drums
Wheelbase (in.):	117.0
Overall length (in.):	208.0
Shipping weight (lbs):	3,998
Top speed (mph)::	115.5; 123.0 with 340-bhp engine
0-60 mph (sec):	8.1; 7.7 with 340-bhp engine
Production:	1963 40,000 1964 37,958 1965 34,586

[1]1963 model

The '65 Riviera featured the hidden headlamps that designer Bill Mitchell had wanted in the first place. Also new was the Gran Sport package, which came with the 360-bhp V-8, specially calibrated transmission, 3.42:1 positive-traction rear axle, firmer suspension, and faster steering.

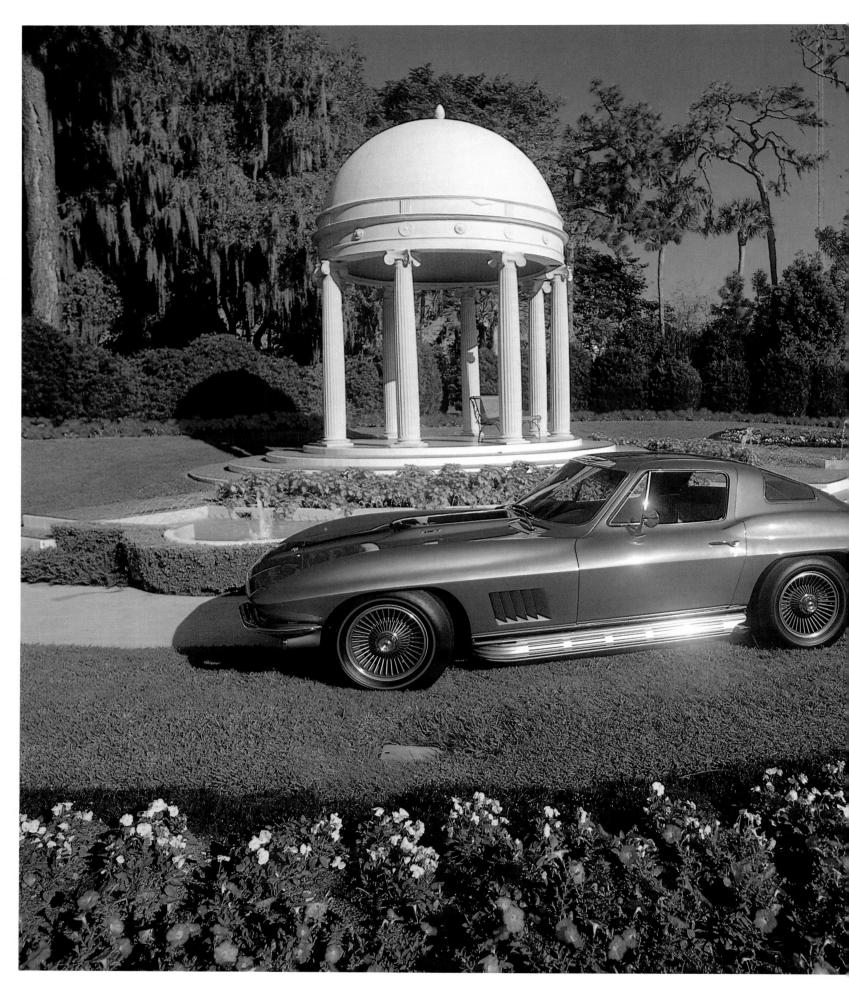

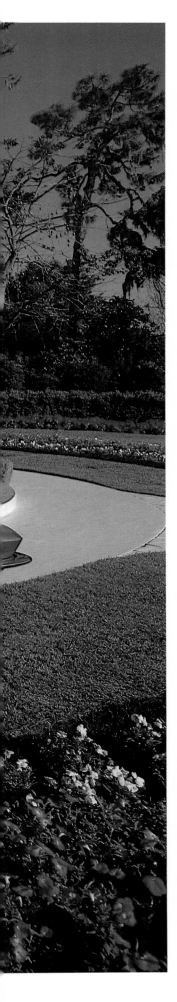

Enormous impact then and high appeal now explain why the Corvette Sting Ray is most always mentioned whenever "great cars" are discussed. The most changed Corvette since the 1953 original, it was the most exciting to look at—and the most rewarding to drive. In fact, many still rank this 1963-67 generation as the best Corvette ever.

The Sting Ray took both its name (but as two words) and general shape from the sleek late-Fifties Stingray racer built by General Motors design chief Bill Mitchell on the rescued "mule" chassis from the unsuccessful 1957 Corvette Super Sport program. Mitchell privately entered this Stingray Special in Sports Car Club of America C-Modified events, and Dr. Dick Thompson drove it to the 1959-60 class championships. Partly because it wowed the public, this car became the styling template for project XP-720, begun in 1959 to deliver a new road-going Corvette with more room, better ride and handling, and even higher performance.

The result was a very different Corvette: shorter in wheelbase (pared four inches) and overall. Despite a new steel "cage" that made for a stronger cockpit, curb weight was also slimmed, via thinner fiberglass body panels and a new ladder-type frame that was lighter—yet stiffer—than the previous X-braced design. Though the engine/transmission package again rode behind the front-wheel centerline for optimum weight balance (47/53 percent front/rear), the center of gravity was lowered by putting passengers within the frame instead of on top of it.

But the big departure was independent rear suspension, a first for a modern U.S. production car. Conceived by Corvette chief engineer Zora Arkus-Duntov, it comprised a frame-mounted differential with U-jointed halfshafts acting on a transverse leaf spring; diff-mounted control arms ran laterally and slightly forward to the hub carriers to limit fore/aft motion, and a pair of trailing radius rods was fitted behind. Relatively cheap, yet highly effective, this arrangement was much lighter than the 'Vette's old live axle, significantly reducing unsprung weight.

Steering was improved via faster gearing, a new vibration damper, and a first-time power option (except with the two most powerful engines). Brakes remained cast-iron drums, but were made wider in front and self-adjusting. Sintered-metallic linings returned at extra cost, as did finned aluminum drums, but power brakes were another new-to-Corvette option, along with air conditioning and leather upholstery.

Chevrolet's masterful small-block V-8, the heart of Corvette power since 1955, was enlarged from 283 to 327 cubic inches for 1962, and the four Corvette versions continued in the Sting Ray: carbureted 250- and step-up 300-horsepower units (hydraulic lifters, 10.5:1 compression, dual exhausts); solid-lifter 340-bhp (bigger four-barrel carb, larger intake valves and exhaust manifolds); and top fuel-injected 360-bhp

The '67 Corvette sported a five-slot vent in each front fender. Otherwise changed only in minor details, it would be the last of the Sting Ray generation. This car sports the optional wheels and side-mounted exhaust system. Note also the bulged hood.

Among the Sting Ray generation Corvettes, only the '63 coupe had the split rear window. The '67 seen here has the one-piece unit, and no decklid, of course.

option. Standard three-speed manual and optional Powerglide automatic transmissions returned, but the overwhelming enthusiast's choice remained the manual four-speed option, available with wide- or close-ratio gearsets depending on engine.

Styling accounted for much of the Sting Ray's huge introductory impact: basically Mitchell's sharp-lined racer with hidden headlamps and some non-functional doo-dads. Equally dramatic was the new "boattail" fastback coupe that joined the expected traditional convertible. Duntov opposed the coupe's striking, vertically split rear window as hindering driver vision. Mitchell countered that "If you take that off, you might as well forget the whole thing." They did take it off for '64, leaving the split-window '63 a highly prized one-year-only model. Predicting the "aero look" of two decades hence, the coupe's doors were cut into the roof for easier entry/exit. Alas, cost precluded trunklids on both body styles.

The Sting Ray was as wonderful to drive as it was to behold. Though no faster than a '62 Corvette engine for engine, it had an edge in both traction and handling with its new rear suspension. And somehow, Chevy's high-winding small-block was better than ever. Testing a four-speed fuelie with a 3.70:1 axle, *Motor Trend* clocked 0-60 mph in just 5.8 seconds and a 14.5-second standing quarter-mile at 102 mph. Considering that, fuel consumption was reasonable at 14.1 mpg overall. Yet there was no less value here than in previous 'Vettes. A fuelie coupe with a few extras ran to around $5,300, a sensational deal. Sales reflected this and the superb overall design; model-year production jumped 50 percent above the '62 total (itself a Corvette record).

Though change was hardly needed, the Sting Ray was nicely spruced up for 1964. Besides the coupe's backlight divider bar, Chevy erased the dummy hood vents, opened up the coupe's fake B-pillar vents, simplified the wheel covers, switched steering wheels from color-keyed to simulated walnut, and altered instrument bezels from chrome to non-glare flat black. Springs went from fixed- to progressive-rate for a smoother ride, shock absorbers gained small bags of cooling freon gas to prevent fluid bubbling and loss of damping, more sound insulation was added, body and transmission mounts were revised, and there were more bushings in the shift linkage. A big new Holley carb and high-lift camshaft upped the solid-lifter 340 engine to 365 bhp; the fuelie went to 375. The Borg-Warner four-speeds gave way to a similar pair of GM "Muncie" manuals with stronger synchronizers. Sintered-metallic brakes now cost a whopping $629.50, but included aluminum drums. Positraction limited-slip differential, still bargain-priced at $43.05, went into more than 80 percent of production—which set another new Corvette record.

The '65 Sting Rays sported smoothed-out hoods, three vertical front-fender vents (no more decorative "speedlines"),

and new wheel covers and rocker moldings. More welcome was the advent of optional four-wheel disc brakes: four-piston units with two-piece calipers and finned rotors that increased swept area from 328 to 461 square inches. Per pending Federal regulation, there was also a new master brake cylinder with separate front and rear reservoirs and lines. Though diehards could still have drums as a credit option, discs went into all but 316 of the '65 models.

Responding to persistent demands for more power, Chevrolet issued the first Corvette big-block V-8 at mid-'65, officially titled Mark IV but marketed as the "Turbo-Jet." A 396 wedgehead design that immediately ousted the fuelie small-block, it followed the so-called "mystery" 427 NASCAR engine of 1963 in having "porcupine" valvegear—pushrods set at odd angles. Hydraulic lifters, four-barrel carb, 11.0:1 compression, and premium features including impact-extruded alloy pistons with chrome rings and a cross-drilled crankshaft yielded a thumping 425 horsepower. To handle it, Chevy threw in a heavy-duty suspension with a rear sway bar. An aggressive hood bulge and optional side-mount exhaust pipes identified the beast at rest. Though it weighed some 650 pounds, the big-block actually improved weight distribution to 51/49 percent. With all this, the 396 'Vette could pull standing quarter-miles of around 14 seconds at 102-104 mph and sail on to nearly 140 mph, even with a tame axle ratio.

But Ford had an impressive 427 V-8 that one Carroll Shelby was stuffing into his sparse two-seat Cobras. Corvette kept pace for 1966 by boring out the 396 to 427 cubes, which yielded 390 bhp on 10.25:1 compression or 425 bhp via 11.0:1 compression, larger intake valves, solid lifters, and a big four-barrel Holley on an aluminum manifold. Of course, horsepower was often understated in those days to placate insurance companies, so the actual figures here were more like 420 and 450 bhp. Positraction and the close-ratio four-speed were mandatory options, but that did include the uprated 396 suspension plus stouter shot-peened halfshafts and U-joints.

Any 427 Sting Ray was an incredible performer. The short 4.11:1 gearset could produce 0-60 mph in an unbelievable 4.8 seconds; even the modest 3.36:1 axle was good for 5.4 seconds and a standing quarter of 12.8 seconds with a trap speed of 112 mph. Because 427s made 327s less necessary, small-blocks were cut to the 300- and 350-bhp versions. All '66 Sting Rays wore a new eggcrate grille insert, and coupes were shorn of their roof vents. This relative lack of change did not reflect a fall-off in demand. Indeed, '66 was another record-busting sales year.

The 'Vette's optional Turbo-Jet 427 V-8 came in three forms, the top one with triple two-barrel carbs and 435 bhp.

A new Corvette had been planned for '67, but was delayed by unexpected problems, so the Sting Ray carried on for a final year. Many judged it the best yet. Styling was cleaner still, with five small front-fender "gills," flat-finish rockers, and handsome slotted "Rally" wheels with chrome beauty rings. Both small-blocks and the 390-bhp big-block (hulking beneath a redesigned hood scoop) were unchanged, but there were two new triple two-barrel 427s belting out 400 and 435 bhp. The latter, RPO L71, had solid lifters and transistorized ignition; a special RPO L89 version with special aluminum heads and huge exhaust valves carried the same grossly underrated horsepower.

But the ultimate '67 Corvette engine was coded L88, an even wilder L71 built close to pure racing specs. A still-hotter cam, towering 12.5:1 compression,

and a single 850-cfm Holley carb gave it a staggering 560 bhp. But it required hard to get 103-octane fuel, couldn't be ordered with radio or heater, and cost a cool $1,500 extra. With that, the L88 wasn't a serious proposition even for would-be dragsters, so only 20 such Sting Rays were built (of which at least three are known to survive today).

It was an explosive finish for what would be the one truly new Corvette before the still-distant 1984 model. The Sting Ray was widely mourned, mainly because its 1968 replacement was just a more gimmicky, less practical car with the same basic chassis. But that chassis would endure for another dozen years, eloquent testimonial to the expertise of Duntov and his team.

As was the Sting Ray itself. It was—and is—the kind of car that happens only once in a lifetime.

The cockpit of the Sting Ray Corvettes was a bit tight, but it continued with a twin-cove theme, and placed a large speedometer and tachometer in front of the driver. The seating was low, though comfortable. For 1967, the handbrake lever was moved from beneath the dash to between the seats.

Specifications	
Engine:	V-8, ohv **1963** 327 cid/5,359 cc (4.00 x 3.25-in/101.6 x 82.6-mm bore x stroke) 340 bhp @ 6,000 rpm, 344 lbs/ft torque @ 4,000 rpm; 360 bhp @ 6,000 rpm, 352 lbs/ft @ 4,000 rpm **1963-65** 327 cid, 250 bhp @ 4,400 rpm, 350 lbs/ft @ 2,800 rpm; 300 bhp @ 5,000 rpm, 360 lbs/ft @ 3,200 rpm **1964-65** 327 cid, 365 bhp @ 6,200 rpm, 350 lbs/ft @ 4,000 rpm; 375 bhp @ 6,200 rpm, 350 lbs/ft @ 4,400 rpm **1966-67** 327 cid, 350 bhp @ 5,800 rpm, 360 lbs/ft @ 3,000 rpm **1965** 396 cid/6,489 cc (4.09 x 3.75-in./103.9 x 95.3-mm), 425 bhp @ 6,400 rpm, 415 lbs/ft @ 4,000 rpm **1966** 427 cid/6,997 cc (4.25 x 3.75-in./108 x 95.3-mm) 425 bhp @ 6,400 rpm, 460 lbs/ft @ 4,000 rpm **1966-67** 427 cid, 390 bhp @ 5,400 rpm, 460 lbs/ft @ 3,600 rpm **1967** 427 cid, 435 bhp @ 5,800 rpm, 460 lbs/ft @ 4,000 rpm
Transmission:	3-speed manual; 4-speed manual and 2-speed Powerglide automatic opt. with most engines
Suspension, front:	Independent unequal-length A-arms, coil springs, tube shocks, anti-roll bar
Suspension, rear:	Independent halfshafts, lateral arms, trailing radius rods, transverse semi-elliptic leaf spring, tube shocks (anti-roll bar with 396 or 427 engines)
Brakes:	Hydraulic, front/rear drums; front/rear discs opt. 1965-67
Wheelbase (in.):	98.0
Weight (lbs):	3,050-3,270
Top speed (mph):	105-150
0-60 mph (sec):	5.4-8.0
Production:	1963 21,513 1964 22,229 1965 23,562 1966 27,720 1967 22,940

The '63 Avanti was a bold move by a failing automaker. Unfortunately, it was rushed to market too quickly, causing problems, such as ill-fitting fiberglass bodies initially. Still, it was a stunning car from a design standpoint, and performance was impressive as well.

Raymond Loewy had been six years absent from South Bend when Studebaker president Sherwood Egbert phoned him in January 1961. Egbert wanted a new car—something, he said, as earth-shaking and revolutionary as the Loewy Studios' 1947 Starlight coupe or 1953 Starliner hardtop: a personal sports model to begin with, but with lines that might lead to a new generation of Studebaker family cars. Sensing a return of the important contract he'd last held in 1955, Loewy assured Egbert he could produce just the ticket—and in no time flat. A few weeks later he assembled the design team: young designers Bob Andrews and Tom Kellogg, and John Ebstein from Loewy's New York design office. The four secreted themselves at a ranch house in the desert near Palm Springs, California, which Loewy had rented for the purpose.

Work proceeded at a breakneck pace. "It was like a cloak and dagger movie," remembered Bob Andrews. "We had no idea what was up except that it was terribly secret and we'd have to develop the thing in a very short time. Once we got there, R.L. closed us up tight. He wouldn't even let us out for a night on the town. He disconnected the telephone, stopped the clocks, banned wives and girl friends. We worked sixteen hours a day every day for weeks. It was so grueling that I took to fooling around, walking up behind Tom making loud heel clicks in imitation of The Boss. Tom would drop his butt or coffee and bend over the drafting board. I'd lean over his shoulder and whisper obscenities in his ears. He'd groan and chew me out. It kept us from going balmy."

The shape that emerged was off the professional pens of Andrews and Kellogg, but the concept was 100 percent Raymond Loewy. "Pininfarina could never have produced a body with the nervous, histrionic surface development of the Avanti," one latterday reviewer said. Neither could your everyday car stylist. Admittedly, the style "worked" very hard. *Road & Track* magazine said it was "contrived, straining for visual impact to the exclusion of utility, or efficiency, or grace," while admitting that it was "mercifully free of excrescent ornamentation" and "not a copy of anything."

The last remark was right, anyway. Significantly, the Avanti was more Loewy than the 1953 Starliner, than the 1947 Starlight, than the 1939 Champion—his earlier Studebaker successes—in that it expressed his personal flair, interpreted and tempered by skilled designers. Contrary to his public persona, Loewy in his later years was not a designer but a salesman of concepts. The cars he designed himself were amateurish. The Avanti's shape was most closely influenced by the "Loraymo," a weird BMW 507 Loewy had customized, with the same extruded, bulging fenders, Coke-bottle waist, radical wrapped and curved greenhouse, and asymmetrical hood scoop. But on the Avanti, Loewy's stylists made all

The '64 Avanti sported square headlight bezels and an under-bumper grille. The instrument panel featured full instrumentation, and its ends curved toward the driver. A big console carried controls for heating and ventilation plus the shift lever.

a spacious cockpit with red-lit instruments angled under a modernistic steering wheel; bucket seats swiped from the Alfa Romeo Giulietta, but thinner to provide more rear knee room. A big console carried controls for heating and ventilation plus the shift lever. Aircraft influence was apparent in the light controls: a row of rocker switches mounted in the center of the cockpit above the windshield. The Avanti, as Bob Andrews said, was "very aircraft."

By mid-year the car was named "Avanti," the Italian word for "forward"—which was exactly right, given the schedule. Egbert was pushing for a late 1962 introduction—partly because Studebaker desperately needed something to spice up a line of dowdy Larks and aging Hawks, and partly because he had cancer, and didn't have a lot of time himself.

The decision to make the Avanti out of fiberglass was prompted by the need for speed—there was no time (or money, for that matter) to tool for steel dies.

these disparate ideas work with each other. That was the difference.

Incredibly, Loewy was in South Bend with a small scale model and sketches of the interior on April 2, 1961. Egbert was delighted. A few months later, with Studebaker styling chief Randy Faurot and designer Bob Doehler pitching in at South Bend, they had a full-size clay model and were finalizing the interior:

The Avanti's sensuous curves still look good nearly two decades later. Note the large backlight and thick C-pillars.

Studebaker had no fiberglass facilities, so Egbert contracted with Molded Fiberglass Products of Ashtabula, Ohio, which already supplied Corvette bodies. The frame was from the Lark convertible, with new front/rear sway bars and rear radius rods. Front disc brakes and a built-in roll bar were also part of the Avanti spec. Independent rear suspension with inboard discs would have been nice, but costs interfered. Studebaker engineer Gene Hardig settled for a conventional rigid axle and finned drum brakes—adequate but hardly exotic.

The only available performance engine was Studebaker's old but reliable cast-iron 289 V-8. Hardig gave it a three-quarter race cam, heavy-duty valves and crankshaft bearings, dual breaker distributor, viscous fan drive, four-barrel carb, and dual exhausts. Like Rolls-Royce, Studebaker smugly refused to divulge this "Jet-Thrust"—or R1—engine's horsepower, but estimates put it around 240 bhp, good for 0-60 mph in about 10.5 seconds and a top speed of 115 mph.

With the help of Andy Granatelli, four special Avanti engines were developed. By far the most common was the R2, with Paxton Supercharger and 290 bhp, which reduced the 0-60 time to about 7.5 seconds and gave at least 120 mph. The other three, bored to 304.5 cubic inches, were low-production exper-

imentals: supercharged R3 with 9.6:1 compression and 335 bhp; the unblown R4 with twin four-barrel carbs, 12.0:1 compression, and 280 bhp; and the experimental R5, with two Paxton blowers, Bendix fuel injection, a dry-sump oiling system, and specially ground camshaft. This "due cento" powerhouse turned 575 horsepower at 7,000 rpm—an amazing two horsepower per cubic inch.

Though Studebaker built only nine R3 Avantis, one of them, driven by Granatelli, broke 29 stock car speed records at Bonneville in early 1962. Finely tuned (they thought it had about 400 bhp), with a low axle ratio, and flush wheel covers but little other body alterations, this R3 racked up 168 mph in the flying mile. A year later Egbert himself drove an Avanti 168 mph for his personal flying mile, while Granatelli broke more records with the R3 and did 196 mph with the "due cento"—quite something for 305 cubic inches.

On paper the Avanti seemed a sure winner, but it proved a disaster. Deliveries were held up because of ill-fitting fiberglass panels, the result of improper or premature curing—the rush to get into production had finally backfired. This cost Studebaker many a canceled order—but the fact is, there weren't that many orders. Studebaker customers were pretty thin on the ground by 1963—most people thought the com-

pany was a bad risk by then—and tended to buy Larks, not Avantis. At $4,500 base, the R1 Avanti was competing with such established personal luxury cars as the T-Bird and Buick Riviera.

A late '63 facelift involving square headlamps, a radiator grille, and a more elaborate interior with dummy wood veneer didn't help, and ultimately Studebaker built only 3,834 '63s and 809 '64s. The last '64 had barely rolled out of South Bend in December 1963 than Studebaker closed, moving a rump assembly—not including the Avanti—to its Ontario plant, where the firm survived only two more years as a car producer. The Avanti will thus be remembered as the last great Studebaker.

Specifications	
Engine:	V-8, ohv **R1** 289 cid (3.56 x 3.63-in. bore x stroke), 10.25:1 compression ratio, ¾-race cam, heavy-duty valves and crankshaft bearings, dual breaker distributor, 4-bbl carburetor, 240 bhp. **R2** 289 cid, 9.0:1 c.r., Paxton supercharger, 285-290 bhp **R3** 304.5 cid (3.65 x 3.63-in.), 9.75:1 c.r., supercharger, 335 bhp **R4** 304.5 cid, 11.0:1 c.r., 2 4-bbl carbs, 280 bhp **R5** 304.5 cid, special cam, magneto ignition, fuel injection, twin superchargers, 575 bhp @ 7,000 rpm (experimental)
Transmission:	4-speed manual or 3-speed automatic
Suspension, front:	Independent, unequal A-arms, coil springs, tubular shock absorbers, anti-roll bar
Suspension, rear:	Rigid axle, longitudinal leaf springs, radius rods, tubular shock absorber, anti-roll bar
Brakes:	Hydraulic, front discs/finned rear drums
Wheelbase (in.):	109.0
Overall length (in.):	192.5
0-60 mph (sec):	**R1** 10.5 **R2** 7.5
Top speed:	**R1** 115 **R2** 120 +
Production:	1963 3,834 1964 809

The '64 Pontiac GTO made history by being the first of what would soon be called the "muscle car." Imitators were quick to follow.

For several years, Pontiac had been carefully cultivating a performance image. During the 1961 season, for example, Pontiacs racked up 21 NASCAR victories. Ten more followed in 1962, including the Daytona 500, and then Pontiac went on to set six new world records at Indianapolis and the Darlington Motor Speedway. In stock car competition and on the drag strips as well, Pontiac was the car to beat.

The effort did good things for sales, boosting the division's standing in the industry from fifth place in 1960 to third rank two years later. But then the word came down from no less a personage than James Roche, president of General Motors: Pontiac was to get out of racing. No arguments, no exceptions. The party was over.

This left Elliott "Pete" Estes and John Z. DeLorean, Pontiac's general manager and chief engineer, respectively, with a difficult dilemma: How best to preserve that hard-won reputation for speed without bringing down upon themselves the wrath of the corporate brass?

It happened that General Motors was about to introduce a new group of intermediate-sized cars for the 1964 season. Logic suggested that if Pontiac wanted to turn its version, known as the Tempest, into a real stormer, the trick would be simple enough. The Tempest's 326-cubic-inch V-8 was basically an under-bored version of the big Pontiac's 389, meaning of course that the Bonneville V-8 would drop into the smaller car's engine bay with no modification whatever, thus providing the little car with a tremendous increase in horsepower. Trouble was, a further announcement from corporate headquarters had declared that the maximum engine displacement allowable for any of the new intermediates would be 330 cubic inches.

But then somebody at Pontiac thought of a way to get around that regulation. Perhaps it was DeLorean, who had always been something of a rebel. Or maybe it was Jim Wangers, who worked for Pontiac's advertising agency. Or Pontiac engineer Bill Collins. Or it could be that the three of them cooked it up together. In any case, the ploy was a simple one—don't list the larger engine as standard equipment. Rather, carry it on the options list. And so late in 1963, a performance package became available—for $295 extra—on any of the three upscale Tempest LeMans models: coupe, hardtop, or convertible. Borrowing its title from Enzo Ferrari (who probably took a dim view of the idea) Pontiac called it the GTO: Gran Turismo Omologato. Or in unvarnished English, Grand Touring Homologated. Signor Ferrari had coined the term (quite accidentally, some say) to describe a competition coupe approved for racing. This wasn't a very accurate description of what Pontiac was doing, to be sure, but the name certainly had a nice ring to it.

317

The 1965 GTO was even sexier than the first edition. It featured a single hood scoop, curvier "Coke-bottle" styling on its flanks, and vertically stacked quad headlights. At this point, the GTO was still listed as a package option, not a separate series.

The GTO was more than a Tempest with a Bonneville engine, by the way. Although its powerplant was basically that of the Bonne, for this application a high-performance camshaft and special hydraulic valve lifters were fitted. Cylinder heads were borrowed from the big 421-cid Pontiac engine, which provided larger valves for better breathing, and a seven-blade, 18-inch fan and dual exhausts were added. Taken together, these modifications raised the horsepower from 303 in the Bonneville to 325 in the GTO.

Then to complete the package Pontiac added a heavy-duty suspension, including wide-rim wheels, firmer springs, stouter shocks, and a beefier anti-roll bar. U.S. Royal "Red Streak" tires were part of the deal, and extra heavy springs and sintered metallic brake linings were available on special order. Identifying trim items included twin simulated hood scoops, an engine-turned dash insert, and special GTO emblems.

Given that the Tempest was nearly 600 pounds lighter than the Bonneville (which was no slug in its own right), the GTO package turned Pontiac's new intermediate into a full-blooded tiger. And for those who wanted even more vitamins there was yet another version

of the 389 engine, this one featuring Tri-Power: three two-barrel Rochester carburetors. So equipped, the GTO Tempest put out 348 horsepower.

There were three transmission choices, the same three that could be had with any Tempest model. Standard issue was a three-speed manual. A two-speed automatic was optional, but those who were serious about performance opted for the four-speed manual—a Warner T-10 at first, later superseded by a GM Muncie gearbox. Both manual boxes featured Hurst shifters.

GTO features for '65 included sporty wheels and unique louver-style taillights. The standard engine, with re-cored cylinder heads, was boosted to 335 horsepower at 5,000 rpm, while a Tri-Power option boosted bhp to 360 at 5,200 rpm.

Frank Bridge, Pontiac's veteran sales chief, didn't like the sound of the whole menu, but he reluctantly agreed to accept 5,000 cars with the GTO package. They sold out in a hurry, and in the end 32,450 examples were produced during the 1964 model year. Sales might well have been double that figure had it not been for the hesitant start, combined with a crippling strike during the critical third quarter.

The motoring press was generally enthusiastic. *Car and Driver* found it "a better car, in some respects, than most current production Ferraris," which was quite a recommendation for a car whose prices began as low as $2,757. *Car Life*, road-testing a GTO hardtop with the Tri-Power engine, four-speed transmission, and standard 3.23:1 axle ratio, blasted from 0-60 mph in 6.6 seconds and recorded a top speed of 135 miles per hour, which was a good deal better than adequate by anyone's standards.

Meanwhile, out in Royal Oak, Michigan, "Ace" Wilson's Royal Pontiac dealership was modifying GTO's for even greater performance. Carburetion, throttle linkage, spark advance, and lifters were all diddled a bit, and 3.90:1 cogs were used for maximum acceleration. Testing one of these "Royal Bobcats," *Car and Driver* scrambled from rest to 60 mph in just 4.6 seconds! The standing quarter-mile was covered in 13.1 seconds, topping out at 115 mph.

Still, there were criticisms. Steering, for example, was slow, requiring too many turns of the wheel for high-performance work where turns were involved. And with 56.5 percent of its 3,126 pounds carried over the front wheels, the GTO had a distinct forward weight bias. *Road Test* magazine took the GTO to task for its brakes, which provided only 150.2 square inches of effective area—less, even, than the 2,540-pound Plymouth Valiant. Less, for that matter, than the little Volvo PV-444. And the supposedly "firm" suspension was firm only in relation to the spongy springing found in the normally suspended Tempests.

The GTO was still an option package, rather than a separate series, when the 1965 models were introduced. A single

The '65 GTO sported a backlight recessed into the sail panels, a styling motif that would be used by other automakers as well. GTO output more than doubled for '65, with the hardtop coupe easily being the most popular body style: 55,722 were built.

false hood scoop replaced the dual dummies previously employed, and the cylinder heads were re-cored to improve the flow of gases. Standard horsepower was increased by 10, to 335 @ 5,000 rpm. Tri-Power, priced at $115.78 including a special 288-degree camshaft, boosted that figure to 360 at 5,200 rpm. Which should have been ample for most people, but reportedly a few new GTO's were delivered to lead-footed buyers with dealer-installed 421-cid engines.

By this time Frank Bridge had retired, and production of the GTO option during 1965 more than doubled the initial year's output. Larger brakes were fitted, though they still appeared to be no better than marginal. And the weight distribution was adjusted to relieve a little of the forward bias that had been the cause of some complaints. But still, the GTO was at its best in straight-line, down-the-road high-speed travel. Driven that way, the GTO provided most of the performance of a Corvette at a savings of about a thousand dollars.

For 1966, the GTO was officially listed as a Tempest sub-series, doing away at last with the fiction that this was simply an option package. By that time, General Motors had abandoned its limitation on engine displacement for its intermediate cars, and any objections that may have been raised were lost amid the ringing of GM's cash registers.

Another point was that Pontiac had, in effect, come up with a brand new *genre:* the Muscle Car. Jim Wangers, as

quoted by Jan Norbye and Jim Dunne, said it all: "GTO was the first really true, hot street-machine. It started in cold weather. It had an automatic choke, and it used hydraulic valve lifters, despite a rev limit as high as five-five. But the reality of that vehicle is far more significant than almost anybody has given it credit for. It was a social statement. It appealed to youth. It was something they could identify with. Car songs got popular at that time, starting with one called 'Lil GTO' by Ronnie and the Beach Boys [sic]."

And best of all, it came at a very reasonable price.

Specifications[1]	
Engine:	V-8, ohv, 389 cid (4.062 x 3.75-in. bore x stroke), high-performance camshaft, 10.75:1 compression ratio, Carter 500-cfm 4-bbl carburetor, hydraulic valve lifters, 325 bhp @ 4,800 rpm **Tri-Power:** 3 Rochester 2-bbl carbs, 348 bhp @ 4,900 rpm
Transmission:	3-speed all-synchro manual with Hurst shifter; 2-speed automatic or 4-speed manual with Hurst shifter opt.
Suspension, front:	Independent, unequal length wishbones, coil springs, anti-roll bar
Suspension, rear:	Rigid axle, coil springs, two upper and two lower trailing arms
Brakes:	Hydraulic, front/rear drums
Wheelbase (in.):	115.0
Overall length (in.):	203.0
Tread, front/rear (in.):	58.0/58.0
Weight (lbs):	3,200-3,500
Tires:	7.50 x 14 red-stripe on 6-in. wheels
0-60 mph (sec):	6.6
Top speed (mph):	135
Production:	1964 spt cpe 7,384 htp cpe 18,422 cvt cpe 6,644 1965 spt cpe 8,319 htp cpe 55,722 cvt cpe 11,311

[1]1964 model

Superb to begin with, the Porsche 911 has stayed remarkably contemporary despite more than 25 years of automotive progress and no fundamental changes to its basic design. The reason is the same relentless, yearly updating that kept the 356 Series ever youthful. Then, too, the rear-engine 911 came to be so regarded as the one "true" Porsche that the firm simply couldn't let it die. In fact, the 911 still outsells its one-time replacement, the newer front-engine 928.

The 911 was initiated in 1959 as essentially a faster, more agile, slightly larger 356. Basic construction was unaltered, but wheelbase was stretched 4.4 inches and the torsion-bar suspension received MacPherson struts and lower wishbones in front and semi-trailing arms in back. Also on hand were all-disc brakes, rack-and-pinion steering, and a five-speed transaxle with racing-style gate (first to the left of the other four gears, with reverse above it). The engine remained an air-cooled horizontally opposed unit sitting behind the rear axle, but now had six cylinders instead of four, as well as one chain-driven overhead camshaft per bank instead of pushrods and rockers. Designed by Ferry Porsche's nephew, Ferdinand Piech, this 1,991-cc unit also employed a cast-aluminum crankcase, eight-bearing forged-steel crankshaft, and dry-sump lubrication. With two triple-choke Solex carbs, horsepower was an impressive 130.

Wrapped around all this was a more angular new fastback coupe body designed principally by Ferry's son "Butzi," still with definite 356 overtones. When the 356C was discontinued in 1965, about a year after the 911 debuted, its engine went into this shell to create the 912, which at around $5,500 cost some $1,000 less, thanks also to fewer standard features.

Though somewhat pricey, the 911 was an instant hit. *Car and Driver* was not alone in judging it "a worthy replacement for all the models that preceded it. Race breeding and engineering development ooze from [its] every pore.... More important, the 911's appeal should be considerably wider...." Prescient indeed.

Porsche moved quickly to keep that appeal strong. Space here only permits highlighting the myriad changes which were to come. They began with the Targa—a companion semi-convertible with a fixed rollbar and a removable roof panel above the front seats—announced in 1966. The following year brought the high-performance 911S, with a tuned 160-bhp engine, plus rear anti-roll bar, vented brakes, and five-spoke alloy wheels.

New U.S. safety and emissions standards for 1968 began a confusing parade of "Federal" 911s with specific tuning and equipment to meet them. But these suffered only against their European counterparts, and advancing technology would ultimately permit something like "universal" specifications once more.

The secret to the longevity of the Porsche 911 is that it has been continually updated. The inaugural '64 model was basically a faster, more agile, slightly larger 356. The wheelbase was 4.4 inches longer and the flat-four engine made way for a flat-six.

Though seen here as a '67 model, the 911 Targa had actually debuted for the 1966 model year. A semi-convertible, it had a fixed rollbar, a removable panel above the seats, and a fold-down rear plastic window.

The '69 models rode a 2.2-inch longer wheelbase, owing to longer semi-trailing arms and reangled halfshafts. Offerings now comprised coupes and Targas in base, T, luxury E (replacing an interim L model), and S form, with the last returning to the U.S. after a year's absence. All sported newly flared wheelarches. Bosch mechanical fuel injection benefitted performance and driveability on E and S, and the Targa's rear window changed from a leaky zip-out plastic section to fixed wraparound glass.

A bigger bore expanding displacement to near 2.2 liters upped 1970 performance across the board. Front suspension attachments were relocated for reduced steering effort and kickback, and limited-slip differential became optional. Two years later, a stroke job took capacity to 2,341 cc, mostly to bolster low-end power being lost to tightening U.S.-mandated smog controls. Also new that year were a stronger, easier-shifting five-speed with conventional gate (fifth on the dogleg to the right of the H), a modest "chin" spoiler for the S (optional elsewhere), and an external oil-filler (abandoned after '72 because people confused with it with the fuel-filler). For no apparent reason, wheelbase was stretched a mere 0.1-inch.

But 1972's most exciting news was the return of the Carrera name—last seen on 1967's mid-engine Type 906 Makes Championship car—for a 911-based racer with a 2,687-cc engine. Called 911RS, it was lightened in every possible way. Alas, it couldn't be driven on U.S. roads for lack of detox gear, but became available for track use in 1973 when approximately 1,600 were built, of which 600 were trimmed to 911S specs for European roads.

The 1974 models boasted a revised look that would persist for the next 15 years. The impetus was the new U.S. requirement for five-mph basher bumpers front and rear. Porsche met it beautifully with body-color bumpers that looked liked they'd been there all along. Other changes included high-back front seats, dash vents, and a larger fuel tank. Another bore job swelled displacement to near 2.7 liters, and fuel injection switched to Bosch CIS electronic for emissions and driveability reasons. The T and E vanished, but there was now a road-legal U.S. Carrera. Relegating the S to mid-line status, this was essentially the European RS with the new 167-bhp U.S. engine, plus bold lower-body identification, racing-style "ducktail" engine-lid spoiler, and rolling stock that was wider aft than fore.

America's bicentennial year brought new excitement via the rapid Turbo Carrera. Sometimes known as the 930, it was the roadgoing result of a decade's turbocharging work that had produced the mighty competition 917 flat-12. Its heart was a 3.0-liter version of the amazingly adaptable 911 flat-six engine, the larger size chosen for better off-boost performance with the lower compression then necessary with turbocharging. That performance was prodigious, what with 234 U.S.-legal horsepower and torque so ample that only a wide-ratio four-speed gearbox was required. One magazine reported just 4.9 seconds from 0-60 and 156 mph all-out, yet the Turbo was surprisingly tractable in daily driving. Inside was most every convenience Porsche could pack in; outside rode the famous "whale tail" spoiler introduced on the '75 S, plus wider rolling stock for a suitably beefed-up chassis.

Regular 911s were pared to S and Carrera, but features had proliferated greatly, running to luxuries like cruise control, tinted glass, and optional automatic air conditioning. Prices kept pace—a minimum $14,000 by now, versus $9,950 in 1974.

For 1978, Porsche offered just the Turbo and a new normally aspirated 3.0-liter 911SC, the latter essentially the old Carrera with quieter styling and 20 less horsepower but a fuller, flatter torque curve that improved low-end response. Accompanying it were a stronger crankshaft, bigger bearings, and the return of an aluminum crankcase (replacing the pressure-cast magnesium sump of 1968-77). U.S. 911s were now nearly identical with European ones save emission controls. Power brakes became standard for '79, when the never-popular semi-automatic "Sportomatic" transmission offered since '68 was finally canceled. The Turbo, meantime, was bumped to 3.3 liters and, via an air-to-air intercooler, 253 SAE horsepower. Go didn't change much, but its stopping ability did, thanks to cross-drilled four-piston discs from the 917.

Save more yearly technical improvements and steadily expanded standard amenities, the SC changed little through

1983, when Porsche introduced its first factory-built Cabriolet in 18 years. For 1984, the SC coupe, Targa, and Cabrio became 911 Carreras powered by a stroked, 3.2-liter six boasting Bosch's new "Motronic" management system with integrated electronic ignition. Horsepower was back to 200, yet mileage was better than ever. Other alterations included thicker brake rotors, standard fog lights, and a "Turbo Look" option offering the panache and chassis prowess of the awesome 930 at an equally awesome price.

The 930 itself was also relatively untouched, but Porsche didn't sell it in

America from 1979 to 1985, partly in deference to a second energy crisis. But the crisis soon passed, and by 1986 Zuffenhausen had taken control of its U.S. distribution (from VW of America) and largely returned to a "world" specification for all models. A "Federal" Turbo thus returned that year, and was more like its European cousin than ever. There was more rated power, if not actual performance, but interim chassis refinements had made the beast more predictable and safer in really fast work. And for the first time, the Turbo could be ordered in Targa or new Cabriolet form. A 1987 slant-nose modification

The 1972 911T Targa looked little different than the 911 Targa on the preceding page, but note the different wheels. Note also the interior differences, particularly the steering wheels. By 1972, meeting U.S. federal regulations was a primary concern of Porsche.

The Carrera name returned to Porsche for 1972. In 1987, the Carrera ran with a 3.2-liter flat six that developed 214 bhp. Alas, Porsche prices had been skyrocketing, and the Carrera ragtop listed at $44,500.

The '91 911 Turbo coupe's 3.3-liter flat six boasted 315 horsepower. However, the price was up to a cool $95,000.

provided the looks of Porsche's late-Seventies 935/936 GT-class racers for a stupefying $24,000—*not* counting the car! This then became a separate model called 930S.

Following such improvements as an expanded warranty, improved shifter and climate system, and a further 14 bhp for Carreras, the 911 was thoroughly overhauled to become the 1989 Carrera 2 and Carrera 4. Both featured reshaped front and rear ends, a still-larger 3.6-liter six, and revised all-coil suspension. The 2 also boasted Tiptronic, a "thinking" self-shift transmission option with manual and fully automatic modes. The Carrera 4? Nothing less than a more affordable version of the late, high-tech 959, with a simpler version of its variable-torque-split full-time all-wheel drive. And just for fun, Porsche produced a handful of 911 Speedsters, with a cut-down windshield and unlined top in the image of the fondly remembered 356 model. The Carrera 4's anti-lock brakes and dual airbags became standard for 1990 Carrera 2s. The Turbo was brought into line the following year (after a year's absence from the U.S.), with a Carrera-type facelift, coupe-only body choice, 33 more horsepower (via freer breathing), and bigger new ABS brakes.

Compared to its Sixties ancestors, today's 911s are faster, more socially responsible, far more luxurious, and much costlier—prices at this writing range from $61,000 for the Carrera 2 coupe to a cool $95,000 for the Turbo. They're also less intimidating in tight corners as the original, oft-criticized snap-oversteer tendency has been gradually transformed into mild understeer as the basic handling trait. How long can the 911 go on? Given the record, this unique and seemingly ageless thoroughbred sports car should be delighting and thrilling us well into the 21st Century.

Specifications

Engine:	Flat six, sohc (DIN ratings unless otherwise stated) **1964-69** 2.0 121.5 cid/1,991 cc (3.15 x 2.60-in./80 x 66-mm bore x stroke) **911/911L** (1964-68): 130 bhp @ 6,100 rpm (148 bhp SAE), 125 lbs/ft torque @ 4,200 rpm **911S** (1966-68): 160 bhp @ 6,600 rpm (180 bhp SAE), 127 lbs/ft @ 5,200 rpm **911/911T** (1967-69):110 bhp @ 5,800 rpm (125 bhp SAE), 112 lbs/ft torque @ 4,200 rpm **911E** (1969): 140 bhp @ 6,500 rpm, 125 lbs/ft @ 4,500 rpm **911S** (1969) 170 bhp @ 6,800 rpm, 130 lbs/ft @ 5,500 rpm **1970-71** 2.2 134 cid/2,195 cc (3.31 x 2.60-in/84 x 66-mm) **911T** 125 bhp @ 5,800 rpm, 126 lbs/ft @ 4,200 rpm **911E** 155 bhp @ 6,200 rpm, 137 lbs/ft @ 4,500 rpm **911S** 180 bhp @ 6,500 rpm, 142 lbs/ft @ 5,200 rpm **1972-73** 2.4 142.9 cid/2,341 cc (3.31 x 2.77-in./84 x 70.4-mm) **911T** 130 bhp @ 5,600 rpm, 140 lbs/ft @ 4,000 rpm **911E** 165 bhp @ 6,200 rpm, 147 lbs/ft @ 4,500 rpm **911S** 190 bhp @ 6,500 rpm, 154 lbs/ft @ 5,200 rpm **1974-77** 2.7 164 cid/2,687 cc (3.54 x 2.77-in./90 x 70.4-mm) **1974 911** 150 bhp @ 5,700 rpm (143 bhp SAE net), 168 lbs/ft @ 3,800 rpm **1974 911S/Carrera** 175 bhp @ 5,800 rpm (167 bhp SAE net), 168 lbs/ft @ 4,000 rpm **1975-77** 165 bhp @ 5,800 rpm (157 bhp SAE net), 161/168 lbs/ft @ 4,000 rpm **1978-83** 3.0 182.6 cid/2,993 cc (3.74 x 2.77-in./95.0 x 70.4-mm), 172 bhp (SAE net) @ 5,500 rpm, 189 lbs/ft @ 4,200 rpm **1984-88** 3.2 193 cid/3,164 cc (3.74 x 2.93-in./95 x 74.4-mm) 200/214 bhp (SAE net) @ 5,900 rpm, 185/ 195 lbs/ft @ 4,900 rpm **1989-91** 3.6 219.7 cid/3,600 cc (3.94 x 3.01-in/100 x 76.5-mm), 247 bhp (SAE net) @ 6,100 rpm, 228 lbs/ft @ 4,800 rpm **1975-77 Turbo 3.0** 182.6 cid/2,993 cc (3.74 x 2.77-in./95.0 x 70.4-mm), 234 bhp (SAE net) @ 5,500 rpm, 246 lbs/ft @ 4,500 rpm **1978-85 Turbo 3.3** 201.3 cid/3,299 cc (3.82 x 2.93-in./97 x 74.4-mm), 253 bhp (SAE net) @ 5,500 rpm, 282 lbs/ ft @ 4,000 rpm **1986-89 Turbo 3.3** 282 bhp (SAE net) @ 5,500 rpm, 278 lbs/ft @ 4,000 rpm **1991 Turbo 3.3** 315 bhp (SAE net) @ 3,750 rpm, 332 lbs/ft @ 4,500 rpm
Transmission:	4/5-speed manual, Sportomatic semi-automatic (1968-79, exc. Turbo), Tiptronic automatic (1990-91)
Suspension, front:	Independent, MacPherson struts, lower A-arms, longitudinal torsion bars (concentric coil springs from 1989), tube shocks, anti-roll bar
Suspension, rear:	Independent, semi-trailing arms, transverse torsion bars (concentric coil springs from 1989), tube shocks, anti-roll bar
Brakes:	Hydraulic, front/rear discs
Wheelbase (in.):	1964-68 87.1 1969-71 89.3 1972- 89.4
Weight (lbs):	2,270-3,275
Top speed (mph):	125-160 Turbo 150-165
0-60 mph (sec):	5.5-9.1 Turbo 4.8-5.3
Production:	1964 235 1965 4,865 1966 5,381 1967 17,676 1968 9,118 1969 14,446 1970 10,234 1971 12,422 1972-73 15,061 1974 11,624 1975 7,824 1976 7,981 1977 10,308 1978 5,183 1979 4,067 1980 3,715 1981 4,096 1982 4,780 1983 6,095 1984 4,554 1985 5,890 1986 8,084 1987 7,889 1988 5,842 1989 5,713 1990 5,465 (calendar year)

The original Corvair, announced in 1960 as Chevrolet's answer to the demand for "compacts," was a disappointment. That's because it was almost effortlessly outsold by its far more conventional—but cheaper and far more on-the-target—rival, the Ford Falcon. As Chevrolet soon realized, rear-engine, air-cooled cars were going nowhere as mass-production vehicles. Even Volkswagen, which failed to produce a successful car of this type after the Beetle, was forced to admit that there was a limit to how far the idea could be pushed after trying with the Fastback and Squareback and the slow-selling 412. VW ended up talking about future front-drive, water-cooled models even as the Beetle dominated the import car market, and would ultimately be forced to move in that direction in the mid-Seventies.

But in the early Sixties, what saved the Corvair temporarily was its sporting image. Almost by accident (so it's told), Chevrolet brought out a slick little demi-sports model called the Monza, and thereby uncovered a much vaster market than its product planners had suspected.

On the outside, one could argue that the Monza was just another upside-down, sharp-edged bathtub like the other Corvairs. But in mid-1960, Chevy dressed its interior with bucket seats, snazzy vinyl upholstery, and carpets—instead of the usual "cheap-car" bench seats and rubber mats. By 1961, the Corvair could boast about a four-speed manual gearbox, and even a convertible. There were also Monza sedans and wagons, but the coupe and the convertible were what mattered. Before long the Monza was outselling all the other 'Vairs combined—and planting in Ford's Lee Iacocca the germs of the idea that led to the phenomenally successful Mustang.

When Bill Mitchell's designers gave the Corvair a handsome new suit of clothes for 1965, they created one of the most beautiful forms of the Sixties. At the top of the 1965-66 line was the Corsa, which was all of the above and then some: a Monza with real power, great brakes, fine handling. It was the best Corvair ever built.

Corsas were offered in two advanced states of tune: 140 horsepower with quad one-barrel Rochester carbs, and 180 horses with the then-novel turbocharger. The technology that produced the latter was a product of Chevy's search for performance in the rear-mounted, air-cooled flat six that Ed Cole had originally designed to be a kind of American Volkswagen. Such engines didn't respond to conventional performance mods, and there was a limit to displacement increases. But a supercharger/turbocharger seemed to offer interesting possibilities.

The first supercharged Corvair was the 1961 Sebring Spyder, an experimental show car designed under Bill Mitchell. A svelte two-seater on a short wheelbase, the SS was only 162 inches long and a mere 37 inches high. Its Paxton supercharger was the same unit used on the

Very few cars had turbos in the mid-Sixties, but the sporty Corvair Corsa did. With it, the 164-cid flat six cranked out 180 bhp.

Like other Corvairs, the Corsa—offered as a hardtop or convertible—rode a 108-inch wheelbase. The hardtop weighed a modest 2,519 pounds.

Studebaker Avanti, but its main disadvantage was soon clear: it drew power constantly.

Chevrolet engineers next considered the turbocharger, a concept that actually dates back to the early Twenties and is today found in many high performance cars. A turbocharger may be compared to a waterwheel, where exhaust gasses replace the waterfall. Like a jet engine or turbine, the gasses spin the "wheel" or impeller. Power is then transferred by a shaft, running not to a gristmill but to another impeller (compressor), which in turn pressurizes the fuel/air mixture. As the exhaust flow increases and its temperature rises, the turbine spins faster, adding positive manifold pressure or "boost." Its only real disadvantage was that it had a lag period before it began spinning fast enough to make a difference, a problem that still

plagues automakers using turbos.

Turbochargers first appeared on heavy diesel truck engines, where they're virtually standard today. The higher exhaust gas temperature in a gasoline engine posed some engineering problems, but Chevrolet thought these could be surmounted through the use of heat-resistant alloys. The turbo offered obvious advantages: no mechanical drive, no noise or vibration, efficient use of space, and boost only when required (thus propping-up fuel economy). Against a slight loss of fuel economy, depending on how driven, the turbo offered serious power for relatively low cost. J.O. Brafford and R.E. Thoreson were the engineers assigned to develop it for the production Corvair.

The Corsa turbocharger, ultimately manufactured by Thompson Valve Division, had an 11-blade exhaust im-

peller or "turbine" with a three-inch diameter, made from heat-resistant cobalt-base alloy. Exhaust flow began through the engine's twin manifolds and traveled through a lower crossover pipe mounted in front of the engine, then up into the turbine chamber, exiting through the muffler. A conventional Carter YH sidedraft carburetor with three concentric venturis was selected, the same instrument having been used on the six-cylinder Corvettes.

The first turbocharged production Corvair, the 1962-64 Monza Spyder, batted out 150 horsepower—a 48-percent increase over the 102-bhp engine from which it had evolved. Torque shot up 64 percent to 210 pounds/feet. With the Corsa, a displacement increase dating to 1964 plus increases in the air/fuel mixture ingested by the turbo gave a remarkable 180 bhp and 265 lbs/ft of torque, which is as much as any production Corvair ever delivered. The Corsa turbo thus delivered a 115-mph top speed and 17-second quarter-mile times. The 140-bhp version, with its four carburetors, new cylinder head, larger valves and intake manifold, was close behind. Of course, both cars had appropriate alterations to deal with this kind of power, including heavy-duty springs and shocks, larger brakes, and quicker steering.

Corsas came only as a two-door hardtop or convertible, complete with all the luxury Chevrolet could reasonably throw at them: oversize speedometer and tach, smaller gauges for head temperature, fuel, clock, and manifold pressure, set into brushed aluminum panels. The Corsas looked fantastic with the optional wire wheel covers—and they cost under $3,000! Amazing....

The most important 1965 mechanical change, present on other models as well as the Corsas, was the new rear suspension. The controversial Corvair swing-axle setup (though it had been improved after a few years) was finally gone, replaced by a sophisticated four-link independent rear suspension with trailing arms and coils instead of a transverse leaf spring. "This new setup made for some impressive geometry changes," wrote Mike Knepper in his excellent book, *Corvair Affair.* "Roll center was reduced from a huge thirteen inches to just five, and roll stiffness was increased by eleven percent. The Corvair's back end was now and forevermore under complete and efficient control."

What we had in the 1965-66 Corsa was the Corvair idea at its highest state of development—ironically destined for oblivion by GM (in favor of the '67 Camaro) just as soon as the tooling was amortized. In point of fact, this turned out to be 1969, but no Corsas were built after 1966. The Corvair's greatest nemesis, Ralph Nader, rose to fame as the nation's nanny by attacking the unimproved swing axle of the 1960-61 model. Perhaps it deserved it, but when one of Nader's people attended a Corvair Club meet in the Seventies to see if it was some kind of GM front, he didn't even have the barest idea of how the suspension had been changed.

Inside, the Corsa featured bucket seats and full instrumentation. The base engine was the 164-cid flat six with four single-barrel Rochester carbs and 140 bhp, but collectors prefer the turbocharged unit, which was clearly labeled under the "hood."

But when is all said and done, it was the Mustang—not Nader—that convinced Chevrolet to produce a "conventional" ponycar, the Camaro. It was a much easier car to modify, improve, and hot rod as the market required. And so easy to grab off the Chevy II chassis and economical to produce, as indeed Ford had in large measure based the Mustang on Falcon components. In any case, it was probably Ed Cole himself, always the businessman, who issued the Corvair's formal death notice.

Too bad, because the 1965-66 Corsa was one of the nicest cars of the decade: perfectly sculpted, elegantly curved and strikingly beautiful, great fun to drive, and utterly safe. *Car and Driver* magazine summed it up nicely: "It is undoubtedly the sexiest-looking American car of the new crop and possibly one of the most handsome cars in the world... it unabashedly borrows from the best of the already established foreign and domestic coachwork without losing any of its identity as a Corvair."

Specifications		
Engine:		Aluminum six, horizontally opposed, ohv, 163.6 cid (3.438 x 2.938-in. bore x stroke), 4 main bearings, hydraulic valve lifters **Standard** 9.25:1 compression ratio, 4 1-bbl Rochester carburetors, 140 bhp @ 5,200 rpm **Optional** 8.25:1 c.r., turbocharger, Carter carb, 180 bhp @ 4,000 rpm, 265 lbs/ft torque
Transmission:		4-speed manual, 2-speed Powerglide automatic
Suspension, front:		Independent, wishbones, coil springs, tubular shock absorbers
Suspension, rear:		Independent, upper axle half-shafts, lower unequal-length control arms, rubber-bushed rods, coil springs, tubular shock absorbers
Brakes:		Hydraulic, front/rear drums
Wheelbase (in.):		108.0
Overall length (in.):		183.3
Tread, front/rear (in.):		55.0/56.6
Weight (lbs):		htp cpe 2,475/2,485 cvt cpe 2,710/2,720
0-60 mph (sec):		10.0 (Turbo)
Top speed (mph):		115 (Turbo)
Production:		1965 htp cpe 20,291 cvt cpe 8,353 1966 htp cpe 7,330 cvt cpe 3,142

The '65 Mustang, which bowed on April 17, 1964, was an instant hit across America because of its styling, low price, and huge options list.

I f the 1955-57 Bel Air is the so-called "Classic Chevy," the 1965-66 Mustang has to be the so-called "Classic Ford." Neither term would appeal to the Classic Car Club of America, whose definition applies to expensive, limited-production luxury cars built between 1925 and 1948. But if we use "classic" in the generic sense, as something of significant and permanent value, the Mustang fits.

It you judge a car's significance by its effect on the market, the Mustang was the most singular model of the Sixties, or most any other decade for that matter. It certainly set every kind of sales record. Introduced on April 17, 1964 (contrary to whatever you've heard there was never an official "1964½" model), it was priced at $2,368 base for the six-cylinder hardtop. It drove people to distraction. One San Francisco trucker reportedly stared so hard at a Mustang in a dealer showroom that he drove right through the window. A Chicago dealer had to lock his doors to keep people from crowding in and crushing his cars or each other. It was the same everywhere. Ford had hoped to sell 100,000 in the first year, but sold 100,000 in four months. The extended 1965 model run (April 1964-October 1965) racked up 680,992 sales—a still-unsurpassed record for a new model in its first year.

The Mustang was conceived, as most everyone knows, primarily by Lee Iacocca, the sales-wise Pennsylvania hotshot who had rocketed to the presidency of Ford Division. Certainly his predecessor, Robert F. McNamara, could never have had such a vision. But the Mustang was produced by an army of people honing Iacocca's original idea. Marketing was the name of the game.

The idea was sound: a sporty car with a long-hood, short-deck configuration, which sold new for under $2,500, and had a huge range of options so each buyer could "tailor" his or her car to suit himself/herself.

Basic equipment was the 170-cubic-inch Falcon six, a three-speed manual floorshift, full wheel covers, padded dash, bucket seats, and carpeting. From there you started personalizing—and spending your money. Typical options included Cruise-O-Matic, four-speed manual, or overdrive transmission; a bigger six, or three different V-8s; limited-slip differential; Rally-Pac gauges (tach and clock); special handling package; power brakes; disc front brakes (from late 1965); power steering; air conditioning (except on "Hi-Performance" 271-bhp engines); console; deluxe steering wheel; vinyl roof covering; pushbutton radio; fake knock-off or wire-wheel wheel covers; 14-inch styled steel wheels; and whitewalls.

There were also option packages, which really tempted people: the Visibility Group (mirrors, wipers); Accent Group (pinstriping, rocker panel moldings); Instrument Group (needle gauges for fuel/water/oil/amps and a round speedo); GT Group (disc brakes, driving lights, and

In the fall of '64 a semi-fastback model called the 2+2 joined the hardtop and ragtop in the Mustang lineup. It sported louvers in place of rear side windows and a folding rear seat, and like all other Mustangs a galloping pony grille, triple taillights, and mildly recessed headlights.

The '65 Mustang 2+2 listed at $2,633, about halfway between the hardtop and soft top. A total of 77,079 were built for the model year.

special trim). The Mustang took up the personal car theme pioneered by the Thunderbird and delivered it to the Common Man—or Woman, as the female sex loved it and bought it in vast numbers (encouraged by Ford advertising). For less than $3,000 one could order an exciting, individual car. Hardly any two Mustangs were exactly alike.

In addition, Ford's thinwall Fairlane V-8 was a classic engine design: light, efficient, powerful. The lightest cast-iron V-8 on the market, it was capable of being truly tweaked to deliver formidable performance. The best factory mill in 1965-66 was the Hi-Performance 271, developing .95 bhp per cubic inch and whacking out 312 pounds/feet torque to pull stumps and insult all those snobs in their English sports cars.

Comparisons are noteworthy: the standard Mustang 289 with 200 bhp would do 0-60 in about 10 seconds, the standing quarter-mile in 17 seconds at 80 mph, and top out at 110 mph. The

271 changed those numbers to eight seconds, 15.5 seconds, 85 mph, and 120 mph. With optional quick steering, stiff springs/shocks, beefy sway bar, and 5.90 x 15 Firestones, the softly sprung, mild-mannered stock Mustang was transformed into the wild horse it was named after. All it needed was disc brakes, and these arrived nine months into production. They completed the specifications of a genuine GT car—priced at a fraction of legendary European Gran Turismos.

Of course, if the 271 wasn't enough, one could buy "Cobra equipment" off the shelf at Ford dealerships: special camshafts, heads, and intake manifolds; dual four-barrel carbs; or even Webers. All this hardware was considered factory stock, although it wasn't actually installed at the factory. Mustang-runners at the dragstrip and on the race track were thus able to meet their organizers' rules for "factory stock" competition classes. Exactly how much horsepower

could be wrung out of Cobra equipment is uncertain—but 350 gross horsepower seems within reason.

The original hardtop and convertible were created by the Ford Studio under Joe Oros, who later became executive director of Ford and Lincoln-Mercury Design, assisted by Gail Halderman and David Ash. "We said what we would and wouldn't do," Oros remembered. "We didn't want the car to look like any other car. It had to be unique." They considered—but rejected—a two-seater, like the original Mustang show car that wowed fans at the Watkins Glen race track in New York. But Iacocca figured that two-seaters would appeal only to "the buffs, the true nuts," and was convinced that Ford needed to woo families as well as singles. The long-hood, short-deck appearance was the most important element inherited from the Mustang show car.

A third body style, a semi-fastback called the "2+2," was announced in

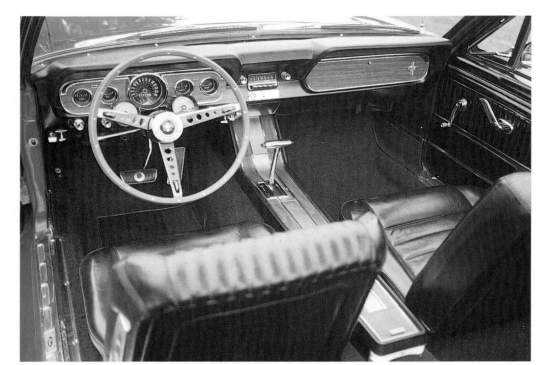

To the basic Mustang, driving enthusiasts added the GT package (disc brakes, special ID, and more), the Rally-Pac gauges (tach and clock), special wheels, and the 289 V-8. In top form, it developed 271 bhp, but "Cobra" equipment was also available off the shelf at Ford dealers.

Convertibles don't generally sell near as well as closed models, but the '65 Mustang ragtop found 101,945 eager buyers during the long '65 model year. Though priced at $2,789, most carried $500-$1,000 in options.

the autumn of 1964. Rear legroom was scanty in this body style—and it was by no means generous in the other models either. Unlike the coupe or convertible, however, the aptly named 2+2 had a folding rear seat. With it down and a trunk partition lowered, a long platform was created to accommodate things like skis or fishing rods. The sleek fastback lacked rear quarter windows, but had small air vents which allegedly provided flow-through ventilation.

With sales breaking every record in the books, Ford hardly even bothered to facelift the 1966 'Stang, making only minor detail changes. The single horizontal grille bar disappeared and the background mesh was changed, the fuel cap was redesigned, windsplits were added to the dummy rear-wheel scoops, wheel covers were new, and script and badges were shuffled. Inside, the cheap-looking Falcon-style 1965 instrument panel yielded to the five-gauge arrangement used in the '65 GT. The Rally-Pac tach/clock combination remained optional. Six-cylinder Mustangs got 14-instead of 13-inch wheels, and the larger 200-cid six was standardized. The 289 V-8 with

200, 225, and 271 bhp continued.

Sales of the '66s were not technically as high because of the longer 1965 model year, but comparing 12-month periods they actually rose by 50,000 units. Mustang, after all, still had no serious competition. The beautiful but unorthodox Corvair had shot its load in 1965 and wasn't even in contention, while the Camaro and Firebird were a year away. Plymouth's Barracuda, meanwhile, was still limited to a Valiant-based fastback model.

The Mustang's shape wasn't, in fact, new—Studebaker arguably had used the same format with its Hawk in 1956. But Ford's was the most effective use of these proportions in history. Combined with the arm-long options list and that wonderful small-block V-8, it was for a time unique and inimitable. By the end of the decade, every American car company was copying what came to be known, in Mustang's honor, as the "ponycar." Alas, the ponycar market folded at the same time muscle cars became extinct, but the Mustang lives on—a testament to the rightness of Iacocca's original idea.

Specifications	
Engine:	1965 I-6, ohv, 170 cid (3.50 x 2.94-in. bore x stroke), 8.7:1 compression ratio, 1-bbl carburetor, 101 bhp @ 4,400 rpm; V-8, ohv, 260 cid (3.80 x 2.87-in.), 8.8:1 c.r., 2-bbl carb, 164 bhp @ 4,400 rpm 1965-66 I-6, ohv, 200 cid (3.68 x 3.13-in.), 8.7:1 c.r., 1-bbl carb, 120 bhp @ 4,400 rpm; V-8, ohv, 289 cid (4.00 x 2.87-in.), 9.3:1 c.r., 2-bbl carb, 200 bhp @ 4,400 rpm; 289 V-8, 10.0:1 c.r., 4-bbl carb, 225 bhp @ 4,800 rpm; 289 V-8, 10.5:1 c.r., solid valve lifters, 271 bhp @ 6,000 rpm
Transmission:	3-speed manual; overdrive, 4-speed manual, and 3-speed Cruise-O-Matic opt.
Suspension, front:	Independent, coil springs mounted over the upper A-arms, tubular shock absorbers
Suspension, rear:	Solid axle, longitudinal semi-elliptic leaf springs, tubular shock absorbers
Brakes:	Hydraulic, front/rear drums; front discs opt.
Wheelbase (in.):	108.0
Overall length (in.):	181.6
Weight (lbs):	2,488-2,789
0-60 mph (sec):	9.0 (225 bhp)
Top speed (mph):	110-115 (225 bhp)
Production:	1965 htp cpe 501,965 cvt cpe 101,945 fstbk cpe 77,079 1966 htp cpe 499,751 cvt cpe 72,119 fstbk cpe 35,698

I n the stock car contests of the 1930s, Ford was the car to beat. Except, of course, that it was rarely beaten. And as the only V-8 in the low-price field it maintained its performance image through the 1940s.

But then in the postwar world the Oldsmobile Rocket "88" and Hudson Hornet became the newest track champions on the fledgling NASCAR (National Association for Stock Car Automobile Racing) circuit. Chevrolet followed a few years later with a 225-horsepower Corvette—which of course proved to be only the beginning for that breed. Then in the early Sixties there were some blazing MoPars from Chrysler and the hot-footed Pontiac GTO, among others. It was a whole new ball game. It's not that Ford had suddenly become a slug—it's just that the make from Dearborn no longer had the field to itself.

Then Carroll Shelby got into the act. His credentials as a racing driver were more than impressive—he had won at Le Mans in 1959 in a Ferrari, for example. And he had achieved competitive success with his Cobra roadster, in which he had married the lightweight aluminum body of the British-made AC Ace to a super-heated small-block Ford V-8. By 1963, he was turning out these hot little items at Lance Reventlow's ex-Scarab plant in Venice, on the southern California coast. But at six grand a pop—enough in 1962 to buy two full-sized Ford Galaxie 500s—the road-and-race Cobra's market was obviously a limited one.

Shortly after the Mustang's April 1964 introduction, some anonymous performance buff at corporate headquarters evidently got what Ford later used in its advertising as a "Better Idea." If a reasonably priced, high-speed version of this new "ponycar"—as it would soon come to be called—could be developed, the resultant publicity would do good things for sales of the Mustang, as well as the entire Ford line.

And so it followed that early in 1965 the Mustang GT-350, better known as the Shelby Mustang, was introduced. Partially completed Mustang fastbacks, finished in Wimbledon White and minus rear seats, hoods, and exhaust systems, were shipped to the Shelby plant in California. There Carroll Shelby's staff worked magic on the 289-cid Ford engine, already a notable performer rated at 271 horsepower in high-output form.

A high-rise aluminum intake manifold was fitted, together with a four-barrel carburetor with 1.7-inch venturis and center-point floats to prevent cut-out during hard cornering. There was an aluminum oil pan with half again the capacity of the standard steel unit, along with special Tri-Y exhaust headers and a pair of straight-through mufflers that exhausted just ahead of the rear wheels. There was nothing modest about this car—it loudly announced itself wherever it was driven. But then, to add a touch of class, finned aluminum valve covers were installed

Carroll Shelby's AC Cobra was a successful racer using Ford V-8s, so it's hardly surprising that he was the one to develop the race-and-drive Shelby GT-350. Though based on the '65 Mustang, it was thoroughly reworked for higher performance, and its looks were altered as well. Seen here is a '66 GT-350. The first 252 were actually leftover '65s updated to 1966 specs.

The heart of the GT-350 was its reworked 289, which after massaging was good for 306 bhp. It was mated to a Borg-Warner T-10M four-speed manual gearbox. Over-the-car racing stripes and various scoops were seen on the exterior.

bearing plates that read "COBRA—Powered by Ford."

As revised, Shelby rated the engine at 306 horsepower and red-lined it at 6,500 rpm, though it would easily spin at 7,000 without complaint. Coupled to it were a heavy-duty 10½-inch clutch and a Borg-Warner T-10M all-synchro, close-ratio, four-speed manual transmission. A Detroit Locker limited-slip differential completed the driveline.

Chassis modifications were equally significant. A brace was stretched across the engine compartment between the upper shock absorber mounts to avoid body flex. Special Pitman and idler arms were fitted for better steering response. Over-the-axle traction bars helped to counteract wheel-hop during hard acceleration. A rock-solid, one-inch sway bar replaced the smaller-diameter stock unit. Big Koni shocks were adjusted for maximum firmness. Kelsey-Hayes front disc brakes were combined with 10-inch rear drums, borrowed from the Ford station wagons and fitted with sintered metallic linings which virtually eliminated any tendency to fade under hard use. And low-profile 7.75 x 15 Goodyear Blue Streak tires were installed.

An 8,000 rpm tachometer and an oil pressure gauge, housed in a special dashboard pod, were added to the standard instrumentation, while a genuine hardwood steering wheel with a cobra pictured on the hub replaced the stock unit. No provision was made for a horn button at the wheel; instead, the hooter was activated by a toggle switch on the dashboard. Air Force-style seat belts equipped with quick-release mechanisms were supplied, and the rear seat was replaced by a fiberglass shelf on top of which the spare tire rested in plain sight.

The Mustang's exterior appearance was substantially altered as well. A fiberglass hood, complete with functional scoop, was held in place by NASCAR-style hood pins. The grille was modified and the Mustang emblem was moved to the far left side. A side stripe on the lower rocker panel carried GT-350 lettering, while blue over-the-body stripes, beginning at the front valance and ending at the rear one, became a popular option.

In 1965-66, the GT-350 was available only as a fastback coupe, and at around $4,600 it wasn't cheap. The brake scoops and rear quarter windows were added for 1966.

Autolite 600-cfm carburetor was substituted for the 715-cfm Holley, but otherwise these cars were virtually identical to the other GT-350's. One can readily imagine the abuse these machines must have taken at the hands of weekend cowboys, so it's hardly surprising that Hertz is said to have lost money on them. But perhaps the attendant publicity made the project worthwhile, for the company purchased some additional Shelby Mustangs during 1968 and '69.

The Mustang GT-350 remained in production through 1970, joined in 1967 and thereafter by a big-block version called the GT-500. But it is the original version of 1965-66 that is remembered most affectionately by aficionados, and sought after most avidly by collectors.

Car and Driver, whose editors were not always easily impressed, had high praise for the Shelby Mustang. "It is, if nothing else, certainly the most sporting street machine we have driven in a long while," its road testers wrote. "And anyone who tells you it isn't a genuine sports car is nuts. The Mustang GT-350 may have a most unsophisticated suspension, but it goes around corners furiously fast, and has speed and brakes to match. . . ."

The GT-350 was not by any means an easy car to drive. Clutch and brake pressures were very heavy. Steering had no power assist, and of course the stiff suspension guaranteed a bone-shaking ride. But it would go! The quarter-mile, according to *Car and Driver*, could be covered in 14.9 seconds, topping out at 95 mph. Meanwhile, zipping from 0-60 took just 6.5 seconds and top speed at the red line was 127 mph. Among its numerous race victories, the Shelby Mustang won its class in the Sports Car Club of America's 1965 national road race championship—and repeated the performance in 1966 and '67.

For those who were totally into competition, there was a full-race version known as the "R" model. This was powered by a blueprinted engine, fitted with a racing cam, oil cooler, and extra-capacity radiator—and rated at 350 horsepower. Plexiglas rear and side windows reduced the weight of the Rs, and a front apron helped direct cooling air to the radiator and brakes. A 32-gallon fuel tank, additional instrumentation, special racing seats, fireproof

interior trim, and rear side scoops with brake cooling ducts were supplied. In addition, 15 x 7-inch American Racing mags were fitted. At $1,500, the package was a bargain, but only 37 of the cars were so equipped.

An optional Paxton supercharger became available on the 1966 GT-350, giving it even better acceleration. Side scoops were added to all models in order to duct air to the rear brakes, and Ford's C-4 automatic transmission joined the options list. Quarter windows replaced the Mustang's standard vents, adding a stylish touch, and several new color options were offered in addition to the original Wimbledon White.

Production, which had amounted to only 562 cars for 1965, was stepped up to 2,380 units for 1966. Included among that number were six convertibles and 936 GT-350H models, the latter specially built for Hertz Corporation, to be used as rental cars.

Most of the "Rent-a-Racers" were painted black and sported gold stripes, and nearly all of them were equipped with the automatic transmission. An

Specifications	
Engine:	**1965-66** V-8, ohv, 289 cid (4.00 x 2.87-in. bore x stroke), 10.0:1 compression ratio, high-riser intake manifold, welded tube headers, 4-bbl 715-cfm Holley carburetor, 306 bhp @ 6,000 rpm, 329 lbs/ft torque @ 4,200 rpm **"R" model** 289 cid, blueprinted engine, racing cam, oil cooler, 350 bhp **1966** Paxton supercharger opt.
Transmission:	4-speed all-synchro manual; 3-speed C-4 automatic opt. 1966
Suspension, front:	Independent, upper wishbones, lower control arms and drag struts, coil springs, 1-in. anti-roll bar, Koni shocks
Suspension, rear:	Rigid axle, semi-elliptic leaf springs, torque rods, Koni shocks
Brakes:	11.3-in. front discs, 10-in. rear drums (non-powered)
Wheelbase (in.):	108.0
Overall length (in.):	181.6
Tread, front/rear (in.):	57.0/57.0
Curb/dry weight (lbs):	2,850/2,551
0-60 mph (sec):	5.7[1]
Top speed (mph):	133[1]
1/4-mile (sec/mph):	14.5/98[1]
Production:	1965 562 1966 2,380, incl. 936 Hertz models and 6 cvt

[1]Per Shelby American

The 206 GT wore no Ferrari nameplates—it had a "Dino" badge up front—but it served as a preview of future mid-engine Ferraris.

What separates "great cars" from merely memorable ones? Some point to timeless styling, balanced overall dynamic ability, a distinguished pedigree, maybe even a competition connection. Others simply point to Ferrari's mid-Sixties Dino 206 GT and its evolutionary successor, the 246GT/GTS. But more than just embodying all those desirable qualities, these cars are historically significant as the first road-going Ferraris with fewer than 12 cylinders, as well as a preview of future mid-engine Ferraris and, indeed, the "sensible supercar" we would come to embrace by century's end, exemplified by the 1990 Honda/Acura NSX.

Of course, no one could know any of this when the Dino itself was first previewed as a special exhibit on the Pininfarina stand at the 1965 Paris Salon. Titled "Dino 206 S Speciale," this shapely coupe intrigued showgoers with a twincam, 65-degree Ferrari-designed 2.0-liter V-6 mounted amidships behind a two-seat cockpit. Though built on a racing chassis (number 0834), it was strictly a design exercise, right down to its non-functioning engine. But a running prototype followed soon enough, at the 1966 Turin show. Dubbed "Dino Berlinetta GT," this bore new PF styling that was just a slightly exaggerated rendition of that being planned for the production model, which bowed a year later, again at Turin, as the Dino 206 GT.

It was a big departure for a Maranello road car: the first with V-6 power and the first with the competition-inspired mid-engine configuration then predicted to be the wave of the future in production sports-car design. Then again, the Dino was not obviously from Maranello, as it wore neither the Ferrari name nor a prancing-horse badge anywhere. Still, most observers were quick to recognize its link to the earlier V-6 sports/racing Ferraris named in honor of Enzo Ferrari's deceased son. This would also be *Il Commendatore*'s first and only attempt at a "companion" marque.

Like the '66 prototype, the production 206 employed the 2.0-liter V-6 (hence the numerical designation) originally developed for racing. But instead of sitting longitudinally, it was now mounted transversely, "sidewinder" fashion, driving the rear wheels via a transfer drive and on to a five-speed gearbox housed beneath the sump.

Somehow, word got around that the Dino engine was built entirely by Fiat. It wasn't. Not only had Ferrari engineer Franco Rocchi designed it, but Maranello built the lower section, including the sump, as well as the transaxle and halfshafts. The Italian giant merely supplied the block, heads, manifolds, and accessories to Ferrari's specifications. One reason for the misperception was undoubtedly the fact that Fiat appropriated this V-6 for its own new sports car, the front-engine Fiat Dino, announced in 1967. Then, too, collaboration between automakers of such disparate size seemed mighty strange—at least until Fiat bought a controlling interest in Ferrari in 1969, a move that would have vast implications for Maranello's future products and production methods.

There was no question about the 206 chassis, crafted in Maranello as well as designed there. Predictably for an Italian, it was a tubular-steel affair (to which separate steel exterior panels were attached) and featured all-independent suspension in the classic mold: upper and lower wishbones and coil springs at each wheel, plus front and rear anti-roll bars. Also on hand were the all-disc brakes and rack-and-pinion steering expected in a "proper" sports car. As with so many previous Ferraris, the house of Scaglietti was again tapped as body supplier, and also carried out assembly.

To the joy of marque loyalists everywhere, Ferrari's new "junior" GT reflected the many lessons Maranello had learned in racing, where the firm was by now running nothing but mid-engine cars (save for front-engine 275 GTBs). Front/rear weight balance was almost ideal. With the heaviest components

almost in the middle the design achieved a desired low polar moment of inertia that made the Dino extremely maneuverable, a car with quick transient responses that made for a willing partner on tight, twisty roads.

But there were trade-offs, as in other "middies," mainly a lot of cockpit noise and marginal luggage space (albeit in a separate, easily accessible compartment behind the engine). Dino owners learned to travel light, and likely did more miles in cities and suburbs than on the open road.

Dino styling predicted that of future Ferraris mainly in its "flying buttress"

roofline, a treatment rapidly gaining favor in the late Sixties and destined to appear on the flat-12 Berlinetta Boxer and V-8-powered 308 of the Seventies. Vision forward and laterally was thus good, but terrible astern and over-the-shoulder. Still, owners didn't seem to let this or any other drawback overshadow their car's many good points—not the least of which was the fact that it was a true Ferrari. Even if it didn't have 12 cylinders, the Dino certainly acted like a Ferrari.

The 206 didn't last long, being phased out in late 1969 for the more powerful and refined 246. Most of the 100 or so built were sold in Europe (though a few found their way to other countries), so the 206 wasn't as well known in the U.S. as the 246. Indeed, it was conceived mainly for Europe, where smaller engines meant a smaller tax bite on buyers. (Still true.)

Ultimately, though, Ferrari couldn't ignore the U.S., where a larger engine was almost mandatory given the much longer distances between major population centers. It was also deemed a

Succeeding the Dino 206 GT at the end of 1969 was the 246 GT. All but indistinguishable from the 206, only the sharp-eyed may have noticed its 2.1-inch longer wheelbase. For a "low-line" car, the cockpit was comfortable and relatively plush.

relatively practical proposition given America's seemingly unlimited supply of low-cost fuel. Porsche and Lotus offered stylish coupes, and many Yankee enthusiasts drooled at the prospect of being able to buy a lower-cost Ferrari. The 246 would answer their prayers—and the competition.

Previewed in 1969 and in production by year's end, it was all but indistinguishable from the 206, though the sharp-eyed may have noticed its 2.1-inch longer wheelbase or, more likely, the extra legroom resulting from it. A more obvious difference—really the only other one of note—was signaled by the change in nomenclature. Sure enough, the twincam V-6 had been enlarged (via increased bore and stroke) to 2.4 liters for a gain of 15 horsepower (on 9.0:1 compression). But it was also made of cast iron now, instead of Silumin alloy, this for greater reliability, an important consideration in the increasingly critical U.S. market. A single dry-plate clutch continued to transfer power to an all-indirect five-speed transaxle pulling a 3.62:1 final drive. Otherwise, all was as before. Scaglietti continued as body supplier, Fiat the main engine contractor.

Again, there was no Ferrari insignia, the reason for which has never been clear. Some claim the Dino was denied its heritage because of the Fiat-built engine, others because it had only six cylinders instead of 12. The former seems more plausible. After all, Enzo had used Dino on his Grand Prix V-6 to honor the son who'd been working his way up through the Ferrari organization and would likely have taken it over one day had he not been killed. Then, too, the old man had put his own name on cars with inline fours, straight sixes, V-6s, and V-8s. Now that *Il Commendatore* is gone, his reason for not doing so here must forever remain a mystery.

The Dino 246 GT received only minor changes over the years, the most visible being the mid-1970 substitution of five-bolt Campagnolo alloy wheels for the original Cromodora center-lock knock-off rims, a change made to most examples sent to the U.S. A more major development arrived in 1972, an open version titled 246 GTS (S for "spyder").

The 206 GT's V-6 was increased to 2.4 liters for the 246 GT, gaining 15 horsepower to 195 at 7,000 rpm and boosting torque to 160 lbs/ft at 5,500 rpm.

It wasn't a full convertible, though, being a "targa" design with a lift-off panel above the cockpit. The GTS also eschewed the coupe's rear-quarter windows for metal panels bearing three small louvers, which contributed to its different look.

For a "low-line" car, the 246 cockpit was comfortable and relatively plush. The instrument panel, in fact, was almost identical with that of the contemporary 365 GTB/4 Daytona, albeit suitably scaled down, encompassing eight instruments in an elliptical binnacle set just ahead of the steering wheel.

Still, not all was bliss. In testing a 1972 coupe, *Road & Track* found the 246 "noisy in the extreme. The sounds are exciting to be sure: busy tappets, whining cam chains and transfer drive, a raucous exhaust system. . . . Even on a slow run to the corner drugstore, the Dino seems to be working, snarling, racing. The exhaust note at low speeds gives away its 6-cylinder configuration, but as the engine climbs into its effective rev range (little happens below 3000 rpm). . . it takes on the characteristic Ferrari sounds despite having only half the number of cylinders."

Of course, with a little less than two-thirds the weight but only half as many horses, even a 246 couldn't match the Daytona in a straight line, but the Dino could still outmaneuver almost any car on a winding road. Even better, it proved

reasonably well-made and reliable. One weak point was the front-cylinder-bank cam chain, which had to be regularly checked for proper tension. It was tricky to reach, so some mechanics didn't bother, but the wages of neglect were potentially disastrous: a chain slipping a tooth on a sprocket could destroy the engine.

Nowadays, you're apt to see some of these Dinos wearing Ferrari badges. Purists may sneer at such lily gilding, but it says much about pride of ownership, which the Dinos deserve as much as any "real" Ferrari. They did Maranello proud—great "little" cars among Enzo's many giants.

Specifications	
Engine:	V-6, dohc **1967-69** 121 cid/1,987 cc (3.39 x 2.25-in./86 x 57-mm bore x stroke), 180 bhp @ 8,000 rpm **1969-74** 145 cid/2,418 cc (3.64 x 2.36-in./92.5 x 60-mm), 9.0:1 compression ratio, 195 bhp @ 7,000 rpm, 160 lbs/ft torque @ 5,500 rpm
Tansmission:	5-speed manual (in rear transaxle)
Suspension, front:	Unequal-length A-arms, coil springs, tube shocks, anti-roll bar
Suspension, rear:	Unequal-length A-arms, coil springs, tube shocks, anti-roll bar
Brakes:	Hydraulic, front/rear discs
Wheelbase (in.):	**206GT** 90.0 **246GT/GTS** 92.1
Weight (lbs):	1,980-2,800
Top speed (mph):	140-142
0-60 mph (sec):	7.1-8.0
Production:	**206GT** 100 (some sources list 150) **246GT** 2,800 **246GTS** 1,200 (all figures approx.)

Audi of Germany likes to take credit for pioneering all-wheel-drive road cars with anti-lock braking systems (ABS), but it shouldn't. Some 15 years before Audi's first Quattro, a tiny producer in the British Midlands proffered a high-performance 2+2 with both those advanced features, plus svelte Italian styling and red-blooded American muscle. Its name: Jensen FF.

The FF was the crowning achievement for the firm of brothers Richard and Alan Jensen, who took over the old West Bromwich coachbuilder W.S. Smith & Sons in 1934. Like William Lyons of Jaguar fame, they specialized in custom bodies for British production chassis, but bodied U.S. Ford V-8, Lincoln V-12, and Nash straight-eight chassis. Dick was chief engineer, Alan the administrator, which may explain why some of their designs weren't all that attractive. Still, they found favor among monied types who wanted to drive something different.

Following World War II, the Jensens used six-cylinder Meadows engines and Moss gearboxes, then switched to a four-liter Austin six for the lumpy but appealing Interceptor fastback coupe of 1949. Its successor, called 541, appeared four years later, and was notable as the first production four-seater with a fiberglass body. The Jensens soon began earning most of their money as contract body suppliers for the new Austin-Healey sports car, but they evolved the 541 into improved, higher-power R and S models (significant as early users of all-disc brakes, by the way) before introducing the replacement CV8 in 1962. This was basically a facelifted 541 packing a 361-cubic-inch Chrysler V-8 with 300 horsepower, linked to the American maker's responsive three-speed TorqueFlite automatic transmission.

Though far from pretty, the CV8 sold well for a specialty car on its attractive combination of coachbuilt exclusivity, reasonable price, and high performance. Performance went even higher in 1964 with the adoption of Chrysler's four-barrel 383 V-8, whose 330 bhp was good for 130 mph. Jensen was going great-guns financially too, still turning out Healeys as well as Volvo's new P1800 coupe (which it assembled in 1961-64). With the future looking very rosy—and the CV8 looking very dated—the firm began planning a brand-new Interceptor in 1965. Even more ambitious, there would be a derivative model built with the "Ferguson Formula," the full-time four-wheel-drive system that inventor Harry Ferguson had been developing since the early Fifties. Perhaps as a preview, Jensen displayed a Ferguson-converted CV8 at the 1965 Earls Court Motor Show.

While there was never a doubt that the new models would retain the basic CV8 chassis, styling was hotly debated. The original pattern was an experimental in-house convertible called P66, but its lines didn't suit chief engineer Kevin Beattie, who insisted that the new, more upmarket

The all-wheel-drive Jensen FF could be distinguished from the standard rear-drive Interceptor by its twin front fender vents and four-inch-longer 109-inch wheelbase.

The rarest of the Jensen FFs was the Mark III, of which only 15 were built in 1971 before production was halted. Note the huge rear hatch window and deluxe interior.

Jensens needed the Italian touch to compete with Latin exotics and Aston Martin. Beattie carried the day and, after shopping at Ghia and Vignale, chose a proposal from Carrozzeria Touring: a shapely fastback coupe of largely squarish appearance save for a rounded tail capped by a huge, compound-curve backlight hinged hatchback-fashion. Alas, Touring was in no position to finalize this design, let alone build it, so Vignale was contracted to supply both the prototype and production bodies, which would be rendered in steel.

After some 18 frenzied months, the new Jensens bowed with a flourish at the annual London show in October 1966. The handsome Interceptor would

have been achievement enough for such a small firm, but its companion, simply called the Jensen FF, was a sensation: the world's first production road car with all-wheel drive—and great, loping big-inch performance to boot. Moreover, the FF marked the showroom debut of Dunlop's "Maxaret" anti-skid braking system, lately added to the Ferguson Formula.

Though not unusual now, the FF's drive system was quite extraordinary for a late-Sixties road car. Its heart was a special center differential-cum-transfer case bolted to the TorqueFlite automatic. This sent power to the rear wheels in the normal way, and to the front wheels via a second propshaft driven from the diff by chain. Torque was apportioned

in a fixed ratio of 37/63 percent front/rear to approximate the handling of a normal rear-drive car. The rear differential was contained in a conventional Salisbury live axle with "Powr-Lok" limited-slip capability. The front diff was a chassis-mounted affair with double-jointed halfshafts. Two multi-disc clutches permitted the front wheels to overrun the rears by up to 16.5 percent and the rears to overrun the fronts by up to 5.5 percent to account for differences in wheel rotation rates through turns, as well as to preclude driveline "binding." To accommodate the extra hardware, the wheelbase was extended four inches ahead of the cowl. Apart from that and an extra front-fender air slot, the FF was easily mistaken for the new Interceptor.

Until one encountered snow or rain, that is. Road testers praised the all-wheel drive for its near fail-safe traction and correspondingly increased safety reserve even on dry roads. But Britain's *The Autocar* magazine really demonstrated its worth by persuading an FF to climb a snow-covered 1-in-4 ski slope— this on ordinary bias-ply tires. Given the laws of physics, an FF could be made to slide eventually, but it did so much later than conventional cars and at far higher speeds. Even then, it tended to gentle four-wheel drifts that were easily "catchable" on most any surface other than glare ice. In routine driving, the FF behaved like a well-

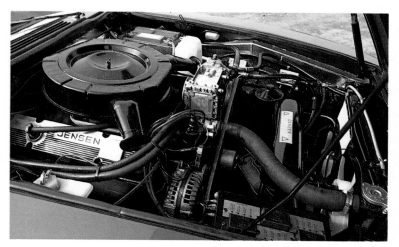

The '71 FF Mark III was powered by Chrysler's 383 V-8 mated to a three-speed TorqueFlite automatic. Maxaret anti-lock brakes were standard.

balanced rear-drive car, exhibiting mild initial understeer that could be changed to oversteer with a judicious wheel-twitch and throttle-poke.

Though the all-wheel drive virtually eliminated wheelspin in hard takeoffs, the FF proved about as fast as the new Interceptor despite being some 330 pounds heavier. *The Autocar* ran the benchmark 0-60-mph sprint in 8.4 seconds; then-rival *Motor* reported 8.1—more than fair going.

Mixed reviews attended the anti-lock brakes. These worked from a sensor on the transfer case that detected incipient wheel locking; in the event, the sensor triggered the brake servo (via a solenoid) to apply and release hydraulic pressure to the affected brake until normal wheel rotation was restored. All much like today's electronically controlled ABS systems except that, in those pre-chip days, Maxaret was purely mechanical and thus slow, cycling only 2-3 times a second versus the 15-20 cycles now common. Nevertheless, Maxaret did its intended job, and did it well. But most drivers disliked the brake-pedal "kick-back" it produced (again not unlike today's ABS systems), and *The Autocar* was unnerved by the thought that emergency stops might force the driver to "leave himself in the hands of the unit." *Motor* groused that Maxaret "bounced the whole car on its springs" when operating, and said that, plus the kickback, could "under certain circum-stances . . . put the car off balance."

These quibbles aside, the FF repre-sented an unprecedented marriage of speed and safety, and *Autosport*'s John

Bolster spoke for many in terming it "the world's safest car." But it came at a price: initially some $15,000, fully 35 percent more than the Interceptor, which crimped sales as much as the FF's visual similarity to its orthodox brother. The FF was also hampered by the sheer complexity of its driveline, which proved trouble-prone. As *The Autocar* noted in a 1983 retrospective, "every single production FF had to be 'set-up' in the experimental department of Jensen before delivery. . . ." No wonder, then, that only one FF was sold for every 10 Interceptors.

The FF might have had more of a future had it not been for blossoming American safety regulations and the growing need for Jensen to certify its cars for U.S. sale to make up for the loss of its Volvo and Austin-Healey business. Though the FF received the late-1969 "Mark II" updates accorded the Interceptor—a tidier "safety" dash-board designed with U.S. rules in mind, plus minor cosmetic changes and stand-ard radial tires—minuscule sales and Jensen's fast-worsening cash situation soon rendered it a liability. The FF was thus quietly phased out in late 1971 after a handful of "Mark III" models were built with the same nice new wheels and seats given to Interceptors.

The Autocar mourned the loss of the "historic" FF, "fallen under the safety axe, its production volume being insuf-ficient to justify full-scale crash testing and development. Ironically, and in total ignorance, Ralph Nader has been respon-sible for killing the safest high-perfor-mance car ever built." Of course, that

was written before the Quattro and other all-drive/ABS cars appeared in the Eighties. A shame the FF was never recognized in its own time as the trail-blazer it turned out to be.

At least it's honored today as a prime collector car, and for the same things that made it so desirable when new: outstanding dynamic safety, terrific go, and *grand luxe* appointments (full Con-nolly leather, electric windows, and AM/FM/tape player, to name a few). It's still not for everyone—high asking prices and low original production (320 total) see to that—but we can all appre-ciate its important contributions to motoring progress. They're more than sufficient reasons to rank the Jensen FF among the truly great cars of the 20th Century.

Specifications	
Engine:	Chrysler ohv V-8, 383 cid/6,276 cc (4.25 x 3.38-in./106 x 86-mm bore x stroke), 10.0:1 compression ratio, 5 main bearings, hydraulic valve lifters, 4-bbl Carter carburetor, 325 bhp (SAE gross) @ 4,600 rpm, 425 lbs/ft torque @ 2,800 rpm
Transmission:	Chrysler Torqueflite 3-speed automatic
Suspension, front:	Independent, upper and lower wishbones, coil springs, tubular shocks
Suspension, rear:	Live axle on semi-elliptic leaf springs, Panhard rod, Armstrong Selectaride tubular shocks
Brakes:	Front/rear discs with Dunlop Maxaret anti-lock system
Wheelbase (in.):	109.0
Weight (lbs):	4,030
Top speed (mph):	130
0-60 mph (sec):	7.7-8.1
Production:	Mk I 196 (1967-69) Mk II 109 (1969-71) Mk III 15 (1971)

1966-67 OLDSMOBILE TORONADO

For most periods in American automotive history, there have been companies whose styling led the field and dictated the shape of everything else. In the late Forties it was Raymond Loewy's Studebaker; in the late Fifties it was Virgil Exner's "Forward Look" Chrysler Corporation. The rest of the time it was General Motors—hands down. When American cars passed out of the age of chrome and tailfins, GM led the way, showing the rest that there was life after Virgil Exner. By 1966 there wasn't one GM car that represented anything less than state-of-the-art styling. But some models, like the Olds Toronado, were more equal than others.

Forget for a moment the Toro's innovative engineering—the first application of front wheel drive to a large postwar American automobile. Pretend that it had a conventional drivetrain, and dwell instead on its lines. Those lines were strictly beyond reproach. As Don Vorderman wrote at the time in *Automobile Quarterly*, "a radically different look has been achieved with a minimum of fuss. There are no loose ends, no unresolved lines. . . . The result is logical, imaginative and totally unique."

Toronado styling was mainly the work of young David North, a designer in the Oldsmobile Studio headed by Stanley Wilen, who reported to GM chief of design Bill Mitchell—the man who had returned GM to the styling lead after its stagnant years of the late Fifties. That North's ideas actually led to a production car was one of the traits of Mitchell's era, so uncommon after he retired. Mitchell liked designers to be given their heads, to produce the wildest cars imaginable. He'd pick the best of them and sell them to management, going at them hammers and tongs not to water down a really exciting, producible idea. At other companies, selling a good idea to management meant getting it past a battery of critics from Sales, Engineering, and Product Planning— the moral equivalent of raining up. But nobody ignored Mitchell.

North's styling came from an idea car known at GM as the "flame red job," a stunning scarlet airbrush rendering against a jet black background. A personal coupe of fairly compact proportions, it was magnificent. The roofline fell gently toward the edges of the roof, then dropped in an unbroken curve over the windows, sides, and rocker panels. Only boldly flared wheel arches relieved the shape of the curved fuselage. The front and rear were ultra-clean, wrapped as tightly underneath as at the sides.

It's easy to draw impressive cars, harder to produce them. When Wilen and Mitchell fell in love with his design, they told North that he had to make it fit GM's E-body. That meant it had to share the long hood/short deck "personal-car" body with the Buick Riviera, which was also a styling *tour de force*, but rear-wheel drive and quite different

The '66 Oldsmobile Toronado was a response to Ford's successful four-seater Thunderbird and Buick's Riviera. Though based on the same "personal-luxury" theme and with long-hood/short-deck proportions, the styling of the fastback Toronado was unique—and outstanding. Enough so, in fact, that the 1966-67 Toro is a recognized "Milestone" car.

348

The '66 Toronado's sleek styling hid the fact that it was the first mass-produced front-wheel-drive American car since the Cord 810/812 of 1936-37. Olds chose front drive because it wanted American-size power with the outstanding handling and traction of the best European GTs.

looking. North thus drafted his four-seater on a mammoth 119-inch wheelbase, resulting in a design nearly 80 inches wide and nearly 18 feet long. And GM built it without altering his lines!

Among postwar American cars, the ones that stand out for superb styling generally emerge with something close to their originally intended dimensions, like the 1953 Studebaker coupes, the '56 Continental Mark II, and the '51 Kaiser. None of these were changed so drastically in size between the first sketch and the completed product, so the Toro really did them one better.

Many a reader will notice another interesting characteristic of these Toronados: they took considerable inspiration from the classic Cord 810/812 of 1936-37. The wheels were virtual copies; the uncluttered front end with the thin horizontal-bar grille stood as a modern interpretation of the Cord's famed "coffin nose" grille. However, the Toronado didn't attempt to copy the Cord so much as invoke its spirit, undoubtedly because it was the last front-drive American car until the Toro, 30 years later.

Against its great styling, the Toronado's engineering was equally impressive. The object of the front-drive project

was traditional, though it took GM to try it on a car this big. Oldsmobile wanted a chassis-drivetrain that would combine traditional American-size power with the outstanding handling and traction of the best European GTs. The work was done by Oldsmobile's engineering staff largely because Olds had been GM's "experimental division" ever since it had developed Hydra-Matic in the late Thirties. It was a natural assignment. "We had a choice between turning the project over to our regular design and development groups or assigning it to a smaller group of specialists," said former chief engineer and general manager Harold Metzel. "We

decided to give all departments their share of the Toronado responsibility."

The Olds' front-wheel drive combined with a 425-cubic-inch, 385-horsepower V-8 with a split transmission: the torque convertor was separate from the gearbox, connected by a chain drive and sprocket. The silent chain, developed by Hydra-Matic and Borg-Warner, was the key. Unbreakable, flexible, light, and not expensive, it made possible a very compact engine-drivetrain package via the split transmission. The torque convertor was in its usual place behind the V-8, but the gearbox was located under the left cylinder bank. The chain was pre-stretched prior to installation

The Toronado was powered by Oldsmobile's huge 425-cubic-inch V-8, which developed 385 bhp and 475 lbs/ft torque. It was mated to GM's three-speed Turbo Hydra-Matic, but in this instance the torque converter was separate from the gearbox—they were connected via a chain drive and sprocket.

so as to never need an adjustment, an idler, or a tensioner. The concept was ingenious. While other front-drive systems put the engine behind the transaxle, Olds stacked the entire unit over the front wheels, yet managed a reasonable 54/46-percent front/rear weight distribution.

The Toronado understeered, of course, but only slightly and with plenty of warning. It handled well and was utterly silent at 100 mph. Its top speed was a dramatic 135. You had to live with the automatic gearbox, but a manual would have been superfluous in a car of its character anyway. Altogether, this was a big, fast, comfortable, luxurious grand touring automobile, one of the outstanding cars of the Sixties.

The Toronado's technology was soon borrowed by Cadillac, which released its own front-drive "personal-luxury" car, the Eldorado, in 1967. By then the Toronado had changed from its horizontal-bar grille to an eggcrate affair, but this did little to mess up the design — it was still a near-perfect shape on a chassis this large. But post-'67 editions became progressively vulgar, culminating in a hulking great beast of a Toro by 1971. Ditto the Eldorado. The early ones are more fun to drive, far more nimble in the handling department, breathe better through their pre-emission-control engines, and are stunning to look at. Yet a good clean original example is still not expensive — making it a fine investment in history and fine design.

The grille, hidden headlights, and the wheels of the '66 Toronado took their inspiration from the 1936 "coffin-nose" Cord. As might be expected of a $4,311 car, the interior was luxurious. Output for 1966 came to 40,963 units.

Specifications	
Engine:	V-8, ohv, 425 cid (4.125 x 3.975-in. bore x stroke), 10.5:1 compression ratio, 5 main bearings, hydraulic valve lifters, Rochester 4-bbl carburetor, 385 bhp @ 4,800 rpm, 475 lbs/ft torque
Transmission:	3-speed Turbo Hydra-Matic
Suspension, front:	Independent, with torsion bars, lower control arms, anti-roll bar, tubular shock absorbers
Suspension, rear:	Dead axle, longitudinal single-leaf springs, angled shock absorbers (2 per side)
Brakes:	Hydraulic, front/rear drums
Wheelbase (in.):	119.0
Overall length (in.):	211.0
Weight (lbs):	4,311-4,366
Tires:	8.85 x 15
0-60 mph (sec):	8.5
Top speed (mph):	135
Production:	1966 htp cpe 6,333 Deluxe htp cpe 34,630 1967 htp cpe 1,770 Deluxe htp cpe 20,020

I t's not every car that establishes its maker's name while leaving its own indelible impression, but the Lamborghini Miura did both with decisive passion. It was, as British writer Graham Robson observed, "one of those rare and wonderful supercars that hardly disappointed anyone." As such, it single-handedly elevated the Lamborghin' name to the exalted realm of Ferrari, Porsche, and Jaguar.

First shown as a bare chassis at the 1965 Turin Auto Show, the Miura simply astonished the motoring world. A midships V-12 was exotic enough, but its transverse mounting was the real eye-opener. This was a *road* car? No way!

Yet what else from the stocky, flamboyant tycoon whose life and style ever testified that he was a Taurus. Born to a farming family in 1916, Ferruccio Lamborghini grew up amidst Italy's premier automakers, and an early fascination with machinery spurred him to an industrial arts degree. World War II cut short an apprenticeship in Bologna, but provided a chance to hone native fix-it skills, first for the Italian army, later for the British forces occupying the island of Rhodes. He then successfully hammered swords into plowshares by building much-needed farm tractors, opening his own factory in 1946. By the late Fifties, Lamborghini was one of Italy's largest tractor makers, its founder a widely respected man with the wherewithal to pursue new ventures.

Commercial and home heating equipment was one, and success there earned Ferruccio two government honors: an "Order of Merit," making him a *Commendatore*, and a "Knight of Labor" or *Cavaliere de Lavoro*. But *Il Cavaliere*, the title he came to prefer, remained a rabid car enthusiast—he'd even raced little Fiat Topolinos back in the Forties. In 1962, he set himself a new challenge: a car to out-do anything by the famed *Il Commendatore*, Enzo Ferrari.

Ferruccio quickly assembled a stellar team unsurprisingly composed of experienced—and young—Ferrari engineers: Giampaolo Dallara (also a Maserati veteran), Paolo Stanzani, and a lanky New Zealander named Bob Wallace. Talented free-lance engineer Giotto Bizzarrini contributed a splendid 3.5-liter 60-degree V-12 derived from a 1.5 Formula 1 powerplant he'd devised, and it went into the first prototype Lamborghini, a semi-fastback 2+2 with conventional engineering but somewhat unconventional looks (by ex-Bertone hand Franco Scaglione). Still, this 350 GTV made a sufficient impression on its 1963 Turin debut that Ferruccio committed funds to a new factory at Sant'Agata, near Ferrari's home in Modena, and to modifying the design for series production. The resulting 350GT, unveiled at Geneva in spring 1964, was enthusiastically received for its excellent handling and 150-mph performance from 280 horsepower. Demand grew rapidly once word got around, and Ferruccio stoked it further with a 400GT boasting 320

The Miura, here a '67, established Lamborghini's name with its straight-out-of-tomorrow styling and transverse-mounted midships V-12.

bhp, near 160-mph capability, and more coherent styling. By the time this series ended in 1968 (with 393 built), *Automobili Ferruccio Lamborghini S.p.A.* had passed Ferrari in prestige without ever passing it on a racetrack.

The reason was the spectacular Miura, which had a second "premiere" at Geneva 1966, fully bodied this time, but still far from finished. Though Ferruccio's "Three Musketeers" had looked to the Ford GT40, Ferrari 250 LM, and other exemplars of the mid-engine revolution then sweeping world-class competition, the Miura was always planned as the ultimate *road* car. Though a racing version was considered, *Il Cavaliere* ultimately decided not to challenge the more experienced Ferrari in that business. Besides, the Miura hardly needed a competition connection; it already looked like a racer.

Bertone's Marcello Gandini, another talented youngster, is credited with that shape, one of Italy's loveliest—which is saying something. Sexy, and somehow both masculine and feminine, it looked straight out of tomorrow. A "sidewinder" V-12 (basically the 400 GT unit) seemed equally futuristic, but was prompted by the very practical need for adequate cockpit space within a fairly short wheelbase.

Bodywork and drivetrain aside, the Miura was typical mid-Sixties Italian supercar. Its chassis was a sheet-steel monocoque fabricated from small panels and welded joints—a little rough, but effective. The suspension employed classic all-round double wishbones and coil springs, plus the expected all-disc brakes and rack-and-pinion steering (both *sans* power assist). Aluminum outer body panels weren't new either, though as on the latest endurance racers, the entire front and rear ends were hinged to tilt up for chassis/drivetrain access.

Despite its racy nature, the Miura was a perfectly liveable everyday car, offering a surprisingly good ride and amazing engine flexibility. But pavement-peeling acceleration and towering top speed were its implied *fortes*, and it didn't disappoint. Though horsepower was initially advertised at 350, the actual figure was more like 320. Still, 0-60 mph took just 5.5 seconds, the standing quarter-mile 14 seconds at 100 + mph. Top speed? Over 170 mph.

Alas, these supercar strengths were offset by the usual supercar weaknesses— and some that weren't so usual. Most serious was considerable high-speed lift, a function of the curvy snout and suspect aerodynamics. Chassis flex

was a problem in really hard driving, the cabin was tight *and* noisy, shift effort high (due to the complex linkage needed to "get around" the engine), ventilation poor, luggage space nil, and vision limited to any quadrant except dead-ahead. Workmanship also left much to be desired, thanks to the handbuilt methods typical of small Italian specialty makers, not to mention obvious "cut-and-try" solutions to several engineering problems.

Yet the Miura's well-heeled owners didn't mind any of this, perhaps because they *were* well-heeled and thus able to take it all in stride. Most were convinced they'd simply bought the world's greatest car—easily one of the most charismatic.

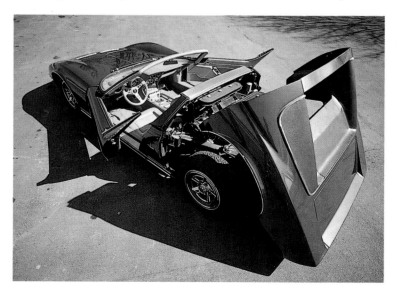

Road & Track doubtless spoke for many in calling the Miura "one of those beautiful experiences every enthusiast owes himself."

Experience was what it was all about. You bought a Miura to be noticed, to savor the engine's delicious whoops and wails each time you poked the throttle, to thrill at the neck-snapping go and colossal cruising ability whenever conditions and space permitted. No American muscle car ever took on a Miura more than once. Who cared that it cost more than other Italian thoroughbreds? This was motoring at its fastest and finest.

But not fine and fast enough for Ferruccio Lamborghini. Thus, the original P400 Miura (P for *posteriore*, mid-rear engine) gave way in 1970 to the P400S with 370 bhp (via higher-lift cam and larger carburetors and manifolds), needed structural reinforcements, revised rear suspension geometry, fatter tires, vented brakes, and factory air conditioning and radio options. The ultimate P400SV of 1971-73 boasted even more chassis stiffening, bulged fenders enclosing still wider rolling stock, no finned "eyebrows" above the layback headlamps, and a hiked rear-end that lowered the nose and finally tamed the dreaded high-speed lift. Though power went to 385 bhp (courtesy of still-bigger carbs and altered cams), the SV was heavier and thus little, if any, faster than previous Miuras. Still, its 175 + mph bested Ferrari's Daytona; no wonder Enzo put the rush on a mid-engine reply, the Berlinetta Boxer. SVs also benefited from tidier ergonomics and standard full-hide upholstery (replacing leather-look vinyl).

Though Sant'Agata never built an open Miura, Bertone did a one-off targa-style spyder for the International Lead-Zinc Research Organization (ILZRO) in 1969—predictably with zinc instead of other metals in every possible place. A few closed Miuras were similarly converted by private owners.

Then there was the Jota, a lightweight Miura-based special commissioned by Wallace in 1969 as a "hobby car." Aimed squarely at competition ("J" was for FIA Appendix J rules), it packed 440 bhp and weighed 770 pounds less than standard, which added up to an honest

The '72 Miura SV upped the horsepower ante to 385 at a high 7,850 rpm. Torque likewise was increased, to 294 lbs/ft at 5,750 rpm. Only 140 P400SVs were built from 1971-73.

186 mph. The factory later built four replicas to special order, but these were more like the regular article, lacking the original Jota's dry-sump oiling, high-tech Avional body, flared fenders, super-wide wheels and tires, and other features. Predictably perhaps, the Jota touched off a spate of Miura "customizing," some of it dubious.

Happily, this work of art has come to be appreciated as far more than another toy for the ultra-rich. Consider this ode by Lamborghini authority Pete Lyons from 1988: "She is old, but she has not aged. . . . Her achingly lovely body can haunt your dreams. As, in another way, her voice haunts the air. A full mile distant, you can hear her engine clearly. Strapped inside, you can hear nothing else. . . . [But the] Lamborghini V-12 is an engine to live for . . . an uncanny blend of savagery with civility. It trickles along sweetly in traffic at idle rpm, yet it responds to the throttle with the instant *whing* of a superbike engine and its power builds like the long, smooth slope of a volcano. . . .

"The Miura is not a car for everyday use. It is fragile. It is finicky. It is expensive. . . . They didn't build the Miura to race, but they built a lot of racer into it. Like a high-performance motorcycle, [it] requires . . . your whole attention. . . . Nor is it a car for today.

Look at it: It's naked. No bumpers. No door beams. [No rain gutters, either.] No shoulder belts. No emissions controls. No *cruise control*. In its innocence it is charming, but it is also wearing . . . born in a distant time, and for another place.

"Ah, but watch as the liquid light pours over her, so pretty it actually hurts. What sweet contrasts it reveals: her sensual, soft skin, her muscled wheels. *Contrappunti!* How lovely she is. How young. In such a light, she is perfection."

Specifications	
Engine:	V-12, dohc, 239.8 cid/3,929 cc (3.23 x 2.44-in./82 x 62-mm bore x stroke) **Miura** (1967-70): 350 bhp @ 7,000 rpm, 278 lbs/ft torque @ 5,000 rpm **Miura S** (1970-71): 370 bhp @ 7,700 rpm, 286 lbs/ft @ 5,750 rpm **Miura SV** (1971-73): 385 bhp @ 7,850 rpm, 294 lbs/ft @ 5,750 rpm (advertised bhp and torque)
Transmission:	5-speed manual in rear transaxle
Suspension, front:	Upper and lower A-arms, coil springs, tube shocks, anti-roll bar
Suspension, rear:	Upper and lower A-arms, coil springs, tube shocks, anti-roll bar
Brakes:	Hydraulic, front/rear discs
Wheelbase (in.):	98.4
Weight (lbs):	2,850-3,000
Top speed (mph):	170-175 +
0-60 mph (sec):	5.5-6.7
Production:	Miura P400 475 P400S 140 P400SV 150

I f prophets are without honor in their own time, it may be
because of the way they deliver their messages. Consider the
NSU Ro80. Announced in 1967, it was, with the telling exception of its
Wankel rotary engine, an amazingly accurate forecast of the typical
middle-class sedan 20 years hence: largish but light, sleekly aerodynamic,
roomy (thanks in part to front-wheel drive), rewardingly roadable, even
fuel efficient. But like some other visionary cars now regarded as "greats,"
the Ro80 was seriously flawed at first, plagued by unexpected (though
perhaps avoidable) problems that still stigmatize it as just another
overreaching failure. It was bad news for its maker, too. In fact, the
Ro80 virtually bled NSU to death.

The maker had died in the town of its birth long before:
Neckarsulm, upstream of Stuttgart on the River Neckar in the southwest
German state of Baden-Württemburg. Having made its name with bicycles
and motorcycles, *Neckarsulmer Fahrradwerke* turned to building cars
in 1905, four-cylinder models that sold quite well. A vertical twin was
added after World War I, along with large 2.6- and 3.3-liter offerings,
but 1.3- and 1.6-liter models remained NSU's mainstay cars; they even
did well in competition. Then, inexplicably, NSU erected a new auto
plant in nearby Heilbronn, only to sell it to Fiat of Italy in 1933. But
this left Neckarsulm free to concentrate on building some grand new
bikes; by the eve of World War II, their renown had made NSU one of
the largest and most respected companies in the business.

NSU haltingly resumed motorcycle production after the war,
but its new president, Gerd Stieler von Heydekampf, was quicker than
most to see the inevitable decline of the two-wheeler market in the Fifties.
NSU's future, he felt certain, lay in the car business, which was already
starting to boom in the economic "miracle" of the new postwar West
Germany.

Thus did NSU return to the automotive fold after 25 years with
the 1958 Prinz, a boxy minicar whose two-cylinder engine was air-cooled
and rear-mounted, aping the increasingly popular Volkswagen Beetle.
Larger, more powerful four-cylinder variants soon joined the basic 500-cc
Prinz. Heydekampf, meantime, had become interested in the experiments
of one of his staff engineers, Dr. Felix Wankel, and soon committed NSU
to further development of his embryonic "rotary-combustion" engine.

Wankel's concept was simplicity itself. Instead of pistons pumping
within cylinders to generate rotary motion through connecting rods, a
curved-sided triangular rotor spun inside a housing shaped roughly like
a slice of bread, the rotor's tips scraping past a mixture intake, through
a "combustion chamber," and on to an exhaust port to complete the
customary four-stroke cycle. Because it produced rotary motion to begin
with, the Wankel made more power than reciprocating engines of like

**Not only did the
1967-77 NSU Ro80
boast the only
Wankel rotary
engine in
production, it also
featured modern
aerodynamic
styling. With a
compact overall
length of 188.6
inches, the Ro80
rode a longish 112.6-
inch wheelbase,
which allowed for
exceptional interior
space.**

The Ro80's styling was dominated by a huge upwardly curved windshield, conservative but flowing lines, and dart-like profile. The '77 soft top was a "special."

junior Mercedes/BMW size—and became far more complicated than first envisioned.

It was nevertheless stunning, especially coming from an outfit so lately returned to automaking—a genuine technical *tour de force*. Aside from its advanced new engine, the Ro80 boasted space-saving front-wheel drive, fully independent suspension (via long-travel coil-sprung MacPherson struts at each corner, plus rear trailing arms), power steering (ZF rack-and-pinion), and four-wheel assisted disc brakes—inboard at the front, to minimize unsprung weight. Though familiar now, these features were far from common in the late Sixties, even in Europe.

So was the Ro80's aerodynamic styling, dominated by a huge, upwardly curved windshield, conservative but flowing lines, and dart-like profile. Drag coefficient came in at a sensationally low 0.36; only the Citroën DS could match it among volume production cars. The 112.6-inch wheelbase was quite long for a mid-size European, but combined with short overhangs for exceptional interior space and the proverbial velvet ride.

Front drive and a fairly broad stance gave the Ro80 agile handling and die-true straightline stability despite skinny tires (175-14s on five-inch-wide rims). Performance was hampered by a three-speed semi-automatic transaxle with fairly short final gearing (4.857:1, giving 18.8 mph/1,000 rpm in top), but was still reasonable. This testified to the slippery shape, a decent power-to-weight ratio of 115 bhp for 2,700 pounds, and a good, though hardly exceptional,

displacement. It was also more compact and had far fewer parts to wear out. The design also offered an appealing, cost-effective manufacturing advantage: the relative ease of bolting several housings together to create multi-rotor engines of suitable size and power for various applications.

To gain production and field experience with the new engine, NSU installed a single-rotor 50-horsepower unit in a Prinz-based two-seat convertible styled by Italy's Carrozzeria Bertone. The result, called Wankel Spider, saw some 5,000 copies built in 1964-66. But though NSU was then selling upwards of 100,000 Prinzes a year, Heydekampf knew his firm could no more live on minicars than motorcycles. What NSU needed was a larger, nicer product to

compete in the lucrative, fast-growing German family car market then dominated by the Opel Rekord and Ford Taunus. So while boldly selling off motorcycle operations (to Marshall Tito in Yugoslavia), Heydekampf not only ordered up a new "big NSU" but decreed that it be designed expressly for a Wankel engine. The Ro80 was underway.

Initially, Heydekampf and chief engineer Ewald Praxl felt the new model need only be two steps up from the Prinz in size, price, and performance, so they planned it for 80 bhp (hence the name) and a curb weight of around 1,750 pounds. But when its intended new two-rotor engine proved more potent than expected, engineers ignored the scales. The Ro80 thus ballooned to about *five* steps beyond the Prinz—to

The most avant-garde feature of the Ro80 was its engine: a Wankel twin rotary. A four-stroke unit, its two chambers displaced only 995 cc—60.6 cubic inches. Still, it turned out 115 smooth horsepower and 116 lbs/ft torque. Alas, early engines suffered with short-lived rotor seals and oil leaks.

116-pounds/feet torque. Healthy Ro80s could hit 112 mph flat out and do 0-100 km/h (62.5 mph) in under 14 seconds. Overshadowing all was the refinement of the new two-rotor Wankel engine: revvy, very quiet, nearly vibration-free—a revelation to a public weaned on rough, noisy reciprocating fours.

What NSU called a "Selective Automatic" transmission was chosen by Praxl to enhance driving ease. It was supplied by Fitchel & Sachs, which also built Porsche's later "Sportomatic" option, a four-speed version. Like VW's similar "Automatic Stickshift," the Ro80 unit combined two-pedal convenience with stir-it-yourself flexibility. Grasping the floor-mounted lever tripped a solenoid within the knob to disengage a vacuum-operated clutch (here supplemented by a hydraulic torque converter); the clutch re-engaged once the shift was made and the knob released. It was a good idea in theory, but most drivers never got the hang of it even with practice.

Poor mileage was another sore point, especially at first, but the Ro80's widespread reputation for gas-guzzling was undeserved. Yes, consumption *seemed* excessive, but only in relation to engine size—combined chamber volume was just 995 cc (60 cubic inches)—not engine power. Early models typically returned only 15.7 miles per gallon, but writer Jan Norbye got 20.6 mpg from a '74 model on a hard 3,100-mile trip, and logged some 25 mpg at a steady 62 mph with a '76. Early Ro80s definitely swilled oil—up to a quart every 140 miles—but engine changes later reduced that to normal levels.

All things considered, the Ro80 program went quite smoothly. But advanced design usually means high production costs that get passed along to buyers, and the Ro80 was no exception. At an initial $3,500, it cost as much as a small Mercedes or BMW. Yet though undeniably more modern, it could equal neither their performance nor prestige.

But what really hurt sales was the early raft of engine problems that branded the Ro80 notoriously unreliable. Most highly publicized were short-lived rotor-tip seals and resulting oil leaks, plus chamber-wall distortion and other maladies that could necessitate a

Early teething problems held down Ro80 sales, so only 47,400 were built from 1967-77. Because of the Ro80, NSU became unprofitable; VW took over in 1969. Twin headlamps were a feature of early Ro80s.

rebuild or replacement engine as early as 30,000 miles. While total failures were rare, complaints about gradual power losses and rising fuel/oil consumption were not. A tune-up and new seals (claimed to last 60,000-80,000 miles) usually put things right, but few believed it. Interestingly, NSU backed the entire car for 30,000 miles—*triple* the German norm.

And to its credit, NSU kept faith with Ro80 owners once the problems appeared, replacing many engines free of charge—even some that simply needed minor attention. Yet this generosity did little to change the now-tainted image of the car, its engine, and its maker, and sales continued languishing even after the engine problems were largely cured by modifications in 1969 and '71.

In the end, it didn't matter. The massive warranty expenses on top of the Ro80's formidable development and tooling costs had left NSU hemorrhaging red ink, so the firm was relieved to accept a takeover by Volkswagen in February 1969. But though merged with just-acquired Auto Union into a new Audi-NSU Division (a title that would last through 1984), NSU soon lost its minicars as well as the K70, then nearing completion as a sort of junior Ro80 with conventional power. The latter, seized upon as the answer to Wolfsburg's

own upmarket woes, belatedly appeared in 1971 as a new "big VW," but found scant acceptance as such, and was dropped within a few years.

The Ro80 itself somehow survived all the way through March 1977, with production ending at 47,400 units (after which the Neckarsulm plant was retooled for Porsche's new 924). Yet given that, and its forward-looking design, the Ro80 must be judged a winner, if not a very big one. It's a shame it started out looking like such a loser—but then, prophets seldom have it easy.

Specifications[1]	
Engine:	Wankel twin rotary, alloy, 4-stroke, 60.6 cid/995 cc total displacement, 9.0:1 compression ratio, 115 bhp (DIN) @ 5,500 rpm, 116 lbs/ft torque @ 4,000 rpm
Transmission:	3-speed semi-automatic with hydraulic torque converter
Suspension, front:	Independent, MacPherson coil spring/telescopic shock absorber struts, lower articulated wishbones, anti-roll bar
Suspension, rear:	Independent, semi-trailing arms, coil springs, telescopic shock absorbers
Brakes:	Hydraulic, 4-wheel disc, inboard-mounted at the front
Wheelbase (in.):	112.6
Overall length (in.):	188.6
Tread, front/rear (in.):	58.3/56.5
Weight (lbs):	2,844
0-60 mph (sec):	13.0-14.0
Top speed (mph):	112
Production:	47,400 (1967-77)

[1]1977

Between 1968 and '71, BMW turned out some 16,448 2000ti—*turismo internationale*—sport sedans. With twin carbs, it developed 120 DIN horsepower.

Max Hoffman, the sales-wise Austrian who ran Hoffman Motors from New York's Park Avenue, has been mentioned several times already in these pages, and he is unavoidable. Hoffman probably imported, and certainly influenced the design of, more great European makes sold in the United States than any other single individual. Marque after famous marque—Mercedes-Benz, BMW, Alfa Romeo, Lancia, Facel-Vega, Jaguar, Porsche, Cisitalia, Lagonda, Delahaye, Allard, Le Francis, Healey—Hoffman imported and introduced them to Americans.

Toward the end of his life, in the 1970s, he was the U.S. distributor of BMWs, a business that he finally sold for many millions to a subsidiary of the Munich company. He was certainly responsible for transforming BMW from a peripheral vendor of oddballs to one of the most respected imports in America. He did it with cars like the BMW 2002.

The 2002 was a development of the BMW 1600, which "Maxie" brought in during 1966. His idea was to offer BMW's already respected engineering expertise and quality of construction at an unprecedented low price, hooking thousands of people on what he knew was habit forming. Once the 2002 was established, Hoffman and his successor, BMW of North America, got what the market would bear. By 1970, the BMWs typically came in "loaded." Automatics stickered near $4,000 against a base price closer to $3,400.

The BMW 1600 had the price of a Chevy Nova, the quality of a Benz, and the performance of a Mustang. *Car and Driver* called it "the best small sedan we ever drove." Hoffman couldn't lay his hands on enough of them, but starting in 1968 the federal government threw a monkey wrench at his happy little operation: emissions controls. Hoffman, who obviously hadn't got where he was for nothing, promptly had BMW slap a single-carburetor two-liter four into the 1600—thus raising its displacement by 25 percent and getting the emissions controlled without compromising performance.

The resulting 2002 was one great little car. There are still people abroad in the land pining over its demise in 1975 and bemoaning its replacement, the 3-Series. Most of them will tell you there was never a better Bimmer. The 2002 comfortably held four people and a weekend's worth of luggage in a modestly proportioned box that looked like a Studebaker Lark and went like an Austin-Healey. It would outrun, outride, and outhandle anything in its class. Yet it was a flexible car, demanding nothing in everyday city driving, not even vigorous use of the shift lever. Let a TR4 or an MGB get out of line, though, and you could blow it off the road. Remarkably, too, the 2002 was just as fast with the three-speed ZF automatic which arrived as an option (called 2002A) in 1969: road testers found that it made only a 0.3-second difference in the quarter-mile times.

The ultimate BMW 2002 was the 1973-74 turbo, a modified tii. Never exported to the U.S., it zipped from 0-60 mph in eight seconds flat and topped out at 125 mph. Early models sported large mirror-image "turbo 2000" lettering in the blue portion of the front spoiler. The interior was of course designed for the enthusiast driver.

Only 10 months after the 2002 came the 2002ti — *turismo internationale* — with twin carbs and 120 DIN horsepower, but this one didn't pass the U.S. regulations and was reserved for Europeans. Its successor, which did make the U.S. market, was the 1971 2002tii, with fuel injection and 130 horsepower. With the tii, Hoffman made the plain 2002 his base car. Though this meant dropping the 1600, evolutions of that model continued in Europe through 1975.

The tii took care of any lingering worries over the little rocket's performance in the emission control era, returning top speeds near 120 mph. Temporarily, in 1972, BMW had to lower compression to meet the regs, like everybody else. But in 1973 the firm introduced trispherical combustion chamber heads, meeting the law while restoring the old performance — while nearly everybody else was reducing compression further. Unfortunately, the 2002 couldn't cope with the "safety" regulations, and was yoked with heavy, ugly bumpers beginning with the 1973 U.S. models.

A number of permutations not often seen should be noted. Karosserie Baur was a coachbuilding house which pro-

duced a cabriolet version of the 1600 and a semi-cabriolet version of the 2002. The latter sported a Targa-top affair on the order of Porsche's, a sunroof and fold-down rear section with a rollbar in between. Neither was imported into the United States, though several got in privately; they are relatively desirable, though the Targa is a bit odd looking.

Odder yet was the "Touring hatchback," which carried 1600, 1800, and 2000 designations until 1972, when it became the 1602, 1802, 2002, and 2002tii. On paper this seemed like the perfect idea: it resembled an Alfa Giulia

Sprint, afforded a capacious cargo area behind the front seats, and did away with the upright, chunky rear window-line that had begun to look so aged on the 2002 by the Seventies. For some reason, though, it didn't sell. The last Tourings were built in 1974, and total production of that body style was less than 30,000 over five years. There hasn't been a BMW hatchback since—once burned, twice shy.

Other European variations were the 1502, a stripper coupe sold in Europe only during the oil crisis (1975-77) with a single-carburetor 1.6 engine and 75 DIN horsepower, and the 1802 (1971-75) with a 1.8-liter engine, Solex carburetor,

and 90 horses. Neither is likely to be encountered in the United States.

Unfortunately, 2002s are complicated restoration projects and an all-out salvaging campaign on one is sensibly to be avoided. But people love 'em, and the trade in fine originals is very strong 15 years since the last new ones were sold. Nostalgia is a funny thing: 2002s were beautifully built, but certainly not works of art; they were fine performers, but hardly the only cars that would deliver 115 mph and 0-60 times under 10 seconds. As much as anything, their attraction to Bimmerfolk is their status as the last "affordable" BMWs. After they were gone, the 3-Series rose rapidly to $8,000 and above. But this was largely a matter of timing—everything doubled in price during the late 1970s, including BMWs. Had the 2002 been kept on, it too would have been a five-figure car by 1980.

That still doesn't explain why 2002 owners spend unconscionable sums keeping their cars on the road. Firms like Automotive Import Recycling (AIR), of Belvidere, New Jersey, actually exist

to make dog-eared 02s "brand new" again, and will even hang on four-wheel disc brakes and Recaro bucket seats. In the mid-Eighties, AIR was producing about 20 remanufactured cars a month at about two-thirds the price of a new 3-Series. People bought 'em, too. Such was— and is—the magic of the BMW 2002.

Specifications[1]	
Engine:	I-4, sohc, 1,990 cc (89 x 80-mm bore x stroke), 9.5:1 compression ratio, mechanical fuel injection, 130 DIN bhp @ 5,800 rpm
Transmission:	4- or 5-speed manual, 3-speed ZF automatic (opt. beginning 1969)
Suspension, front:	Independent, MacPherson struts, coil springs, anti-roll bar
Suspension, rear:	Independent, semi-trailing arms, coil springs
Brakes:	Hydraulic, front disc/rear drum
Wheelbase (in.):	98.4
Tread, front/rear (in.):	52.8/52.8
Weight (lbs):	2,227
0-60 mph (sec):	approx. 10.0
Top speed (mph):	118
Production:	2002 cpe 339,084 (1968-76) cabriolet 4,199 (1971-75) **Touring** 5,705 (1971-74) **2002ti** 16,448 (1968-71) **2002tii cpe** 38,703 (1971-75) **Touring** 5,783 (1971-74)

[1]2002tii

Good for 170 horses, the 2002 turbo's KKK compressor was held to eight psi. Turbo touches included bodyside stripes and flared fenderwells.

Defiantly upholding Ferrari's front-engine tradition in a world filling quickly with mid-engine exotics, the 365 GTB/4 Daytona burst out at the '68 Paris Salon. The car's exaggeratedly conventional sports-car proportions—a long hood sheltering a big V-12 and a short rear deck—shouted Enzo Ferrari's homily that "The horse does not push the cart, it pulls."

Aside from the early-Sixties 250 GTO and Berlinetta Lusso, and the conquering late-Eighties F40, the 365 GTB/4, popularly known as the "Daytona," ranks as the most coveted Ferrari ever built. It's certainly one of the most remarkable of the roadgoing Ferraris. First shown at the 1968 Paris Salon, it was not only the costliest such car to that point in Ferrari's 21-year history (just under $20,000), but the fastest. *Road & Track* magazine verified the factory's claimed 174-mph top speed and ran the standing quarter-mile in a blistering 13.8 seconds at 107.5 mph. The Daytona was, in short, a "muscle car" Italian-style.

And what muscle. Replacing the 275 GTB/4, the Daytona rode a similar chassis, right down to wheelbase and rear-transaxle configuration, but carried an evolutionary version of the long-running "Columbo" V-12, bored and stroked to 4.4 liters. Blessed with dual overhead camshafts, no fewer than six twin-choke Weber carburetors, and a fairly high (for the day) 8.8:1 compression ratio, the car that Ferrari designated as the *Tipo* unleashed 352 thoroughbred horses at 7,500 rpm. As on the 275, a single dry-plate clutch connected to a torque-tube drive and five-speed transaxle.

Work toward the Daytona began in 1966, when Pininfarina, Maranello's long-time primary coachbuilder, began sketching ideas for a new "deluxe" two-seat berlinetta on the existing 330/365 GTC chassis. Though somewhat difficult to fathom now, the result initially divided opinion among both Ferrari fans and the motoring press. More than 20 years later, those who merely liked the Daytona then seem to love it, while those who didn't care for it have at least come to like it. "Aggressively elegant" describes it; so does "influential." In fact, many Daytona features have since shown up on a number of lesser cars—and several unauthorized replicas, most built on latterday Corvette chassis, were so close to the original in appearance as to prompt cease-and-desist lawsuits, which Ferrari ultimately won.

There was certainly no mistaking the Daytona's intent. As Pete Lyons observed in *Ferrari: The Man and His Machines*, this car, with its exaggerated long-hood/short-deck proportions, was a defiant statement that "Ferrari's flagship would hold fast to its heritage one more time." Not coincidentally, it was also a slap in the face of rival Lamborghini, whose recently launched Miura embodied the "latest race-think" in a midships V-12, and looked sensational to boot.

Lyons records that the most controversial aspect of the Daytona's appearance was the "axe-blade" nose, particularly the four headlamps behind a full-width plastic cover. The latter, which Europeans judged gimmicky in the extreme, was prohibited by U.S. law, and prompted at least two alternative proposals, both with the lamps fully exposed in very ugly fashion. The final solution was not only far more elegant but

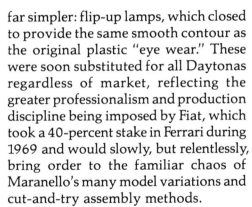

Fashionable as the Daytona coupe was in the late '60s, Pininfarina created a positively haute Spider simply by slicing off its roof.

far simpler: flip-up lamps, which closed to provide the same smooth contour as the original plastic "eye wear." These were soon substituted for all Daytonas regardless of market, reflecting the greater professionalism and production discipline being imposed by Fiat, which took a 40-percent stake in Ferrari during 1969 and would slowly, but relentlessly, bring order to the familiar chaos of Maranello's many model variations and cut-and-try assembly methods.

It was in 1969, more than a year after the prototype was shown at Paris, that the Daytona finally entered production, again the province of Scaglietti per usual Ferrari practice. Incidentally, the press—not the factory—was responsible for the Daytona name, but it stuck, perhaps because it had long been legendary the world over. And really, what better handle for this fastest-ever Ferrari than the name of the Florida beach city that bills itself as "The Birthplace of Speed"?

Well, they might have used "International"—as in truck, because that's how the Daytona felt, at least at lower speeds. Its chassis remained a solid Ferrari platform composed of oval-section tubes supporting a body structure of round and square members, but there

was a new wrinkle in a "bathtub" of fiberglass panels that were bonded to the body skeleton to form the cockpit (construction that would continue into the Nineties). Though exterior sheetmetal was mostly steel, doors, hood, and trunklid were rendered in weight-saving aluminum. For all this, the Daytona flattened the scales at a hefty 3,600 pounds, so it was just as well that the quad-cam V-12 produced an equally hefty 315 pounds/feet torque, spread over a very wide rev range before peaking at 5,500 rpm.

It was that broad-banded torque more than top-end power that gave the Daytona its lightning acceleration. And though the car was undeniably heavy, at least the weight was ideally distributed 50/50 front and rear. One result was exceptional high-speed stability. Noted Ferrari expert Dean Batchelor recalls that when *Road & Track* ran its Daytona flat-out, the car was "smooth as glass at that speed"—which turned out to be a genuine 173 mph. "It was easy," Batchelor said. He was even able to take a photograph of the main instruments at the telling moment.

But if the Daytona was a rocket, as author Lyons noted, "it was also a rocket *sled*... a truck. Where the 275 had

impressed everyone with its light steering, at least at low speeds, the 365's struck everyone as heavy. So did the throttle and clutch pedals, though by unpleasant contrast, the brakes were over-assisted. The brakes themselves would sometimes fade in hard stops from high speed, a shortfall blamed on the [high] weight."

Still, given enough time, the Daytona driver could learn to go indecently fast on both straight and twisty roads alike. Author Lyons fairly quoted the book *Daytona*, in which Pat Braden and Gerald Roush observed that the car "really only begins to come into its own at about 70 mph and hits its stride above 140 mph.... [B]elow 80 mph the car is a bit bumpy, but the suspension begins to work smoothly as speed builds, and steering becomes appropriate. Owners who complain of heavy steering should remember their baby was designed for precise control at 174 mph. Parking lots were low on the priority list"—as evidenced by a clumsy 39-foot turning circle.

Yet not everyone judged the Daytona "trucky." European journalist Paul Frere reported that "on its big fat tires, the Ferrari could be flung around the corners, quite irrespective of [a] none-too-well-maintained surface. It certainly did not feel very big and its agility belied its weight. . . . The general cornering attitude is that of a slightly understeering car, with a small tendency to tuck into the bend as the throttle is closed. . . . There is practically no trace of roll, and the moderately light steering is very precise." The Daytona was far from quiet; no Ferrari was in those days. But neither Frere nor anyone else minded an engine that made "the finest music of all [for] the enthusiast. . . a music he can enjoy in the comfort of a well-sprung car, fitted with such amenities as electric window lifters, air conditioning (that could be improved) and a really capacious luggage locker—a Grand Touring car *par excellence.*"

Happily, Ferrari had the good sense to keep its hands off the Daytona during the model's half-dozen year production run. Besides the aforementioned headlamp change, the only notable development was the advent of a companion "spider" convertible, unveiled at Frankfurt 1969 as the 365 GTS/4. It would account for only 127 of the more than 1,300 Daytonas built.

Low production and timeless, high appeal explain why Daytona asking prices would soar into the million-dollar stratosphere by the late Eighties. Convertibles, of course, generally command bigger bucks than coupes—by a factor of 20-100 percent among Ferraris—

The 4,390 cc (268 cid) V-12 used in the 365 series Ferraris boasted six Weber two-barrel carbs—and a mighty 352 bhp.

which explains why several shops got into Daytona spider conversions. While some were done for enthusiasts who simply wanted an open car and really wanted it to be a Daytona, most were doubtless motivated by the spider's higher market value and the prospect of further appreciation. The irony is that this top-chopping might one day leave berlinettas scarcer and thus more valuable than spiders, original or otherwise.

True to tradition, Ferrari built 15 special lightweight Daytona coupes for racing by authorized factory distributors. Interiors were stripped, roll cages and other necessary racing hardware added, underpinnings suitably fortified, and engines tweaked to as much as 450 bhp. Some also sported fully aluminum bodies with opening fiberglass panels. All were formidable performers—top speed approached 200 mph—and some

ran with distinction. Competition Daytonas finished first in class at both Le Mans and Watkins Glen in 1972, at Le Mans in 1973 and again in '74, and—appropriately enough—at Daytona Beach in '73, '75 and, impressively, 1979. Alas, braking remained a weakness throughout because the racers were just as portly as roadgoing models, their larger rolling stock and heavier fuel loads (from bigger tanks) offsetting the some 400 pounds saved through bodywork and componentry.

Not that it mattered much, because midships racers were here to stay, and the Daytona was to be Ferrari's last two-seat GT in the classic mold—though not its last front-engine car, as witness the later 365 2 + 2 and its 400/412 and 512 America successors. But these were much gentler front-engine Ferraris, almost "sedans" in the words of one writer, so the Daytona still marks the end of an era—or rather Ferrari's historic transition from a builder of macho, barely tamed race cars for the street to a "mature" automaker specializing in plush, well-equipped—but still blindingly fast—*gran turismos.*

That also explains today's lofty asking prices. Quite simply, there was never anything like the Daytona before, and we shall not see its mighty like again. For that reason alone, it will always be counted among the greats.

This 365 GTC Speciale featured the running gear of the of the 365 GTB/4 Daytona, but it was strictly a one-off built for a member of the Dutch royal family.

Specifications	
Engine:	V-12, dohc, 268 cid/4,390 cc (3.19 x 2.79-in./81 x 71.3-mm bore x stroke), 7 main bearings, 8.8:1 compression ratio, 6 Weber 2-bbl carburetors, 352 bhp @ 7,500 rpm, 315 lbs/ft torque @ 5,500 rpm (competition model: up to 450 bhp)
Transmission:	5-speed manual in rear transaxle
Suspension, front:	Independent, unequal-length A-arms, coil springs, tube shocks, anti-roll bar
Suspension, rear:	Independent, unequal-length A-arms, coil springs, tube shocks, anti-roll bar
Brakes:	Hydraulic, front/rear discs
Wheelbase (in.):	94.4
Overall length (in.):	174.2
Tread, front, rear (in.):	56.6/56.1
Weight (lbs):	approx. 3,600
Tires:	215/70VR-15
Top speed (mph):	170 + (competition model: 195 +)
0-60 mph (sec):	5.0-5.9
Production:	berlinetta: approx. 1,285 (incl. 15 competition models) spider: 127

It's not as though Plymouth was new to the performance field in 1968. As far back as 1956 the original Plymouth Fury had been a hotfooted favorite, and by 1962 Plymouths were showing their muscle in competitive events all over the country. The top engine option that year, so far as factory installation was concerned, was a 305-horse-power version of the 361-cubic-inch Chrysler V-8. But available over-the-counter were the 383- and 413-cid Chryslers, the latter fitted with 15-inch "short-ram" induction tubes—all perfectly legal for competition purposes, of course.

By 1964, there was the Stage II wedge engine, rated at 425 horsepower when the 13.5:1-compression heads were fitted. At Daytona that February, that one derailed Ford's string of 10 consecutive NASCAR (National Association for Stock Car Automobile Racing) victories as Plymouths placed 1-2-3, and Richard Petty set a new 500-mile stock-car record at 153.34 miles an hour.

But despite its many victories on the track and at the drags, Plymouth didn't really get serious about the "muscle car" market until three years after Pontiac started it all with the GTO. That was in 1967, the year the GTX appeared as a separately catalogued Plymouth model. An upscale version of the division's mid-sized Belvedere, the GTX came standard with Chrysler's big 440-cid "wedge" engine, rated at a lusty 375 horsepower.

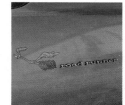

Pontiac may have "invented" the muscle car in 1964, but it took Plymouth to bring out the first *budget* muscle car, that in 1968. Its name was Road Runner, and it listed at just $2,870, although the '69 coupe seen here was bumped to $2,945, still a bargain by any enthusiast's reckoning.

Or, for the driver who really took this sort of thing seriously, the 426-cubic-inch, 425-horsepower "Street Hemi" was optional at extra cost. Plymouth was officially out of the racing game that year, though independently sponsored cars continued to give an excellent account of themselves on the nation's tracks. But the pitch was obviously being made to performance enthusiasts.

All of which was simply prologue. For 1968, Plymouth's intermediate models featured sensational new styling, replacing the squared-off look of earlier years with what would shortly become known as the "coke bottle" shape: smooth, sleek, and sexy. The public responded enthusiastically, boosting sales of the Belvedere and its derivatives an impressive 63 percent for the model year.

In its handsome new dress the GTX was more popular than ever. But it was clearly upstaged by a new performance machine called the Road Runner, the industry's first bargain-priced muscle car. It was a clever piece of work. What Plymouth planners had done was simply to take the bottom-of-the-line Belvedere coupe—"El Cheapo," one might say—and outfit it with enough standard performance goodies to please almost any lead-footed driver. Then they added a very effective gimmick: a decal of the Road Runner, one of the most popular figures among the animated cartoons of the day. Plymouth even tuned the horn to exactly

The '69 Road Runner roster included a convertible. It cost $3,313 and weighed 3,790 pounds (355 more than the coupe), but it was the fastest ragtop around.

match the "beep-beep" sound so familiar to cartoon fans.

The engine was Chrysler's justly famed "383," fitted with heads and camshaft borrowed from the "440 Super Commando" V-8 and nourished by means of a big four-barrel carburetor and a special intake manifold. An extra-duty cooling system with viscous-drive fan was included, as well as an unsilenced air cleaner, while dual exhausts completed the package. Horsepower was rated, no doubt conservatively, at 335 at 5,200 rpm, while the torque measured 425 pounds/feet at 3,400.

A four-speed manual transmission was standard issue, though a heavy-duty version of the excellent TorqueFlite automatic cost just $39 additional. Heavy-duty springs—torsion bars in front, semi-elliptics at the rear—were supplied, along with stiff shocks and an anti-roll bar.

Fifteen-inch wheels, fitted with wide-oval F-70 x 15 red-line tires, were substituted for the usual 14-inchers, and

11-inch heavy-duty drum brakes took the place of the standard 10-inch jobs. Front discs were available for a few dollars extra, and a wise investment. Also on the options list were such items as a heavy-duty Sure-Grip axle (expensive, at $146, but worth the money), power steering, power brakes, "air-grabber" hood, and sport stripes.

But apart from the performance-related goodies, the identifying decals, and the goofy horn, this car was strictly a low-level automobile. Upholstery has been described as "early taxicab," and chrome trim was applied sparingly. Introduced on September 14, 1967, along with the rest of Plymouth's 1968 lineup, it came only as a pillared coupe at first. At mid-year, however, a hardtop was added, and by 1969 there was a convertible as well.

The best part of all this, of course, was the Road Runner's price: $2,870 for the coupe, $3,034 for the hardtop. *Car Life* magazine called it "a sort of Scotsman's Supercar," adding that it "emulates what a young, performance-minded driver might do on his own, if properly experienced and motivated." By way of comparison, the far more luxurious '68 GTX hardtop listed at $3,416. Not surprisingly, the Road Runner outsold the fancier version by a margin of well over two-to-one.

The 426-cubic-inch, 425-horsepower Street Hemi engine was available to Road Runner buyers from the start, though the price was a stiff one: $813.45. And in the spring of 1969 another hotshot performer joined the options list: the "440 Six-Pack," Chrysler's 440-cid V-8, fed by three two-barrel carburetors and rated at 290 horsepower. Much more affordable than the Hemi, it was priced at $250.

Base prices for the '69 coupe and hardtop rose to $2,945 and $3,083, respectively, while the new ragtop stickered at $3,313. Still a bargain! In fact, *Motor Trend* selected the 1969 Road Runner as its "Car of the Year," noting that it "offers the highest ratio of driving sensation per dollar of any domestic made."

Explaining its selection in greater detail, the editors added, "The Road Runner is a pleasure to drive. Nearly everybody on the staff preferred this

Compared to 33,743 coupes and just 2,128 convertibles, 48,549 sales made the hardtop the most popular '69 Road Runner. Each and every one came with the now-famous "beep, beep" Road Runner horn. The standard engine was a 335-horsepower 383 V-8.

Some Road Runners were more equal than others, and the most equal of all was the $4,298 Superbird. This out-and-out 1970 racer sported fender vents atop the front wheels, hood pins, a standard 375-bhp 440 V-8 (Hemi optional), styled steel wheels, and Road Runner decals in appropriate places. Bucket seats were optional.

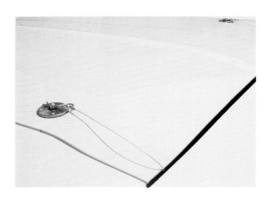

car to all the others whether they were driving freeways, curves, bumper-to-bumper rush hour traffic, or taking out-of-town guests to dinner at one of our better restaurants. It's not a hot rod but it will give a darn good imitation of one if you ask it to. It handles extremely well on mountain curves, rides securely at high speed on all types of roads, has reserve power for passing situations at any speed, stops straight and quick, and has good room for both passengers and luggage. . . .

"When you get right down to the marrow, the Road Runner is one hell of a nice, solid, responsive, good handling machine offering more to start with for under three grand than anybody else in Detroit. It's that simple."

Even Managing Editor Ellen Merlo, admittedly no "car nut," was enthusiastic: "Wow! What a sensational car. Here was I, driving around in one of the most exciting automobiles I've ever sat in. It wasn't just a car anymore. I'd found love. . . . For a week I made up lies about my car being out of commission so that I could continue driving the Road Runner."

And Technical Editor Eric Dahlquist, who had been trying out a Road Runner powered by the Street Hemi, called it "probably the fastest production sedan made today."

Road Runner production for 1969 nearly doubled the 1968 total, but that year would prove to be the car's high point as far as sales were concerned. The numbers dropped by nearly half for 1970 — as they did for practically all muscle cars — this despite the addition of the flashy Superbird, identified by a wind-splitting nose cone up front and a wild-looking airfoil stabilizer at the rear. By 1971, the bottom had completely fallen out from under the muscle car market, this because of government-mandated safety and emmissions regulations and prohibitive insurance premiums for muscle cars, particularly for young drivers. The mood of America had changed, but the brief heyday of the muscle car will never be forgotten — and neither will the Road Runner, the muscle car that captured the spirit of the times better than any other.

The '70 Superbird sported an aerodynamic nose cone, streamlined backlight, and an outrageous rear wing, which quickly earned it the name "Winged Warrior."

Specifications[1]	
Engine:	V-8, ohv, 383 cid (4.25 x 3.38-in. bore x stroke), 10.0:1 compression ratio, 5 main bearings, hydraulic valve lifters, Carter 4-bbl carburetor, 335 bhp @ 5,200 rpm, 425 lbs/ft torque @ 3,400 rpm **Hemi** 426 cid (4.25 x 3.75-in), hemispherical combustion chambers, 10.25:1 c.r., 2 4-bbl carbs, 425 bhp @ 5,000 rpm, 490 lbs/ft @ 4,000 rpm (opt.)
Transmission:	4-speed manual; 3-speed Torque-Flite automatic opt.
Suspension, front:	Independent, heavy-duty torsion bars, anti-roll bar, tube shock absorbers
Suspension, rear:	Rigid axle, extra heavy duty semi-elliptic springs, tube shock absorbers
Brakes:	Hydraulic, front/rear drums; front discs opt.
Wheelbase (in.):	116.0
Shipping weight (lbs):	3,405
0-60 mph (sec):	7.3
Top speed (mph):	122 (383, per *Car Life*, 5/68)
Production:	1968 cpe 29,240 htp cpe 15,359 1969 cpe 33,743 htp cpe 48,549 cvt cpe 2,128 1970 cpe 15,716 htp cpe 24,944 cvt cpe 824 Superbird 1,920

[1]1968 coupe

The Datsun 240Z burst onto the American sports car scene with neat styling, plenty of power, excellent handling—and a remarkably low price.

People who whine about the way the Japanese have taken over the car industry tend to ignore all the reasons why that has happened. Some facts deserve criticism: the "export subsidy program" by which the Japanese government reduces the price of export Toyotas compared to identical home models, and restrictions on imports hidden behind environmental or health regulations come to mind. Neither of these are, however, responsible for the Japanese automotive success. They've earned that—by simply building great automobiles.

The Datsun 240Z was one early example. As *Automobile Quarterly* said, it "hit its particular import market bulls-eye with such a wallop that its competitors will probably never recover." Ron Wakefield, of *Road & Track*, enthused that "We think Datsun had a real winner." *Car and Driver* named it the "Car of the Year" in 1971. Meanwhile, *Motor Trend* concluded that "Datsun has created a real sports GT which . . . should be around for a long time. . . ." Notably, the Z-car's competitors— the Opel GT, the MGB GT, the Fiat 124 Sport—never did recover. The only car that would hold a candle to it, *AQ* suggested, was the GTV Alfa, but that was beginning to show its age and cost almost $1,000 more: "The Datsun itself could quite justifiably cost $1,000 more than it does."

It was price, of course, that got everybody excited. Style-wise, the 240Z was competent enough, designed, allegedly, by Albrecht Goertz, creator of the famous BMW 507. Mechanically, too, it was up to date, with a reliable and smooth overhead-cam inline six, coil-spring independent four-wheel suspension, power front disc brakes, fine handling, and more. Okay, great. But it sold for $3,526 when it first arrived in the U.S.! To get a similar package elsewhere in those days, it took $2,500 more for an E-Type Jag or a Corvette.

Of course, this dawned on people right away—and showed very early how carefully Nissan's product planners were gauging the American market. Comparison: one of the Studebaker Avanti's excuses always was that Stude dealers didn't attract Avanti customers. Well, Datsun dealers hardly seemed a likely place to find 240Z customers. The only sporting car they'd had up to the Z was the 1961-69 SP/SR-series "Fairlady," a two-seater similar to—but not copied from—the MGB right down to its mock-SU carburetors, and just about as exciting. The difference with the Z-car was product planning. Nobody had really needed the Avanti, which was going up against established rivals like the Thunderbird and Riviera. But everybody needed, or at least wanted, the Z-car, which landed plumb in the middle of a market almost bereft of competition. As a result, people soon were paying $1,000 over sticker for one, from "brokers" or the occasional unscrupulous dealer who accepted premiums to guarantee early delivery by leap-frogging waiting lists.

Here's another difference between the failed Stude project and Datsun's glittering Z-car success story: corporate attitudes. Nissan lifted the franchise of any dealer caught flogging 240Zs at inflated prices. Not that demand was ever comparable for Avantis, but there wasn't anything a Stude dealer wouldn't do to make a sale, and Studebaker couldn't have cared less.

Bob Sharp Datsun, of Wilton, Connecticut, explained his policy to this writer on a visit when the Z-car was brand new: "People come in and ask us how much it will cost to move up a few places on the waiting list. They seem pretty surprised when we tell them we're not interested." An official waiting list was posted in plain view in the showroom so customers could watch their names moving up. It's no surprise that Sharp is still in business.

If the name Sharp seems familiar, it ought to be. One of the first American racers to take Datsuns seriously, he had been running and winning in SCCA production racing since the early Sixties.

When we interviewed him, Bob was racing a new 240Z in Class C-Production, a beautifully prepared car that regularly showed its heels to the pack.

Sharp's personal road-going 240Z was the one we drove and photographed that day back in 1970, when it was the hottest new car since the Mustang. The car was immaculate and very carefully optioned—with air conditioning and the seven-inch lightweight wheels with 175/SR x 14 Bridgestone radials (Japanese Firestone), a slightly stiffer than standard anti-roll bar at the front, and the optional non-polluting dual exhausts.

The first impression behind the wheel was one of relaxing order. There are some cars you never feel at home in, but this one felt like an old friend immediately. The seating position and placement of the wheel were just right, and the pedals had long, smooth throws and were well separated.

Twisting the key produced one of the most sensuous automotive noises we'd heard since the XK-120. The dual-exhaust system cost around $200 includ-

Powering the 240Z was a 2,393-cc (146-cid) inline six with a single overhead cam and dual carbs. Horsepower was rated at 151, enough to accelerate the 2,238-pound Z-car from 0-60 in 8.0-9.0 seconds. The styling probably sold as many Zs as the power, however.

ing manifolds, mufflers, pipes, and installation, but it was certainly money well spent. With that kind of music built in, who needed a radio?

Of course, the 240Z was a joy to drive. There's no point in filling these pages with a plethora of g-loads and acceleration times. The Z was thoroughly tested and retested by the new-car monthlies during its four years of production. (It was succeeded by the 260Z and 280Z, which became considerably heavier and far less lively.) The fact that it was by far the fastest imported car in anywhere near its price class was known far and wide.

But we did add our voice that day to the chorus singing the praises of the 240Z's handling. We'd never driven a front-engined machine that felt more nimble and stable under very hard braking and cornering. It was an extremely safe, beautifully balanced car that deserved every bit of the praise that was heaped upon it. As it stood with all those options installed, it retailed for $4,636. That sounded incredible then. It seems impossible now.

Japanese cars have not come of age among collectors. For the Z-car, the 20 years that seems necessary before nostalgia sets in and produces collectibility is only just up. But we can expect the 240Z to become one of the first Yokohamas to be collected and restored during the 1990s.

Bob Grossman, veteran race driver and longtime purveyor of European exotics, once delivered a Ferrari to a dealership and drove home in a borrowed Toyota. "Somewhere along the way it suddenly dawned on me that this bargain-basement people-hauler was one of the best cars I'd ever driven," he said. The Japanese made their first American inroads by showing people that economy cars didn't mean strippers with park-bench seats, cardboard upholstery, and rubber mats underfoot—that cheap cars could provide quality and be fun to drive. With the 240Z, they raised our expectations in the area of sports cars. Today they're doing the same with our concept of luxury cars. What'll they think of next?

The fastback styling of the 240Z embraced the practicality of a rear hatch, which swallowed up a generous load of luggage for *gran turismo* touring. And with a top speed of up to 125 mph, the touring could be grand indeed! This Z sports aftermarket wheels.

Specifications[1]	
Engine:	I-6, sohc, 146 cid/2,393 cc (3.26 x 2.90-in. bore x stroke), 9.0:1 compression ratio, dual carburetors, 151 bhp @ 5,600 rpm, 146 lbs/ft torque @ 4,400 rpm
Transmission:	4-speed manual; 3-speed automatic opt.
Suspension, front:	MacPherson struts, lower wishbones, coil springs, anti-roll bar
Suspension, rear:	Chapman struts, lower wishbones, coil springs, anti-roll bar
Brakes:	Hydraulic, front discs/rear drums, power assisted
Wheelbase (in.):	90.7
Overall length (in.):	162.8
Tread, front/rear (in.):	53.3/53.0
Weight (lbs):	2,238
0-60 mph (sec):	8.0-9.0 (later models slower)
Top speed (mph):	up to 125
Production:	130,000 + (U.S. sales 1970-73)

[1]1970 model

Some might dispute the DeTomaso Pantera as a great car of the 20th Century, but there's no disputing its significance: the first affordable mid-engine exotic. It was fairly successful as such, though not in all respects, especially numbers. But it's still being built two decades on, which surely testifies to its inherent "rightness," if not greatness.

As most enthusiasts know, the Pantera came together from two quite distant points in the late Sixties. In Dearborn, Michigan, was Lee Iacocca, soon to become president of Ford Motor Company after engineering a string of successes as head of Ford Division, most notably the Mustang "ponycar." In Modena, Italy, Alejandro DeTomaso, a one-time race-car driver/builder from Argentina, was trying to establish himself as a *bona fide* purveyor of high-performance road cars *a la* Ferrari, Maserati, and Lamborghini.

Iacocca had taken due note of DeTomaso's first serious production effort, the mid-engine Mangusta ("Mongoose"). Announced in 1966, it featured a Lotus-like "backbone" chassis drawn by famed engineer Giotto Bizzarrini (but derived from that of DeTomaso's earlier, stillborn Vallelunga) and wicked-looking coupe bodywork drawn by the talented young Giorgio Giugiaro of Ghia (recently moved from Bertone). What particularly intrigued Iacocca was the powerplant: a small-block 289 Ford V-8 parked behind a two-place cockpit beneath wild gullwing-style covers and tuned as for Carroll Shelby's hot GT-350 Mustang. This also happened to be the engine that had recently powered Ford's factory GT endurance racers to impressive wins at Le Mans and elsewhere.

What Iacocca had in mind was a replacement for the limited-edition road-going GT40 being sold in Europe, as well as an exotic new "image car" for U.S. Lincoln-Mercury dealers to sell alongside their imported Capris. Alas, the Mangusta was plagued by excessive chassis flex, and was just plain impractical for everyday American use (though Ford briefly considered selling a rebadged version as a new "Shelby Cobra"). Accordingly, Iacocca asked DeTomaso to give him something better—and in unheard-of quantities for a small Italian specialist: 2,500 a year.

But by then, Alejandro was quite able to respond. Flawed though it was, the Mangusta had proved saleable. Moreover, his wife's brother, a director in the American firm Rowan Controls, was persuaded to have Rowan buy not only DeTomaso's factory but Ghia too—and the old-line coachbuilder Vignale. By 1970, some 300 Mangusta sales in Europe had given Alejandro the wherewithal to complete Iacocca's car, which was dubbed Pantera.

Revealed at the New York Auto Show that March, the Pantera sported a new unitized steel structure—which would later cause a lot of pain for restorers—designed by consultant engineer Giampaolo Dallara.

Originally seen at the New York Auto Show in March 1970, DeTomaso's Pantera has seen remarkably little change over two decades. The clean and original lines were penned by American Tom Tjaarda at Ghia.

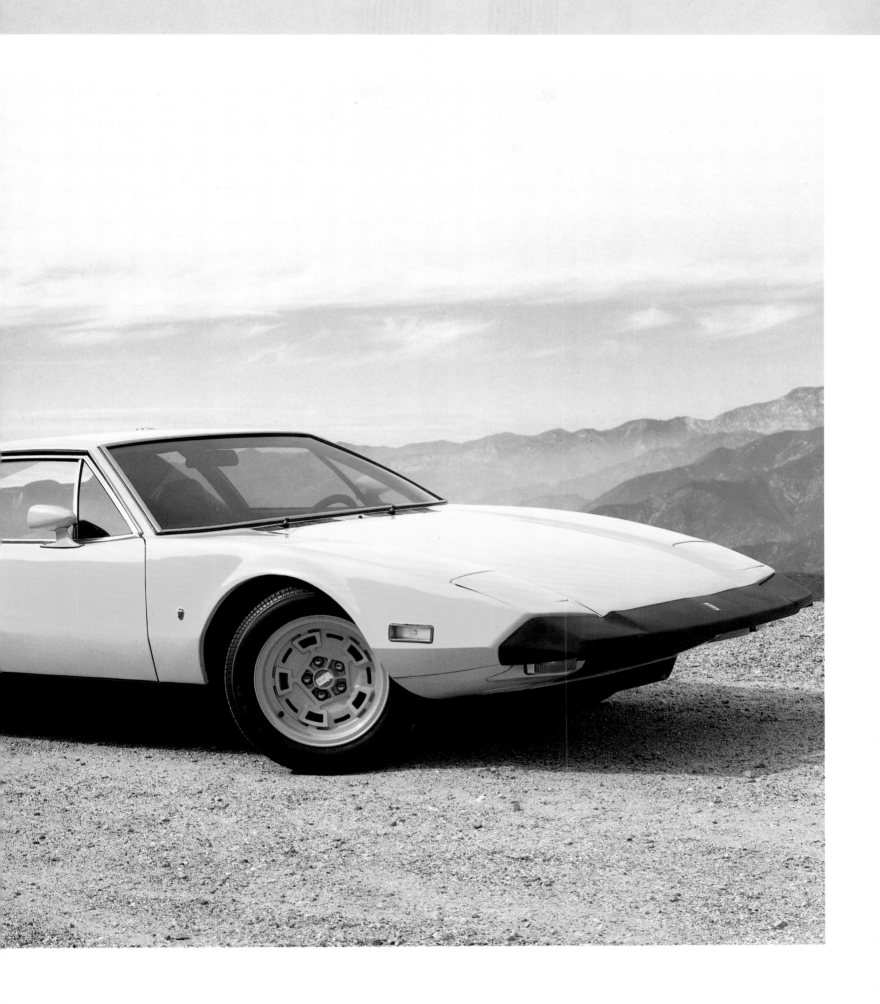

A large lid opened hatchback-style to reveal a midship-mounted Ford V-8 underneath. At first these were U.S. 351s, but beginning around 1980 Australian-produced 351s were installed. The engine used in 1991 was the U.S. Ford 302 with 225 bhp, as used in 1989-91 Mustangs.

first 300 or so Panteras needed substantial post-build corrections before they were literally fit to sell. Though this delayed initial U.S. deliveries until 1972, the Pantera was still big news. The reason was price—at around $10,000, it cost far less than other high-buck Italians, mid-engine or no, yet offered all their panache plus a rugged, well-known engine that could be serviced most anywhere. It even came with Ford's normal new-car warranty. Alas, complaints of marginal engine cooling and excess cabin heat surfaced early, and performance wasn't all it should have been in U.S. form. European models unfettered by "detox" gear could beat 160 mph, but American Panteras weren't nearly as fast. Then too, the simple Yankee iron was hardly a bragging point, and the driving position seemed downright peculiar to many prospects.

Moreover, the Pantera had been designed with a curious disregard for pending U.S. safety and emissions standards. An ugly black-rubber nose guard and bigger back bumpers went on to meet 1973-74 requirements, but meeting the '75 standards would have meant a major redesign, including a new powerteam. Ford bean-counters deemed all that too costly given the modest sales rate, which was rendered even more modest by the 1973-74 gas crisis. As a result, U.S. imports were halted after '74, though not before Dearborn stylists had mocked up a full-size proposal for a rebodied replacement. Though Lincoln-Mercury allegedly sold 6,091 Panteras over four calendar years, some historians think that exaggerated; one source, in fact, lists only 5,629.

Regardless, the Pantera would carry on for Europe, proving especially popular in Germany. Changes would be remarkably few through 1990: a switch to Ford Australia engines once Dearborn quit making 351s; production trimmed to 50-100 units annually, all to special order; commensurately improved quality; and two high-powered derivatives: the mid-Seventies GTS with 350 bhp, and a bespoilered, beskirted 1980 replacement called GT5, a 300-bhp reply to the Lamborghini Countach. The GT5 lost its "ground effects" apparel in 1983 but went to 330 bhp and gained an S

Dimensions were little changed from the Mangusta's. So was weight distribution, little more favorable with a 58-percent rearward bias, so unequal-size tires were retained: 185/70-15s front, 215/70-15s rear. Dearborn's desire for easy servicing and high reliability dictated more "standard Ford" components than in the Mangusta. Among these was the HO (high-output) version of the new 351-cubic-inch "Cleveland" V-8, hooked to the usual five-speed ZF transaxle. Horsepower was initially 310 in U.S. form and 330 for European models. Emasculating emissions controls would bring the former down to 250 bhp by 1973.

Though hardly spacious by absolute standards, the Pantera was at least

roomier than the Mangusta. Reflecting Ford input, detail engineering was more thorough and professional, equipment more complete. Even air conditioning was included, unusual for a low-volume Latin, but necessary to satisfy U.S. consumers. Practicality also dictated more conventional body construction, with a single engine lid, hinged at the cockpit end. Predictably, bodies were to be supplied by Vignale from Turin, with final assembly at DeTomaso's Modena works. The styling assignment went to Ghia—again no surprise—only this time the designer was American Tom Tjaarda. His handsome work still speaks for itself.

Unfortunately, quality suffered mightily in the rush to production, and the suffix. Within a few years, though, Europe's own environmental movement had prompted power cuts to 212 for the basic Pantera L and 247 for the GT5 S.

Meanwhile, Alejandro regained control of DeTomaso Automobili in 1976, two years after he sold both Ghia and Vignale to Ford (as implied in his original deal with Iacocca). A bit later, American sales resumed on a limited basis under private auspices, the Pantera being recertified in 1981 by a small Santa Monica, California, firm called Panteramerica. Distribution then passed to Stauffer Classics, Limited, of Blue Mounds, Wisconsin.

Today's Pantera is a much-modified GT5 S built in annual lots of 75 or less under the watchful eye of Alejandro's son, Santiago. Highlighting a substantial and visually arresting exterior overhaul—by no less than master stylist Marcello Gandini—are a tidier nose with a new combination bumper/spoiler; two large, functional radiator air vents in the hood; an odd-looking aerodynamic "winglet" at the base of the windshield; and husky new bulged rear flanks capped by a Ferrari F40-style loop spoiler, with an integral underbumper tray whose contour runs forward to mate with revived, differently shaped rocker skirts.

In addition, sourcing has been changed for some minor components—and a few major ones. Take the engine, which is again American: the familiar Ford 302, with electronic multiport fuel injection and 225 bhp as used in 1989-91 Mustangs. DeTomaso retains its catalytic converter but massages intake manifolding, cams, cylinder heads, valves, and pistons to extract an additional 70 bhp and 33 lbs/ft torque. Putting it all to the pavement are big new 17-inch alloy wheels wearing monster Z-rated Michelin performance radials sized at 235/45 fore and 335/35 aft. The two-inch gain in rim diameter makes room for larger brakes: racing-type Brembo self-venting units with four-piston aluminum calipers, also massively sized at 15.7/14.8 inches front and rear. To accommodate the beefier rolling stock, the suspension has been treated to longer wishbones all-round.

Despite its checkered history, the Pantera is still a great drive. Outward vision remains poor (really worse than ever on the "Series II" '91, thanks to that big rear wing), and the cockpit is as tight and disorganized as ever, though it's much better finished these days and has even acquired a not inconsiderable amount of hide and genuine tree-wood.

But such mundane matters are forgotten as soon as you fire up that Ford small-block and persuade the burly ZF five-speed into gear. Though it lacks the ultimate grip and dynamic agility of newer GTs like Ferrari's 348, the Pantera doesn't drive like a 20-year-old machine. Even the steering—still manual—can be managed without raising a sweat (except at parking pace), and the ride is more than acceptable for a supercar. Noisy? What else with the engine right behind your ear? Happily, performance also recalls the "good old days." Despite less displacement (but little change in weight), the latest GT5 can top 167 mph—not the ultimate in exoticar velocity, but certainly more than adequate.

The only real problems are price—would you believe close to $112,400 now?—and availability: the '91 GT5 S isn't certified for U.S. sale, though it may be someday soon (it's already passed crash tests).

Let's hope so. We Americans deserve another new Pantera. After all, it was meant for us in the first place.

Specifications	
Engine:	**1970-90** Ford ohv V-8 (U.S., 1971-80; Australian, 1980-90), 351 cid/5,763 cc (4.00 x 3.50-in/101.6 x 88.9-mm bore x stroke), 250-350 bhp (SAE net) @ 5,400-6,000 rpm, 325-330 lbs/ft torque @ 3,600-3,800 rpm **1991** Ford (U.S.) ohv V-8, 302 cid/4,942 cc (4.00 x 3.00-in./101.6 x 76.2-mm), 305 bhp @ 5,800 rpm, 333 lbs/ft @ 3,700 rpm
Transmission:	ZF five-speed manual in rear transaxle
Suspension, front:	Upper and lower wishbones, coil springs, tube shocks, anti-roll bar
Suspension, rear:	Upper and lower wishbones, radius rods, coil springs, tube shocks, anti-roll bar
Brakes:	Hydraulic, front/rear discs
Wheelbase (in.):	99.0
Weight (lbs):	3,100-3,300
Top speed (mph):	140-167 +
0-60 mph (sec):	5.2-7.5
Production:	est. 9,500 through 1990

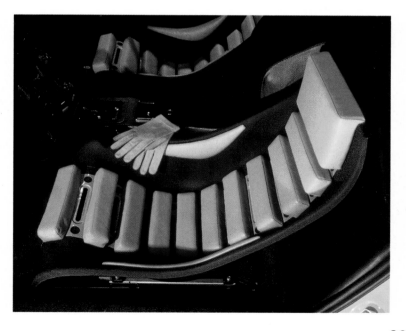

The interior of the Pantera was always a bit tight, but it was well fitted out with all the proper gauges, sport seats, and even air conditioning for U.S.-bound cars. Since the mid-Seventies, about 50-100 units have been built per year.

The Countach, here a '75 LP400, was designed to inherit the "ultimate supercar" mantle from the Miura, and indeed it did. One writer described it as "Outlandish, unreal, otherworldly," which it was from the wild looks to its throbbing 375-bhp dohc V-12.

So much hysteria attended the Lamborghini Countach over its 16-year life span that it's difficult to get a true picture of the beast. Perhaps the most even-handed assessment comes from Pete Lyons, author of CONSUMER GUIDE®'s *Complete Book of Lamborghini*: "Outlandish, unreal, otherworldly. That was how most everyone viewed the Countach. As an expression of the designer's art, [this] ultracar was a triumph. Yet . . . that far-out styling did an injustice to the car beneath it. On the road, the [Countach] was brilliant in a way its coachwork was not."

To the more cynical, the Countach merely proved that fantasy styling and shattering performance were all a car needed to generate widespread wonder and fascination. But many "great" cars have been masses of contradictions both as machines and in the reactions they illicit. In that, the Countach was absolutely without peer.

It was, of course, designed to inherit the "ultimate supercar" mantle from the pretty Miura. It was also supposed to address that car's most glaring faults—namely high-speed nose-lifting, snap-oversteer in fast corners, tiring shift action, and a hot, noisy cockpit. But "improved" and "more practical" were the last thoughts on people's minds when the Countach prototype stopped the 1971 Geneva Auto Show. The reaction was more akin to the meaning of the name (pronounced COON-tahsh), which translates roughly to "Good Lord!"

Except for being a mid-engine two-seat coupe with the famous quad-cam Lambo V-12, the Countach differed from the Miura as chianti from claret. Starting with the proverbial clean sheet, engineer Paolo Stanzani discarded the Miura's pressed-steel chassis for a complex multi-tubular space-frame, which was easier to fabricate for a small firm like Lamborghini and made more sense for the very limited production envisioned. Like the Miura, Sant'Agata didn't see Countach demand being very high or prolonged.

More important, the powerteam was resituated from "east-west" to "south-north," the V-12 facing backwards and the gearbox running forward into the cockpit to permit a short, direct linkage for easy, positive changes. Alas, this fundamental alteration slightly raised the center of gravity and, with a two-inch shorter wheelbase, left the front wheels eating up a lot of footwell space, something the Miura had successfully avoided. But there were compensations in more favorable positioning of major masses—though not fore/aft weight balance, which was little changed—and easier isolation of the cockpit from noise and heat.

What everyone noticed, of course, was the strikingly sharp-edged, almost pyramidal body, another effort of Bertone's Marcello Gandini. General proportions and the wild "beetle-wing" articulated doors—which swung almost straight up—were clearly taken from Bertone's 1968

Carabo show car (built on the Alfa Tipo 33 racing chassis), but the Countach was more muscular and menacing. Luggage space? Virtually none. Outward vision? Difficult at best, what with the super-sloped windshield, ultra-low seat position, and blind-quarter "tunnelback" roofline. But who cared? Just looking at a Countach was almost as good as driving it—or being seen in it. This time, Bertone would supply just the body in aluminum, like the Miura's, but a scant 1-mm thick; Sant'Agata itself would handle assembly, paint, and trim.

Although the prototype mounted a V-12 bored and stroked to 5.0 liters, the initial production Countach carried the well-known "4.0-liter" unit (actually a 3.9) with 375 DIN horsepower. It was designated the LP400, "LP" for "longitudinal posterior" engine. The Countach also bore numerous changes made during what turned out to be a lengthy three-year gestation (unlike the Miura, which had been a one-year rush job). Among these were a race-car-like steel-tube suspension with basic Miura geometry, a nose recontoured for *less* downforce, and a slightly higher roofline for more livable headroom. Along the way, a pair of air scoops was added to the car's "shoulders" and NACA ducts cut into its flanks, both to make the side-mounted radiators more effective. After two more prototypes, the second of which was shown as the production version at Geneva '73, the Countach finally went on sale in early 1974. Only 23 were delivered that year, but all were 175-mph cars capable of roaring from 0-60 mph in less than seven seconds—and turning *every* head. From the first, handling, braking, and stability were all of competition caliber—as well they needed to be given the searing performance.

Four years into its career, the Countach was further evolved into the LP400S. Giampaolo Dallara had come back from his successful free-lancing business to supervise the updates, which included modified suspension geometry, super-wide Pirelli P7 tires on broader "five-hole" wheels (shared with Lamborghini's contemporary mid-V-8 Silhouette), wheelarch extensions to accommodate them, and a front spoiler. One new

The wild "beetle-wing" articulated doors drew plenty of attention to the Countach, even in '88, and so did the strikingly sharp-edged, almost pyramidal body.

option ended up on most S-models, and many later Countachs as well: a huge rear wing flying on twin struts, which only made the car look even more like a ground-running missile. By 1980, there was a Series 2 S with a tidier, redesigned instrument panel.

European emissions standards were by now beginning to take a performance toll, so Lamborghini upped displacement to 4.75 liters in 1982 for a further evolution, the LP500S. But horsepower was still 375 due to lowered compression. Accordingly, in March 1985, Lamborghini unleashed the 5000 Quattrovalvole, the surname denoting four valves per cylinder, as on Ferrari's contemporary 308. But here, "5000" really meant larger cylinders, as capacity grew to 5,167 cc. With a genuine 455 horsepower in European tune, the Countach was again king of the top-speed hill—over 180 mph—though its status as "the world's fastest car" was shaky, usually due to mechanical difficulties with various cars tested, and endlessly debated by the automotive press.

Alas, American enthusiasts unwilling to deal with "gray market" importers missed out on the Countach from the

mid-Seventies through about 1982. This was, of course, a reflection of Lamborghini's difficulties in those years and its inability to keep pace with changing U.S. rules, something it hadn't planned to do with the Countach anyway. But the rules were relaxed during the Reagan years; and Sant'Agata's financial future looked decidedly brighter once Chrysler bought the place in 1987.

Lamborghini's 25th Anniversary as an automaker came in 1988, and the company marked the occasion with a special edition Countach—the final variation in the car's history. The 25th Anniversary Edition was at once noticeable by its exterior modifications. Straked air intakes, new exterior panels over the engine bay and gracefully integrated radiator units replaced various tacked-on scoops. This not only softened the Countach's shape, but helped cool the engine. While the engine remained unchanged, the interior of the Anniversary Edition also included refinements. Power seats and windows combined with more sound insulation to make the interior a more habitable place.

A number of other alterations occurred over the years, some good, some less so. There were useful, periodic detail revisions to the brakes and suspension. There were also patchwork solutions to U.S. safety standards: most depressingly, blocky black-rubber bumpers slapped on in the Eighties by an interim U.S. importer, then by Sant'Agata itself. Equipment was progressively upgraded; even air conditioning could be factory-installed by the time a fully certified Countach reached U.S. shores in 1988.

Compared to the '82 S, the federalized model packed 420 SAE net horses (against 325), did 0-60 mph in 5.2 seconds (versus 5.7), and reached 173 mph (compared to 150). Price naturally escalated along with performance: from "only" $52,000 in 1976 to near $120,000 a dozen years later.

And what did you get for it? A rocky ride, engine noise approaching 747 levels, a driving position only Plastic Man could comes to terms with, and controls only an Arnold Schwarzenegger could manipulate. But oh, that body and, oh, that go!

Author Lyons echoed the general consensus when he termed the Countach "absolutely useless for anything a citizen of America is allowed to do. It's guaranteed, therefore, to bring lust swelling up in your heart. It's the sort of object you long to possess for all the wrong reasons. . . . Yet when doing what it was built to do, the immense competence of the thing banishes all thoughts of everyday absurdities. . . . Driven the way Paolo Stanzani and [test engineer] Bob Wallace intended—hard and sharp, with spirit but with feeling—it is a marvelous ride: perhaps the most exciting one outside a race course."

One of the features of the Lambo's dash was a 200-mile-per-hour speedometer (320 kph).

The Countach predictably demanded, as Lyons observed, "certain skills from those who [would] master it. Not the least of these was decisiveness." Given that, the Countach would reward you with what British writer Doug Blain termed "perfection in performance and behavior." But woe be unto the timid, who could find it exhausting. "To be effective," said Blain, "you must get in there and boss the thing, using muscle but not force, urging it deeper and deeper into corners with little twitches of the wheel, banging the gears home, stomping on brake and clutch till you ache all over." But this was only part of the "no-wimps" mystique that grew up around the thing.

The Countach was undeniably hard-riding around town, yet Blain's colleague Mel Nichols found it "not uncomfortable, merely reassuring. At speed in bends this stiffness means that the car stays extraordinarily flat. It snaps around curves like an electric slot racer, answering the steering with lightning quick

response and precision and displaying a honed sharpness. . . . There is never any understeer, and only oversteer when you want it with power." So for all its bluster and bravado, and despite the inherent penalties of its 21st-Century looks, this was, in Nichols' view, a "purposeful car" you could drive "with an easy precision and a clear, relaxed mind." Amazing.

But while such contradictory views will also ever be part of the Countach mystique, one thing remains indisputable. As *Road & Track* put it, the Countach was "bigger than its performance figures, bigger than the sum of its automotive qualities. . . . The Countach's sole reason for existence is that somehow, according to some magic formula, it's bigger than life. The fact that after all these years that is still true, that this car still works the same soul-stopping spell on nearly everyone who sees it, is testament to the success of the Lamborghini concept and the original Bertone design. In fact, if you think it over, it's just a bit miraculous."

Like the car itself.

Specifications	
Engine:	V-12, dohc **LP400/LP400S** (1974-78/1978-82):239.8 cid/ 3,929 cc (3.23 x 2.44-in./ 82 x 62-mm), 375 bhp (DIN) @ 8,000 rpm, 286 lbs/ft torque @ 5,000 rpm **LP500S** (1982-85): 290.3 cid/4,754 cc (3.37 x 2.72-in./ 85.5 x 69-mm), 375 bhp (DIN) @ 7,000 rpm, 302 lbs/ft @ 4,500 rpm (U.S. version: 325 bhp [SAE net] @ 7,500 rpm, 260 lbs/ft @ 5,500 rpm, **LP5000S Quattrovalvole, 25th Anniv. Ed.** (1985-89): 315.3 cid/5,167 cc (3.37 x 2.95-in./85.5 x 75-mm), 455 bhp (DIN) @ 7,000 rpm, 369 lbs/ft @ 5,200 rpm (U.S. version: 420 bhp [SAE net] @ 7,000 rpm, 341 lbs/ft @ 5,000 rpm)
Transmission:	5-speed manual with rear transaxle
Suspension, front:	Independent, unequal-length A-arms, coil springs, tube shocks, anti-roll bar
Suspension, rear:	Independent, upper lateral links, lower A-arms, upper and lower trailing arms, dual coil springs, tube shocks, anti-roll bar
Brakes:	Hydraulic, front/rear discs
Wheelbase (in.):	96.5
Weight (lbs):	2,915-3,285
Top speed (mph):	173-192
0-60 mph (sec):	4.9-6.8
Production:	**LP400** 150 (1974-78) **LP400S** 235 (1978-82) **LP500S** 323 (1982-85) **LP5000S QV** 610 (1985-88) **25th Anniversary Edition** 650 (1988-90)

Cabin space wasn't a strong point of the Countach; outward vision was hampered by the super-sloped windshield, ultra low seats, and blind-quarter "tunnelback" roofline.

The midships Ferrari V-8s began with the 308 GTB in late 1975, but seen here as the later Quattrovalvole model. Styling was by Pininfarina: taut and muscular, yet smooth and sensuous. The functional concave scoop on the sides was a design element destined for future Ferraris. The 308 retained the fiberglass cockpit "tub" first used on the big Daytona.

The midships V-8 Ferraris beginning with the 308 GTB of late 1975 would be on anyone's "great cars" list if only for being Ferraris. But they also merit inclusion as the most popular products in Maranello history. They're certainly among the most recognized cars in the world, thanks to stunning Pininfarina styling that still receives wide exposure on TV's *Magnum P.I.* Then too, this series includes an exciting spinoff in the race-and-ride mold of the famed early-Sixties 250 GTO. Today's 348tb picks up where the interim 328 models left off and carries this thoroughbred line proudly into the Nineties.

The line had begun inauspiciously in late 1973 with the Dino 308 GT4, the belated replacement for the beloved 206/246 two-seaters. Though blessed with a similar chassis and a new V-8—a first for a production Ferrari—it was hooted not only for being a 2+2 but one of the least attractive Ferraris ever. Angular and ill-proportioned, the GT4 was one the few Maranello road cars not penned by Pininfarina, coming instead from the usually able house of Bertone. Actually, source was not the problem so much as the design's origins in a rejected Bertone prototype for the rival, just-introduced Lamborghini Urraco. Still, the GT4 would see a respectable 7,500 sales over a seven-year life span despite unfortunate styling and a plethora of shortcomings, including poor fuel economy and workmanship, wooden steering, and "+2" accommodation that was token at best.

Ferrari more than made amends with the 308 GTB, a two-seat, short-wheelbase derivative of the GT4 unveiled more than a year behind it (a delay never fully explained, by the way). Styling was by Pininfarina this time, and it was terrific: taut and muscular, yet smooth and sensuous. Even better, the form followed function, being refined in the wind tunnel for low drag and high-speed stability. And Maranello fans were pleased to note the Ferrari nameplates and prancing-horse insignia—no dubious heritage here.

A "flying buttress" roofline provided a visual link with the V-6 Dinos, but everything else was new, from sharply cut nose to crisply clipped "Kamm" tail. Spicing up the sides was a concave wedge leading to a functional scoop just ahead of and above each rear wheel, an element destined for future Ferraris. Overall, the GTB was thoroughly modern, yet not faddish in the least. The first few bodyshells were rendered mostly in fiberglass, the most extensive use of this material yet seen on a road-going Ferrari. Though finish was excellent, conventional steel construction took over very early in production; Ferrari customers just weren't accustomed to "plastic cars." However, all GTBs retained the fiberglass cockpit "tub" first used on the big Daytona.

As on the GT4, "308" denoted an all-aluminum, 90-degree, 3.0-liter V-8. In cylinder dimensions and several other respects, it was "two-thirds of the contemporary 365 V-12," as author Pete Lyons observed. Again transversely mounted ahead of the rear-axle centerline, it retained four overhead camshafts, but with drive by a toothed rubber belt instead of a chain. With a quartet of twin-choke Weber carburetors and 8.8:1 compression, initial rated horsepower was 205 at 6,600 rpm. Drive still passed from a single-plate clutch to a five-speed all-synchromesh transaxle, here with 4.06:1 gearing. Chassis specs were much like the 246's, right down to the wheelbase.

Unlike the GT4, the GTB met immediate critical acclaim. "Dino 246 fans... now have a worthy successor to their favorite car," wrote Paul Frere, "as the 308 GTB is even faster, quieter and more comfortable." Though understeer dominated handling, there was power enough to kick the tail out in tight corners, high-speed stability was superb, and additional wheel travel made ride uncommonly good. Performance was first-rate, Frere reporting 6.4 seconds for the 0-60-mph romp and 153.5 mph flat out. Alas, the emissions-tuned U.S. version was appreciably slower, with *Road & Track* clocking 9.4 seconds and 132 mph. Even so, *R&T* was impressed by the "balanced blend of styling, performance, comfort, ride and handling that few cars can match. [The GTB also provides] a blending of man and machine that makes the two feel and act like one. That's what makes [it] such a great car."

An open GTB was inevitable, and it duly appeared at the 1977 Frankfurt show as the 308 GTS, sporting a 246-style removable roof panel and louvered rear side windows. Meantime, Ferrari introduced debored 208 models for the Italian market, where taxes on engines over 2.0-liters made their cost prohibitive.

The next big development occurred in 1981, when Bosch K-Jetronic fuel injection replaced carburetors for emission-prompted driveability reasons, and an "i" was added to model names. *R&T* thought the letter also meant "improved," as the magazine's U.S. GTSi ran 0-60 mph in 7.9 seconds and topped 145 mph. (Simultaneously, the 208 received a KKK turbocharger to go from 170 to 220 bhp). The following year brought

The 308/328/348 were all powered by an all-aluminum 90-degree V-8. Over time, horsepower ranged from 205 to 394, and a four-valves-per-cylinder layout was adopted along the way. The 328 GTS (*below*) ran with an enlarged 3,185-cc V-8, and could thunder from 0-60 mph in under six seconds.

a revised *Quattrovalvole* V-8 with four valves per cylinder and 240 bhp, 10 bhp less in America. Accompanying this was a styling update comprising a small lip spoiler at the aft roof edge, transverse hood louvers, and body-color bumpers (replacing black and integrated with the lower body).

Reflecting the production discipline imposed by parent Fiat, Ferrari was by now evolving its cars with almost Porsche-like regularity. New proof arrived in 1985 with the 328 GTB/GTS, sporting a 3,185-cc V-8 with increased power and torque. Fuel injection was retained, but the Marelli Digiplex electronic ignition was switched to the new Multiplex system, said to be more versatile. At the same time, the wheelbase was lengthened a token 0.4-inch. Performance was better than ever, with *Car and Driver* reporting 5.6 seconds

0-60 and a 153-mph maximum. So was the interior: handsomely reworked to correct the 308's messy ergonomics. Though *C/D* judged its test GTS a bit too flexible on bumpy roads, and more prone to lift-throttle oversteer than 308s, one editor declared that the 328 "deserves to wear its prancing horse as proudly as the best of the 12-cylinder cars"—high praise indeed.

Somewhat overshadowing the 328's debut was the 1984 announcement of a new GTO—not a reissue of the hallowed original, but a very special derivative of the 308/328 GTB. Though broadly similar in appearance and chassis specs, this 288 GTO rode a new 96.5-inch wheelbase necessitated by an engine reoriented to longitudinal. The four-cam V-8 itself was considerably different: resized to 2,855 cc and sporting twin turbos, each with an intercooler giving

a denser air charge for mixing with fuel from Weber-Marelli port-electronic injection. Rated horsepower was a smashing 394, delivered by a twin-disc clutch to the usual five-speed transaxle. Long-legged 2.90:1 final gearing gave a verified maximum of 190 mph, and *Road & Track* timed 0-60 mph at a blistering five seconds flat, the standing quarter-mile in a sizzling 14.1 at 113 mph.

The 288's primary mission was FISA Group B, which specified a minimum production run of 200 units. Ferrari built that many, but no more. As a competition car, this GTO was never certified for the U.S., though a few inevitably found their way in via the infamous "gray market." All were fully equipped for road use, and a package option delivered air conditioning, AM/FM/cassette stereo, and electric windows for $1,800, which was steep only if you blanched at the $83,400 sticker price.

Though Group B ended almost before it began, the 288's racing-inspired, "instant collectible" aura rubbed off on its production sisters. That was one reason their platform was used as its starting point, though cost and time constraints were the main ones. But the 288 was more significant for influencing the next iteration of the roadgoing V-8 Ferrari, the 348tb of 1990.

Styled along the husky lines of the mighty, contemporary flat-12 Testarossa, the 348 had a GTO-type wheelbase and longitudinal powerplant, but deployed its transaxle crosswise, beneath the engine, to lower drivetrain mass and thus the center of gravity. Another twin-plate clutch transferred power through shafts and bevel gears to a differential at the extreme rear. Displacement was up, as the model number indicated. Thanks to a more sophisticated Bosch Motronic engine management system and new two-stage intake

The 348, here a '91 tb, boasted updated styling more akin to the 12-cylinder Testarossa and an even larger 3,405-cc V-8. The 0-60-mph sprint now took just 5.4 seconds.

manifolding, output was up too: by almost 30 bhp over the U.S. 328 and to 296 total bhp in non-catalyst form.

Car and Driver judged the 348 a great success. Not only faster than a 328 — Ferrari claimed 5.4 seconds 0-60, 171 mph all-out — it could keep up with a Testarossa on the track, yet was "perfectly content if, for some reason, you choose to putter about in high gear at low speeds." *C/D* also reported "plenty of grip. . . . [D]riven carefully, mild understeer will signal the limit of adhesion. But you can cause the tail to step out smartly in a hard corner by either applying or lifting the throttle. Once the tail's out, keeping it there becomes a simple matter of planting your right foot. [But be] aware that the car is a challenge to keep under control. Overdo things and you'll need quick reflexes and plenty of muscle to twirl the high-effort, arms-out steering wheel rapidly enough."

But it has ever been thus with Ferraris, which is why even these "little ones" will always be desired over machines of lesser breeding and character. There's no substitute for experience, and Ferrari has been building superlative sports/GT cars for over 40 years now. Enzo Ferrari left us in 1988, but his legacy is in caring hands, and his great work

will continue well into the 21st Century — a heartening prospect indeed for all all who cherish his matchless automobiles.

Specifications	
Engine:	V-8, dohc **308 GTB/GTS** (1975-80): 179 cid/2,927 cc (3.19 x 2.79-in/81 x 71-mm bore x stroke), 205-255 bhp @ 6,600-7,700 rpm[1], 181 lbs/ft torque @ 5,000 rpm **308 GTBi/GTSi** (1981-82): see 308 **308 GTB/GTS Quattrovalvole** (1982-84): 230/240 bhp @ 6,800 rpm[1], 188 lbs/ft @ 5,500 rpm **328 GTB/GTS** (1975-89): 194.4 cid/ 3,185 cc (3.27 x 2.90-in./83 x 73.6-mm), 260/270 bhp @ 7,000 rpm[1], 213/224 lbs/ft @ 5,500[1] rpm **348 tb** (1990-date): 208 cid/3,405 cc (3.35 x 2.95-in./85 x-75-mm), 296/288 bhp @ 7,200 rpm[1], 238 lbs/ft @ 4,200 rpm **288 GTO** (1984): 174.2 cid/2,855 cc (3.15 x 2.80-in./80 x 71-mm), 394 bhp @ 7,000 rpm, 366 lbs/ft @ 3,800 rpm
Transmission:	5-speed manual in rear transaxle
Suspension, front:	Independent, unequal-length A-arms, coil springs, tube shocks, anti-roll bar
Suspension, rear:	Independent, unequal-length A-arms, coil springs, tube shocks, anti-roll bar
Brakes:	Hydraulic, front/rear discs
Wheelbase (in.):	308s 92.1 328 92.5 348, GTO 96.5
Weight (lbs):	2,555-3,350
0-60 mph (sec):	5.0-9.5
Top speed (mph):	130-190
Production:	308 (1975-80): 3,665 (incl. 208) 308i NA **308** QV NA **328** NA **348** continues at this writing **288 GTO** 200

[1]Variously quoted within this range depending on year and engine tune.

The first-generation Mazda RX-7 changed only in detail from 1978-85; it is seen here in its mildly updated 1981-85 guise. The RX-7 was powered by a 70- or 80-cid rotary engine good for 100 or 135 bhp. Initially, prices started at $6,995, making it a bargain, so sales were brisk.

Three significant qualities mark the first-generation Mazda RX-7 as a great car of the 20th Century. First, it almost single-handedly kept the Wankel rotary engine alive. Second, to the delight of enthusiasts everywhere, it was the first truly affordable sports car since the Datsun 240Z took the world by storm in 1970. Last but not least, the RX-7 was simply a terrific sports car.

Toyo Kogyo, as Mazda was known in the Seventies, had taken up the rotary-engine cause from Dr. Felix Wankel in Germany, via a licensing agreement. The firm then set about doing what Wankel and his cohorts at NSU apparently couldn't: making the thing both durable and reliable. Mazda's main work centered on the vulnerable apex seals of the engine's main moving part, its epitrochoidal rotor. Those seals, which had been a principal downfall of NSU's own Ro80, were switched from a special carbon material, which was relatively soft and hence short-lived, to a sturdier iron-based metal.

But as we in the West were coming to learn as typical of the Japanese, Mazda made many other improvements, too. Among them: a rotor housing whose face was made of die-cast aluminum-alloy bonded to the metal; pinpoint porous chrome plating on the rotor (for better oil adhesion and hence wear); gas-nitriding for the housing's inner contact surfaces (same reasons); and uprated oiling capacity. Because the engine used a small amount of oil for internal lubrication, oil consumption remained high relative to piston engines (about 1,500-2,000 miles per quart), so Mazda fitted an oil-level sensor with a warning light.

Alas, the Wankel's fuel consumption also remained relatively high—or so it seemed in the otherwise bog-ordinary sedans where Mazda first chose to offer it. Which is precisely why the rotary almost sent TK the way of NSU. The problem was basically one of image. Though more powerful than piston engines of the same nominal displacement, the rotary wasn't—and still isn't—as thrifty. But this distinction was lost on consumers in the panic of the first Energy Crisis. Americans, especially, saw the rotary-powered RX-2 and RX-3 as "economy cars," judged them too fuelish, and quit buying. By 1975, Mazda was on its knees, retreating from rotaries, and relying more on piston-engine cars like the simple little 323/GLC.

But Kenichi Yamamoto, the rotary's patron saint in Hiroshima (and destined to be Mazda president), kept the faith. If the rotary was confusing in sedans, why not limit it to sports cars? There was even a precedent. Eight years after the Wankel surfaced in Germany, Mazda began building the Cosmo 110S sport coupe (previewed at the '64 Tokyo show), which garnered much press, if not many sales, between 1967 and '72. Market research provided further impetus by showing strong demand, especially in the U.S., for a reasonably priced rotary sports car.

Both the floor and lift-over height were high, but there was space for luggage for two under the rear hatch. For large people, the cabin was a bit cramped.

All this came together in Project X605, initiated in 1974 and completed by late '76. The result, designated RX-7 (following the large RX-4 sedans and a new Cosmo coupe called RX-5) went on sale in Japan in early 1978 and reached U.S. shores that May.

Engine apart, the RX-7 was conventional, but thoroughly modern. A small hatchback coupe with the expected unitized body/chassis, it rode an all-coil suspension with front MacPherson struts and a live rear axle securely located by trailing arms and a Watt linkage. Steering was recirculating-ball (and exclusively manual through 1983), brakes vacuum-assisted front discs and rear drums. Styling was orthodox, too, mixing elements of several other contemporary sports cars without looking like any one of them—except maybe around the nose, which evoked thoughts of Porsche's 924. The 95.3-inch wheelbase limited seating to two Americans, though laughably small "+2" rear seats were offered in Japan and Europe.

Mazda's then-current twin-rotor engine, the 12A, derived from the earlier RX-3 unit, was small enough to sit behind the front-wheel centerline, making the RX-7 a "front/mid-engine" car *a la* the 240Z and Chevrolet Corvette—and with the same fine fore/aft weight balance (initially 53/47 percent). As ever, the Mazda Wankel packed a lot of power

for its size: 100 bhp in U.S. form from just 1,146-cc nominal displacement. But also as ever, it was weak on torque, especially at low rpm, which is why the RX-7's standard four-speed and optional five-speed overdrive manual transmissions were overwhelmingly preferred to the optional three-speed automatic initially offered. Besides, what self-respecting sports car "nut" would be caught with a self-shifter?

But purist or *poseur*, nobody minded the RX-7's long list of standard amenities.

These ran to the relative sports-car luxuries of full carpeting, AM/FM stereo radio with electric antenna, an electric rear-window defroster, quartz clock, and tinted glass, plus flip-up headlamps and decent, if not generously sized, tires (initially 165HR-13s). And that was the base S model. An additional $500 put you into a GS version with the five-speed transmission standard, plus beefier tires (185/70s), rear anti-roll bar, padded steering wheel, and nicer cabin appointments. Factory options were few, but

encompassed the obligatory air conditioning plus a nifty tilt/takeout manual sunroof (later made standard on some models), and a Porsche-style "ducktail" spoiler encircling the hatch. Who said sports-car ownership dictated a spartan existence?

With all this, the RX-7 was, as they say, greeted with enthusiasm. Zesty, nimble, and solidly built, it was long on fun, yet quite practical for a sports car. Even better, events soon proved it boringly reliable—especially the engine, thus easing many consumers' fears. And at an initial U.S. POE price of just $6,995, it was a sensational value. Indeed, one U.S. magazine judged the RX-7 "a major breakthrough for the enthusiast."

Not that it was perfect, of course. The ride was a bit stiff, the cabin cramped for larger folks (especially in headroom), cornering could be a tail-happy exercise on bumpy surfaces or in the wet, and maintaining momentum sometimes dictated keeping the rev-happy rotary in the upper reaches of the rpm band, an unfamiliar drill for Americans weaned on big, lazy, high-torque V-8s. But these things were hardly major flaws, and the RX-7 sold like hot cakes.

It continued to do so for the next six years despite an often difficult market. Most annual changes were of the evolutionary sort. Transistorized ignition and a larger brake booster improved the '79s, while 1981 brought a revised dash, tidier nose, full-width taillight ensemble, a larger fuel tank, and more efficient emissions-control measures, such as a catalytic converter to replace the relatively crude thermal reactor that often produced unwanted backfiring in earlier Mazda rotaries. That same year, the existing S and GS models were joined by a new top-line offering called GSL, with standard rear-disc brakes, limited-slip differential, alloy wheels, and power windows, plus optional leather upholstery. Responding to demands for more power, Mazda brought over a larger 13B engine for an even plusher 1984 entry, the GSL-SE, packing 135 bhp, more generous low-end torque and, by most accounts, sub-8.0-second 0-60 acceleration. At the same time, rear control arms were relocated on all

The rotary engine in the RX-7 established a good record for reliability. Its major weakness—at least to some people—was that it had to be revved to keep the car moving briskly because torque was weak at lower rpm.

RX-7s, and power steering with speed-variable assist was offered optionally for the GSL-SE.

Unfortunately, American inflation and an appreciating yen had pushed top-line RX-7 prices beyond $15,000 by then, so this budget sports car no longer fit into as many budgets as before. But there was still nothing that could touch the RX-7 for anywhere close to the money; most rivals, in fact, cost considerably more.

To no one's great surprise, RX-7s went went racing around the world in a big way. In America they dominated the GTU class (GTs under 2.0 liters) in IMSA (International Motor Sports Association) endurance events, then started challenging Corvettes and Porsches in GTO. RX-7s also did well in rallying, ran with distinction in SCCA (Sports Car Club of America) races, and even set a few speed records at Bonneville. Reflecting these exploits as well as a burgeoning owner body was the growing number of aftermarket companies that catered to RX-7s with a plethora of "go-faster" parts and accessories—everything from special shock absorbers to flashy wheels, tune-up kits to custom-tailored nose guards.

But time and changing tastes wait for no car, and the RX-7's huge success inevitably prompted competitors. So although sales remained healthy all along, Mazda knew as early as 1981 that the RX-7 would have to be changed. It was, for 1986, and improved in many ways, but this second-generation model

wouldn't be nearly so popular, perhaps because it was bigger, heavier, and less "light-footed" as a result—and more derivative in appearance.

A pity, that, because the original RX-7 had not just advanced the rotary engine at a time when the concept was being abandoned everywhere else, it advanced the state of the sports-car art without losing the essential, timeless sports-car magic. As *Car and Driver* put it in 1984, the RX-7 "sings an irresistible song, begging to be revved to its redline and thrown into corners. . . . [I]t communicates the joys of the sports-car experience to its driver." If that doesn't define a great car, what does?

Specifications	
Engine:	2-rotor Wankel, 70 cid/1,146 cc, 100 bhp @ 6,000 rpm, 105 lbs/ft torque @ 4,000 rpm **GSL-SE** (1984-85): 80 cid/1,308 cc, 135 bhp @ 6,000 rpm, 133 lbs/ft @ 2,750 rpm
Transmission:	4-speed manual, 5-speed overdrive manual, 3-speed automatic, 4-speed automatic
Suspension, front:	Independent, MacPherson struts, lower lateral links, compliance struts, coil springs, tube shocks, anti-roll bar
Suspension, rear:	Live axle on lower trailing links, upper angled links, Watt linkage, coil springs, anti-roll bar
Brakes:	Hydraulic, front disc/rear drum **GSL/GSL-SE** 4-wheel disc
Wheelbase (in.):	95.3
Weight (lbs):	2,440-2,640
0-60 mph (sec):	7.8-9.7
Top speed (mph):	115-125
Production:	1978 72,692 1979 71,617 **1980** 56,317 1981 59,686 1982 59,686 1983 57,864 1984 63,959 1985 63,105

Greatness comes in all shapes and sizes, and it is both shape *and* size, plus extraordinary popularity, that qualify Chrysler's late-Eighties Dodge Caravan/Plymouth Voyager minivans for inclusion in this book. Arriving in the wake of a second world fuel shortage, these T-115s—Chrysler's internal designation—were an instant sellout that kept right on selling, appealing strongly to cost-conscious commercial users, diehard "vanatics" grown weary of full-size vans, and families seeking a more practical alternative to the conventional station wagon. Deliveries topped a million units within three years and two-million within six, a key factor in helping transform a moribund, me-too producer into a prosperous Detroit innovator.

Though hailed as revolutionary, the T-115 was not a wholly new idea. Germany's Volkswagen had sold a compact, Beetle-based van, the Type 2 Microbus, since the mid-Fifties; Chevrolet offered slightly larger copies in 1961-65 Corvair models; and Ford's first Econoline, a contemporary front-engine reply to the rear-engine Chevys, was another "cab-forward" design of similar size to the eventual T-wagons. What set the Chrysler products apart were their front-wheel-drive configuration—a world first—plus many car-like qualities that made them far more pleasant than previous small vans.

Those qualities weren't surprising, because the Caravan/Voyager was also derived from a car: Chrysler's new-for-1981 K-body. That do-or-die compact was midwifed by chairman Lee Iacocca, the legendary, lately fired president of Ford Motor Company who'd fathered the enormously popular Mustang. Intriguingly, Dearborn had developed a "garagable" van under his aegis in the early Seventies, only to abandon it at the mock-up stage when planners decided the market wasn't ready yet. Iacocca remembered this idea when he shocked the industry by riding off to rescue Chrysler in 1978, but Highland Park barely had enough money then to bring out the K-car, let alone a minivan. So although the T-115 was locked up and production-approved within two years of Iacocca's arrival, the whopping investment for requisite tooling delayed it until 1984, by which time encouraging K-car sales had provided the necessary funds.

Most of the ultimate $660-million expenditure went toward new automated equipment for the firm's Windsor, Ontario plant. It would prove to be money well spent. Indeed, initial sales projections proved grossly conservative, and Windsor couldn't keep up with demand. For Iacocca and the many colleagues he'd lured over from Ford, the T-115 was Mustang *redux*.

The T-115 was basically a "tall-boy" version of the familiar K-car wagon, sharing its space-efficient transverse powertrain but measuring 11 inches taller and some 1.5 inches wider, though no longer

The difference between the '84 Plymouth Voyager (and Dodge Caravan) and other vans was front-wheel drive and more car-like handling.

For 1987 the front-end styling of the Dodge Caravan was altered to include "aero" headlights. Also new that year was a stretched version with a seven-inch-longer wheelbase and 14.6-inch increase in overall length, which expanded cargo volume to 155 cubic feet. Also new was a 3.0-liter V-6 option.

overall despite a foot-longer wheelbase. The one other big departure was rear leaf springs instead of coils to cope with heavier loads than K-wagons could manage. Against the smallest full-size Dodge van, the T-115 at 175.9 inches overall was just three inches shorter, but a significant 15 inches lower and nearly 10 inches slimmer. Like a van, it had a sliding right-rear door, two front doors, and a rear door, in this case a lift-up tailgate. Unlike a van, it was rather attractive, shaped by the capable Roy Axe, later chief designer for Britain's Rover Group. Careful attention to aerodynamic details produced an unusually low drag coefficient for a van— 0.43—and the basic K-car chassis provided step-in height just fractionally more than the passenger car's.

Grilles and minor trim differences apart, the Caravan and Voyager "consumer" models were identical, right down to price. Trim levels would always comprise base, SE (Special Edition), and LE (Luxury Edition), the last distinguished by pseudo-wood side paneling. Five-passenger seating was standard: two in front, three on a bench directly behind; a seven-place package was optional. Effectively, the T-115s replaced the smaller full-size window vans Dodge and Plymouth had been selling. There was also a Dodge commercial version called the Mini Ram through 1987, after which it became known as the Caravan "C/V"; as expected, the interior was stripped and it had no side windows behind the doors. For a time, Dodge pitched the recreational market with a ready-to-customize offering with full headliner and carpeting.

Passenger T-wagons evidenced numerous thoughtful interior touches. Both second and third seats were easily removed via quick-release clamps. Meanwhile, seven-seaters came with a second set of floor slots so that the wider, three-person hindmost bench could be moved up in place of the two-person middle seat. Also for enhanced cargo-carrying, the third-seat backrest could be folded down and pushed forward, while the spare tire was mounted out of the way in a wind-down carrier on the vehicle's underside. Low-effort needle bearings made operating the side door fingertip easy. Side windows were nearly flush with the body, and forward-hinged for low wind noise when open. A clever option was remote operation of the rearmost side windows via handwheels near the rearview mirror.

Powertrains were proven fare: initially the 2.2-liter Chrysler "Trans-4" engine developed for the K-cars driving through a standard five-speed manual or optional three-speed TorqueFlite automatic. A torquier 2.6-liter four from Japanese partner Mitsubishi was optional, offered with automatic only. Unfortunately, the small four was really too small except for running without a load, and workmanship left much to be desired, as one CONSUMER GUIDE® editor confirmed on buying an '84 Caravan.

But the T-115 was definitely more car than truck, and impressive for ride, maneuverability, and overall driving ease. Its only real dynamic lapses were marked body roll (what else from a tall box?) and slight rear-end hop over fast humpbacks. Otherwise, only higher-than-normal seating said you were in something other than a car, and it was this as much as roomy versatility and front-drive traction that would keep T-wagons selling by the carload.

Of course, success inevitably breeds imitators in Detroit, so few were surprised when the similarly sized Chevy Astro bowed for 1985, followed by Ford's droop-snoot Aerostar for '86. But these were both rear-drivers, and far more truck-like than the garagable Chryslers. True, they offered greater towing ability with larger engines, but that was offset by poorer fuel economy. So few were surprised when this new

This '89 Dodge Caravan, the $13,987 LE short-wheelbase model, was optioned with the $1,469 ES decor package, which meant it had the 2.5-liter turbo four (150 bhp), seven passenger seating, 205/70R15 all season tires on alloy wheels, and unique exterior trim, including a "turbo" badge on each front fender.

The '91 Chrysler Town & Country was the "Cadillac" of minivans. For $23,905, the buyer received new interior and exterior styling, leather upholstery, and much more.

competition, and some later import challengers as well, failed to dent Chrysler's huge early lead in minivan sales—prompting Iacocca to boast in magazine ads: "Even when we showed them how, they didn't get the message."

Happily, Chrysler heeded the message about workmanship, though it took a few years. And there were other improvements that helped maintain the T-115's dominance (always 40 percent at least) in the market it had uncovered. A key 1987 development was companion "Grand" models with seven inches added to wheelbase, 14.6 inches to overall length, and 30 more cubic feet of interior volume (155 total). Accompanying this was a Trans-4 enlarged to 2.5 liters and a smooth new Mitsubishi V-6 to replace the rough-and-ready 2.6 four. All models were spruced up with flush headlamps and revised grilles.

For 1988, the V-6 became standard for Grand LEs, while the 2.5 was base power elsewhere. Grands were also treated to a new 4,000-pound trailering option. A sporty new ES decor group for Caravans was matched by a plush LX package for Voyagers. The following year brought an optional turbocharged 2.5 that gave more snap, though in a herky-jerky manner quite inappropriate for a family vehicle. More useful was Chrysler's new four-speed "Ultradrive"

automatic for V-6 models, plus a front suspension modestly reworked for a smoother ride, optional leather interior, and standard air conditioning for LEs. Alas, prices were hiked a substantial $3,000.

The minivan was moved even more upmarket for 1990 with the introduction of a Chrysler version bearing the hallowed Town & Country name: a long-wheelbase seven-seater with the traditional woody-look side trim, leather interior, full-house equipment, and a $25,000 window sticker. But included also was a new Chrysler-built 3.3-liter V-6 teamed with the four-speed automatic, a powertrain newly standard for Grand Caravan/Voyager. Other improvements included fuel tanks enlarged by five gallons (to 20), higher-capacity air conditioner, and standard seven-passenger seating for shorty LEs.

By this time, the new-car market had again turned difficult, forcing Chrysler to offer its first rebates on minivans. Nonetheless, the T-wagons marched into 1991 with their most sweeping revisions yet, most of them for the better. Though unchanged in size or basic appearance, they looked better thanks to all-new exterior panels (save the roof) that also increased glass area for a better look out. Interiors were updated, too, with new seats and a more modern "ergono-

mic" dashboard. Mechanical news began with the automatic transmission being made standard across the board and the first-time availability of anti-lock brakes (standard for the T&C, optional elsewhere with the 3.3 V-6, and available on shorty SEs and LEs shortly afterward). Further, Chrysler added a full-time four-wheel-drive Caravan/Voyager option (also tied to the 3.3). Even more praiseworthy was Chrysler's installation of driver's-side airbags beginning with mid-1991 production, the first minivans to be equipped with this valuable latter-day safety device.

All told, the T-115s stand as a timely idea that has, at least so far, stood the test of time—one of the few instances in living memory where Chrysler has led the industry instead of following it. Of course, one home run does not necessarily win the ball game, and at this writing Chrysler's future is decidedly cloudy once more. But regardless of its long-term fate, the firm would surely not have survived the Eighties so well without these likeable do-everything minivans, and that's something to celebrate.

Specifications	
Engine:	**1984-87:** I-4, sohc, 135 cid/2.2 liters (3.44 x 3.62-in./87.3 x 91.9-mm bore x stroke), 101 bhp @ 5,600 rpm **1984-87:** I-4, sohc, 156 cid/2.6 liters (3.59 x 3.86-in./91.2 x 98.0-mm), 104 bhp @ 4,800 rpm **1987-1991:** I-4, sohc, 153 cid/2.5 liters (3.44 x 4.09-in./87.3 x 103.9-mm), 100 bhp @ 4,800 rpm **1989-90:** I-4, sohc, 153 cid/2.5 liters (3.44 x 4.09-in./87.3 x 103.9-mm), turbocharged, 150 bhp @ 4,800 rpm **1987-1991:** V-6, sohc, 181.4 cid/3.0 liters (3.59 x 2.99-in./91.2 x 75.9-mm), 141 bhp @ 5,000 rpm **1990-1991:** V-6, ohv, 201.5 cid/3.3 liters (3.66 x 3.19-in./93.0 x 81.0-mm), 150 bhp @ 4,800 rpm
Transmission:	5-speed overdrive manual, 3-speed automatic, 4-speed automatic
Suspension, front:	Independent, MacPherson struts, lower A-arms, coil springs, tube shocks, anti-roll bar
Suspension, rear:	Beam axle on parallel leaf springs, trailing arms, tube shocks
Brakes:	Hydraulic, front disc/rear drum
Wheelbase (in.):	112.3 **Grand** 119.3
Overall length (in.):	175.9 **Grand** 190.5
Weight (lbs):	2,911-3,800
0-60 mph (sec):	11.0-14.0
Top speed (mph):	94-98
Production:	2,000,000 built by 1990

Motor Trend called the '86 Porsche 959 "the fastest, most technologically advanced sports car in history." What else needs to be said?

nthusiasts have always dreamed of the "everything" car, the one that has it all. The Porsche 959 was that dream come true, and more. *Motor Trend* magazine rightly called it "the fastest, most technologically advanced sports car in history." Said *Car and Driver*: "The 959 can accomplish almost any automotive mission so well that to call it perfect is the mildest of overstatements."

But like many "dream cars," the 959 proved something of a nightmare for its maker and would-be owners. In fact, the furor it created is a story in itself. But more of that anon.

The 959's progenitor was the fully finished and evidently producible "*Gruppe B*" prototype unveiled at the 1983 Frankfurt Auto Show as Porsche's entry in the new Group B series for factory-experimental racers. Two years later, also at Frankfurt, Porsche announced that 200 production versions, designated 959, would be built to meet series homologation requirements. All were spoken for within weeks despite a price of about 225,000 U.S. dollars. Still, Porsche lost a bundle on every one, as actual unit cost was estimated at a cool $530,000.

That was evident from even a cursory glance at the specifications sheet. Though based on the contemporary 911 Carrera, with the same wheelbase and a similar steel central structure, the 959 was a very different rear-engine Porsche. Distinctions began with a lower body reshaped for good surface aerodynamics, and with a profusion of ducts and vents for controlled airflow *through* it. The distinctions ran beneath it, too, as a bellypan covered the entire underside save the engine. Dominating all was a muscular, ultra-wide tail topped by a large loop spoiler. The results: a drag coefficient of 0.31 (creditable if not startlingly low) and—the real achievement—*zero* lift. To save weight, doors and front lid were rendered in aluminum, the nose cap in polyurethane, the remainder in fiberglass-reinforced Kevlar.

Rolling stock was equally striking: beautiful five-spoke, 17-inch alloy wheels wearing low-profile Bridgestone RE71 tires developed especially for the 959 and chosen over a Dunlop design—which raised eyebrows, as Porsche had not previously sanctioned Japanese rubber. The tires were sized 235/45 fore and 255/40 aft, but were only V-rated, meaning for speeds up to 149 mph—curious, as the 959's claimed maximum was some 40 mph higher. Hollow wheel spokes, first used on Porsche's 1980 Le Mans racers, provided more air for the tires and a smoother ride than was otherwise possible. There was no spare, not because of the size differential but because the tires were designed to run flat for some 50 miles after a blowout. Another innovation was electronic sensors within the wheels to warn of pressure loss.

The soul of any Porsche is its engine, and the 959's was a masterpiece: a short-stroke version of the then-current 3.3-liter 911 flat-six with twin overhead cams per bank, four valves per cylinder, water-cooled heads (air cooling continued for the block), low-mass titanium con rods, and twin KKK turbochargers. Crossover pipes and bypass valves afforded "sequential turbocharging." Only the port blower was active below 4,000 rpm; the starboard unit progressively phased in as exhaust-gas flow increased toward 4,000, thus marrying low-speed tractability with top-end power. Despite modest 8.3:1 compression, DIN horsepower was a heady 450.

Putting it to the ground was a unique full-time four-wheel-drive system with a *six*-speed gearbox. This was basically the five-speed Carrera unit with an extra-low first gear, ostensibly for off-road use—and marked "G" for *Gelande*, or terrain). Power was taken aft in the usual way. Drive forward was via a tube-encased shaft running from the gearbox to a differential employing a multi-plate clutch in an oil-filled chamber. Varying clutch oil pressure determined the amount of front torque delivered, so no center differential was required, though a locking rear differential was provided.

Torque apportioning was accomplished from a steering-column stalk that selected one of four computer programs or full automatic mode. "Traction" locked the front clutch and rear diff for maximum pull in mud and snow. "Ice" split torque 50/50 front rear, while "Wet" provided a static 40/60 distribution that progressively increased to the rear on acceleration. "Dry" also offered a static 40/60 split, but could vary that up to 20/80 in all-out acceleration. All this was accomplished via the Bosch Motronic engine management computer in conjunction with the wheel-mounted speed sensors of the standard anti-lock braking system, the latter developed in conjunction with WABCO-Westinghouse. Electronics apart, the brakes were 911 Turbo with larger front discs.

Departing from 911 tradition, but prefiguring the 1990 Carrera 2 and 4, the 959 suspension featured double wishbones all-round, plus twin shock absorbers and concentric coil springs at each wheel. The shocks in each pair were assigned separate damping roles,

both computer-controlled according to vehicle speed. The driver had a choice of soft, firm, and automatic settings. Also chip-managed was a novel, hydraulic ride-height system offering three degrees of ground clearance—4.7, 5.9, and 7.1 inches—plus automatic lowering as needed from about 95 mph up for improved fuel consumption and aerodynamic stability.

The 959 was offered in two forms. First was the "Comfort" model with air conditioning, electric front seats and windows, 911-type rear seats, and the ride-height control. The second offering was a "Sport" version that deleted these items, and thus weighed 110-130 pounds less. Though the Sport was the 959 given most journalists to try—doubtless because it was just that little bit faster (carrying 6.1 lbs/bhp versus 7.1)—the differences in performance proved slight.

Not that it mattered much. As *Car and Driver* reported: "With rocket-sled acceleration and the highest top speed we've ever measured, the 959 stands alone at the pinnacle of production-car performance. If that sounds like hyperbole, how does a 0-to-60-mph time of 3.6 seconds strike you? Or 100 mph from rest in a mere 8.8 seconds[?] . . . .

The 959 devours the standing quarter-mile in twelve seconds flat, with a terminal speed of 116 mph." Top speed? With boring regularity, *CD* and others confirmed the factory's claim: no less than 195 mph.

Just as impressive, the 959 was as docile in town as any 911, at least as quiet, and so stable on the highway that 100 mph felt more like 60, even in driving rain. In corners, it was simply a revelation. Observed British writer Mel Nichols: "At different times, I lifted off when near maximum power, and all the car did was tighten its line neatly at the front. There was no way that tail—so deadly in these circumstances in a 911—was going to come around. . . . What I liked was the clarity and accessibility of the handling that went with it." A virtual absence of body roll helped immeasurably, as did the twin-turbo engine's smooth, seamless, but relentless power delivery, though Phil Bingham reported an "explosion" of thrust once the second blower cut in.

But life at the pinnacle is often difficult, as so it was with the 959. Troubles with the drive system and anti-lock brakes, plus Porsche's insistence that this stupefyingly complex supercar be

The 959 used the central structure of the 911 Carrera, but it featured a lower body reshaped for good aerodynamics and a muscular, ultra-wide tail with a large loop spoiler.

A profusion of ducts and vents saw to it that airflow was controlled *through* the 959, just as the body shape made sure the air flowed *over* it. The result was a coefficient of drag of 0.31 and zero lift—all of which made the 959 extremely stable at its top speed, which approached 200 miles per hour.

absolutely right, delayed initial deliveries by over a year. Dr. Wolfgang Porsche, youngest son of the firm's founder, got the first one in April 1987, by which time it was clear that the run wouldn't be completed for another year still. One reason was painstakingly slow assembly. Because the 959 was far too involved for Porsche's usual methods, a small shop was set up to build the cars virtually by hand from numerous custom-fabricated components.

Meantime, rich-and-famous folk everywhere scrambled to be among the few chosen for 959 ownership. Tennis star Boris Becker was refused (too young and inexperienced, Porsche said), but not Martina Navratilova, Indy 500 winner Danny Sullivan, actor Don Johnson, and conductor Herbert von Karajan. But money alone was not enough. To qualify, you had to be a Porsche owner already and promise not to sell your 959 for at least six months. You also had to be willing to travel: sales and service were handled only from the Stuttgart factory.

You were out of luck entirely if you lived in America and wanted to drive on public roads. Porsche reneged on its promise to certify 959s for federal safety

and emissions standards, and a later plan to sell 26 of them as "racers" through driver/dealer Al Holbert was stymied by Holbert's untimely death in 1988. So even the wealthiest and most influential Americans could still only dream of owning this engineering triumph, the car that had won the gruelling Paris-Dakar rally not once but twice (1984 and '86, in competition 961 trim).

Some may eventually get the chance, but not many. Though the exact total is in dispute, production came to only some 230, including development prototypes and racing 961s.

Which will only keep the dreams burning bright. As Mel Nichols concluded: "No car has ever affected me as deeply as [the 959]. Its performance alone makes it more thrilling than any other car I have driven, but I love it most because it gave so much and asked for so little. . . . That is Porsche's achievement. It has built a racing car for road drivers. . . . As magnificent as that achievement is, the good news is that . . . other Porsches will gain the 959's technology and degrees of its prowess." And so it would be with 1990's new Carrera 4, essentially a simplified 959 at a far more realistic price.

Nevertheless, the 959 will forever be cherished as that seemingly impossible "everything" automobile. As *Car and Driver* observed: "It is to the ordinary car what the F-15 is to a hang glider. We cannot, in the final analysis, call it perfect. But if you want to call [it] the best car in the world, you will get no argument from us."

Specifications	
Engine:	Flat-six, dohc, 174 cid/2,849 cc (3.74 x 2.64-in./95.0 x 67.0-mm bore x stroke), 4 valves per cylinder, dual turbochargers, 450 bhp (DIN) @ 6,500 rpm, 369 lbs/ft torque @ 5,500 rpm
Transmission:	Full-time 4-wheel drive via a 6-speed manual transmission to front differential and rear transaxle
Suspension, front:	Independent, unequal-length upper and lower A-arms, coil springs, dual tube shocks, anti-roll bar
Suspension, rear:	Independent, unequal-length upper and lower A-arms, coil springs, dual tube shocks, anti-roll bar
Brakes:	Hydraulic, front/rear discs with anti-lock control
Wheelbase (in.):	89.4
Weight (lbs):	**Comfort** 2,977 **Sport** 3,088
0-60 mph (sec):	3.6-3.8
Top speed (mph):	195+
Production:	approx. 230, incl. prototypes and Type 961 competition models

Ferrari SEFAC (*Societa per azioni Escerizio Fabbriche Automobili e Corse*) turned a middle-aged 40 in 1987. Enzo Ferrari, the firm's legendary founder—indeed, its very soul—was in his 89th year. On July 21, as he'd done so many times before, Mr. Ferrari presented his latest Ferrari. Simply called F40, apropos of the anniversary, it was a glorious thing for him to give the world: a snarling, no-compromises race-and-ride sports car in the hallowed tradition of the original GTO. Sadly, it would be the last new car Mr. Ferrari would introduce. A little more than a year later, on August 14, 1988, *Il Commendatore* was dead.

He had told the world press assembled in Maranello that July day that the F40 had been born barely a year before. On June 6, 1986, "I expressed a wish to our executive committee to have a car reminiscent of the original 250 LM. [Managing director] Ing. Giovanni Razelli and his collaborators considered my proposal, which had been approved by [Fiat chairman] Mr. Ghidella." One goal, according to Pininfarina general manager Leonardo Fioravanti, was "to recover the spirit of some of the Ferrari cars of the past; that is, to give our customers the possibility of driving objects that are very similar to the racing cars." Mr. Ferrari put the matter more directly, telling reporters that he'd wanted this car "to be the best in the world." Period. By all accounts, his design team succeeded brilliantly. In fact, many old hands at Maranello shunned the prosaic F40 designation, referring to the new model as "LM" or "Le Mans" instead.

Ferrari's response to Porsche's amazing 959 was the F40. It must be noted, however, that—as might be expected—Enzo made sure the two were very different cars. Whereas the Porsche was a technical *tour de force*, the Ferrari was more akin to the screamers of the muscle car era. Note the ducts, scoops, and vents, as well as the Pininfarina badge.

Actually, the F40 was nothing so much as a "streetable" version of the GTO *Evoluzione*, the extension of the latterday 288 GTO that would have been Ferrari's Group B contender had the FIA not cancelled that racing series after two tragedy-plagued seasons in 1985-86. It also represented a response to Porsche's erstwhile Group B machine, the 959. Italian pride couldn't let Germany lay claim to the world's ultimate sports car, hence this new semi-racer, available to only a handful of "qualified"—namely, expert—buyer/drivers.

Though superficially similar to the *Evoluzione*, 288 GTO, and the 308/328, the F40 differed in numerous ways. Styling was predictably and obviously Pininfarina/Ferrari, with the same sort of greenhouse styling and the identical rear cockpit window of insulating glass. But there were echoes of the 959 in wider, more deeply drawn bodywork marked by a high-flying rear airfoil, wheels and tires of Indy-car proportions, and a profusion of scoops, grids, and louvers. There was even a pair of racing-style extractor ducts beneath the tail to generate "ground-effects" downforce for maximum high-speed stick. Despite extensive testing in the Pininfarina wind tunnel, the resulting drag coefficient of 0.34 was unexceptional by even contemporary road-car standards, but that was a price of the ultra-wide rolling stock and physical dimensions approach-

Businesslike was the best way to describe the F40, whether discussing the high-flying rear airfoil or the bare metal foot pedals inside. Even the side windows were only crude sliding plexiglass units. Businesslike also translated into a claimed top speed of 201 mph, not a bad testament to Enzo Ferrari, who likely knew that the F40 would be his last car.

ing those of the big flat-12 Testarossa. Overall length, for example, was just 2.2 inches less—174.4 inches, 5.5 inches up on the 288—and width was almost as great, an impressive 78 inches. Wheelbase measured the same as the 288's, overall height the same as the Testarossa's, a rakish 44.5 inches. As a semiracer, the F40 was designed for minimum weight, which worked out to 2,425 pounds, fully half a ton less than the beefy Testarossa.

Naturally, there were a few concessions to comfort. Sketchy air conditioning was provided, but only to help keep drivers fresh through hours of three-figure velocities. There was no carpeting, sound system, sound insulation, windup windows (replaced by sliding Plexiglas panels), or interior door handles (simple pull-cords sufficed)—a literal stark contrast to Porsche's lush 959. Furthering the race-car aura were form-fitting bucket seats clad in fire-resistant, day-glo-orange Nomex and supplied in three sizes to suit different physiques. Other competition features included four-point seat harnesses and a pair of safety fuel bladders—big rubber-encased sponges soaking up a combined 31.7 gallons.

The chassis was also racing-inspired, if conventional enough for Ferrari: a steel-tube space-frame carrying classic twin-wishbone all-independent suspension with coil-over-shock units. The remaining basic structure was made of Kevlar and molded carbon-fiber, the latest in composite materials and said to provide three times the stiffness at

20 percent less weight than conventional construction. Composites were also used for outer body panels. Per racing tradition, nose and tail sections were hinged, one-piece affairs for fast trackside servicing. A more high-tech touch was three-position ride-height control. At speed, the car automatically lowered itself 20 mm to reduce drag; to clear steep driveways, it could be manually raised 20 mm from "neutral" height, all very similar to the 959's arrangement.

But the Ferrari again departed from the Porsche in lacking power assistance for its rack-and-pinion steering and brakes. Also missing was an anti-lock brake system. But the brakes themselves were Group-C massive: 13-inch-diameter vented, cross-drilled discs with aluminum centers and cast-iron outers. Those heroic dimensions were made possible by the wheels and tires: modular Speedline five-spoke rims of 17-inch

diameter and 10/13-inch fore/aft width for mounting new ultra-performance Pirelli P-Zero tires of 245/335-mm front/rear section.

The F40's least exotic element may have been its engine: basically a detuned version of the *Evoluzione* V-8, which in turn was a bored, short-stroke derivative of the 288 GTO's twincam *quattrovalvole* unit. Twin air-to-air Behr intercoolers fed dual IHI turbochargers with integral wastegates, which along with ignition and port fuel injection—featuring two injectors per cylinder—were electronically controlled by a Weber-Marelli IAW engine-management system. Compression was a modest 7.8:1, but the maximum boost was no less than 16 psi—so horsepower totaled an eye-popping 471. If that wasn't enough, Ferrari offered a package with different turbos and cam profiles said to deliver 200 bhp *more*. Power reached the

ground via a GTO five-speed manual transaxle, albeit with taller 2.73:1 final gearing, versus 2.90:1.

There remains much confusion about F40 production and prices. Initially, Ferrari announced that only some 400 would be built over a two-year period starting in 1988, but the number was subsequently upped to 700-800, then to 1,000. Price was initially set at $260,000 U.S., which guaranteed that F40s, like 959s, would be known first-hand by only a privileged few. To the delight of American *Ferraristi*, the factory said it would certify the F40 to meet U.S. safety and emissions standards, but the work went very slowly and the first American-spec cars weren't shipped until the summer of 1990—four each to the East and West Coasts. By that time, speculators had inevitably driven prevailing market prices to near museum levels. One Californian paid $400,000, and bids of up to $1 million were not unheard-of. Interestingly, U.S. dealer cost was a reported $325,000 even though each F40 was estimated to cost Ferrari only $125,000. "That's a profit... of around $200,000 per car," said that California buyer to the *Los Angeles Times*. "So on 1,000 cars, Ferrari's profit will be $200 million—incredible."

But then, so was performance: a claimed 201-mph maximum and a sizzling 12 seconds from 0-200 km/h (124 mph). Unbelievable, maybe, but true, as Ferrari performance quotes had become far more accurate since the Fiat takeover in 1969.

Journalists didn't get to drive the F40 until nearly a year after the unveiling, but it was everything they expected—and less. After touring Ferrari's Fiorano test track, *Road & Track*'s Dennis Siminaitis was "amazed by what a friend this marvelously potent F40 could be.... The car did nothing silly... [and it] was prepared to meet me halfway. Its controls communicated in loud clear voices. Its steering told me all I needed to know about grip.... Its brakes hauled the car down embarrassingly quickly. More than once, I found myself puttering through a corner because I got onto the binders way too soon. Throughout, I was agog at how benign the car felt as I probed my limits."

As ever with a Ferrari, the engine was the heart of the car. In the case of the F40, it was a dual-overhead-cam V-8 of a modest 2,936 cc, but it came with twin turbos and had four valves per cylinder, all of which translated into 471 horsepower at 7,000 rpm. With the "hood" open, one could easily see that this was serious business.

Make no mistake: driving an F40 was real work. Shifter and clutch demanded plenty of muscle, ventilation was poor, noise ear-splitting, and the car's sheer size intimidating at times. But as *Car and Driver*'s William Jeanes observed: "Unless you perform some monumentally stupid act, hard driving in the F40 is just as exhilarating as you think it should be."

After 600 miles of precisely that, Roger Bell, writing in Britain's *CAR* magazine, concluded that this Ferrari was "the most exciting...car I have driven in 35 years." Yet he termed it "a magnificently absurd machine. It had thrilled and enthralled, worried and frightened like no other car in my experience. In the wrong hands, it could be lethal. Even in the right ones, it needs respect and understanding. As practical transport it is seriously flawed by excessive (and unpleasant) noise, poor visibility and minimal luggage accommodation. [But as] raw entertainment it is the world's greatest sports car. Isn't that what Ferrari set out to make?"

Emphatically so. Author Pete Lyons records that the "aim wasn't to out-high-tech the...959. No, Enzo probably knew the F40 would be his last Ferrari, and he wanted to take the glove off the fist. It's both touching and fitting that

this was the kind of untamed street racer that made Ferrari's name in the first place. In its simplicity and power, the F40 took Enzo home."

Specifications	
Engine:	V-8, dohc, 179 cid/2,936 cc (3.23 x 2.74-in./82 x 69.5-mm bore x stroke), twin turbocharged and intercooled, 4 valves per cylinder, 471 bhp @ 7,000 rpm, 426 lbs/ft torque @ 4,000 rpm; approx. 670 bhp opt.
Transmission:	5-speed manual; rear transaxle
Suspension, front:	Independent, unequal-length A-arms, concentric coil springs with tube shocks, anti-roll bar
Suspension, rear:	Independent, unequal-length A-arms, concentric coil springs with tube shocks, anti-roll bar
Brakes:	Hydraulic, front/rear discs
Wheelbase (in.):	94.5
Weight (lbs):	2,425; 2,650 fully fueled
Top speed (mph):	201[1]
0-60 mph (sec):	est. 3.0
Production:	1,000

[1]manufacturer's data

Y̲ou can, with little effort, draw some telling parallels between the ultra-high-performance Corvette ZR-1 of the Nineties and its six-cylinder grandfather of 1953. Both were announced prematurely, weren't genuinely available once sales began, and arrived with several features that purists deemed downright inappropriate.

But the comparison shouldn't be strained too much, because the ZR-1 is as far removed from that first Chevrolet sports car as Moscow, Russia is from Moscow, Idaho. The shared similarities are four wheels, two seats, front-mounted engine, and fiberglass bodywork. However, the ZR-1 does maintain one tradition associated with post-1955 Corvettes: outstanding performance value for money. Indeed, *Road & Track* was moved to term it "the most civilized and technologically advanced and [yet] the least expensive supercar in production because it is still a Corvette."

Because the ZR-1 is technically an option package for the sixth-generation Corvette coupe (RPO ZR1), a brief review of that foundation is in order. Unveiled in early '83 as a 1984 model, it was a cleaner, somewhat leaner car than the 1968-82 "shark" series, but still recognizably Corvette in appearance, format, and essential chassis design. Departures comprised a fiberglass-reinforced front transverse leaf instead of individual coils (matching a rear "monoleaf" previously adopted); more sophisticated five-link rear-end geometry (ousting the venerable three-link arrangement introduced with the 1963 Sting Ray); a rigid new "backbone" chassis *a la* Lotus of England, welded to a steel "birdcage" as a structure for attaching outer body panels; suspension hardware rendered as beautiful—and costly—aluminum forgings; and a roomier, more practical body with hatch-type rear window and a front-hinged, Jaguar E-Type-inspired "clamshell" hood/front fender assembly.

This basic package would be steadily refined over the six years leading up to the ZR-1. A key 1985 improvement was switching the evergreen, 350-cubic-inch V-8 from twin-throttle-body fuel injection to multiport, good for an extra 25 horsepower (and a production-code change from L82 to L98). An oil cooler and gas-charged shocks were also standardized that year. Arriving for 1986 were no-cost Bosch anti-lock control for the all-disc brake system and—happily—the first new Corvette convertible since 1975. Roller valve lifters and higher compression boosted 1987 horses to 240. The '88s gained five more via modified heads and cam, and also offered a meaty P255/50ZR17 tire option in lieu of the regular V-rated 16-inch rubber. For 1990, the never-liked "4+3" overdrive manual transmission offered since '84 gave way to a German ZF gearbox with no fewer than six forward speeds. As ever, though, most Corvettes rolled out with the still-respected four-speed Turbo Hydra-Matic self-shifter.

Squarish taillights, a convex rear fascia, and bulged rear wheelwells announced the ZR-1. From the front it looked much like a workaday 'Vette, which of course was hardly bad. Seen here is the 1991 model, which sported four horizontal vents (rather than vertical slots) behind the front wheels and wraparound inserts for the fog lamps and turn signals.

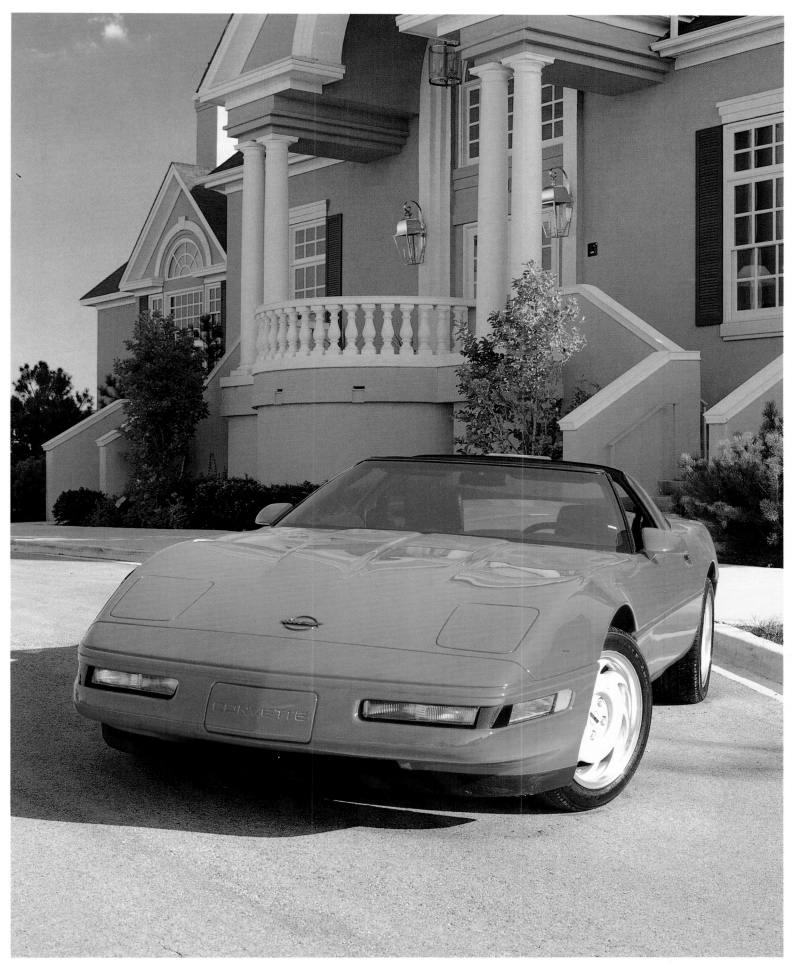

The Corvette's interior was cleaned up for 1990, and carried over for '91. The only digital readout was now for speed, and there was a host of warning lights. A Getrag six-speed was standard.

Meantime, the Corvette engineering group under Dave McLellan had been seeking ways to elevate their car into the rarified performance realm of the Lamborghini Countach, Ferrari Testarossa, and other latterday exotics. After considering—and rejecting—twin-turbo V-6s and V-8s, Chevy turned to Group Lotus in 1985, just as General Motors was moving to take over the famed sports-car and Formula 1 constructor. The result was an all-new, normally aspirated all-aluminum V-8, ultimately designated LT5, that shared nothing with the existing pushrod unit save nominal displacement, bore centers, and physical size, which permitted installation with no alteration to the existing engine bay.

Technically as well as visually, the LT5 was a sight to behold. For each cylinder bank, twin chain-driven overhead camshafts operated four valves per cylinder above dished aluminum pistons running in Nikasil-coated aluminum liners. Integral four- and six-bolt main-bearing caps of sturdy cast iron supported a forged-steel crank. Compression was a high 11.0:1. The big attraction was the induction system: 16 artfully fashioned runners, dual fuel injectors for each cylinder, and a novel three-valve throttle body comprising a small primary butterfly and two larger secondaries. At light throttle, the engine's

electronic "computer" directed mixture through the primary valve and one set of injectors and intake valves; going beyond half-throttle, around 3,500 rpm, opened the larger butterflies and valves as well as the secondary injectors for full power: a smashing 380 emissions-legal bhp (375 for 1991)—no less than 135 bhp above the everyday L98. To ensure that didn't fall into unauthorized hands, Chevy put in a key-operated "valet" switch that locked out the "second-stage boost," thus limiting horses to about 150.

To put all those ponies to the ground, stylist Jerry Palmer flared his original bodywork from the doors back to

accommodate huge P315/35ZR17 tires on 11-inch-wide rims. Meanwhile, 9.5-inchers with P275/40ZR17s continued up front, as on standard 'Vettes with the Z51 handling option. The change was subtle enough unless you were dead astern, where squared taillights in a convex rump gave distinction from the familiar round lights and concave back panel. Also for handling, a slightly thicker rear stabilizer bar was specified, along with the FX3 "selective ride" system optional on lesser 'Vettes. The latter, developed by Delco and Bilstein, provided no fewer than 14 levels of electronically controlled damping across three driver-selectable modes. "Perfor-

As with all exotics, the ZR-1's engine was all-important: a V-8 in the old American tradition, except that it laid claim to twin chain-driven camshafts, four valves per cylinder, and a high 11.0:1 compression ratio—not to mention a 16-runner induction system.

The back end is what most people ever saw of a ZR-1 'Vette, whose huge P315/35ZR17 rear tires rode on 11-inch-wide aluminum rims. Pop-up headlights didn't help aerodynamics at night.

mance" was the setting of choice for Showroom Stock racing—or the Corvette Challenge Series; rough surfaces demanded the mildest "Touring" mode lest your fillings fall out, with "Sport" available for smooth-road handling.

And what handling! Most buff books reported lateral acceleration in excess of 0.9 g—comfortably above that of most European exotics. Yet this was readily "accessible"—and safe—even for those who hadn't been to high-performance driving schools, and quite comfortable all things considered. Obviously, the FX3 suspension did its job superbly. Without it, as *Car and Driver* observed, "the ZR-1 would not be the grand tourer it is."

Grand described the performance—as formidable as you'd expect for a car where each horsepower carried fewer than 10 pounds. Though Chevy said 0-60 mph took just 4.3 seconds, most magazine clockings were about a half-second behind. But who cared? With its two-stage induction and some 370 lbs/ft torque available from as little as 1,500 rpm, the ZR-1, as *R&T* reported, "burbles along happily at practically idle speed. So there's no need to do a lot of shifting...until it's safe to... PASS!" And *CD* timed 0-150-0 in slightly under half a minute—real exoticar agility that testified as much to the arresting capabilities of the brakes as to the mighty thrust of the LT5 V-8.

All was not bliss, however. Because the ZR-1 was offered only with the six-speed manual, it inherited something called CAGS—"Computer Aided Gear Selection"—that forced a shift from first directly to fourth at lighter throttle openings, a real pain in give-and-take driving. There were also ugly rumors about overheating, staunchly denied by Chevy and soon proven false—the LT5 actually ran cooler than the L98

engine. Worst of all, perhaps, the ZR-1 inherited the sixth-generation's squeak-and-rattle propensities and overly busy "video arcade" instrumentation, both consistently criticized since '84.

As it happened, Chevy had a new dashboard ready for all 1990 Corvettes, which helps explain why the ZR-1 didn't reach showrooms for nearly a year after its early '89 world debut at Geneva and splashy press launch in France. The new panel was no less futuristic, but reduced digital readouts to just speed; the tachometer and engine gauges were now analog. Still, *Road & Track* judged the design "less successful than it should be, with its randomly placed gauge pointers...and strange mixture of colors, textures and shapes."

Strange indeed was Chevy's decision to apply ZR-1 tail styling to all 1991 Corvettes (though without the bulged flanks and jumbo tires), thus diluting the SuperVette's exclusivity. The ZR-1 even retained the roof-mount high-center stop lamp that moved nicely into the back panel of the standard coupe.

Changes were otherwise minimal for '91: horizontal strakes instead of vertical slots in the front fenders, lower-restriction mufflers, and standard power-steering-fluid cooler, low-oil warning light, and a "delayed accessory power" feature—all shared with other 'Vettes. At $31,683, the ZR-1 remained the costliest option this side of a custom-built Porsche, and at $64,138 for the entire car, the dearest car GM had ever offered (the original announcement price had been $58,995). That some buyers—really speculators—were willing to pay upwards of $150,000 for early 1990 models says as much for the ZR-1's undeniable charisma and ultimate collectibility as its stellar dynamic

performance.

In December 1990, disaster struck as some LT5 engines were mysteriously seizing at the factory, a problem that was ultimately traced to defective camshafts. As a result, no ZR-1s were built during the first quarter of 1991, and although production resumed early in the second quarter, 1991 output was expected to reach just 1,500 units instead of the planned 3,000—making an already scarce car that much rarer.

"It's bittersweet," *R&T* observed, that the ZR-1 "reaches fruition [just] as tremendous environmental and regulatory forces muster to tackle the serious problems of global warming, acid rain and other specters." In other words, it may not have long to live. But whatever its fate, the ZR-1—roundly and rightly acclaimed a genuine world-class supercar—is certain to be regarded by future generations as historic, not just as a Corvette, but as one of the greatest production cars ever.

Specifications[1]	
Engine:	V-8, dohc, 350 cid/5.7 liters (3.90 x 3.66-in./99 x 93-mm bore x stroke), 4 valves per cylinder, 375 bhp @ 5,800 rpm, 370 lbs/ft torque @ 4,800 rpm
Transmission:	Getrag 6-speed overdrive manual
Suspension, front:	Independent, upper and lower A-arms on transverse monoleaf fiberglass spring, tube shocks, anti-roll bar
Suspension, rear:	Independent, 5 links on transverse monoleaf fiberglass spring, tie rods, tube shocks, anti-roll bar
Brakes:	Hydraulic, front/rear disc
Wheelbase (in.):	96.2
Overall length (in.):	178.6
Curb Weight (lbs):	3,465
0-60 mph (sec):	4.9
Top speed (mph):	170+
Production:	Continues at this writing; approx. 3,000 through the end of 1990

[1]1991 model

The Miata, a '91 model here, has won many awards: "Automobile of the Year" from *Automobile* magazine, one of the "Ten Best Cars in the World" and the "Best Sports Car/GT between $13,000 and $21,000" from *Road & Track*, one of the "Top Ten Performance Cars.

Let's take "sports car" to mean an open two-seater with some kind of top and a personality that says "Drive me just for fun." By that definition, the Mazda MX-5 Miata differs not a jot from all the low-cost sports cars that have preceded it: Austin-Healey Sprites/MG Midgets, MGAs and Bs, Triumph TRs, Austin-Healeys, and all the rest.

Which explains why the Miata was big news long before its public debut in July 1989. Here was nothing less—and nothing more—than the first affordable new "classic" sports car in more than a decade: a traditional, yet fully contemporary, roadster for the tweed-cap and stringback-gloves crowd—a timeless idea reinterpreted for modern times. But though unabashedly patterned on beloved sports cars of yore, the Miata imposed none of their hated drawbacks. As long expected of Japanese products, it was beautifully built, full of thoughtful details, and virtually fail-safe. Most of all, the Miata was one very good sports car. Good value, too, at a base retail price of just under $14,000.

Like its European forebears, the Miata was modest in size and relatively straightforward. A front-mounted 1.6-liter twincam four with an iron block and a 16-valve aluminum head sent 116 horses to the rear wheels via a five-speed all-synchro gearbox. (A four-speed overdrive automatic became available during 1990, but was quickly dismissed by purists as detrimental). At each wheel: a disc brake, coil spring, and double wishbones. Steering, naturally, was the preferred rack-and-pinion. The roadster body—convertible, actually, as there were roll-up windows and a permanently affixed soft top—was a steel *monocoque* of small—but not tiny—proportions.

Beyond this were features unimaginable in the "ironmongery" era. Valves, for example, were actuated by inverted bucket tappets from a sturdy cogged-belt cam drive. Also on hand was integrated electronic ignition/port fuel injection, which with a highish 9.4:1 compression ratio contributed to the fine specific output and good driveability. Hydraulic valve-lash adjusters reduced both noise and maintenance.

More innovative still was what Mazda called the "Power Plant Frame": a truss-like forged-aluminum structure tying the engine/transmission assembly to the final drive. In concert with a body designed with the aid of computerized "Dynamic Model Analysis," it made for an uncommonly rigid open car. In fact, the Miata was likely the stiffest full convertible extant in 1990. Plastic bumpers—with energy-absorbing blow-molded reinforcements—and an aluminum hood helped hold base curb weight to a modest 2,182 pounds. Likewise, the optional lift-off factory hardtop weighed but 40 pounds.

Simple the Miata may have been, but hardly spartan. Standard features included shapely reclining bucket seats, full carpeting, a heater that really worked, integrated ventilation system with dashboard registers,

The interior of the '90 Miata, as seen with the manual folding top down, was hardly spartan, and came with a driver's air bag standard. The 116-bhp dual overhead cam four (with manual gearbox) got the Miata from 0-60 mph in 8.6 seconds. At 3.6 cubic feet, cargo capacity was a bit meager.

two-speed wipers with intermittent mode, and courtesy lights. There was even an airbag. Options ran to anti-lock brakes—an even better high-tech safety device, available as of 1991—as well as air conditioning, limited-slip differential, compact-disc player, floor mats, the aforementioned hardtop, and two equipment packages. The "A" group comprised power steering, alloy road wheels, leather-rim steering wheel, and an AM/FM/cassette stereo. Package "B" added power windows, cruise control, and speakers built into the headrests. Dealer accessories included the ever-popular decklid luggage rack and center-zip tonneau, a trendy protective nose mask, engine-block heater, and an anti-theft system. Purists may have cried that amenities like air and power windows were too fancy for a "real" sports car, but in fact they didn't detract a bit from the Miata's frisky, high-revving, cornering-fool character.

That character was formed over a lengthy gestation that began in 1981 with a chat between Bob Hall, then a writer for *AutoWeek* and *Automotive News*, and Kenichi Yamamoto, the godfather of rotary power in Hiroshima and then head of Mazda Research and Development. Hall, a confirmed Mazda fan, had watched America's sports-car choices wither in the Seventies, but believed that latent demand was still sufficient to support a stylish, reliable, low-cost roadster—if only somebody would offer one. With a new rear-drive economy car at hand, the 323/GLC, Mazda was the company to do it, Hall argued. Besides, the original rotary-powered RX-7 was a hit, and its more ambitious, more expensive replacement being planned for 1986 left room for a lower-cost running mate. By early '82, Hall had accepted a job at Mazda R&D's U.S. branch in Irvine, California, where he could push his dream in earnest.

Investigations toward what was variously called Project 729 and "LWS" ("lightweight sports car") soon commenced in a Lee Iacocca-style intramural design contest under Product Planning chief Michinori Yamanouchi. A Tokyo-based team pursued front-drive concepts *a la* Honda CRX and mid-engine coupes not unlike Toyota's forthcoming MR2. Irvine persisted with Hall's favored front-engine/rear-drive convertible, with sketch work done largely by Mark Jordan, son of GM design chief Charles M. "Chuck" Jordan. The Californians carried the day in an April 1984 review of full-scale models built to evaluate the three configurations. Though Hall had proposed reducing cost and development time by using as much 323 hardware as possible, the Japanese were eager to go further. As he later told Britain's *CAR* magazine: "I was shocked at how willing they were to consider new components at the earliest stages of the car's design—things such as fully independent suspension that were on the early wish lists."

Mazda then commissioned IAD in England to build a running version of the California convertible. Completed by the end of 1985, it was even driven around Santa Barbara (in the company of a Mark IV Spitfire, interestingly enough) for a more accurate assessment in its intended environment. It caused quite a stir. Meantime, Irvine-based designer Masao Yagi, working under Shigenori Fukuda, had completed a slightly larger "Mark II" evolution. This was shown to the Mazda board in early 1986, when Yamamoto, newly ap-

One of the features of the '90 Miata was hidden headlights. The sleek styling helped sales as much as its winsome performance; 35,944 were sold in the U.S. in 1990.

pointed as company president, gave it his full endorsement. Bob Hall's dream was now reality.

Because P729 was always viewed as being mainly for U.S. consumption, production styling was carried out in Irvine, by Tom Matano and Koichi Hayashi, though it was finalized in Tokyo by Shunji Tanaka. Japan took engineering responsibility from day one, assigning the job to Toshihiko Hirai, who'd then just brought forth the first front-drive 323.

Hall is quick to credit the high enthusiasm of these and other team members for the Miata's strong personality. The trans-Pacific back-and-forth "was like doing a car by correspondence," he later said, "but I don't think it's any the worse for it. It didn't get 'commitee'd' to death. That's one reason everything works so well with the car. It didn't have one of these easy, laid-back, simple development times. There were times it was a real struggle. But there were also times when everybody knew exactly what had to be done, and it got done."

Hirai, who sought to imbue the Miata with a feeling akin to that between a horse and rider, merits special praise from Hall. "He's nicknamed by a lot of the Japanese 'Hirai-otoosan,' which means something likes 'Pops' Hirai. He's got this enthusiasm below the surface.

He looks often as poker-faced as any other Japanese engineer, but you see this twinkle in his eye."

And in the Miata. Whether you've already suffered through TRs and MGs or are just discovering such cars, the Miata is sure to bring a smile to your face as it tousles your hair. It's as light and nimble as it looks: safe, controllable oversteer takes only a well-timed wheel-twitch and throttle-prod. It's also fast enough: 8.6 seconds 0-60 mph. And thrifty, too: 30 mpg in town without even trying. Better still, it's surprisingly civilized and even practical for a basic sports car. Six-footers can ride all day without cramping, ride is firm but not teeth-chattering, and the top is so well designed that you can practically raise or lower it with one hand while on the move. About all anyone might wish for is more luggage space.

Mazda introduced the Miata as "an enthusiast's dream come true—again," and the description fit like a driving glove. Even Hall was pinching himself. So were enthusiasts. Buff book reviews were uniformly ecstatic, though there were some snide remarks about the Miata's nasal similarity with the fragile, lilliputian Lotus Elan. That apart, the Japanese car resembled that British one the way saki resembles sherry. If anything, the Miata was a 1990's Spitfire

or MGB, only it wasn't about to leak, rust away before your eyes, or leave you stranded on some dark, deserted road.

Demand was predictably enormous and immediate, especially in Sunbelt states, where rabid buyers eagerly queued to pay upwards of $5,000 over sticker. "Miata mania" continued to run rampant for the first 18 months or so, then cooled, bringing delivered prices down to saner, "suggested" levels.

But three well-deserved cheers for this happy Oriental sports car—and the determined Yankee who dreamed it up. Like many great notions, this one makes you wonder why nobody did it before, though that's easy to say with the blinding clarity of hindsight.

At least some other automakers have been goaded into following Mazda's lead. There's even talk that a new MG roadster will appear well before the millennium. Another great car of the 20th Century? We sincerely hope so.

Specifications	
Engine:	I-4, dohc, 97.45 cid/1,597 cc (3.1 x 3.3-in./78 x 83.6-cc bore x stroke), 4 valves per cylinder, 9.4:1 compression ratio, port fuel injection, 116 bhp @ 6,500 rpm, 100 lbs/ft torque @ 5,500 (9.0:1 c.r., 105 bhp @ 6,000 rpm and 100 lbs/ft @ 4,000 rpm with automatic)
Transmission:	5-speed manual; 4-speed overdrive automatic opt. beginning in 1990
Suspension, front:	Independent, double wishbones, coil springs, tube shock absorbers, anti-roll bar
Suspension, rear:	Independent, double wishbones, coil springs, tube shock absorbers, anti-roll bar
Brakes:	Hydraulic, 4-wheel disc, power assisted; ABS opt. beginning 1991
Wheelbase (in.):	89.2
Overall length (in.):	155.4
Curb weight (lbs):	2,182; 2,264 with automatic
0-60 mph (sec):	8.6
Top speed (mph):	116
Production:	1989 23,052 1990 35,944 (U.S. calendar year sales)

The '91 Acura NS-X looked like it was bred for the race track, and indeed Honda had had great success in Formula 1 competition and learned a lot in the process. In truth, however, the NS-X was an easy car to drive in rush hour traffic, as well as a world-class demonstration of Honda's technology and talent.

I n the early Eighties, a Honda engineer reportedly remarked that his company aimed to offer BMW style, performance, and crafts-manship at half the price. Within a decade, Honda decisively delivered on this promise with the mid-engine NS-X.

Never mind that Honda had built cars for less than 25 years by then, and mostly workaday family models at that. The NS-X was stunning—a perfect example of Japan's inexorable rise to automaking dominance in the last quarter of the 20th Century. Unveiled in early 1989, barely five years after its inception, the NS-X was further proof that Japan could not only bring out new cars faster than anyone else, but exciting, technically advanced designs that begged comparison with world bench marks. Yet tellingly, it was bargain-priced for a latterday exotic. True, at $60,000 in the U.S. ($64,000 with automatic), it was the costliest Japanese car ever, but still thousands less than comparable Europeans, most of which sold at inflated prices, often simply because of "marque heritage," real or perceived.

Not that the NS-X lacked heritage. After all, Honda Motor Company had gone Grand Prix racing in the Sixties even before building its first serious road cars, and was in the midst of winning a third straight Formula 1 constructor's crown when the NS-X went on sale in mid-1990—with the Honda badge except in America, where it was an Acura, a marketing fiction created for status seekers in 1986. It hardly mattered that Honda had never before attempted a mid-engine road car, or that the project initials denoting "New Sportscar Xperimental" were retained. The NS-X, as *Car and Driver* recorded, "behaves like an automobile that's been refined over decades." Which in a sense it had—through progressively smoother, sweeter, and swifter Civics, Accords, Preludes and, more recently, luxury V-6 Legends. In short, there was nothing "xperimental" about the NS-X.

Its design brief was simple but demanding: overall dynamic ability at least equal to that of the world's best sports/GT cars; high reliability/durability; and maximum day-to-day practicality. With their competition experience, and believing with Raymond Loewy that "weight is the enemy," Honda engineers rejected both V-8 and twin-turbo V-6 engines for a normally aspirated V-6 in the Legend mold, albeit with much higher specific output. To achieve the desired weight-to-power ratio (roughly 12:1), they decided to use aluminum as much as possible throughout the car, even for its body and chassis. The resulting unitized structure thus marked a first in production and, at just 462 pounds with all exterior panels in place, weighed fully 40 percent less than if rendered in steel. Because aluminum is more bendable than steel, computer-based finite-element analysis was employed to determine the metallurgy and fabrication needed to give various components comparable rigidity.

To keep it light, aluminum was used extensively in the NS-X, even for the body and chassis. At just 462 pounds with all exterior panels in place, it weighed 40 percent less than if built in steel. The side ducts cooled the midships engine.

Aluminum forgings, not relatively fragile castings, made up the suspension, which also reflected Honda's Formula 1 experience in having classic double wishbones and coil springs all-round, plus an anti-roll bar at each end and a front "compliance pivot." The last, an upright anchoring the forward wishbone pivots, turned about its vertical axis to provide slight rearward "give" on wheel deflection for a smoother ride without compromising camber or toe angles. Steering, the expected rack-and-pinion, was given high caster but minimal caster trail for good on-center feel and strong self-centering action. The mechanism was manual unless you ordered the four-speed automatic transaxle (unusual for a midships exotic), in which case you got power assist, which was variable with road speed and used an electric motor instead of hydraulics, an American-market first (though Pontiac had prepared something similar for its late, unlamented Fiero). Brakes were the expected four-wheel assisted discs, vented and large (11.1-inch diameter), and sporting Honda's latest four-channel electronic anti-lock control for skid-free stops even anchors-out on slippery surfaces.

Mounted transversely behind the two-seat cockpit in established midships-supercar fashion was a new all-alumi-num 90-degree V-6 with twin overhead camshafts operating four valves per cylinder, sequential multiport electronic fuel injection, and distributor-less "direct ignition" (individual coils fired the plugs). Costly titanium was used for connecting rods as another weight-saving measure—and another production first—and there were two power-boosting innovations. One was VVIS, "Variable-Volume Intake System," a magnesium plenum beneath the main intake chamber with six butterfly valves that opened by manifold vacuum above 4,800 rpm to create a single large passage for optimum top-end breathing. The other was VTEC, the "Variable Valve Timing and Lift Electronic Control" pioneered on Honda motorcycles in 1983. This comprised a pair of primary rocker arms on a conventionally profiled cam lobe, and an in-between rocker arm following a secondary lobe giving greater lift and longer duration. The latter came into play at 5,800-6,000 rpm when hydraulic pressure, actuated by the engine's management computer, locked the three rockers together to follow the more

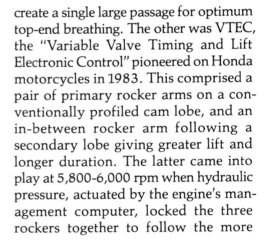

The seats inside the NS-X were deeply bucketed affairs with one-piece aluminum frames and variable-density foam padding—and covered in hand-stitched leather. Automatic-climate-control air conditioning and a Bose sound system were standard.

aggressive secondary cam. All told, VTEC was said to be worth 20 extra horsepower. Total output was a smashing 270 bhp at a dizzying 7,100 rpm—nearly 91 horsepower per liter, a world road-car record.

A twin-disc clutch transferred drive to the aforementioned four-speed automatic transaxle or a manual five-speed unit; a "torque-control" limited-slip differential then distributed power to the rear wheels. Maximizing grip was TCS, Honda's new Traction Control System. Like similar setups elsewhere, this used the ABS wheel-speed sensors to detect tire slip, but differed in that instead of braking the wheels, it reduced power to them according to calculations of road speed and steering angle, thus doing as much to enhance cornering stability as straight-line traction. The NS-X system also differed in having a defeat switch for drivers "who want to think for themselves," as *Road & Track* put it.

Enveloping all this high tech was the slickest body this side of an F16 fighter—which was, in fact, the design inspiration. The tail was deliberately very long, both for high-speed stability (though claimed drag coefficient was a so-so 0.32) and to leave room behind the engine for a trunk (useful, if rather limited at just five cubic feet). Rolling stock was smaller fore than aft—205/50ZR15 tires on 6.5-inch-wide rims versus 225/50ZR16s on eight-inchers—to minimize footwell intrusion, though it was appropriate for the tail-heavy weight distribution of 42/58 percent front/rear. Aircraft influence was also evident in the integral rear loop spoiler, neatly housing a full-width LED stoplamp, and a glassy, rounded canopy atop the "cab-forward" cockpit. Critics chided the stubby, ground-sniffing nose for lacking "character," but it provided a terrific view in concert with Honda's typical low beltline/high-window architecture. Vision elsewhere was good, too—even over the shoulder, usually a bane of "middies."

In fact, the only real cockpit problem was clearing the low roof on entry/exit, though taller types wished for a bit more cranial clearance. Otherwise, the NS-X cabin could have been a shortened version of the big Legend's interior. Instruments and controls had

The NS-X's advanced all-aluminum 90-degree V-6 featured VTEC: "Variable Valve Timing and Lift Electronic Control."

the familiar Honda look and were mastered in a trice. Seats, deeply bucketed affairs with one-piece aluminum frames and variable-density foam padding, fit most bodies in all the right places; the driver's seat even boasted a four-way power adjustment. Hand-stitched leather was everywhere. So were luxury conveniences like automatic-climate-control air conditioning, Bose sound system, power windows and door mirrors, and a tilt/telescope steering wheel with airbag.

If the NS-X looked too cushy to be a serious performer, it quickly proved otherwise in action. CONSUMER GUIDE®'s early manual example ran 0-60 mph in just 5.8 seconds and averaged a short 104 feet in panic stops from that speed—right up there with the world's best supercars. Yet mileage worked out to near 22 mpg despite the hard charging this car encouraged.

Yet the NS-X was as much at home on freeways and city streets as high-speed straights and twisty back roads—and so capable as to make even couch potatoes look like race driver Ayrton Senna. Clutch effort was low for a high-power machine, the shifter snicked with light-switch precision, and the manual steering, though heavy for parking, was marvelous at speed: properly weighted and quite informative. Predictable for a Honda, handling was forgiving, cornering tenacious, if not the absolute tops.

And through it all, you reveled in one of the most thrilling engines outside a race car: super-smooth, unobtrusive in gentle driving (thanks in part to a sound-insulating double-pane window between cockpit and engine bay), and always ready to zing beyond 7,000 rpm to the expensive-sounding accompaniment of four cams and a wailing exhaust. The aural delights alone were almost enough to justify the car's existence.

Honda, of course, had a more serious reason for spending over $140 million to design and build the NS-X. This was to be its showcase car, a demonstration of technology and talent to cement its reputation as one of the world's foremost automakers. The NS-X played that role superbly, while serving notice that Porsche, Ferrari, and all the rest must look to their laurels in earnest.

Like Mazda's winsome Miata, another late-century Japanese sports car that set enthusiast tongues a-wagging, the NS-X made up for any lack of "heritage" with overwhelming excellence. As *Road & Track* concluded: "Technically, it's brilliant. Dynamically, it's outstanding. And its chameleon-like character, that of equally competent soul-stirring road ripper and comfortable, relaxed long-distance tourer, has raised the ante markedly in the exotic, high-end sports/GT marketplace." But then, that's what happens when ability is your most important product.

Specifications	
Engine:	V-6, dohc, 4 valves/cylinder, 181.6 cid/2,977 cc (3.54 x 3.07-in./90 x 78-mm bore x stroke), port fuel injection, 270 bhp (SAE net) @ 7,100 rpm (252 bhp @ 6,600 rpm with automatic), 210 lbs/ft torque @ 5,300 rpm
Transmission:	5-speed overdrive manual; 4-speed overdrive automatic opt.
Suspension, front:	Independent, upper and lower A-arms, compliance pivot, coil springs, tube shocks, anti-roll bar
Suspension, rear:	Independent, upper and lower A-arms, coil springs, tube shocks, anti-roll bar
Brakes:	Hydraulic, front/rear discs with ABS
Wheelbase (in.):	99.6
Overall length (in.):	173.4
Weight (lbs):	3,010/3,098 (manual/automatic)
0-60 mph (sec):	5.8
Top speed (mph):	165+
Production:	Continues at this writing; announced 5,000 per year, 3,000 for the U.S. market

A

Abbott, 221
AC Ace, 168, 259, 297, 336
AC Cobra, 276, 297-299, 303, 311, 336
Acura, 414
    Legend, 417
    NSX, 341, 414-417
Ahrens, Don, 134
Alfa Romeo, 49, 116, 157, 167, 193, 361
    8C 2900, 116-117
    Spider, 55
Allard, 361
Alpine Trials, 126
Alvis, 221
American Automobile Association, 240, 245
American Bantam Car Company, 152, 153
American Motors Corporation, 153, 203, 211
Ames, Harold T., 66, 118
Anderson, Gil, 41
Andrews, Bob, 312, 314
Anibal, Ben, 144
Arkus-Duntov, Zora, 264
Arnold, Graham, 282, 285
Arnolt, 259
Ash, David, 333
Aston Martin, 298, 346
    DB4/DB5, 274-277
Auburn, 64, 66-67, 123-125, 149
    Speedster, 118-121
Audi, 344, 359
Austin A30/A40, 176
Austin-Healey, 265, 344, 347, 361
    Sprite, 411
    100/100 Six/3000, 221-223
Austin-Rover, 281
Austin/Morris Mini, 20, 177, 279-281
Austrian Alpine Trials, 22
Auto Union, 194, 205, 221, 359
Autocar, The, 106, 112, 114, 156, 218, 248, 289, 346, 347
Automobile Manufacturer's Association, 124
Automobile Quarterly, 115, 146, 148, 348, 375
Automobile Racing Club of America, 157
Automobile, The, 46
Automotive News, 412
AutoWeek, 412
Axe, Roy, 396

B

Baits, Stuart, 208
Barr, Harry, 183, 264
Batchelor, Dean, 303, 366
Beattie, Kevin, 344, 346
Bel Geddes, Norman, 107
Bell, Roger, 405
Bennett, Frederick S., 16, 18, 19
Bentley, 92, 216, 218, 259
    R-Type Continental, 216-219
Bentley, John, 16
Benz, Karl, 6, 7, 8, 112
Berlin Auto Show, 112
Bertone, 168, 248, 358, 383, 384, 385, 387
Bertoni, Flaminio, 110
Biondetti, Clemente, 117, 167
Bizzarrini, Giotto, 302, 303, 352, 378
Blatchley, J.P., 216, 218
BMW (Bavarian Motor Works), 259, 260
    2002, 360-363
    507, 258-261, 282, 375
Bond, John R., 180, 183, 306
Bonneville Salt Flats, Utah, 98, 106, 121, 315, 393
Bonsall, Tom, 141
Bordinat, Eugene, 293
Boregeson, Griff, 95
Bourke, Robert, 188, 228, 230, 231
Boyer, Bill, 250, 252, 253
Breech, Ernest R., 186
Breer, Carl, 51, 104

Bricklin, 235
Bridge, Frank, 319
Bridgehampton, Long Island, 157
Briggs Manufacturing Company, 85, 130, 213
British Leyland, 175, 177, 281
British Motor Corporation (BMC), 175, 177, 221, 222, 279, 281
Brock, Pete, 298
Brooklands track, 20
Brown, David, 275
Brunn, 66, 86, 89, 93
Brush, Alanson, 73
Budd, 48, 85, 108, 110
Buehrig, Gordon, 66, 67, 118, 123, 124, 125, 228
Bugatti Type 41 Royale, 52-55
    Type 57, 100-103
Bugatti, Ettore, 53, 54, 55, 100, 103
Bugatti, Jean, 55, 100, 102, 103
Bugatti: Les Pur-Sang des Automobiles, 103
Buick, 50, 143, 145, 190, 305
    Century, 242
    Master Six, 57
    Riviera, 304-307, 315, 348
    Roadmaster, 144, 192
    Series 40 Special, 143
    Six, 59, 242
    Skylark, 226
    Special, 192, 213
    Super, 144, 192
    XP-300, 214
Burrell, Gilbert, 190

C

Cadillac, 29, 57, 58, 59, 73, 78, 80, 84, 88, 90, 96, 102, 130, 134, 144, 146, 160, 190, 192, 193, 234, 253, 256, 267, 295, 305, 306
    1949 Model, 183-185
    Eldorado, 224-227, 244, 254, 351
    Eldorado Brougham, 270-273
    Fleetwood Sixty Special, 185
    Imperial Landau Sedan, 73
    Model 30, 36, 38, 39
    Model K, 16-19
    Series Sixty, 59, 125, 134
    Series Sixty-One, 133
    Series Sixty-Two, 134, 184, 192
    Sixteen, 72-77, 81, 90, 96, 114
    Sixty Special, 134-137, 148
    V-12, 76, 90, 96
    V-16, 76-77, 90, 96, 114, 270
    V-8, 36-39, 45, 54, 64, 184, 242
Caffrey and Judkins, 47
Caleal, Dick, 188
Canaday, Ward M., 152
Car and Driver, 233, 234, 303, 319, 320, 329, 339, 361, 375, 388, 389, 393, 399, 400, 401, 405, 409, 414
Car Life, 295, 306, 319, 370
CAR magazine, 405, 412
Car of the Year, 286, 371, 375
Carrera Panamericana Mexican Road Race, 169, 193, 206, 210, 234, 267
Carrozzeria Touring, 116, 168, 276, 346
Chapin, Roy, 13
Chapman, Colin, 282, 285
Chappell, Pat, 237
Chapron, Henri, 249
Chevrolet, 7, 27, 57, 59, 71, 84, 189, 202, 218, 228, 240, 260, 305, 394
    1955-57, 236-241
    Astro, 396
    Bel Air, 203, 237, 239, 331
    Camaro, 329, 335
    Caprice, 213
    Corvair, 335
    Corvair Corsa, 326-329
    Corvette, 102, 250, 262-265, 286, 297, 303, 305, 319, 336, 365, 375, 392, 393
    Sting Ray, 298, 308-311, 406

ZR1, 406-409
    Firebird, 335
    Fleetline DeLuxe, 189
    One-Fifty, 239
    Special Deluxe, 144
    Styleline, 189
    Two-Ten, 239
Chicago Automobile Show, 50
Chicago World's Fair, 90
Chinetti, Luigi, 169
Chrysler Corporation, 7, 51, 106, 108, 123, 130, 153, 160, 161, 201, 213, 215, 275, 336, 348, 384, 394, 396
    58, 51
    300, 240, 256
    Airflow, 104-107, 242
    Airstream, 107
    B-70, 50-51
    C-300, 242-245
    Custom Imperial, 242
    Minivans, 394-397
    New Yorker, 242
    Royale, 193
    Saratoga, 208, 218
    Town and Country, 158-161, 397
    Windsor DeLuxe, 244
Chrysler, Walter P., 50, 51, 104, 107, 242
Circuit of La Spezia, 49
Cisitalia, 163, 249, 276, 282, 361
    202 Gran Sport, 163-165
Citroën, 15, 173, 177, 272, 358
    DS, 246-249, 286
    Traction Avant, 108-111, 247, 248
Citroën, André, 48, 108, 111, 247
Classic Car Club of America, 7, 225, 331
Clymer, Floyd, 269
Cole Motor Company, 43
Cole, Edward N., 180, 237, 264, 329
Collectible Automobile®, 259
Collier, Miles and Sam, 156, 157
Colombo, Gioacchino, 167, 300
Complete Book of Lamborghini, 383
Complete History of Chrysler 1924-1985, 107
CONSUMER GUIDE®, 7, 115, 300, 383, 396, 417
Conway, H.G., 103
Coppa d'Oro, 164
Coppa Inter-Europa, 169
Cord Corporation, 67, 118, 124
    810/812, 31, 121, 122-125, 350
    L-29, 90, 110, 123
Cord, Errett Lobban, 64, 67, 118, 121, 123, 124, 125, 148
Corvair Affair, 329
Cousins, Cecil, 155-157
Coventry Climax, 284, 285
Crawford, Charles S., 43
Csere, Csaba, 233, 234, 235
Cugnot, Nicholas, 6
Cunningham, Briggs, 55, 289

D

D'Ieteren Freres, 207
Dahlquist, Eric, 259, 372
Daimler, 9, 15, 31, 36, 54, 92
Daimler, Gottlieb, 6, 7, 8, 14, 112
Daimler, Paul, 8, 60
Daimler-Benz, 60, 62, 112, 115, 205, 234, 235
Dallara, Giampaolo, 352, 378, 384
Daniels, Jack, 175, 176
Darlington Motor Speedway, 240, 317
Darrin, Howard A. "Dutch," 93, 146, 213, 214
Datsun 240Z, 374-377, 390, 392
Daytona track, 245, 298, 343
Daytona, 366
Daytona 2000 Kilometers, 303
Daytona 500, 317
Daytona Speed Weeks, 240, 265
de Levaud, Seneaud, 110
de Sakhnoffsky, Count Alexis, 81

DeDietrich, 53
DeDion, 36
Deeds, Edward, 36
Delahaye, 100, 193, 361
DeLaRossa, Don, 293
DELCO, 36, 408
Delling, Eric, 35
DeLorean, John Z., 235, 305, 317
DePalma, Ralph, 35, 42, 51
Derham, 47, 66
DeSoto, 102, 104
DeTomaso Pantera, 378-381
DeTomaso, Alejandro, 378, 381
Deutz, 53
Dewar Trophy, 16, 19
Dietrich, Inc., 86, 93, 267
Dietrich, Ray, 81, 86, 146
Dodge, 145, 267
    Caravan, 394, 396
Dorris, 51
Dort, 51
Drexler, Arthur, 164
Dreyfus, René, 102, 103
Drogo, Piero, 303
Duesenberg, 7, 64, 81, 118, 123, 125
    J-Series, 7, 64-67, 114
    Model A, 64
Duesenberg, August, 64, 67, 118
Duesenberg, Fred, 64, 66, 67
Dusio, Piero, 163, 164

E

Earl, Harley J., 58, 59, 67, 134, 136, 148, 225, 263, 264, 270, 305
Earls Court Auto Show, 128, 175, 344
Eastman, Frank, 46
Eckermann, Erik, 194
Edison, Thomas, 71
Edmundson, Carolyn, 106
Edsel (car), 269
Egbert, Sherwood, 312, 314, 315
Elkhart Lake, Wisconsin, 157
Engel, Elwood, 293
ERA, 221
Erdmann & Rossi, 114
Erskine, Albert Russel, 99
Estes, Elliott "Pete," 317
Evans, Dave, 297
Evernden, H.I.F., 216, 218
Exner, Virgil, 242, 245, 348

F

F.R.P. (car), 35
Facel Vega, 197, 259, 361
Farina, Battista, 49
Farina, Nino, 117
Faulkner, Roy, 98
Federation Internationale de l'Automobile (FIA), 300
Ferguson, Harry, 344
Fergusson, David, 36
Fernandez, 148
Fernandez et Darrin, 66
Ferrari, 169, 211, 234, 239, 275, 276, 286, 319, 336, 341, 352, 354, 381, 384, 389
    166/195/212, 166-169
    250 GTO, 300-303
    308/328/348, 386-389
    365 GTB/4 Daytona, 364-367
    Dino 206/246, 340-343
    F40, 402-405
    Testarossa, 389, 404, 408
Ferrari, Enzo, 53, 116, 117, 167, 169, 300, 303, 317, 341, 343, 352, 355, 389, 403, 405
Ferrari: The Man and His Machines, 300, 365
Fiat, 53, 163-164, 194, 341, 343, 356, 366, 375, 388, 403, 405
Fioravanti, Leonardo, 403
Fisher Body, 57, 58, 59, 75, 76, 144, 145
Fisher, Lawrence P., 57, 58, 73, 75
Fitch, John, 157, 265

Fitzgerald, Warren, 116
Fleetwood, 47, 58, 59, 75, 86, 136
Flint (car), 51
Ford, 19, 24, 83, 84, 130, 132, 152, 153, 186,
    188, 189, 201, 213, 228, 231, 237, 240
    250, 264, 267, 268, 269, 270, 293, 295,
    297, 305, 326, 336, 378, 380, 381, 394
    1949 Model, 186-189
    Aerostar, 396
    Econoline, 394
    Fairlane V-8, 297, 333
    Falcon, 326, 329, 331
    Model A, 27, 64, 68-71, 83, 84, 85, 108,
        140, 186
    Model B, 85
    Model K, 83
    Model T, 7, 20, 24-27, 30, 68, 70, 71, 83,
        108, 138, 186 199, 281
    Mustang, 141, 326, 329, 330-335, 336,
        338, 378, 394
    Skyliner, 294
    Taurus, 352, 358
    Thunderbird, 249, 250-253, 264, 293, 294,
        305, 306, 315, 333
    V-8, 82-85, 99, 121, 132, 138, 203, 344
    Vedette, 188
Ford, Edsel, 27, 70, 84, 85, 86, 130, 132, 138,
    140, 141, 148, 153, 267, 268
Ford, Henry, 24, 26, 27, 29, 35, 53, 68, 70,
    71, 83, 84, 85, 86, 100, 108, 116, 130,
    138, 140, 141, 175, 188, 205
Ford, Henry II, 186
Ford, William Clay, 267, 268, 269
Franay, 66, 219
Frankfurt Auto Show, 367, 388, 399
Frazer-Nash, 259
Frere, Paul, 366, 388
Friederich, Ernest, 53
Frontenac, 43
Frostick, Michael, 48, 49

G
Gabelbach hillclimb (race), 63
Gandini, Marcello, 354, 381, 383
Gangloff, 102, 103
Ganz, Joseph, 194
General Motors, 12, 13, 50, 58, 67, 75, 130,
    134, 136, 143, 144, 183, 185, 190, 192,
    201, 218, 219, 225, 237, 263, 264,
    265,270, 272, 298, 305, 309, 317, 319,
    329, 408, 409
    Art & Colour studio, 58,
    Bendix Division, 186
Geneva Auto Show, 383, 384
Ghia, 168, 346, 378, 380, 381
Ginther, Richie, 157
Giugiaro, Giorgio, 378
Glaser, 206
Goertz, Albrecht, 259, 261, 375
Gordon, John F. "Jack," 305
Graber, 219
Graham, 118
Granatelli, Andy, 315
Grand Prix du Mans, 53
Grand Prix of Pau, 8
Great American Cars of the 50's, 7
Great Book of Sports Cars, The, 7
Gregorie, E.T. "Bob," 132, 138, 140
Grisinger, Buzz, 158, 213-214
Gross, Ken, 253
Grossman, Bob, 377
Gurney Nutting, 66

H
H.C.S. (car), 43
Halderman, Gayle, 293, 333
Hall, Bob, 412, 413
Hardig, Gene, 315
Hardy Spicer, 279
Hare Motors, 35
Harper's Bazaar, 106

Harrah Collection, 55
Haspel, Vilhelm, 233
Hassan, Wally, 172
Hayashi, Koichi, 413
Hayes Body Company, 81
Healey, 222, 361
Healey Silverstone, 221, 223
Healey, Donald, 221, 222
Hedge, Frank, 208
Henney Company, 254
Henry Ford Museum/Greenfield Village,
    55, 83, 89
Hershey, Franklin Quick, 81, 250, 252
Heuer, 206
Heynes, Bill, 126, 171, 172, 173
Hibbard & Darrin, 75, 146
Hill, Phil, 157, 169
Hirai, Toshihiko, 413
Hispano-Suiza, 58
Hitler, Adolf, 115, 194, 196, 197, 205, 259
Hoffman, Max, 197, 206, 234, 259, 261, 361
Holbert, Al, 401
Holbrook, 66, 86
Honda
    Accord, 414
    Civic, 414
    CRX, 412
    Prelude, 414
Hudson Commodore, 210
    Hornet, 208-211, 336
    Super Eight, 211
Hudson Motor Car Company, 13, 201, 203,
    208, 240
Humber, 126
Hurlock, Derek, 297
Hydra-Matic transmission, 144, 145, 184,
    185, 190, 193, 210, 219, 350

I
Iacocca, Lee, 297, 326, 331, 333, 335, 378,
    381, 394, 397, 412
Ideal Motor Car Company, 41, 42
*Illustrated Rolls-Royce and Bentley Buyer's
    Guide*, 22
Indian Tourist Trophy, 49
Indianapolis Speedway, 41, 81
Indy 500, 35, 41, 42
International Motor Sports Association
    (IMSA), 393
Irish Grand Prix, 63
Isbrandt, Ralph, 215
Isotta-Frachini, 53
Issigonis, Alec, 175, 176, 279, 280

J
Jacobs Aircraft Company, 178
Jaguar, 173, 265, 344, 352, 361
    90 Model, 171
    E-Type, 7, 233, 286-291, 297, 375
    SS Jaguar 100, 126-129, 171
    XJ-S, 126, 291
    XK-120, 155, 171-173, 218, 222, 263, 286,
        298
Jano, Vittorio, 116
Jeanes, William, 405
Jellinek, Emil, 8, 9
Jenkens, Ab, 98, 121
Jensen FF, 344-347
Jensen, Alan and Richard, 222, 344
Jordan, Charles M. "Chuck," 412
Jordan, Mark, 412
Judkins, 86, 89, 267

K
Kaiser, 153, 203, 212-215, 350
Kaiser, Henry, 213, 215
Kanzler, Ernest, 27
Karmann, 199, 207

Karosserie Baur, 362
Keller, K.T., 242
Kellner, 55, 93
Kellogg, Tom, 312
Kessler, John, 261
Kettering, Charles F., 12, 36, 136, 192
Kimber, Cecil, 155
Kimes, Beverly Rae, 193
Kirwan-Taylor, Peter, 282
Knepper, Mike, 329
Knudsen, William S., 27, 136
Koto, Holden "Bob," 188, 228
Krebs, Albert, 15

L
La Turbie hillclimb, 9
Lagonda Cars Ltd., 275, 361
Laird, Ray, 83
Lamborghini, 365, 387
    Countach, 382-385, 408
    Miura, 352-355, 365, 383-384
Lamborghini, Ferruccio, 352, 354
Lamm, Michael, 181, 230
Lanchester, 29, 92
Lanchester, Frederick, 29, 30, 31
Lancia, 49, 361
    Lambda, 48-49
Lancia, Vincenzo, 48, 49
Langworth, Richard M., 107, 115, 193
LaSalle, 56-59, 71, 132, 137, 144
Le Mans race, 53, 116, 168, 234, 235, 270,
    289, 297, 298, 302, 303, 336, 367
Lea Francis, 197
Leamy, Al, 123
LeBaron, 64, 66, 86, 89, 93, 146
Lefebvre, 110
Leland, Henry M., 16, 18, 29, 36, 38, 57, 86,
    88, 132
Leland, Wilfred, 86, 89
Levassor, Emile, 14, 15
Levegh, Pierre, 235
Lincoln, 85, 133, 146, 184, 185, 193, 202, 206
    Continental, 7, 137, 138-141
    1956-1957 models, 266-269
    1961-1963 models, 292-295
    Mark II, 237, 270, 272, 273, 282, 350
    K-Series, 86-89, 141
    Model L, 70, 86
    Premier, 269
    V-12, 90, 96, 344
Lincoln Motor Company, 86, 130
Lincoln-Zephyr, 89, 130-133, 138, 141
Locke, 86, 267
Locomobile, 35, 50, 152
Loewy, Raymond, 188, 228, 259, 261, 312,
    348, 414
London Motor Show, 221
Lord, Leonard, 221
Los Angeles Auto Show, 141
Los Angeles Times, 405
Lotus, 282, 343, 408
    Elan, 413
    Elite, 282-285
Ludvigsen, Karl, 265
Lycoming Engine Company, 66, 118
Lyons, Pete, 300, 355, 365, 366, 383, 385,
    388, 405
Lyons, Sir William, 126, 128, 171, 172, 173,
    286, 344

M
Macauley, Alvan, 90
MacKichan, Clare, 237
Maguire, Bob, 250
Marathon de la Route, 248
Marion Motor Car Company, 41
Marmon, 78-81, 90, 96, 146
Marmon, Howard, 36, 73, 78, 80, 81

Marshall, George C., 151
Maserati, 117
Mason, Edward R., 64
Mason, George, 201, 202, 203, 221
Mathis, 53
Maxwell Motor Company, 51
May, Dennis, 219
Maybach, Wilhelm, 8
Mazda
    MX-5 Miata, 411-413, 417
    RX-7, 390-393
McCahill, Tom, 157, 245, 250, 306
McCall, Walter, 74, 185, 273
McCuen, Charles, 144
McLellan, Dave, 408
McNamara, Robert F., 297, 331
McRae, Duncan, 213
McVay, Bob, 307
Mechanix Illustrated, 157, 245, 250, 306
Mercedes-Benz, 35, 42, 117, 225, 233, 259,
    361
    300 SL, 232-235, 260, 265
    35 HP, 8-9
    500K/540K, 112-115
    Model 24/100/140, 60
    Model K, 60, 62
    Model S, 60, 62, 63, 112
    Model SS, 62, 112
    Model SSK, 62, 63, 112
    Model SSKL, 63, 112
Mercedes-Benz: The First Hundred Years, 115
Mercer Raceabout, 32-35, 42
Mercury, 185, 188, 250
Metzel, Harold, 144, 350
MG, 222, 279
    MGA, 411
    MGB, 155
    Midget, 155, 411
    TC, 155-157
Miles, Ken, 157, 298
Milestone Car Society, 7, 230, 273
Mille Miglia, 49, 116, 117, 164, 167, 169,
    234
Mitchell, William L. "Bill," 134, 136, 137,
    148, 305, 307, 309, 310, 326, 348
Monte Carlo Rally, 128, 221, 248
Montgomery, Robert, 77
Montlhery (race), 218
Monza (track), 163
Moon, Dean, 297
Morris Minor, 155, 174-177, 279
Mors, 108
Moss, Stirling, 172
MoToR, 106
Motor Life, 265, 267, 272
Motor Sport, 102
Motor Trend, 183, 189, 210, 247, 306, 307,
    310, 371, 375, 399
Motor, The, 63, 115, 175, 289, 347
Motorama shows, 263, 264, 270, 305
Mulliner, J.J., 218, 219, 275
Mundy, Harry, 291
Murphy, 66, 98, 267
Murray, 85
Musee Nationale de l'Automobile, 55
Museum of Modern Art (New York), 138,
    164

N
Nacker, Owen, 73
Nader, Ralph, 329, 347
Najjar, John, 293, 294
Napier, 36
Nardi, Enrico, 167
Nash, 181, 211, 213, 344
    Model 600, 106
    Ambassador, 203, 221
    Rambler, 200-203
    Statesman, 203
Nash, Charles W., 50
Nash, Lyman N., 151

419

National Association for Stock Car Auto Racing (NASCAR), 193, 208, 210, 240, 245, 297, 310, 317, 336, 338, 369
National Automobile Museum, 77
Neubauer, Alfred, 233, 235
New York Auto Show, 18, 51, 73, 78, 98, 124, 141, 234, 378
New York Salon, 64, 81
New York to Paris race, 16
Nibel, Hans, 60, 62, 112
Nice-Aix-Senas-Nice race, 8
Nichols, Mel, 385, 400, 401
Nickles, Ned, 305
Norbye, Jan, 107, 319, 359
Nordhoff, Heinz, 197
North, David, 348
NSU, 194, 205
    Ro80, 356-359
Nurburgring 1000 Kilometers, 302
Nuvolari, Tazio, 164, 165

O
Oldfield, Barney, 35
Olds, Ransom Eli, 10, 12, 13
Oldsmobile, 10, 12, 19, 59, 75, 84, 107, 130, 183, 186, 193, 208, 242, 305
    88, 190-193, 208, 210, 336
    90, 143-145
    Curved-Dash, 10-13
    Fiesta, 226
    Toronado, 348-351
Olympia Motor Show, 20
Opel, 108, 197, 358
Oros, Joe, 333
Otto, Nicholas Gustav, 6, 14

P
Packard, 39, 51, 57, 73, 77, 96, 130, 148, 184, 185, 201, 225, 231, 267
    Caribbean, 244, 254-257
    Custom Super Clipper, 267
    Model 38, 38
    One Sixty, 138
    One Twenty, 132, 146
    Pan American show cars, 254
    Single Six, 57, 73
    Thirty, 45
    Twelve, 90-95, 114
    Twin Six, 44-47, 57, 90, 96
Packard-Darrin, 146-149
Pagnibon and Barraquet, 169
Palmer, Jerry, 408
Panhard, 14-15, 20, 31
Panhard, Hippolyte and René, 14-15
Paris Exhibition, 14
Paris Salon, 48, 111, 169, 247, 250, 268, 341, 365
Paris-Dakar Rally, 401
Park Ward, 55, 219
Pebble Beach Concours, 265
Peerless, 39, 146
Petty, Richard, 369
Peugeot, 15, 108
Piech, Ferdinand, 320
Pierce-Arrow, 36, 39, 66, 80, 96, 99, 146, 152
    Twelve, 96-99
Piggins, Vince, 240
Pininfarina, 163, 164, 165, 168, 169, 177, 219, 276, 300, 312, 341, 365, 387, 403
Pintacuda, Carlo, 116, 117
Plymouth, 51, 158, 189, 203, 237
    Barracuda, 335
    Fury, 369
    Road Runner, 368-373
    Special Deluxe, 189
    Voyager, 394
Pontiac, 84, 143, 305, 319
    GTO, 316-319, 336, 369
    Torpedo Eight, 144
Popular Mechanics, 269

Popular Science, 153, 189
Porsche, 29, 110, 343, 352, 361, 393, 401, 403, 404
    356 Series, 204-207, 249
    911 Series, 320-325
    959, 233, 398-401
    962, 233
    Speedster, 259
    SSK, 261
Porsche, Ferdinand, 60, 62, 112, 130, 164, 165, 194, 196, 199, 205
Porsche, Ferry, 165, 205, 320
Porsche, Wolfgang, 401
Porter, Finley Robertson, 33, 35
Praxl, Ewald, 358, 359
Premier, 51
Probst, Karl, 152
Purdy, Ken, 53, 54, 55, 67, 118

Q
Quai de Javel, Paris, 108

R
RAC Rally, 126, 128
Rathmann, Dick, 240
RdA (Society of German Automakers), 194, 196
Renault, 108
Reo Motor Car Company, 13
Reutter, 206
Reventlow, Lance, 297, 336
Revere, 51
Riley, 221
Road & Track, 63, 114, 121, 180, 286, 312, 343, 355, 365, 366, 375, 385, 388, 389, 405, 406, 409, 417
Road Test, 319
Roberts, Bob, 208
Robillard, Bob, 213
Robinson, Peter, 110
Roche, James M., 273, 317
Rodger, Bob, 244
Roebling family, 33, 35
Rollert, Ed, 305
Rolls, Charles S., 20
Rolls-Royce, 22, 31, 54, 55, 92, 216, 218, 219, 225, 259, 275, 305, 315
    Silver Ghost, 20-23
Rollston Body Company, 92
Rollston Body Company, 92
Romney, George, 203
Roos, Delmar G. "Barney," 80, 152-153
Roosevelt, Franklin D., 71, 89, 151
Roush, Gerald, 366
Routes du Nord, 248
Routes Pavees (race), 49
Rover, 92, 396
Royal Automobile Club, 18, 19, 20, 175
Royce, Henry, 20, 22
Ruxton, 90
Ryder, H.A., 155

S
Saoutchik, 66
Sarazin, Edouard and Louise, 14
Saturday Evening Post, The, 39
Sayer, Malcolm, 286
Sayers and Scoville, 149
Scaglietti, 261, 303, 342, 343, 366
Scaglione, Franco, 352
Scandinavian rally, 248
Schultz, Carl, 83
Scott-Moncrieff, David, 8
Scottish Automobile Club, 19
Sebring, 157, 298, 302, 303
Sedgwick, Michael, 176
Sedgwick, Stanley, 216
Semmering (race), 63
Senna, Ayrton, 417
Sharp, Bob, 376
Shelby Cobra, 168
Shelby GT-350, 336-339

Shelby, Carroll, 157, 297, 298, 303, 311, 336, 338, 378
Sheldrick, Lawrence, 84
Shelsley Walsh hillclimb, 128
Silverstone Track, 301
Siminaitis, Dennis, 405
Simplex, 35
Skelton, Owen, 51, 104
Skinner, Sherrod E., 193 .
Sloan, Alfred P., 57, 136
Smith, Fred, 13
Smith, Samuel L., 10
Snow Rally (Finland), 248
Societa per azioni Escerizio Fabbriche Automobili (SEFAC), 403
Society of Automotive Engineers, 78
Sorensen, Charles, 84, 130
Sparrow, Edward W., 10
Spencer, Carleton, 214
Sports Car Club of America, 157, 265, 298, 309, 339, 376
Sports Car Illustrated, 265
Standard Motor Company, 126, 172
Stanzani, Paolo, 383, 385
Stein, Ralph, 15, 29, 30, 33, 34
Stevens, Brooks, 213, 214, 230
Stevens-Duryea, 51
Steward, Gilbert, 261
Steward, Mark, 280
Steyr, 62
Studebaker, 98, 99, 152, 188, 201, 249, 312, 314, 315, 348, 350
    Avanti, 261, 312-315, 328, 375, 376
    Champion, 203, 228, 230
    Commander, 228, 230
    Gran Turismo Hawk, 230
    Hawk, 230, 335
    Starlight/Starliner, 228-231, 237, 282
Studebaker-Packard Corporation, 257
Stutz, 41-43, 146
Stutz Bearcat, 40-43
Stutz, Harry C., 41, 42, 43
Sullivan, Danny, 401
Sutton, Ron, 172
Swallow Sidecar and Coachbuilding Company, 126, 171
Swiss Grand Prix, 100

T
Targa Florio, 60, 167, 301
Taruffi, Piero, 164, 165, 169
Taylor, Rich, 165, 261
Teague, Dick, 254
Teague, Marshall, 208, 210, 211, 240
Teague, Walter Dorwin, 81, 140
Thomas B. Jeffery Company, 202
Thomas, Bob, 293
Thomas, Herb, 210, 240
Thomas Flyer, 16
Thompson, Earl W., 144
Thompson, Richard, 265, 309
Thoreson, R.E., 328
Thoroughbred and Classic Sports Cars, 15
Tickford, 221, 222, 275, 276
Time, 138
Tjaarda, John, 130, 132
Tjaarda, Tom, 380
Toivonen, Pauli, 248
Tokyo Auto Show, 390
Tombs, Montague, 156
Tour de France, 169, 303
Tour of Sicily, 169
Tourist Trophy (race), 172
Toyo Kogyo, 390
Toyota, 375, 377
    MR2, 412
Tremulis, Alex, 178, 213
Triumph, 221, 265
    TR, 411
    TR2, 222
Trow, Nigel, 48
Tucker, 102, 178, 213

Tucker, Preston, 178, 180, 181
Tunis-to-Tripoli (race), 49
Turin Auto Show, 341, 352

U
Uhlenhaut, Rudolph, 233, 234
Union City Body Company, 66

V
Van Ranst, Cornelius, 90
Vance, Harold, 228, 230
Vignale, 168-169, 253, 261, 346, 378, 380, 381
Viking, 190
Villoresi, Emilio, 117
Villoresi, Luigi, 169
Vincent, Jesse, 45, 46, 90
Voisin, Gabriel, 110
Volkswagen, 62, 165, 205, 206, 282, 323, 326, 359, 394
    Beetle, 7, 20, 130, 175, 177, 194-199, 281, 326, 356
    Karmann Ghia, 249, 282
    Kombi, 177
Volvo, 344, 347
von Heydekampf, Gerd Stieler, 356, 358
Voorhies, Carl, 98
Vorderman, Don, 115, 116, 348

W
Wakefield, Ron, 114, 115, 375
Walker, George, 188, 250, 293
Wallace, Bob, 352, 355, 385
Walter M. Murphy Company, 81
Wangers, Jim, 317, 319
Wankel rotary engine, 356, 358, 359, 390, 392
Wankel, Felix, 356, 390
Ward's Automotive Yearbook, 307
Warner, Graham, 285
Waters, Tony, 183
Watkins Glen, 157, 333, 367
Weinberger, Ludwig, 55
Weis, Bernard J., 98-99
Weissinger, Herb, 213-214
Welsh Rally, 128
Werner, Wilhelm, 8
Weslake, Harry, 126, 171, 172, 173
White Motors, 99
White, D. McCall, 36
Widman, John, 215
Wilen, Stanley, 348
Williams, George M., 80
Willoughby, 66, 86, 89
Wills, C. Harold, 24
Willys Jeep, 150-153
Willys-Overland, 50, 51, 151, 152, 153
Wilson, "Ace," 319
Wood, Damon, 250
Wood, Jonathan, 15
World War I, 15, 22, 31, 53, 64, 96, 108, 356
World War II, 29, 95, 111, 116, 126, 134, 144, 151, 155, 158, 167, 173, 185, 190, 225, 267, 275, 344, 352, 356
Woron, Walt, 210
Woudenberg, Paul, 22, 89, 138
Wright, Jim, 306
Wright, Phil, 98

Y
Yagi, Masao, 412
Yamamoto, Kenichi, 390, 412
Yamanouchi, Michinori, 412
Youngren, Harold, 186

Z
Zagato, 276
Zeder, Fred, 51, 104
ZF (Zahnradfabrik Friedrichshafen), 275, 277, 282, 358, 361, 381, 406
Zoerlein, Emil, 83